TEN TON DREAMWEAVER

Geoff Blake

Peachpit Press

Ten Ton Dreamweaver

Geoff Blake

Peachpit Press
1249 Eighth Street
Berkeley, CA 94710
510/524-2178
800/283-9444
510/524-2221 (fax)

Find us on the Web at: www.peachpit.com
To report errors, please send a note to errata@peachpit.com
Peachpit Press is a division of Pearson Education

Peachpit Editor: Cary Norsworthy
Development Editor: Judy Ziajka
Production Editor: Susan Rimerman
Technical Editor: Demian Holmberg
Compositor: Melanie Haage
Indexer: Valerie Perry
Cover design: Mimi Heft
Original interior design: Geoff Blake

ISBN 0-321-37412-6

9 8 7 6 5 4 3 2 1

Printed and bound in the United States of America

Acknowledgments

My many thanks spread far and wide, across borders and time zones. However, it all begins on the home front. My endless appreciation, love, and praise for Tracy and Ronan. A guy couldn't ask for a tighter support system. Never lose your innocent curiosity for the world, Ronan. And Tracy...how is it that I'm so lucky? I'll always know where to find you—right by my side, ready to back me up, ready to go through hell with me. No questions. No complaints. You are the home-run hitter, tougher than anyone I know. Your unwavering strength, support, and patience, and your willingness to believe in an idea—in a world much larger than the accepted norm—is something that simply doesn't compute with most people, even those who think they're the smartest in the room. You are the rock upon which I stand; you are the sea upon which I float. Green eyes, the spotlight shines upon you.

Then there's Mom and Dad. What a pair! Mom has that warm smile, gentle way about her, and the unconditional love that only a mother can possess. And Dad? He's a breed all his own. No one is more misunderstood, more underestimated, or more overlooked than him. Yet he travels this journey with the patience of Gandhi, the wisdom of the Buddha, and the divinity of Christ. Most people just don't get him, because his is a mind on a completely different level. It is my life-long goal (as it should be every son's goal) to trump you, sir. That is evolution.

Then there's the rowdy gaggle who make every family get-together a blast: Jon, Laura, little Allison, and of course, the genius of the family, Tim. This kid is an incredible talent and will one day be a famous author (check him out at sterilized-dirt.com). Thanks so much for making wonderful memories, you guys. Also a quick shout to all my friends and extended family for all the love and support; you continually enrich my life and keep things challenging.

With all the weepy sobby stuff out of the way, I gotta thank all the people who made this project a reality, from the initial silly idea scribbled on scraps of paper, to the bound and finished product that you hold in your hands. It all started with Lee Rickwood at Newmedia.pro, who gave me a break and got me started. Then there was the endless support from my homie, Bill Dunlop. Who says worldly philosophy can't be discussed at 5 a.m. on the way to work? And Jason Allin—thanks for all the support. And many, many thanks to Marjorie McAneny for the belief in and refinement of this project early on, and also thanks to Colin Smith for his early help. A huge, *Ten Ton* thanks to Dan Dinicolo for all the help at the beginning and the encouragement along the way. Laura Lewin, my agent, needs endless praise and thanks for all her assistance and patience, too. And of course, lots of thanks to the Peachpit crew: Marjorie Baer, Cary Norsworthy, and Judy Ziajka. Also to Brian Brasher (etherbrian.com) for absolutely killer icons. Nano-phonic!

I should also take this opportunity to thank all my teachers, whether they practice the profession or not; and whether they realize they're teaching me or not. I'd like to point out a few favorites: Andrew Burke, Scott Cameron, Anna Moniz (see, I did something with my grade 9 English!), Pierre Light (can't we spend just a little more time in the shop together before you have to go?), and of course, Jean Luc Picard, Big Bobby Zed, and all my heroes.

Keep your head up and your stick on the ice. The game is still on...

Dedication

For the team and the game that we play.

Contents

PART I: GETTING STARTED WITH DREAMWEAVER

Part I

GETTING *Started* with DREAMWEAVER

Chapter 1

A COLOSSUS *called* Dreamweaver

STUFF YOU'LL LEARN IN THIS CHAPTER

Welcome to the colossus called Dreamweaver! I hope you're up for having some fun here, 'cuz that's what this book is all about. To start things off, we'll have a quick history lesson (relax, there's no test) and find out where Dreamweaver came from and why it's so popular. Then we'll talk a bit about how Dreamweaver fits into the overall design puzzle. Finally, we'll go on a walking tour of the book, so you'll know what you're in for. Your wait for a fun computer book has finally ended: it's ***Ten Ton Dreamweaver***! For your personal safety, please keep all arms and legs inside the ride at all times!

Do You Mean That Gary Wright Song?

Yes, the seventies. Who can forget? Studio 54, fat Elvis, and Sergio Valenti jeans. Who would have thought back then that we'd all be connected by an obscure idea called the Internet? Adult contempo's living legend Gary Wright, that's who. What—you don't remember Gary Wright? You know the airy tune "Dream Weaver," Garth's dream-girl song in ***Wayne's World***. Ah-ha! That's the one, and now it's in your head!

Wright released his classic tune back in 1976, a full 16 years before Macromedia existed, but what vision! However, his classic tune really has nothing to do with this book—so from this point forward, when we mention Dreamweaver, it's the software, not the international hit single we're talking about. Sound good?

All right. With that out of the way, what is the software, what does it do, and why is it so happening?

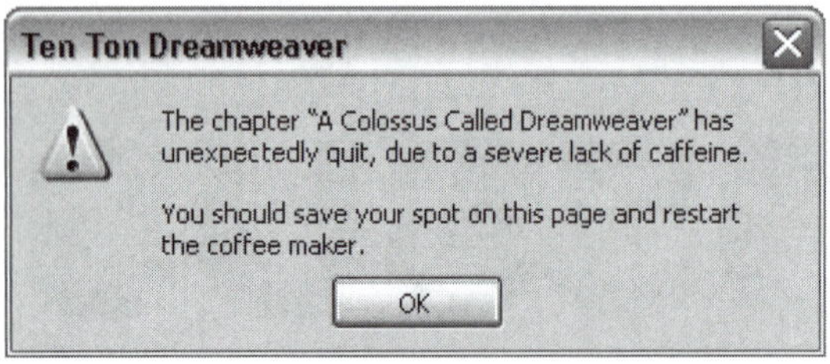

Aww, whaddya go and do?

Web Design History: 1995–2005

First, a quick bit of history. Back in the Stone Age of web design (not Wright's 1976; more like 1995—remember, we've moved on), web sites were coded entirely by hand using basic text editors. Imagine coding an entire page by hand, let alone an entire site? Lordy! One missed bracket or missed space, and entire page components wouldn't function properly. Pass the aspirin.

Ten Ton Dreamweaver will take you onwards and upwards to even newer horizons.

Then a few clever software companies issued programs that made it easier to code HTML using a text-based mode. This enabled designers to use buttons to build page blocks, taking at least some of the agony out of hand coding.

NOTEWORTHY

Even though most design is done with Dreamweaver, you can still make use of older-style editors if you'd like to work more closely with code. Check out "Using External HTML Editors" Chapter 17 for details.

Finally, programs called WYSIWYG editors (because What You See Is What You—should—Get) were built to take the headache out of hand coding—and Dreamweaver was a part of this generation. These HTML editing programs gave web designers a visual environment to work in, similar to desktop publishing—while the code was written in the background for them.

Because of these programs, designers could work much faster and build much more elaborate sites than ever before. Out of this first generation of HTML editors, many have fallen forgotten by the wayside, while others have earned a place as honorable—albeit obsolete—historical landmarks on the timeline of web design. Today's HTML editors have capabilities leagues beyond those of earlier programs. With the sophistication of contemporary sites, pure hand coding just isn't an option any more.

Dreamweaver and other WYSIWYG editors have taken the headache out of hand coding by providing a visual environment to work in—similar to desktop publishing programs.

As for Dreamweaver in particular, it's gone on to become one of the most widely used web design programs in the industry. Its ease of use, straightforward interface, and simple-to-high-end functionality is unmatched, making it the program of choice for many of today's top web designers.

So Why Dreamweaver?

Sure, there are other web design programs available, so why Dreamweaver? What makes it so special? Quite simply, nothing else comes close to it. Don't know a thing about HTML, JavaScript, Cascading Style Sheets, or other scary web technologies? Dreamweaver rides to the rescue—and that's why it's such a popular tool. On a basic level, using Dreamweaver is almost as simple as using a word processor, but you can quickly and easily get into much higher-end functionality without knowing a thing about coding. Dreamweaver writes it all for you in the background. This saves designers massive amounts of time and frustration, and at the same time lets them build some pretty amazing sites.

Pure hand coding an entire web site is thankfully a thing of the past. With the tediousness involved and the high rate of human error, it's just not an option in today's fast-paced world.

Dreamweaver holds the heavyweight title as an industry-standard tool because it can pretty much handle it all: from basic personal home pages, to corporate sites, to heavy e-commerce and data-driven sites that require entire design teams to work together. In other words, with Dreamweaver in your toolbox, there won't be a whole lot you can't tackle.

Using Dreamweaver is almost as simple as using a word processor, but you can quickly and easily get into much higher-end functionality.

If you've ever done any hand coding yourself, or if you have the stomach for delving into the HTML in your pages, you're welcome to go behind the scenes in Dreamweaver and dig in. With its double identity as both a visual design tool and a straight code editor, Dreamweaver provides an array of functions and commands to assist you, whether you want to work visually or directly with the code. You can even take advantage of both environments with a split-screen view. So build pages, build sites, build web applications—and build 'em in a way that suits you. That's what Dreamweaver is all about.

A final note before moving on: Dreamweaver is just one component of a much larger picture—Macromedia's Studio suite, which includes a few other programs to help out in your web design adventures. If you've purchased the full Studio suite, you'll also have other programs such as Macromedia Flash and Fireworks. And if you've got the Studio 8 version of the suite, you'll also get FlashPaper 2 (Windows only), Contribute 3, and ColdFusion Developer Edition. See the sidebar "A Macromedia Studio 8 Primer" for more on the suite. We won't go into these tools in too much detail, but just know that if Flash and Fireworks have your back, there'll be nothing stopping the mad designer you're sure to become!

GEEK'S DELIGHT

Even though Dreamweaver is known for its design capabilities, many programmers use Dreamweaver purely for its professional code-handling tools, making it a standard tool for both designers and coders in various fields.

New to Dreamweaver and web design? Then check out www://virtuallyignorant.com and http://macromedia.com/devnet/dreamweaver

NOTEWORTHY

The short-and-sweet: Raster graphics are made up of millions of colors, as in photographs and paintings, and are built out of pixels. Vector graphics, such as clip art and logos, consist of solid blocks of color and are built out of mathematical lines.

NOTEWORTHY

If you're looking to purchase a word processor, Microsoft Word is really the only choice. There are others out there, but you'll want something that's widely used, whose files you can easily share with the outside world. Word is without a doubt the standard.

A MACROMEDIA STUDIO 8 PRIMER

Macromedia's Studio 8 suite provides everything the professional web designer needs to develop, construct, and maintain web sites, all in one box. In addition to Dreamweaver, you'll be treated to Flash, FlashPaper 2, Contribute 3, and Fireworks. These fellas are all heavyweights in their particular areas of expertise, and because they're all built with the web in mind and share similar interfaces, they integrate easily to make site design a breeze.

Flash Professional: You've no doubt heard of Flash. This groundbreaking program single-handedly changed the way the Internet functions, bringing the world a much more interactive and entertaining web experience. Flash allows you to build vector-based movies, interactive environments, and a whole lot more. Flash's only limit is the designer's imagination. This monster comes in two flavors: Flash Basic and Flash Professional. Both integrate graphics, sound, and the interactive language ActionScript on a controllable timeline. But Professional goes further, with raster image effects, authoring for mobile devices, and high-quality video support. It's a web designer's delight. Fire up Flash at http://macromedia.com/software/flash.

Fireworks: Fireworks is the hub for manipulating graphics to use in the other Studio suite applications. Take on raster and vector images with ease and prepare them for online use. Go further by creating rollovers, buttons, and image slicing. If it's graphics related, Fireworks has the tools. Go pyro with Fireworks at http://macromedia.com/software/fireworks.

Contribute: Are you a busy designer having a tough time managing site content and updates? Wouldn't it be nice if you could just have others in your organization—even those with zero web design experience—handle site content and updates? Think it's a pipe dream? Well think no further than Contribute! This handy little tool makes it easy for literally anyone who can use a keyboard and mouse to handle site content, without messing up a site's design. Let others contribute to your site with Contribute, at http://macromedia.com/software/contribute.

FlashPaper (Windows only): FlashPaper allows tech-savvy and nontechnical users alike to easily convert printable documents— Word files, spreadsheets, and so on—to either PDF or Flash files for use on the web. FlashPaper even integrates with Microsoft Office, making the process of converting documents even easier for those unfamiliar with Flash or PDF. Check out the goods at http://macromedia.com/software/flashpaper.

How Dreamweaver Fits into the Web Design Puzzle

So how does Dreamweaver fit into the overall design puzzle? Well, you can think of Dreamweaver as the piece of the puzzle that sits right in the center, with all the other pieces connecting to it. Dreamweaver is where you bring in and stylize your text, import images and multimedia files, and arrange your other content. To maximize your web-design experience, though, a few other types of programs may be helpful. The pieces you'll most commonly want to complete your puzzle are a word processor and a raster image editor. After you've become comfortable building web pages, you may also find some other pieces useful, such as a vector image editor, a web animation tool, or tools for creating a database-driven site.

Think of Dreamweaver as the piece of the puzzle that sits right in the center, with all other pieces connecting to it.

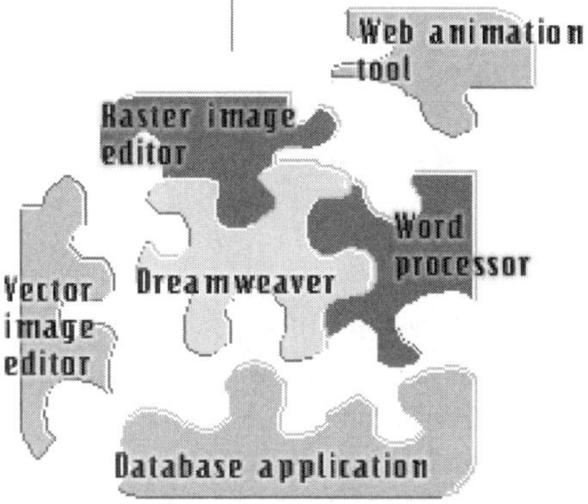

See how nicely everything dovetails together? You certainly don't have to have all the pieces to the puzzle—just the ones that you'll use most.

Word Processors

To prepare the text for your web site, a word processor is always useful. You can type and edit text directly in Dreamweaver, but most folks find it easier to write their text in a program like Microsoft Word and then later bring it into Dreamweaver for formatting. That's actually my preferred way of working, too. Word's text tools, like AutoCorrect, AutoText, and a few other goodies make it a cinch to type up some copy (and share it with others for editing and approval). Check out "Word vs. Dreamweaver: A Steel Cage Match Extraordinaire!" in Chapter 6 for more on the word processing issue.

Raster Image Editors

What would the web be without graphics? As exciting as the 24-hour smelt-fishing channel, that's what. We need some energy and excitement on our pages, so some image-manipulation software is essential. A raster image editor is a program that can handle photographs, scans, and other pixel-based graphics and can take care of sizing, cropping, and color manipulation duties. Don't rely on the free software that came with your digital camera or scanner. It's usually okay for the kids, but the pros employ programs with a lot more horsepower. The biggie is Photoshop, the heavyweight champion of them all. It's the print and web designer's mainstay. If Photoshop's price tag is a turnoff, you could certainly use Fireworks (which comes with Dreamweaver in the Studio suite, remember) or a slew of others that are out there, such as Paint Shop Pro.

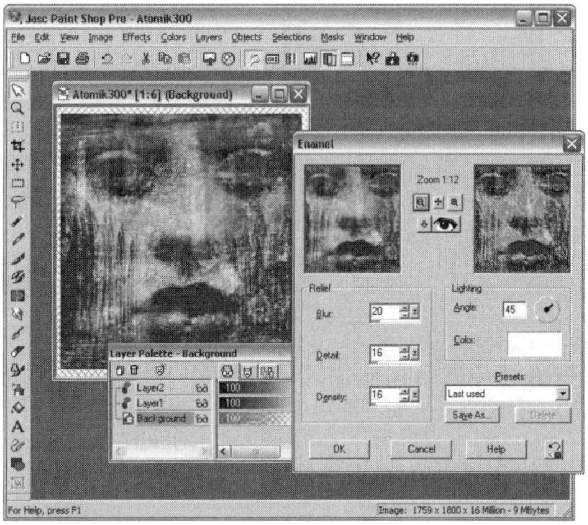

Although it doesn't have an interface as sleek as Photoshop's, Paint Shop Pro is still a compelling tool in any designer's arsenal, especially for the price.

IMMINENT DOOM

Don't be cheap with your image editing software. The free programs that came with your digital camera or scanner just don't have the firepower that web design calls for.

A basic image editor is a must—something that sizes, crops, and manipulates color in your images.

THE LOWDOWN ON IMAGE EDITORS

The App	**The Deal**	**The Damage**
Photoshop CS2	The biggest and baddest of them all, Photoshop is used by print and web pros all over the world. PC and Mac. (Adobe.com)	$599
Fireworks 8	A part of Macromedia's Studio suite. Although it's possible to use Fireworks for print, it's really built for web use. PC and Mac. (Macromedia.com)	$299
Paint Shop Pro 9	With a loyal fan base due to its ease of use, Paint Shop Pro offers many features, even though it isn't as heavy duty as other image editors. Windows only. (Corel.com)	$149
Photo Impact 10	Geared toward web designers and photography enthusiasts, Photo Impact packs plenty of punch behind its easy-to-use interface. Windows only. (Ulead.com)	$89
Satori Photo XL	Packed with special effects, color control, and a price that can't be beat, Satori is a great solution for those who want the features without the aching bank account. Windows only. (Satoripaint.com)	$10

Vector Image Editors

Not up for learning the intricacies of Flash? Check out a much simpler program called SWiSH (www.swishzone.com).

You may want to consider a vector drawing program to help with tasks like creating logos and illustrations. Adobe Illustrator (adobe.com/products/illustrator) would do the job. A vector image editor isn't an absolute necessity, but it can make life easier down the road, once you're a web design pro.

Web Animation Tools

If you want your site to include web animation, you'll need a specialized program to handle those duties—typically Macromedia Flash. Flash allows designers to build pages that incorporate full motion and sound, while producing small files that download quickly. It's really cutting-edge stuff. No doubt you've seen a lot of Flash animation on the Internet already, but don't let those pesky Flash intro pages and wiz-bang advertisements sway your opinion—a lot of people misuse the technology. When they use Flash appropriately, designers can build incredible environments that push web design to the farthest frontiers.

For a great example of a killer Flash site, check out www.terminator3.com. Boy, that movie stunk, but they made up for it with a site that really shows off what Flash—and a little creativity—can do.

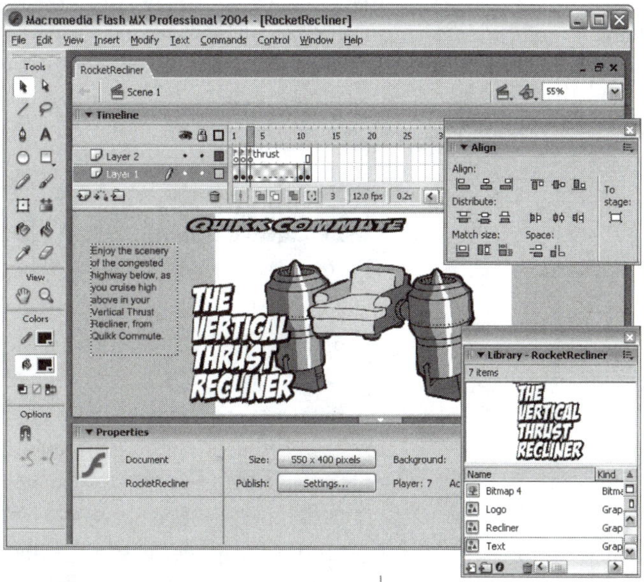

One direction your web design skills can take is to Macromedia Flash, which takes web design to a whole other level. If Jennifer Beals used Flash, her web site would really dance! No takers? Well, it was 1983.

STICKIN' WITH INDUSTRY STANDARDS

My personal thinking is this: If you're going to lay out your hard-earned money, you may as well purchase industry-standard software. Nothing's worse than getting stuck with a program that isn't compatible with the outside world. A few years back, a lot of government agencies were stuck with WordPerfect. It's incredibly frustrating when you can't share files or communicate on common issues with the rest of the planet. So here's a list of standard programs to complete the web design puzzle:

Area of Expertise	And the Winner Is...	Runners-Up
Word processing	Microsoft Word	Corel WordPerfect
Raster image editing	Adobe Photoshop	Macromedia Fireworks, Corel Paint Shop Pro
Vector image editing	Adobe Illustrator	Macromedia Freehand, Corel Draw
Web animation	Macromedia Flash	SWiSH, Macromedia Director

Tools for Database-Driven Sites

Dreamweaver can also build database-driven sites. Massive sites like eBay and Amazon are not built page by page. They use databases running in the background to fill in page content based on the information the visitor requests. This sort of site is beyond our scope here, but just know that you can incorporate server technologies such as ASP, ASP.NET, JSP, ColdFusion, and PHP as you're building pages and sites with Dreamweaver.

DREAMWEAVER'S SYSTEM REQUIREMENTS

We're assuming here that you have Dreamweaver installed and working on your machine—either a Windows PC or a Mac. If you haven't installed the program yet, just follow the installation screens—the process is easy.

Before you get going with Dreamweaver, make sure you have enough horsepower to actually run the program. Your trusty old Pentium I 133 MHz system with 32 megs of RAM just won't cut it this time around. Below, you'll find Dreamweaver's system requirements for both the Windows and Macintosh platforms, but keep one thing in mind: These are the ***minimum*** system requirements. If you actually want Dreamweaver to move a touch faster than a stubborn mule, then you should consider adding as much RAM to your system as you can swing. TV dinners for two months straight will be well worth it!

Windows

- 800 MHz Intel Pentium III processor or equivalent
- Windows 2000, Windows XP SP2, or Windows Server 2003
- 256 MB RAM (1 GB recommended)
- 650 MB available disk space

Macintosh

- 600 MHz Power PC G3 processor or later
- Mac OS X 10.3 and 10.4
- 256 MB RAM (256 MB recommended)
- 300 MB available disk space

The Giddyup: About *Ten Ton Dreamweaver*

So now you're ready for the next step: *Ten Ton Dreamweaver*.

What's worse than learning a new piece of software? Okay, maybe accidentally inhaling a grasshopper. I was shooting for the manual, though—that ridiculously thick tome that makes astrophysics seem like a sudden career possibility. Before you break out the science books, try *Ten Ton* on for size. *Ten Ton* is all about taking the throes out of learning a new program—and having fun in the process!

The Delights That Await Just Around the Bend

There's a lot to get to in *Ten Ton Dreamweaver*. Throughout our time together, we'll laugh, we'll cry, and we'll console each other in those moments when all hope seems lost. So to get a sense of where we'll go and what we'll see, let's take a look at the thrills that await in *Ten Ton Dreamweaver*.

Ten Ton is *all about taking the throes out of learning* Dreamweaver.

PART I—COMMENCE COUNTDOWN: GETTING STARTED WITH DREAMWEAVER

Part I is all about getting you started with Dreamweaver, including planning and implementing your first site. In fact, you've already started Part I with this chapter, which is all about Dreamweaver, web design tools, and what this book is about. In Chapter 2, we'll travel the highways and byways of the interface. We'll walk through the toolbars, panels, menus, and other interface elements, and get a good sense of how everything's laid out. We'll even get into a bit of customization, so stick around for that.

***Part I* is *all about getting you started* with Dreamweaver.**

> **IMMINENT DOOM**
>
> Although you may be eager to begin building web pages, don't skip the first part of this book. It covers a lot of information critical to web design that you'll need to understand before beginning your design work.

Then the work begins! We'll get up to our elbows in site planning in Chapter 3, which covers everything from navigation, to branding, to site structure, to coffee. It's critical info, so get a good night's sleep beforehand.

Chapter 4 provides the details on setting up a site. When you embark on your first web site with Dreamweaver (a momentous occasion filled with toasts, speeches, and power-wedgies), one of your first orders of business will be to define the site. This is sort of the upfront paperwork that needs to be looked after before really breaking ground. We'll discuss how

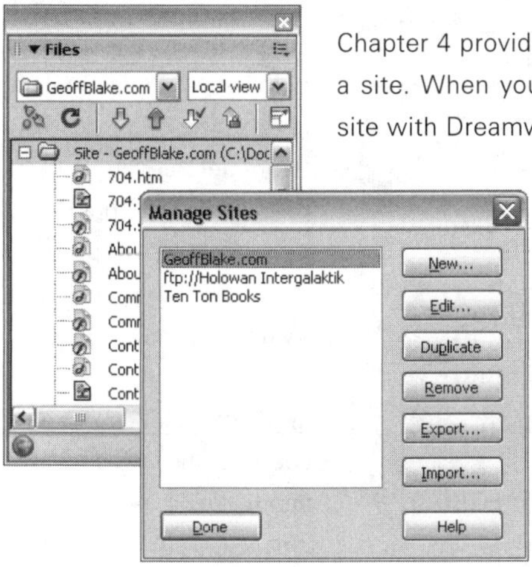

Before going anywhere or doing anything in Dreamweaver, you need to define your web site. We'll talk more about this in Chapter 4.

to set up a local folder on your computer and a corresponding remote folder where you'll publish your live site. You'll also see how to transfer and synchronize local and remote sites and how to handle more than one site at a time. Then you're good to actually start building pages.

PART II: BUILDING YOUR SITE STARTS RIGHT NOW

The second part of the book is all about building pages using Dreamweaver's mighty design elements.

The second part of the book is all about building pages using Dreamweaver's mighty design tools. In Chapter 5, you'll be shipped off to Dreamweaver boot camp, where you'll get a run-through of page construction from start to finish. You'll see how to control page layout with layers, and you'll get a primer on everything from text and images to hyperlinks and libraries. Chapter 5 is a whopper, where things really start happening!

Once you've been through Dreamweaver 101 in Chapter 5, you're ready for the big leagues. In Chapter 6, you'll learn to build your own page layouts with layers. You'll see not only how to build the primary containers for your page elements, but also how to control them externally via Cascading Style Sheets, or CSS. You'll also take a look at div tags, which open up even more design possibilities. Layers and div tags are the modern way, so if you thought web design meant learning HTML, think again—and make a beeline to Chapter 6.

NOTEWORTHY

The second part of Ten Ton Dreamweaver gives you everything you need to know to develop, build, and maintain sites that use a variety of components and technologies.

Chapter 7 covers tables and frames. Now there's something important that you need to know about tables upfront: You can use them to display information—that's the plain-vanilla way to use them—but you can also use them to control page layout and manage content, although they're not as flexible as layers. Framesets provide another layout option: They offer a unique way to build site navigation so that the visitor can see more than one web page at a time within a browser's window. There are pluses and minuses to both tables and frames, but it's a good idea to explore them before you start to build your site. They might be exactly what you need for a particular effect you're trying to achieve.

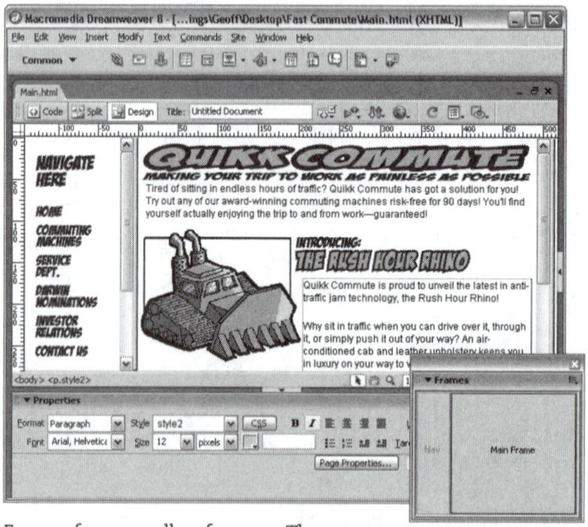

Frames, frames, endless frames... There are many ways to design your site, and frames are but one approach.

In Chapter 8, you'll really see what the CSS buzz is all about. You'll learn how to create and apply Cascading

Style Sheets for your text. Then you'll get to the heart of CSS: You'll see how to build an external style sheet to control multiple styles throughout your entire site, so you can update all your pages simultaneously and maintain the integrity of your text formatting sitewide. CSS is one tasty topic, so tie on your Boss Hogg bib, lick your chops, and get ready for a meal!

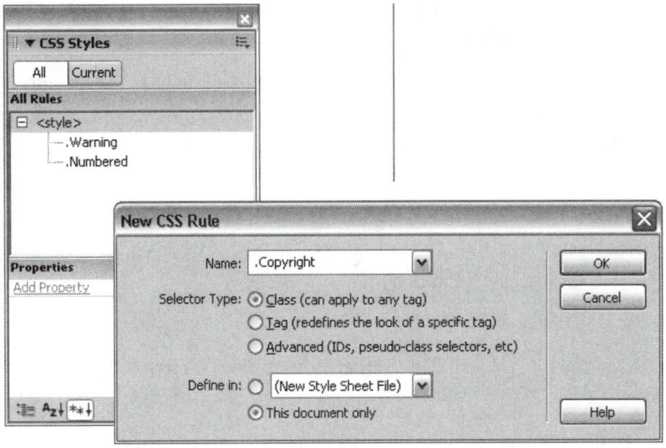

The cat's meow for consistent text formatting, Cascading Style Sheets get put under the microscope in Chapter 6.

At this point, your site is all dressed up without anywhere to go. Chapter 9 provides your limo to the prom, with the inside scoop on everything there is to know about hyperlinks: how to set them up, how to manage them, and possibly most important, what to do when they don't work. You'll see how to link to many different types of web content, including PDF files, MP3 files, e-mail addresses—and (oh yeah) other web pages.

GEEK'S DELIGHT

As the second part of the book progresses, topics get more and more high-end. We even get into looking at and understanding code and how it works on your pages.

Once you have some text and hyperlinks happening, the next logical step is to add some graphics—the topic of Chapter 10. Visuals are critical to web design, so you'll spend some time learning about the types of graphics you can use and what you can do with them. Dreamweaver even lets you do some basic image manipulation on the fly, such as simple cropping and sharpening, so you'll take a look at that. You'll see how to create Flash buttons and navigation bars, too.

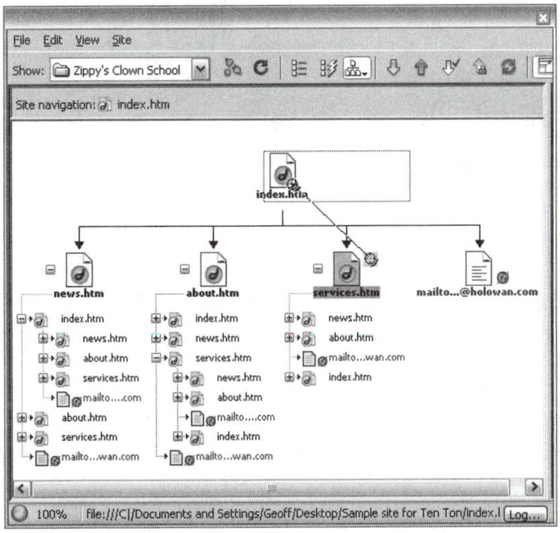

Hyperlink high jinks, seen here in the Files panel's Site Map view—one of many ways to connect your pages to one another. You'll get the hyperlink who's your daddy? *in Chapter 9.*

Chapter 11 digs into multimedia and interactivity—some of the coolest features of web pages. You'll learn to insert audio, video, and Macromedia Flash files and set their properties. Then you'll see how to add interactivity—pop-up

At the www. tentonbooks.com web site, you'll find lots of extra features to accompany your brand-new book!

windows, rollovers, and other dynamic elements. Dreamweaver makes creating these elements easy with ready-made actions called behaviors, which you can apply to your pages without having to know how to write the underlying JavaScript code. In addition, you'll take a look at timelines, which you can use to control the movement and timing of objects on the screen.

Chapter 12 introduces forms, so you can build a worldwide e-commerce empire! You'll take see how to create and lay out forms of all types, from simple surveys to the framework for an e-commerce setup.

There are lots of resources out there. Be sure to check out Dreamweaver's online forums at http://macromedia.com/cfusion/webforums/forum/index.cfm?forumid=12.

Now comes one of the best features of Dreamweaver. Templates, discussed in Chapter 13, are simply mind blowing—these have gotta be my favorite part of the Dreamweaver experience. They're a bit tricky at first, but if you're as neurotic as I am about consistency from page to page throughout an entire site, templates are the sure-fire way to go. You may want to read up on templates before building your whole site. Check 'em out—they are madness!

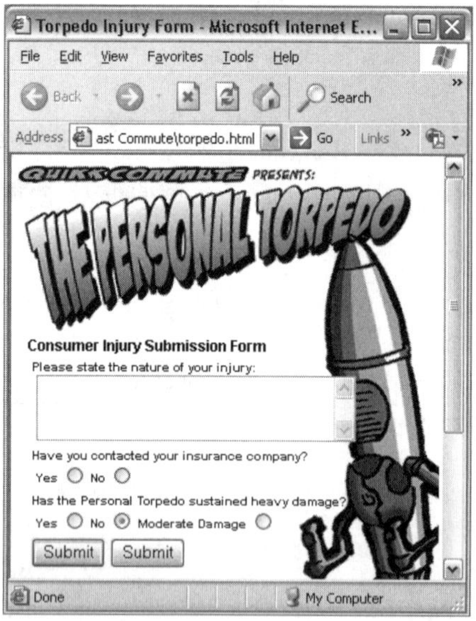

Forms are great for interactive sites such as e-commerce setups, contact systems, and online surveys, as seen here. Learn good form in Chapter 12.

Finally, in Chapter 14, you'll learn about the high-level aspects of managing and maintaining a site. You'll learn how to prepare your site for publishing to the web and how to maintain your site once it's live and running. You'll also find out about some nifty tools that you can use if you're working with a group of web designers.

Lots More on the Ten Ton Web Site

What about the deleted scenes, the outtakes, the Spanish version, and the tricks for going even further with Dreamweaver? That's what the ***Ten Ton*** web site, www.tentonbooks.com, is all about. You'll find lots of extra stuff to accompany the very book you're holding—things like online articles, tutorials, cheat sheets, and lots of free stuff!

The site also discusses many additional features of Dreamweaver. Keep your eyes peeled as you read, and you'll find web references to specific topics.

HEY, THERE'S MORE THAN ONE *TEN TON*!

There's certainly more than one thing that weighs in at a hefty 10 tons. Get glazed, dazed, and amazed at this weighty stuff!

Super Croc

Paleontologist Paul Sereno unearthed the remains of *Sarcosuchus imperator*, otherwise known as Super Croc. Weighing in at an estimated 10 tons and with a skull measuring a menacing 6-feet long, Super Croc is thought to have lived 110 million years ago. Get prehistoric at http://nationalgeographic.com/supercroc.

"Ten Ton Hammer," by Machine Head

Machine Head's thunderous metal anthem "Ten Ton Hammer" kicked off the band's 1997 offering, *The More Things Change...* For lots more on Machine Head, heralded as one of metal's last true groups, check out www.machinehead1.com.

The Millennium Falcon

Ten times 10 tons makes 100 metric tons, and that's the cargo capacity of the most notorious smuggling ship in the business, the Millennium Falcon. All those who knew this already, please put up your hands. Yup, as always, I'm the only geek...

RAF Harrier Jump Jet

Featured in James Cameron's *True Lies,* the British Aerospace Harrier is the only Western combat aircraft possessing a vector-thrust engine, giving the jet its unique vertical takeoff ability. Its maximum vertical lift is just shy of the 10-ton mark, making it an impressive battle machine. Take off to http://en.wikipedia.org/wiki/BAE_Sea_Harrier for more.

What Makes *Ten Ton* Different?

Most computer books are so dry they're a fire hazard. You've probably already flipped around through *Ten Ton* a bit and realized that things are a little unconventional here. Don't be frightened—this is a good thing. I think you'll find this book a whole lot different from other computer books, not just in its layout and design, but also in its approach, content, and style.

Having fun while learning about computers? How is this possible? What is he thinking? He'll destroy us all!

So from this point forward, imagine that you and I are sitting on a big comfy couch in one of those hip downtown coffee pubs. There's some jazz happening in the background (or trip hop, if that's your thing). I brought my laptop, and you brought all your questions about Dreamweaver and web design. Lenny Kravitz just walked in, and after you and I have made fools of ourselves telling him how cool he is, we finally sit down for some Dreamweaver talk. That's what this book's about—chillin' with coffee, Lenny, some background tunes, and big comfy couches.

NEW STUFF IN DREAMWEAVER 8

Wanna know what's up with the new version, Dreamweaver vets? Even if you're new to Dreamweaver, it's still a good idea to find out what's new and improved. While not a comprehensive list, here's some major stuff to look for.

Paste Special showdown: Dreamweaver now has a Paste Special command. This allows you to control the formatting of content being pasted onto the page. Things get sticky in "Retaining Formatting with Paste Special" in Chapter 5.

Synch up with site synchronization: When you're working with local and remote sites (that is, sites that are stored both on your computer and on a web server), keeping both updated and exactly the same can be tough. See "Sync Everything—Even the Kitchen Sink" in Chapter 14 for synching synchronicity.

Linking with root-relative paths: When setting hyperlinks, you can now use root-relative paths rather than Dreamweaver's default document-relative paths. The path to hyperlink mastery starts in Chapter 9.

Get a better look with the Zoom tool: Dreamweaver now lets you zoom in and out on your pages, making it easier to place and align objects more precisely.

Compile in style—The Style Rendering toolbar: Here's a useful tool. Use the Style Rendering toolbar to see how your page will look on different web-capable devices, like television sets, Blackberry devices, and computer projectors. Tool up in "One Eye on the Map: The Style Rendering Toolbar" in Chapter 2.

Life gets easy with the Coding toolbar: Code with ease using Dreamweaver's new Coding toolbar. Highlight invalid code, select parent tags, and adjust the way the code is viewed.

Get more done with background file transfer: In previous versions, Dreamweaver was out of commission when files were being transferred. With background file transfer, you can continue working while files are being moved. Get uploaded in "The End of Coffee Breaks—Forever!" in Chapter 4.

Go miles with comparing files: Can't remember what you did yesterday? Me neither. Now you can compare one file against another and view their differences—very handy if you find your local and remote sites get out of synch.

The deal with document tabs (Mac only): Rather than having separate floating document windows for each open file, Mac users can now enjoy something called document tabs, which Windows users have enjoyed for quite a while. Put it on your tab in "Document Tab Detour" in Chapter 2.

Workspace layout lowdown: Hate having to always reset and rearrange panels and toolbars? Save entire workspace arrangements in Dreamweaver with this handy little function.

Should I Be Reading This Book?

Is this book for you? If you're just getting started in web design, perhaps making the leap from the print world, you're in the right spot. Even zero experience will get you in the door. Or perhaps you're in a situation where you've been working in web design for a while, maybe with another program or even a previous version of Dreamweaver, and you already have some experience under your belt. If that's the case, there's lots here for you to pick up.

***Just the Gist* summarizes each chapter's material in a bulleted format, giving you just the main points.**

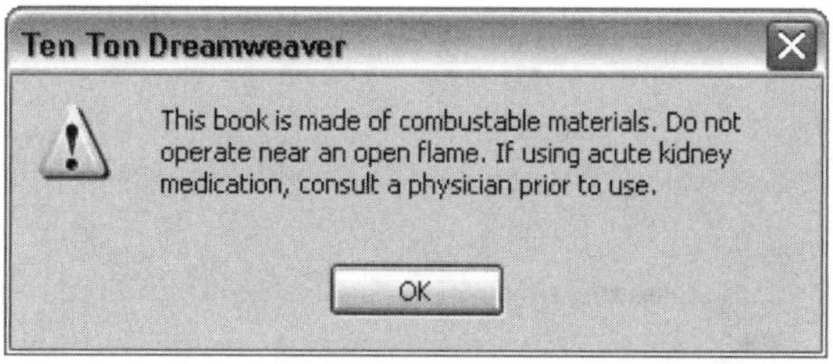

One other thing: A lot of authors want you to read from start to finish. Me, I don't care. Skip chapters, make notes in the margins, highlight stuff, dog-ear pages, destroy the book, read it backwards for demonic passages . . . whatever. The book is meant to adapt to your life, not the other way around. So rain down a firestorm of Post-it notes, paperclips, highlighters, and anything else that'll help you along the way. Read it on the subway, at church, during your kid's dance recital—wherever and whenever works for you.

Some people have an ego that weighs 10 tons. Could you imagine your head weighing that much? Why carry all that weight around? One wrong step and you're on your back, squirming like a turtle.

Stuff to Look For in Each Chapter

Each chapter opens in the same way: with a rundown of what the chapter covers and a table of contents for the chapter. If you wanna skip ahead to different parts (or skip the entire chapter), go for it.

The chapters themselves have lots of visual content—sidebars, notes, tips, and fun stuff all jammed in. One thing to watch out for is a recurring sidebar called Just the Gist. Just the Gist summarizes each chapter's material in a bulleted format, giving you just the main points. Use this sidebar as a reference to find the info you want on a particular topic.

Mark my words: With this book, you don't have to feel tied down—make every day your own personal casual Friday!

Just Three Icons to Remember

I remember thumbing through a book at a local computer training center. In the front was a full page describing all the icons used throughout the manual. There were tons. I should have done an official count, but there had to be at least 15 icons. A lot of them were the old standards. You know them: the light bulb, the graduation cap, the exclamation point, and so on. How original. Others were ridiculously complicated. A stopwatch beside a bomb, a happy face with a paintbrush, a box with an arrow going into it. So not only were readers faced with learning a new program, but they also had to memorize a bunch of goofy icons, too.

Ten Ton keeps things easy and simple. Even though there's a lot of visual content here, there are actually only three regularly occurring icons to remember:

Imminent Doom, a.k.a. The Skull and Crossbones. The deal: If something's gonna blow up, destroy your hard drive, or crash and burn all your hard work in a fiery heap, I'm gonna let you know ahead of time. Not so much so you can mentally prepare yourself, but so you can avoid it!

Noteworthy, a.k.a. The Dagger and Note. The deal: If there's some detail that's interesting, factual, or important, I'll highlight it with one of these guys. This could be where you'll want to dog-ear a page or jot a note in the margin.

Geek's Delight, a.k.a. The Geek. The deal: These icons point to information that, while technical and geeky, may be important to know. You'll see this icon when we're discussing why things work in certain ways or when you need to understand a particular component where a slightly tech-ish—though not too jargony—description is necessary.

OTHER THINGS YOU CAN DO WITH THIS BOOK

With so many possibilities, why limit yourself to just reading this book? Check out these crafty contraptions, or brainstorm your own!

Whatcha Do	Recommendation
Turn the book into a helmet. Open the book at about the halfway point; then, using a belt or bailer twine, fashion a chin strap to fix the opened book on top of your head. Add a cool tinted visor for a techy sci-fi look, or perhaps a plume.	If you're about to get into a head-on collision with a block of JavaScript code, what could be better for cranial protection than this book atop your lid?
Make double-ply paper towel. Carefully cut out all the pages and staple them to each other in groups of two, thus forming the double-ply. Next, daisy-chain them all together at their edges, one after another. Packing tape should hold. Finally, roll up all the pages and place in a handy spot.	A great idea in theory, but it lacks practicality. Imagine this: You wipe out while transporting your sloppy joes to the TV tray. You grab your extra-strength ***Ten Ton*** paper towel and cleanup's a snap. But the next day, you find yourself stumped on the Property Inspector—and it just so happens that the section you wanted was the one you used to sucked up your slop. Now that's a mess!
Build a squadron of paper airplane bombers. Again, this project involves carefully cutting out all the pages in the book. Once all the pages have been freed from their binding, stack them neatly to one side. Take the first page off the top and let the origami fun begin. Make sure folds are crisp and tight, and leave room for cool lightning bolt insignia and shark teeth on the nose cone.	Very labor intensive, although if you put in the time, you'll have air superiority over your entire office. In addition to the time required to build up such a huge strike force though, casualties in your paper Luftwaffe mean a loss in Dreamweaver learning. Consider a fleet of paper cranes instead.
Create laminated placemats. Using a craft knife (get an adult to help), cut away the front cover of your book. Then head down to the local copy store and run off a few color sets, and have the clerk laminate them in the thickest gauge your pocketbook can handle. Arrange appropriately on the dining room table. Wait 'til grandma sees!	Anything that helps get Dreamweaver into dinner conversation is a good thing. Prove to Mom and Dad that you're doing something worthwhile! Not only that, but you can review your Dreamweaver material over your Cheerios in the morning. How can you beat that?

Chapter 2

A Scenic Tour of the INTERFACE

STUFF YOU'LL LEARN IN THIS CHAPTER

Pack up the kids—it's time for a nice Sunday drive through rolling Dreamweaver countryside. There's a lot of scenery here, very picturesque, so we'll be sure to stop for postcards. In this chapter, you'll have a chance to get to know Dreamweaver a bit better as we tour the environment. You'll get a sense of what makes up the Dreamweaver workspace, how to customize the interface, and how to access commands. We'll definitely pull over for pictures. This will be your chance to see what all those blinky-flashy buttons and commands do in Dreamweaver's numerous panels, toolbars, and inspectors. And as we begin, if you feel like you're looking at what seems as cluttered and complicated as the cockpit of a Boeing, don't' fret—by the end of this chapter, you'll feel much more comfortable. So get packing those suitcases—we're goin' on a Dreamweaver getaway!

Heading Out on a Dreamweaver Expedition

Are you eager to get going? Or does the thought of learning Dreamweaver send you running with stomach-twisting pangs of terror? Relax and remember your breathing! When you're ready, let's get started.

In Windows, choose Start > All Programs > Macromedia > Dreamweaver 8, or double-click the Dreamweaver icon on your desktop, if you chose to place one there when you installed the program.

Mac users won't see this, but the first time that you launch the program in Windows, Dreamweaver presents you with the Workspace Setup dialog box. Here, you can choose how you want Dreamweaver's initial interface to be laid out: either in Designer mode or Coder mode. It doesn't really matter which way you go, because you can always change your workspace later. For the sake of this chapter, choose Designer for now (so that your screen is similar to the ones shown here) and click OK. Dreamweaver fires up.

Speaking of long road trips, did you know that classic rockers Journey received a star on the Hollywood Walk of Fame in 2005? Don't know who Journey is? Ask your parents. Or better yet, ask mine.

If you're using a Mac, double-click your hard drive's icon on the desktop, open your Applications folder, double-click the Macromedia Dreamweaver 8 folder, and double-click the Dreamweaver program icon. You can also double-click the Dreamweaver icon on your desktop, if you chose to place one there when you installed the program. Dreamweaver launches by displaying its splash screen. You'll have a few moments to daydream here—then it's back to our road trip!

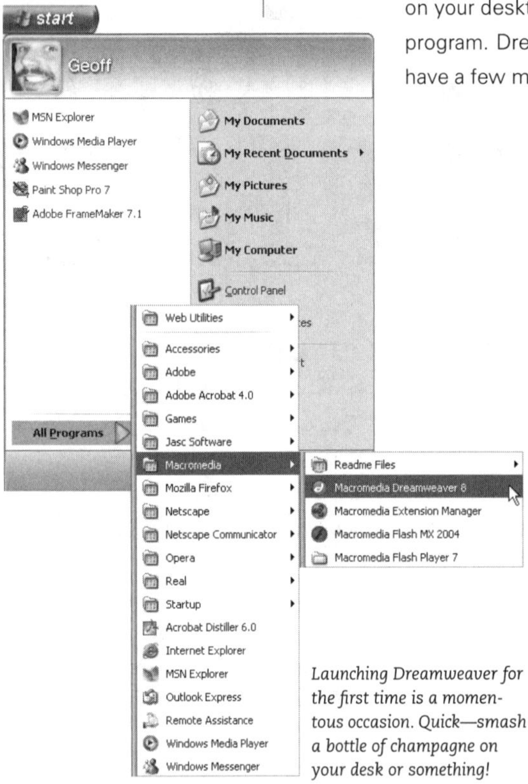

Launching Dreamweaver for the first time is a momentous occasion. Quick—smash a bottle of champagne on your desk or something!

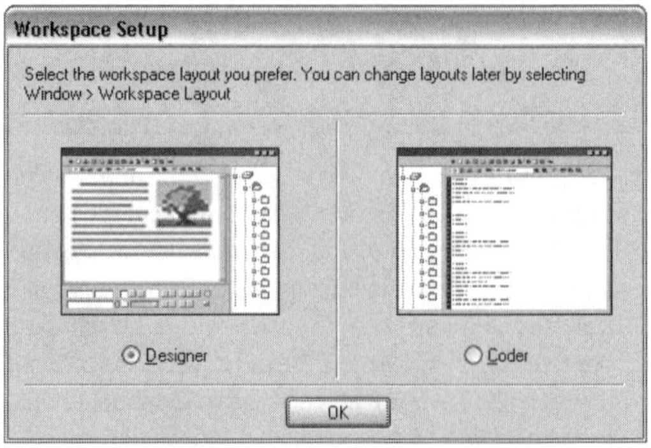

In Windows, when you launch Dreamweaver for the first time, you'll be presented with this Workspace Setup dialog box. It doesn't really matter which of the two options you choose, because you can customize the interface later.

NOTEWORTHY

If you're upgrading from a previous version of Dreamweaver and still have that old version installed, Dreamweaver 8 will automatically import any sites that you've previously defined. However, you'll have to re-enter any usernames and passwords for your sites in the Site Definition dialog box.

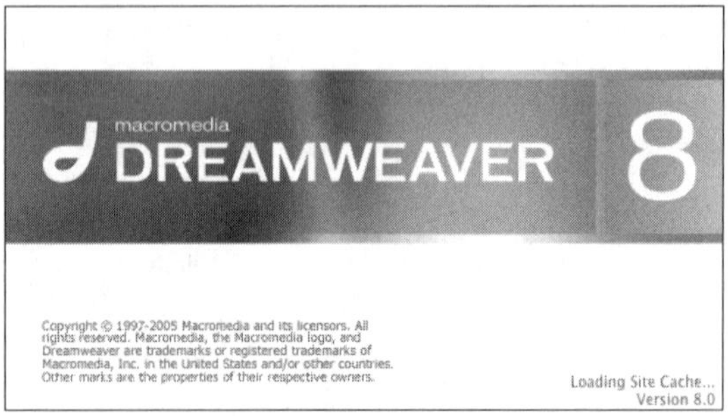

Dreamweaver's launch screen. Feel the anticipation build!

A Trip Through Dreamweaver's Start Page

Once Dreamweaver is running, the Start Page appears—the first stop on our journey. Here, you can either open an existing file or create a new, blank document. As you can see, the Start Page is made up of three main columns: Open a Recent Item, Create New, and Create from Samples.

From Dreamweaver's Start Page, you can either open an existing file or create a new blank document.

If you've been opening and playing with files a little bit, you'll see your most recently used files listed in the Open a Recent Item column. The next column, Create New, lists many of the document types that Dreamweaver can handle, such as JavaScript, PHP, and XML. The last column of the Start Page lists sample document types that come with Dreamweaver, called Design Files, which are a great place to start when building your new pages.

Dreamweaver ships with several online tutorials, which are great for getting your feet wet if you're just getting started in web design.

At the bottom of the Start Page window, you'll see that you can take a Dreamweaver-led tour or run through a tutorial. If you're a Dreamweaver newbie, you'll find the tutorials very helpful for getting started.

At this point, you might find the list of options daunting, particularly in the Create New list—an Acronym Dream Team of possibilities—but for this chapter, choose HTML to start a blank web page.

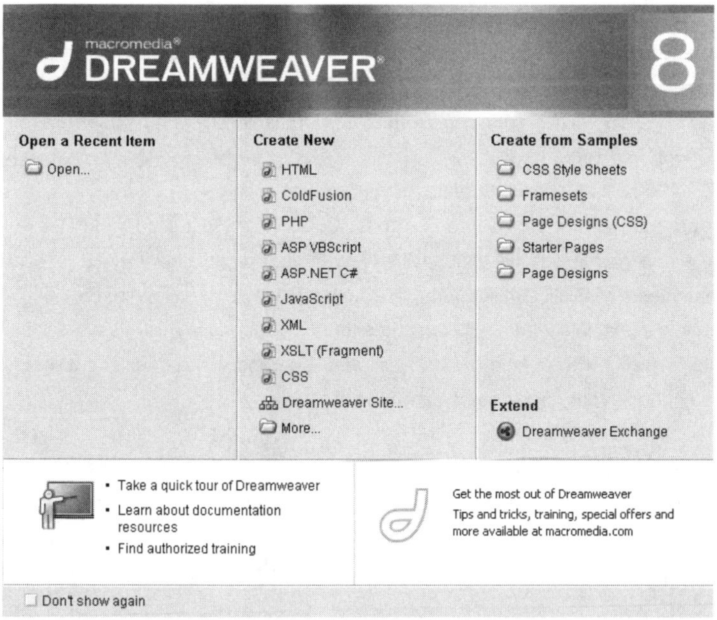

The Start Page, where you can begin a new document based on a variety of technologies, create a page based on a Dreamweaver sample, or even dig into a few tutorials if you're new to all this.

Surveying the Dreamweaver Landscape

If you're running Dreamweaver on Windows, by default all your panels and toolbars are docked.

Once you've created a blank HTML page from Dreamweaver's Start Page, you're ready to tour the main interface. The Dreamweaver window has lots of scenery—panels, toolbars, and inspectors—all waiting to get to know you. Especially note the Insert and Document toolbars at the top, the Property Inspector at the bottom, and the column of panels on the right. The main viewing area is where the current page is displayed. At the top of the window, you'll see the Dreamweaver title bar. This displays the path to where the file is saved (called the document path), the name of the document, and also the technology being used (XHTML by default in Dreamweaver).

On the Mac, all the panels and other window elements float over everything else on your screen.

As usual, the scenery will differ a little depending on whether you're on Windows or Mac. In Windows, by default all your panels and toolbars are docked—that is, they're attached to the sides of your screen. Later you'll see how to undock the panels, move them around, and begin to customize your workspace a little more.

On the Mac, all the panels and other window elements float over everything else on your screen, just as in any other program on the Mac. Again, later you'll see how to rearrange the elements on your screen.

Everybody Outta the Car—It's the Document Toolbar!

The Document toolbar, which appears by default at the top of the Dreamweaver window, contains several buttons and pop-up menus to assist you in managing sites, previewing your work, giving your page a title, and uploading files. It has some tools for working with raw code, too.

Most important is the first set of three buttons: Code View, Split (Code and Design) View, and Design View. Each will change the view of your page, allowing you to work in a way that suits you. We'll talk about these three page views later. Toward the middle of the toolbar is a text field where you can add a title for your page. This title will appear in the visitor's web browser title bar and will also be used when your site is bookmarked—so choose your page names carefully!

If you'd like to turn off the Document toolbar, choose View > Toolbars or right-click (Windows) or Control-click (Mac) any other toolbar. Repeat this process to bring it back.

THE DREAMWEAVER ENVIRONMENT (WINDOWS VERSION)

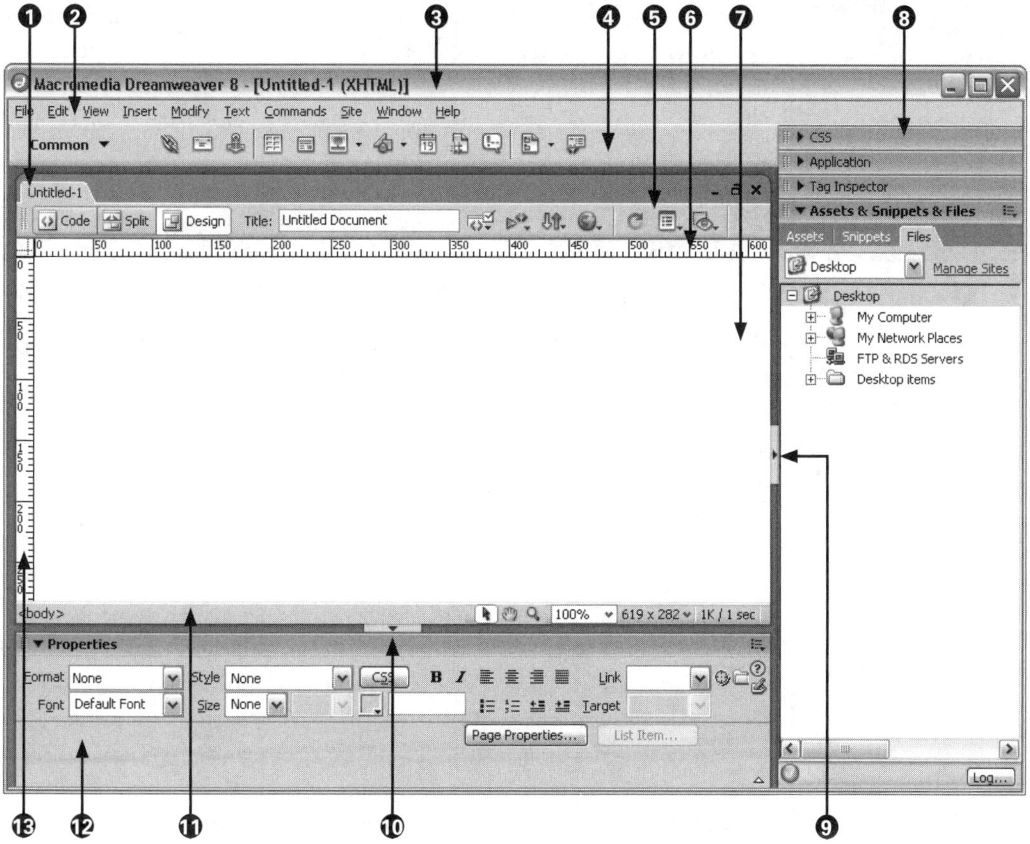

(1) Document tabs **(2)** Menu bar **(3)** Title bar **(4)** Insert toolbar **(5)** Document toolbar **(6)** Horizontal ruler **(7)** Current document **(8)** Panel groups **(9)** Expand/Collapse horizontally (Windows only) **(10)** Expand/Collapse vertically (Windows only) **(11)** Status bar **(12)** Property Inspector **(13)** Vertical ruler

THE DOCUMENT TOOLBAR

(1) Show Code View **(2)** Show Split (Code and Design) View **(3)** Show Design View **(4)** Document Title field **(5)** Check Errors **(6)** Validate Markup **(7)** File Management **(8)** Preview/Debug in Browser **(9)** Refresh Design View **(10)** View Options **(11)** Visual Aids

25-Mile Rest Stop: The Insert Bar

To toggle the Insert toolbar off and on, choose Window > Insert from the main Dreamweaver menu bar.

The Insert bar also appears by default at the top of your screen. This toolbar contains groups of layout elements organized into categories, which are available from the pull-down menu on the left. The Insert bar is one of the most common means of placing images, tables, form elements, scripts, and all kinds of other objects on your page. In fact, think of it as your Swiss Army knife, packed full of diverse tools for a variety of purposes.

THE INSERT BAR

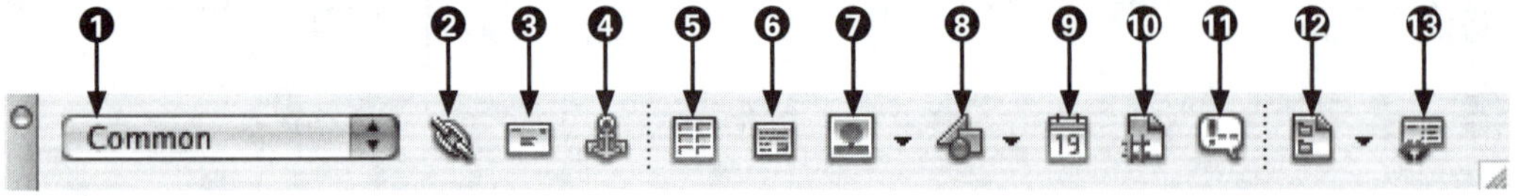

(1) Category menu **(2)** Hyperlink **(3)** E-mail Link **(4)** Named Anchor **(5)** Table **(6)** Insert Div Tag **(7)** Images **(8)** Media **(9)** Date **(10)** Server-Side Include **(11)** Comment **(12)** Templates **(13)** Tag Chooser

The Insert bar has two modes: a menu mode (what you're looking at right now), and a tabbed mode. Both allow you to insert the same objects; the only difference is the way the bar is organized. You may find the tabbed mode a bit easier to use. If you'd like to try it, choose Show as Tabs from the pull-down menu. Now you can move through the Insert bar's categories using the tabs that appear across the top, and even expand and collapse the toolbar by using the arrow that appears in the top-left corner. If you want to go back to the menu mode, in addition to toggling the menu option, you can right-click (Windows) or Control+click (Mac) the tabs at the top and choose Show as Menu.

Whichever mode you prefer, remember that the Insert bar is a multipurpose tool for building your pages—so keep an eye out for it as you make your way through the remaining chapters.

Stick or Automatic? The Standard Toolbar

The Standard toolbar contains buttons similar to those found in Microsoft Word and Excel. If you're familiar with either of those programs, this will be a road-trip cake walk. The toolbar contains common buttons for creating a new document, opening, saving, undoing, and performing other typical commands.

THE STANDARD TOOLBAR

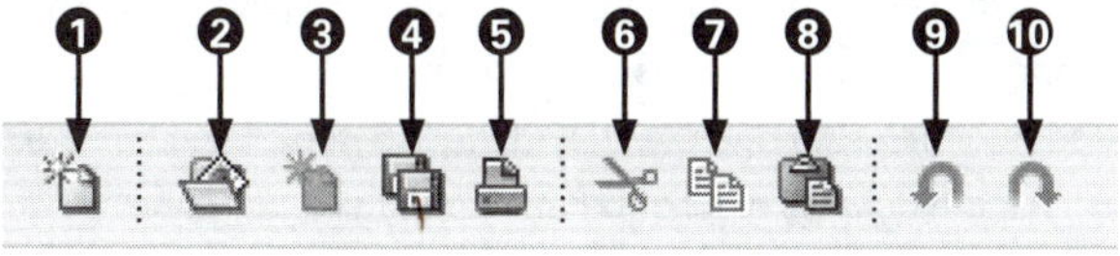

(1) New **(2)** Open **(3)** Save **(4)** Save All **(5)** Print Code
(6) Cut **(7)** Copy **(8)** Paste **(9)** Undo **(10)** Redo

If you want to use the Standard toolbar, you'll have to turn it on first. Choose View > Toolbars > Standard. Or just right-click (Windows) or Control-click (Mac) either the Insert or Document toolbar at the top of the screen and choose Standard from the contextual menu that appears. You'll also be able to show or hide any of the other toolbars that Dreamweaver has to offer from this same menu.

When you right-click (Windows) or Control+click (Mac) a toolbar, you'll see the toolbar contextual menu. The checked toolbars are open.

Two commands worth taking a closer look at are Print Code and Save All. Print Code is a handy function for, well, printing your page's code. The Save All command saves all your open files in one shot, which is very handy. When you use Save All, a Save As dialog box appears for any open documents that have not yet been saved. We'll talk more about saving in the sidebar "Saving Savvy" in Chapter 5.

Personally, I don't use the Standard toolbar, but rely on keyboard shortcuts instead.

Into the Status Bar Countryside

The Status bar at the bottom of the Dreamweaver window relays information about the current page and download speeds and also includes a few navigation and selection tools, some of which are new to Dreamweaver 8.

THE STATUS BAR

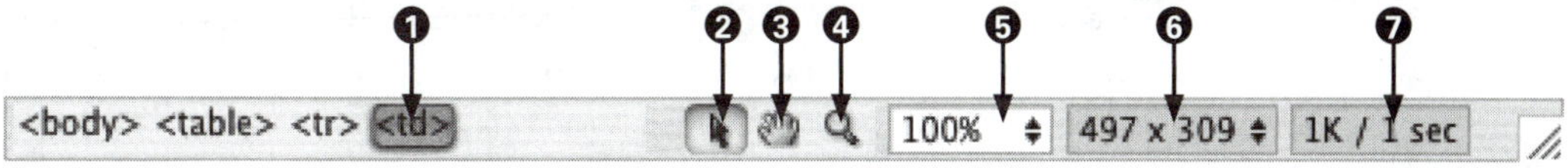

(1) Tag Selector **(2)** Select tool **(3)** Hand tool **(4)** Zoom tool **(5)** Set Magnification **(6)** Window Size **(7)** Load Time

At the far left of the Status bar, you'll see the Tag Selector, one of the most useful components in the Dreamweaver interface. The Tag Selector keeps track of your cursor position on the page, and you can also use it to select blocks of HTML code. At this point, it will say only <body>, because there's nothing on your page. But once you start building layouts—adding tables, images, text, and the like—you'll see this area fill with tag blocks. Clicking a tag block will highlight that element on your page.

> **NOTEWORTHY**
>
> If you're a Windows user and you've maximized your Dreamweaver project window, you won't be able to resize it (all your resolution choices will be grayed out).

Toward the right side of the Status bar, you'll see the Select, Hand, and Zoom tools, which allow you to zoom in on your page, navigate, and work with objects. These tools work pretty much the same way as similar tools you may have worked with in page layout or graphics programs.

At the bottom right of the Status bar are the Window Size menu and the load time indicator—great tools that give you an idea of how your page will look at different monitor resolutions and how long your page will take to download and open at different modem speeds. To change the monitor resolution, just choose a size from the Window Size pull-down menu, and the Dreamweaver window resizes. You can also customize the window sizes and the download speed through the Status bar preferences (choose Edit > Preferences in Windows or Dreamweaver > Preferences on the Mac), although you may want to leave the default connection speed set to 56k. Even though 56k isn't reflective of modern connection speeds, if your download time is good at this speed, it'll blaze at warp factor 8 on anything faster.

To be honest, I don't use either the monitor resolution or connection speed settings. I rely on my results when I vigorously test my sites once they're live online. In other words, I check different window sizes and download times manually. However, if you want to use these settings, go for it.

Document Tab Detour

Document tabs, which are turned on by default, appear in a row across the top of your screen. When you have more than one file open at a time, each file is given a tab. This makes switching between your open files fast and easy, and the tabs help keep your workspace tidy and uncluttered.

> **NOTEWORTHY**
>
> If monitor resolution is a new concept for you, then definitely check out "Metric? Imperial? It's All about Pixels and Browsers Now"—in Chapter 3.

If you want to turn off this tabbed environment and have your open documents appear in separate windows, choose Window > Cascade. Each document will now have its own window, and the tabs will disappear. To revert to a tabbed workspace, click the document window's Maximize button (Windows) or choose Window > Combine as Tabs (Mac).

ONE EYE ON THE MAP: THE STYLE RENDERING TOOLBAR

Most of us build our web sites to be viewed on a computer screen. However, with the explosion of Internet-capable gadgetry like cell phones, Palm Pilots, and WebTV, who knows what folks might be using to view your site—which opens up a whole range of issues. It's hard enough to build sites that look decent in the various web browsers available these days, but now you have to wrestle with these new web-ready devices, too. It's a recipe for an asylum vacation.

Check out smartwebby.com/web_site_design/dreamweaver_tips.asp for tons of Dreamweaver tricks!

Dreamweaver's new Style Rendering toolbar saves the day (and your sanity). This handy little fella will give you an idea of how your page will appear on different media displays, including handheld devices, printers, and television sets. To turn on this toolbar, choose View > Toolbars > Style Rendering. You'll see buttons for switching to different output types, and you'll even be able to toggle the display of Cascading Style Sheets. It's always important to preview your work to see how it will appear, and it's much easier with Dreamweaver's Style Rendering toolbar.

NOTEWORTHY

Try right-clicking (Windows) or Control-clicking (Mac) a file's tab. You'll see a pop-up menu with some helpful options such as Close All, Close Others, and Save All.

THE STYLE RENDERING TOOLBAR

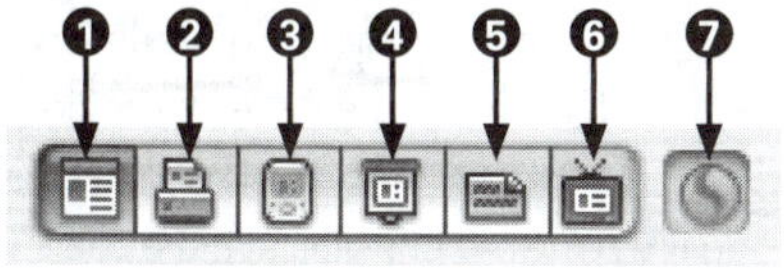

(1) Render Screen Media Type **(2)** Render Print Media Type **(3)** Render Handheld Media Type **(4)** Render Projection Media Type **(5)** Render TTY Media Type **(6)** Render TV Media Type **(7)** Toggle display of CSS styles

A word of caution, though: Because web-ready technology is so new, those who are jumping into it are not expecting sites to look perfect on their Blackberries and cell phones. Besides, most of your visitors will be viewing your site from a computer. The point here is that while it's good to keep these new gadgets in mind, don't murder yourself trying to build the perfect site that'll run on any conceivable device. That's a one-way trip to the loony bin for sure. In the next few chapters, we'll talk more about building sites that are compatible with today's most popular computers, browsers, and settings, so stick around to see what's involved.

Road Trip Toolbox: The Property Inspector

The Property Inspector is the heart and soul of Dreamweaver. It's a dashboard of controls, where you can set fonts, manipulate tables, set hyperlinks, and much, much more. What's great about the Property Inspector is that it's contextual—that is, its commands change to reflect whatever you select on the page. Want to adjust an image? No problem, just select it on the page and look in the Property Inspector. Adjusting a table? Select away and then look down below. Neat, huh?

Dreamweaver's Property Inspector is your dashboard of controls for manipulating content.

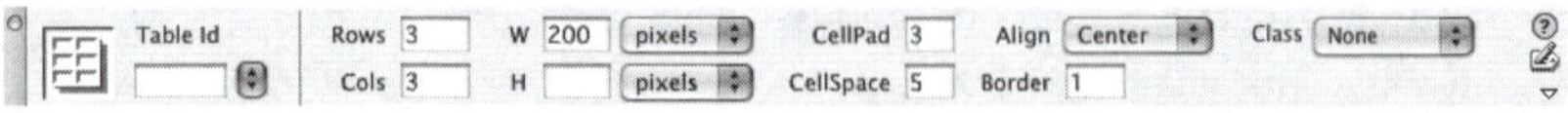

When a table is selected, the Property Inspector offers the most common table manipulation options.

The Property Inspector gives you the most common options for the selected content, though you might not see all options at first glance. To see more options for each category, click the expander arrow at the bottom right of the inspector. Another way to expand the Property Inspector is to double-click anywhere in an empty gray spot.

NOTEWORTHY

To move the Property Inspector around, just drag the vertical bar on the left side.

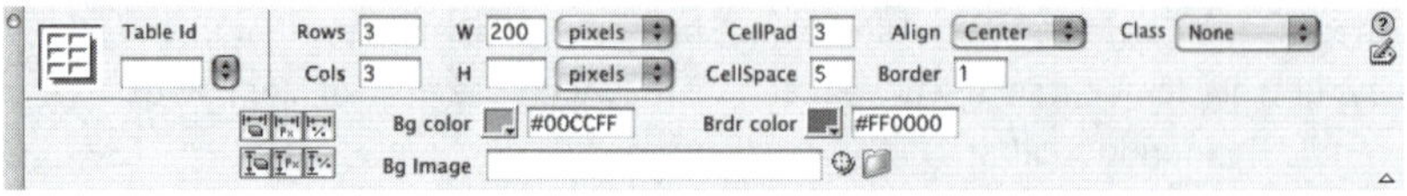

Here's the Property Inspector with the same table selected, but now in expanded mode. Look at all those additional options—see what happens when you keep drinking your milk, kids?

NOTEWORTHY

If you accidentally close the Property Inspector, just choose Window > Properties to resuscitate it.

If you're using Dreamweaver on the Windows platform, the Property Inspector is docked at the bottom of the screen by default. If you want the inspector to float over your page instead, drag the dotted gripper area in the top-left corner to pull the inspector free. To put the inspector back, just drag it downward until you see the black frame indicating that it's about to dock; then release the mouse button. You can even dock the Property Inspector at the top of your screen if you like, by dragging it upward.

Setting Vistas with Document Views

As you saw earlier, Dreamweaver's Document toolbar offers three ways to view your work in the main window: Code view, Split (Code and Design) view, and Design view. You may be relieved to find that you don't have to hand code at all with Dreamweaver, in which case you can stick with Design view. But if you've got the iron stomach needed to get under the hood and tinker with code, you definitely can work that way, too.

Dreamweaver offers three ways to view work: Code view, Split (Code and Design) view, and Design view.

To switch views, click the three buttons at the far left of the Document toolbar. If you want to work entirely in a code environment, go for Code view. If you're more of a visual person, then Design view might suit you better. Even though I prefer visual layout, quite often I find myself using Split view, so that I can work in the code and see the layout as I go. In Split view, when you select a page element in the layout, the corresponding code highlights, too—great, huh?

A look at Dreamweaver's Split view: Code view on the top, Design view on the bottom.

> **NOTEWORTHY**
>
> Try pressing Ctrl+~ (Windows) or Command+~ (Mac) to flip between the document views. The tilde key is the squiggly guy underneath the Esc key.

Dreamweaver's online help is very thorough and is an invaluable resource for web designers.

Help: Your Emergency Roadside Assistance

Dreamweaver's online help is very good. It's thorough and serves as an invaluable resource when things get tricky.

To get help is very simple. Choose Help > Using Dreamweaver. You'll then be presented with a window where you can search, use the index, and so on. If you're really new at web design, choose Getting Started and Tutorials from the Help menu to get a feel for the road and log some mileage with Dreamweaver.

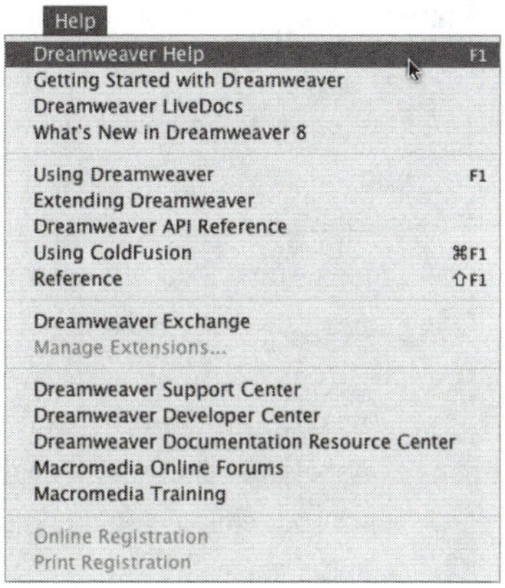

Mayday! Mayday! Thankfully, help is only a few clicks away.

> **NOTEWORTHY**
>
> Before sounding the alarm and having panic ensue, press F1 to activate Dreamweaver's online help. Then rest easy and search for your answer.

Taking in the Panel Panorama

Panels contain many commands that relate to specific tasks in *Dreamweaver*.

Now let's take a look at Dreamweaver's vast array of panels, all available from the Window menu. By default, panels are grouped in a column on the right side of the screen. Panels contain many commands that relate to specific tasks in Dreamweaver, such as working with Cascading Style Sheets or with the files for your site. If you've worked with other graphics programs, then the concept of panels may be familiar.

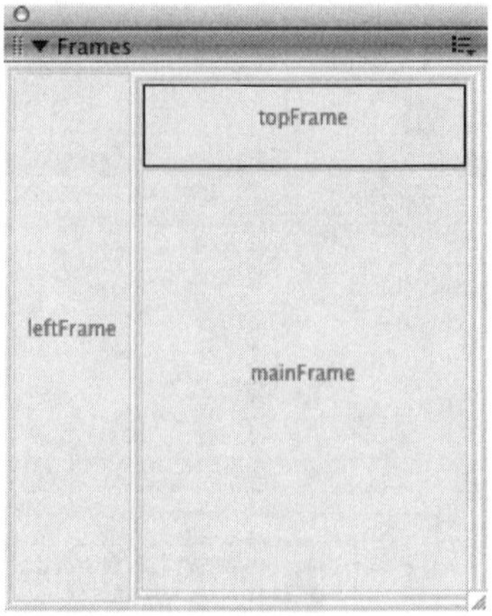

The Frames panel, poised for heavy page layout action.

A Traveler's Guide to Dreamweaver Panels

Ever notice how tomatoes look like really mad oranges?

Sorting out panels in Dreamweaver can be a little confusing, because at times there seems to be no consistency in how they've been organized. Some panels sit on their own, while others are a part of what are referred to as panel groups. Still others look and smell like panels, but are actually called inspectors. Confused? Take a nap and come back.

The panel descriptions that follow begin at the top of the Window menu and proceed on down:

CSS Styles (Window > CSS Styles or Shift+F11): You can use the CSS Styles panel to create, edit, and delete internal and external style sheets.

Layers (Window > Layers or F2): As mentioned in the first chapter, layers allow you to position objects wherever you want on your page.

Behaviors allow you to add a lot of interactivity to your page—and you do it all right here.

Behaviors (Window > Behaviors or Shift+F4): Whoa, Sally! This is where the good stuff is. Here you can add all sorts of interactive JavaScript functionality to your page…without knowing JavaScript!

Files (Window > Files or F8): The Files panel lets you view and manage the files—both local and remote—for your site. This is one of the most important panels Dreamweaver has to offer.

Assets (Window > Assets or F11 [Windows], Option+F11 [Mac]): The Assets panel contains all the elements and components that you've set up for your site, including graphics, Macromedia Flash files, templates, scripts, and color—very cool.

Snippets (Window > Snippets or Shift+F9): Snippets are huge timesavers. Use this panel to insert code for common page items such as tables, headers, and navigation elements.

Tag Inspector (Window > Tag Inspector or F9 [Windows], Option+F9 [Mac]): The Tag Inspector contains the Behaviors panel (described earlier) plus the Attributes panel. The Attributes panel lists the tags you've used on your page and also allows you to make changes to the tags' attributes.

GEEK'S DELIGHT

Have money to burn? Consider purchasing a second monitor to hold Dreamweaver's many panels. This way, they won't be getting in the way while you work, but they'll still be easily accessible. Your friends might think you're a geek, but it'll be so sweet!

Results (Window > Results or F7): The Results panel lets you perform several commands at the site level—for example, you can perform a sitewide Find and Replace operation or check your site in popular web browsers.

Reference (Window > Reference or Shift+F1): The Reference panel is a built-in resource for looking up definitions of code blocks. Remember that we discussed this briefly when we talked about Dreamweaver's online help? Use the Reference panel to find out what a particular piece of code does, how it works within a page, and much more. It's an incredible resource.

History (Window > History or Shift+F10): Are you familiar with History in Photoshop? Same deal. If you're not into Photoshop, here's the scoop: The History panel tracks all your movements as you work. You can then use the panel as a sort of über-undo, and even save steps as a command—sort of like a macro. Great for those repetitive tasks that even the intern refuses to do.

Not only is History Dreamweaver's mega-undo, but you can also use it when you create macros.

Frames (Window > Frames or Shift+F2): Unless you're working with a frameset, the Frames panel will come up blank. Once you've actually built a frameset, you'll see how the Frames panel helps you keep organized and also make changes to your frames-based layouts.

Code Inspector (Window > Code Inspector or F10 [Windows], Option+F10 [Mac]): The Code Inspector gives you another way to view the source code behind your page. If you've set yourself up with two monitors, you can have Dreamweaver's Design view on the main screen and the Code Inspector stretched out nice and big on the other. That way, you can see your visual layout and your code at the same time—an awesome way to work.

Timelines (Window > Timelines or Alt+F9 [Windows], Option+F9 [Mac]): Timelines allow you to control the movement and timing of objects on the page. Have logos zoom across your page or have a layer slowly scroll downward. It's fun stuff.

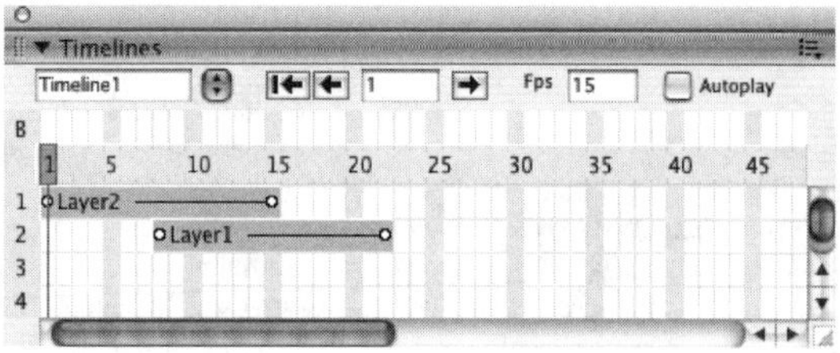

Dreamweaver's Timelines panel, always ready to add animation to your pages.

Exploring the Locale: Managing and Customizing Panels

If you live in a town where the local roadhouse has heifer, wild, nest, or "...and plumbing" in its name, it's time to move.

The panels are all organized into panel groups based on tasks. For example, the Files panel is grouped with Assets because both handle sitewide tasks. Or the Reference panel is grouped with Snippets as these two panels provide assistance with source code. The active panel is the one in the group with the tab at the top. To open another panel in the group, try clicking its name, which is also at the top. When your mouse hovers over a panel name, it will become underlined (Windows) or bold (Mac), indicating that the panel's ready to come out and play. You can expand and collapse panel groups to make way for other panels or simply to open up your workspace. Just click the twisty arrow or the name of the panel group (both at the top of the panel), and the entire group collapses. Click again, and the group expands.

NOTEWORTHY

Too many panels getting in your way? Press F4 to temporarily hide all of Dreamweaver's panels and inspectors. Press F4 again to bring everything back.

COMMON PANEL ELEMENTS

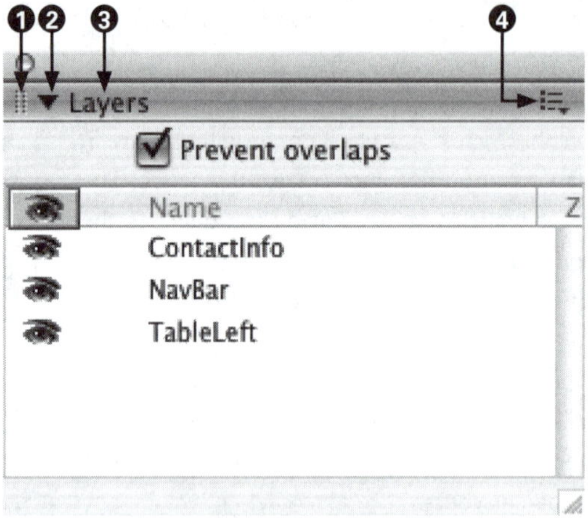

(1) Gripper handle **(2)** Expand/Collapse arrow
(3) Panel name **(4)** Panel Options menu

In Windows only, the panels are docked, or connected, to the right side of the screen, as we discussed earlier. If you want to free up a bit of screen real estate, try clicking the Expand/Collapse arrow on the border that divides the panels from the main work area. This collapses all the panels to the right and opens up the work space. Click that same arrow, and the panels expand back. If you want to expand your work area vertically, click the Collapse/Expand arrow just above the Property Inspector.

In Windows, Dreamweaver provides a horizontal and vertical Collapse/Expand button so you can easily increase your workspace.

If you want to close a panel group, choose Close Panel Group from the Option menu, found in the top-right corner of the panel. To open a panel again, choose the panel name from the Window menu.

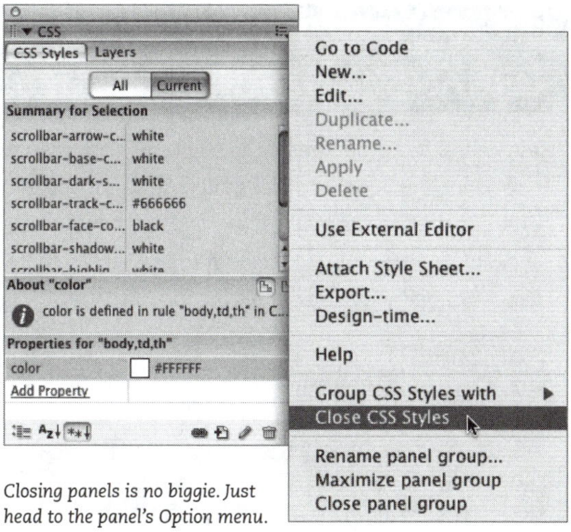

Closing panels is no biggie. Just head to the panel's Option menu.

Also, you can always tear away panels from the main group by dragging the gripper area in the top-left corner of the panel and dragging toward the middle of the screen. Voilà—a floating panel. If you want, you can even have a combination of floating and docked panels in your interface. Personally, I'm not a big fan of docked panels. I don't like having all the panels jammed together in a narrow column, especially for panels like Files and Assets, which require a little more elbow room.

After a panel has been torn away, try making it larger by dragging any of the four sides (Windows) or the bottom-right corner (Mac).

To redock a floating panel, just drag it back into the docked panels. Dreamweaver indicates with a black frame (Windows) or blue line (Mac) that the panel is about to be docked. And in Windows, you can even dock panels on the left side of the screen. Oooo!

To stretch out a panel to its full size, right-click (Windows) or Control+click (Mac) a panel's title bar and choose Maximize Panel Group.

NOTEWORTHY

To make working with panels easier, I pull all my panels apart so that they float on their own. Then I turn off the display of any that I don't use on a regular basis to free up my workspace.

NOTEWORTHY

Dreamweaver's so flexible, it'll even let you rename panel groups. Go to the panel's Option menu and choose Rename Panel Group. Y'all can even use cuss words if ya like.

NOTEWORTHY

Once you've organized Dreamweaver's interface to your liking, save your arrangement as a workspace layout.

TRAVELING IN GROUPS: ORGANIZING PANEL GROUPS

You can always reorganize the layout of your workspace. If you want to move one panel into another panel group, go to that panel's Option menu and choose Group [panel name] With; then select a new panel group from the menu that appears. For example, to move the Files panel into the CSS panel, go to the Files panel Option menu and choose Group Files With > CSS.

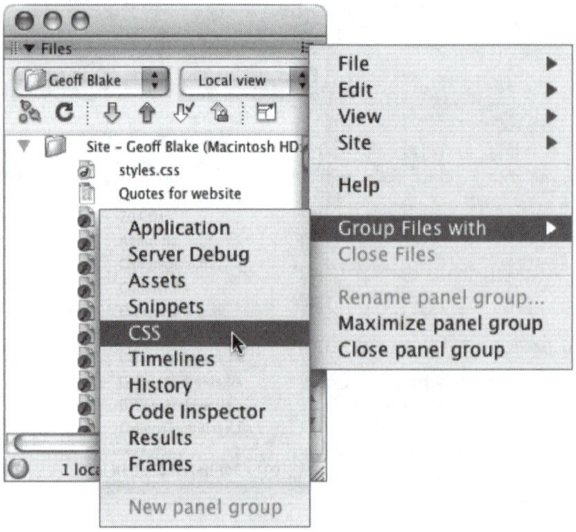

You can organize your panels any way you like. Here, Files and CSS are about to make a love connection.

You can also reach commands in Dreamweaver through the menus.

You can even create your own custom panel groups. Without getting too loopy here, try going to a panel's Option menu and, from the Group With submenu, choose New Panel Group. This creates a new, undocked panel group to which you can add other panels.

NOTEWORTHY

Another great way to access common commands in Dreamweaver (or any program for that matter) is to use contextual menus—that is, the good old right-click (Windows) or Command-click (Mac).

Stopping for Lunch: A Look at Dreamweaver's Menus

You can get to the commands and functions you're after in Dreamweaver in many ways. You've already taken a look at Dreamweaver's toolbars and panels, but you can also reach commands through the menus. There are many options hiding in the menus, so keep your eyes open as we take a quick hike through them to see what's in store—and make sure you're wearing comfy shoes!

The File menu is always at the ready to assist with common functions.

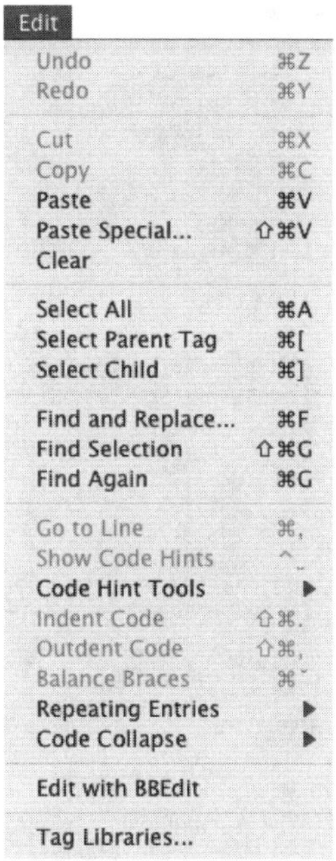

Edit provides many features, some you may already be familiar with.

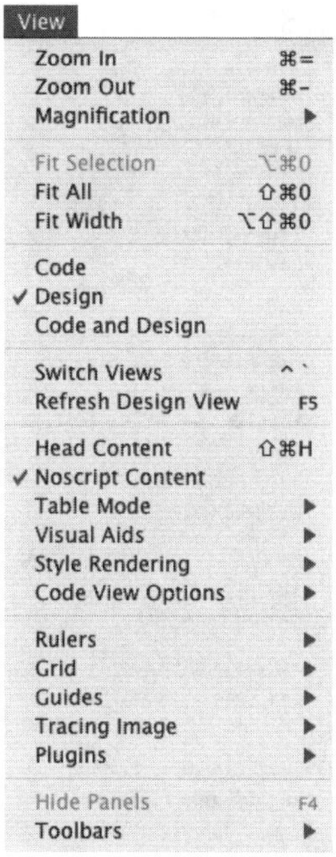

If it's related to display, it's on the View menu.

NOTEWORTHY

One of the most common commands on the Edit menu is Undo. By default, Dreamweaver lets you undo your 50 most recent actions (also called History Steps — remember the History panel?), but if you think you may be too accident prone, you can change this to another number. Choose Edit > Preferences (Windows) or Dreamweaver > Preferences (Mac) and click the General category on the left.

File menu: In addition to the File menu regulars, such as New, Open, and Save, this menu offers handy commands such as Preview in Browser and the Check commands on the Check Page submenu. Use these options to see how your page appears in popular browsers and to have Dreamweaver check various components of your page respectively.

Edit menu: The Edit menu also offers a lot of regulars. Undo, Copy, and Paste are all here, as well as Find and Replace and Tag Libraries.You'll also find a batch of selection commands, as well as a few other handy tools for working with code, such as Code Hints and Code Collapse.

View menu: The View menu contains the commands for controlling the visibility of many Dreamweaver elements, such as rulers, guides, and panels, and lots of other good stuff, such as zooming, the Table Mode, and the workspace view commands. If it's related to display, chances are it's on the View menu.

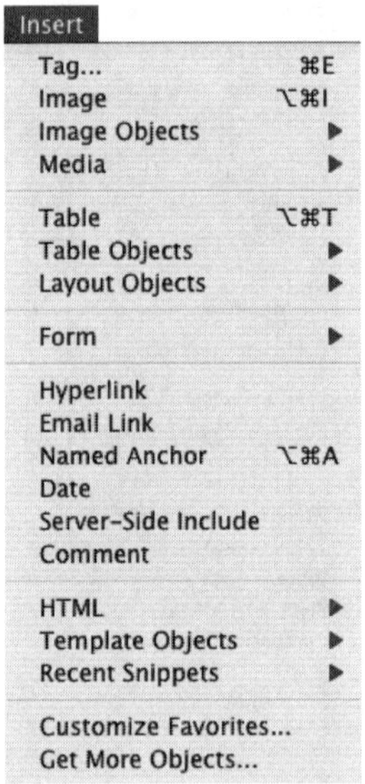

The Insert menu is all about getting different types of content onto your page—but this is just one of several methods.

The Modify menu is always ready to help manipulate selected page elements, such as tables and templates.

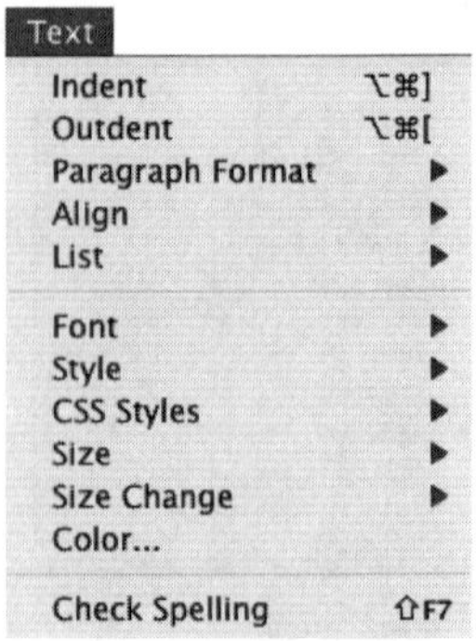

Handle your text with ease with the Text menu.

Insert menu: Getting content placed on your page couldn't be easier with the Insert menu. You'll find it all there—images, media elements, tables, forms, and on and on. In many ways, the Insert menu options mirror those available on the Insert bar, so you can use whichever approach you prefer to insert your page content. Check out the Tag option, which fires up the Tag Chooser (this allows you to pop in code for common page elements), or Template Objects, which opens up the vast world of Dreamweaver templates.

Modify menu: The Modify menu is similar to the Property Inspector in that it allows you to make changes to selected page content, but there're also some additional commands you may find useful, like the table, template and frameset options, for example. Further, the first command, Page Properties, will let you specify settings for the current page.

Text menu: If you want to modify text on your page, the Text menu is the place to be. Changing font, size, and color options couldn't be easier, and this is where you'll find the Spell Checker, too. Also use this menu to handle your HTML heading tags and your Cascading Style Sheets.

Take the repetitiveness out of everyday tasks with the Commands menu.

It's all about setting up a site ahead of time, and that's where the Site menu comes in.

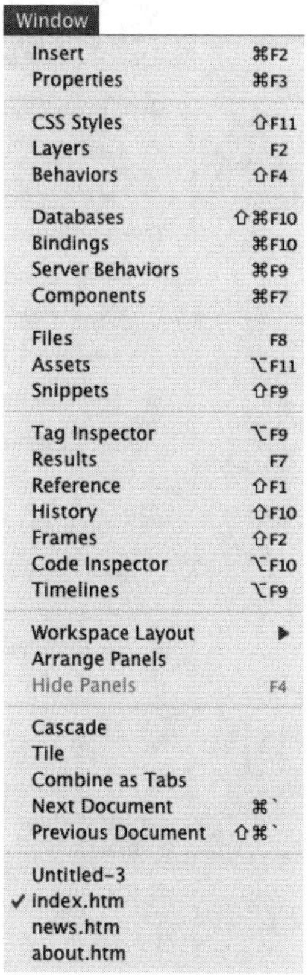

The Window menu: where panels go when they're on vacation—plus a few other nifty goodies.

Commands menu: The Commands menu ties into the History panel. As discussed earlier, you can use the History panel to create and save commands—a process similar to creating macros. The Commands menu is where you actually do this. Record commands, edit them, and run some preexisting commands, too.

Site menu: The Site menu may seem short, but it's a big subject. Pack an overnight bag and head for Chapter 4, where we really get into it. Essentially, you'll be using this menu to create new sites, edit existing ones, and upload your work.

Window menu: As you saw in the previous section, the Window menu stores all of Dreamweaver's panels. It also has a few other goodies packed in. For example, you'll find a handful of commands for managing open documents and for saving and organizing workspaces.

Help menu: As discussed earlier, the Help menu is where you get assistance with Dreamweaver. Dreamweaver's online help is packed with great content in an easy-to-navigate format. If you're a newbie, definitely check out Dreamweaver's built-in tutorials.

Never feel left alone again. The Help menu is your warm blanket on a stormy day.

JUST THE GIST

Dreamweaver's Start Page

- Use the Start Page to open an existing file or to create a new document.

The Toolbars and Inspectors

- The Standard toolbar contains buttons for common commands such as Open, Save, and Undo.
- The Document toolbar contains buttons and pop-up menus to assist you with managing sites, previewing your work, and uploading files.
- The Insert bar contains categories of web elements that you can place on your page.
- Use the navigation tools on the Status bar to zoom in and out.
- The Property Inspector offers you a dashboard of controls.

Getting Help

- If you're new to Dreamweaver, make use of the tutorials available from the Help menu.

Panels

- Panels provide a way to access commands for specific Dreamweaver functions.
- The layout and organization of panels is always customizable.
- If you've closed a panel and want to reopen it, you can do so from the Window menu.
- Every panel has a keyboard shortcut that can be used to open it.

Dreamweaver's Menus

- Menus provide an easy and fast way to reach common commands.
- Many toolbar and panel commands can also be found as menu items.

Chapter 3

Designing a *Site from* Scratch

STUFF YOU'LL LEARN IN THIS CHAPTER

Site planning and file structure can get a little cranial, but it's really important to know this stuff to build efficient, well-designed web sites. This chapter will help cure any web-induced migraine, so stay tuned. We'll start where all planning should start—with coffee. Then we'll talk about your site's audience, have a look at some typical navigation models, try to quantify the various types of web sites, and look at a typical site construction workflow. After that's squared away, we'll talk navigation design and page layout and then wrap up with a discussion of how to structure and organize your site's files. So pass the head cheese and let's go!

Prepare to Plan to Prepare for a Development Plan

Nobody ever wants to plan anymore. People don't have the time. They just want to get going. It's like that scene in *Spaceballs* where Dark Helmet says to Colonel Sandurz, "What are you preparing? You're always preparing. Just go!" Then he gets dumped into his seat. Good news, though: There's coffee!

I'll admit, planning isn't the most glamorous thing to do, but I really enjoy parts of the process, like organizing content and especially coming up with a design template for the entire site. The more you can determine upfront, the easier the actual site construction will be. Most people are really eager to start building pages right away and don't bother with any planning at all. Trust me, this results in a lot of extra time spent reworking pages, changing navigation structure, and so on. But before we get into the nitty, let's cover a most important subject...coffee!

This chapter is more theory based, so we won't be using Dreamweaver much. You may want to save this chapter for the bus ride to work, your next court hearing, or any other time you're away from your computer.

NOTEWORTHY

Cut down the time it takes to develop a site by planning as much as possible up front. Get away from the computer and use two of humankind's most greatest inventions: a piece of paper and a pencil.

FIRST THING'S FIRST: COFFEE!

How can anything be planned without everyone's favorite drink? Sure, some medical experts say coffee could be a health hazard, but they've obviously never built a web site before! So what if coffee's been linked to anxiety, bipolar disorder, and schizophrenia—doesn't that describe every designer you've ever met? So get yourself buzzed with this tasty treat: Irish coffee!

What You'll Need

- One Irish coffee glass or a 5 or 6 fl. oz. glass
- One long shot of good espresso (some people use black coffee—go big or go home)
- Two fingers of decent Irish whiskey (check your boot flask)
- Two tablespoons of brown sugar
- Fresh heavy cream with a dollop of white sugar, beaten until it's the thickness of custard—but don't whip it to fluffiness (store-bought will do in a pinch)

What You Do

1. Warm the glass by pouring in warm water. Once the glass is warm, remove the water and insert a spoon.
2. Pour the brown sugar and Irish whiskey into the glass at once. Stir to dissolve the sugar.
3. Flame the whiskey for just a second or two with a match (get Mom or Dad to help). Experts say this adds a *je ne sais quoi* and brings the whiskey and caffeine into balance.
4. Pour in the espresso. Your glass should be three-fourths full at this point.
5. Add the cream overtop by carefully pouring it down the back of the spoon resting inside the glass. Enjoy.

There's a whole lot more brewing at coffeefaq.com.

If you drink more than eight cups of coffee a day, your head could explode.

What Do You Want to Say and Who Do You Want to Say It To?

There's a cold, hard fact in marketing, and I think it applies here. It may come as a surprise, but here it is (brace for impact): Not everyone wants what you have to give. It's true. When asked who would buy their product, many inexperienced entrepreneurs immediately say "Everyone! Everyone will want my widget!" That's why we see shotgun marketing like spam, mass flyer distribution, and telephone blitzes. The truth is, there's a very specific group of people who will want an entrepreneur's widget, and the same goes for your web site. Not everyone is as exited as you are about guinea pig migration patterns, conspiracy theories behind your neighbor's vegetable garden, or the Travel Buddy comb/toothbrush/nasal trimmer toolkit.

If you can define who your site is for, you can focus your site's design on that.

If you can find out who your niche audience is, you'll build a much better site. So ask yourself: Who specifically am I trying to reach, and what am I trying to say? Once you know that, then you can begin to tailor site content, navigation, and functionality to what your audience wants, not what you want. Would the Granny's Club of St. John's Anglican Church appreciate thundering death metal intro music? Well maybe. You know those wacky granny clubs... But seriously, design it for them. The idea is that if you can define who your site is for, you can focus your site's design around that.

It's slanted toward do-gooder sites, but hey, it's free and full of good stuff for sites of any kind. It's all yours at championsofphilanthropy.com/downloads/Nonprofit-Websites(revised).pdf.

Get the Glue—We've Gotta Build a Navigation Model

Consider which nav model best for your site—or consider using several.

There are four traditional models of navigation used online. These have been morphed and mashed together for different sites, depending on the content being presented. Have a look at each and consider which is best for your site—or consider using different models for different parts of your site as content requires. What do all those different page icons mean? See the sidebar "Web Page Types" later in this chapter.

KEEP 'ER STRAIGHT WITH THE LINEAR APPROACH

Before the web was born, our media was linear. A book has a page-by-page sequential order. A movie has a definite beginning and a definite end. But when the web came along, suddenly information could be conveyed in whatever order the visitor wanted. However, many sites still want to control the sequence of content, maybe for an online tutorial or a slideshow. These examples require a specific, orderly web page sequence that doesn't provide a way for the visitor to jump to different topics or locations.

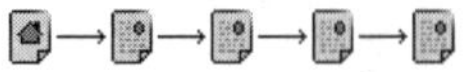

The linear nav model.

LONG LIVE THE QUEEN: THE HIERARCHICAL MODEL

Also called a tree structure, the hierarchical model the most popular navigation model online. With this structure, a site would begin with an opening page that provides several choices that link to main category pages, called landmark pages. Landmark pages provide links to more specific subsections. From this point, the site might branch into more subpages, getting more and more specific as the structure continues.

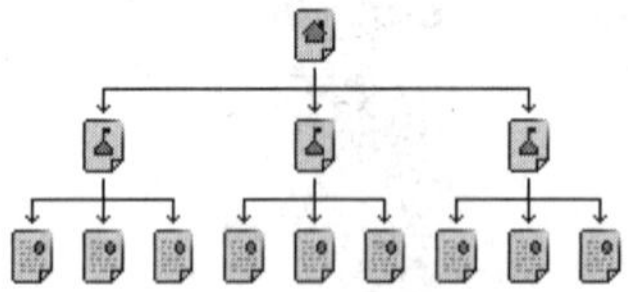

The hierarchical nav system.

BURNING RUBBER WITH SPOKES AND HUBS

In a spoke-and-hub structure, the home page is at the center, with spokes linking to the different categories of the site. From these categories, the site might be organized into deeper structures, depending on the organization and content.

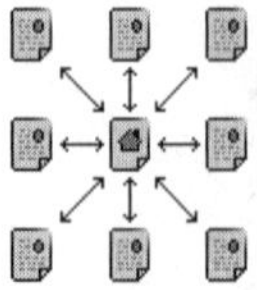

Spoke-and-hub navigation.

GET YOUR FILL WITH THE FULL-WEB DESIGN

The full-web or full-mesh style uses virtually no structure at all, with each page linking to every other page. This is great in that it allows visitors to explore the site in any way that they want, but navigation can get complex and frustrating.

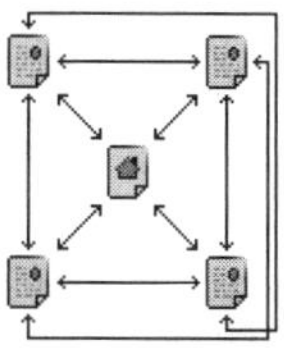

The full-web model.

Public sites are available to anyone online; intranet sites are used within an organization; extranet sites are available online, but users must have access privileges.

Sorting Out the Types of Sites

There are all kinds of web sites, large and small, online. Here, we'll take a look at the major types and the audiences they target. These site types are certainly generalized, and there are countless sites that fall into more than one category, or none at all. In addition, sites can be grouped into three categories according to who can access them: public sites, intranet sites, and extranet sites.

Public sites are the most common. They're available on, and useable by, anyone on the Internet. There are no restrictions as to who can access a public site. Intranet sites are sites used within a company or organization to provide internal information to employees. Extranet sites are accessible on the public Internet, but users must have access privileges, usually a username and password are needed to log in.

The site types that follow typically fall into the public site classification, but theoretically they can occur in all three.

CASHING IN ON COMMERCIAL SITES

A commercial site is one whose primary purpose is to generate profits by providing goods and services to a body of customers. Some companies build commercial sites to support their "bricks and mortar" locations, while other companies are based entirely online, with no physical store that a customer could visit. Good commercial sites provide multiple ways to browse, search, and shop their catalog of goods. Consider, for example, the king of them all: Amazon.com.

GET INFORMED WITH INFORMATION-BASED SITES

If a site's main purpose is to inform and educate, then it's considered an information-based, or content-based, site. Such sites include government service sites, the sites of nonprofit organizations, travel information sites, and news sites. A small site for your church would count, but so would a massive news site. An interesting thing about news sites is that they all have a similar look and feel in their design and navigation. Compare cnn.com with cbc.ca.

Bust a gut and learn something too at storewars.org.

TV'S DEAD—ENTERTAINMENT SITE TAKEOVER

Many everyday people have made names for themselves by creating sites that simply entertain the rest of us. An entertainment site might be the site of a funny online comic, a sports analysis site, or even a site where you can watch web-based movies. There are lots of them out there—but check out www.storewars.org, a site that delivers a great message in a very funny and entertaining way.

FIND YOUR WAY WITH NAVIGATIONAL SITES

Search engines, community portals, and online directories are considered navigational sites, because they help people find their way around. Unless you know the exact site you want to visit, a navigational site will be your starting point. Many nav sites are now offering additional services to gain surfer loyalty. For instance, Google.com now offers e-mail, catalog searching, maps, and a zillion other very useful services.

JOIN THE CLUB—COMMUNITY SITES

Community sites provide a centralized place for people with similar interests to meet and interact, usually in online forums. Here, they can discuss current events, ask and answer questions, and share information. Whatever your niche or unique interests may be, there's a group out there sharing ideas about it. If you're a Lego nut (or if you'd just like a good example of a community web site), click on brickfilms.com, an online community of Lego movie makers.

EXPRESSIVE ARTISTIC SITES

Artistic sites may provide content and information, but often these sites are a work of artistic expression themselves. Many artistic sites are simply a place for someone to express his or her opinion, feelings, or interests, with no economic considerations. My own site, geoffblake.com, is entirely artistic—just a fun place to express myself creatively.

The home page of yours truly. Geoffblake.com is an example of an artistic site.

PERSONAL SITES (GETTING TO KNOW YOU...)

Sometimes called a person's home page, personal sites are often a forum for personal expression. Often, they're used to share photos, stories, and recent events with friends and family members. Others use their sites to test and experiment as they learn HTML and web design. My friend Jason Allin has a great personal home page that he uses to keep others up-to-date on what's new with his acting endeavors. Say hi at jasonallin.com.

NOTEWORTHY

Consider registering your own name as a URL, making it easy for friends, family, and clients to find you online. Once you register your URL, it's yours for life, as long as you keep renewing it.

Visual Site Design

When you put pencil to paper to plan your site, you should make your designs as detailed as possible. But most important, you need to decide two things. First, you need to choose your overall navigation structure: how pages will link together, how sections will be organized, what content should go on which page, and how visitors will move throughout the site. Second, you need to decide on a design layout for the individual pages: the look and feel, the content layout, and what you want appearing on each page.

GEEK'S DELIGHT

Ever wondered how to register your own domain name? Go to networksolutions.com. Registration is fast and easy.

When embarking on planning a site, I like to get away (far away) from the computer and find a quite place where I can think clearly, a place without the distractions of phones, e-mail, or Beverly Hillbillies marathons. I go for bell towers, hunting lodges, or the crow's nest of a clipper ship. You might want to do the same.

Unwritten Web Design Conventions

There are some unwritten laws that surfers have come to expect web sites to obey.

Before actually getting into the down and dirty of site design, let's get some tried-and-tested web conventions out of the way. In web design, nothing's hard and fast, but there are some unwritten laws that surfers have come to expect web sites to obey. When things don't work as expected, visitors tend to get frustrated and eventually surf somewhere else. I'll bet you've come to expect most of these unwritten rules as you surf from site to site, too.

Blast off with this great example of good site navigation. There's lots to look at, plenty of buttons, and a search field, too, making it easy for visitors to explore the final frontier.

Most conventions are navigational, so let's get those out of the way first. A standard on virtually all sites is a main menu, which should appear on every page either across the top or down the left side. Menu buttons link to the landmark pages of the site and then branch off from there. Try to keep your buttons simple and easy to follow. Some sites use indecipherable icons or text captions that don't clearly indicate where links go. It may make perfect sense to you what "Mehta Meyhem" is, but no one else will understand your devotion to the Three Tenors (Didn't get that gag 'cuz you don't know the Three Tenors? Exactly the point. Now get going and look it up!)

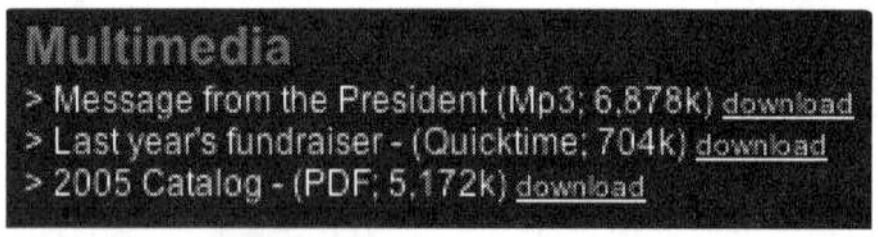

Whenever you're providing files for download, let your visitor know what they're in for by indicating the file size.

The links in a main menu should also be repeated as text links across the bottom of the page, which I'm sure you've seen. These text links, and all text links on your page for that matter, should be underlined so visitors know that they're clickable. Another navigation convention is a site's logo that appears in the upper-left corner. This logo should always link back to the site's home page. Finally, whenever a long page is used, perhaps a directory page or a glossary, always include back-to-top links so visitors can easily make their way back to where they started. It's just a convenience for them.

Two more conventions: First, if you're providing files that visitors can download, maybe MP3 or PDF files, always include the file size in brackets so they know what they're in for. Last but not least, if you have a page that visitors may want to print, provide a printer-friendly version of the page—that is, a clean page without a colored background, a lot of superfluous graphics, and so on. Even better, provide a PDF version of the page for printing purposes. That way, you can be sure your visitors will get a perfect printout.

Navigation 101

So you know the essential conventions. Now it's time to sit down and work out your navigational structure on paper. The key idea here, when you begin thinking about navigation is that you want to build a site that's easy to get around in. This means being sensitive to the needs of both novice and experienced users. Good sites don't rely on the web browser's Back button for navigation. Instead, they provide several methods to move through the site, and the best sites keep each of these methods simple and easy to follow.

A main menu is a must, and think seriously about including text links at the bottom of the page. Another way to employ text links is to use something called breadcrumbs. Breadcrumbs usually appear toward the top of the page and provide a trail of links leading back to where the visitor started.

HOW TO DRESS LIKE A DESIGNER

So now that you're getting into Dreamweaver, it's time to look the part. Find out exactly what it takes to look like a designer, even if you can't draw stick-men to save lives. So grab Daddy's credit card and hit the mall—here's how to dress like a designer!

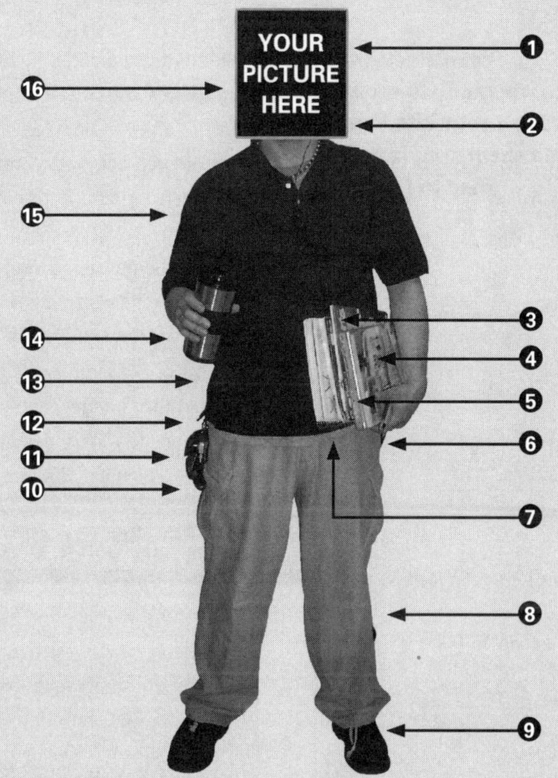

(1) Funky hairdo (consider color) **(2)** Facial hair (men only) **(3)** Graphic design magazines **(4)** 2006 Ikea catalog (to furnish the loft apartment) **(5)** Notebook computer (operating system of choice) **(6)** Markers, HB and 2B mechanical pencils **(7)** 100-page wirebound sketchbook **(8)** Brand cargo pants **(9)** Oxford shoes **(10)** Cellphone **(11)** USB keychain drive **(12)** Car keys (something compact and imported) **(13)** MP3 player **(14)** Brushed-aluminum coffee mug **(15)** Brand golf shirt **(16)** MP3 player headphones (connected to MP3 player)

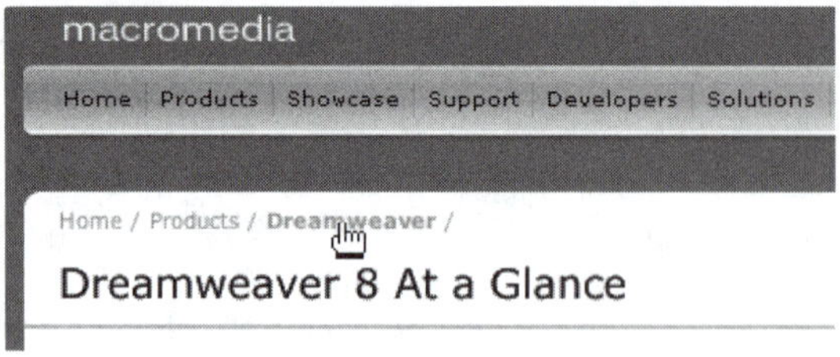

Breadcrumbs are a great navigation tool, helping surfers pinpoint where they are.

Provide several methods to move through your site, and keep them simple and easy to follow.

Another element to consider including is a site map. A site map gives a structural list of all of the pages within a site, providing a very fast way for visitors to find the information they're after. In addition to being an alternative navigation system, site maps are great for search engines, which love all the text links within a site map, which can improve your rankings in search results.

Whatever navigation systems you choose, keep them consistent throughout each page and simple to use, and also make sure they allow visitors to get back to previous levels easily. As you start your planning, consider storyboarding or flowcharting your site to help stay organized. Sort of like filmmakers do for movies, literally draw out your pages on paper. Figure out what text, images, and other content you'll need, and start thinking about how the pages in your site will connect to one another. This whole process is called *information architecture.* It's a nice, fat, 50-cent term that'll get you in good with the boss.

WEB DESIGN RESOURCES

Check out these web design resources:

- Get a head start with Dreamweaver and web design at macromedia.com/devnet/mx/dreamweaver/best_practices.html.
- Want to know more about information architecture? Read Louis Rosenfeld and Peter Morville's book *Information Architecture for the World Wide Web.*
- There are lots of resources on the web regarding information architecture. To get started, check out jjg.net/ia.
- Visit usableweb.com for nearly endless resources on structure design, interfaces, conventions, and a bazillion other topics.
- For help building your own site maps—and lots more—check out XtREEME SiteExpert (xtreeme.com).
- Visit webpagesthatsuck.com/mysterymeatnavigation.html for examples of what not to do!

WEB PAGE TYPES

Here's an overview of required and optional pages for your site. Use these icons and descriptions with the nav models described in "Get the Glue—We've Gotta Build a Navigation Model" earlier in this chapter.

Splash page: You can use an optional splash page to introduce your site. More often than not, splash pages contain Flash intro movies that are, quite frankly, useless. Often, all a Flash intro does is give the designer a chance to show off his or her skill and cause an unwanted download for the viewer. If you do use a splash page, it should be to give visitors an idea of what to expect inside the site, and also to provide site requirements, such as monitor resolution, plug-ins, or other settings. The intro page for robzombie.com is an example of a well-used splash page.

Home page: A site's home is its main opening page. If you don't use a splash page, you must give the home page a default name such as index.htm for the site to function (see "What's the Deal with Index Files" in this chapter). The home page serves as the main point where landmark pages link from, and it usually has a unique design to distinguish it from the rest of the site. Also, make sure to provide a way to link back to the home page from all other pages.

Landmark page: You could also call these category pages. Landmark pages are the main pages for the predominant sections of a site, which are normally linked to from the site's main menu. A landmark page links to content pages within its specific category.

Content page: Content pages branch off from landmark pages. This is where information is most specific for the visitor. If you like the analogy of a tree structure, you can think of a these as leaf pages, the pages farthest from the home page.

Contact page: Every site should include a contact page, and it should be accessible from every other page. Give your visitors multiple ways to contact you. Unless you're a business, phone numbers aren't such a good idea. But you could include your e-mail address, a form for visitors to fill in, or even a way to contact you via instant messenger.

Other page types: There are all sorts of other optional pages you can include in your site. If you've been surfing the web for a number of years, you may have noticed trends that come and go. For example, guestbooks and chatrooms used to be all the rage. They're still around, but they've given way to online forums and blogs (short for web logs). If you'd like to add a blog or forum to your site, one option is to use a free online service like bravenet.com. Only bummer is that endless pop-up ads will appear on your site unless you pay for the full service.

IMMINENT DOOM

You are not the user of your site, and the user is not you. The users of your site don't think like you do; they think like they do. Remember that you're building an interface, an environment, for others to use, not for you to use. Any navigation structure that digs deeper than three levels before actually getting to the content is too difficult to navigate.

GEEK'S DELIGHT

Blogs have really risen in popularity. They're basically like an online journal where people can post their rants and opinions. Some are really well written, while others are just soapboxes. Check out guerrillanews.com for an example, or blogger.com to create your own.

But Isn't Content King?

There's an unfortunate fact in web design. Because the web is a visual medium like film or TV, your site's design is the first thing visitors will see and begin evaluating you by. If you're not a designer or visual person, this may not make a lot of sense. Some people think that if they have really well-written content, the masses will come, that the visual design doesn't matter.

GEEK'S DELIGHT

Consider adding a counter, site search, or even local news and weather to your site. Things like shopping carts or a wish list for returning customers are pretty heavy duty, but anything's possible. Check out htmlgear.com to get started, or better yet, when you're signing up for web hosting, make sure your package includes a Cpanel interface. Check out cpanel.net/features-cpanel.html to get the scoop.

Well, there's actually a bit of psychology here. Get this: If you've got killer content in a really badly designed site, the perception in people's minds is that the content has no value. And the opposite is true. If you have really bad content in really, really nicely designed packaging, people immediately think it's of high value. Want a real-world example of this? Watch any top-10 music video countdown.

If you've got killer content in a really badly designed site, the perception in people's minds is that the content has no value.

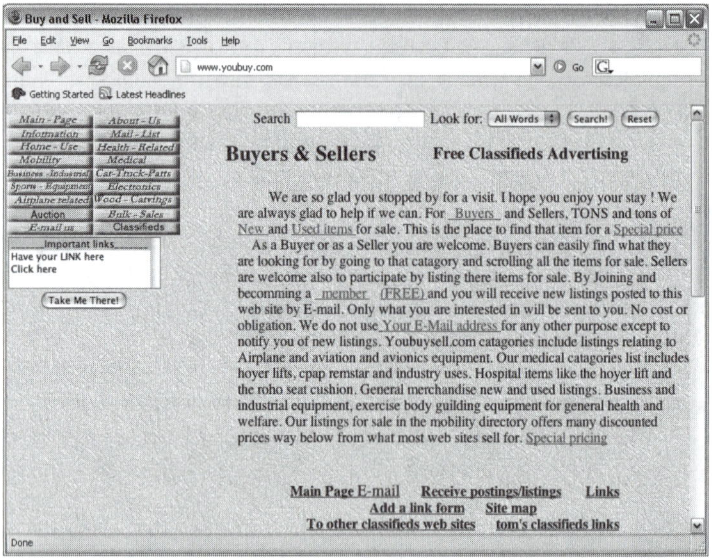

So is content more important than presentation? I don't know about you, but this site doesn't exactly motivate me to soak up its content.

Branding: Your Consistent Message

If you're new to visual design, check out The Non-Designer's Design Book *and* The Non-Designer's Web Book, *both by Robin Williams.*

Remember that building a site is all about communication, and I don't mean through text. Design, color, and images speak. The best-designed sites are those that embody the overall look and message of the organization they represent. In design circles, this is called branding. Branding encompasses everything from the overall look, colors, and fonts of the organization, to more abstract things like attitude and environment. It is the story that an organization is telling.

A site that totally misses its mark in this regard is Ikea.com—sad times, because they're one of my favorite companies. They're all about design and innovation. Everything—from their store, to their catalog, to their products—reflects this. They're consistent in everything they do—except in their web site. Knowing Ikea, I'd expect a site that's as innovative as their products and store layout, something that really makes you go, "Wow, what a cool site." Ikea.com is pretty plain and doesn't even contain the company's entire catalog. Ikea, you're such a cool company. Please build us a site that's as cool as everything else you do!

The best-designed sites are those that embody the overall look and message of the organization they represent.

Just drying my eyes... Okay.

Other times, an organization provides a single page just to establish some kind of web presence. If Bob's Antique Market has an online brochure, it doesn't necessarily mean Bob's on the cutting edge. Can I search his stock, ask him a question, or get some tips on fixing my mother-in-law's nineteenth-century coffee table after playing rugby in her living room? Ultimately, here's what it comes down to: Does the page serve Bob, so he can say his company is online, or does it serve the needs of his clientele? Getting heavy, huh?

Does Bob's web page exist for him or for his clients? As you can see, there isn't a whole lot here to help out his clientele.

We talked about unwritten rules earlier. Here's another: If a company doesn't have a web site, it isn't considered professional. This is like a business not having an answering machine attached to its telephone. If a company does have a site, but the design is very amateur, then people won't take the company seriously. A site has to look good and function perfectly, but also deliver the information that people are after.

Planning Page Layout

Design a template to use throughout the pages of your site.

When beginning the design of that first page, keep this in mind: On the web there's no fixed page size. This means that you can make your pages as long and wide as you like, but be careful. Surfers don't like to do a whole lot of scrolling, especially horizontal scrolling. So make sure that the size of your page is appropriate for the content it's going to hold.

What I find easiest is to design an initial page template to use for the main pages of my site. I decide where I want the main menu, contact information, common links, and so on to appear. This process isn't just about deciding where to put elements on my page, but also how they'll look and what colors to use. As you begin roughing out your designs on paper, think about what you like and dislike about sites that you visit. Are there particular elements that you'd like to incorporate?

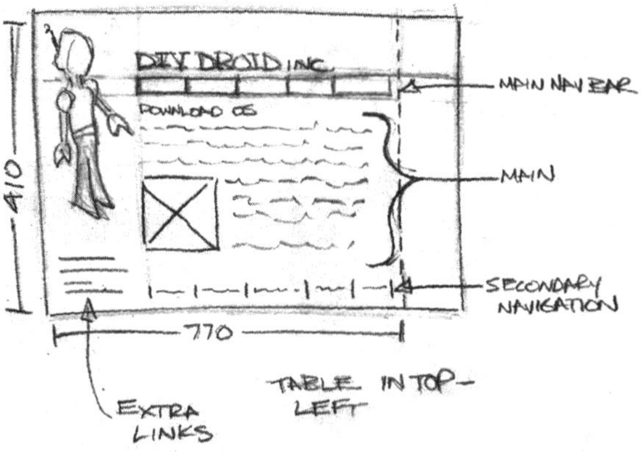

Here's an example of a rough site concept. Even if you can't draw, it's imperative to plan out your page designs on paper. Take as long as you need, and develop your ideas as far as you can.

Metric? Imperial? It's All about Pixels and Browsers Now

In the land of web design, everything's measured in pixels. Why? Because that's how computer monitor resolution is measured. If you're not familiar with monitor resolution, it's the number of pixels horizontally and vertically that are displayed onscreen.

IMMINENT DOOM

Keep contrast high between page elements. If you want to use a dark background, don't plan to use dark text.

COLOR ON THE WEB

One thing that can be tricky when designing your pages is matching colors—knowing what colors go nicely together. Women, I think, have a sort of sixth sense for this kind of thing. They just seem to know what colors go with what. My mom's a killing machine at this. For the rest of us, there's a neat utility called Color Wheel Expert (Windows only) at abitom.com.

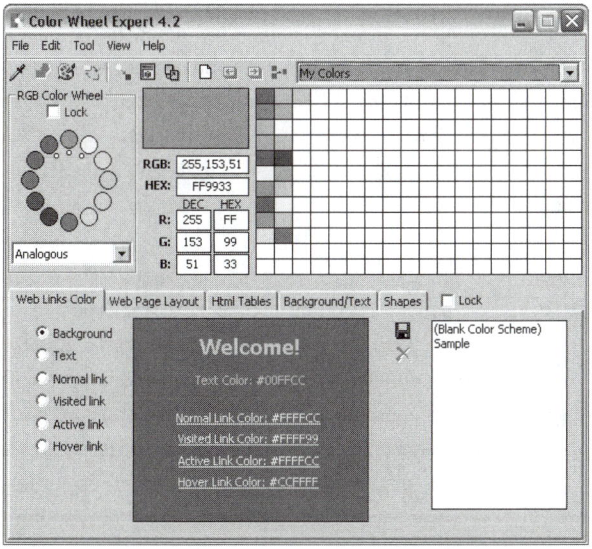

Color Wheel Expert—snappy color coordination for those who haven't a clue!

You pick a color to start, and then Color Wheel Expert gives you a huge range of color combinations to use, all based on correct color theory, so you know all the combinations are right. To really make use of this tool, you have to understand how color wheels work, so go out to your local arts and crafts store and get one for a few bucks; then visit webwhirlers.com/colors/index.asp to get a handle on how it all works.

CHANGING MONITOR RESOLUTION

Have you never changed your monitor resolution before? It's easy. Just follow these steps for your particular operating system.

Windows XP:

1. Minimize all your programs so that all you see is your desktop.
2. On the desktop, right-click and choose Properties from the menu that appears.
3. In the Properties dialog box, click the Settings tab.
4. At the bottom of the tab, drag the Monitor Resolution slider left or right to increase or decrease the screen resolution (Figure 3.9).

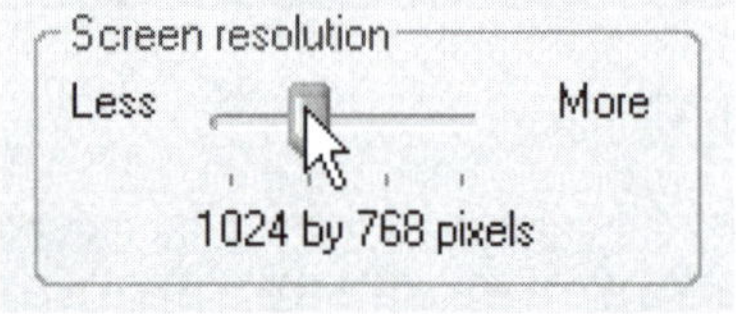

Setting the screen resolution in Windows XP.

Mac OS X:

1. Open the Apple menu and choose System Preferences.

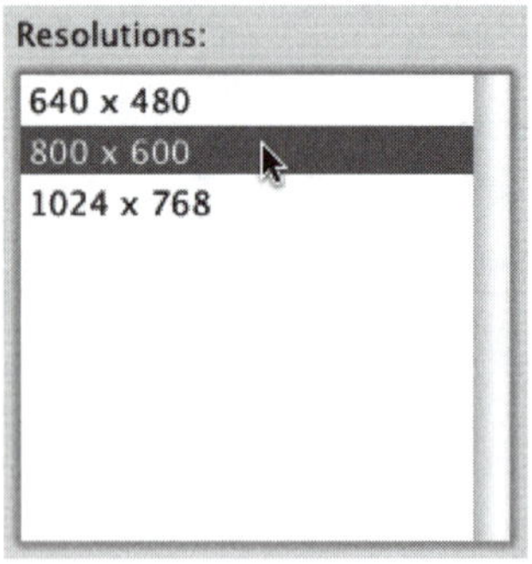

Setting the screen resolution in Mac OS X.

2. In the Hardware category, click Displays.
3. Choose a setting from the Resolutions list (Figure 3.10).

The lowest resolution, and really used only on older computers, is 640x480. One notch up is 800 x 600, which is a good worst-case scenario for web design. The most popular resolution is 1024 x 768. From there, resolutions get pretty high—up to 1152 x 864, 1600 x 1200, 1280 x 1024, and even 1600 x 1280.

When you begin designing your pages (remember, on paper first!), you should keep monitor size in mind. There are a few sharp stabbing pains here. First, you have no idea what resolutions your visitors' computers will be running. Second, you have no idea what web browsers your visitors will be using; different web browsers take up different amounts of screen space with their toolbars, menus, and so on (called the browser's chrome).

First, let's talk about monitor resolution. As I mentioned, there's really no way to know what resolution your visitors will use. However, there are a few workarounds. For example, you can use a bit of JavaScript to detect the resolution being used and then redirect the visitor to a page built specifically for that monitor type. More commonly though, most web designers assume a worst-case scenario: that your visitor will be running the lowest of the common resolutions, 800x600. With this approach, you build your pages to target the 800x600 setting—and your pages will also look good on anything higher. This is a much better way to go. That's why you see something like "This site best viewed running 800x600 or higher" on so many sites.

Echoecho.com seen at 640x480 (left), 800x600 (center), and 1024x768 (right). See what a difference monitor resolution can make?

Now the issue of browser chrome. This'll drive you nuts. First, what browser will people be running? Next, what version of that specific browser will they be running? Finally, what toolbars and extras might they use (like a Google searchbar added in, for example)? It's impossible to know all the variables, and trying to compensate for all the combinations will surely land you in the loony bin. I won't even bring up different operating systems, or Blackberries and cellphones...

"So what do I do?" you plea. "I thought web design was supposed to be fun!" Soothing breath...you are a hollow reed. Here's what you do: You find some kind of lowest-common denominator that tells you what browsers are most popular. Then you test the heck out of your site against those browsers. How do you find out what the popular browsers are? You probably already have a fairly good idea, but for specifics, go to echoecho.com. When the page loads into your browser, scroll down a bit, and on the right side you'll see Surfer Stats. The first box gives some stats for the most popular browsers.

Find a common denominator for screen resolution and browser chrome.

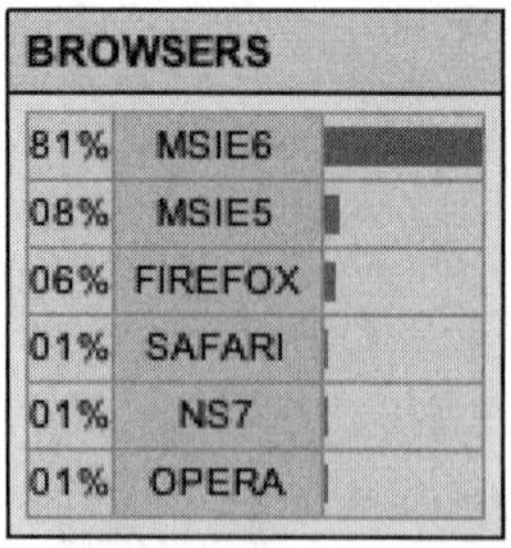

Surfer's browser stats, as seen at echoecho.com.

As you download, install, and test your pages in the various browsers available, keep one important thing in mind: Most web surfers are not interested in web browsers—they're everyday folks who just want to surf (many don't even know what a browser is!). Most will opt to use whatever browser came with their computer (Internet Explorer 6 in Windows XP, and Safari 2 in the latest release of Mac OS X), and unless they're web savvy, they won't want to download and install anything because that's too "technical."

This makes a web designer's job tough, because a browser like Explorer 6 is becoming sadly outdated, while browsers like Firefox and Opera have risen up to support most (if not all) current web standards. So even though these newer browsers will render your pages better, most surfers will be using the outdated Internet Explorer.

Go with the Site Design Workflow

You should have a solid idea of the site you want to build worked out on paper first.

At this point, you should have a solid idea of the site you want to build. You should know exactly how your site will be structured, how pages will connect to one another, what content you'll need, and how your pages will actually look. Once you've ironed all this out on paper, you can finally sit down with Dreamweaver and create your grand vision. I know we haven't really even gotten into Dreamweaver, but now's as good a time as any to get a quick idea of what's involved in actually constructing your monumental first site.

FIRST, DEVELOP THE MOCK SITE

Some designers also call the mock site the alpha site. This is like the first draft of the site. The important thing here is to get the necessary pages built and linked together, so don't worry about filling in any content at this point. All you're after is a workable site with basic navigation that your client or boss can green-light.

SECOND, BUILD A BETA SITE

Once the alpha site receives a passing grade, then you can start putting real content into the pages. You can also start adding things like JavaScript rollovers, a site map, and Flash elements. At the end of this stage, you should have a finished site that's ready to roll off the production line and enter the crushing intensity of site testing.

THIRD, GET TESTING

Now the part everyone skips. You've worked so hard planning, designing, and building that I'm sure you're ready to just wash your hands of this thing and be done with it. Hold up. You've gotta test the heck out of your site to make sure it actually works under a variety of conditions. Most designers take a quick look at the site in a browser or two,

POPULAR WEB BROWSERS

There are many browsers out there, but here's a list of the most popular. Keep in mind that these are the latest versions as of this writing, and new releases come out all the time. Also, I've rounded down the viewable areas for both the Windows and Mac versions. That said, it's always a good idea to give yourself a reasonable margin of error. You can see that the smallest horizontal space is 760 (Internet Explorer 5 for the Mac), and 410 is the smallest vertical space (Netscape 8 for Windows). So a final page size that wouldn't scroll horizontally or vertically on a Mac or Windows computer, plus a bit of a margin of error, would be around 740x390 (depending on how conservative you want to be). Most surfers don't mind vertical scrolling so much, so the first value is the most critical.

Browser	**Viewable Area at 800x600 (with default chrome and vertical scrollbar visible)**		**Get It At**
	PC	**Mac**	
Internet Explorer 6 (latest Windows version)	775x425	N/A	microsoft.com/windows/ie/downloads
Internet Explorer 5 (final Mac version)	N/A	760x425	microsoft.com/mac/downloads.aspx#IE
Firefox 1	780x430	785x475	firefox.com
Safari 2 (Mac only)	N/A	780x505	apple.com/safari/download
Netscape 8	770x410	775x430	browser.netscape.com/nsb/download
Opera 8	775x425	780x495	opera.com
Mozilla 1.7	775x420	780x460	mozilla.org/products
Camino 0.8.4 (Mac only)	N/A	780x460	caminobrowser.org
Avant 10 (Windows only)	775x405	N/A	avantbrowser.com

click a few links, and call it a day. You've gotta be thorough. Punch every link and test every page in a variety of browsers. It may seem tedious, but keep testing and fixing. Upload your site to a testing area and get friends or your dorky kid sister to try it out.

NOTEWORTHY

While in the testing phase, try running your site on an older machine with a much slower connection. If your site runs okay on an older machine, it'll blaze on the latest and greatest. This has given a second life to Huxley, my rusty old PI 133 with his 32k modem.

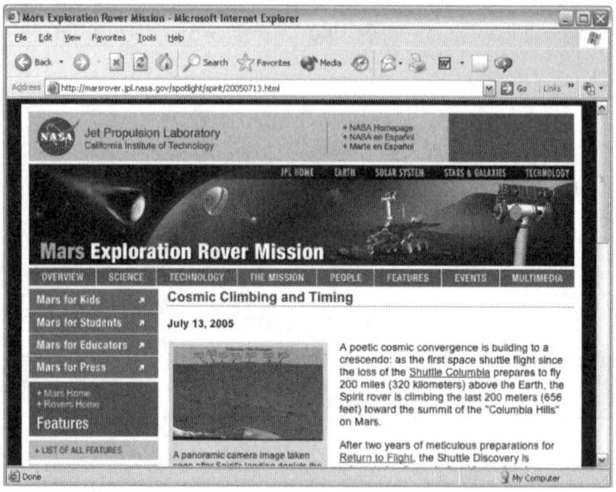

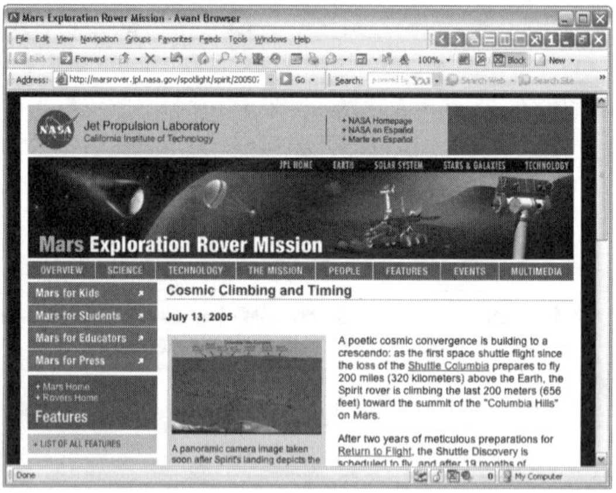

The Mars rover gets off easy here, rendering accurately in Avant, Explorer, and Firefox. However, it's critical that you test your pages in a variety of browsers, under a variety of conditions.

FOURTH, THE GREAT UNVEILING

Okay, you're ready to publish your site live. In the next chapter, we'll go into all kinds of detail about how this is done. But once everything's uploaded, the main bulk of the work is done but there'll be ongoing maintenance and updating. A big deal with sites these days is keeping content fresh and updated. So really, web design is an ongoing job, but if it's a site that you love, it'll never seem like work.

After the release of your site, testing is an ongoing thing, too. Whenever you find yourself in front of a computer (at a friend's, in the jailhouse, wherever), hop onto your site to see how it looks.

IMMINENT DOOM

There's little deadlier to a site than a line that tells your visitors "last site update Sept. 26, 1998." Update your site regularly.

How to Structure Your Site

Navigation structure, file structure, now site structure? What's with all this structuring!?! Of them all, site structure is the most critical to developing your site, and it is this area that causes the most confusion and frustration for newbies.

Web design is all based on references—references to other pages, to images, and to other content. If these references are broken, the site won't function properly. So if you're new to all this, here's one suggestion: After you've decided on a site structure, draw it on paper and keep it beside you as you work to help you stay on track. Okay, let's have a closer look.

What's File Structure?

File structure refers to the way you organize and save all the files used in your site. When you create hyperlinks or use images and other media, you're creating reference paths to other files in your site structure.

***File structure* is the way you *organize* the files used in your site.**

Typically, I create a folder on my hard drive and name it after the project I'm working on. This folder is called the "root" of the site. Inside this folder, I organize all the content related to the site into subfolders. How you decide to organize your own project is completely up to you, but usually simpler is better. I always suggest creating three folders on the root level (the top level) of your site, *htm* for all HTML files, *img* for all images, and *media* for MP3, PDF, and other files.

A basic site file structure ta git ya started.

IMMINENT DOOM

Not organizing your site content into a single folder but instead leaving files scattered all over your hard drive will result in ultimate destruction of your site! When you go to upload your work, those scattered files will be missing, resulting in a site that will not function.

Many times you can begin to understand how a site is structured just by looking at your web browser's address bar—that is, unless the web site is database driven (in that case, you just get a seemingly incoherent line of text). We'll spend more time discussing site structure in the next chapter, where you set up your first site in Dreamweaver.

THE SEVEN DEADLY SINS OF WEB DESIGN

Come children and bear witness to what web design decadence does to those whose fate lies in eternal design damnation. Some artsy or personal sites seek exemption from this fate, and so they are spared for these are sites wrought with creativity and not spoiled by the economic yearnings of man. (That was cool. Did you read that with a boomy Wizard of Oz voice? Read it again!)

Cardinal Sin #1: Solving Your Problems, Not Your Customer's

The absolute worst sin. Does your company have a marketing problem? Do you want to increase sales? A web site is not the solution. Many companies think that even just a single home page is enough, but that does nothing to help your customers fix their problems. To be frank (and it may be hard to hear), customers don't care about your company—they care about fixing their problems. The truth may hurt, so let's hug. Then go build a site to help your customers, not yourself.

Cardinal Sin #2: Thinking Like You Do, Not Like Your Audience Does

It may make perfect sense to you, but make sure the rest of us get it, too. After all, we'll be using your site more than you. Many designers build sites and navigation systems that make sense to them, but make very little sense to everyone else. Remember that unless you're building a personal or artsy site, your site is not for you. It's for your audience. If nobody gets it, somebody else will get your visitors. Chew on that; then answer this nugget: What does your audience want, and why should they surf to your site to get it?

Cardinal Sin #3: Letting Technology (and Trends) Get in the Way

Visitors come to your site for a reason: to fix a problem or to find information they're interested in. Be conscious of what technology and trends you follow. Will they care if your site uses the latest CSS standards? Will your ability to code ActionScript in your sleep enable them to find what they're after? Quite possibly, only don't let it get in their way. Technology for technology's sake is what landed everyone in the meat grinder in Jurassic Park. A great example of this is Flash intros, which aren't as popular any more (thank god). Are Flash intros for the benefit of the designer or for the benefit of the visitor? Give 'em what they came for and get out of their way!

What's the Deal with Index Files?

Okay, this is critical. The opening page of your site (your home page or splash page) is typically called something like *index.htm*, and it has to be placed at the root level of your file structure—otherwise, your site won't work. When you navigate to a site, say geoffblake.com, your web browser will look for an *index.htm* file. If the browser finds it, it'll display it on your screen. If it can't find it, it will display a directory listing or an error message of some sort.

THE SEVEN DEADLY SINS (CONTINUED)

Cardinal Sin #4: Failing to Test

Test, test, and then test some more. Test on your machine. Test on a friend's machine. Pretend you're buying a new computer and test at the store. Test your links. Test your load time. Get your roommate to test. Get the guy at the gas station to test. Get grammy's Aunt Gertrude to test. Test on Macs. Test on PCs. Test in Explorer, Safari, Firefox, and any other browsers you can muster. Test on hi-res monitors. Test on low-res monitors. Have I drilled it in? Good—then test the crud out of your site until it works as best as possible in every conceivable situation.

Cardinal Sin #5: Building a Bad Navigation System

Navigation should be an easy topic. It only has to answer three questions. Where am I right now? Where have I been? Where can I go to next? Always make sure that your navigation system is mindlessly simple, with logical button labels, and you'll make it really difficult for people to get lost. Also, provide at least three different navigation systems—a main menu, a site search engine, and a site map, for example.

Cardinal Sin #6: Believing Computers Design Good Sites

Computers don't design sites—people do. Many graphic designers have a tough time charging the rates they do, because most people just don't get why they should pay for design. But there's an interesting correlation here. The larger the company, the more the company realizes the importance of good design. What percentage of Nike's revenues go into web development versus Floyd's Fish Farm's? For many, making something look good just isn't important. They think content rules over the presentation of that content. But bubblegum pop stars would argue the opposite: style over substance. Truth is, they're both critical, so make sure to balance that act!

Cardinal Sin #7: Using an Inconsistent Design Throughout the Site

You site should have one main look throughout. Obviously, splash pages and home pages will have their own designs, but all other pages should have the same consistent look and feel. Sites that change design and move common elements like logos and navigation buttons around on different pages are frustrating to surf. Keep it simple, and don't expect your visitor to have to learn how your site works. Stick with the standards and be consistent.

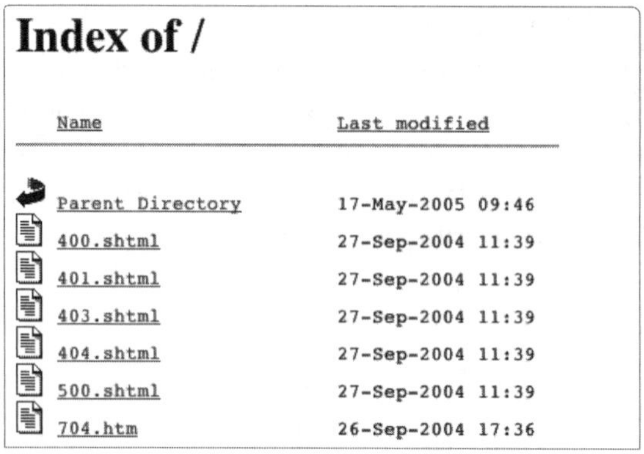

When an index file isn't present, bad things happen, such as nasty warnings—or worse, the contents of the entire directory may be exposed, as seen here.

NOTEWORTHY

There's more than one default homepage name on today's web. Be sure to find out what the page naming convention is for your site's environment. Depending on the ISP, OS, or web server, your default home page might be called index.cfm, index.html, default.htm, or index.jsp, to name a few examples.

You can use this behavior to your advantage. Let's say I want a survey on my web site. I could create the survey page and save it in my *htm* folder, but this would result in the following URL: www.geoffblake.com/htm/survey.htm. Kinda lengthy. To make the URL shorter and easier to remember, I can set up the URL to read www.geoffblake.com/survey. How? Well, I can create the survey page and then save it as *index.htm* inside a *survey* folder in my site structure. When a browser is pointed at a folder, it will try to find an index file to display. A site can have more than one index file, just not in the same directory.

Knowing this, you can make important URLs much more succinct and easier to remember. If I ran into you in the grocery store and asked you to fill out the survey at my web site, the second URL would be much easier for you to remember than the first one. Use your imagination; you can use this approach for a products page, a bio, a resume, or whatever else you want.

Getting rangy with the 'ol index trick.

HOW TO DITCH WORK AND TRAIN FOR A TITLE SHOT

Well, you're on your way to becoming a Dreamweaver heavyweight champion. But there's a nagging thorn that's keeping you away from a chance at the title: the daily grind of a job! So call in sick and play with Dreamweaver instead! Now wrestling the boss can be harder than cinching an arm bar on an alligator, but remember, whenever you're trying to pull one over on the boss, think smart. Your excuse for not making it in has to be believable (space aliens or chemical leaks won't cut it that stuff would be on the news). Further, the boss has caller ID, so you'll need to use your cell phone or a pay phone with the appropriate amount of background noise to make your call convincing.

So think things through and plan ahead before you start dialing. Here are a few excuses to help you get started. A successful pull-off means you'll have an entire day to spend with Dreamweaver rather than commuting to work and pretending you're a team player.

A Fiery Explanation: Say that you headed out nice and early this morning and were making great time until you began smelling smoke. Upon pulling over to investigate, your car burst into flames, leaving you stranded on the side of the highway. Nothing was salvaged, not even your Sammy Davis, Jr., bobble head, so you won't be making it in any time soon.

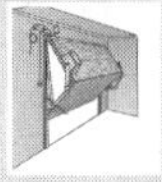

Power-Failure Forgiveness: Explain that early this morning, there was a power failure in your neighborhood, knocking out electricity for three square blocks. You'd love to get a jump on those TPS reports, but the manual release on your power-operated garage door is seized. Besides, no electricity means no coffee. Reminding the boss how grumpy you are without coffee will seal the deal.

Burnt Justification: Another commuter excuse. This time, as you set out to get a head start on traffic, some jerk with Jersey plates totally cut you off. In a tense moment of swerving and braking, you spilled your coffee into your lap, causing second-degree burns. The paramedics said the scarring shouldn't be too bad. Flowers and well wishes from the office staff would be greatly appreciated as you ride the road to recovery.

A Holy Excuse: Explain that last night just before bed, it happened again—you were stung with your stigmata. Although you're feeling okay now and you could come in, you don't feel that you'd be very productive. Typing would be hard, and your hands would be a major diversion for coworkers, sinking everyone's productivity. Rather than cause distraction in the office, you feel that the day would be better spent in spiritual reflection.

JUST THE GIST

Planning and Audience

- The more you can determine upfront, the easier site construction will be.
- Find out who your niche audience is, and you'll build a much better site.
- Tailor your site to what your audience wants, not what you want.

Nav Models

- Most site-navigation models can be categorized as linear, hierarchical, spoke-and-hub, or full-web models

Types of Sites

- Most web sites can be categorized in seven ways: as commercial, information-based, entertainment, navigational, community, artistic, or personal sites

Design Conventions

- The main menu should always appear across the top or down the left side.
- Repeat the main menu as text links across the bottom of the page.
- The site logo should appear on each page and link back to the start page.
- Use back-to-top links on long pages.
- Provide file sizes for documents that visitors will download.
- Give visitors alternate clean versions of pages they may want to print.

Navigation

- Give visitors at least two other ways to get around in your site.
- Carefully plan what content you want on each page and how they'll connect

Design

- Visual design is what visitors use to determine a site's worth.
- Great content in a poorly designed site equals a bad site.
- Build a template to consistently use throughout the site.
- Build sites to fit the lowest common screen resolution.
- Test your site in the most popular browsers.

Branding

- A single page just so a company can say it's online does nothing to help customers.
- For a company to be considered professional, a web site is a must.

File Structure

- Save your site's files and folders in one main folder, called the site's root folder.
- The address bar usually reveals how a site is structured.

Index Files

- The first page in your site must use a standard default name
- Browsers hunt for index files.
- A site can have more than one index file, just not in the same folder.
- Use index files to your advantage by using them to shorten common URLs.

Chapter 4

Setting YOUR *Sights* on Sites

STUFF YOU'LL LEARN IN THIS CHAPTER

Even though Dreamweaver will let you start building pages without setting up a site first, the results would be nothing short of disastrous. In this chapter, we'll look at Dreamweaver's basic site settings and also take a trip through other time-saving features such as cloaking, Design Notes, and Check In/Check Out. With that down, we'll explore how to manage and edit multiple sites and see how the Files panel makes life much easier for file transfer. This chapter also has some extra bits thrown in—about using an external FTP client, choosing a web hosting company, and more. So smash a bottle of champagne on your desk; we're about to set sail with Dreamweaver!

Keep Arms and Legs Inside the Ride—We're About to Define a New Site!

I know, I know. You must be dying to start building pages. But this chapter is absolutely critical to constructing sites. If you remember back in the previous chapter, I said that defining a site in Dreamweaver was imperative. If you skip this part, things will really mess up on you. So tape your eyelids open and pay attention!

When you go through the site definition process, essentially what you're doing is telling Dreamweaver where all the files that are a part of your site will be stored on your hard drive. Every image, every page, even individual sound files and scripts that you use in your site—all must be stored in the same location. Otherwise, your site won't run.

As you define your site, you'll also set up your remote site, the location where you'll be publishing your site online. If you're already set up with a hosting company—or perhaps your site will be hosted internally by your company—you should already have the information you need for this part of the process. If you've yet to sign up for hosting, you can always come back later to fill in the required content. See the sidebar "Finding a Web Host" later in this chapter to learn more about hosting companies.

To get an idea about how to keep yourself organized, check out my approach. I have a folder on my machine called Websites, where all my current sites are stored.

When you define your site, you can use either Basic or Advanced mode. Basic mode (which you get when you use the Site Definition wizard) provides a simplified way to define a site. The Advanced mode may seem overwhelming at first, but it allows you to make full use of all of Dreamweaver's site functions. We'll start with the Site Definition wizard (Basic mode) and then take a look at the Advanced mode.

Shazam! Using the Site Definition Wizard

The Site Definition wizard provides a simplified way to define a site.

With the Site Definition wizard, you'll be sailing smoothly, but because it's so simplified, it may be missing some of the functionality that you might be after. That's where the Advanced mode comes in. But first, the wizard.

Here's the goods on the Site Definition wizard:

1. From the Site menu, choose Manage Sites.

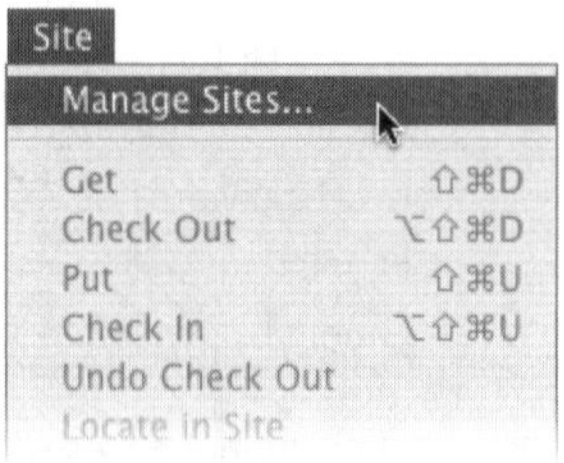

2. In the Manage Sites dialog box that appears, click New; then choose Site from the pop-up menu.

3. If necessary, click the Basic button at the top of the Site Definition window.

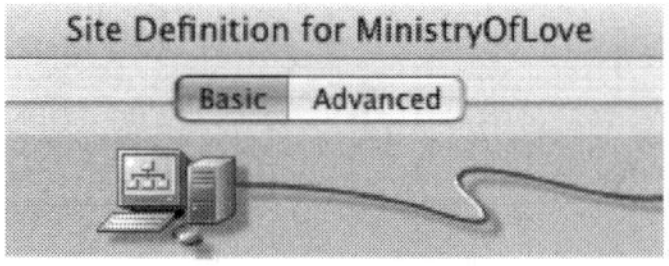

This switches you to the Site Definition wizard.

4. Give your site a name and enter your site's URL if you know it. When you're done, click Next at the bottom of the window.

I suggest giving your site a clear descriptive name. Down the road, you may find yourself working with multiple sites, and it can get really tricky remembering the difference between Unnamed Site 1, Unnamed Site 2, and so on. Also, If you haven't registered your URL yet or don't know what it will be, you can always come back and fill it in later.

5. In the next window, make sure the option No, I Do Not Want to Use a Server Technology is selected; then click Next.

This setting relates to building dynamic pages with Dreamweaver. Find out more in the sidebar "Taking a Drive with Data-Driven Sites."

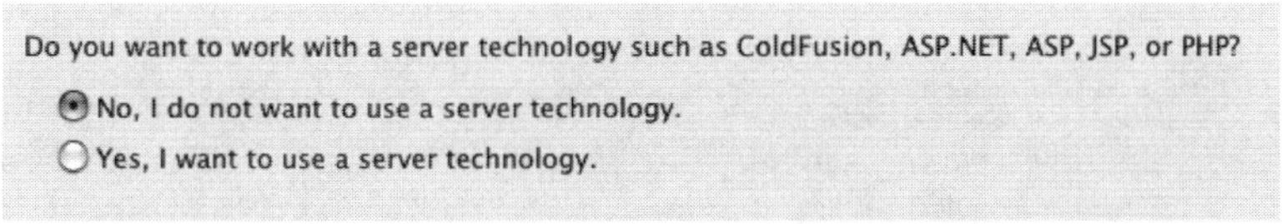

6. On the next screen, choose the way you want to work with your site:

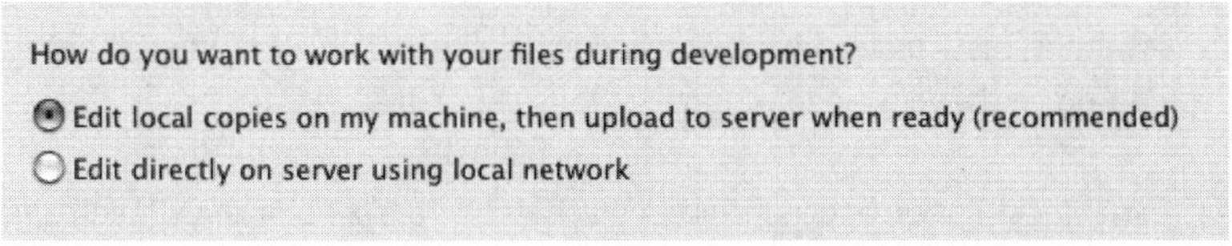

- Odds are you'll stick with the first option, Edit Local Copies on My Machine. Use the folder icon beside the Where on Your Computer Do You Want to Store Your Files field to specify where you'll be saving your web site on your computer.

NOTEWORTHY

A local site is a copy of your web site that resides on your computer. The local site is where you'll be doing the majority of your work, including updating, creating new pages, and adding new content. Once changes have been made to your local site, it will need to be uploaded to your remote site. See "Put Yer Files Up Dar and Git 'Em on Back" later on in this chapter.

IMMINENT DOOM

Every site you define in Dreamweaver should have its own separate local root folder. If it doesn't, working on your sites can get very confusing, or downright disastrous. If you do choose a folder that's already being used by another site, Dreamweaver warns you of the possible problem.

- If you use the second option, Edit Directly on Server Using Local Network, use the folder icon beside the Where Are Your Files on the Network field to specify your site's folder on the network.

7. Click Next. If you selected Edit Local Copies on My Machine, read on. If you're using the Edit Directly on Server Using Local Network option, skip down to step 11.

8. Choose how you want to connect to your remote server; then click Next.

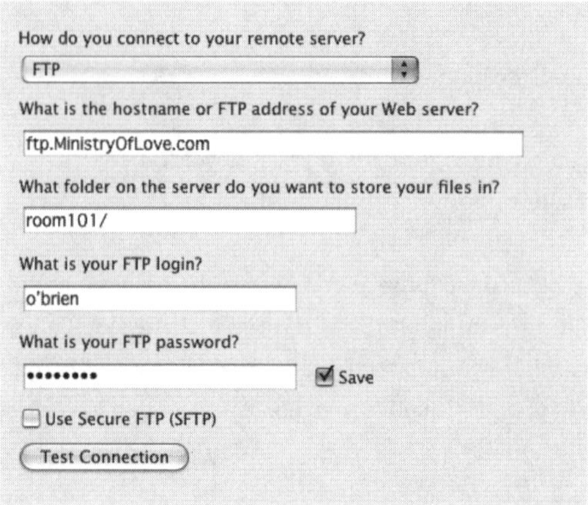

FTP is a common approach, but there are several to choose from. The options below the pull-down list will change depending on the connection type you choose. If you're not sure which you'll use, choose None—you can come back to this setting later.

10. Specify whether you want the ability to check files in and out; then click Next.

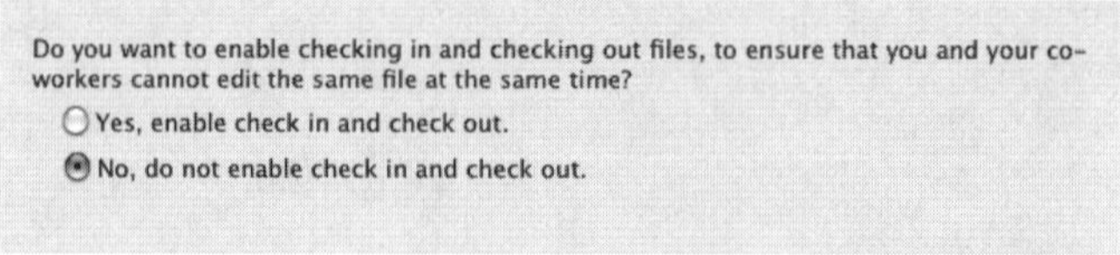

Essentially, enabling Check In/Check Out allows a team of designers to work on a site at the same time without worrying about overwriting each others' files. If you work on your own, you don't need to worry about this.

11. The Summary page appears. Take a quick look to ensure that all your settings are correct; then, when you're good, click Done.

If you want to make a change, use the Back button to return to page you want to fix.

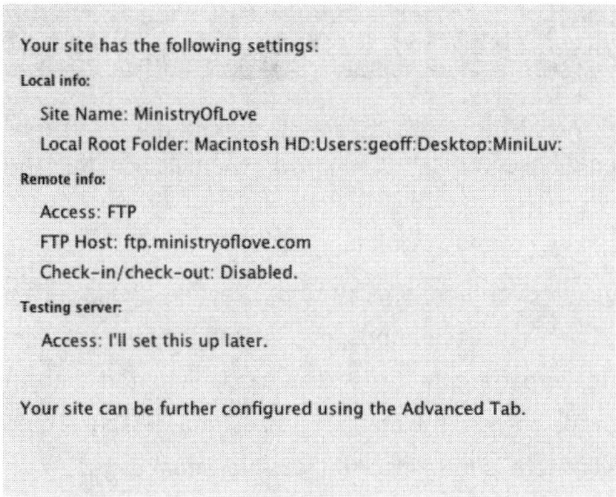

The Summary page in the Site Definition wizard

12. Back in the Manage Sites dialog box, click Done again.

    The Updating the Site Cache window may appear. Let it do its thing—it'll speed up Dreamweaver's work with your site.

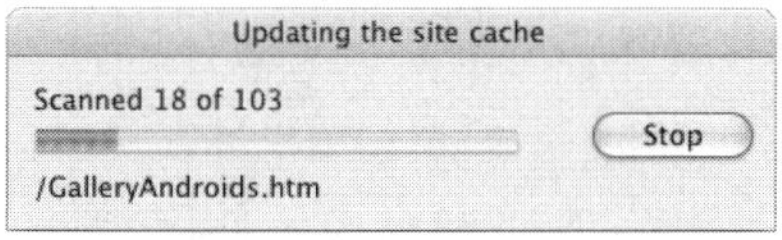

    Once the site definition process is complete, take a gander at the Files panel. It should load in your new site. We'll take a closer look at the Files panel later.

    If your Files panel is empty, that's cuz you don't have any pages or graphics yet. But you will soon.

So that's all there is to setting up a site in Dreamweaver. Didn't hurt too much, right? Now let's take a look at the Advanced mode.

TAKING A DRIVE WITH DATA-DRIVEN SITES

In greater and greater demand these days are web sites that are driven by back-end databases—that is, sites whose content is inserted dynamically, rather than being fixed on the page.

A great example of a database driven site is eBay.com. Creating pages for this massive site by hand would be practically impossible. Instead, all the graphics, descriptions of items, and other page content is dynamically inserted onto the page. When a surfer performs a search, it's actually a back-end database that's being searched, and whose content is then inserted into individual pages.

Although it's beyond the scope of this book, Dreamweaver makes it easy—even for those with little experience—to create dynamic, database driven sites in a variety of server technologies and programming languages, including ASP.NET, PHP, JavaServer Pages (JSP), Microsoft Active Server Pages (ASP), and Macromedia ColdFusion. If you're interested in traveling this route, Dreamweaver's online help is a great place to begin, and there are many resources online to also help you get underway.

Taking the High Road with the Advanced Mode

Using the wizard, Dreamweaver essentially holds your hand through the site setup process. But after a few times through, you may find it a bit tedious. The Advanced mode lets you set up a site with a few clicks (assuming you know where to go) and gives you a wider range of optional site features. Once you're in, the Advanced window lists eight categories of items on the left—but don't freak out; you'll probably use only the first few. Cloaking, Design Notes, Site Map Layout, File View Columns, and Contribute are, for the most part, used only when you're working with a team of designers.

The Advanced mode allows you to make full use of all of Dreamweaver's site functions.

So let's take a look at Advanced mode:

1. Choose Site > Manage Sites. Click New and then Site. At the top of the Site Definition dialog box that appears, click Advanced.

   The Advanced window appears with the Local Info category selected at the far left and the Local Info screen displayed.

SITES OF SIGNIFICANCE

There are many types of sites out there to explore, even beyond the web. Here's a few different types of sites to get you started!

Construction sites: The Big Dig, Boston, MA—The problem: Downtown traffic in Boston that's thicker than Irish Guinness. The solution: The Central Artery/Tunnel Project (CA/T). Beginning in 1991, and on target for completion in mid 2005, Boston's Big Dig is comparable in scale and complexity to the construction of the English Channel Tunnel or the Panama Canal. The project will expand and bury the Central Artery and reunite city areas that have been cut off from the core of Boston since 1959. A little green on the subject? See massturnpike.com/bigdig for more.

Grave sites: Père-Lachaise Cemetery, Paris—The largest cemetery in Paris and the most frequented in the world, Père-Lachaise was opened by none other than notorious French conqueror Napoleon Bonaparte in 1804. At first, the cemetery didn't garner much attention, so the remains of the once famous were relocated as part of a marketing strategy. The plan worked, and now the cemetery is the immortal resting place of over 300 writers, painters, and statesmen. If you're thinking of purchasing a plot, you'll have some stiff competition. See pere-lachaise.com for more.

Web sites: Thematrix101.com—The first movie was great, but the other two were cash cows, right? Think again, and let thematrix101.com be your guide. The site is an online community of Matrix fans and thinkers who attempt to distill the mythos and meaning behind the Wachowskis' work of genius. Suddenly you realize that the masses aren't supposed to "get it." Find out what Colonel Sanders, the Animatrix, and even the video games are really all about. Stay in Wonderland and see how deep the rabbit hole truly goes.

Parasites: Guinea Worm Disease—Hope you're not eating. The Dracunculiasis medinensis, or Guinea Worm Disease, is contracted by those who drink unsanitary water that contains the worm larva. The larva enters the host and heads for the small intestine, where it punctures the intestine wall and makes it's way into the body cavity. There, it can lie undetected for up to a year as it grows to adult size. Here's the tasty part: The worm then punctures the skin of its human host to release its eggs, hopefully into open water. Good news is they're common in only 12 sub-Saharan countries. For yummy pictures, hit up www.biosci.ohio-state.edu/~parasite/dracunculus.html. On that note, lets eat. Who's ready for lunch?

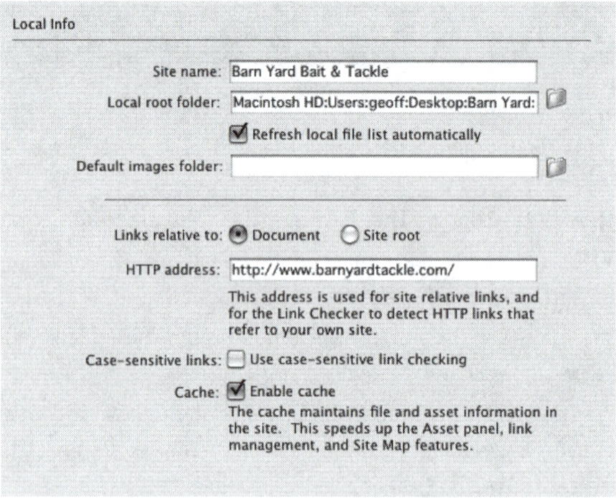

GEEK'S DELIGHT

The folder that you define on your computer is known as your site's local root folder. Once you upload your work, you'll also have a remote root folder.

You'll start by naming your site and telling Dreamweaver where to store it on your hard drive.

2. On the Local Info screen, in the Site Name field, give your site a descriptive name.

3. Click the folder icon at the far right of the Local Root Folder field to specify where you want to store your site on your computer.

4. If you're using the site structure I suggested in Chapter 3, which uses an images folder, specify it in the Default Images Folder field.

NOTEWORTHY

Keep Refresh Local File List Automatically checked. This will automatically update Dreamweaver's Files panel without you having to manually refresh it yourself.

5. Set the Links Relative To option to either Document or Site Root (using the default setting is fine) and if you know the URL for your site, enter it in the HTTP Address field.

If you don't know the URL just yet, you can leave this field blank for now, but know that Dreamweaver will use this URL when it checks the links in your site.

Now you'll tell Dreamweaver where your site will be published. You do this by specifying settings on the Remote Info screen.

6. On the far left of the Advanced window, click the Remote Info category.

The Remote Info screen appears—in the figure, for FTP access.

7. From the Access pull-down menu, select the type of transfer access you want to use. The options include:

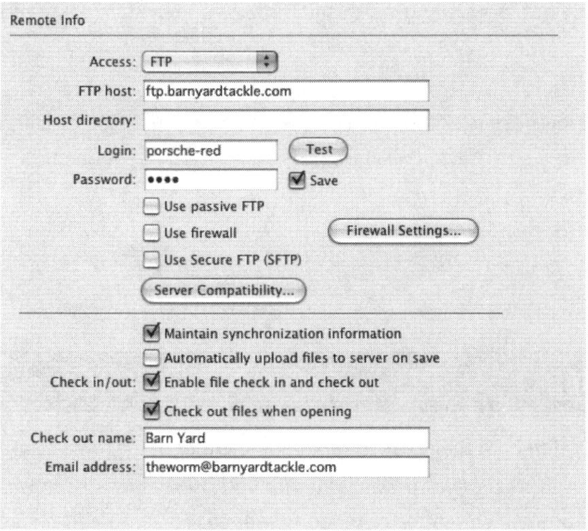

GEEK'S DELIGHT

To ensure that your site will appear on the web exactly as you've created it, you must duplicate your site into your remote web space exactly as it is on your computer.

None: Leave the menu set to None if you're unsure of your access type, or if you only want to develop your site for now and look after publishing it later.

FTP: FTP (File Transfer Protocol) is a common protocol for connecting to web servers. The sidebar "FTP for You and Me" later in this chapter goes into more detail about setting up an FTP connection.

Local/Network: Some companies run their own web servers internally; this option is used in that scenario. See the sidebar "Local/Network Perks" later on in this chapter for more on this type of setup.

WebDAV: If you're using the WebDAV (Web-based Distributed Authoring and Versioning) protocol, use this setting.

RDS: RDS (Remote Development Services) is used most commonly, though not exclusively, with ColdFusion sites.

Depending on the Access option that you pick, Dreamweaver asks for additional information.

8. Specify the rest of the Remote Info settings according the Access option you chose. Then click OK to close the Site Definition dialog box.

9. In the Manage Sites dialog box, click Done.

A Site Cache window may appear. Again, this will speed up your site work later, so just let it run.

Once the site definition process is complete, the Files panel should load in your new site. When you set up a site in Advanced mode, the only two categories you really need to specify are Local Info and Remote Info.

GEEK'S DELIGHT

What's an intranet site? An intranet can be any number of things, including an internal only network. Many intranets are simply closed networks. More at: http://wikipedia.org/wiki/Intranet

STAYIN' LOCAL WITH LOCAL/NETWORK

Larger organizations often host their own intranet sites. Other times, an organization is large enough to host its own public web site and doesn't have to rely on an external hosting company. In either of these two scenarios, you can choose Local/Network from the Access pull-down menu in Dreamweaver's Site Definition dialog box to specify where you'll be transferring your site.

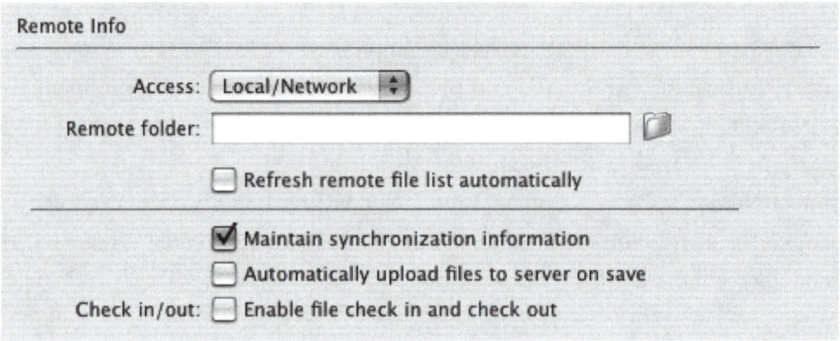

Goin' after some Local/Network access.

In the Remote Info category, click the icon for Remote Folder to navigate to the location where you want the site transferred. Several additional options are also available: You can set the remote list of files to refresh automatically as you're transferring files, and you can take advantage of Dreamweaver's Check In/Check Out command.

TAKIN' THE FTP ROUTE

A common connection to a remote site is via FTP. In the Site Definition dialog box's Remote Info category, choose FTP from the Access menu. Dreamweaver will then ask for the information needed to connect to your remote site. If you've signed up with a web hosting company, the company will provide you with all the information required. (See "Finding a Web Host" later in this chapter for more on choosing a web hosting company.)

To start, enter your FTP host address. This is usually ftp.*url*.com, (where *url* is your site's address). Then enter your username and password and make sure that Save is checked so that you don't have to enter your password every time you connect. All other default settings should be fine, unless you're behind a firewall or want to use Dreamweaver's Check In/Check Out option.

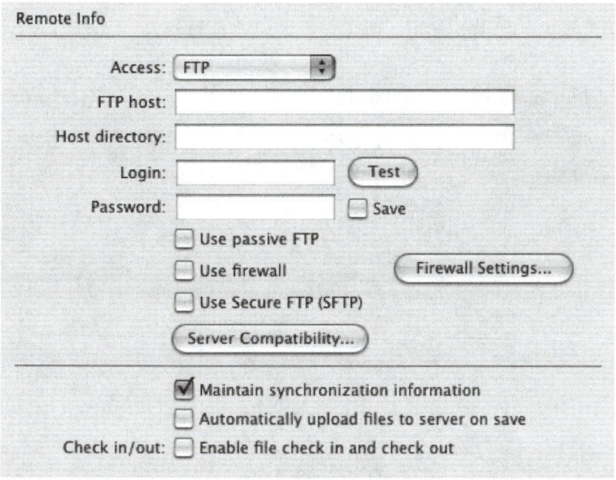

Doin' it FTP style. The kids are all about this one.

Think You've Seen the Sights? Here's Lookin' After Your Sites

You can use Dreamweaver's Manage Sites dialog box not only to create new sites, but also to manage, import, and remove existing sites. You can work with as many sites as you like, as long as they've all been configured in the Manage Sites dialog box—and all sites are always editable. Simply select the site in the list and click the Edit button to open that site's Site Definition dialog box. Here's a few other things you can do...

Been There, Done That: Duplicating a Site

Duplicate all the site's settings, including Local Info and Remote Info.

If for any reason, you want to duplicate an existing Dreamweaver site, you can do so in the Manage Sites dialog box.

1. Choose Site > Manage Sites.
2. In the Manage Sites dialog box, select the site you want to duplicate.
3. Click the Duplicate button on the right.

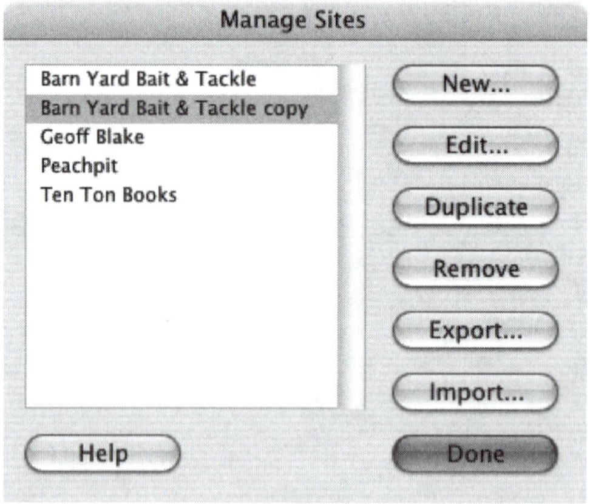

Dreamweaver duplicates the site and adds "copy" to the site name. All the site's settings, including Local Info and Remote Info settings, are duplicated for the new site.

Move Along, Nothing to See Here: Deleting Sites

You're not nuking the entire site. All you're doing is removing the site from Dreamweaver.

Once you're done with a site, you can remove it from Dreamweaver's Manage Sites dialog box. Don't freak. You're not nuking the entire site from your hard drive. All you're doing is removing the site from Dreamweaver. However, once you delete the site, all those settings in the Site Definition dialog box are lost, so be careful!

1. Choose Site > Manage Sites.

2. Select the site that you want to remove.

3 Click the Remove button on the right.

4. When Dreamweaver asks you to confirm, click Yes.

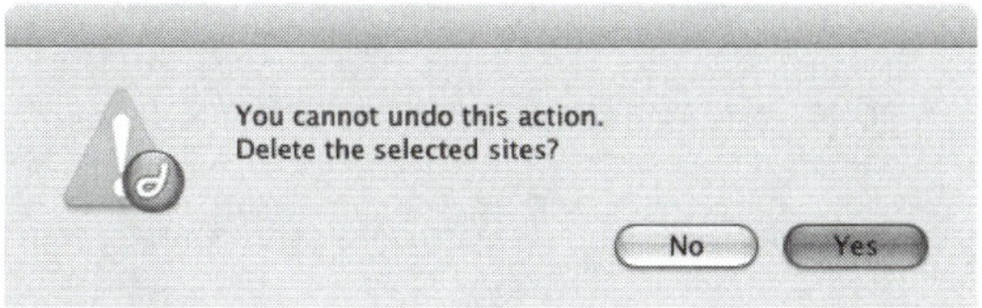

5. In the Manage Sites window, click Done.

Bon Voyage: Importing and Exporting Sites

This is a neat feature. What if a co-worker has set up a site and now you want to import those same settings? Or what if you want to back up your site settings so you'll have them in case your machine blows up? This and more is possible in the Manage Sites dialog box. When you export a site, Dreamweaver saves all the site's settings in an XML file that you can then back up, move to another machine, or e-mail to someone else. That XML file can then be imported back into Dreamweaver, saving you and everyone else from having to reset all those options.

HERE'S HOW TO EXPORT YOUR SITE

It's a really good idea to export your site's settings whenever you're backing up your data, or even to share with others, as previously mentioned.

1. Choose Site > Manage Sites.

2. In the Manage Sites dialog box, click Export.

   If you have remote login and password info set for the site, a dialog box will appear asking you if you're backing up your site or sharing it with others. Essentially, it's giving you the option of exporting the site with or without the remote login info. If this dialog box appears, choose the option you want and click OK.

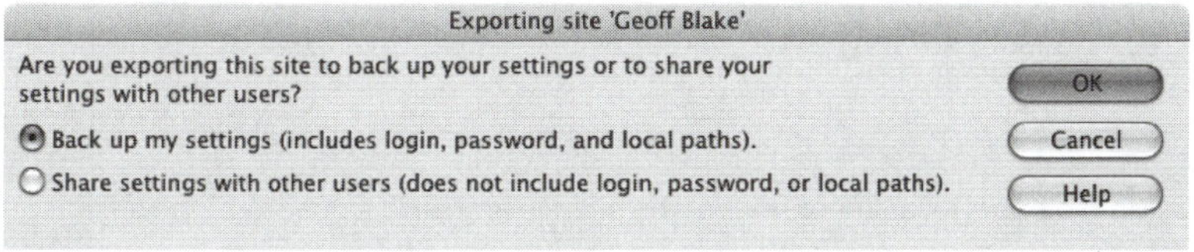

IMMINENT DOOM

Make sure you export a site's settings before removing it from Dreamweaver in case you need the Remote Info settings down the road.

Dreamweaver exports the site's settings in an XML file, which can then be imported back in.

NOTEWORTHY

Paranoia is a sickness most designers suffer from. What if your office explodes? What if ants nest in your CPU? Back up your local sites on a regular basis, and don't forget to export each site's settings and back up those files, too.

When you're exporting a site, Dreamweaver gives you the option of exporting with or without the remote login settings—a nice feature for thwarting evil-doers.

In either case, the Export Site dialog box appears, with a field where you can tell Dreamweaver where you want to save the exported site.

3. In the Export Site dialog box, navigate to a location and click Save.

   The site will be saved with the .ste extension, so keep your eyes peeled for it.

NOTEWORTHY

If you work with multiple sites at a time, as soon as a client's job is complete and you're ready to archive the project, export the site settings and save them in the site folder before removing the site from Dreamweaver's Manage Sites dialog box. That way, you'll always have the site settings if the client wants updates in the future.

AND HERE'S HOW TO IMPORT

So using your computer for a skateboard ramp wasn't your most brilliant idea, huh? Lucky you backed up your stuff. Now be more careful with your new machine.

1. Open the Manage Sites dialog box and choose Site > Manage Sites.

2. Click Import.

   The Import dialog box opens, where you can navigate to the site file (remember, .ste).

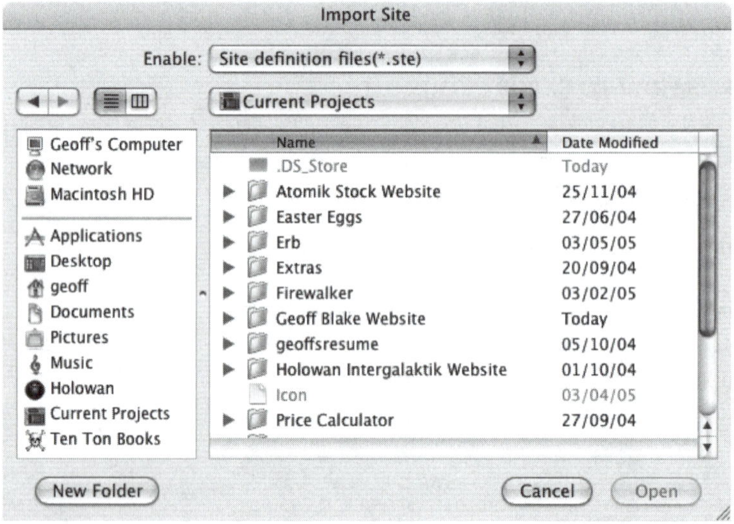

3. In the Import dialog box, select the site file and click Open.

   The site is added to the Manage Sites dialog box, settings and all.

DEFINE A SITE? TOMMYROT—CONNECT DIRECTLY INSTEAD!

Sometimes, defining a site is not necessary in Dreamweaver, especially if you're working with individual pages rather than an entire site. If you find yourself as a part of a design team and your job is to update single pages, then all that's needed is a connection to the remote server.

You manage individual server connections in a way similar to the way you handle sites: through Dreamweaver's Site Definition dialog box. If you want to set up a siteless server connection, follow these steps:

1. From the Site menu, select Manage Sites.

2. Click the New button; then choose FTP & RDS Server from the pop-up menu.

   Dreamweaver will display a message saying that the only two types of server connections allowed are FTP and RDS, and that sitewide functions will not be available.

3. Click OK to close the warning message.

4. In the Configure Server dialog box that appears, enter your server connection information.

   If you're connecting via FTP, enter a name for your connection, the FTP host name, the login name, and the password. If you're connecting via RDS, enter the URL prefix.

5. Click OK when you're done.

The Manage Sites dialog box will list FTP and RDS connections along with any sites you've defined.

You can use these connections just as you would a defined site.

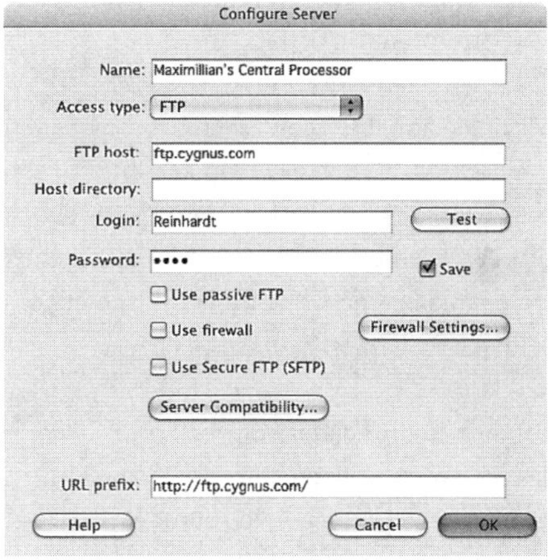

Once the connection has been made, the files on the remote server will be listed in the Files panel. Double-clicking a file will download the file (and all its dependent files) locally to your machine. You can then make your changes and save the document as you normally do. When the file is saved, it's magically transferred back to the remote site, and the local copy is deleted. This is all accomplished without a defined site—pretty spiffy, huh? Look ma, no site!

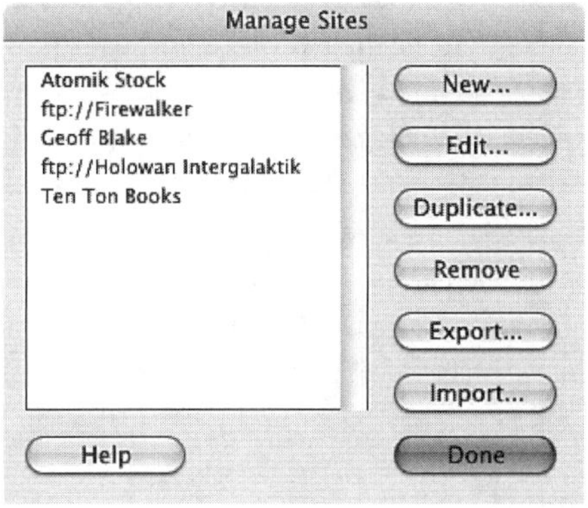

FINDING A WEB HOSTING COMPANY

Still messed up by that whole Guinea Worm Disease thing? Okay, no more talk about parasites. When we discuss hosts, it'll be about web hosts from now on—promise.

A lot of people find the whole issue of web hosting very complicated. It's actually pretty simple (in fact, you probably already have some free web space through your Internet service provider). What trips up most people is registering a URL and then connecting that URL to their web space.

The first step is to register your URL with a company like networksolutions.com. Once the URL is registered, it needs to be pointed somewhere. That somewhere is your web space, and this is done through your URL's Domain Name Server (DNS) settings. These settings can be a bit tricky, but your hosting company should be able to help you out.

Here's a few frequently asked questions to provide further insight into the mystical issue of web hosting:

Who should I choose to host my site?

I don't want to out-and-out plug any specific company, but what you should know is that hosting companies are a dime a dozen. It's not like it used to be during the Internet boom of the late 90's where hosting companies could charge whatever they wanted. Now the competition is unbelievably fierce, and the subscription fees have dropped through the floor. Check out tophosts.com. To sift through the listings, use Fast Find on the main page (center screen—just scroll down a bit).

I suggest choosing a host that offers a cPanel interface, even if you're an experienced designer. It can't be beat. CPanel is an application that runs on a web server, providing a very easy point-and-click interface for you to manage your site. It comes standard with web-based e-mail, built-in FTP functionality, a pile of CGI scripts, and a wealth of other add-ons, like blogs, mini-polls, and online forums. Pretty much anything you want to be able to do with your site, you can do with cPanel. Read up at cpanel.net/features-cpanel.html.

What should I pay?

As little as possible. Again, because competition is so cutthroat, prices are a fraction of what they used to be. To give you a meter stick, one of the sites that I run costs less than 10 bucks a month for 600 MB of space, 10 GB of bandwidth, unlimited e-mail accounts, and about a bazillion other add-ons. You could probably do even better if you hunted around.

Can I host other people's sites myself?

This is another field that's really opened up: reseller hosting. Essentially, if you have a client base, you can offer hosting to them as an add-on service. To do this, you would purchase a reseller plan from a hosting company. Your profits will be the spread between your hosting costs and your earnings from fees—but be careful; you may be lining yourself up for a new job as a *client support specialist*—which could mean more headaches than your hosting is worth to you, and the competition is ferocious. Then again, hosting may be a perfect add-on to your existing services.

A Favorite Getaway: How the Files Panel Works

The Files panel is where you can easily access your site's files and folders within Dreamweaver—you'll see them listed in hierarchical order, as they should also appear on your remote server. You can also view and compare the files on your remote server by clicking the Connect button or by customizing your Files panel, as I'll explain here.

Remember the words of the great George Bernard Shaw: "All professions are a conspiracy against the laity." Regardless as to how complicated co-workers and IT technicians make it sound, web hosting is mindlessly simple—if you've done your homework.

By default, this panel is docked on the right, grouped with the Assets panel. I've always found it difficult to work with sites in such a narrow column, so here's what I suggest: From the Files panel's Option menu, choose Group Files With > New Panel Group. Now the panel is floating on its own, where you can move and expand it, to make viewing a bit easier.

Even still, the Files panel is kinda crammed. At the top are two pull-down menus. The first lets you change the site you're looking at, and the second lets you change the site view.

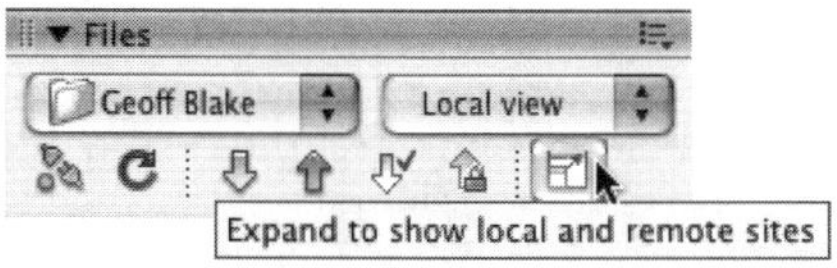

The Files panel is packed tighter than a Japanese commuter train. To get a little elbow room, click the Expand button on the panel's toolbar.

It's all jammed in there, so here's another suggestion. At the top of the panel, click the Expand button. This opens a split-screen view of the Files panel, which you can expand nice and wide. Now you can clearly see your local site on the right and your remote site on the left. Ahhh...that's easier, huh?

If you defined a remote site in the Site Definition dialog box, the left pane displays a message telling you how to see your remote files. Just click the Connect button on the Files panel toolbar. If you didn't specify a remote site, you'll see a message on the left telling you that to see the files on your web server, you must define a remote site. Click the message to set one up. Once you're connected to your remote site, you'll see a listing in each pane, making it really easy to see both the local and remote sites at the same time.

NOTEWORTHY

One thing I love is that if I add files or folders outside Dreamweaver (say through the desktop), the Files panel is smart enough to pick up on this and refresh the site listing automatically, if Refresh Local File List Automatically is turned on in the Site Definition dialog box, that is (it's on by default—no need to hunt!).

PANEL MENU BAR (WINDOWS ONLY)

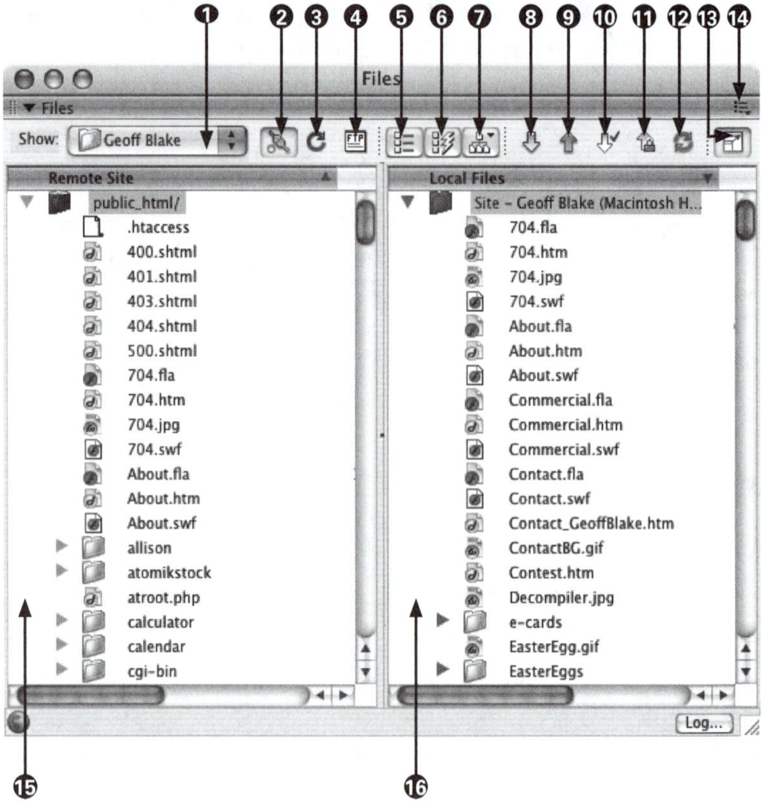

(1) Site pull-down menu **(2)** Connect/Disconnect from Remote Host button **(3)** Refresh button **(4)** View Site FTP Log button **(5)** Site Files button **(6)** Testing Server button **(7)** Site Map button **(8)** Get File(s) button **(9)** Put File(s) button **(10)** Check Out File(s) button **(11)** Check In button **(12)** Synchronize button **(13)** Expand/Collapse Panel button **(14)** Files Panel Option menu **(15)** Remote Site pane **(16)** Local Files pane

SETTING SITE PREFERENCES FOR THE FILES PANEL

You can use the Site Preferences window to customize the way the Files panel behaves when managing your sites. To access the preferences, choose File > Preferences (Windows) or Dreamweaver > Preferences (Mac); then click Site in the category list on the left.

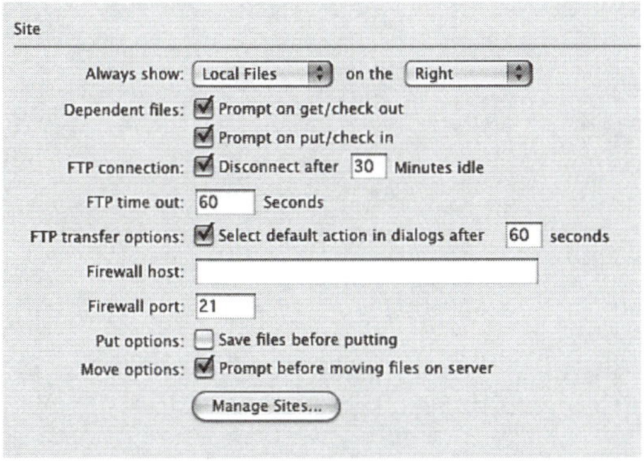

Dreamweaver's Site Preferences window. Customize the behavior of the Files panel and the way that Dreamweaver handles file transfers.

Here are some of the more commonly set preferences:

- **Always Show:** Specify whether local or remote sites are displayed in the right or left pane of the Files panel's expanded view.
- **Dependent Files:** If Prompt on Get/Check Out and Prompt on Put/Check In are checked, a prompt will appear asking you if you want to transfer dependent files whenever you use Get and Put or Check In and Check Out. Remember that a dependent file is a file that's referenced from an HTML page—for instance, a graphic or audio file.
- **FTP Connection:** Specify how long Dreamweaver maintains a remote connection before conking out.
- **Firewall Host:** Here you can insert the address for the server to use to connect to the outside world. If you don't use a firewall, just leave this field empty.
- **Put Options:** Have Dreamweaver automatically save files before they're uploaded.

NOTEWORTHY

A dependent file is any file that's associated with an HTML page. It could be an image, a sound file, or an external style sheet. The dependent file is required for the HTML page to be displayed properly.

Setting Up Camp: Makin' New Files and Folders

When you want to create new files or add folders for your site, you can do so directly in the Files panel.

When you create new files or add folders to your local site, you can do so directly on the Files panel. If you're connected to a remote site, you can create files and folders in the left pane, too.

To delete a file or folder, just select it and press the Delete key on your keyboard. Be careful, though. Deleting files and folders may break or cause errors with hyperlinks you've set.

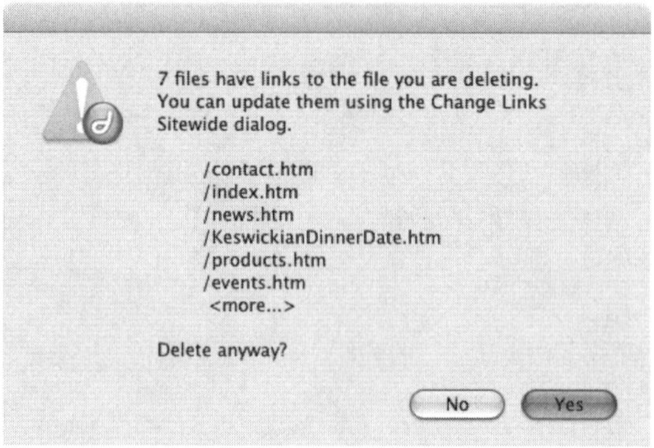

Deleting files and folders from your site may cause massive amounts of destruction if you're hasty. Chill with a chardonnay before making any rash moves.

Don't be a hobo—use keyboard shortcuts! Ctrl+Alt+Shift+N (Windows) or Command+Option+Shift+ (Mac) will create a new folder in the Files panel.

Here's how to add files or folders through the Files panel: Whether the Files panel is expanded or collapsed, just right-click (Windows) or Control+click (Mac) in the panel and choose either New File or New Folder. If you chose to create a new file, you'll get a blank, untitled HTML document.

Here's one approach to web design: Once you know what pages you'll need in your site (remember from the last chapter—what, you fell asleep?), you can create the site's entire structure with blank documents right in the Files panel and then go back later to add in content and linking.

A Home Away from Home: Transferring Your Site Files

Dreamweaver helps you transfer any dependent files, so you have to select only your HTML files when transferring.

You may want to start uploading parts of your site before everything's finished so you can see how everything's working remotely. This will let you test download times and browser support, or maybe just have a look at how things are being displayed before you develop too far. You can also pull content from an existing site and save it locally on your machine.

Obviously, once your site is complete, it will need to be uploaded in its entirety. Every component of your site—every page, every image—will have to go. Everything. Again, this is why you save everything in your local root folder—and why defining a site in Dreamweaver right away is so important: Every component of your site has to stay together for your site to work, and so Dreamweaver can upload the works for you when your site's complete.

When you select your HTML files for transfer to the remote site, Dreamweaver will display a message asking you if you'd like to transfer any dependent files. Click Yes to ensure that all the dependent files for a page will be transferred, which means that you'll never forget to move a GIF image again. (Nor will you ever move an unnecessary file, such as an earlier version of an image, by mistake.) What's more, Dreamweaver automatically creates any subfolders necessary to maintain the site's structure. These two features alone will save you from pulling frantic all-nighters.

One other thing: You don't have to use Dreamweaver to handle file transfer. Many designers opt for an external file transfer utility (called an FTP client) to upload and download their files; see "Using an External FTP Client" later in this chapter. But right now, let's see how Dreamweaver handles file transfers.

IMMINENT DOOM

It's a really good idea to test the various components of your site on a small scale to see if they work before you get too far along with your site. The worst thing in the world is realizing that something doesn't work after it's already been rolled out on a massive scale and used throughout your entire site. Get the sledge hammer—it's time to smash your computer.

UPLOADING FILES

When you're ready to upload your files, follow these steps:

1. In the right pane of the Files panel, select the file (or files) that you want to upload.

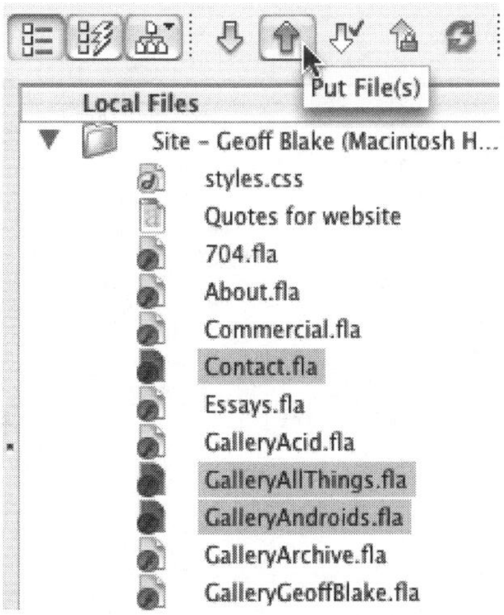

To select multiple files and folders, hold down Ctrl (Windows) or Command (Mac) as you click. To grab a range of files, hold down Shift as you click.

NOTEWORTHY

As you're transferring HTML pages, Dreamweaver may keep asking you if you want to include dependent files. If you keep getting this warning, you can turn it off in Dreamweaver's preferences. Choose Edit > Preferences (Windows) or Dreamweaver > Preferences (Mac), click the Site category on the left, and uncheck the two prompts for dependent files.

2. On the toolbar at the top, click Put Files.

   Now sit back and watch the show.

NOTEWORTHY

The newest version of Dreamweaver has something called Background File Transfer. Check out the sidebar "The End of Coffee Breaks—Forever!" further on in this chapter for more info.

UPLOADING AN ENTIRE SITE

When you're ready to transfer your entire site, don't select all the individual files and folders—try this instead:

1. At the top of the Files panel, select your site's folder.

2. On the toolbar, click the Put button.

   Dreamweaver will ask you if you want to upload the entire site.

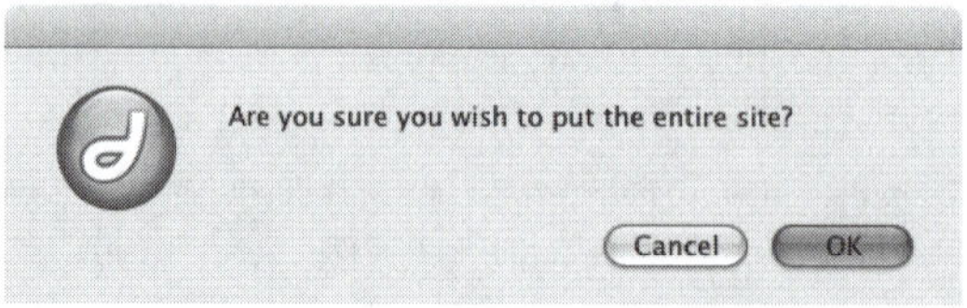

3. Click OK.

NOTEWORTHY

If you move files or folders in your local view, Dreamweaver is smart enough to update the hyperlinks to and from those files. If you do this on the remote side, Dreamweaver first asks for a confirmation.

DOWNLOADING FILES

Downloading files is the reverse of uploading files, so get out that Sabbath record, play it backwards, and give downloading a try:

1. In the left pane of the Files panel, select the file (or files) that you want to download.

   Remember: To select multiple files and folders, hold down Ctrl (Windows) or Command (Mac). Hold down Shift to select a range.

2. On the toolbar at the top, click Get File(s).

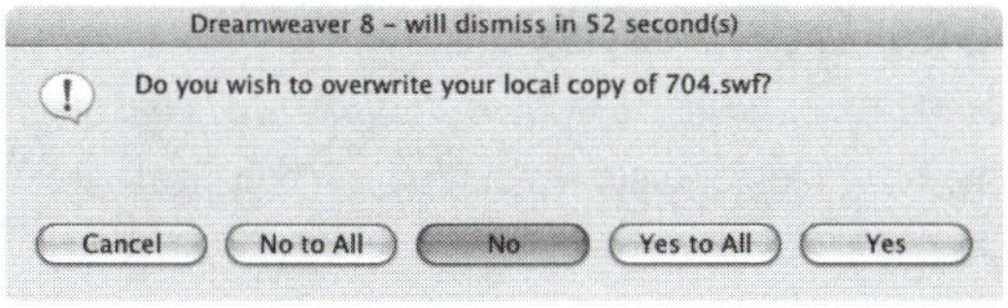

If you're retrieving files that you already have on your local site, Dreamweaver will ask if you want to overwrite them. Think fast—Dreamweaver has you on a time limit!

3. Sit back and contemplate life.

STOPPING A FILE TRANSFER

Did ya goof? It's all good; just don't drink so much at work. To stop an upload or download, simply close the Background Activity dialog box that appears when you start a transfer. Dreamweaver will warn you that closing the window will toast your file activity, which is what you want, so click OK.

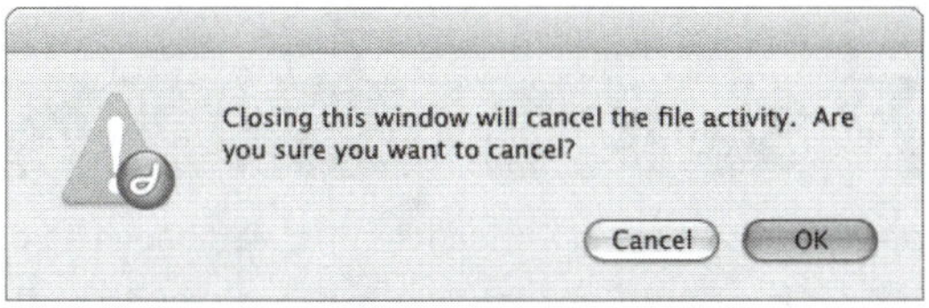

If you ever want to stop a file transfer, just close the Background Activity dialog box and click OK in the confirmation box.

NOTEWORTHY

When you're working on a particular file, you can also use the File Management button on the Document toolbar to get, put, check in, check out, and perform a number of other operations on the file.

THE END OF COFFEE BREAKS—FOREVER!

A new feature in Dreamweaver 8, Background File Transfer gives you the ability to keep working while files are being uploaded or downloaded. In previous versions, this was coffee break time. Now you have to keep working.

Dreamweaver's online help provides a more detailed list of commands that cannot be performed while transferring, but here are a few that won't function: Get and Put are out, as are Check In and Check Out. Most remote functions are unavailable as well—for instance, you can't create new folders, save to the remote site, or delete files. Also out is refreshing the remote location. That being said, when it's crunch-time, you can still get a lot done while stuff's transferring!

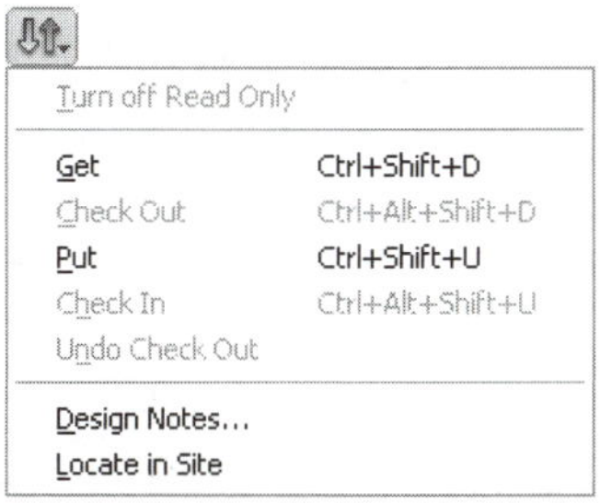

The File Management button on the document toolbar provides another way to get to some of the commands we've been talking about.

NOTEWORTHY

The Files panel isn't only for working with local and remote sites. Often, I need to transfer files to an FTP site for a client or co-worker. Without going through the hassle of setting up a site in Dreamweaver, I use the Files panel simply as a file transfer utility. See the sidebar "Define a Site? Tommyrot! Connect Directly Instead!" earlier in this chapter.

Going at It on Your Own with FTP

If you want to use another program for ***transferring files****, it's not going to cause any problems for Dreamweaver.*

You certainly don't have to use Dreamweaver's Files panel to look after your file transfers. In fact, I used an external FTP client for the longest time just because I was more comfortable with it. I eventually switched to using the Files panel, but I still keep an FTP utility handy. If you want to use another program for transferring files, that's fine—it's not going to cause any problems for Dreamweaver.

Choosing an FTP Client

There are many FTP programs available: some good, some not so good; some free, some not so free. You may want to download a few to try them out and see which you like best. Personally, I like the ones that give you two window panes: one for the remote site and one for the local site. Others have just a single window that you can drag and drop files into, just like a folder window on your computer.

GEEK'S DELIGHT

FTP stands for File Transfer Protocol. It's the method used to transfer files to a remote location.

Tractors are not family vehicles, so park it in the shed mister.

GEEK'S DELIGHT

The term client just means program or application. So an FTP client is just a program that looks after file transfers. Some people refer to their e-mail program as their e-mail client. Same idea.

PICKIN' AN FTP CLIENT

Here are a few FTP programs that you can download and install, depending on your platform. They all work in a similar way and are easy to use, so you shouldn't have trouble with them. For a much greater variety, visit download.com.

FTP Client	Get It At	What's the Deal?
Windows		
WS_FTP	ipswitch.com/_download/wsftppro.asp	Free to try, $35 to buy
FTP Commander	internet-soft.com/download.htm thesecond.net/files/GuildFTPd.exe	Free
Mac		
Fetch	fetchsoftworks.com	Free to try, $25 to buy
Cyberduck	cyberduck.ch/index.php#download	Free

Setting Up the FTP Connection

Most FTP programs are very straightforward to use. The toughest part is usually setting up the connection to your remote site, but even this is fairly straightforward. The programs usually have a New Connection button on the toolbar or something similar in the File menu.

GEEK'S DELIGHT

Often when you're establishing a new connection, the dialog box will contain a field labeled Host Directory or Initial Path. If your site is stored within a specific folder when you connect (a folder called public, for example) you could enter the path to that folder to connect directly to it, rather than having to navigate to it after you connect. Common host directories are public_html, www, and site. Check with your host.

Cyberduck's New Connection dialog box. Most FTP clients have a similar dialog box for establishing a remote connection to your web space.

When you establish a new connection, you'll get a dialog box that asks you to provide your server address (usually "ftp.*url*.com," where *url* is your site's address), your username, and your password. This information should be provided to you by your hosting service or IT department if you're working within a large organization.

JUST THE GIST

Defining a Site

- Defining a site in Dreamweaver is imperative.
- When you define a site, you're telling Dreamweaver where all the files that are a part of your site will be stored on your hard drive.

Site Definition Wizard

- If you're just getting started with Dreamweaver, the Site Definition wizard provides the easiest way to define a site.
- Experienced users can make use of the Site Definition's Advanced mode.
- Advanced mode contains categories that some users may never use.

Duplicating Sites

- Duplicate a site and all its settings in the Manage Sites dialog box.

Deleting Sites

- Once your work is complete on a site, you can remove it from Dreamweaver's Manage Sites dialog box.
- Removing a site from Dreamweaver does not delete it from your hard drive.

Importing and Exporting Sites

- Dreamweaver gives you the option to export your site's setings with or without sensitive remote login info.

Creating New Files and Folders

- You can add new files and folders directly in the Files panel or through your OS.

Uploading and Downloading

- By default, the Files panel displays your local site on the right and your remote site on the left.
- Use the Put and Get buttons on the Files panel toolbar to upload or download.

Stopping a Transfer

- To stop a file transfer, close the Background Activity dialog box.

Choosing an FTP Client

- You don't have to use Dreamweaver's Files panel for uploading and downloading.
- There are many external and inexpensive FTP programs available online.

Setting Up the Connection

- FTP programs usually have a New Connection button; when you click it, you'll be prompted to enter your site's remote info.
- Most programs allow you to save your remote connections as bookmarks or favorites.

Part II

Building Your SITE Starts *Right Now*

Chapter 5

Building *your first* Site

Building a Simple Web Site—Dreamweaver Boot Camp

All right, no more tiptoeing through the tulips! It's finally time to get to work with Dreamweaver. In fact, think of this chapter as your Dreamweaver boot camp. Here, you actually get to build something: your first, simple web site.

So what awaits you in boot camp? Here, you'll step you through the whole process: You'll start by defining your site—that's always the first step. Then, without further delay, you'll jump headlong into basic training, building and adding components to your page. You'll add and format some text, insert a graphic, set some hyperlinks, and make use of Dreamweaver's Library panel.

STUFF YOU'LL LEARN IN THIS CHAPTER

Do you have a six-point harness handy? Good. Fasten it—you're in for a ride! In this chapter, you'll finally get some hands-on design time. We'll start by defining a site. Then we'll bulldoze into Design Files. Then the goods: text formatting, Flash Text, and images. Want more? Good, 'cuz then it's on to the library, hyperlinks, and—best of all—building a fully functional site. Better cinch that harness a bit tighter! Here we go!

Dreamweaver's prebuilt Design Files are a great place to start. You can easily replace the sample text and graphics with your own, insert additional content, create library items, and begin building a multi-page site—all of which you'll learn how to do in this chapter.

You'll skip through rubber tires, climb ropes, and crawl under barbed wire. By the end of all this, you'll have a simple three-page site that's ready to be tested and uploaded live to the web. You'll be a lean, mean, Dreamweaver machine—able to tell the difference between the friendlies and the bad guys like any proud soldier can. All right—lace 'em up, and let's move out!

Defining Your Site and Structure—Packin' Up and Heading Out

Getting dropped off at basic can be hard on mom, but let's get going. If you're going to make it through boot camp, there are certain things you've gotta bring with you, and web design is no different. While coffee is always a great start, there are a few other things you need to prep and pack—namely, you need to define a Dreamweaver site and organize your structure.

Before we start, Dreamweaver should be running, with no open files. With nothing open, you should be looking at Dreamweaver's Start Page. Ready? Okay, let's get started.

Defining the Site

Before anything else happens, you have to define a site in Dreamweaver.

If you recall from Chapter 4, the first thing you have to do before anything else happens is define a site in Dreamweaver. When we looked at this topic before, it was pre-basic training. Now you're actually in the field with your boots on the ground, so you'll see how site definition works with a real site.

Stowin' gear starts right here:

1. On Dreamweaver's Start Page, in the Create New column, select Dreamweaver Site.

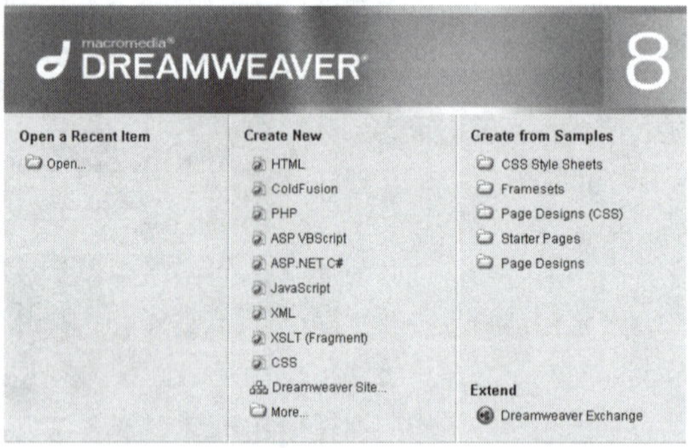

2. In the Site Definition wizard that appears, name your site—for example, `My First Site`; then click Next.

3. Make sure that No I Do Not Want to Use a Server Technology is selected; then click Next.

4. On the next screen, make sure that Edit Local Copies on My Machine is selected; then in the Where on Your Computer Do You Want to Store Your Files? field, click the folder icon.

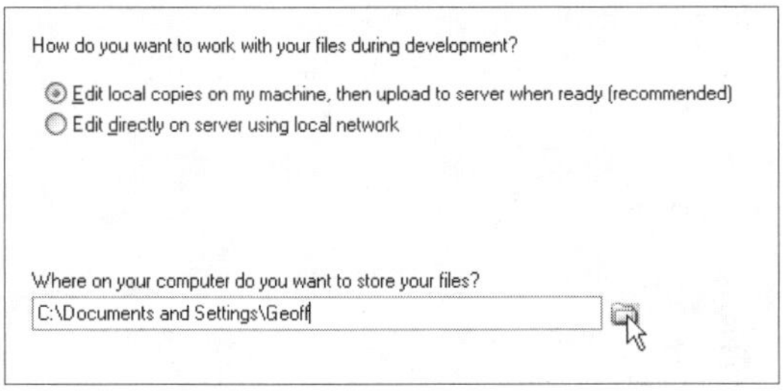

Here, you'll tell Dreamweaver where your site will be stored on your computer.

5. In the Choose Local Root Folder window that appears, navigate to your desktop.

You can specify a folder anywhere on your computer, but for simplicity, you'll create a folder on the desktop for now.

6. Create a new folder on your desktop.
   - In Windows, click the Create New Folder button and name the folder `My Site`. Then click Open and then Select. Click Next when you're done.

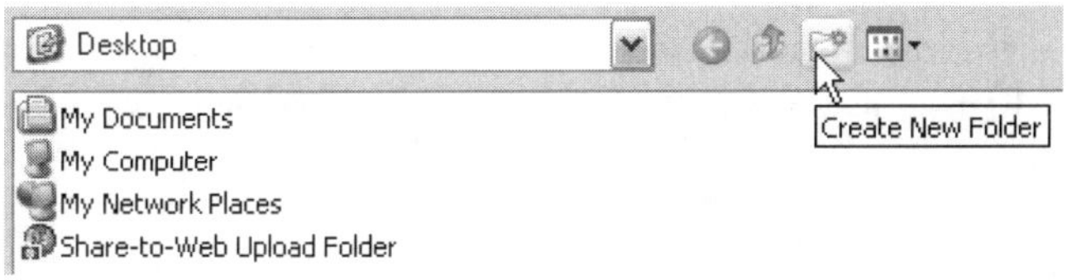

   - On the Mac, click the New Folder button, name the folder `My Site`, and then click Choose. Click Next when you're done.

7. From the How Do You Want to Connect to Your Remote Server menu, choose None; then click Next.

Usually, you'll connect using FTP; then you'll have to enter your FTP information. For this example, just choose None. You can always come back later and enter your FTP information if you want to connect to a remote site.

8. Review your settings on the Summary page; then click Done.

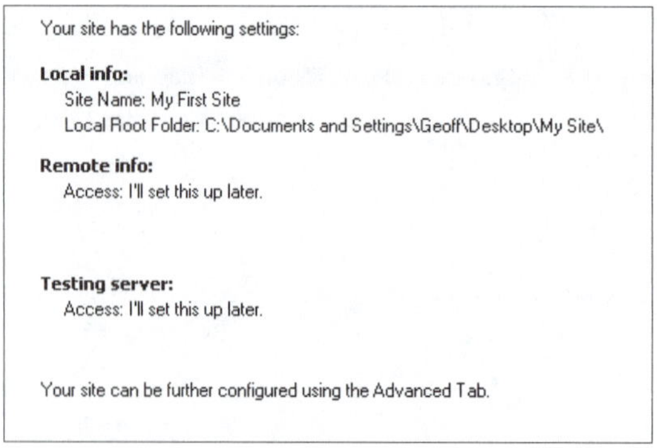

Creating Site Folders

You can create a site's structure directly in the Files panel.

Once your site is defined, Dreamweaver's Files panel loads your site (choose Window > Files if you don't have the Files panel open). However, because your site is empty, there isn't a whole lot to look at—so we'll create a basic site structure directly in the Files panel. In fact, this site structure will be the same one suggested back in Chapter 3.

In addition to defining your site structure in Dreamweaver's Files panel, you can define it in Windows Explorer (Windows) or the Finder (Mac). Just make sure to refresh the Files panel when you come back to Dreamweaver.

If defining a site is like packing up your gear, then creating the site structure is like getting your footlocker, duffle bag, and backpack ready—you're getting containers ready to hold your site's content. Leave the suede designer suitcases at home—they don't cut it in the army, son!

Here's how to create a site structure:

1. In the Files panel, right-click (Windows) or Control+click (Mac) and choose New Folder from the menu that appears. Name the folder `htm` and press Enter (Windows) or Return (Mac).

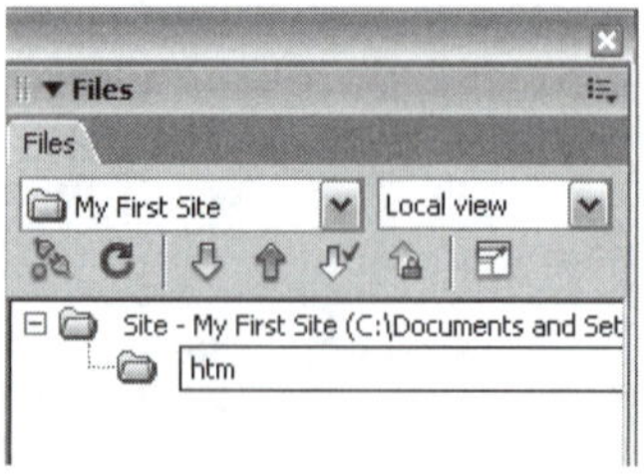

You'll use this folder to store all your web pages. Next, you'll create another folder for images.

NOTEWORTHY

You can use the Files panel to open files, too. Just make sure you're looking at the correct site (use the Show menu at the top right of the panel); then double-click the file you want to open.

2. Click the topmost folder in the Files panel (here, it's Site – My First Site); then right-click (Windows) or Control+click (Mac) and choose New Folder again. This time, name the folder `img`.

Designing Your Site Using Dreamweaver Design Files

The moment has arrived: It's finally time to create your first page. To get started, you'll use Design Files, which are prebuilt pages that come with Dreamweaver. Each Design File provides a layout, plus sample graphics and text, all ready for you to work with—they're the perfect place to start if you're new to the web design world. There are lots of Design Files to choose from, but we'll keep things simple here by sticking with a straightforward example.

Design Files are prebuilt pages that come with Dreamweaver—perfect for those just starting in web design.

Have you ever used templates in other programs? Design Files are based on the same idea—although don't confuse Design Files with Dreamweaver's template commands. Templates in Dreamweaver are totally different from Design Files. Templates allow you to control and drive the layout and content of a number of pages from a single file. We'll tackle Dreamweaver templates in Chapter 13.

So are you ready to go? Saddle up your gear and fasten that chin strap!

Check out dreamweaver-templates.org, where you'll find tons of prebuilt Dreamweaver pages to help you get started.

To use a Design File, follow these steps:

1. From the Start Page, click Page Designs (CSS) in the Create from Samples column.

   The New Document dialog box appears with the General tab displayed and the Page Designs (CSS) category selected in the Category list. If you're not using Dreamweaver's Start Page, just choose File > New and then click Page Designs (CSS) in the Category list in the New Document dialog box.

START YOUR MISSION WITH DREAMWEAVER'S START PAGE

By default, whenever you start Dreamweaver (or whenever you don't have any files open), the Start Page appears. If you find this window vying a little too much for your attention, you can disable it. To turn it off, click the Don't Show Again check box at the bottom left. The next time Dreamweaver launches, the Start Page won't appear.

If you've turned the Start Page off and want to get it back, you can do so through Dreamweaver's preferences.

1. Choose Edit > Preferences (Windows) or Dreamweaver > Preferences (Mac).
2. Make sure the General category is highlighted on the left and click Show Start Page in the Document Options section at the top.

NOTEWORTHY

Dreamweaver offers many other Design Files besides those in the Page Designs (CSS) category. In the New Document dialog box, you can explore the CSS Style Sheets, Framesets, Starter Pages, and Page Designs samples, which are all available from the Category list in the New Document dialog box.

IMMINENT DOOM

If you navigate outside your site's local root folder when you're saving, links to dependent files (such as graphics and style sheets) will be lost when you upload your site to your web server. It's very important to save all your files within a Dreamweaver-defined site.

2. In the Page Designs (CSS) column, choose Halo Left Nav.

   Dreamweaver displays a preview of the page at the right, with a description of the page below.

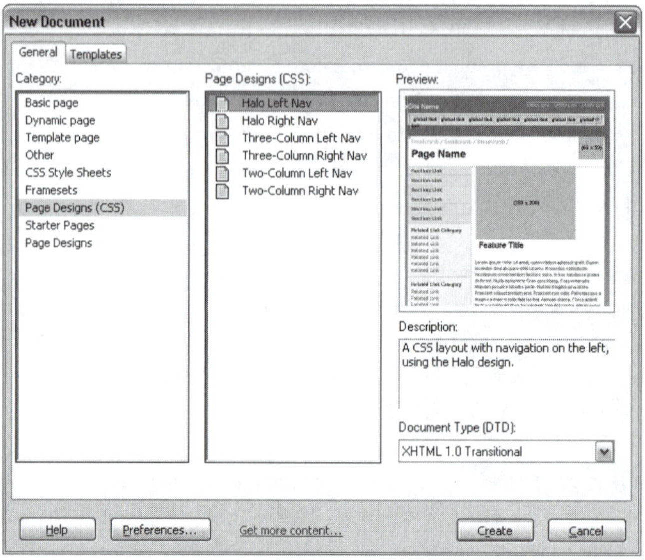

3. Click Create.

SAVING SAVVY

When you work with Dreamweaver's Design Files, usually you'll be prompted to save as soon as you create them. However, when you're building a page from scratch, it'll be up to you to save on your own. Saving in Dreamweaver is no different than saving in any other program—just choose File > Save.

When you're saving your files, steer clear of special characters, punctuation, and spaces. Most web servers don't understand them, and they may prevent your pages from being displayed correctly.

Here's a neat feature in Dreamweaver: If you've made a change to your page and have not yet saved it, an asterisk appears on the document tab and in the title bar beside the file name. This is just a friendly reminder letting you know that the document has been changed and hasn't yet been saved. Once you save the file, the asterisk disappears.

Dreamweaver opens the page and also prompts you to save. Because this page will be the opening page to your site, make sure to save it as `index` at the top level of the site (again, called the site's root directory).

4. In the Save As dialog box, name the page `index.html` and save it in the My First Site folder.

   Because this Design File page already has images and some text formatting, it uses several dependent files. Dependent files are files that the page needs for it to be displayed properly—for instance, graphics and style sheets. So after you click Save, the Copy Dependent Files dialog box appears.

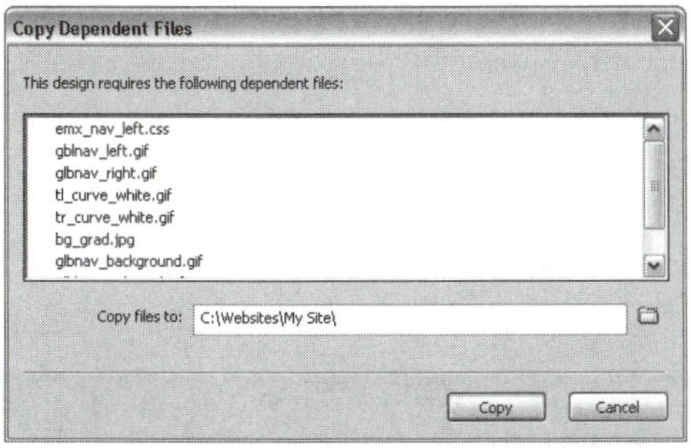

5. In the Copy Dependent Files dialog box, click Copy to bring all the dependent files into your site.

   The Files panel will now list your *index.html* file, but it may not list the dependent files you just copied. That's because the panel needs to be refreshed.

6. Click the Refresh button at the top of the Files panel to have the dependent files appear.

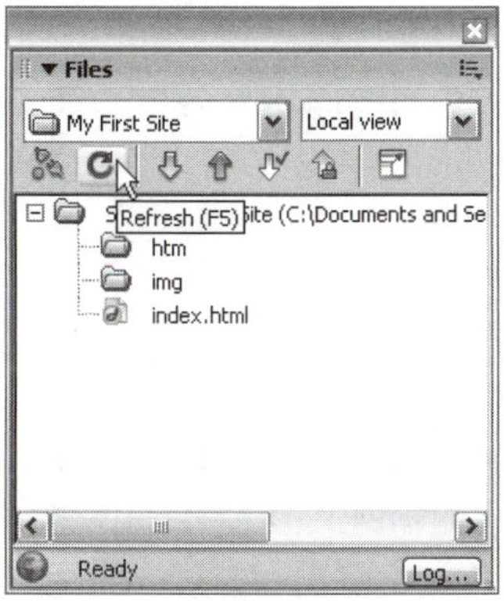

Next, you'll give your page a title, which will appear in your visitor's browser title bar.

Personally, I go with .htm. The way I see it, the shorter extension saves me 1/16 of a second when typing the file name, which could easily add 20 minutes to my life—and I'm gonna savor those 20 minutes!

NOTEWORTHY

When you save a file, by default Dreamweaver uses the .html extension. But recall from Chapter 3 that .htm will work just as well. If you like, you can switch Dreamweaver to use .htm, but be careful—building a site can get frustrating if you have a mix of pages, some using .html and others using .htm, especially when you start working with hyperlinks. Make things easier on yourself by sticking with either .html or .htm. Use the New Document category of Dreamweaver's preferences to set the default extension that you want to use.

7. On the Document toolbar, highlight the Untitled Document text in the Title field, type a new title, and then press Enter (Windows) or Return (Mac).

Keep in mind that the page title is also used when a visitor bookmarks your site, so you may want to make your title descriptive, to make it easy for surfers to find your site again in their list of Favorites.

The particular Design File that you've created uses something called layers to help control your page layout. Layers are areas on a page that are isolated from other content, and they make controlling and managing your page layouts really easy. There's lots more to know about layers, so we'll take a closer look at them in the next chapter.

Now, with a page created and a title added, you'll want to take a look at how your page and title will appear in your visitor's browser. In a moment, you'll preview your page in your web browser. But first, a little bit of housekeeping is in order.

STARTING FROM SCRATCH: CREATING A BLANK PAGE

Often, you won't be starting your work with a Dreamweaver Design File, but creating your pages from scratch instead. Creating a page from scratch may seem a bit daunting at first, because it's hard to know where to start, especially if you're new to web site design. At least with a Design File, you have something to work with. Now you're staring down a page that looks like the Winnipeg frontier in July.

But fear not. In the next chapter, you'll find out how to build your own layouts from scratch using Dreamweaver's CSS layers. In the meantime, though, you may want to know how to create a brand-new, blank document.

To create a blank page, follow these steps:

1. Choose File > New.

2. In the New Document dialog box that appears, on the General tab, choose Basic Page from the Category list on the left. Then, from the Basic Page list in the center, choose HTML.

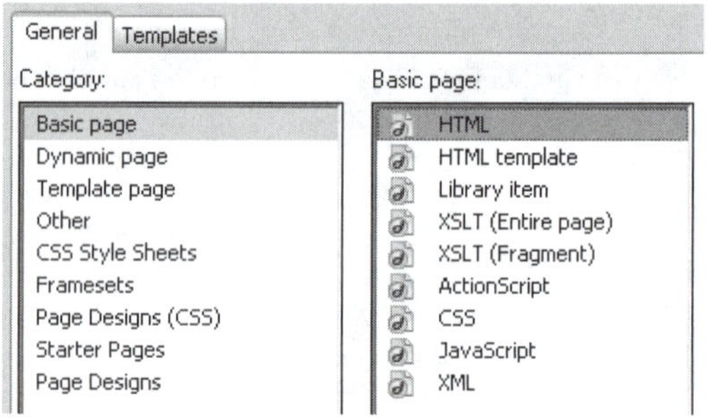

3. Click Create at the bottom right.

   Your new page opens, and you're ready to roll.

Dreamweaver allows you to work with many document types and technologies, but nine times out of ten, you can stick with the Basic Page category and choose HTML for the pages you create.

Organizing Your Files

When you copied those dependent files when you set up your Design File page, Dreamweaver dumped them all into the top level of your site. In other words, you've got some loose gear, so you'd better stop and tie it down.

Sort your pages and images directly in Dreamweaver's Files panel.

For the Halo Left Nav Design File, you should see one CSS file, six GIF files, and two JPG files. The GIF and JPG files are images, so they should be moved into your *img* folder. As for the CSS file, that's your Cascading Style Sheet file that's helping to format the text on the page and control the page layout. You can leave it where it is for now. You can sort your pages and images directly in Dreamweaver's Files panel.

Here's how to organize your site files:

1. Ctrl+click (Windows) or Command+click (Mac) each of your GIF and JPG files.

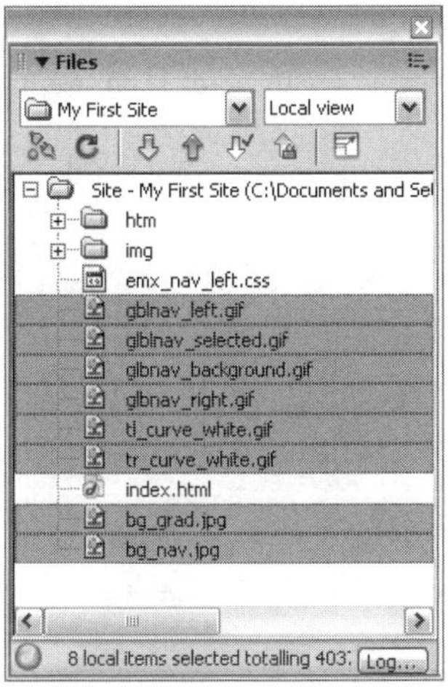

2. Drag the files into your *img* folder.

   The Update Files dialog box appears. Because the images you're moving are referenced from both the *emx_nav_left.css* file and the *index.html* file, Dreamweaver asks if you want to update the links.

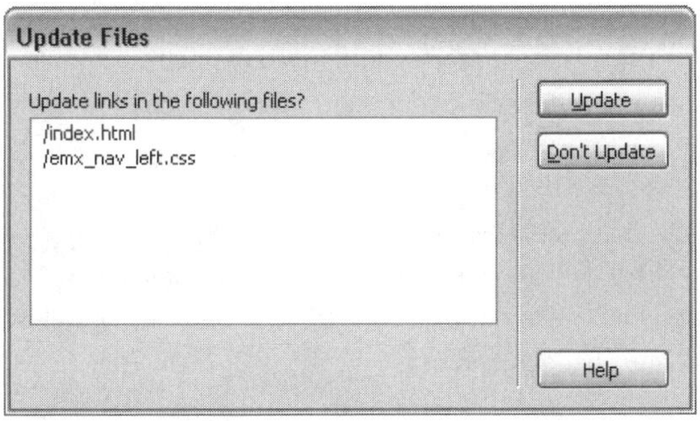

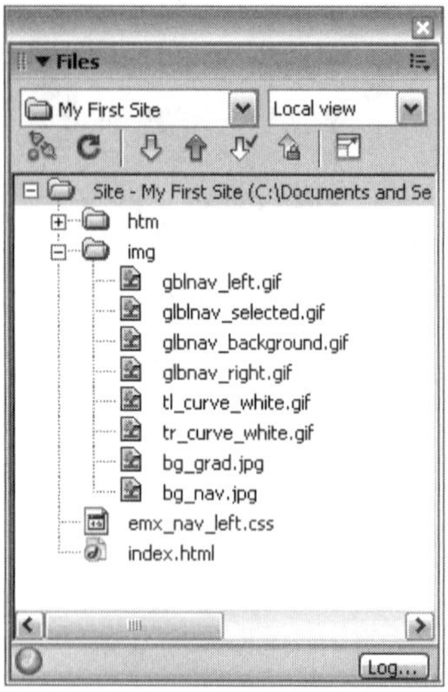

3. In the Update Files Dialog box, click Update.

Dreamweaver updates the links after moving the files into the *img* folder.

All right—with everything squared away, it's time to see how your page will look to your visitors.

Previewing Your Page

Even though Dreamweaver's Design view approximates the way your pages will appear in a browser, it's just not the real thing. So as you build your pages—adding text, graphics, and other page elements—you'll want to check periodically to see how your pages will appear in an actual web browser .

Follow these steps to preview your work:

1. To preview your page, choose File > Preview in Browser; then select your browser.

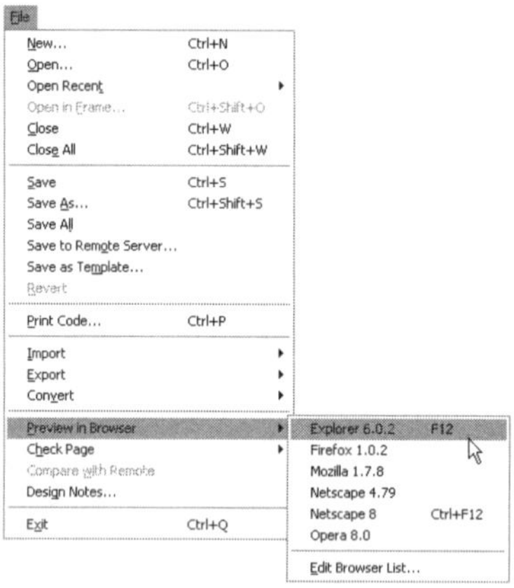

It's a good idea to have several current browsers set in Dreamweaver and to preview your work often in all of them.

Periodically view your pages in a variety of browsers to see how they'll look to your visitors.

2. You may be prompted to save. Make sure you do so.

   Dreamweaver opens the page in your browser, giving you a much clearer idea of what your visitors will see when they view your page. You'll also see the title that you added to your page earlier in the web browser's title bar.

After you've previewed your page, don't close your browser window—keep it open in the background as you work in Dreamweaver. Then you can make changes to your page in Dreamweaver, save your page, and flip back to your browser and click the Refresh button to see how your changes turn out.

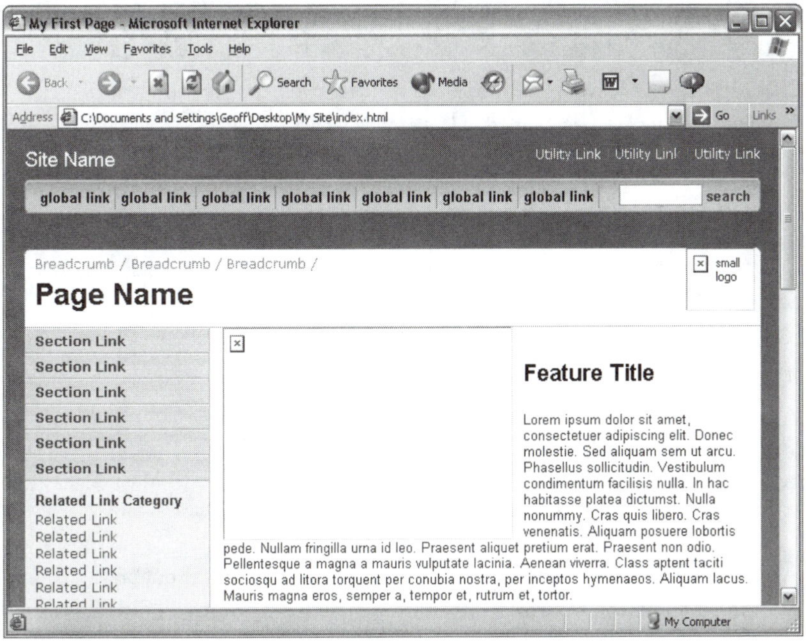

It's always a good idea to preview your work in a web browser to see how it will render for your visitors. In fact, keep your browser running in the background as you're working in Dreamweaver. That way, when you save your page, you can simply flip back to your browser and click the Refresh button to see how things are looking.

Another way to preview your work is to use the Preview/Debug in Browser button on the Document toolbar. Just pull down the menu and select the browser you want to use. If you don't have many to choose from, see the sidebar "Adding Browsers to Dreamweaver."

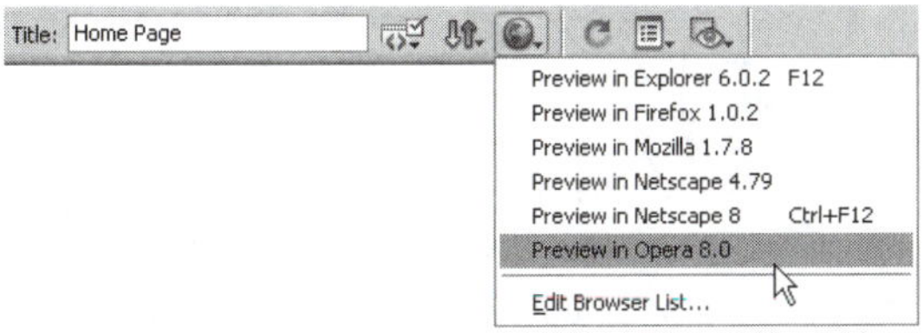

Get previewing that page! Just select your target browser from the Preview/Debug in Browser pull-down menu on the Document toolbar.

NOTEWORTHY

I like to keep the page I'm working on open in my browser as I go. I also sometimes run several browsers simultaneously, all with the same page open, so I can see how the page is being treated by each browser.

IMMINENT DOOM

Previewing your work is an absolute must. Remember: Users don't blame their browsers when a web page doesn't work—they blame the web page.

ADDING BROWSERS TO DREAMWEAVER

Dreamweaver's Preview in Browser menu (available from the File menu) lists all browsers that have been added to Dreamweaver's preferences. This list can contain up to 20 browsers (if you can scrounge up that many), and you can also set one browser to be the primary browser and another as the secondary browser. You'll first want to download and install the most common browsers available (see the sidebar "Popular Web Browsers" in Chapter 3). Then follow these steps to add more browsers to Dreamweaver:

1. Choose Edit > Preferences (Windows) or Dreamweaver > Preferences (Mac).

2. In the Category list on the left, click Preview in Browser.

3. In the Preview in Browser preferences, click the plus button to add a browser.

4. In the Add Browser dialog box that appears, click the Browse button to locate the browser you want to add.

5. If you want to make the browser either the primary browser or the secondary browser, click the appropriate check box.

6. When you're naming the browser in the Add Browser dialog box, type the version of the browser, too. It's always a good idea to have a few versions of major browsers installed.

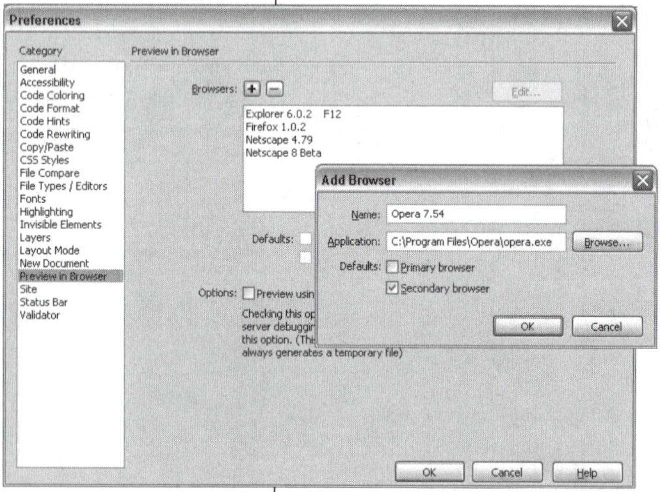

7. Click OK.

The browser is added to the list of browsers.

If you set the browser to be the primary browser, you'll see the F12 (Windows) or Option+F12 (Mac) shortcut beside the browser's name. Use this shortcut to automatically launch the browser and preview your page. Similarly, for any browser set as the secondary browser, you can use the Ctrl+F12 (Windows) or Command+F12 (Mac) shortcut.

Putting Text on Your Page—At Ease, Soldier

You can add text in to your web page either by typing it directly on the Dreamweaver page or by creating it first in another application and then copying it to your page. You can also create something called Flash Text, which is graphical text that is perfect for artsy or decorative headings.

Dreamweaver's Design Files provide sample text that you can easily replace with your own. You can type directly over it, paste in text from another program, or use Flash Text, which allows you to create decorative headings.

To create text in Dreamweaver, just click in the Document window and begin typing. All normal typing functions work just as they do in a regular word processing program—for example, to replace the sample copy in the Design File you're working on, you can select it and then enter your own text.

Most often, though, you'll be working with copy written outside Dreamweaver—either created by you or by clients or co-workers. If you use text written in a word processor, you'll have to employ a different strategy: copy and paste.

When the text is pasted onto your page, most—if not all—the formatting gets stripped away, leaving plain copy that you'll then need to reformat manually in Dreamweaver. This isn't necessarily a bad thing, though, as you'll probably want to reformat a lot of the text anyway.

Here's how to paste text into Dreamweaver:

1. In your word processor, select the text you want to copy.

2. Still inside your word processor, choose Edit > Copy.

3. Switch to Dreamweaver and place your insertion point where you want the text to appear.

NOTEWORTHY

Whenever you enter text in Dreamweaver, it's a good idea to run Dreamweaver's spell checker (Text > Check Spelling), which works just like the spell checker in your word processor. And remember, the only thing worse than missing spelling mistakes in your work is having your boss or even worse, your client—catch them for you. Save yourself the embarrassment by taking 30 seconds to spell check your pages.

NOTEWORTHY

Another way to move text on a page is to select the text and then drag it to a new location.

Even though there's a lot of crossover among software programs these days, I try to keep clear distinctions among my tools: one handles web design, one handles word processing, and one handles image editing. Even though Dreamweaver has word processing and image manipulation features, it simply isn't dedicated to those types of work. It's like, even though my Swiss Army knife contains a thousand tiny tools, most are completely useless when compared to their full-sized counterparts. Ever try chopping down a tree with that stupid mini-saw tool?

*When text is **pasted** into Dreamweaver, the **formatting** is stripped away.*

4. Choose Edit > Paste.

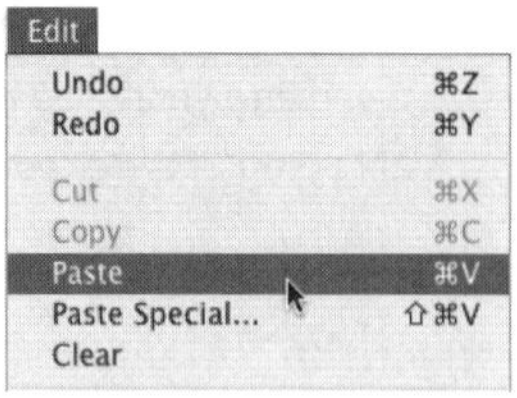

The copied (and now unformatted) text is placed where you clicked, ready to be formatted.

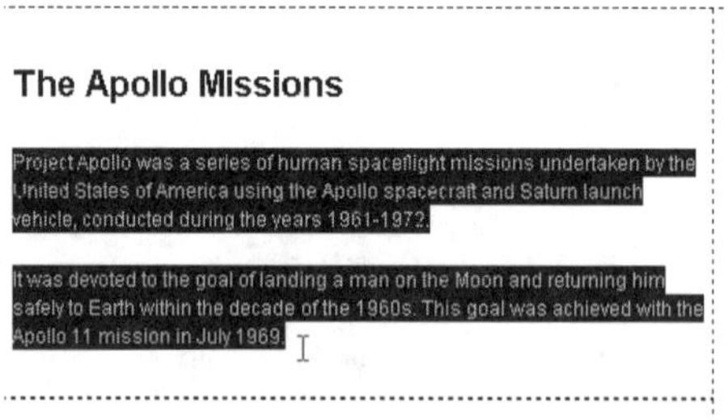

NOTEWORTHY

If you don't want to be bothered with all the text reformatting you'll have to do when you paste content into Dreamweaver, consider saving your Word file as HTML. When the file is opened in Dreamweaver, most of the text formatting should be retained.

Applying Basic Formatting

*Many text **formatting** options are found on the **Property Inspector**.*

Formatting your text requires a little firepower. Thankfully, you have Dreamweaver's Property Inspector along for the mission—it contains many of the text formatting options you'll want to use. Dreamweaver uses CSS text formatting by default, so as you begin applying fonts, text sizing and color, styles will be created for you automatically.

Some types of formatting, however—bold, italics, text alignment, ordered and unordered lists, and indenting and outdenting—are not included in the CSS styles that are created, even though they're available from the Property Inspector. You can manually apply them from the Property Inspector if you want, but be aware that you'll also have to maintain them manually, rather than automatically via CSS. In Chapter 8, we'll delve much deeper into how to use CSS styles to control text formatting.

Here's how to apply basic text formatting:

1. Select the text on your page that you want to format.

2. From the Font menu in the Property Inspector, choose a font list.

When someone visits your site, the browser will try to display your page using the first font listed. If that font cannot be displayed, the browser will try to use the second font, and so on. For more on how fonts work, see the sidebar "How Fonts Work on the Web."

When you choose a font, the text is reformatted. Note too that the Style menu in the Property Inspector displays Style1—an automatically created style.

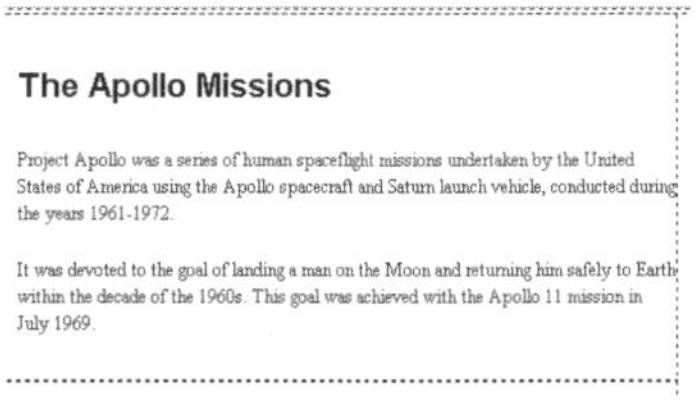

NOTEWORTHY

As you're working in Dreamweaver, you sometimes may goof up. Hey, nobody's perfect. Although you can use Edit > Undo to correct a mistake, Dreamweaver packs an even better tool: History (Window > History). The History panel tracks all the steps you perform as you're working. If you want to go back a number of steps, just drag the vertical slider on the left to literally step back in time.

3. With your text selected, open the Size pull-down menu in the Property Inspector and choose a size. To change the unit of measurement being used, select an option from the Font Unit menu.

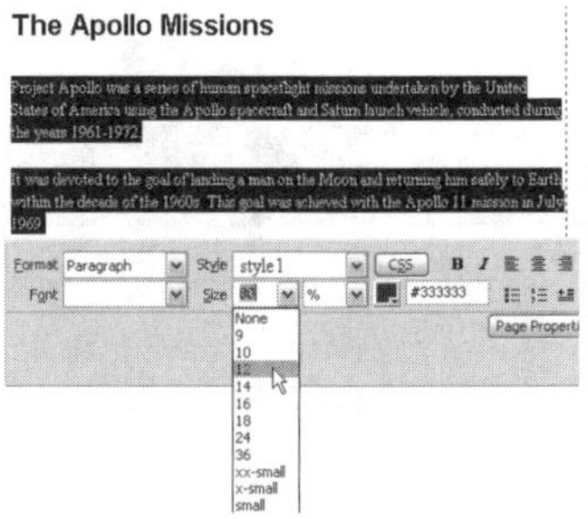

You can also type a value directly in the Size field. The menu also offers relative sizing (xx-small, medium, larger, and so on), but it's best to stick with values.

Next, you'll apply some color to your text.

NOTEWORTHY

It's good design practice to keep fonts to a minimum on your page. Use only two or three fonts to help visitors distinguish among headlines, body copy, and navigation elements.

4. Select the text on your page.

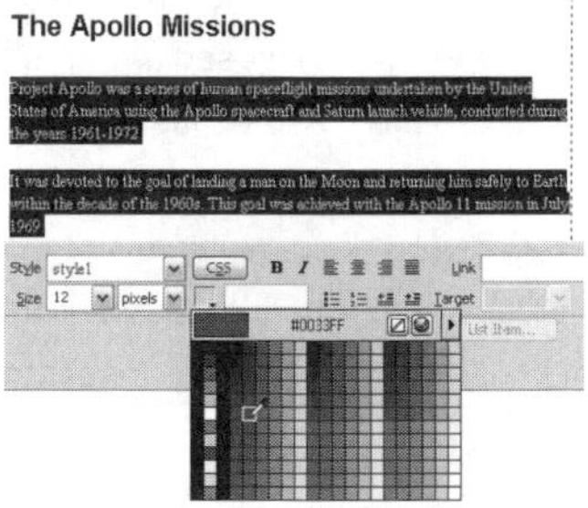

5. In the Property Inspector, click the Text Color box to open Dreamweaver's web-safe color palette.

When Dreamweaver's color palette is open, your cursor changes to an eyedropper. With the eyedropper, you can not only pick a color from the color palette, but you can sample a color from anywhere onscreen. For more on working with web-safe colors, see the sidebar "Choosing Web-Safe Colors."

Having the ability to sample a color that's used in another piece of text or in a graphic helps keep color consistency throughout your pages.

6. Choose a color from Dreamweaver's color window, or sample a color from another area of your screen.

If you want to set the font color back to the default, open Dreamweaver's color palette in the Property Inspector and click No Color in the top-right corner. Another way to set the color back to the default is to delete the hexadecimal code from the Text Color field in the Property Inspector. The default text color is determined either by the page properties dialog box or, if Page Properties aren't being used, the visitor's web browser preferences.

NOTEWORTHY

To ensure that your text appears in your visitor's web browser just as it does in yours, stick with sizing text in pixels.

HOW FONTS WORK ON THE WEB

Unless you use Flash Text or save your text as a graphic, if you want your text to appear as you designed it, you can use only fonts that your visitors have installed on their machines. To understand why, you've gotta understand how fonts work in web design.

Whenever you apply a font to text on your page, a reference to that font is created in your page's background code. Fonts are not embedded—they're not uploaded to your web space when you publish your site. That's critical to remember. When a surfer opens your web page, the person's browser reads the code and looks for font references. When a reference is found, the browser looks for the font on the surfer's hard drive. If the browser can't find the font, it uses a default font instead, usually something like Times New Roman or Courier. So if you've used a font that isn't very common, there's no way for the visitor to see the font (because the visitor won't have it on his or her computer).

To make sure that you use only fonts that everyone else has, just choose one from Dreamweaver's font list. Open the Font menu in the Property Inspector to take a look. The list consists of groups of fonts that are common to both Windows and Mac machines. When someone visits your site, the browser will look for the first font, and if it can't find that font, the browser will look for the next font, and so on.

So trust Dreamweaver's font list for your text, and whenever you want to throw in some artsy or decorative text, use Flash Text or save your text as a graphic in a program like Photoshop or Fireworks.

GEEK'S DELIGHT

Even though Windows and Mac OS X machines have similar fonts (such as Arial and Times), the fonts can still be quite different. Fonts on Macintosh computers are usually slightly smaller than their Windows counterparts, making it important to test your site on both platforms.

RETAINING FORMATTING WITH PASTE SPECIAL

Using the regular Paste command blows away the formatting that your original text had. Paste Special, which is new to Dreamweaver 8, lets you control the formatting of the text as it's being pasted. This command provides four formatting options that take some of the aches out of reformatting your pasted text.

Here's how to paste with Paste Special:

1. In your word processor, select the text you want to copy and choose Edit > Copy, just as you did before.

2. Switch back to Dreamweaver and place the insertion point where you want the text to appear.

3. Choose Edit > Paste Special.

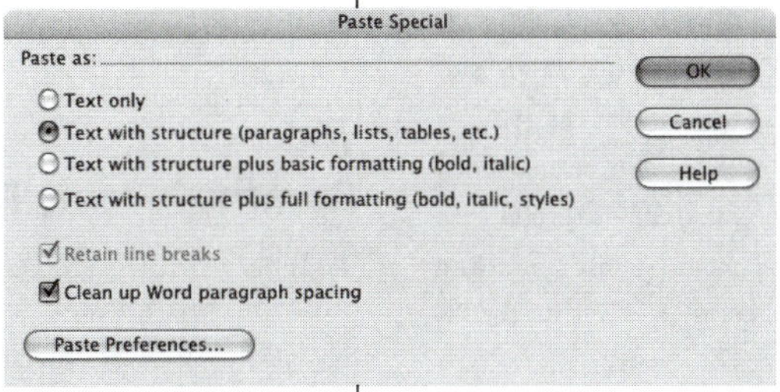

4. In the Paste Special dialog box that appears, choose how to format the text that's being pasted:
   - **Text Only:** This option strips away any formatting from the copied text. It also removes paragraph breaks, giving you one single block of text.
   - **Text with Structure:** This option removes all the text formatting while retaining any structure (paragraphs, tables, and so on).
   - **Text with Structure Plus Basic Formatting:** This option retains the structure and also keeps any simple formatting, such as bold and italics.
   - **Text with Structure Plus Full Formatting:** This option keeps all structure, plus all HTML and CSS formatting that has been used.
   - **Retain Line Breaks:** Select this option to keep line breaks as they were before the text was copied.
   - **Clean Up Word Paragraph Spacing:** When you choose either the Use Text with Structure or Text with Structure Plus Basic Formatting option, select this option to remove the white space between the paragraphs.

5. Click OK when you're ready.

The text is placed on your page using the formatting setting you specified. If your text appears formatted in a way that you didn't expect, then you may have to choose Edit > Undo and try again, selecting a different Paste Special option.

It is the visitor's web browser that ultimately determines the overall look of your page. That's why previewing your work is so important.

CHOOSING WEB-SAFE COLORS

Consumer-grade monitors are terrible at displaying color. If you have a print design background, I need not say more. But if this is news to you, try previewing your site on a variety of computers in a variety of lighting conditions. Your reds and blues may look like scarlets and purples. Don't be alarmed—that's just the way it is.

To get around this limitation, a palette of 216 web-safe colors was created. These colors remain consistent on monitors and accommodate the color differences between Windows and Macs.

Thankfully, technology has progressed, and sticking with web-safe colors is not as important as it used to be. Still, some designers strictly limit their color work to the 216-color palette. By default, Dreamweaver plays conservative and sticks to web-safe colors, but these days you can use pretty much whatever colors you like.

GEEK'S DELIGHT

In web design, color is determined using something called the hexadecimal color system. If you happen to know the hexadecimal value of the color you want to use, you can type it directly in the Text Color field.

Creating Flash Text

Another way to use text in Dreamweaver is to create it as Flash Text. Flash Text is graphical text rather than normal, selectable text. This distinction means that you can use a much larger range of fonts, which is especially nice for headings and titles.

Even though Macromedia Flash is traditionally used to build animation and interactivity into your site, Flash Text itself is static. Don't know a thing about Flash? No worries—you don't have to (you don't even need to have the Flash software installed on your computer).

NOTEWORTHY

If you're working with a blank new document and haven't saved it yet, Dreamweaver won't let you use Flash Text. Make sure to save your file first—then you can get started with Flash Text.

Flash Text is stored as a small SWF (Shockwave Format) file, with the fonts embedded, just as if you had saved the text as a graphic. This means that you can use artsy or decorative fonts and rest easy knowing that the Flash Text you see on your monitor is exactly what your visitor will see—which is certainly not the case with regular text.

Here's how to create Flash Text:

1. Click your Dreamweaver page where you want your text to appear.

2. Choose Insert > Media > Flash Text.

3. In the Insert Flash Text dialog box that appears, type your text in the Text field, or paste in text from elsewhere. Press Enter (Windows) or Return (Mac) to set any line breaks you want.

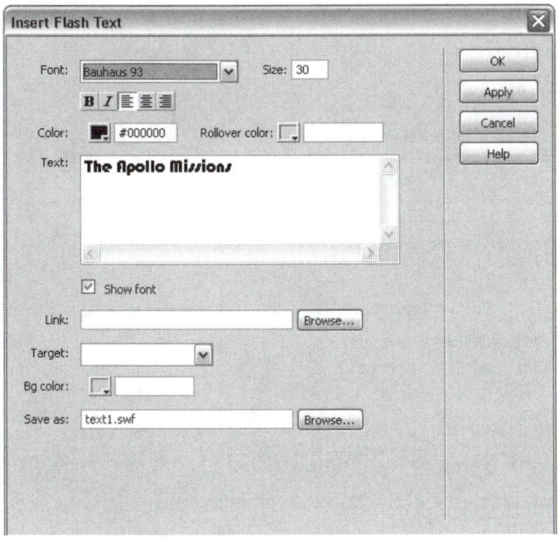

4. Use the formatting options at the top of the dialog box to set the look of your text.

   Set the font options as usual. Click the swatch in the Color field to set the color of your text. To change the color of your text when the visitor's mouse rolls over it, select a color for Rollover Color. Then click the Apply button on the right to see how your text will appear on your page.

5. If you want to set a hyperlink for the text, enter the link's URL in the Link field.

   We'll talk more about hyperlinks shortly.

6. If you want, set a background color for your Flash Text by clicking the swatch in the BG Color field and choosing a color.

7. In the Save As field at the bottom of the dialog box, name your Flash Text file (or you can use the default name) and click OK.

8. If you have Accessibility turned on (it's on by default), set the Title, Access Key, and Tab Index information in the Flash Accessibility Attributes dialog box that appears, or just leave the fields empty for now and click OK.

   Your Flash Text appears on your page.

IMMINENT DOOM

As you type or paste text in the Insert Flash Text dialog box, make sure to press Enter (Windows) or Return (Mac) at the end of each line, before you click OK. Otherwise, your Flash Text will appear as a very thin gray line on your page (in other words, Dreamweaver will try to fit all the text in the paragraph onto a single line). Once you click OK, this cannot be fixed—the only solution is to delete the text and start again.

GEEK'S DELIGHT

By default, Flash Text SWF files are saved at the root level (the top level) of your local site. If you want to save the SWF file in a different location in your site, click the Browse button at the bottom of the Insert Flash Text dialog box to specify where you want the file stored.

IMMINENT DOOM

When you upload your site live to the web, make sure to upload all the SWF files for your Flash Text, too. Otherwise, they won't appear on your pages.

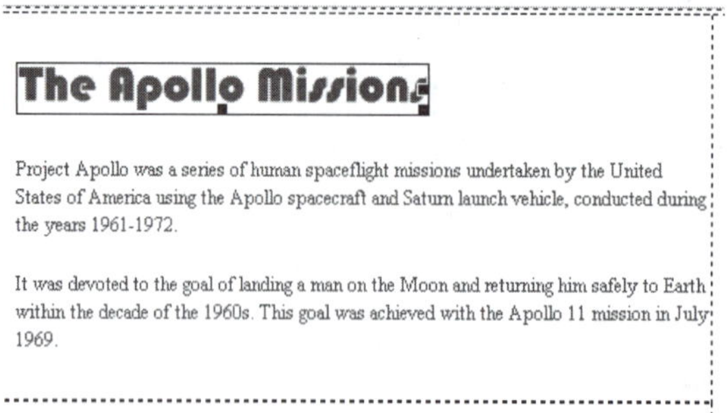

With Flash Text, you can use many fonts that would otherwise be unusable on the web. As you can see here, Flash Text selects as a page object—just like a graphic.

Even though it may be tempting to use Flash Text for the main body text on your page, this type of text isn't really suited for that purpose. Remember that line breaks have to be manually inserted as you enter text in the Insert Flash Text dialog box.

If you click your Flash Text on your web page, you'll notice that it's not selectable like regular text—it selects as a block because it's a graphical object.

And what if you want to edit your Flash Text? The process is just as easy as entering the text in the first place. Double-click your Flash object to return to the Insert Flash Text dialog box. Make any text or formatting changes that you want and then click OK.

Adding Graphics—and Making Your Boots Shine!

All right soldier, you've made it this far. Now let's see how to insert images. Normally, you insert images by choosing Insert > Image, but you'll do something a bit different here—you'll insert a graphic using the Assets panel, which is a much faster way to work.

Inserting a graphic from the Assets panel is much faster than going through the menus.

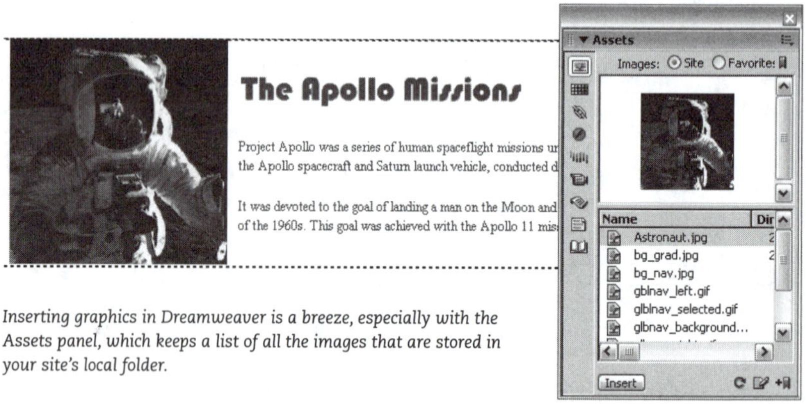

Inserting graphics in Dreamweaver is a breeze, especially with the Assets panel, which keeps a list of all the images that are stored in your site's local folder.

For this process to work, you'll need an image file on your computer. Minimize Dreamweaver and locate a graphic on your hard drive that you can use (a sample file or a photo that you have on your computer will work just fine). When you find an image, copy it to your site folder's *img* folder.

Here's how to insert an image:

1. On your page, select the gray box that's labeled 280x200.

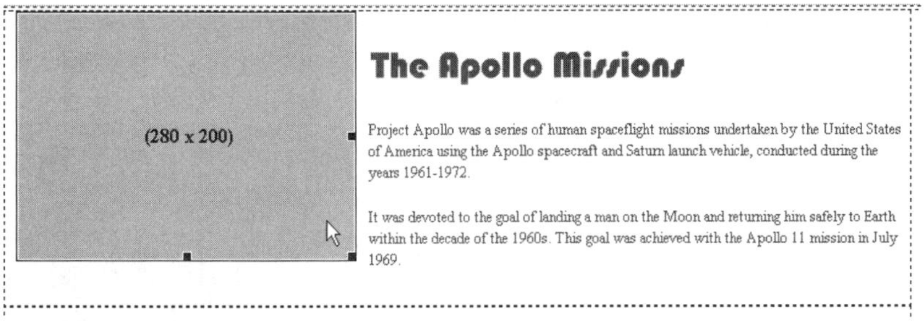

   This gray box is an image placeholder. You'll replace it with your image.

2. Remove the image placeholder by pressing the Delete key.

3. Choose Window > Assets to open the Assets panel; then in the column of buttons on the left, make sure that Images is selected.

   The Images category of the Assets panel lists any graphics that are stored in your site's local folder. When you select an image, a preview appears at the top of the panel.

   You should see a list of images that the Design File is using (remember those dependent files?) as well as your graphic that you copied to your site folder. If you don't see your graphic, click the Refresh button at the bottom of the panel.

4. Select your graphic from the list of images; then at the bottom of the panel, click Insert.

   The image is inserted into your page. Notice too, that with your image selected, the Property Inspector changes to offer image-related options. We'll get to all these options and a whole lot more in Chapter 10.

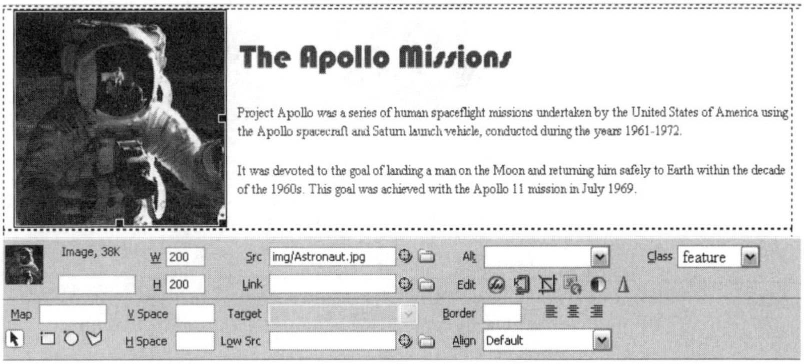

To replace the other image placeholders on your page, just repeat the preceding steps.

A useful option for images (especially images that are hyperlinks) is to include alternative text. Alternative text provides a brief message for visitors when they roll their mouse over the image. This message is also picked up by screen readers.

5. Select the graphic that you want to add alternative text to.

6. In the Property Inspector, in the Alt field, type a short message.

   Alternative text won't appear in Dreamweaver. To test it, you'll have to save your page and preview it in your web browser.

7. Save your file, go back to your web browser (which should still be running in the background), and click the Refresh button to see your changes.

   If you closed your web browser, in Dreamweaver choose File > Preview in Browser, or use the Preview/Debug in Browser menu on the Document toolbar.

8. To see your alternative text, roll your mouse over the image.

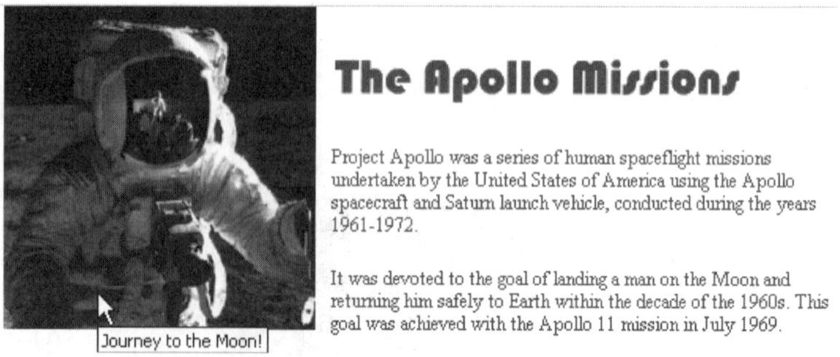

To test your graphic's alternative text, save your page and preview it in your browser; then hold your mouse over the image for a moment. Alternative text is especially useful when a hyperlink has been set for an image. The text can tell your visitors, before they click, where the link will take them.

Now that you have the basics of text and graphics down, boot camp's gonna get a little more heavy duty. What we're talkin' about here is building a basic site, complete with hyperlinks and a library item. Still proud to be in the corps, soldier? Great. Now drop and gimme twenty!

Building a Library—Stockpiling Ammo

Here's one of the best parts of boot camp: Dreamweaver's library. With this handy tool, you can take any element on your page (or group of page elements) and save it for future use on other pages in your site. In fact, utilizing the library to its fullest extent will help you maintain design consistency throughout your pages, right across your site.

Libraries* let you save *any page element for future use* on other *pages at your site.

In this section, you'll see how to take an item from your page and save it as a library item. A little later, in the section "Linking Your Pages and Updating Library Items," you'll see how to edit your library item and have it automatically update on any pages within your site that use it—the real power of libraries.

Before we begin, if you closed the Assets panel after the previous task, open it again by choosing Window > Assets.

Here's how to add an item to the library:

1. Click within the text at the top of your page that reads *Site Name*; then in the Tag Selector on Dreamweaver's Status bar, click <div#masthead>.

   The Tag Selector is very useful for selecting page elements.

   When you click `<div#masthead>`, Dreamweaver highlights the page header that appears at the top of your page, including the main navigation bar.

2. In the Assets panel, click the Library category in the list of buttons at the left.

3. At the bottom of the Library pane, click New Library Item.

   Dreamweaver warns you that your library item may not appear correctly when inserted on other pages because it uses CSS. In this example, you won't have a problem, but watch out when you're working on your own pages. For the library item to work correctly, the page that it's inserted into must use the same style sheet that the library item uses. You'll find out more about CSS style sheets in Chapter 8.

4. Click OK to continue.

   The header content and navigation bar are added to the library. Notice that in the Library pane's preview area, the header content looks different than it does on your page. Again, this is because of the CSS formatting that the header uses.

When an item is added to the library, you're prompted to name the item. It's a good idea to not only name your library items but to use some descriptive text to help you remember what's what.

5. Enter a descriptive name for your library item.

6. If Dreamweaver displays the Update Files dialog box, click Update.

   Notice back on your page that your header content now contains yellow highlighting. This is a visual indication that this area of your page is a library item. In fact, you can't even highlight any text in this area—it's entirely locked.

   Now you can make changes to your library item, and it will update automatically on any pages where it's being used, as you'll see once you've created some additional pages and linked them.

NOTEWORTHY

As you begin adding items to the library, Dreamweaver automatically creates a Library folder in your site folder where it saves each library item as a separate file (take a look in your Files panel to see).

In this chapter, you're adding only one library item, which is placed on a single page (your *index.html* page). But when you're working on your pages, you can add as many items to the library as you want: navigation bars, copyright notices, buttons with hyperlinks—anything. Once you've added an item or two to your library, you can start lobbing them onto your pages like grenades into a pillbox. And you certainly don't have to limit yourself to Design Pages. You can drop library items right on new, blank pages, too. In this chapter though, we'll stick with Design Files so you can get a feel for how the library works.

Now it's time begin building a web site—albeit a small and simple one—so you can see how everything ties together.

Creating Additional Web Pages

You have a single page that's shaping up nicely. Now it's time to expand your site. To create additional pages for your site, you could start all over again with a Design File and repeat all the steps that you've performed so far, inserting and formatting text, placing a graphic or two, setting up library items, and so on. But that would be a lot of work.

Instead, if you want your new pages to look similar to your first one, you can start by duplicating the single page that you've created to create as many new pages as you want. Then you can put in new text and graphics, just as you did before.

Here's how to create new pages from an existing one:

1. Toward the top of your page, select the text "Page Name"; then type `Home Page.`

   The new text replaces the old.

2. Save your page by choosing File > Save.

   Your *index.html* file is saved. Now you'll save two duplicate pages, each with its own page title.

3. Select the Home Page text that you just entered; then type About Us.

4. Choose File > Save As.

   The Save As dialog box that appears should display your site's local root folder. If it doesn't, navigate to it.

5. Double-click your site's *htm* folder.

6. At the bottom of the Save As dialog box, name your page `AboutUs.html`; then click Save.

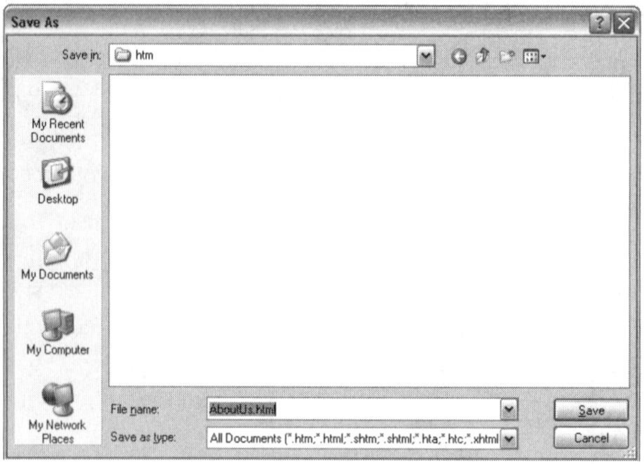

7. Dreamweaver displays a message asking you to update links. Click Yes to continue.

8. Select the *About Us* text and type **News and Events**; then choose File > Save As.

9. In the Save As dialog box that appears, name your file **Events.html**; then click Save.

   You should now have three identical pages: *index.html*, which resides on your site's root level, and *AboutUs.html* and *Events.html*, which reside in your site's *htm* folder. You can now open each page and add text graphics and other elements appropriate to the page.

   But your pages are not connected with hyperlinks, so really, you don't have a web site yet. All you have are stand-alone pages. You'll take care of that next by creating links to each page from the main navigation bar. To do this, you'll have to edit your library item, which was copied along with everything else—and which contains the site's main navigation bar.

Linking Your Pages and Updating Library Items

Hyperlinks are based on file paths, so you'll have to be careful when working with them.

Now you're ready to pull it all together. Hyperlinks are based on file paths (a connection between the current page and the hyperlink's destination), so you'll have to be careful—this is a live-fire exercise. One wrong path, one missed file, and your links won't work—they'll be sending you home to mom with a broken leg and a lollypop.

With Dreamweaver, though, it's really hard to mess up. While it's important to understand file paths (which we'll delve into in Chapter 9), you're not going to be creating them by hand. With Dreamweaver, it's just a matter of pointing and clicking.

To see how the overall process works, you'll open your library item for editing and then set three text-based links on your main navigation bar: one for each of your pages. Like magic, when you save your library item, each page will automatically update. To make sure everything works, you'll then test your site in your web browser. Setting links in a library item is exactly the same as setting links directly on your page, so after this section, you'll be able to set links wherever you want. Ready? Let's move out!

Here's how to set hyperlinks and update a library item:

1. Close any pages that you have open in Dreamweaver; then in the Assets panel's Library category, double-click your library item.

   Dreamweaver opens the library item as if it were a web page.

   As before, the library item looks totally different than it does on the pages that it's inserted on—in this example, it looks like a mess. Remember, though, that the pages that use the library item also use the CSS style sheet that controls the look and positioning of this header content, so in your actual web site, it will look fine.

   You'll begin by typing text that will serve as the hyperlink.

2. Select the first instance of the placeholder text "global link"; then type **`Home`**.

   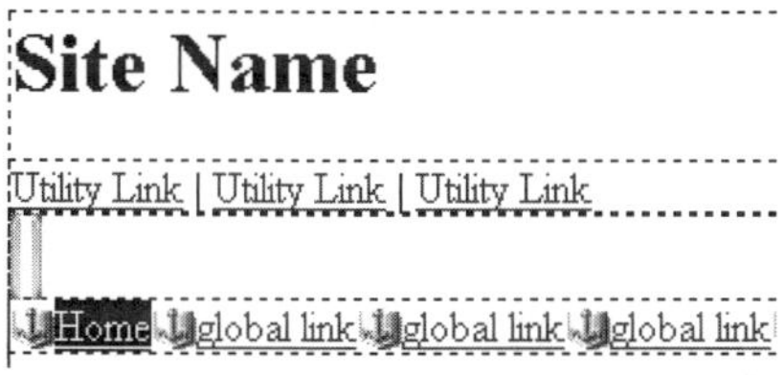

3. Select the second instance of "global link" and type **`About Us`**; then select the third instance of "global link" and type **`News and Events`**.

   Now that you have the link text inserted, you're ready to begin setting hyperlinks to your three pages.

4. Select the Home text that you typed.

5. In the Property Inspector, click the Browse for File icon beside the Link field.

6. In the Select File dialog box that appears, navigate to and select your index.html file; then click OK.

   Dreamweaver creates a hyperlink from the Home text to your index.html file. It's as easy as that.

7. Select your About Us text; then click the Browse for File icon to set a hyperlink to your AboutUs.html page. Repeat these steps to set a link from the News and Events text to the Events.html file.

   When you're done, you should have three hyperlinks: one to each of your pages. Now there's just a few loose ends to tidy up before you can try out your new site.

8. At the top of your library item, select the Site Name placeholder text and type a name for your web site.

9. Select all the subglobal links at the bottom of the library item; then press Delete.

   You're not creating any more links right now.

   Now your library item is ready to roll. This is the cool part—you're going to automatically update the three pages that use this library item. Updating is easy. In fact, it's as simple as saving.

10. Choose File > Save.

11. In the Update Library Items dialog box that appears, click OK.

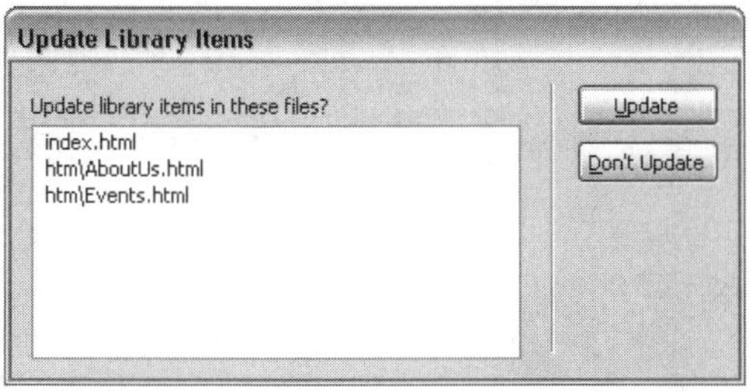

Dreamweaver displays the Update Pages dialog box and updates your pages. If you'd like to see a log for the update, select the Show Log option.

12. When Dreamweaver completes the update, click Close.

Now for the moment of truth. Did your pages really update? Will the hyperlinks actually work? In the next section, you'll take a look!

Testing Your Site

With your hyperlinks set to each of your pages and your library item updated, you now have a web site! It's small; it needs more content—but hey, it's a start. And what you've seen in this chapter is a microcosm of the process for building much larger, much more sophisticated web sites—which you'll learn how to do throughout the rest of this book. But for now, are you ready to test your new site?

To test your new site, follow these steps:

1. Choose File > Open; then navigate to and open your *index.html* file.

   When the page opens, you'll notice—somewhere in all that yellow highlighting—the changes that you made to your library item. Ooh and ahh as you feel appropriate.

2. Choose File > Preview in Browser; then select a browser to view your page in.

   The browser launches, and your page opens. There are the changes you made to your library item, but now for the moment of truth—your hyperlinks!

3. In your browser, click the About Us link.

   The About Us page opens. Even if you haven't added new content and graphics to the new pages and all your pages look the same, you can tell that your hyperlink worked by the title you added just below the Breadcrumb text.

4. Try out your other two links to make sure they work.

Now if you really want to see your site in action as your visitors would see it, you could upload it to your remote web space. However, for you to do this, a number of things will need to be in place. The biggest issue you'll need to resolve is how you will be connecting to your remote site. Recall the remote access options discussed in Chapter 4. Typically, you'll connect via FTP, but that depends on the type of site you're working on. Of course, you'll also need remote space to publish to. If you're connecting via FTP, for example, you'll need space on a remote web server to transfer your site to—again, as discussed in Chapter 4.

But if you know your connection type and if you do have remote space, go for it—upload your site and see how it will look for your visitors. Just follow the steps in Chapter 4 to set your site's remote info, and you're away. And remember: It's imperative to test your live site not just on your computer, but on other machines, too, to make sure everything runs smoothly.

So there you go: a simple, straightforward web site. It isn't a terribly exciting one just yet, but in the coming chapters, you'll learn much more about the topics introduced here, as well as some new ones, such as controlling your page layouts, working with multimedia, adding interactivity, and managing your site once it's complete. There's lots more to see, so stick around for more Ten Ton Dreamweaver!

JUST THE GIST

Defining a Site and Setting Up Structure

- Your first step is to define a site in Dreamweaver.
- You can build a structure for your site—and reorganize your site's files—directly in the Files panel.

Using Design Files

- Design Files are pages that have already been laid out with text and graphics—perfect for newbies.
- Most Design Files use dependent files—that is, files that are required for the page to be displayed properly. Usually, dependent files are graphics and style sheets.

Previewing Your Page

- Dreamweaver's Design view only approximates what your page will look like online. It's much better to preview your work in an actual browser.
- Keep your browser open as you work, so that you can periodically save your pages and preview them to see how they're rendering.

Inserting and Formatting Text

- Typing text in Dreamweaver is no different than typing text in a word processor.
- Most basic text formatting can be done with Dreamweaver's Property Inspector.
- Flash Text allows you to use artsy or decorative text for headings without having to worry about fonts not displaying properly.

Working with Graphics

- Normally, you insert graphics by choosing Insert > Image.

JUST THE GIST (CONTINUED)

- A faster way to insert graphics is through the Assets panel (Window > Assets).

Using Libraries

- You can save any page element as a library item and use it on other pages in your site.
- Library items highlight in yellow, helping you differentiate between them and other sorts of page objects.
- To edit a library item, double-click it in the Assets panel. When the changes are complete and the library item is saved, any pages that use it are automatically updated.

Hyperlinking

- Hyperlinks can be set for either text or graphics using the Property Inspector.
- To set a basic hyperlink, click the Browse for File icon beside the Link field in the Property Inspector.

Chapter 6

BUILDING a *Layers*-Based Layout

STUFF YOU'LL LEARN IN THIS CHAPTER

Layers are containers on your page that you can use to structure and control your web site layout. And because layers tie tightly with CSS, they're becoming increasingly popular with today's top designers. In this chapter, you'll see how to build a layers-based layout; then you'll see how to control that layout entirely with CSS. You'll also see how to insert content into your layers and how to work with layers' twin sister, div tags. Bring your spill-proof travel mug—you're in for a ride!

Getting Started with Layers

The fundamental problem with web design is that HTML wasn't built to handle page layout or design. It was developed to structure text-based content and to provide a way to jump between documents via hyper-linking. For years, web designers have wrestled with HTML, trying to get it to do something it wasn't meant to do: control a page's layout. Early on, innovative designers began using HTML tables as a way to build a grid of rows and columns on a page. While tables did offer a way to control a page's layout, this approach made maintaining and updating pages a real pain.

But with the development of Dreamweaver's layers, controlling and maintaining page layout has gotten much easier. Layers are containers that you can place on your page to hold content. Anything that you can normally place directly on a page—text, graphics, Flash movies, and so on—can sit inside a layer. You can then position the layers on your page by dragging and dropping them—a luxury that the print design world has enjoyed for nearly two decades. Typically, a layers-based design uses multiple layers for each major region in the layout and is oriented to the top-left corner of the page.

*Layers are **containers** that you can place on your page to **hold content.***

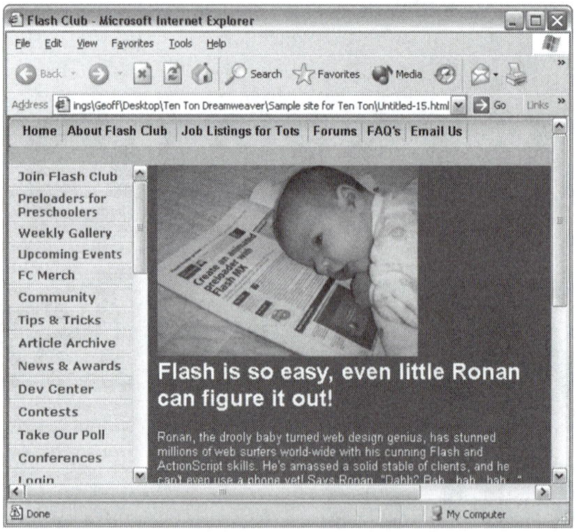

Layers are perfect for controlling page layout. Typically, layers are used to contain the major regions of a layout. In this example, the navigation bars on the left and across the top are each on a separate layer, as is the main content area.

GEEK'S DELIGHT

Dreamweaver's layers are actually div tags, or what some designers call layout blocks. There's lots to know about Dreamweaver layers and div tags, as you'll see later in this chapter.

By using layers to handle page design, you can essentially lock down your layout—and more important—control it via CSS. Layers are actually a component of CSS (called CSS-P—the P stands for positioning). CSS layers allow you to separate content from structure. This means that you can control a page's layout independent of its content. To give you a sense of how layers work, this chapter will show you how to build a basic page layout using Dreamweaver's CSS layers. You'll start by building the layers that your particular layout needs. Typically, you'll need a layer for each major region of your design: one to hold a nav bar at the left, one to hold the header, one to hold the main content in the middle of the page, and so on. Then you'll see how to control and manipulate your layout with CSS.

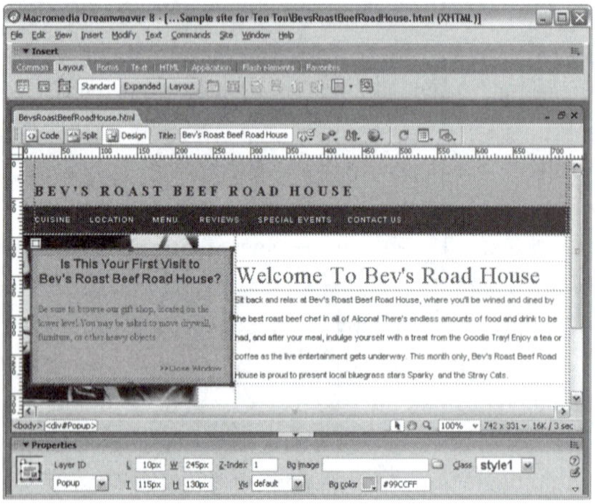

Page layout isn't the only use for layers. For instance, you can insert graphics or text within a layer that floats above other content on your page and then apply Dreamweaver's behaviors, which you'll learn about in Chapter 11, to create interactive objects such as pop-up menus or messages and control their visibility or even have them zoom across your screen! It's pretty cool stuff.

Layers add a huge amount of versatility to sites, even beyond structuring layouts. Here, a layer hovers above the left side of the page and has been combined with Dreamweaver's behaviors to create an interactive pop-up message. Be sure to drop by for the best roast in all Alcona!

Inserting Layers on Your Page

So are you ready for this brave new world of layers? Getting layers onto your page and inserting content into them is very easy. In this section, you'll learn how to insert layers onto your page. You'll actually be drawing them just like you draw a shape in a graphics program. Once your layers are drawn, you can size and position them in your layout. You'll also see how to nest layers—that is, how to place a layer inside another layer for even tighter layout control.

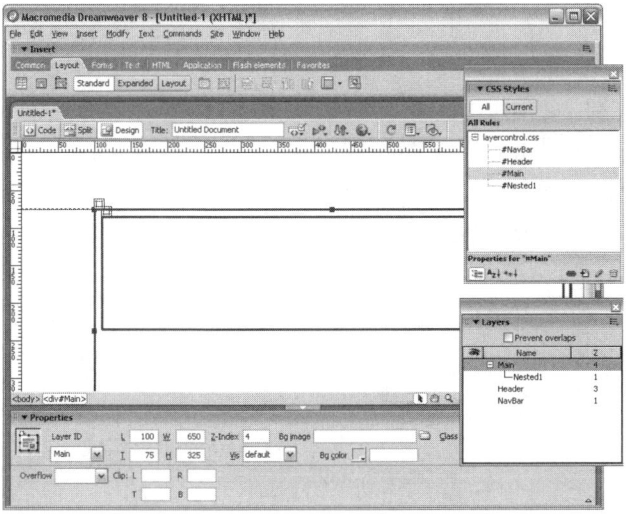

Layers form the skeleton and provide the empty containers for your page's layout. As you begin adding layers to your page, keep an eye on the Layers panel, which tracks the layers on your page, and the CSS Styles panel, which tracks the layer IDs that identify your layers.

As you're creating your layers, keep in mind the layout that you want to create, as discussed in Chapter 3. Each of your page's main elements, or regions, will require its own layer, so if you want a header across the top of your page, you'll need a layer that spans the top, if you want a nav bar running down the left side, you'll need a layer running down the left side of your page, and so on. Once you've created the layout containers, you'll be able to control them via CSS. Then you'll be ready to start inserting content.

As you're creating your layers, keep in mind the layout that you want to create. Each of your page's main elements, or regions, will require its own layer.

You'll be using the Layers panel to keep track of the layers that you've drawn on your page. You can also use the Layers panel to control your layers' stacking order and visibility, as you'll see in the sidebar "Controlling Layer Stacking and Visibility" later in this chapter.

Here's how to build the layers for your web page:

1. Create a new, blank web page in Dreamweaver.

As you're drawing layers, you might find Dreamweaver's layout grid helpful. To turn it on, choose View > Grid > Show Grid.

2. Open the Layers panel by choosing Window > Layers.

   The Layers panel is empty because there are no layers yet on your page.

3. If it's not already onscreen, open Dreamweaver's Insert bar (choose Windows > Insert); then switch to the Insert bar's Layout category.

NOTEWORTHY

To draw more than one layer at a time, hold down Ctrl (Windows) or Command (Mac) before you click and drag. This will keep the Draw Layer button activated, allowing you to draw additional layers without having to reclick the button.

4. In the Layout category, click the Draw Layer button.

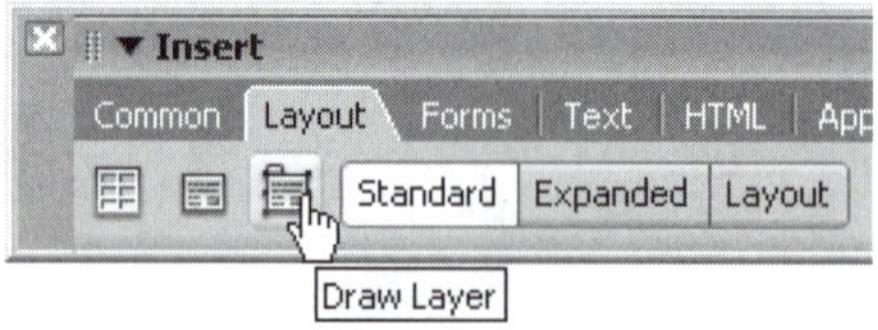

   The cursor changes to a crosshair.

5. Click the cursor on your web page and drag a rectangle to draw a layer.

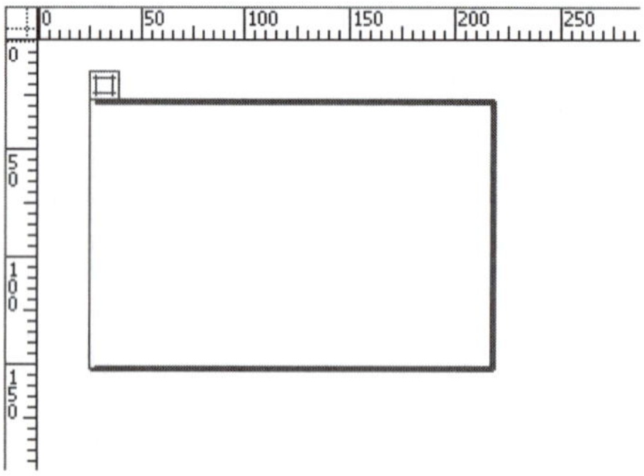

   Don't worry about precision right now, when you're drawing your layers. You'll set their size and position in a moment, so the initial size and placement don't matter.

   A blue box appears on your page, representing your new layer. If you click outside the layer, the blue highlight disappears. To make it reappear, click inside the layer again. In the Layers panel, you'll see Layer 1, which also represents your layer.

An alternative way to draw a layer in Dreamweaver is to place the insertion point on your page and then choose Insert > Layout Objects > Layers. The size and properties of the layer are determined by Dreamweaver's layer preferences—choose Edit > Preferences (Windows) or Dreamweaver > Preferences (Mac); then click Layers in the Category list.

6. Select the layer by clicking the layer's selection handle—the box above the layer's top-left corner.

   Alternatively, you can Ctrl+Shift+click (Windows) or Command +Shift+click (Mac) a layer to select it.

   When a layer is selected, resize handles appear on all four sides and in all four corners of the layer.

   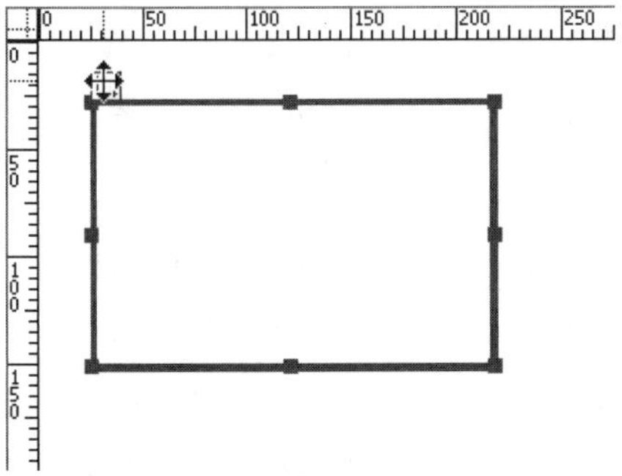

To select more than one layer at a time, hold down Shift and click the layers, the same way you select multiple objects in a word processing program.

7. In the Property Inspector's Layer ID field, give the selected layer a unique name.

   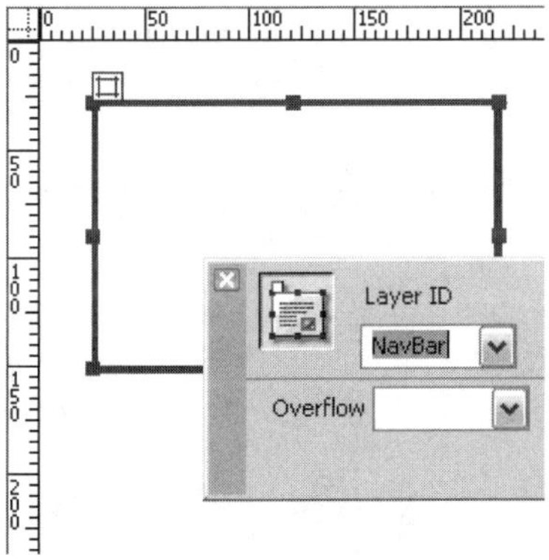

   Dreamweaver sequentially names your layers for you as you draw them. Every layer on your page must have a unique layer ID. Layer IDs are used when controlling layers with CSS or when using Dreamweaver's behaviors to manipulate layers. You can leave the layer's default layer ID, or you can replace it with a more descriptive name. For example, if your layer will hold a navigation bar, you might name it NavBar to help you remember what the layer is for. Layer IDs must begin with a letter and can consist of only numbers and letters.

When you change the layer ID in the Property Inspector, the Layers panel changes to reflect the new name.

8. Set the position of your layer on the page by doing one of the following:

   - Drag the layer's selection handle to place your layer visually.

   If you're coming from a print design background, you'll find dragging layers very similar to moving objects around in a page layout program. Yay—web design finally catches up to circa 1986 desktop publishing!

   - Use the arrow keys on your keyboard to move the layer in one-pixel increments.

   Hold down Shift and use the arrow keys to move your layer incrementally according to Dreamweaver's layout grid.

   - Use the Property Inspector's L (left) and T (top) fields to set the position of your layer in relation to the left and top edges of your page.

   This is the most precise way to position your layer—not only can you enter positive values, but you can use negative ones, too. If you're familiar with X-axis and Y-axis positioning, perhaps from the print-design world, then you should be right at home here.

9. To size your layer, pull any of the layer's resize handles that appear around its outside edge.

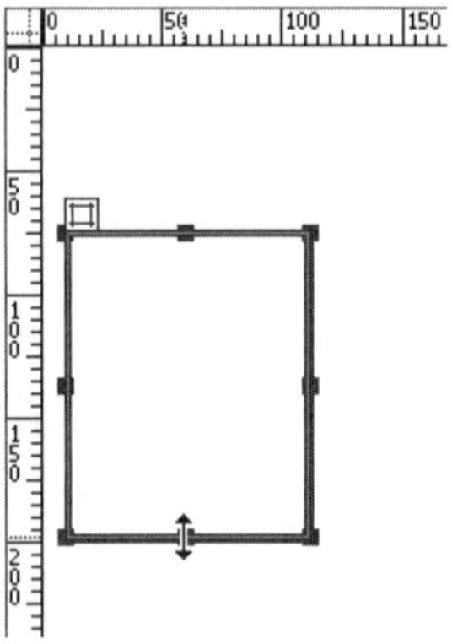

Alternatively, you can enter values in the Property Inspector's W (width) and H (height) fields—a much more precise way to size your layers than eyeballing them.

As you're sizing your layers, keep in mind the discussion in Chapter 3 about the visible area within web browsers. Essentially, your layers will be dividing up the visitor's browser window, so be sure to create them so that they appear on the screen in a way that suits the goals of your web site layout.

10. Save your work.

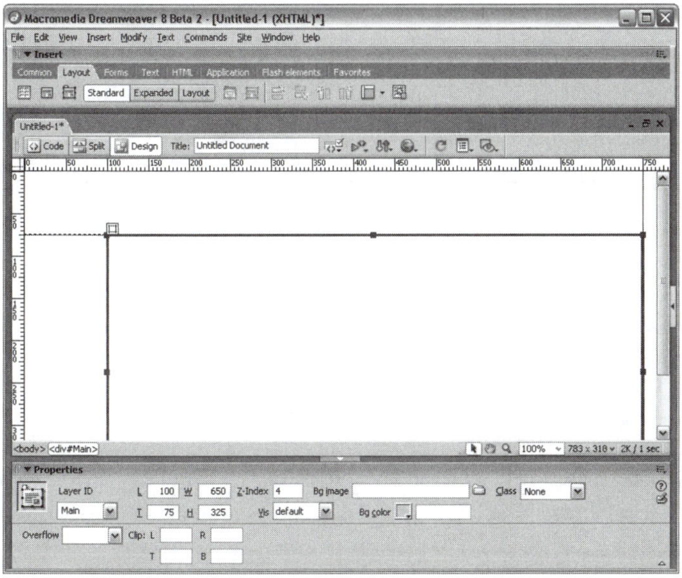

11. Repeat steps 4 through 10 to continue drawing the other layers that you need for your layout.

12. To remove a layer from your page, select it by clicking its selector handle and then press Delete.

Creating Nested Layers

For more design possibilities, you can nest one layer within another layer—that is, place one layer inside the boundaries of another layer. Doing so groups the layers together: wherever one goes, the other follows.

The position of nested layers is determined by the top-left corner of the parent layer (that is, the outermost layer). So, for instance, you could design a page element that contains a logo, a navigation bar, and a heading, each on its own layer nested within a parent layer, and then move all the layers as a unit to wherever the element is needed on the page. The nested layers will remain in position exactly as you created them.

NOTEWORTHY

When you set values in the Property Inspector to position a layer (the L and T fields) and resize a layer (the W and H fields), the values are measured in pixels (px). However, you can also use millimeters (mm), centimeters (cm), picas (pc), points (pt), inches (in), or percentages (%). Just type the appropriate abbreviation directly after your numeric value in the Property Inspector.

If you have multiple layers that you want to make the same size, hold down the Shift key and click the layers to select them. Then choose Modify > Arrange and then either Make Same Width or Make Same Height.

NOTEWORTHY

If you want to align two or more layers to one another, hold down the Shift key and click the layers to select them; then choose Modify > Arrange and choose an alignment option: Align Left, Align Right, Align Top, or Align Bottom. All selected layers align with the border of the last selected layer. Sure beats eyeballing it!

1. To nest a layer inside another layer, place the cursor inside an existing layer; then choose Insert > Layout Objects > Layer.

You can nest one layer within another layer. Doing so groups the layers together: wherever one goes, the other follows.

Dreamweaver inserts a layer within the existing layer and highlights it in blue. In the Layers panel, the nested layer is shown indented under its parent layer.

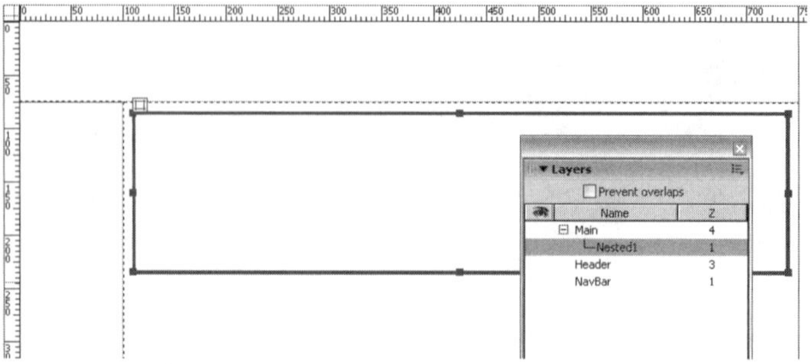

2. Set the layer ID. Use the L and T positioning fields in the Property Inspector to position the nested layer within its parent layer.

3. Save your nested layer.

Now you can move the outer layer to wherever you want on your page. The layers will move all together. The outer layer also controls the visibility of nested layers.

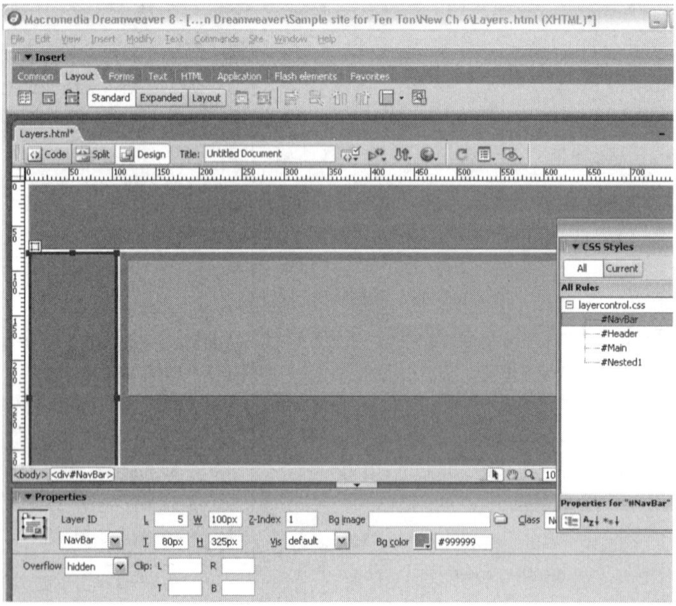

Formatting Layers with CSS Styles

Because layers are a component of CSS-P (remember, P stands for positioning), you can control the page layout of layers with CSS. Whenever you draw a layer on your page, the layer ID appears in the CSS Styles panel, allowing you to control your layers through the CSS Styles panel rather than the Property Inspector. Using CSS instead of the Property Inspector to control your layers opens a whole new

Because Dreamweaver's layers are part of the CSS-P specification, you can control your page's entire layers-based layout—and even the layout of your whole site—very easily. With CSS on the job, maintaining and updating a web site is truly a breeze!

range of possibilities. Not only does the CSS Styles panel offer many more options than the Property Inspector, but for site maintenance, CSS is unmatched.

The CSS rules that control a page's layout can reside in either an *embedded* style sheet or an *external* style sheet. An embedded style sheet is contained within the current page and applies to that page only. An external style sheet is much more powerful. An external style sheet can be attached to multiple web pages to control and maintain their layouts *simultaneously*—making updating your site as simple as opening a single file (the external style sheet) making your adjustments, and then resaving the file. All pages that use the external style sheet are then updated automatically. No previous web page layout method, such as tables or frames, offers this capability.

NOTEWORTHY

You can nest one existing layer on your page inside another. In the Layers panel, Control-drag (Windows) or Command-drag (Mac) a layer into another layer. Remember, though, that the nested layer's position is oriented by the outer layer's top-left corner. For example, if you drag Layer 2, which is positioned at 150x50, into Layer 1, which is positioned at 50x50, Layer 2 will now be positioned at 150x50 from the position of Layer 1—meaning that Layer 2 is now at 200x100.

So let's see what can be done with CSS and layers. As you begin drawing layers on your page, by default Dreamweaver begins building an embedded style sheet. However, you want to be able to control your entire site via an external style sheet. To do this, you first export the layer IDs that control your layers. Then you link your current page to the external style sheet. Once that's done, you can create additional pages that use the external style sheet. Then, whenever you want, you can update your style sheet file, and the changes will be reflected on all your pages.

Here's how to export an internal style sheet to create an external style sheet:

1. Choose Window > CSS Styles to open the CSS Styles panel.

   When the CSS Styles panel opens, you'll see the layer IDs for each of your layers.

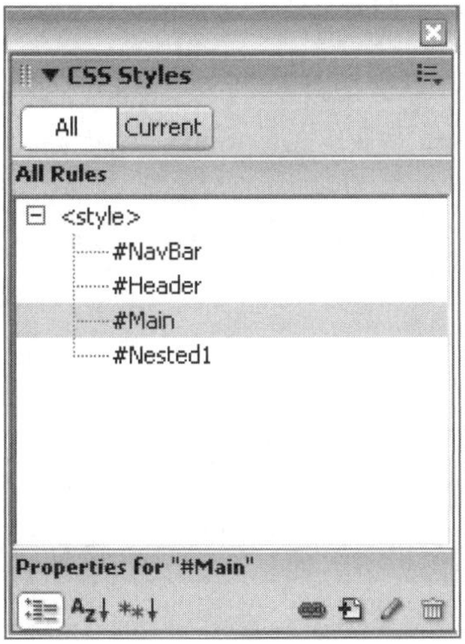

An external style sheet can be attached to multiple web pages to control and maintain their layouts simultaneously—making updating your site a breeze.

2. Choose File > Export > CSS Styles.

3. In the Export Styles as CSS File dialog box, navigate to the location where you want to save your external style sheet, give the file a name, and click Save.

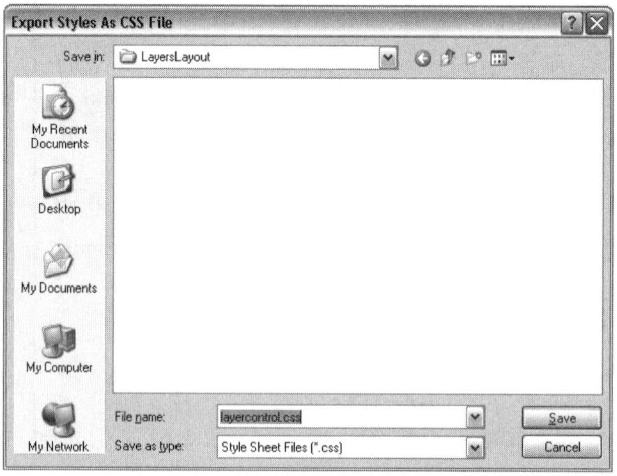

Although the style sheet has been exported, the layer IDs remain in the document they were created in. You need to remove the internal style sheet that contains the layer IDs. Then, when that's done, you'll need to link the document to the external style sheet.

4. In the CSS Styles panel, click the <style> expander heading at the top of the panel (this header represents your embedded style sheet); then click the Delete Embedded Style Sheet button at the bottom of the panel.

   The embedded style sheet is removed. On your page, it appears as though your layers are removed, too. They're still on your page, however; they're just not being controlled by a style sheet. You need to connect your page to the external style sheet that you created.

5. At the bottom of the CSS Styles panel, click Attach Style Sheet.

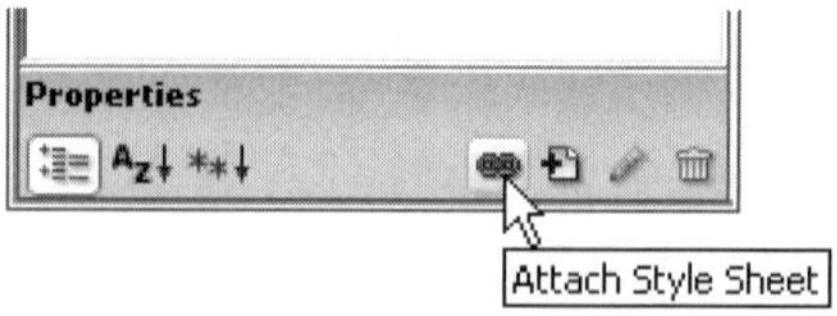

6. In the Attach External Style Sheet dialog box, click Browse and navigate to the external style sheet you saved earlier.

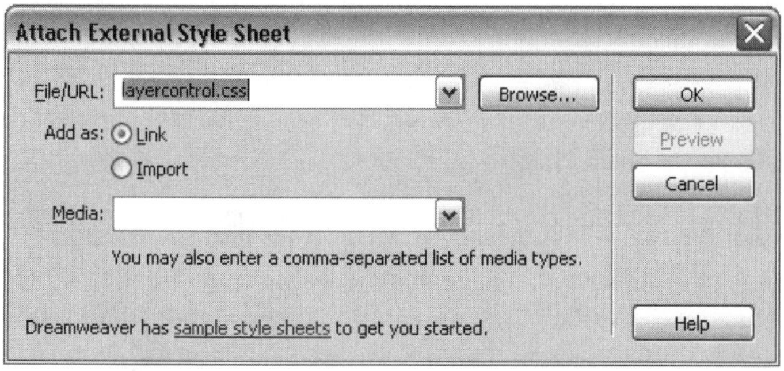

7. Set the Add As option to Link; then click OK.

   Link is Dreamweaver's default. This setting creates a reference to the style sheet from your page.

   When you click OK, the layers on your page revert to their previous formatting. The layers are now being controlled by your external style sheet, as you can tell by looking at the CSS Styles panel. Notice that your external style sheet has been added (its name ends in .css), as have the layer IDs that the style sheet contains.

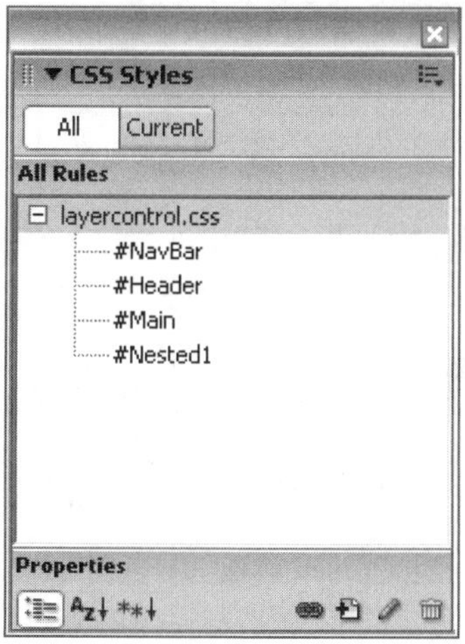

Easy, right? Now to really see the power of using CSS to control your page layout, you'll make changes to the external style sheet and watch the updates appear on your page right away.

Editing an External Style Sheet

Now that your page layout is being controlled by an external style sheet, you can make changes to it, and the changes will take effect right away. You can make changes to an external style sheet in either of two ways. One way is to open the style sheet file directly in Dreamweaver by double-clicking the .css file in the Files panel. The .css file opens in Code view. You can then edit the code by hand if you like, or you can make your changes through the CSS Styles panel.

With your page layout controlled by an external style sheet, you can make changes to it, and the changes will take effect right away.

You can also edit an external style sheet within any page that uses it. As you saw in the previous section, if a page is linked to an external style sheet, the style sheet name (ending in .css) appears in the CSS Styles panel. You can then edit the external style sheet through the CSS Styles panel. This is the method we'll use here.

Here's how to edit an external style sheet using the CSS Styles panel:

1. On your Dreamweaver page, in the CSS Styles panel, double-click the layer ID associated with the layer that you want to manipulate.

2. In the CSS Rule Definition dialog box that appears, in the list on the left, click the category of the settings that you want to change. For this example, click the Positioning category.

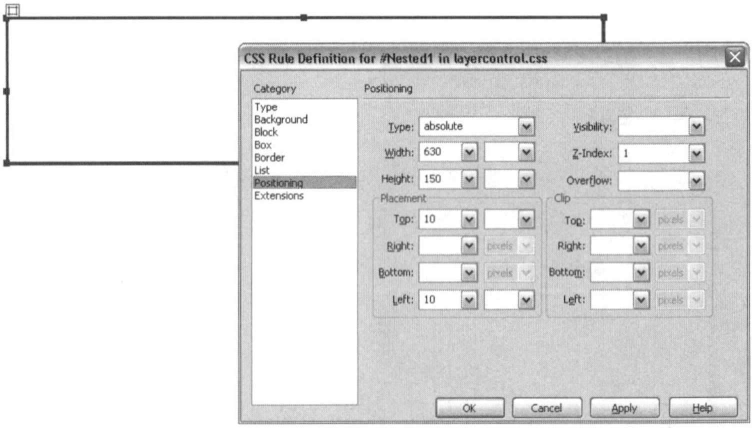

The Positioning category contains many commands that the Property Inspector also contains, such as width, height, and positioning controls.

3. Enter new values for the settings you want to change. Here, change the width and height of your layer by entering new values in the Positioning category's Width and Height fields. To preview your changes, click Apply at the bottom of the dialog box.

4. To change the position of the layer on the page, enter new values in the Positioning category's Placement fields.

   Normally, a layer's placement is set in relation to the top-left corner of the page, so that you can simply enter values in the Top and Left fields. However, you can further control a layer's position by entering values for Right and Bottom.

   Next, you'll set the way that content behaves on the layer. By default, layers display their entire contents, even if the contents are larger than the layer itself. But you can use the Overflow pull-down menu to determine how the layer handles content that's placed in it.

> **IMMINENT DOOM**
>
> When you're using CSS to control layers, make sure to leave the Positioning category's Type pull-down menu set to Absolute. Even though there are three other options, making any choice other than Absolute creates a div tag, and you'll no longer have what Dreamweaver calls a layer. You'll learn more about div tags in "Inserting Div Tags" later in this chapter.

5. Open the Positioning category's Overflow menu and choose an option.

   Visible: Ignores the layer's width and height settings. The layer expands to accommodate it's content. This is Dreamweaver's default, and not the best choice when using layers for layout because you'll want fixed control in your layout. You might use this option if you're using a layer in other ways—for a pop-up message, for example.

   Hidden: Applies the layer's width and height settings. Any content that exceeds this area is hidden. This setting is good when using layers to control page layout, as it creates a fixed container.

   Scroll: Forces the layer to display horizontal and vertical scrollbars, even if the content fits within the layer. The scrollbars are not visible in Dreamweaver. To see them, you need to preview your page in a browser.

   Auto: Adds scrollbars to the layer, but only if the layer contains content that exceeds its boundaries. To see the scrollbars, you need to preview your page in a browser.

   The Positioning category also contains several other options, such as Visibility and Clip, which we'll talk about shortly. Now, though, we'll set a background color or image for the layer.

> **NOTEWORTHY**
>
> Watch those target browsers when it comes to Overflow. Be sure to preview your page in popular browsers to ensure that your setting makes your pages appear as you intend.

6. To set a background for your layer, click the Background category in the CSS Rule Definition dialog box; then use the Background Color field to choose a color, or click the Browse button beside the Background Image field and select an image.

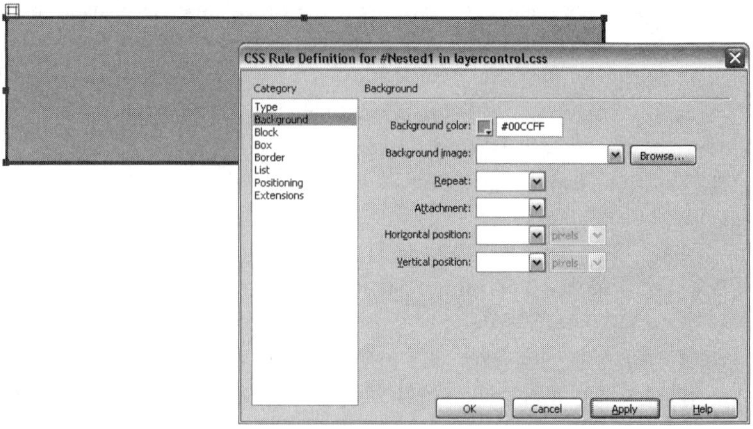

If you don't set a background image or a background color, then your layer's background will be transparent.

Layers primarily make use of the Positioning and Background categories, as you just saw. However, that doesn't mean that you can't use the other categories in the dialog box. For example, maybe you want to set a border for your layer or control the look of any text that appears on the layer. With CSS, it's all fair game—just be sure to preview your settings in as many browsers as you can to make sure that your layout looks as you expect.

7. Using other categories in the CSS Rule Definition dialog box, set any other options that you want for your layer. When your changes are complete, click OK.

   When you click OK, the settings that you specified are applied to your layer.

8. Use this same process to make changes to the other layers on your page.

   Instantly, your page is updated.

Now suppose your web site contains 50, 100, or 200 pages that all need to be updated. Maybe you need to add a new element to a navigation bar that appears on every page. If you're using an external style sheet to control all of your pages, you can update the whole site—every single page—in a matter of seconds. That's how powerful external style sheets are.

Attaching an External Style Sheet to Create Additional Pages

Once you've created CSS layers and an external style sheet, you can quickly build out your site to as many pages as you need. Whether you're creating a five-page personal web site or a massive commercial site with thousands of pages, the process is the same.

Here's how to use CSS layers and an external style sheet to create additional pages:

1. Create a new, blank web page.

2. Using the Draw Layer button on the Insert bar, draw the layers you need for your layout.

   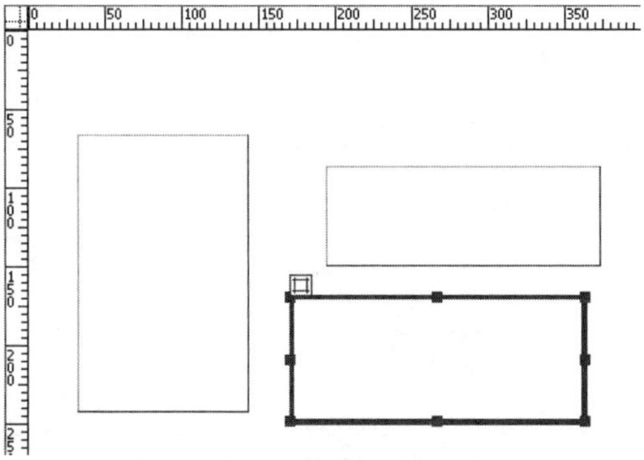

   As before, you can draw your layers anywhere. However, each layer that you want to control with the external style sheet must use a layer ID that's defined in the style sheet.

3. Select each layer in turn and, in the Property Inspector's Layer ID field, type the name of the layer ID that you want to control each layer.

4. Choose File > Save As and save your new web page. You can name your page whatever you like—just make sure to save it in your local site folder.

   Now you're ready to attach your new page to the external style sheet. Here's where the magic happens.

5. At the bottom of the CSS Styles panel, click Attach Style Sheet.

6. In the Attach External Style Sheet dialog box that appears, click the Browse button beside the File/URL field; then navigate to your external style sheet. Make sure that Add As is set to Link; then click OK.

   Presto! Your three new layers resize and snap into the same position as the layers on your previous page. They also take on any other properties that you've set.

   How'd they know to do that? Look at your CSS Styles panel. You'll see <style>, which is the embedded style sheet, and you'll also see your external style sheet (ending in .css). The layer IDs in the external style sheet are overriding the ones in the embedded style sheet.

NOTEWORTHY

If you'd really like to wrap the 'ol cranium around layers and their use in controlling page layout, explore Dreamweaver's CSS-based design files to see how they were built. Choose File > New; then in the Category list on the left, click Page Designs (CSS). You'll see a list of six very well-designed pages, which you can pick apart.

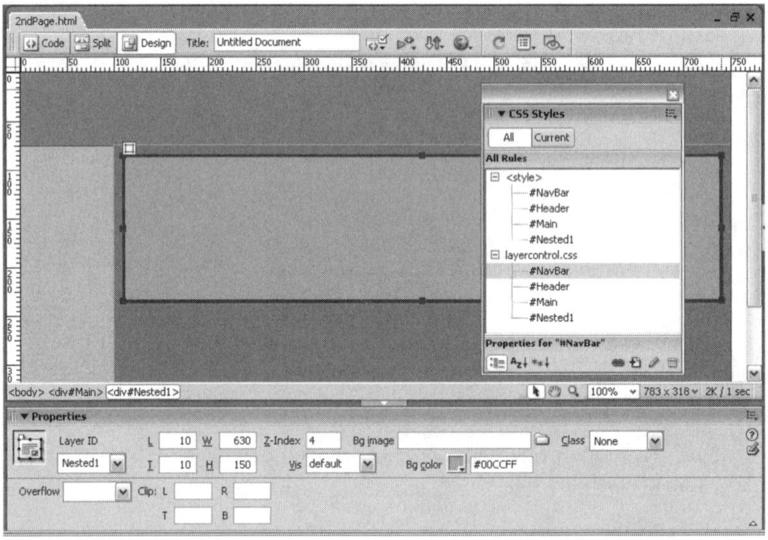

7. Your embedded style sheet is no longer needed. Select it and click Delete Embedded Style Sheet at the bottom of the CSS Styles panel.

Even though this is a simple example, you can see how amazing layers can be when they're controlled by an external style sheet. What's even better is that now you can open your external style sheet in Dreamweaver and make whatever changes you want, and the pages that are connected to your external style sheet will all update automatically. With CSS, you can control the layout of your entire site from a single teeny-tiny text file. Now that's the cat's meow!

PROFESS YOUR DEVOTION TO CSS: GET INKED FOR LIFE!

Badass dudes ride choppers, smoke filterless cigarettes, and drink milk straight from the carton—and girls dig dangerous dudes.

Web design isn't dangerous, unless you consider not backing up your work a walk on the wild side. Fed up with getting pushed around? Tired of being called a Ctrl+Alt+Dweeb? Show 'em you're a badass with one of these killer CSS tattoos. Once the guys in the cellblock see you sporting one of these, nobody will wanna mess with you. In each case, these tats were taken right from the author's own body!*

Let 'em know where you stand with CSS or Death.

Let co-workers know you're serious with the Keep Coding skull and crossbones.

Nobody messes with the External Breathes Fire dragon!

The IE sunburst. Contemporary, yet sophisticated.

The snake death-choke. Show this to the fellas at the AOL booth at the next tradeshow!

Pledge your allegiance to CSS with the CSS Forever heart.

*Tattoos taken from the author's body were temporary transfers, but that doesn't mean he's not a badass.

Inserting Content into Layers

So you've set up the containers needed for your page layout, and everything's being controlled by an external style sheet. You've also begun creating additional pages for your site. Perfect. You're now ready to begin inserting content into your pages.

You insert content on a layer just as you insert content directly on your page.

Layers can hold any content that can normally appear on your web page—text, graphics, tables, navigation bars, multimedia elements, and any other page element.

To insert content on a layer, first click inside the layer. With the cursor inside the layer, begin inserting content just as you would insert content directly on your page. For nested layers, the process is exactly the same: just click inside the nested layer, and you're away. Knock yourself out.

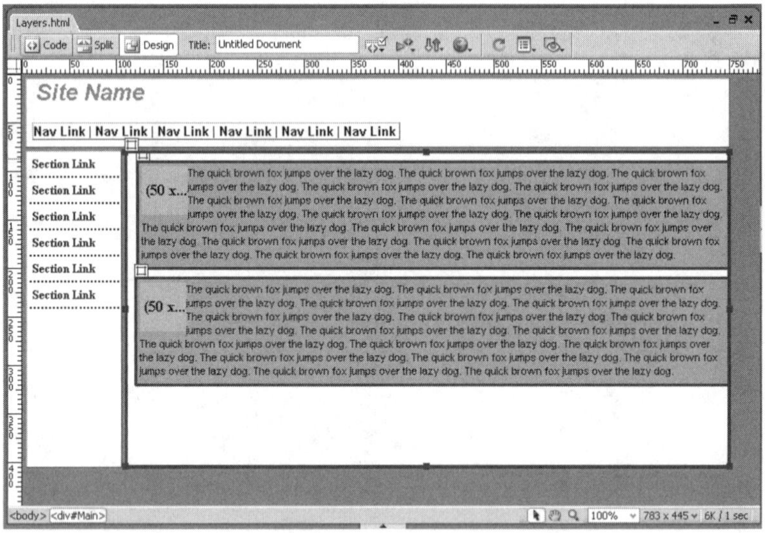

With your page's structure built and under firm control with CSS, you can begin inserting content into your layers. Inserting text, graphics, and other content into layers is just as easy as inserting it directly on your page.

After you have your content on your layers, you can set additional CSS options for your layers to help control their contents. For example, you might want to mask part of a layer, add some padding to a layer, or put a margin around a layer to separate it more from other layers on your page.

Here's how to insert and control content on a CSS layer:

1. Click in the layer where you want your content to appear. Then insert the content just as you would if you were inserting it directly on the page.

2. In the CSS Style panel, double-click the style that you want to change.

3. In the CSS Rule Definition dialog box that appears, click a category on the left. For the example here, click the Positioning category.

4. Enter the values you want. For instance, to crop the content on your layer, enter values in the Clip fields.

   The values in the Clip fields determine the area within the layer's width and height is visible; any content outside that area is masked, or hidden. You set the layer's visible area by entering values in the L (left), T (top), R (right), and B (bottom) fields. Each of these values sets a corner point of a rectangle; each corner point's value is set relative to the top-left corner of the layer.

   For example, if your layer contains a photograph that's 300x200 and you want to shave off 10 pixels all the way around the image, you'd enter 10 px in the L and T fields, 290 px in the R field, and 190 px in the B field. These values create a box inside your layer that's 280x180. Any layer content that falls outside this box is hidden.

   Remember that clipping just masks layer content. You aren't permanently deleting anything—you're just hiding it.

5. To add space between the edge of your layer and its contents, click the Box category; then set values in the Padding fields.

Use the Clip fields in the Property Inspector to mask part of your layer's contents. Be sure to preview your page, and watch those target browsers—some don't play nice with this setting.

NOTEWORTHY

If you use the Clip settings to mask part of your layer's contents, watch those target browsers. Even some popular browsers won't show it.

Keep Same for All selected if you want to use the same setting for all four sides of your layer; uncheck Same for All if you want to set individual values for each side.

6. To control the distance between the layer and other objects on the page, enter values for the Margin field.

   Again, keep Same for All selected to use the same value for each side, or deselect it to set individual values.

CONTROLLING LAYER STACKING AND VISIBILITY

Even though layers are great for controlling page layout, you can use them for many other things, too. For example, maybe you'd like to create a pop-up message that appears and disappears, or have some content that floats above the rest of your page. With layers, these sorts of things are possible by making use of layer stacking order and layer visibility.

Stacking order is the order in which multiple objects (in this case layers) are stacked on top of one another on your page. Dreamweaver calls stacking order a layer's *Z-Index,* and it's good to understand if you want to be able to stack layers upon one another. A layer's visibility setting determines whether the layer is visible or hidden when your page opens in a web browser.

Here's how to control layer stacking order and visibility:

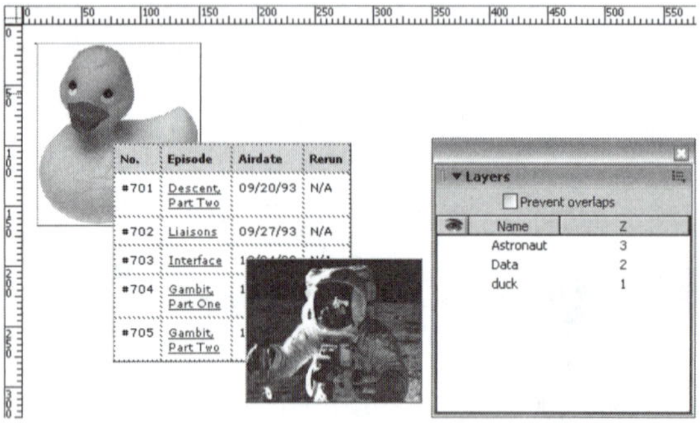

With Prevent Overlaps turned off in the Layers panel, you can move layers above and below each other, changing the layer's stacking order. The stacking order is determined by each layer's Z-Index, as can be seen in the Layers panel.

1. If it's not already open on your page, open the Layers panel by choosing Window > Layers.

2. To change the stacking order of your layers, in the Layers panel, drag a layer above or below other layers in the panel.

This is the easiest way to change your layer's stacking order. Alternatively, you can enter a value in the Z-Index field on the Property Inspector. Layers with lower Z-Index values appear behind layers with higher values. However, choosing a Z-Index value isn't very intuitive.

CONTROLLING LAYER STACKING ... (CONTINUED)

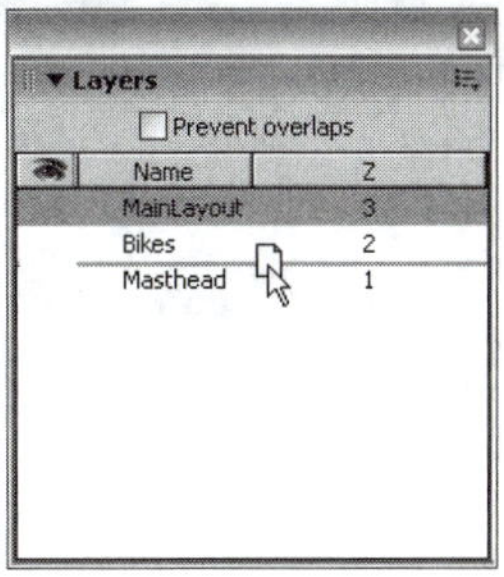

3. If you want layers to overlap one another, uncheck the Prevent Overlaps option at the top of the Layers panel.

   With Prevent Overlaps turned off, you can now stack several layers above one another.

4. To set the visibility of a layer, choose an option from the Vis pull-down menu in the Property Inspector.

   The Vis menu determines the initial visibility of a layer when the page opens in the visitor's browser. You may want the contents of a layer hidden until a Dreamweaver behavior is triggered to show it. Or perhaps you want a pop-up message to appear when your page loads, which can then be closed by the visitor.

   Default: Allows the visitor's web browser to determine the layer's visibility. Most browsers use Visible by default (but if the layer is nested, most browsers use Inherit).

   Inherit: Sets the visibility of a nested layer to that of its parent.

   Visible: Displays the layer when the page is opened.

   Hidden: Hides the layer when the page is opened.

   Even though a layer may be hidden when your page opens in the visitor's browser, the contents of the layer are still there and still have to load; hidden content takes up just as much download time as visible content.

   You can also control a layer's visibility directly in the Layers panel. In the eye column on the left, click once to make a closed eye appear, indicating that the layer is hidden. Click again to make an open eye appear, indicating that the layer is visible. Click a third time to make the eye disappear, indicating that the layer's visibility is set to Default.

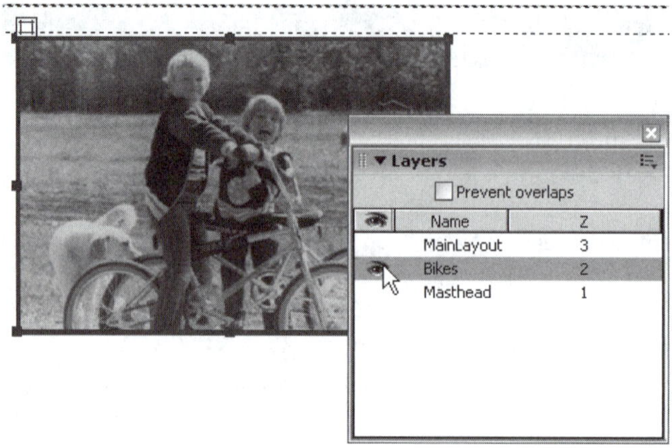

Inserting Div Tags

Now you're ready for div tags. Div tags are very similar to Dreamweaver layers. Both act like containers on your page, both can be used to control your page layout, and both can be controlled via CSS. However, div tags offer much more flexibility in terms of where and how they can be used.

NOTEWORTHY

The big diff between div tags and layers: if you're working with div tags, you won't be able to drag and drop them in the same way that you could drag layers. Div tags are controlled entirely by CSS, so you'll have to go back and edit your style sheet if you want to change your div tag's position in the layout.

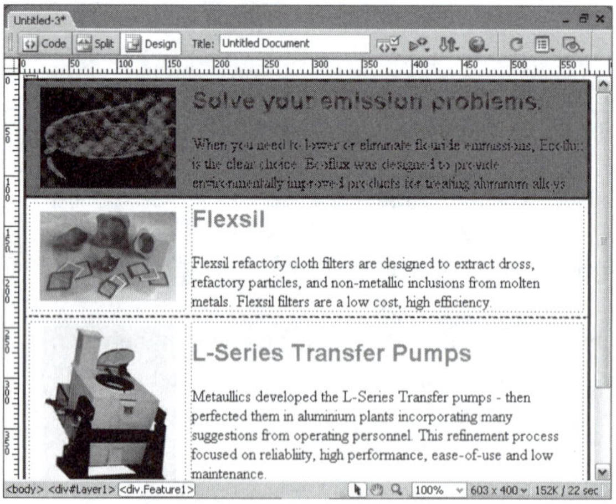

Div tags offer a wide range of flexibility. They can be used for pop-up messages, boxes containing information, and much more. Here, they're being used to help control a simple layout, just like a Dreamweaver layer.

For example, earlier in this chapter, you saw how X- and Y-axis coordinates can be used to determine the position of a layer in relation to the top-left corner of the page. X- and Y-axis coordinates can also be used to determine the position of div tags, but instead of the top-left corner of the page, the coordinates are based on the location of another object on the page, like text or a graphic. This feature makes div tags suitable for elements such as pop-up messages and floating information boxes. For more on the differences between div tags and Dreamweaver layers, check out the sidebar "The Truth About Dreamweaver Layers" later in this chapter.

Div tags are very similar to Dreamweaver layers.

Before you insert a div tag, you'll create a CSS style to help control it. You don't have to work this way, but you might find this approach helpful while you're getting started with div tags because you'll be asked what CSS style you want to use to control your div tag when you insert it.

Here's how to insert and manipulate div tags:

1. At the bottom of the CSS Styles panel, click the New CSS Rule button.

2. In the New CSS Rule dialog box that appears, set Selector Type to Class; then enter a name for your new style.

   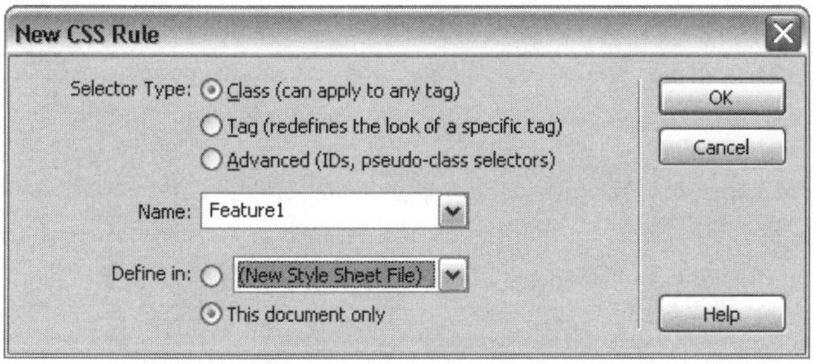

   Choose Class because, in a moment, you'll be telling your div tag which CSS style to use—and that style has to be a Class style.

3. Use the Define In settings to indicate whether your new style sheet will be stored in an embedded or an external style sheet; then click OK.

   The CSS Rule Definition dialog box opens; however, you may find it tricky (especially if this is your first time out with div tags) to set properties for an object that hasn't yet been inserted onto your page. So before you set any options for your div tag, you'll insert it on your page.

4. Click OK to close the CSS Rule Definition dialog box.

5. Click your page where you want to insert the div tag.

6. Choose Insert > Layout Objects > Div Tag.

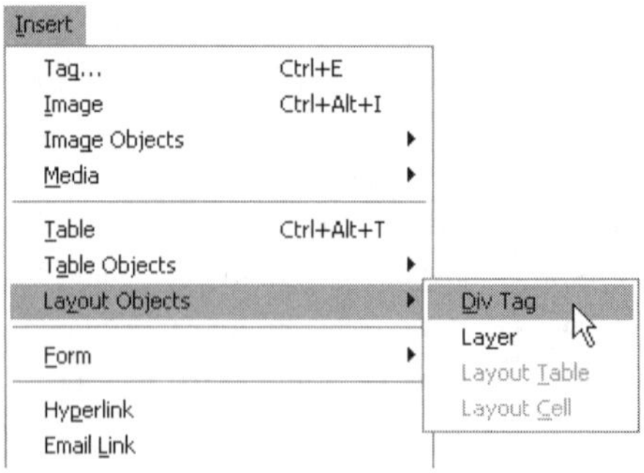

7. In the Insert Div Tag dialog box that appears, use the Insert pull-down menu to specify where you want the div tag inserted:

   At Insertion Point: Places your div tag exactly where you've positioned your cursor in the code.

   Wrap Around Selection: Places any selected content inside your div tag. This option is available only if you've made a selection before inserting the div tag.

   After Start of Tag: Allows you to position the div tag directly after your page's opening <body> tag, ensuring that the div tag appears at the very top of your page. If other tags in your document are being controlled by ID selectors, you can position the div tag in relation to their location by selecting them from the adjacent pull-down menu. For example, if you've already inserted a few layers or div tags on your page, you may see <div id="Layer1"> in the pull-down menu. The div tag will be inserted directly after the selected tag's opening code, meaning that the div tag will be placed inside the tag that you selected, before any content that the tag holds.

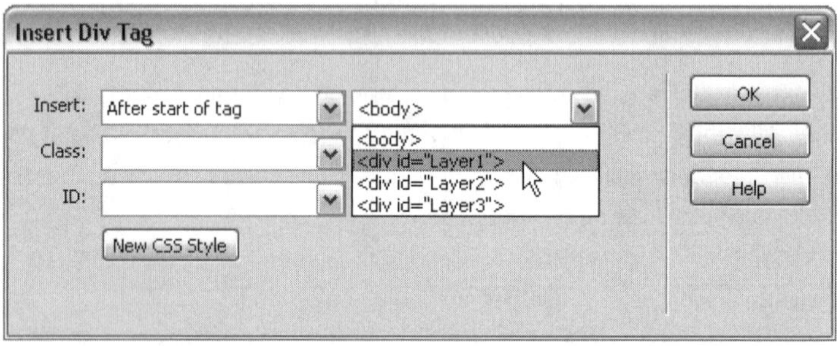

   Before End of Tag: Inserts the div tag just before your page's closing <body> tag, placing the div tag at the very bottom of your page. Again, if other tags in your page have ID selectors, you can place your new div tag within them, after any content that they may contain.

Before Tag: Places the div tag before the tag that you specify. This option is available only if other tags on your page have ID selectors applied to them.

After Tag: Inserts your div tag after the tag that you specify. This option is available only if other tags on your page have ID selectors applied to them.

WHAT'S UP WITH ID SELECTORS?

Dreamweaver offers two types of CSS styles to help control your layouts: Class styles, which we discuss in Chapter 8, and a new type of style, called an ID Selector. Both offer unique advantages.

With Class styles, you can control multiple layers or div tags in your layout. So if you want all layers and div tags on your page to take on certain characteristics—maybe you want to control their Visibility or Overflow settings, for example—then controlling them with Class styles would be the way to go. Think of Class styles as having global control over your layout.

ID Selectors are a means of assigning unique identifiers to layers and div tags, allowing you to control them individually, independent of other layers or div tags in your layout. When you name a layer (creating what Dreamweaver calls a layer ID), you're actually using an ID Selector. . Each layer or div tag, then, has its own ID Selector (which always begins with a # sign), which cannot be assigned to any other layer or div tag on your page. How are ID Selectors useful? Well, each layer or div tag in your layout can have a unique position or size, which can then be controlled through its ID Selector.

If you want maximum control over your layout, you can apply both a Class style and an ID Selector to a single layer or div tag. For example, the Class style could control the layer's or div tag's global properties, while the ID Selector controls its local properties. Best of all, both Class styles and ID Selectors can be used in an embedded or external style sheet, giving you total control over your site.

8. From the Class pull-down menu, select the CSS style that you just created; then click OK.

   You can also specify a layer ID for your div tag from the ID pull-down menu, if the Layer ID is not already being used by another layer. If you specify both an ID and a CSS style, then your div tag will be controlled by both. You can also click the New CSS Style button to create a new style or layer ID.

NOTEWORTHY

The Insert options in the Insert Div Tag dialog box may seem overly complicated at first, especially if you're still getting used to handling your page's background HTML code. You may want to stick with At Insertion Point until you're feeling more comfortable.

When you click OK, Dreamweaver inserts a div tag on your page, which appears as a dotted frame with some sample text in it.

Don't forget that you can click Apply in the CSS Rule Definition dialog box to preview the effects of your settings.

Now you're ready to begin manipulating your div tag.

9. In the CSS Styles panel, double-click the new CSS style that you created for your div tag.

10. In the CSS Rule Definition dialog box, open the Positioning category.

11. In the Positioning category, choose an option from the Type pull-down menu.

    The Type pull-down menu determines the behavior of your div tag onscreen.

    Absolute: Converts your div tag to a Dreamweaver layer. This means that the position is then determined by the values in the Placement fields in relation to the top-left corner of your page, as described earlier in this chapter.

    Fixed: Locks the div tag on the page, so that when the visitor scrolls on the page, the div tag remains in its current position. Fixed positioning is helpful when you want an object—for instance, a logo—to appear in the same position on every page, even if the page is scrolled.

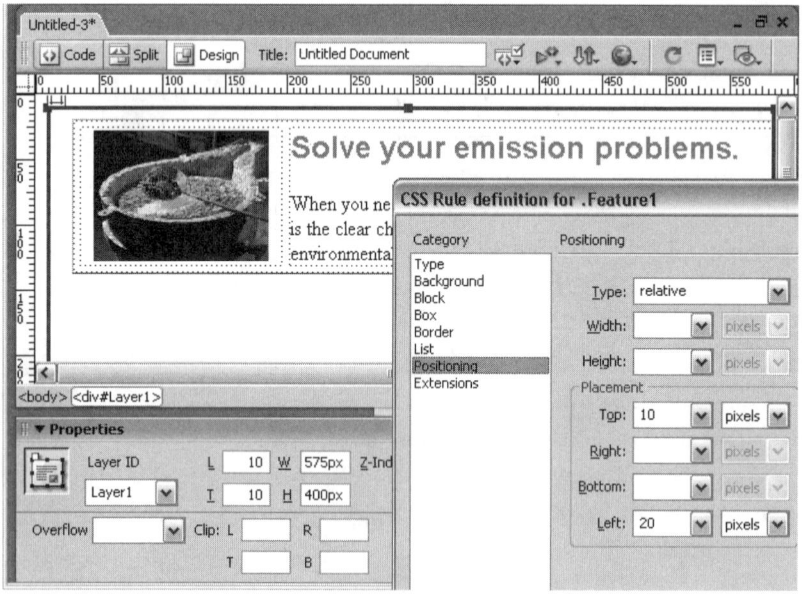

Relative: Positions the div tag in relation to where it was inserted on your page, rather than in relation to the top-left corner of your page (as with Dreamweaver's layers). For example, you might use Relative if you want a div tag to appear within a table or within a paragraph of text. Using Dreamweaver's behaviors, you can then control the appearance of the div tag so that it appears as a pop-up message on your page.

Static: Places the div tag on your page where you inserted it, just like Relative, but tells Dreamweaver to ignore any values inserted in the Placement fields in the Positioning category. This means that your div tag will appear exactly where it was first inserted.

12. Set any other options in the Positioning category—or in any other categories in the dialog box. When you're done, click OK.

    Now that your div tag is placed on your page, you can begin inserting content into it, just as you did with layers.

THE TRUTH ABOUT DREAMWEAVER LAYERS

There's layers, and then there's div tags—what the heck is going on? You've been working with layers long enough—you're ready for the truth. What Dreamweaver calls "layers" are actually div tags. You've been working with div tags for the entire chapter, whether you were aware of it or not. It may be hard to accept, but it's the truth. Should we hug now?

So why does Dreamweaver provide two separate commands if they're the same thing? That's a good question. Personally, I think they could be combined into one. The term layer harkens back to an obsolete HTML tag that Netscape created, which allowed content to float over other objects. Back in the day, Netscape went ahead with a lot of tags without waiting for consent from the web community. Netscape's <layer> tag never really hit the big time—it was replaced with the then up-and-comer CSS. Yet Dreamweaver adopted the name to describe floating page elements. Really though, this just confuses the subject of div tags. Many new designers aren't sure of the differences among div tags, layers, layout blocks, and content blocks. The fact is, they're all the same—and all can be controlled by CSS, either by a Class style or an ID selector, or both.

Other than how they're inserted onto your page, the only difference between div tags and layers is their positioning. Dreamweaver layers are div tags with position set to Absolute, whereas the Insert > Layout Objects > Div Tag command uses Fixed, Relative, or Static positioning. This is why in "Formatting Layers with CSS Styles" I said not to change your layer's positioning type: Doing so would convert your layer to a div tag.

So that's what's really going on in Dreamweaver with layers and div tags. Now that you've received this sensitive information, this book will self-destruct in five seconds.

JUST THE GIST

Getting Started with Layers

- Layers are containers that you can place on your page to hold content.
- Dreamweaver's CSS layers make maintaining and updating a web site very easy.
- To insert a layer, use the Draw Layer button in the Layout category of Dreamweaver's Insert bar.
- Select a layer by clicking its selection handle; then use the Property Inspector to set any options you want.

Formatting Layers with CSS Styles

- When you draw layers in Dreamweaver, the CSS Styles panel keeps track of the layer IDs. Double-click a layer ID in the panel to set properties for that layer.
- Exporting all your embedded styles to an external style sheet allows you to control the layout of your entire site from a single file.
- To attach an external style sheet to a page, click the Attach Style Sheet button at the bottom of the CSS Styles panel.

Inserting Content into Layers

- Add content to your layer just as you add content directly on your page.
- Use the CSS Rule Definition dialog box to set options to control the behavior of content that resides in a layer.

Inserting Div Tags

- Div tags are identical to layers except for their positioning type.
- Before inserting a div tag, you may want to create a CSS style that will control it.
- To insert a div tag, click in your page's background code; then choose Insert > Layout Objects > Div Tag.

Chapter 7

Creating *Layouts* with Tables and Frames

STUFF YOU'LL LEARN IN THIS CHAPTER

In this chapter, you'll learn about two other tools for creating web page layouts: tables and frames. These two approaches provide less flexibility than CSS layers, but you'll still find them useful for certain tasks. You can use tables to build a grid-like layout, for instance, and frames can be great for displaying more than one web page in your visitor's browser. You'll also learn to create page layouts using image slicing, which makes use of tables as well as CSS.

When to Use Tables and Frames

Unlike in traditional graphic design, you can't just start slapping down your page elements on a blank Dreamweaver page. You need something to control your layout—some containers on your page to hold those page elements. In Chapter 6, you learned about the latest (and best) way to lay out web pages: create layers. Another approach to page layout is to use tables. You can also use tables and layers together.

Regardless of whether you use tables or layers (or tables and layers together), the pages that you build can be contained within a frameset. A frameset allows you to display multiple web pages in a browser window at once, which can be useful for glossaries, FAQs, or indexes, for instance. Framesets are an older technology, and as useful as they can sometimes be, they present some search engine and browser compatibility issues you'll need to watch out for, which we'll talk about later.

Getting Started with Tables

In web design,* tables pull double *duty:* they are used both to *hold data* and to *control page layout.

Tables were originally used simply to present data, much as they are in a word processor. Tables are still used quite often on web pages for organizing information—statistics or price lists, for example. But in web design, tables pull double duty.

Rather than using tables just to hold data, early web designers realized that they could use tables—or more specifically, the grid of rows and columns that make up a table's structure—to hold graphics, paragraphs, headings, and so on. Though more sophisticated page layout methods—such as CSS layers—are now available for controlling web pages, tables remain a mainstay of web design—plus they're easy for budding web designers to use.

No.	Episode	Airdate	Rerun	Review	Parody	Rating
#701	Descent, Part Two	09/20/93	N/A	N/A	N/A	N/A
#702	Liaisons	09/27/93	N/A	N/A	Yes	N/A
#703	Interface	10/04/93	N/A	N/A	Yes	N/A
#704	Gambit, Part One	10/11/93	N/A	N/A	N/A	N/A
#705	Gambit, Part Two	10/18/93	N/A	N/A	N/A	N/A
#706	Phantasms	09/25/93	N/A	N/A	Yes	N/A
#707	Dark Page	11/01/93	N/A	N/A	N/A	N/A
#708	Attached	11/08/93	N/A	N/A	Yes	N/A
#709	Force of Nature	11/15/93	N/A	N/A	Yes	N/A

Here's a table in its more traditional role: displaying data.

NOTEWORTHY

Not too sure about table structure? No worries. Tables are made up of rows, columns, and cells. Rows run horizontally, columns run vertically, and cells occur wherever rows and columns intersect.

But whether you're using tables to present data or to control your page layout, a lot of the table commands and features in Dreamweaver are the same. If you know the commands for tables that hold data, you'll also have 'em down for tables that control layout.

You'll start here by inserting a basic table to hold data on your web page. This will get your feet wet for what comes next: using tables to structure your page layout.

Inserting a Basic Table

So you're ready to start setting up a basic table, right? Before you begin, you should have a fairly good idea of the number of rows and columns you think you'll need. If you're going to be building a complex table, you may want to figure out your table on paper first, before you begin building it in Dreamweaver. That way, you'll know how many rows and columns to create. If you're building a table that will be used to control page layout, think about how many main areas you want on your page. For example, you may want a header across the top, a nav bar on the left, and a main area taking up the rest of the screen—which means you'll need a table that contains two rows and two columns.

Whether you're using a table to help lay out your page or simply to hold text-based data, the process for inserting a table on your page is the same. Getting your table to look and do what you want is another matter, but we'll discuss that in a bit.

If you're building a table that will be used to control page layout, think about how many main areas you want on your page.

Here's how to insert a table on your page:

1. Place your cursor where you want to insert the table.

2. Choose Insert > Table.

3. In the Table dialog box that appears, set the number of rows and columns that you want in your table.

   If you find that you'll need more rows and columns in your table after you've inserted it, you can always add more. You'll see how to do this shortly.

If you've spent some time with your word processor's table feature, then the concepts and processes here should be familiar. A lot of the terminology and functionality of Dreamweaver tables is the same as in popular word processors.

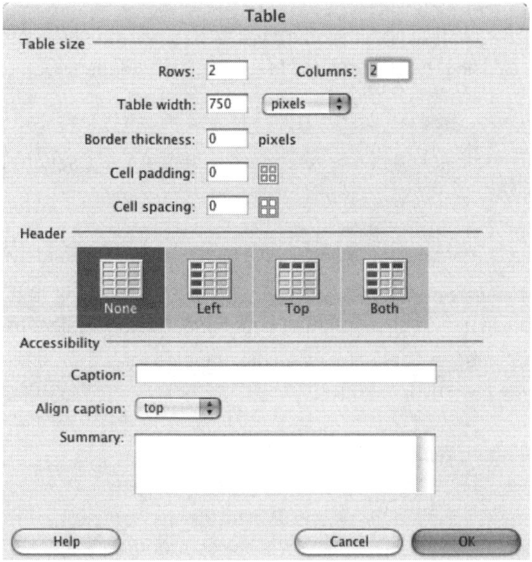

4. Use the Table Width field to set the total width of your table, and Border Thickness to set the appearance of the table border.

   You can set the table width using either a pixel value or a percentage. If you use a pixel measurement, the width of the table will be fixed—it will appear the same on any computer—whereas if you set a percentage, the width of the table is relative to the size of your visitor's browser window. We'll talk more about table width in "Setting Table Properties" later in this chapter.

If you don't want your table to have a border, set Border Thickness to zero rather than leaving it blank. If you leave this field blank, some web browsers interpret this setting as a border thickness of 1.

> **NOTEWORTHY**
>
> If you leave the Cell Padding or Cell Spacing setting blank, most web browsers will use a cell padding of 1 pixel and a cell spacing of 2 pixels. To ensure that no cell padding or cell spacing is used, set each option to zero.

5. Set values for your table's cell padding and cell spacing.

   Cell padding is the distance from the edge of a cell to the cell's contents. This is sometimes called the cell margin in word processors and desktop publishing programs. Cell spacing is the distance between the cells within a table. When you use a table for page layout, you might want to consider these settings to help space out your page's content.

6. If you want to use column headers in your table, select an option in the Header area of the Table dialog box.

   Choose None, Left, Top, or Both to specify where the header will appear in your table. Of course, if you're using a table for page layout, column headers won't be needed.

7. If you want to add accessibility features, set the Caption, Align Caption, and Summary options.

   Caption displays a line of text, which can serve as a table title, outside your table. Position your caption with the Align Caption menu. In the Summary field, you can provide a brief description of your table, for use by screen readers. These options are not useful when using tables for layout, but they're a good idea for tables that display data.

> **NOTEWORTHY**
>
> If you set your table's border to zero, Dreamweaver will display a dotted line to indicate where the table border falls. These dotted lines are for design purposes only and will not be displayed in your visitor's web browser. If you used a border of zero and don't see dotted lines, choose View > Visual Aids > Table Borders.

8. When you're done, click OK.

Dreamweaver inserts the table on your page as a grid of rows and columns. You'll notice that the width of each column is scaled proportionally to maintain the overall width of your table. Later in this chapter, in "Setting Row, Column, and Cell Properties," you'll see how to precisely control the column widths to make individual columns wider or narrower in your table.

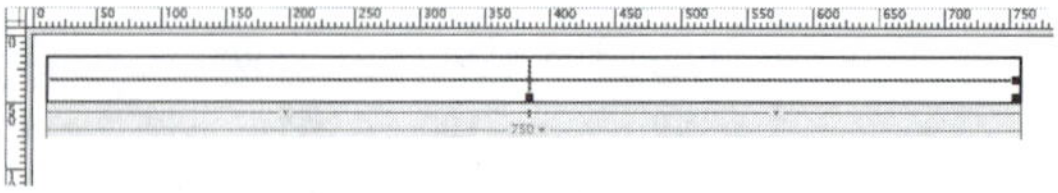

So that's how to get a table on your page—and if you're using tables in the traditional way, you can begin inserting data. You'll often use tables in this way on your pages.

But you can also use these same tables to lay out your web pages—our next topic. Remember, though: Whether you're using your table to display data or to control page layout, all the commands are the same.

Using Tables for Layout

All right—you have a table on your page, and you're ready to go. Because tables form a grid, they make it easy to align objects to one another on your page. Many times, tables are used not only to align content horizontally, but also to create multiple vertical columns on a page, each holding its own content, just like a newspaper page.

Because tables form a grid, they make it easy to align objects to one another on your page.

But when you use tables to control your page layout, it's really important to start at the beginning. First, you have to decide what elements you want to include on your page. Will you have a navigation bar, a header bar, your site's logo? What other content might you want? After you've decided ***what*** you want to appear on your page, you have to decide ***where*** you want it to appear.

This is where you break out the pencil and paper and begin planning your layout. Sketch out where you want your nav bar, your logo, the main content, so on. Then draw a rough grid over your sketch—that's going to be the table that you insert into Dreamweaver to control your layout.

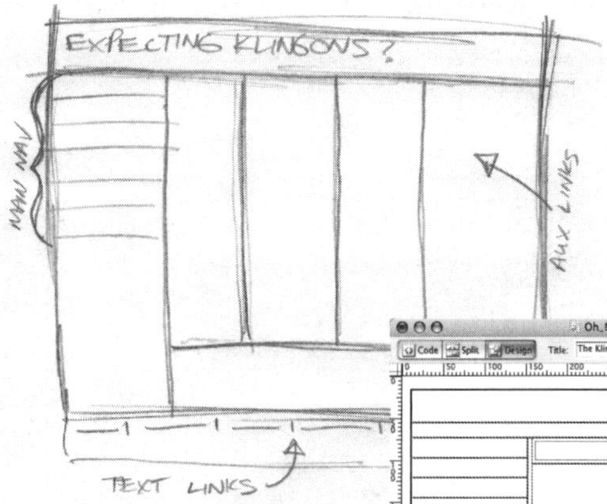

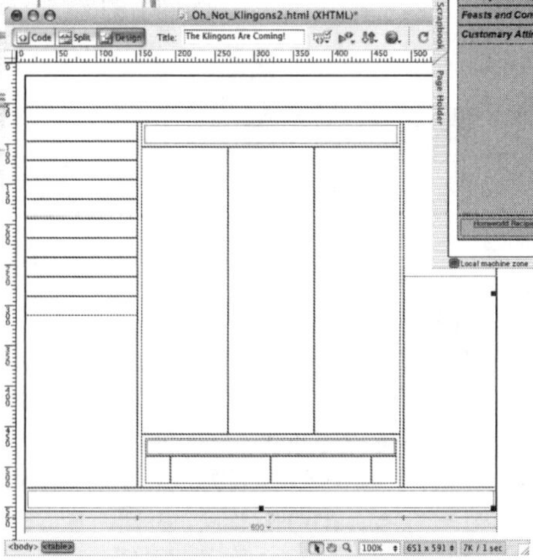

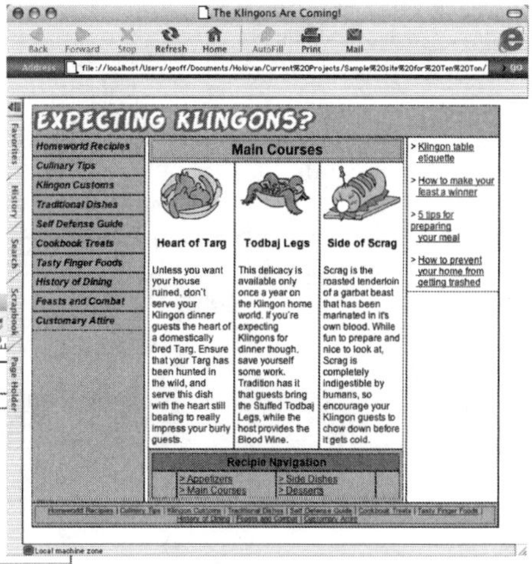

When using tables to control your layout, start by planning the content you want to include and the size of table you'll need. Then you can begin building your layout in Dreamweaver.

NOTEWORTHY

Dreamweaver has an additional command—Layout Mode—to assist you in creating tables specifically for page design. With Layout Mode, rather than working with rigid HTML-based tables, you can draw tables visually.

Now use your sketch to determine how many rows and columns your table will need. Then insert a table into Dreamweaver and begin setting properties for it. Finally, insert your logos, nav bars, and other content.

DREAMWEAVER'S FORMATTING HIERARCHY

As you set formatting options for your tables, Dreamweaver uses a hierarchical approach to determine what formatting takes priority. For example, say you set a background color for a single cell in your table, as well as a background color for an entire row. The cell's formatting would override the row's formatting. Row formatting then overrides any table formatting. So the formatting priority goes like this: cells, then rows, then the table.

Keep this hierarchy in mind as you format your cells and content. If you encounter any formatting problems, odds are it's due to this formatting order.

DREAMWEAVER'S EXPANDED TABLES MODE

If you want like to apply preset formatting to your table, you can use Dreamweaver's Format Table command, which works well with data tables.

If your tables get too crowded to easily select and manipulate, use Dreamweaver's Expanded Tables Mode to temporarily add cell padding, cell spacing, and a border to the tables on your page.

Choose View > Table Mode > Expanded Table Mode. Dreamweaver displays the Getting Started in Expanded Tables Mode dialog box, which explains that this mode makes it easier to select and edit tables. Click OK to continue. Dreamweaver expands all the tables on your page, including nested tables, making it much easier to make selections and table edits.

With your tables expanded, you can more easily work with your table elements.

Once you make your selection or change, head back to Dreamweaver's Standard mode by choosing View > Table Mode > Standard Mode.

Setting Table Properties

To set table properties, you'll start by selecting your entire table. Selecting an entire table is useful when you want to set table-wide options, or when you want to copy and paste an entire table in one shot. In addition, once your table is selected, you can remove it and all of its contents from your page by pressing Delete.

You can easily select a row, column, cell, or entire table with just one mouse click.

Dreamweaver makes selecting table components—rows, columns, cells, and tables themselves—fairly intuitive. You can easily select a row, column, cell, or entire table with just one mouse click. Once you have a selection, you can then make any changes that you want in the Property Inspector, which will display different options depending on which table component you have selected.

Here's how to set properties for your table:

1. Select your table by clicking one of its inner horizontal or vertical lines.

   Before you click, as you hover your mouse over table components, Dreamweaver outlines the components in red so that you know what you're going to select—very handy.

   When your table is selected, Dreamweaver highlights it with a black frame (just as it does a selected graphic), and the table and column widths appear in green above or below the table. The green down-pointing arrows beside the widths are pull-down menus that provide additional column- and table-related commands.

   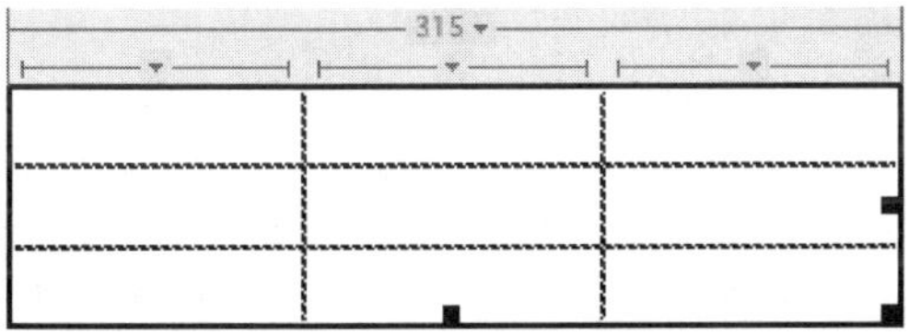

   To deselect the table, click anywhere outside the table.

2. If you want to adjust the number of rows and columns in your table, type new values in the Rows and Cols fields in the Property Inspector.

3. If you want to change the width of your table, adjust the value in the Property Inspector's Width field.

NOTEWORTHY

Another way to select a table is to click anywhere inside it and then click <table> in the Tag Selector on the Status bar.

IMMINENT DOOM

If you reduce the number of rows or columns in your table using the Property Inspector, Dreamweaver won't warn you if the rows and columns that are being removed contain content—it will simply remove them.

Setting a percentage for your table width scales it in relation to Dreamweaver's window, which is often larger than most browser windows. This means that as you work, you won't have a good sense of how your table will actually appear for your visitors.

Dreamweaver resizes the table on your page, scaling the column widths in your table proportionately. When entering values for your table's width, you can use either a fixed pixel value or a percentage. If you want to set a percentage for the width, type a percent sign (%) after your value. Remember, if your width is a percentage, your table's size is then determined by the size of the visitor's browser window, which you have no control over.

Alternatively, you can resize your table visually. Just drag the table's resize handles, which appear on the right, bottom, and bottom right of your table when it's selected (just as with graphics).

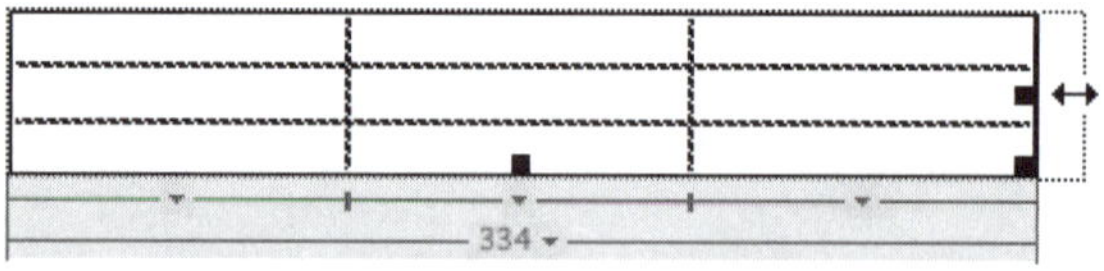

NOTEWORTHY

Below the Width field in the Property Inspector, you'll see a field for controlling your table's height. Normally, you don't need to specify a table's height, so you can leave the Height field blank. A table's height is usually determined by the table content.

4. To adjust the amount of cell padding and cell spacing in your table, use the Property Inspector's CellPad and CellSpace fields.

   Remember that the cell padding is the spacing within a cell, and cell spacing is the spacing between cells in the table.

5. To change your table's horizontal position on the page, choose an option from the Align menu.

   The alignment options are Default, Left, Center, and Right. Choosing Default uses the visitor's web browser default setting, which normally is left alignment and doesn't allow text to flow around the table. Left positions the table on the left side of your page and allows text to wrap around the right side of the table, Center positions the table in the middle of the page with no text wrapping, and Right moves the table to the right side of the page and allows text to wrap on the left side of the table.

Keep in mind that as you're building your overall web page, you can make structural changes to your tables at any time, whether they're filled with content or not.

6. If you want to set a background color and a border color for your table, use the color window that appears when you click the swatches beside Bg Color and Brdr Color.

7. Rather than using a background color, you can set a graphic for the background of your table by using the Property Inspector's Bg Image option.

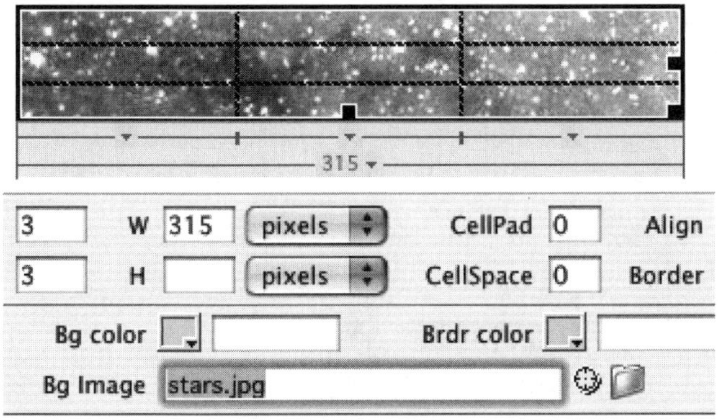

When you set a background graphic for your table, the image appears behind all the cells in your table. Be careful with background graphics, though. Text inserted in your table cell may be difficult to read.

These settings all apply to your entire table. Next, you'll set some options for the cells within it.

ADDING (AND REMOVING) ROWS AND COLUMNS

As you're working with tables in Dreamweaver, you may find that you have more content than you thought and that you need to add rows and columns to hold it all.

You can adjust the size of your table using the Property Inspector, but you may find Dreamweaver's other options for adding rows and columns (and deleting those that are no longer needed) even easier.

Here are some ways to add rows or columns to your table:

- Choose Modify > Table > Insert Row or Insert Column to add a row above your current selection or a column to the left of your current selection.
- Choose Modify > Table > Insert Rows or Columns. In the Insert Rows or Columns dialog box that appears, enter the number of rows or columns that you want to add.
- Click the green down-pointing arrow beside the column's width and, from the pull-down menu that appears, choose Insert Column Left or Insert Column Right.
- Click the last cell of your table and then press the Tab key. Dreamweaver automatically adds a row to your table.

To remove unwanted rows and columns from your tables, click inside a cell that's within the row or column that you want to delete. Choose Modify > Table and then choose Delete Row or Delete Column.

Setting Row, Column, and Cell Properties

In addition to setting options for your entire table, you can format rows, columns, and individual cells to control their look. Selecting rows and columns is useful when you want to make property changes that affect only a specific row or column. Selecting individual cells is handy when you want to change only a specific cell or group of cells and leave the rest of the table unchanged.

Selecting cells, rows, and columns is useful when you want to make property changes that affect only a specific group of cells and leave the rest of the table unchanged.

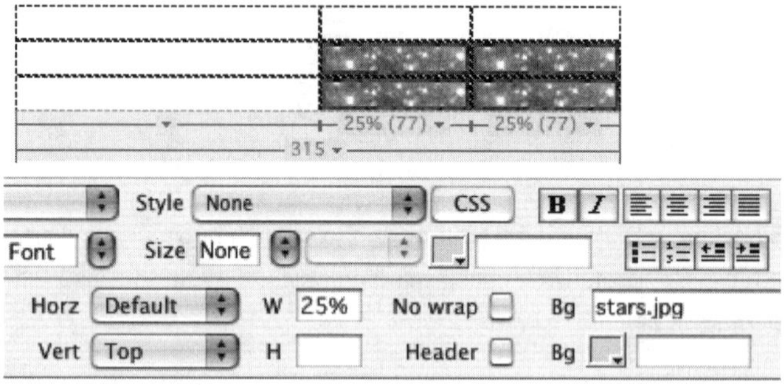

Select individual cells to set options specifically for them, including their width and background graphic, to exercise finer control over your table's appearance.

You can also individually resize the columns in your table. Unlike in some word processors, you cannot make a cell wider or narrow than the column it sits in. When a cell is resized, so is its entire column. If you find yourself getting into hot water setting your column widths, just head for the sidebar "Resetting Column Widths" later in this chapter.

As you're formatting cells, rows, and columns, don't forget Dreamweaver's table formatting hierarchy: cell formatting overrides row formatting, and row formatting overrides table formatting.

Unlike rows, columns can't be changed in one shot. If you select an entire column, you're actually manipulating a group of cells.

Here's how to set properties for cells and rows:

1. In your table, select the cell or row that you want to manipulate by doing one of the following:

    - To select a single cell, hold down Ctrl (Windows) or Command (Mac) and click inside it.

A black border appears around the cell, indicating that it's selected.

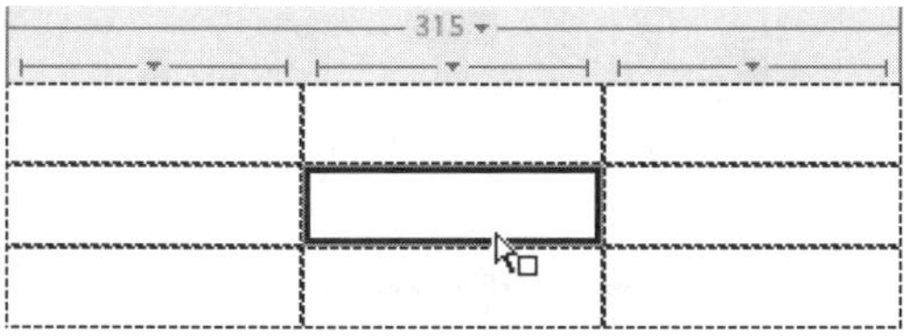

- To select a row or column, position your cursor on the left or top edge of your table; then click.

Dreamweaver selects the entire row or column, indicated by the black frame that appears. Again, just before you click, Dreamweaver uses a red outline to indicate what you're about to select. If you want to select additional rows or columns, just drag into neighboring cells.

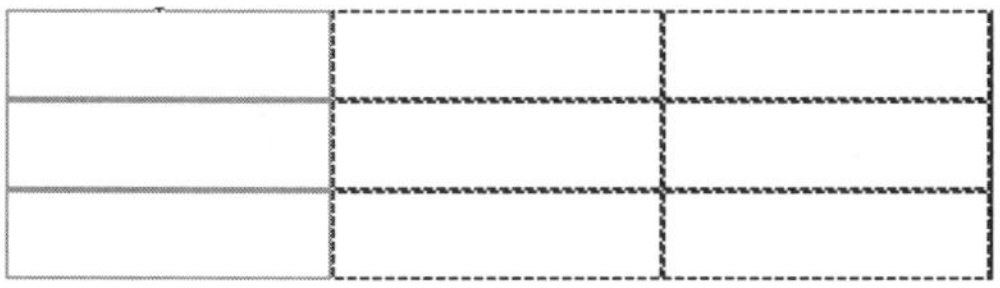

- To select multiple cells, rows, or columns, drag within your table to select them.

2. To resize your columns, use the Property Inspector's Width field.

Typing a value by itself fixes the width using pixels. If you want to resize the column width as a percentage of the overall table, type a percentage sign (%) after your value.

You can also visually size your columns. Drag the edge of a column to increase or decrease its width. You'll find that when you change column widths, other columns in the table may be affected, so you may have to perform more resizing to get your table right.

Although you can increase row height using the same methods as you used to size your columns, normally row height is determined by the table contents—just like table height.

If you're trying to select a row or column and you're finding it tricky to get your cursor to change to a selection arrow, try moving the cursor outside your table and then slowly bringing it toward the table's edge.

As you begin formatting tables in Dreamweaver, you may find it difficult to know what's selected, and therefore what's being affected. The Property Inspector will help you out here. After you make a selection, look in the bottom-left corner of the Property Inspector. Just to the right of the table icon and above the Split and Merge buttons, you'll see either Row or Cell. You can then proceed to add formatting knowing what's being affected.

After you select a row or column, you can remove it and all of its contents from your table by pressing the Delete key. If you press Delete while a single cell is selected, the cell won't be removed from the table—only its contents are deleted.

NOTEWORTHY

If you want to change a column's width without affecting other columns in your table, hold down Shift as you drag a column's border. Other column widths in the table will remain as they are, and your table's overall width will expand or contract to accommodate the selected column's new size. Keep in mind that if you're building a fixed-width design, using this resizing method will likely trash your layout table.

3. In the Property Inspector, set the horizontal and vertical alignment for the selected cells by choosing options from the Horz and Vert pull-down menus.

NOTEWORTHY

Think of the widths you set for the columns in your table as minimum widths. If you add wide content (like a large graphic or a long URL, or if No Wrap is used, for example), the column that holds the content will expand, accommodating the wider content. When this happens, the original column width that you set is overridden. Therefore, if you're creating a fixed-width layout, you'll want to be careful about the size of the content your table will hold.

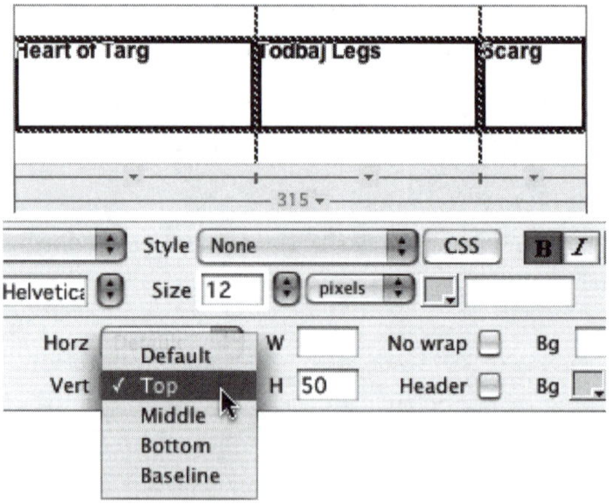

The Horz menu sets the horizontal alignment of cell contents. Its options are Default, Left, Center, and Right. Vert sets the cell's vertical alignment; options are Default, Top, Middle, Bottom, and Baseline.

If you leave these two settings blank, cell contents will align left horizontally and in the center of the cell vertically.

NOTEWORTHY

If you're using tables to lay out your pages, it's a good idea to set your table cell's vertical alignment to Top. With this setting, content will shift toward the top of your page, and you'll be able to control the space on your page more easily.

4. If you don't want content (typically text) to wrap within the cell, turn on No Wrap.

   If you turn on No Wrap, the cell's contents will remain on a single line, preventing any line breaks, and the width of the column will increase to accommodate the contents.

5. If you want the selected cells formatted as table headings, select Header in the Property Inspector.

   Normally, table headers appear across the top of a table or in the leftmost column. By default, table headers are centered and bold.

6. If you want to add a background graphic to a cell, click the Browse button beside the Bg field.

   A graphic specified for a cell's background will override a graphic or colored background that's set for the whole table.

7. If you want to set a solid-color background instead of a graphical one, choose a color using the Property Inspector's Bg color picker.

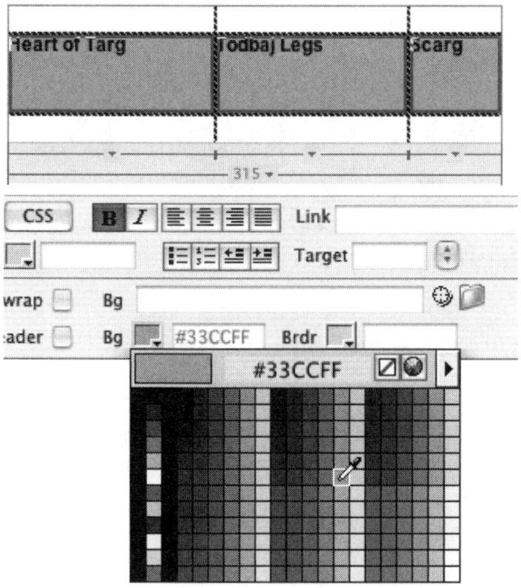

It's kinda confusing: the Property Inspector has two Bg fields. The one on top sets a background graphic, and the one on the bottom sets a background color. There are a few places where the Property Inspector's interface could be improved, and this is one of them.

8. If you want to set a border color for your selected cells, use the Brdr color picker.

   As you make your settings in the Property Inspector, your selected cells and rows take on the new formatting.

RESETTING COLUMN WIDTHS

If you've turned your lovely table into a dog's breakfast, you may find it easier to just pack it in and start over again. But before deleting your entire table and starting from scratch, try clearing your table's column widths. Doing this will collapse your table and column widths to make them as narrow as they can be. If the table contains any content, the column widths will be reset to the size of the widest content in a column.

Once your table size has been reduced, you can begin resetting your column widths. This process may be tedious, but it can be a lot easier than rebuilding your entire table from the ground up.

Here's how to clear all column widths in a table:

1. Select the table by clicking any of its inside borders.

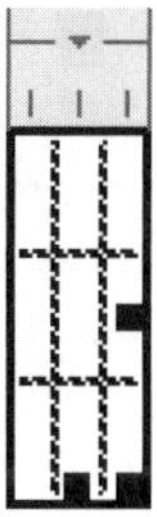

2. Choose Modify > Table > Clear Cell Widths.

   Your table is reduced to its smallest possible size. Now you can begin resetting your column widths using the Property Inspector.

Merging and Splitting Cells

Sometimes you'll want to make one cell wider than the others—for a title, for example. Other times, you'll want to divide a single cell into two—to accommodate subcategories, perhaps. To help you out, Dreamweaver provides merging and splitting commands in the Property Inspector. When you merge cells, you join two or more neighboring cells to form a single cell. When you split a cell, you divide it into a number of rows and columns, the opposite of merging.

To merge cells in your table, do the following:

1. Drag in your table to select the cells that you want to merge.

   You can merge cells horizontally or vertically in your table, as long as your cells are all in a continuous line.

   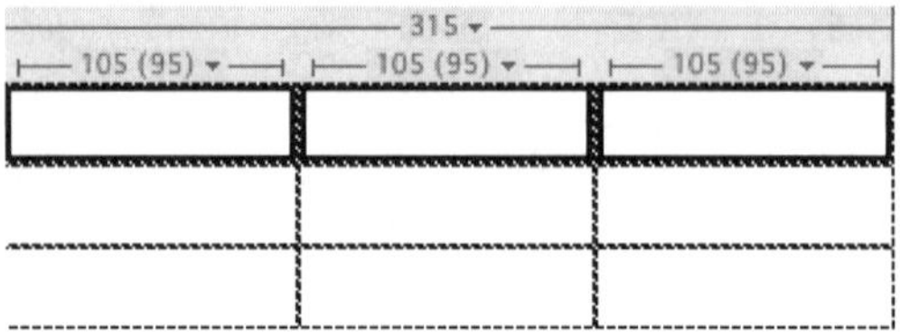

2. Choose Modify > Table > Merge Cells.

   Alternatively, you can click the Merge Selected Cells Using Spans button in the Property Inspector.

   The cells are merged into one larger cell that spans multiple rows or columns, depending on your original selection. If the cells contained any text or graphics, the content now appears in the merged cell.

   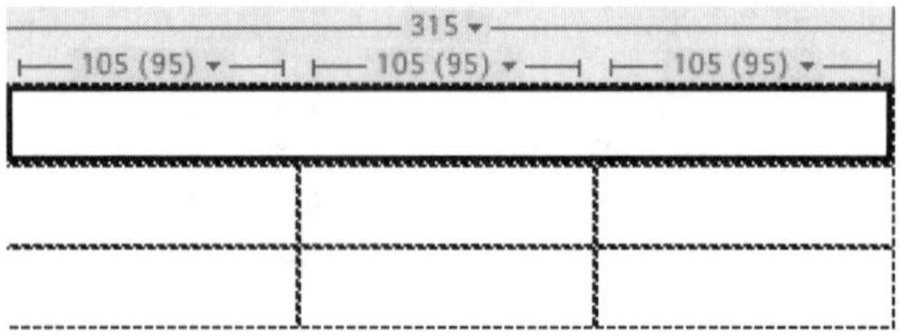

To split a cell, do this:

1. Click in the cell that you want to split.

2. Choose Modify > Table > Split Cell.

   Alternatively, you can click the Split Cells into Rows or Columns button in the Property Inspector.

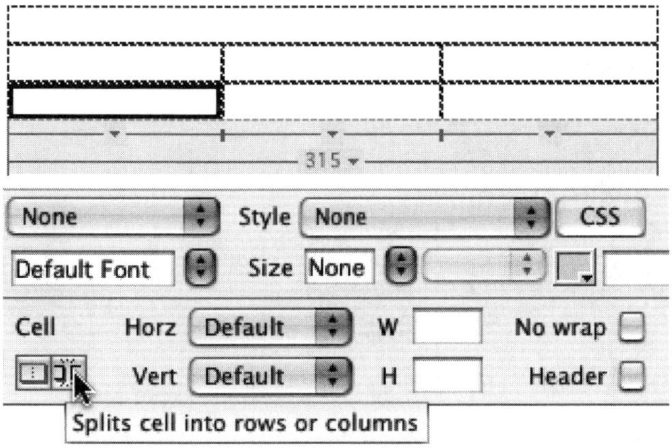

You can split a cell into as many rows or columns as you like, but if you insert too many, you may find your table tricky to work with. Usually, I keep these settings at a minimum. If you do need a lot more cells, consider using nested tables, discussed later in this chapter.

3. In the Split Cell dialog box that appears, set the way that you want the cell split by choosing Rows or Columns.

   Selecting Rows splits the cell horizontally; selecting Columns splits the cell vertically.

4. Set the number of rows or columns that you want to split the cell into.

5. Click OK.

   The cell splits into the number of rows or columns you specified.

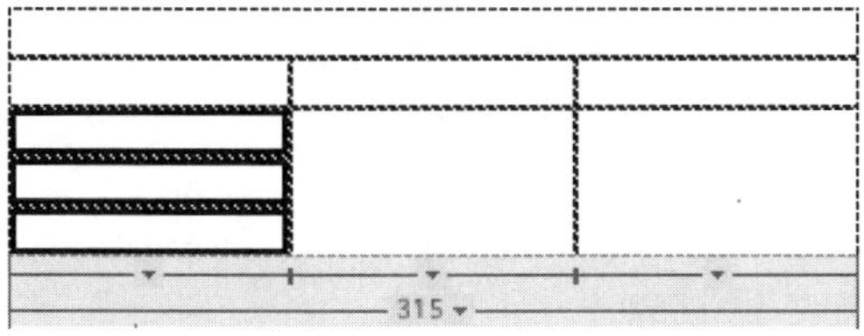

Cutting, Copying, and Pasting Cells

In Dreamweaver, if you want to move content around in your table, you can always do so by cutting and pasting it rather than deleting and re-creating the content manually. You can cut or copy a single cell, or a group of cells, such as an entire row or column.

Here's how it works:

1. Select a single cell or group of cells to cut or copy.

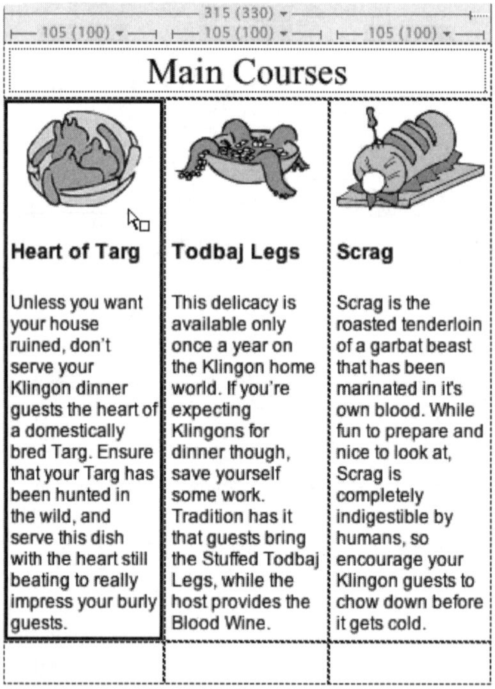

2. Do one of the following:
   - Choose Edit > Cut to remove the content from the table. If you have an entire row or column selected, then the row or column is completely removed from the table; otherwise, just the cell content is removed.
   - Choose Edit > Copy to leave the content in the table. This places a copy of the content on your system's clipboard.
3. Place the cursor where you want to paste the content.

   If you want to paste over existing cells, select them in your table. The selection that you make must match the structure of the cells being pasted. For example, if you cut or copied three cells in a column, you must make a similar selection before pasting.

If you're pasting an entire row or column, click in the cell where you want the row or column to appear. Pasted rows appear above the current cell, and pasted columns appear to the left.

4. Choose Edit > Paste.

The pasted content is added to your table.

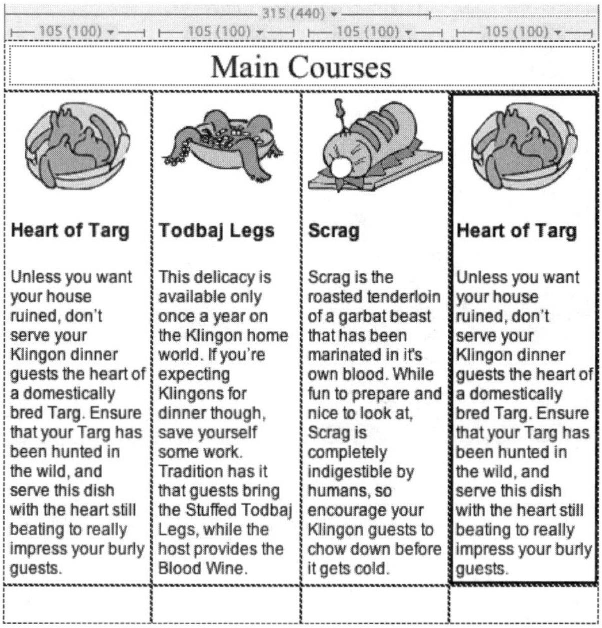

Nesting Tables

Very simply, nested tables are tables that sit inside another, larger table. Think of the outermost table as the "parent" table, and the nested table as a "child" table.

Nested tables allow you to very precisely control your page design. For instance, you can insert a fine grid of rows and columns within a single table cell to hold thumbnail graphics or a group of buttons.

Nested tables are tables that sit inside another, larger table.

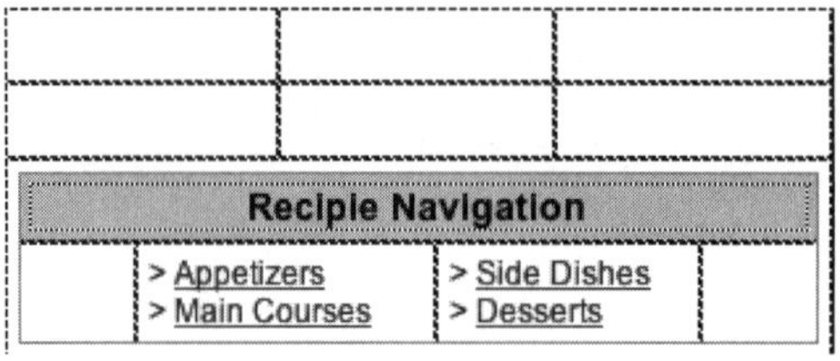

Nested tables are tables that sit within the cell of another table, like this navigation bar here.

Although Dreamweaver lets you nest as many tables inside one another as you want, nesting too many can make it difficult to discern what column is a part of what table.

Here's how to nest a table:

1. Click in the cell where you want to insert a nested table.

2. Choose Insert > Table.

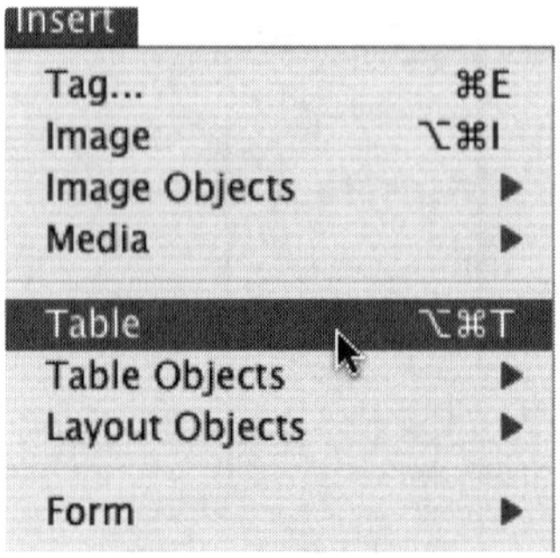

NOTEWORTHY

I find it easiest to set a nested table's width using a percentage, because my outer table's column widths are often set using a pixel value. If you set a nested table's width to a pixel value that's wider than the column that the table sits in, the column will scale to accommodate the extra size.

3. In the Insert Table dialog box that appears, set the number of rows and columns, the width, and other table options just as you would for a regular table. Click OK when you're done.

   Normally, you'll use just a few rows and columns in a nested table and keep its size to a minimum—there isn't much room inside a table cell.

   When you click OK, Dreamweaver inserts the new table in the current table cell.

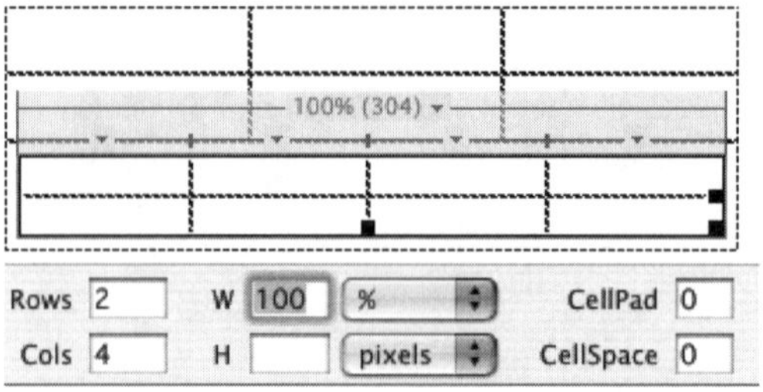

4. To distinguish between your nested table and your parent table, hold down Ctrl (Windows) or Command (Mac) and move the cursor over the table's edge.

   Dreamweaver highlights the nested table's rows and columns in red. Single-clicking selects your nested table.

   You format nested tables exactly the same as you format a regular table. Just select the table element that you're after and make your settings in the Property Inspector.

To *add content* to your table, simply *click inside a cell;* then enter whatever content you like just as for any web page.

Inserting Content into Your Table

How's your table looking—is it ready for some content? Actually, now that you've built a table on your page and set it up for your design, this is the easy part.

You don't have to set up your table's structure before inserting content, but this is often the easiest approach. It can just get too complicated fiddling with column widths, splitting cells, and adjusting other table options with content in the way.

To add content to your table, simply click inside a cell; then enter whatever content you like. Text, graphics, Flash movies, or pretty much anything else that you can normally insert directly on your page is all fair game inside your table, even inside a nested table.

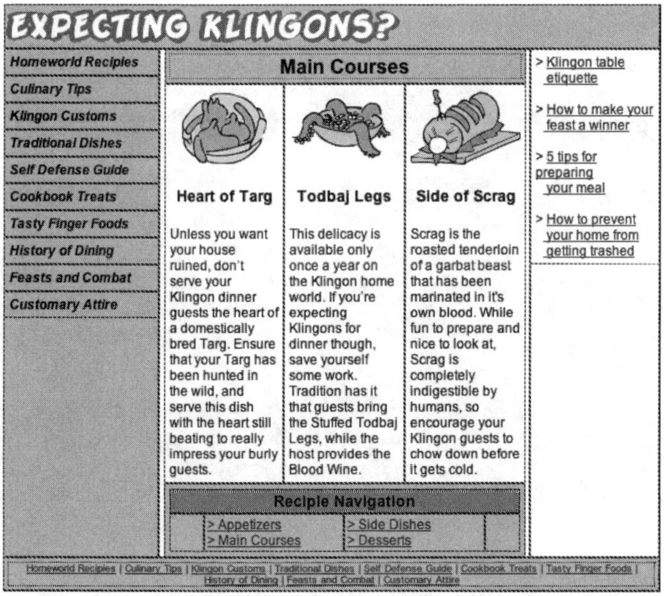

Adding text, graphics, and other content to your tables is a cinch! Just place your insertion point inside a table cell and let 'er rip! This table includes a navigation bar, some links across the bottom, and some text and graphics. All right—who included the Heart of Targ?

So go ahead and place a nested table in the far left column to tightly control button graphics for a navigation bar. Use a large cell toward the center of your table to hold the page's main content. Merged cells across the bottom of your cell work perfectly to hold text links—a great secondary navigation option for your visitors. If you wanna get fancy, you can copy and paste content directly into a table cell.

As you're inserting content into your table, press the Tab key to move your cursor one cell to the right, or press Shift+Tab to move one cell to the left. You can simply click within a cell with your mouse, too.

Building a Layout with Image Slicing

With *image slicing*, you build your page's structure with tables, but you start with a single, *flat image that you slice up* to create your layout.

Image slicing is another way to use tables to build a web page layout. With image slicing, you build your page's structure with tables, but you start with a single, flat image. You first create a large image in your graphics program that looks exactly as you want your web page to look. Then you cut out all the page components—title bars, buttons, navigation menus, and so on—and save them as individual graphic files. Then you bring everything into Dreamweaver and reassemble it to build your page design. It's a very cool technique, and one of the most popular methods for building web pages.

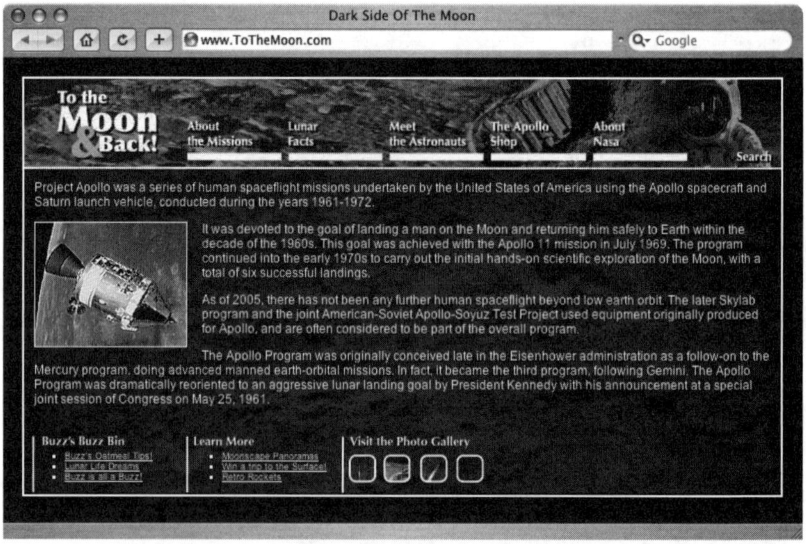

Image slicing allows you to create your web page in a graphics program and then reassemble it in Dreamweaver for tweaking and formatting. This whole page layout started as a single graphic.

I usually build my page design in Adobe Illustrator and then use ImageReady to slice up my layout. ImageReady's various slice commands make it very easy to break a layout into individual files. You can also use Fireworks 8, which makes image slicing very easy.

The following sections describe how to build a layout, slice it up, and then reassemble it in Dreamweaver, regardless of what graphics program you're using.

Step 1: Designing the Full Page

To implement image slicing, you first have to build a single page design using your graphics program. Here's where you take all those concepts, ideas, and designs that you drafted way back in Chapter 3 and build them into a single page layout.

In your graphics program of choice, start with a blank page with dimensions set to the lowest common width and height that you've decided to use. As you'll recall, 750x400 is a good rule of thumb for modern web browsers.

Once your page's dimensions are set, it's a matter of building your design. Design and lay out all your buttons, background graphics, logos, and so on, building up your page's design. Don't worry about actual page content—the text and other objects that would appear on the individual pages of your site. Imagine you're building a template. What you're after is the overall look of all the pages in your site.

It's usually these initial layouts that freelance designers present to their clients for approval.

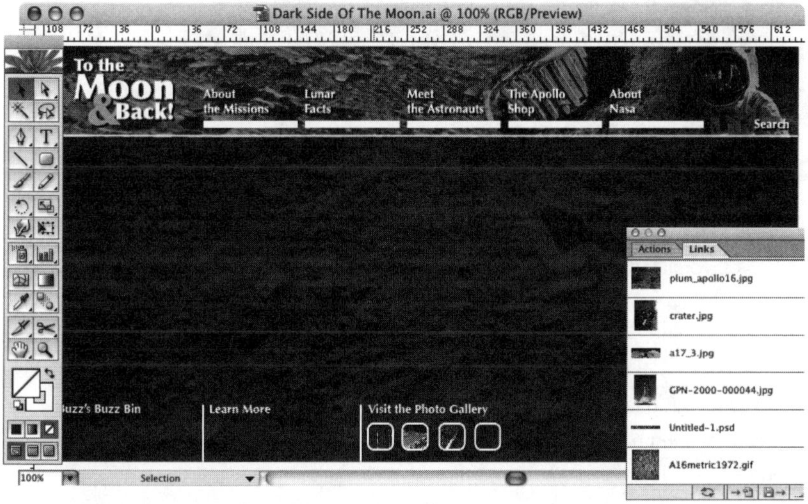

Here's the original page design as created in Adobe Illustrator. I prefer using Illustrator and ImageReady for my image slicing, but you can use your graphics program of choice.

Step 2: Slicing and Saving

With your page design created, it's time to begin slicing. Most modern graphics programs provide a function for image slicing. For instance, Photoshop and ImageReady provide a slice tool, and Fireworks provides slicing commands, too.

Slicing up your design is the fun part. What you're doing is taking your overall layout and cutting it into smaller pieces. This means you'll be isolating buttons, logos, and background areas on your page by slicing them away from the rest of the layout.

Don't get frustrated if you have to start over a few times: image slicing does takes a bit of patience. Knowing where and what to slice is a matter of practice.

Once your page design is complete, begin slicing it apart using your graphics program's slicing commands. Every slice you create will be saved as an individual graphic.

As you're saving your images, your program should give you options for controlling the HTML code that will be saved. For example, your program may let you save a table-based layout or a CSS layout. You may have to dig for these options, but they should be there.

Once you've sliced up your image, you're ready to save your images. Now here's the icing on the cake: Not only will your graphics program save all your sliced images in one shot (meaning that you don't have to save them all individually), but it's also going to build your page's underlying structure for you. In other words, when you save your slices, your graphics program will also save all the necessary HTML code, so that you can reassemble your layout in Dreamweaver. Therefore, when you save all your image slices, you'll also get an additional HTML file. That's the file that you'll want to open in Dreamweaver. Awesome is an understatement here, folks—it doesn't get much sweeter than this!

Step 3: Havin' at It in Dreamweaver

Once you've saved everything in your graphics program, get opening that HMTL page—it's all Dreamweaver from here on in. With your page open, you'll see that your original layout is being controlled by a table, with each of your slices occupying a cell. You can now make any tweaks and adjustments to your page that you want. For example, you can center your table and set your page's background and title. You can delete any image slices that were simply holding spots for page text. You can build any CSS styles that you'll need, and insert other content on your page.

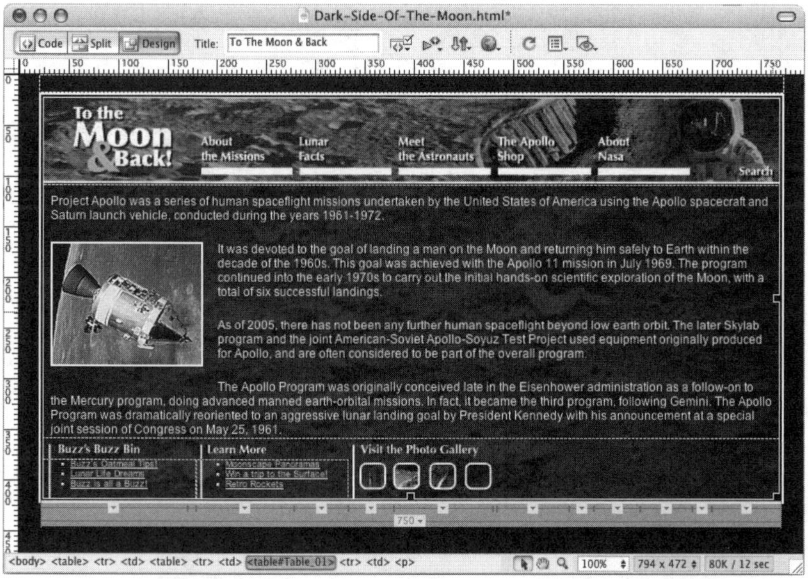

Once your design has been sliced apart, open it in Dreamweaver. Voila! Compare this graphic to the first one in this section, which shows the same layout in a web browser. See how closely they match?

From here, it's all tweaking—adjusting CSS styles, text, and other page elements within your design. If you want a graphic to appear behind the text in a table cell (which you can see was done in the sample page design, which uses a crater background behind the text), remove a graphic from its table cell and set it as the cell's background image, just as you did earlier in this chapter. Then insert your text in the cell as you normally would. As you work, don't forget to preview your page to see how your design is looking.

And here's one more trick: With your page working well in Dreamweaver and previewing nicely in those target browsers, use it as the basis for the other pages in your site by resaving it under a different file name for each page. Even better, you can use your page as a Dreamweaver template—something you'll see how to do in Chapter 13.

Frames are areas within a browser window, each of which can display a separate web page. Several frames being used together are collectively called a frameset.

Getting Started with Frames

Frames offer another approach to web page construction. Frames are areas within a browser window, each of which can display a separate web page—each containing its own, text, graphics, and other content, and even a table or CSS-based layout. Several frames being used together are collectively called a frameset. The frameset file isn't displayed in the visitor's browser window as content, but it's needed to control the other frames in the layout.

Think of frames as like the rows and columns in a table—they essentially divide the browser window into a grid. Think of the frameset itself as the table that contains those rows and columns, holding everything together. So a frameset that contains four frames, for example, actually needs five web pages to work. C'est bon?

If you've been surfing the web for a while, you've probably encountered a site that uses frames, so you may be familiar with them. Usually, a frames-based layout contains a narrow frame on the left that contains the site's main navigation, and a larger frame that contains content. With this arrangement, the site's navigation will always be available, even if the visitor scrolls down through the main content.

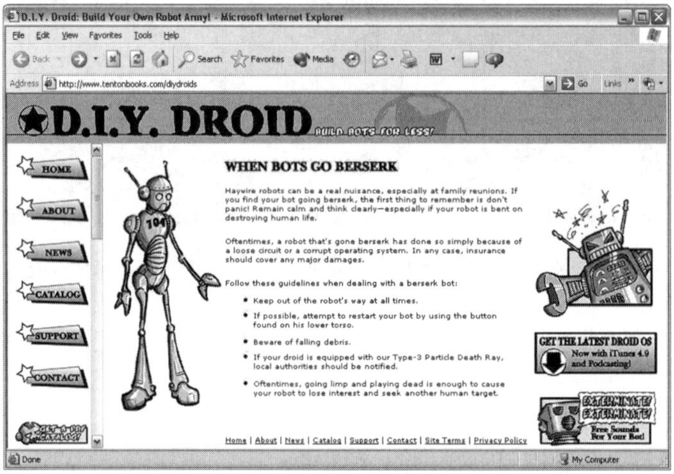

Three frames are being used in this frameset: a frame that spans the top of the browser window, a narrow frame on the left that contains the site's navigation controls, and a larger frame that occupies the rest of the browser window.

Just as you can nest a table within a table, you can nest framesets—that is, you can insert a frameset within the frame of another, larger, frameset. For example, imagine you have a frames-based layout with a frame spanning the top of the window and two horizontal frames beneath it. This layout actually uses two framesets. The first frameset divides the browser window horizontally into two rows: one frame above and one below. The second frameset is placed in the lower row and divides the screen vertically: one frame on the left, and the other on the right. With nested framesets you can achieve very precise layouts, and best of all, Dreamweaver does all the hard work for you. In fact, many of Dreamweaver's predefined framesets (which we'll get to shortly) use nesting.

Many times, nesting is required to build the frameset you want. However, Dreamweaver makes nesting framesets very easy and even uses nesting in many of its predefined framesets.

You can also nest framesets.

As interesting as frames may sound, carefully consider whether you want to use them in your site. Frames-based sites can get complicated not only to build, but also for surfers to navigate. Many times, a more straightforward approach like, layers or tables, achieves the same objectives better than frames.

Still, for some layouts, frames may be exactly what you need—maybe not for your entire site, but perhaps for a component of it, such an online store or a web-based presentation.

Even though frames are terribly out of date, they do allow you to divide the visitor's web browser window into multiple regions, so that content such as logos and navigation bars that appear every page don't have to reload every time new page content is loaded. Because this content sits in another area of the page, it can always remain onscreen. Further, each section of the screen is completely independent of other sections within the layout and can be customized independently, so that each frame can have its own scrollbar, its size can be locked in, and it can have its own unique colors, fonts, and other page formatting. These features make frames perfect for an index or glossary within your site, for example.

However, frames don't fit the way that surfers have come to conceptualize the web. Normally, one web page has one URL—that's how we all expect the web to work. But in a site that uses frames, several pages use the same URL. Instant headache? You betcha. Here's why. Say you have a promotional flyer or brochure that directs potential clients to a specific page in your site—a survey page, for example. For that page to appear correctly, it would have to be part of a frames-based layout. If it isn't, then it will appear in the browser window without the rest of the frames layout—in other words, your site's navigation bar, logo, and other layout elements that are a part of the overall frames-based layout will not appear. We'll talk more about this when we discuss saving frames a little later.

Also, because frames-based layouts are made up of several pages, they can be difficult to bookmark or print. Bookmarks and printers handle only one file at a time, and framesets use several. Search engines also have a hard time handling framed pages, as do the Forward and Backward buttons in a web browser. Frames don't support accessibility features well, either. And as with many other web design elements, different browsers handle frames slightly differently, so your meticulously crafted frameset may look like something out of the bottom of a dumpster by the time a noncompliant browser gets hold of it.

Building a Frames-Based Layout

You can build your frameset files using predefined framesets that come with Dreamweaver, or you can create your own from scratch by dragging and dropping frame areas.

You can create a frames-based layout in either of two ways. You can build your files using predefined framesets that come with Dreamweaver, or you can create your own from scratch by dragging and dropping frame areas. Going with a predefined frameset is the easiest way to get started, and once the frameset has been created, you can easily customize it however you like. Once you've created a frameset or two, you may wish to visually create your layouts using dragging and dropping. This approach is fast, but also a little more advanced. By the end of this section, you'll know how to tackle both approaches.

Either way, Dreamweaver provides lots of tools to help you. With Dreamweaver, you can view all the documents in your frameset at once, just as they'd appear in a browser, or you can view individual pages that appear within frames on their own—after all, they're just regular web pages.

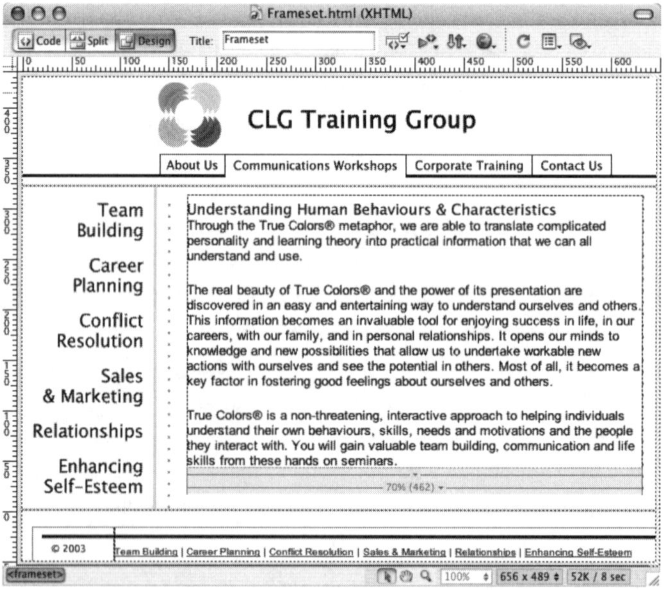

A well-thought-out, well-constructed frames-based layout can support a web site's navigation rather than hinder it—the whole point behind frames. This site's navigational elements have been placed in the frames that surround the layout's main content frame—separating navigation from content.

Here's how to create a frameset from Dreamweaver's prebuilt framesets:

1. Choose File > New.

2. In the New Document dialog box that appears, click Framesets in the Category list on the left.

3. From the Framesets list that appears, select the style of frameset that you want to create.

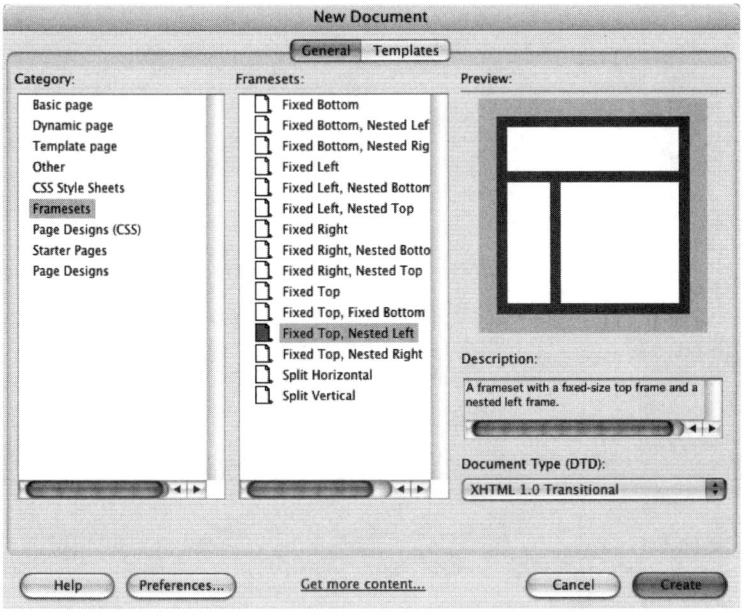

As you select a frameset style from the Framesets list, you'll see a preview on the right side of the dialog box with a brief description beneath it.

Dreamweaver provides a variety of framesets. Some framesets are fixed, meaning that frames within the frameset have set widths or heights, and other framesets will scale to match the size of the visitor's browser window. Other framesets come prebuilt with nested framesets that appear within fixed layouts. The last two choices, Split Horizontal and Split Vertical, divide the layout into two equal frames that scale to fit within the visitor's browser window.

4. When you've found a frameset style that you want to use, click Create.

   Dreamweaver creates your frameset document.

5. The Frame Tag Accessibility Attributes dialog box appears. In the dialog box, enter a name for each of your frames; then click OK.

You can hide the frame borders in Dreamweaver by choosing View > Visual Aids > Frame Borders. However, with frame borders hidden, you may find it difficult to work in Dreamweaver. Choose View > Visual Aids > Frame Borders again to bring them back.

Gray lines appear in the Dreamweaver window. Even though the view may look like a single page that's been divided into regions, each line indicates the borders of the frames in your frameset, and thus the various web pages in your layout. These frame borders will not appear when your frameset is viewed in a browser, unless you want them to.

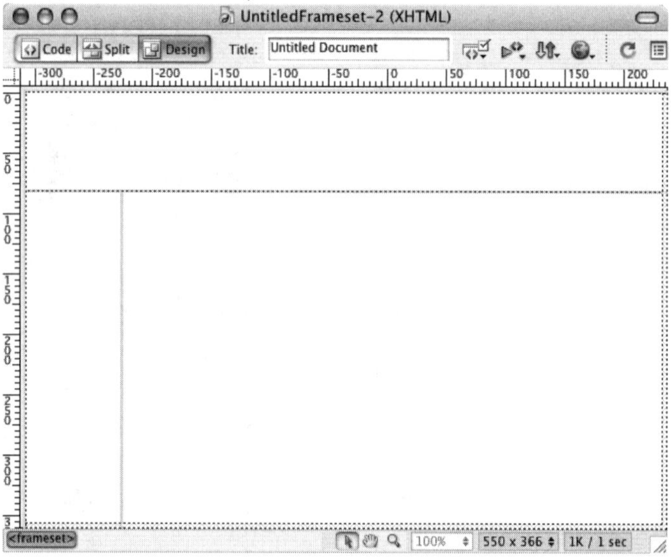

Now save your frameset.

6. Click any frame border within Dreamweaver to select the frameset. Then choose File > Save Frameset As.

7. In the Save As dialog box that appears, give your frameset file a name, navigate to where you want to save it, and click OK.

Remember that the frameset file is the background file that controls the structure of your layout. If you want your frame layout to appear as soon as someone navigates to your site, make sure to name your frameset file ***index.htm*** and save the file at the root level of your site, as discussed in Chapter 3. As you work on your frameset and change its properties, make sure to save the frameset file periodically. Just click a frame border as you did here and choose File > Save Frame.

Adding and Deleting Frames

You can add frames to your structure by splitting existing frames into smaller ones, just as you can split a table cell. Frames that you decide you don't need can be deleted.

NOTEWORTHY

Because a frameset file is just a normal HTML-based page, it can be hard to tell frameset files apart from other pages in your site. To help distinguish them from other pages, use frameset or FS in the frameset's file name. For example, you might call your frameset Catalog_FS.htm.

Here's how to add a frame to a frameset:

- Position your cursor over the frame border that appears around the outside edge of the Dreamweaver window; then click and drag inward.

  When you bring your cursor over the frame border, it changes to a two-headed arrow. As you drag inward, a gray line appears, indicating where your new frame will appear.

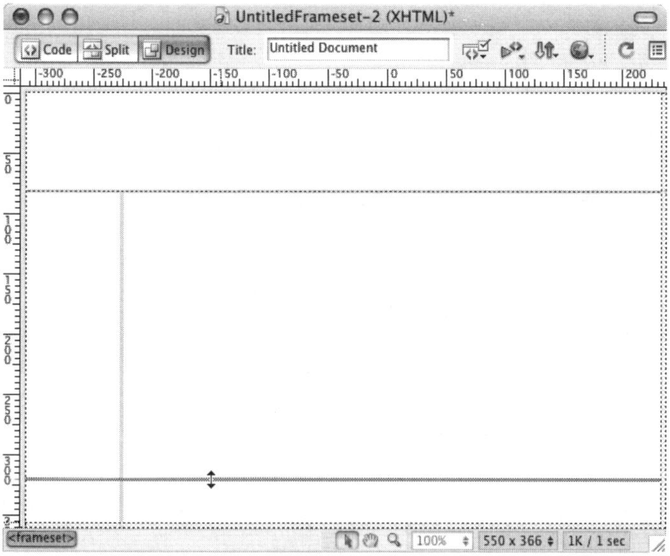

  Rather than adding new frames visually, you can choose Modify > Frameset and then choose Split Frames Left, Split Frames Right, Split Frames Up, or Split Frames Down. The direction that you choose determines where the current page is placed in the frameset. For example, if you choose Split Frames Left, the Dreamweaver window will split vertically, and the current page will appear on the left.

Here's how to delete a frame from a frameset:

1. Drag the border of the frame you want to delete toward the edge of the Dreamweaver window until the frame disappears.

2. If you're removing a frame that contains unsaved content, Dreamweaver will ask you if you want to save it. If you want to use the content in the future, click OK; then in the Save As dialog box that appears, give the page a name and save it in your site's local root folder, where you can retrieve it for future use.

CREATING FRAMESETS FROM THE INSERT BAR

If you've already created a web page in Dreamweaver, complete with tables, some CSS styles, and maybe a graphic or two, you can easily build it into a frameset using the Insert bar. Your preexisting page can contain as much or as little content as you like. Keep in mind that when building a frameset from an existing page, the page that you start with will always serve as the frameset's main frame, and that you'll be adding frames around it.

Here's how to create a frameset from an existing page using the Insert bar:

1. Open the page that you'll be using as the main frame in your frameset by choosing File > Open.

2. Choose Window > Insert to open Dreamweaver's Insert bar, if it's not already open.

3. Switch the Insert bar's category to Layout.

   Recall that the Insert bar has two modes: menu mode and tabbed mode. If you're in menu mode, choose Layout from the pull-down menu on the left. If you're in tabbed mode, click the Layout tab at the top.

4. In the Layout category, open the Frames pull-down menu; then choose one of the frame layouts.

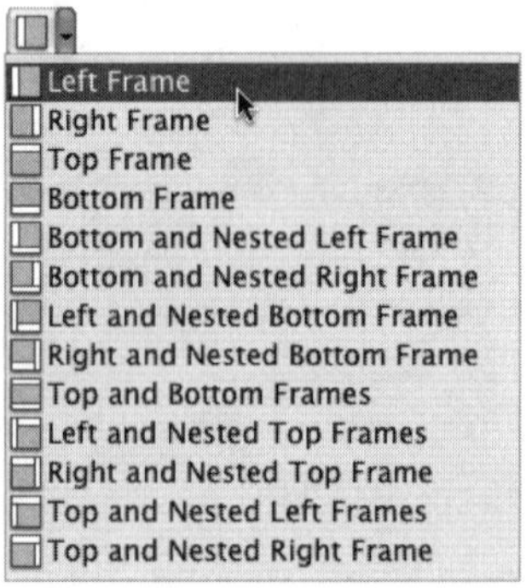

The icons in the Frames pull-down menu help you choose the type of frameset you want to create, and as you can see, there's no shortage of choices. The blue area in each icon indicates where your current page will appear in the frameset.

CREATING FRAMESETS ... (CONTINUED)

When you choose an option from the pull-down menu, Dreamweaver creates your frameset document.

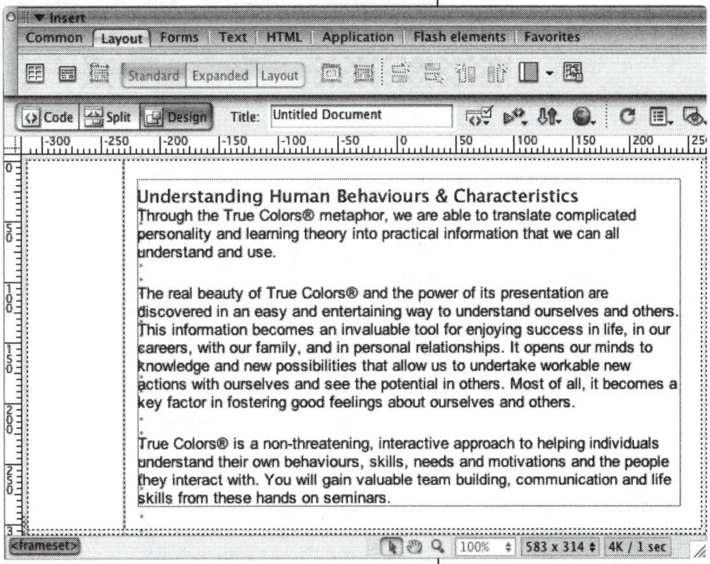

5. If you have Dreamweaver's accessibility option turned on, the Frame Tag Accessibility Attributes dialog box appears. In the dialog box, enter a name for each frame; then click OK.

   Your page now is a frameset.

Setting Properties to Customize Your Frameset

You control some of the formatting of your individual frames via the Property Inspector—size and scrollbars, for example. You control other formatting through Dreamweaver's Page Properties dialog box, just as you've already seen. So if you want to set a background graphic or color or control the look of your hyperlinks, it's all the same as before. Just click the frame that you want to change, choose Modify > Page Properties, and you're on your way.

As you're working on your layout, be sure to save the pages that appear within the separate frames. Click inside the frame that you want to save; then choose File > Save Frame. In the Save As dialog box that appears, give your file a name and save it as you would a regular web page. As you make changes to your individual frames—whether you're adding content or changing the frame's properties—you'll need to save the frames. Also, because you're working with multiple web pages, you'll need to save each file individually for your frameset to function properly when it's live on the web.

Here's how to customize your frameset by setting its properties:

1. Choose Window > Frames to open the Frames panel.

2. Do one of the following:

> **NOTEWORTHY**
>
> Pages that appear within frames are just ordinary HTML-based web pages. This means that you can open them in Dreamweaver by themselves (without the rest of the frameset) to make any changes or additions that you want. Once you're done, just save the pages as you would any other web pages.

- To customize your main frameset, select the frameset by clicking the outside edge of the frameset pane in the Frames panel.

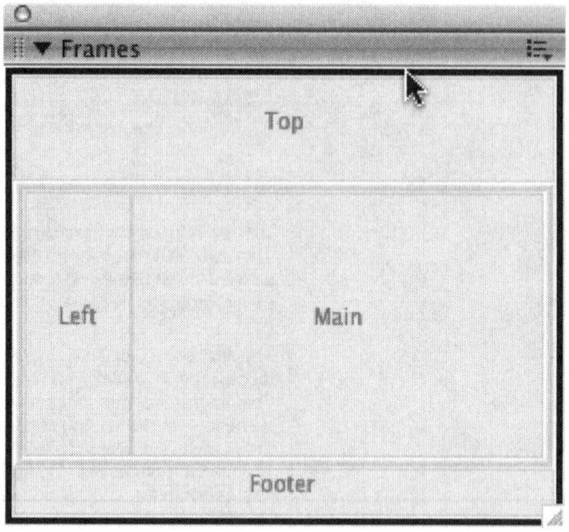

NOTEWORTHY

Rather than saving framesets and the pages that appear within them separately, you can simply choose File > Save All. Choosing Save All saves all the web pages in the frameset, as well as the frameset file itself. A Save As dialog box appears for each unsaved frame file and for the frameset file, one after the other. A heavy dotted line appears around the frame in the Dreamweaver window, so you'll know which frame you're currently saving.

As you saw earlier, you can also select a frameset by clicking a frame border within the Dreamweaver window or by using the Tag Selector on Dreamweaver's Status bar. When a frameset is selected, the Frames panel's outline highlights.

- To customize a nested frameset, select the nested frameset by clicking a frame border in the Dreamweaver window. In the Tag Selector on the Status bar, you'll see <frameset> <frameset>. Click the right <frameset> tag to select the nested frameset. This is the easiest way to select nested framesets. If you have framesets nested within nested framesets, select them by clicking the gray lines in the Frames panel where your nested frameset appears. To see what you've selected, keep your eye on the Tag Selector at the bottom of your screen.

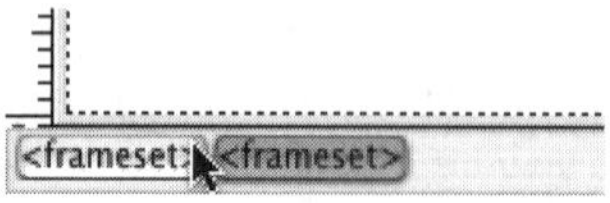

Once your frameset is selected, you're ready to set options for it.

3. In the Document toolbar's Title field, give your frameset file a title.

   Remember that your web page's title will appear in the visitor's browser title bar. Because your frameset will contain multiple web pages, the web browser cannot display all their page titles. Rather, your visitor's browser will display the title that you enter for your frameset file.

4. If you want the frameset borders to appear in your visitor's browser, choose Yes from the Borders pull-down menu and use the Property Inspector's Borders, Border Width, and Border Color options to set them.

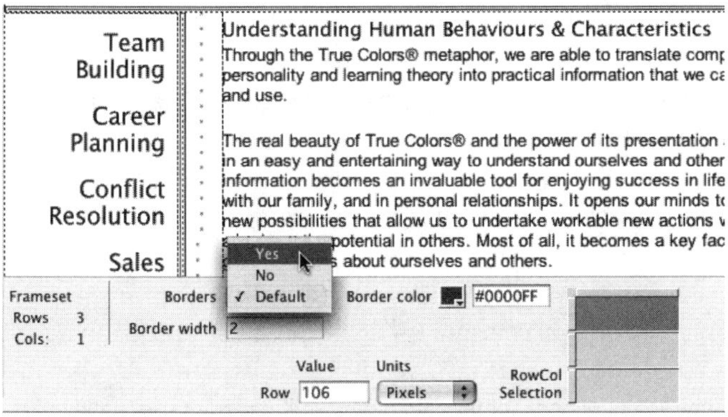

Because browsers handle border settings inconsistently, if you want borders to appear, make sure to choose Yes from the Borders pull-down menu and enter a pixel thickness in the Border Width field. Use the Border Color option to select a border color from Dreamweaver's color palette.

If you later decide that you want to make the borders in your frameset invisible, set the Borders pull-down menu to No and enter `0` in the Border Width field. You have to set both options to shut off your borders because of browser incompatibilities with frames. Some browsers understand the first option, and others understand only the second.

You can also control frame borders for just specific frames, which you'll see in a moment—but again, browser inconsistencies will drive you mental. Probably the best approach is to shut off borders entirely.

5. To resize your frames, in the RowCol Selection box in the Property Inspector, select the row or column in your frameset that you want to resize; then do one of the following:

    - To set the size of your frame in pixels, enter a number in the Value field and set the Units pull-down menu to Pixels.

    - To set the size of your frame as a percentage of the visitor's browser window, type a percentage in the Value field and set the Units pull-down menu to Percent.

IMMINENT DOOM

If you leave the Property Inspector's Borders pull-down menu set to Default, you run a high risk of disastrous results. The Default setting allows the visitor's web browser to determine whether borders will be visible or not, meaning that you'll have no idea how your frameset will actually appear for your visitors.

- To set the size of your frame relative to other frames in your frameset, set the Units pull-down menu to Relative and type 1 in the Value field.

The Relative option is useful for occupying any remaining space in your visitor's browser that isn't being occupied by other frames. For example, say your frameset has two frames: a narrow frame on the left that holds navigation buttons, and a wide frame on the right that holds content. The left frame's width is set to 100 pixels, and you want the frame on the right to occupy the rest of the screen. You could then set the main column's width to Relative so that it expands or contracts to fill the available width in the visitor's browser window.

The down-and-dirty way to change frame sizes is to drag their borders.

Repeat this step to size other frames in your frameset.

Now that you've set options for your frameset, you're ready to set options for the individual frames within your frameset.

6. In the Frames panel, click a frame in your frameset.

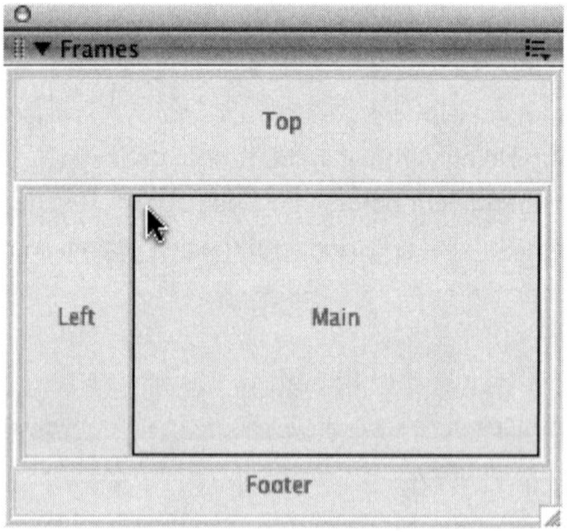

Alternatively, you can Alt-click (Windows) or Option-Shift-click (Macintosh) inside a frame in the Dreamweaver window to select it. The frame in the Frames panel highlights with a thin black line. The options you select next will apply to that frame.

7. In the Property Inspector, in the Frame Name field, enter a name for your selected frame.

Frame names are used to differentiate your frames when you add hyperlinks within a frameset, so that when your users choose a link, the new page will load in the correct frame—don't confuse them with the file name that you used when you saved your frame. The two are completely different.

Dreamweaver provides frame names by default (like leftFrame and mainFrame). You can leave them as they are or change them to suit your design. You may wish to use even simpler names like Top and Left. The names themselves don't matter so much, as long as you know what each frame is called so you can refer to them in Dreamweaver.

> **NOTEWORTHY**
>
> Whatever names you use for your frames in the Property Inspector, they'll appear in the Target pull-down menu. Then, when you create a hyperlink in one of your frames, you'll not only select the file name for your targeted page and add it to the Link field, but you'll also choose a target page (where your linked page should appear) from the Target menu. If you don't, the new page will load in the same frame in which your users clicked the hyperlink, which is usually wrong.

8. If you want to display a different web page in the frame, use the Src field in the Property Inspector to change the page.

   You saw earlier how to open an existing web page in your frameset. You can use the Property Inspector's Src field to do the same thing.

9. Use the Scroll menu to specify whether you want scrollbars to appear for the selected frame.

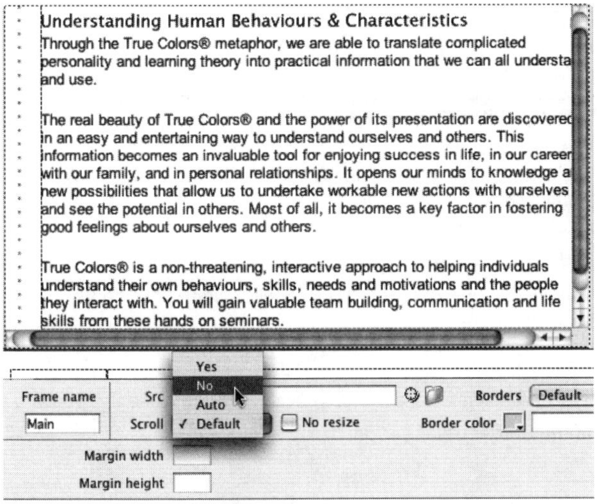

Scrollbars appear whenever the content of a frame is too large to fit within its specified size. Choosing Yes from the Scroll pull-down menu enables or disables scrolling within the frame. Choosing No disables scrolling, even if the content is larger than the frame—meaning that some of your content will not be viewable. Page content reflows depending on the browser, monitor resolution, and platform that your visitor is using, so you may want to remove a frame's scrollbars to ensure a more unified look, especially for a frame that contains a navigation menu or your site's logo, or if you're concerned that font sizes may change. Using Default allows the visitor's web browser to determine whether scrollbars appear, although most browsers use the equivalent of Auto, which displays scrollbars only when they're needed.

10. If you don't want your visitors to resize the frames in their browser window, select No Resize.

    It's probably a good idea to select this option. Allowing the visitor to change the interface is, well, an open invitation to destruction.

11. To add an inside margin to your frame, use the Property Inspector's Margin Width and Margin Height fields.

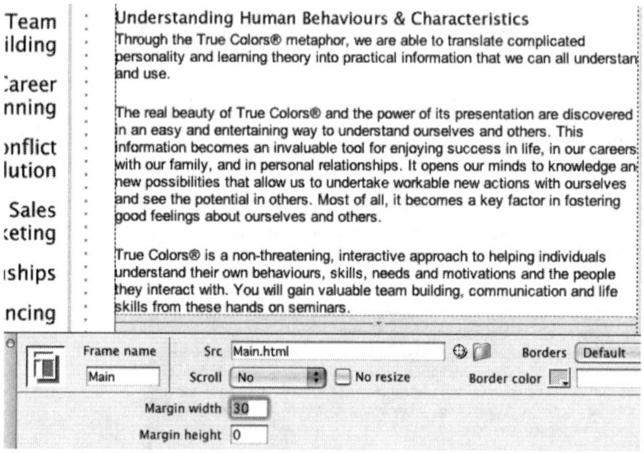

    The Margin Width and Margin Height fields pad the inside of the frame, pushing its contents away from the frame borders, similar to cell padding in a table cell.

12. To set the visibility and color of borders for individual frames, use the Borders pull-down menu and the Border Color option.

    Typically, borders set for individual frames override the border settings for the overall frameset—at least that's how it's supposed to work. Depending on the browser being used and even the computer platform, though, the frameset's overall border setting may override the frame's border setting. With this level of erratic browser support, again it's best just to leave borders off.

13. With the options set for one frame, select the next frame in your frameset and repeat steps 7 through 12 to set its properties.

Remember: To select a frame just click it in the Frames panel or Alt-click (Windows) or Option-Shift-click (Macintosh) inside the frame in the Dreamweaver window.

14. Once the properties for all your frames have been set, save the entire layout by choosing File > Save All; then choose File > Preview in Browser to view your work.

    Choosing Save All saves your frameset file and all the pages that appear within it. With the frameset saved, the files opened within it will now appear whenever the frameset file is displayed.

Paranoid about making sure all your work's been saved? Chill out! Just make sure to always choose File > Save All. That way, you'll know that everything in your frames-based layout has been saved.

Opening an Existing Page Inside a Frame

Often, you'll want a page that you've already created to open in one of the frames in your frameset. Perhaps you've already built a page in Dreamweaver, and now you want to add it to your frameset, perhaps so that it appears beside a frame that contains your site navigation. No problem.

NOTEWORTHY

In addition to working with rigid frames within a frameset, you can insert floating frames—that is, a floating area within one web page that displays the contents of another web page. Floating frames work similarly to layers.

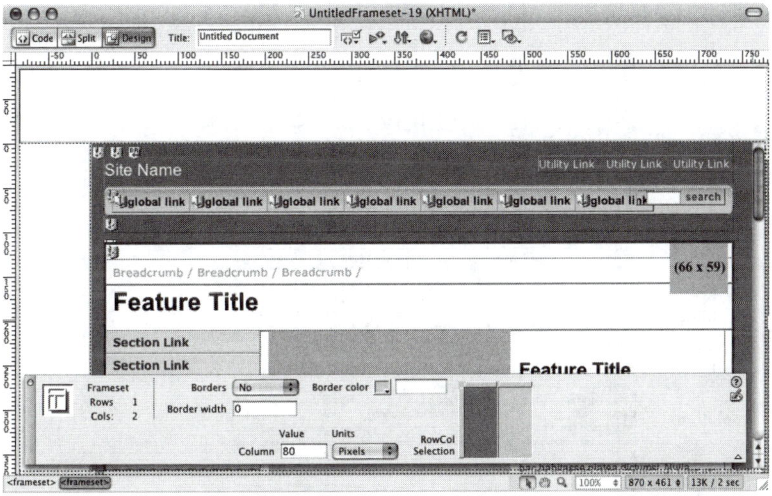

Working with pages that appear within frames is no different from working with regular web pages—except now, you can see more than one page at a time. Control the various aspects of your frames with Dreamweaver's commands, including the Page Properties dialog box, to set background graphics and colors.

Here's how to open an existing page inside a frame:

1. Place your cursor in the frame that you want to open your page in.

2. Choose File > Open in Frame.

3. In the Select HTML File dialog box that opens, navigate to the page that you want to open; then click Open (Windows) or Choose (Mac).

   Dreamweaver opens the page inside your frame.

4. If you want to continue opening existing pages in other frames, click in the next frame; then choose File > Open in Frame again to repeat the process.

5. Once you have the pages open or created in your layout, save your frameset file.

   Saving ensures that the pages currently displayed within your layout will appear whenever the frameset file is opened.

Because a frame holds a regular web page, you insert content just as when you're working with a regular Dreamweaver page.

Getting Content into Your Frameset

Because a frame holds a regular web page, you insert content just as when you're working with a regular Dreamweaver page. So if you want to use a frame to hold a navigation bar, go for it. Use a table to help control your page layout. Toss in some buttons, text, and CSS formatting just as you've done before. Just click inside the frame that you want to add content to and go nuts—everything's the same, only this time the visitor can see more than one page at a time.

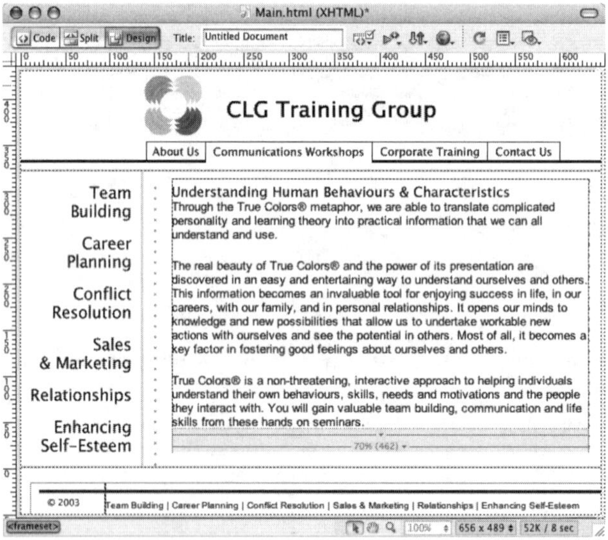

Getting content into the pages that appear within your frameset is easy—they're just regular web pages. Therefore, you can insert any content that can normally be inserted into a stand-alone page.

Setting Frameset Hyperlinks

Hyperlinking is really what framesets are all about. You learned a bit about hyperlinking in Chapter 5, and you'll learn a lot more in Chapter 9. Here, though, you'll be setting up links in one frame, with destinations that will then open in another frame. In other words, links in one frame will control the content of another frame. But before we get to that, you need to know a bit about how to display a frameset file in the first place.

> **NOTEWORTHY**
>
> Smaller frames in a frameset are normally used to control the content of larger frames. This means that most of the hyperlinks you'll be creating will be in smaller frames, and their destinations will be set to open in your frameset's main content window.

For a browser to display a frames-based layout properly, the browser needs the URL of the frameset page, not the URL for the individual pages within the frames. That's why it's a good idea to add "frameset" or "FS" to your frameset file name—so you'll know what file controls your frameset. Here's an example: Say your site has an opening splash page (remember, called *index.htm*, because it's the opening page of your site) that links to your frames-based layout. On your opening page, you have to place a hyperlink that then links to the frameset file itself. If your link connects to just any one of the pages that appears within the frameset, only that frame will appear. So when linking to a frames-based layout, link to the frameset file, not to the pages that appear within the frameset.

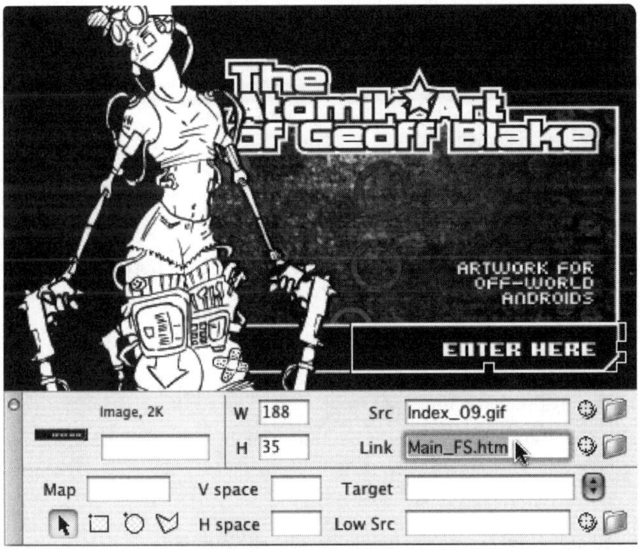

If your site includes an opening splash page that links to your frameset, make sure to link to your actual frameset file, not to a page that appears within your frameset.

When linking to a frames-based layout, link to the frameset file, not to the pages that appear within the frameset.

If you don't want to use a splash page, but instead want your frameset to open right away when a visitor navigates to your site, remember that you must name the frameset file itself using the default document name of the web server.

Also, linking to your frameset file is fine when you're creating a hyperlink from your splash page, but when you're setting links within your frameset, whatever you do, don't link to your frameset file! If you do, you'll end up with ***recursive framing***. Recursive framing occurs when a frameset opens within itself—a huge mess that even the savviest of web surfers can't dig out of.

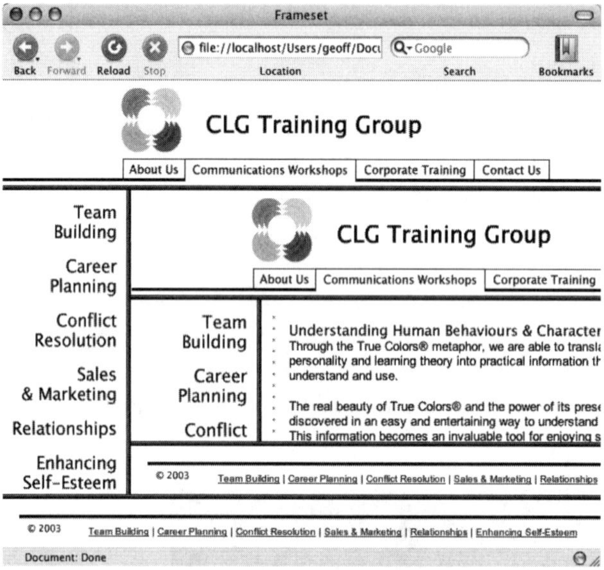

Another tricky aspect of working with frames is recursive framing, which occurs when a frameset opens within itself multiple times. This happens when hyperlinks within frames are not set correctly.

Probably the biggest goof people make when they're working with frames-based layouts is not setting their links correctly. Links in framesets use the Property Inspector's Target menu, which specifies where a hyperlink's destination should open. It's an easy setting to miss, and that's why it's so easy to goof.

Here's how to set hyperlinks within a frameset:

1. Within a frame in your frameset, select the text or graphic that you'll be using as the hyperlink's source.

   The object that you select will be a clickable element on your page.

2. Click the Browse for File icon beside the Link field in the Property Inspector; then navigate to the page in your site that you want to link to.

3. Using the Target pull-down menu in the Property Inspector, specify the frame in which you want your hyperlink's destination to open.

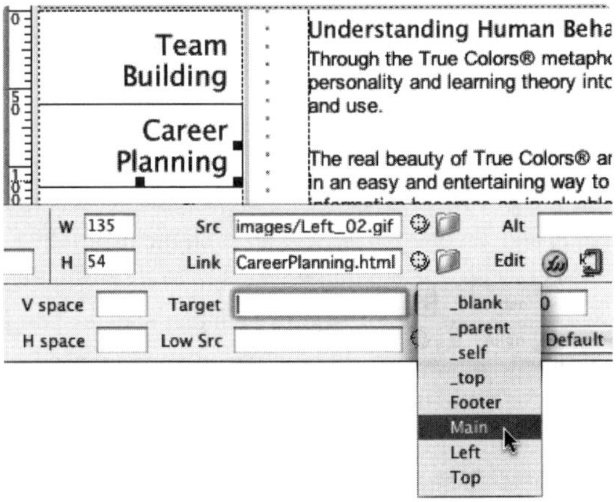

If you named your frames in the Property Inspector as we discussed earlier in this chapter, you'll see them listed in the Target pull-down menu; otherwise, you'll see Dreamweaver's generic frame names appear. Just choose a frame name to set the hyperlink's destination. You'll also see _blank, _parent, _self, and _top.

_blank: The _blank option opens the hyperlink's destination in a new browser window, leaving the current browser window open in the background.

_parent: If you're linking from a frame within a nested frameset, _parent will open the hyperlink's destination within the frame that the nested frameset occupies. In fact, _parent always opens a hyperlink's destination in the parent of the current frame.

_self: Using _self will open the hyperlink's destination in the current frame, which is Dreamweaver's default if the Target menu is left unset.

_top: The _top option opens the hyperlink's destination within the current browser window, replacing the entire frameset.

4. Continue setting hyperlinks for your layout, using the Target menu in the Property Inspector to specify the frame where the hyperlink's destination should open.

When you're done, don't forget to save and preview your work.

IMMINENT DOOM

When setting links in frames, make sure to link to regular web pages, not frameset files. If you were to link to a frameset file, then your link would open a frameset within a frameset. This is another reason why it's important to use "frameset" or "FS" in your frameset file's name—so you'll know not to link to them. If for some reason you do need to link to a frameset file from within an existing frame, make sure to set the link's target to _top in the Property Inspector.

BROWSERS THAT DON'T LIKE FRAMES

Although most browsers these days can handle frames, they can still stump some search engines. If you're concerned about these issues, here's what to do: With your frameset open in Dreamweaver, choose Modify > Frameset > Edit NoFrames Content. You'll then be switched to a blank page, with "NoFrames Content" appearing across the top. This blank page is actually located within your frameset file (trippy, huh?). Here, you'll be able to add content and work with Dreamweaver's commands and panels just as you can in an ordinary web page. Any content that you insert will appear in noncompliant browsers and will be available for search engines, but will be ignored by browsers that understand frames. Once you're finished adding content to your Noframes page, choose Modify > Frameset > Edit NoFrames Content again to return to your frameset.

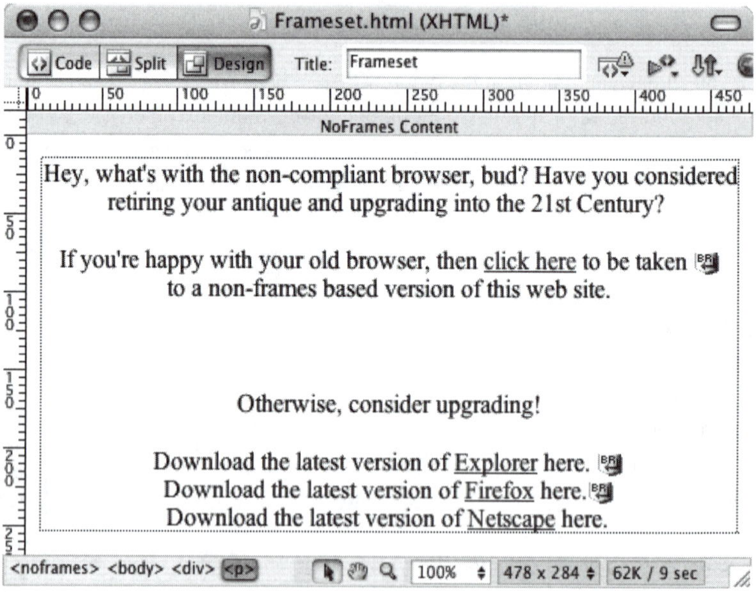

So what sort of content would you want to add to your Noframes page? Well, if you're concerned about noncompliant browsers, you can provide a link to a nonframe version of your site (of course, this means that you'll have two sites to manage now rather than one), or you can include links for visitors to download the newest versions of popular browsers. If it's search engines that you want to accommodate (which every frameset should do, by the way), then you should insert links to the top-level pages (the landmark pages, as we discussed in Chapter 3) in your site and include meta data, which search engine spiders feast on.

JUST THE GIST

Getting Started with Tables

- Tables pull double duty in web design. They're used to hold data and also to lay out pages.
- Tables that hold data and tables that control page design both use the same commands, so mastering one means also mastering the other.
- To insert a table on your page, choose Insert > Table.

Using Tables for Layout

- Tables that are used for layout can either use a flexible width or a fixed width.
- To set properties for your table, select it and then use the options in the Property Inspector. To set properties for individual cells, select them and then use the options in the Property inspector.
- A nested table is a table that's inserted into the cell of a larger table.
- To insert a nested table, click inside an existing table's cell and choose Insert > Table.
- Inserting content into a table is the same as inserting content in an ordinary web page in Dreamweaver.

Building a Layout with Image Slicing

- Use image slicing to build a page that's made up of graphics controlled by an overall layout table.
- Start by building your page layout in your graphics program of choice; then use your program's slicing tools to divide your page layout into individual images. When you save your slices, your graphics program will write the HTML code needed to reassemble your layout into a table in Dreamweaver.
- Once your layout is open in Dreamweaver, you can tweak it and insert any additional graphics, text, and so on.

JUST THE GIST (CONTINUED)

Getting Started with Frames

- Frames allow you to split the visitor's browser window into multiple areas, or frames, which are contained in a frameset.

- Each frame, plus the frameset file, is a separate HTML-based file.

Building a Frames-Based Layout

- To use a predefined Dreamweaver layout, choose File > New; then in the Category list in the New Document dialog box, click Framesets.

- To visually create a frameset, drag inward from the outside edge of the Dreamweaver window.

- Inserting content into a frame is the same as inserting content in an ordinary web page in Dreamweaver.

- To open an existing page in a frame, choose File > Open in Frame.

- Choose File > Save All to save all the contents of your frameset. All pages in your frameset, plus the frameset file itself, must be saved for the frameset to work properly.

- Use the Frames panel (Window > Frames) to select the components of your frameset.

- Use the Property Inspector to set scrollbars, borders, frame size, and other options for frames and framesets.

Setting Hyperlinks in Framesets

- When linking to a frameset, make sure to link to the actual frameset file.

- When you set a link within a frameset, you can set it so that its destination opens in a different frame.

- To set a link in a frameset, create your link within the Property Inspector; then use the Target pull-down menu to specify where the link's destination should open.

Chapter 8

Controlling Your Site with CSS Styles

STUFF YOU'LL LEARN IN THIS CHAPTER

CSS and web design were made for each other—give CSS a whirl, and your dating days are over! You'll first see how to edit and update your styles in CSS. Then you'll learn to create new CSS styles for your specific needs. Then comes the big moment: working with external style sheets to control multiple styles throughout your entire site. So pick out a nice outfit—it's time for your first date with CSS!

Getting Started with CSS Style Sheets

Ready for a night out on the town with CSS? Are you looking sharp? You didn't have your parents drop you off, did you? Okay, off we go!

A style is just a set of formatting rules for your text to follow. A style sheet is a file that holds a group of styles. These files are called Cascading Style Sheets because of the way the styles flow, or cascade, through your page, or even your entire site.

In Chapter 5, you saw how Dreamweaver uses Cascading Style Sheets to build a library of styles for you in the Property Inspector as you work. By default, Dreamweaver creates styles that apply to a single page at a time: an ***embedded*** style sheet. An embedded style sheet is stored within your current page. But to really get the most out of style sheets, you should create one that applies to ***all*** of the pages in your web site: an ***external*** style sheet. External style sheets are stored outside of your web pages. You'll learn how to create both kinds of style sheets in this chapter.

Make a simple change to a CSS style, and instantaneously the entire site is updated—no matter how many pages your site includes.

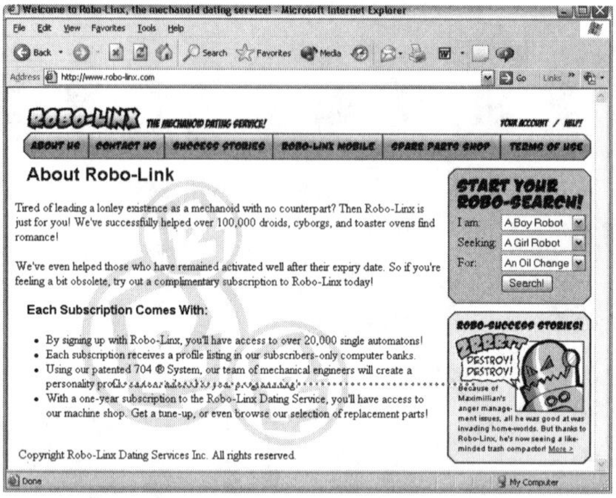

Any page, whether it's a simple text-based layout or something a little more complex, can benefit from Cascading Style Sheets, which add a whole new level of typographic control to your layouts.

CSS provides the ability to control an infinite number of pages in a web site.

So that's the theory. Now imagine this: You have six headings on your page. The boss comes along at 4:45 p.m. on the Friday before a long weekend and wants you to change the font, size, and color being used for the headings. If you're using CSS, you make the requested change in just one spot: in the CSS style that controls the headings. In under 30 seconds, you're done and off for the beach. The boss is so impressed, you'll be up for an executive parking spot in no time!

And that's just a basic example. What if you had six headings per page and a 200-page web site? Same deal. Make a simple change to the style, and instantaneously the entire site is updated. Believe it—CSS is one serious catch!

How does this work? Well, when you format a piece of text using a style, CSS creates a reference from the formatted text to the style. The text simply follows the formatting rules defined for the style. If the style says to use Arial, the text uses Arial. If the rules for the style change so that the font for the style is now Times, the text follows the new rules and changes to Times. Whatever the style says to do, the text just follows along.

You'll see how to use CSS to control an entire site later in this chapter. But first, let's look at what's involved in editing styles that you've already created. Put on a dinner jacket and pop a mint so I can introduce you two lovebirds.

Getting Started with Dreamweaver's Sample Style Sheets

Here's a great way to get started with CSS: Use Dreamweaver's sample style sheets. Dreamweaver comes loaded with many style sheets that you can browse through and apply to your pages. Once you apply a style sheet to your page, you can use the CSS Styles panel to edit and change the styles as much as you like.

With your page open in Dreamweaver, follow these steps to give the sample style sheets a try:

1. At the bottom of the CSS Styles panel, click Attach Style Sheet.

   If your panels aren't visible, you can reopen the CSS Styles panel via the Windows menu.

2. In the Attach External Style Sheet dialog box that appears, click the Sample Style Sheets link.

3. In the Sample Style Sheets dialog box, browse through the list of sample Dreamweaver style sheets.

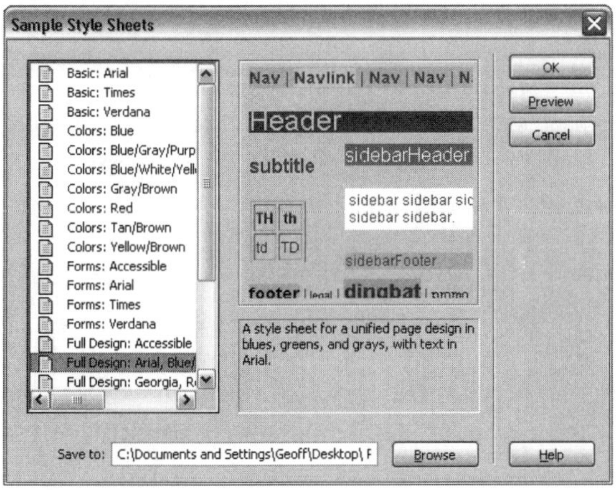

   When you click a style, a preview and description appear at the right. To see how the style sheet will look when applied to your page, click the Preview button.

4. When you find a style sheet that you want to use, click OK to apply it to your page.

Once you've applied a sample style sheet, Dreamweaver adds it to your site's local folder as an external style sheet—something we'll be discussing later. For now, know that you can add, edit, and apply these styles just as you normally would. And once you're used to the sample style sheets, you can move on to bigger and better fish: creating your own customized styles.

NOTEWORTHY

When you use Dreamweaver's sample style sheets in your site, Dreamweaver saves an external style sheet in your site's root folder, inside the CSS folder. We'll talk more about external style sheets later in the chapter.

CSS'S DIRTY LITTLE SECRET

There's trouble in paradise! Even though CSS has it all—power, beauty, prestige, and a hot car—it does carry some baggage. Most notably, CSS is not supported by all web browsers (Boo! Hiss!). You build what you think is an amazing web site, only to find out that it looks like a spaghetti train wreck when you preview it in older browsers.

Remember our web designer motto: Check your target browsers! In fact, early CSS features aren't fully supported until IE6 and NN6. The sixth-generation browsers (as well as newer browsers such as Firefox and Safari) support quite a lot of newer CSS features—but even these browsers don't all display CSS formatting in the same way. But there are a few options for getting around CSS's browser-support problems.

One possibility is to insert some JavaScript into your page to redirect noncompliant web browsers to a page that relies on older formatting techniques. The only problem is that now you have two sites to maintain, not one. Have you ever tried going steady with two people at once?

Another approach is to post your site's compatibility info on your opening page—a common addition to sites these days. Be careful here, though. On the one hand, you want to save your visitors the headache of wondering why your site doesn't work right for them. But on the other hand, what you're really telling your visitors is, "Upgrade your browser, you freaks!" You're transferring responsibility for your site's poor performance to your visitor. Ouch—read that one again.

You can validate your CSS to ensure that it will work properly in most web browsers. Choose File > Check Page > Validate as XML.

It's a balancing act. You want a large body of people, under a variety of conditions, to be able to surf your site. This is why testing your site in many browsers under an array of conditions is so important.

GEEK'S DELIGHT

As stated at the World Wide Web Consortium web site, CSS code "degrades gracefully." What the heck does this mean? It means a rusty old browser won't display a broken link icon or code gibberish if it doesn't understand the CSS code. It just ignores the problem and renders the page the best it can. Find out more about CSS at w3.org/tr/rec-css1.html (CSS1 specifications) and w3.org/tr/rec-css2 (CSS2 specifications).

Editing Your Styles

In Chapter 5, you created a few basic styles, renamed them, and applied them to your page. Now what if you want to make changes to your styles? If you try making changes using the Property Inspector, Dreamweaver creates a new style for you rather than editing the existing style—which isn't what you want.

Style editing ***takes place in the*** ***CSS Styles panel.***

THE CSS STYLES PANEL

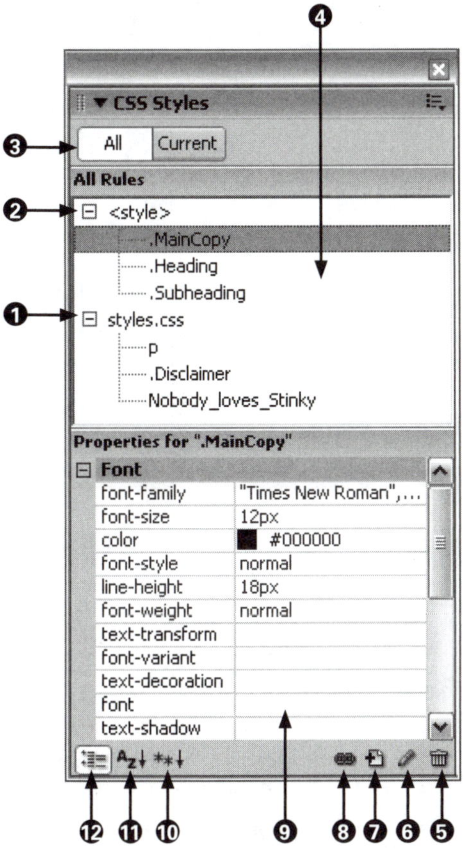

(1) External style sheet **(2)** Embedded style sheet **(3)** Panel mode buttons **(4)** All Rules pane **(5)** Delete Embedded Style Sheet/Unlink CSS Style Sheet/Delete CSS **(6)** Edit Style Sheet/Edit Style **(7)** New CSS Rule **(8)** Attach Style Sheet **(9)** Properties pane **(10)** Show Only Set Properties **(11)** Show List View **(12)** Show Category View

So instead of using the Property Inspector to make your changes, head for the CSS Styles panel—where all CSS editing takes place (choose Window > CSS Styles).

The CSS Styles panel is divided into top and bottom sections.

At the top of the CSS Styles panel, you can click the All and Current buttons to control the panel's mode. The mode determines what is visible in the top pane. Stick with the All mode at first—you'll find it easier when you're getting started (we'll talk about the Current mode later). When All mode is active, the top section displays the All Rules pane, which lists all available styles for the current page.

In the bottom half of the panel, the Properties pane is displayed. When a style is selected in the All Rules pane at the top, the Properties pane displays all the

> **NOTEWORTHY**
>
> To expand the size of either the top or bottom pane in the CSS Styles panel, bring your mouse over the area that divides the two panes (your cursor should change to a double-headed arrow) and drag.

settings for that style, and also allows you to make any changes you want. As soon as you edit a style, the style is updated automatically throughout your page (or pages, if you're using an external style sheet).

You can use the CSS Styles panel to create and edit styles whether you're in Design view or Code view.

THE PROPERTY PANE'S THREE VIEWS

The three buttons at the bottom left of the CSS Styles panel—Show Category View, Show List View, and Show Only Set Properties—allow you to control the Properties pane display.

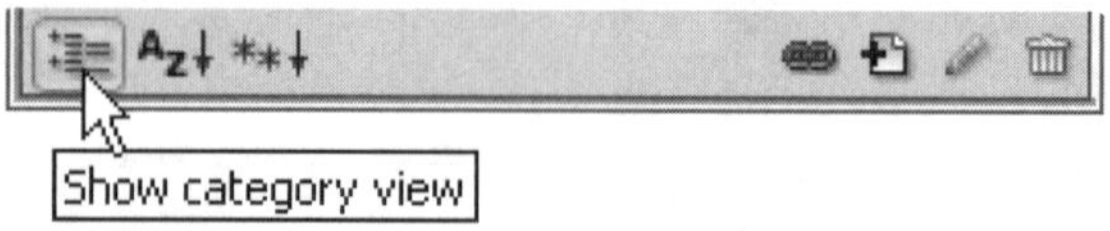

Use the three view buttons at the bottom of the CSS Styles panel to control what the Properties pane displays.

Category view organizes all the available CSS properties into categories that can be expanded and collapsed and has a structure similar to that of the CSS Rule Definition dialog box, which you'll see later in this chapter. List view presents an alphabetized list of all properties, with any currently set properties displayed at the top of the list. Show Only Set Properties displays only the properties that have been set for the selected style.

You may be confused at first about which view to use, especially if you're all nervous and stuff on your CSS date. But remember that these buttons control only the display of the Properties pane—they don't change your styles.

To edit a CSS style, do this:

1. Click the All button at the top of the CSS Styles panel to set the panel's mode.

   If you're working on a page where you've already applied some styles, the panel lists all the styles that you created.

2. In the All Rules pane in the top, select the style that you want to edit.

3. In the bottom-left corner of the CSS Styles panel, click the Show Category View button.

4. In the Properties pane, expand a category by clicking the plus sign (Windows) or the expander arrow (Mac). For instance, expand the Font category to change the font.

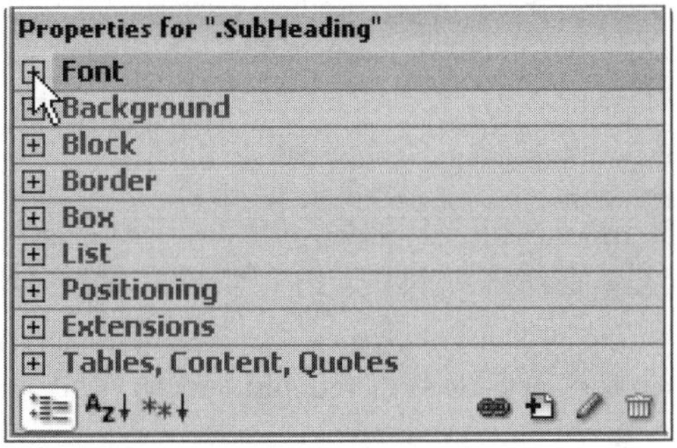

If you've already set font, size, and color formatting for your style via the Property Inspector, then you'll see those settings in the Font-Family, Font-Size, and Color fields. Currently set properties always appear in blue; properties that are not set appear in black.

5. In the right hand column, select the attribute that you want to change and then choose a new setting.

NOTEWORTHY

When editing your styles, you can double-click the style name in the All Rules pane at the top of the CSS Styles panel to open the CSS Rule Definition dialog box. There, you can make your changes. You'll learn more about the CSS Rule Definition dialog box later in this chapter.

Depending on the property you want to change, you'll choose from a color window, a text field, or a pull-down menu. For example, if you want to change the font family, select a new setting from the menu in the Font-Family field.

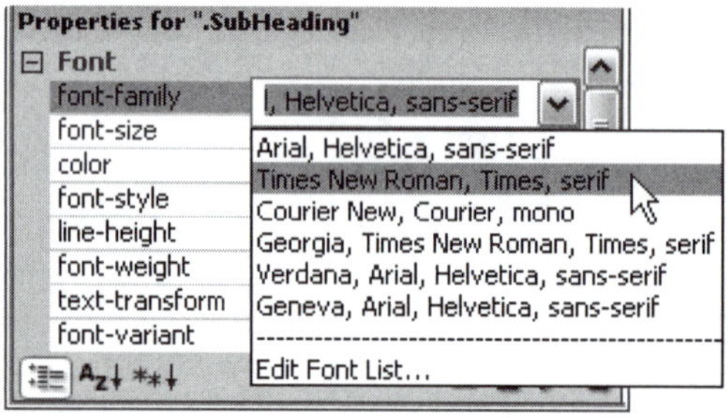

If you want to remove a value, just select it and press the Delete key.

Any changes that you make are applied instantly, meaning that any text on your page that's currently using the style is automatically updated. How's that for speed? Start planning the weekend!

Creating New Styles

Get access to the CSS arsenal of formatting options by creating your styles in the CSS Styles panel.

When you use the CSS Styles panel, you're creating styles in a much more advanced—and functional—way than when you work from the Property Inspector. You'll also see the arsenal of formatting attributes that CSS offers, which goes way beyond the basic font, size, and color settings that the Property Inspector provides. You'll see everything from case and alignment control to line and letter spacing—an array of features rivaling that of even high-end print typography.

As you begin creating styles through the CSS Styles panel, the styles won't be applied to the text on your page just yet. The idea here is to create styles first and then apply them to your text afterward. You can apply styles to your text through the Property Inspector.

To create a style using the CSS Styles panel, follow these steps:

1. At the bottom of the CSS Styles panel, click the New CSS Rule button, or choose Text > CSS Styles > New to begin creating a new style.

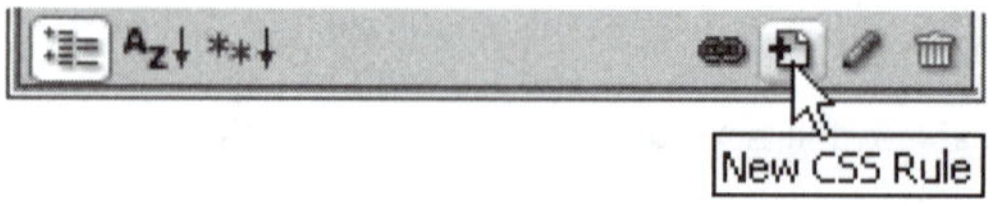

PICKIN' UP STYLES THROUGHOUT HISTORY

CSS ain't the only party in town! Styles have been with us since the dawn of time. Not happy with your current situation? Take a trip through history and get a few style pointers from these folks!

Early Man

The Deal: Even though prehistoric man didn't have much sense of style, he didn't mind running through the woods in animal skins. In fact, it's his uncomplicated style that has kept animal prints on the fashion radar for thousands of years . Sure beats wearing fig leaves. **Last Seen:** Picking stomped squirrel from his toes.

Middle Ages King

The Deal: Medieval kings had it all: hot queenies, servants, and massive armies at their beckon. As sweet pimpin' as they were, they'd bathe only three times in their life: at birth, for their wedding, and for their funeral—major style faux pas. **Last Seen:** Getting soaped up by a mortician who wished the king had married much later in life.

Far East Warrior

The Deal: Artisans of sword play, hand combat, and fine weaponry, the feared warriors of the ancient East were also snappy dressers. Never ones to go for business casual, with their ornate and colorful combat attire, they sure made their opponents feel underdressed. **Last Seen:** All dressed up and ready to conquer.

Victorian Lady

The Deal: Every woman's fantasy life: stately mansions, chauffeured horse-drawn carriages, and gentlemen of noble society. This era lacked but one thing: narcotics control, with snuff being considered a lady's luxury at the time. **Last Seen:** Down at detox.

British Redcoats

The Deal: Never ones to dress down for an occasion, the British army always looked its best, even when facing down a fierce band of American colonists. As was quickly discovered, vibrant red didn't conceal an invasion force well in dense underbrush. **Last Seen:** See that big red blotch about two miles out?

Modern Punk Rocker

The Deal: Safety pins, tattoos, spiked gauntlets, piercings—it's all fair game for anti-establishment types. What was once fresh and full of political angst in the 1970s is now homogenized mainstream big business. Sorry to pop your bubble, kids. **Last Seen:** At the GAP—the whole ensemble for less than $200.

2. In the New CSS Rule dialog box that appears, make sure that Selector Type is set to Class.

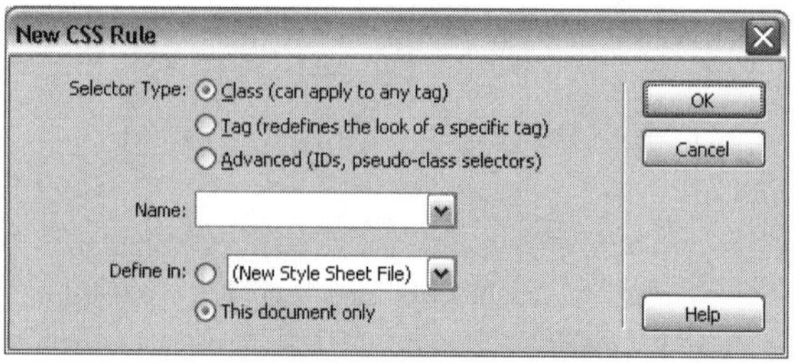

With CSS, you can create three types of styles: class styles, redefined tag styles, and advanced styles.

A class style is a custom style that you create from scratch and apply throughout your pages, as you'll do here (and, in fact, what you've been doing with CSS). A redefined HTML tag style is a great way to make use of those ugly HTML block tags; you'll see how these work in a bit. Advanced styles are useful for creating interactivity with the hyperlinks on your page; for more on how these work, see Chapter 9.

3. In the Name field, type a name for your style, preceded by a period. (If you forget the period, Dreamweaver adds it for you.)

You can use numbers and letters for the name, but you can't use spaces or punctuation, besides the period that precedes the name. Avoid names like title, body, and h1, because these names are used in HTML (if you do, Dreamweaver will warn you to be home by 11 o'clock).

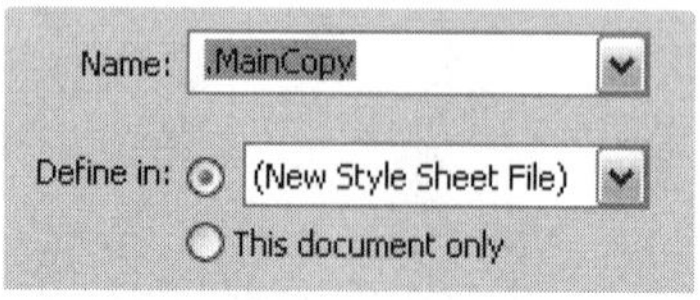

4. At the bottom of the dialog box, set Define In to This Document Only.

Choosing the New Style Sheet File setting will create an external style sheet that will apply to your whole web site. Choosing This Document Only limits the style to the current page.

5. Click OK.

The CSS Rule Definition dialog box appears, where you can set properties for your new style. The eight categories on the left side of the dialog box offer up all available formatting options for CSS (as opposed to the pishy three options available from the Property Inspector).

The next section details the three most common categories in the CSS Rule Definition dialog box: Type, Block, and Border. The remaining categories relate to graphics, hyperlinking, and page layout—all of which are discussed in other chapters.

The dialog box is called the CSS Rule Definition dialog box is because it's here where you set the rules (the formatting options) for your style. Remember that any text that's formatted with the style simply follows the rules and does what it's told.

Exploring the Rule Definition Dialog Box

So you've created a new CSS style, and now you're staring down the CSS Rule Definition dialog box. Don't let all those knobs and buttons make you queasy. Here, you'll get a rundown of all the options available in the Type, Block, and Border categories; then you'll see how to actually put them to work in your own styles.

SETTING THE TYPE OPTIONS

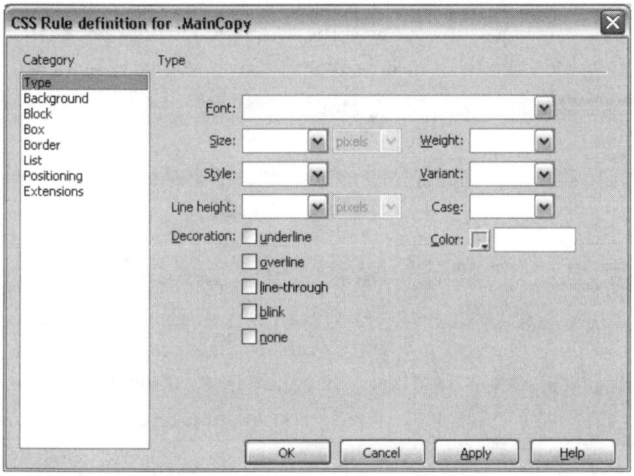

The CSS Rule Definition dialog box contains all the properties available to your new styles. The Type category, shown here, offers up a pile of typographic control.

The Type category is one of the most commonly used, because usually designers are after a lot of typographic control. The best thing about it, though, is support. Even old-timers like Internet Explorer 6 and Netscape Navigator 4 support its options. Here's a rundown of the available settings:

Font, Size, and **Color:** These options work the same as in the Property Inspector. Use the Font menu to set your typeface, the Size menu to set your text's size (remember: sizing in pixels is best), and the Color window to set a text color (you're not limited to the colors in Dreamweaver's web-safe palette; with modern browsers and operating systems, pretty much any color should be fine).

Style: Sets italics for your text. What's the difference between italic and oblique type? Oblique type is sometimes rendered by the browser as a normal font that's just slanted, not as true italicized text.

Line Height: Sets what designers in the print world call leading, which is the space between the lines in a paragraph.

Decoration: Applies visual formatting to your text. However, if you apply the Underline format to your text, you'll confuse at least some of your visitors—they'll think it's a hyperlink. As for Blink, if you want to make your site look like a Niagara Falls wedding chapel, then by all means, knock yourself out. None is one of the more useful options here; you can use it to create a rollover effect for hyperlinks, as you'll see in Chapter 9.

Weight: Adds a degree of boldness to your text. The Weight menu provides a list of values you can use to set the degree of boldness for your text. Normal is about 400, and Bold is equivalent to about 700.

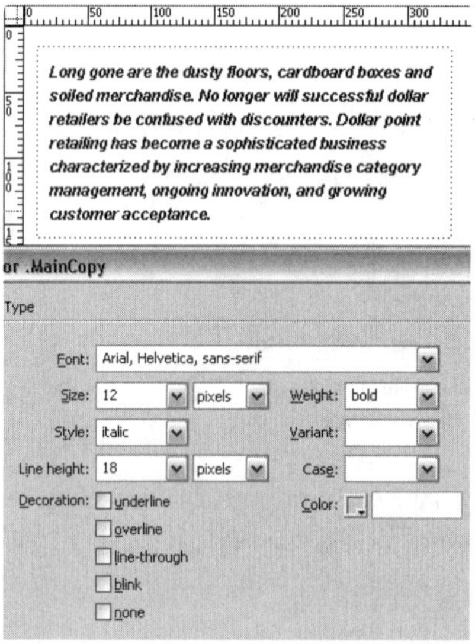

Let your text have it with the CSS Rule Definition dialog box's Type Category! Here, you can see settings for Font, Size, Weight, Style, and—most interestingly—Line Height (known as leading to print designers) being applied to a paragraph. Take that, text!

Variant: Sets your text to either normal type or small caps.

Case: Controls your text's capitalization. The options are Capitalize, Uppercase, and Lowercase. Capitalize capitalizes the first character in each word—same as Title Case in word processors.

WORKING WITH THE BLOCK CATEGORY

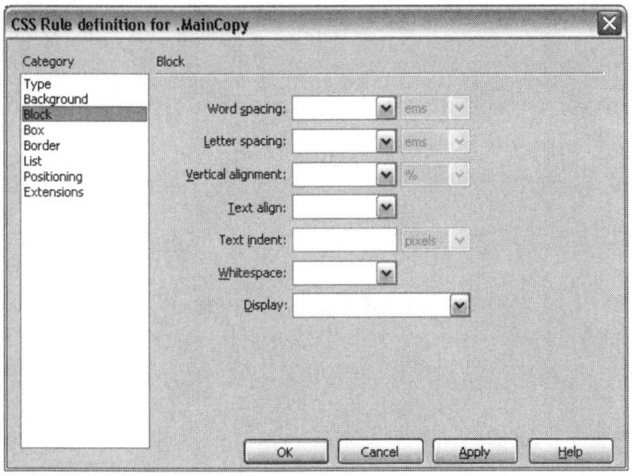

The Block category gives you much greater control over your paragraphs of text than rusty old HTML can. Get settin' those properties!

The Block category contains yet more traditional typography commands, including settings for word and letter spacing, indents, and justification that affect an entire block (or paragraph) of text. Some of these options can't be displayed in Dreamweaver's Design view, so you'll have to preview their effects in a compliant web browser.

Word Spacing: Spreads apart the words in your paragraph. You can use negative values if you want, but just be sure that your target browsers support this functionality.

Letter Spacing: Spreads apart the characters throughout your paragraph. Letter spacing is what print designers call kerning. Use positive or negative values to precisely control the amount of space between your characters. This option is supported by Internet Explorer 4 and Netscape Navigator 6 and up.

Vertical Alignment: Controls the vertical position of the text on your page. Vertical alignment is known as baseline shift in the print world; it controls the vertical position of text in relation to other words on the same line. Make sure you preview this setting in your target browsers.

Text Align: Sets the horizontal position of the text on your page. The menu options are Left, Right, Center, and Justify.

Text Indent: Sets a left indent for your style. You can type positive or negative values (a negative value creates an outdent), but keep your eye on those target browsers.

Whitespace: If your background HTML code contains whitespace—that is, tabs, spaces, and line breaks—then this option controls the way that it's rendered onscreen. Normal disables the display of all whitespace characters on your page. Pre displays all whitespace characters as they were entered into your code, with no line breaks. Nowrap removes all whitespace, like Normal, and displays text on a single line unless a forced line break (created by pressing Shift+Enter) occurs. Normally, code shouldn't contain tabs and additional spaces, so these settings are not commonly used.

Display: Controls the appearance of formatted elements onscreen. Only a handful of these options are supported by current browsers, including Block, Inline, and None, so be sure to test your page if you use these.

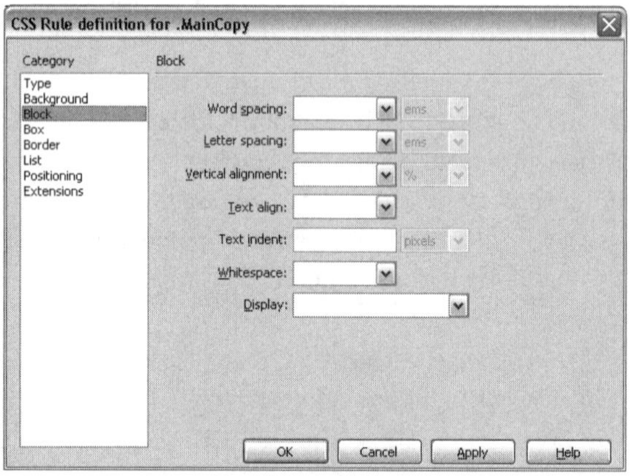

You may not use all the options in the CSS Rule Definition dialog box's Block category, but many come in handy for just the right amount of typographic control, including Letter Spacing, Text Align, Text Indent, and Whitespace, as seen here.

WORKING WITH THE BORDER CATEGORY

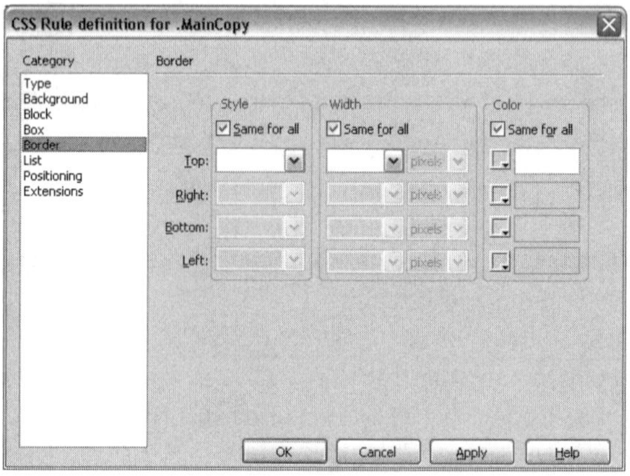

Don't be a square—use the Border category to place a frame around your text! The available settings help control the type, thickness, and color of your frame.

The Border category lets you apply and control border styles, colors, and line widths on text and graphics on your page.

Style: Choose from eight border styles, including solid, dashed, and dotted. The actual display of the border will depend on the browser being used, so be sure to preview your settings. Choose Same for All to set the same style for all four sides of your page element, or use different styles on different sides.

Width: Sets the thickness of the border. Choose Thin, Medium, Thick, or a custom value, or choose Same for All if you want to apply the same setting to all four sides.

Color: Use Dreamweaver's 216-color web-safe palette, or any other color palette, to set the color of your style's border. Again, set the same color for all four sides, or set different colors for each side. Browser display can be touchy, so be sure to preview your work.

NOTEWORTHY

The Dreamweaver developers do a great job of keeping up with the latest CSS standards—which means that the options in the CSS Rule Definition dialog box are right on that bleeding edge, making it imperative that you test your pages in a variety of popular browsers. However, Dreamweaver's code validator will check your CSS and report, via a red wiggly line below the item, any CSS style element that is out of sync with common browsers.

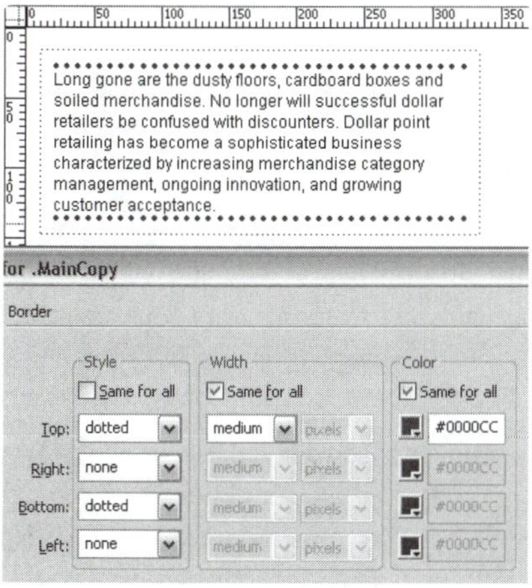

Using the Border category, place a frame around your text. Even better, turn off the Same for All option in the Style area, as shown here, and set different borders for different sides of your text. Then use the Width and Color options to control the border thickness and color.

SETTING FORMATTING FOR YOUR STYLE

Now that you've had a quick tour of the CSS Rule Definition dialog box, you're ready to put some of those settings into action. In this section, you'll see how to set some of the more straightforward options for your new CSS style. It's as easy as delivering a five-cent pickup line.

Before you begin, take a gander at the CSS Styles panel, and you'll see your new stule loaded into the top pane.

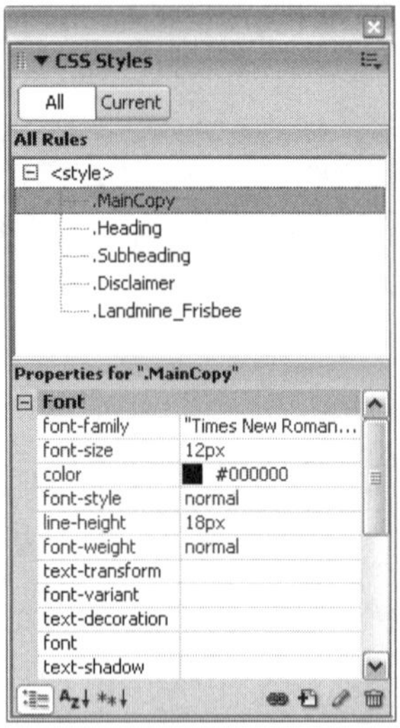

Once your new style is created, Dreamweaver adds it to your list of styles at the top of the CSS Styles panel.

NOTEWORTHY

Some CSS style options can't be displayed in Dreamweaver's Design view, so you may need to preview your page in your target browsers to see the effects of your CSS style settings.

Because your new style hasn't been applied to any text on your page, you won't see any visible formatting changes yet. To actually see your style in action, you have to apply it in your page using the Style menu in the Property Inspector, which is where we'll start, with the Type Options.

Here's how to set options for your style:

1. If the CSS Rule Definition dialog box is open on your screen, click OK to close it; then select the text on your page that you want to format with your new CSS style.

2. From the Style menu in the Property Inspector, choose your style.

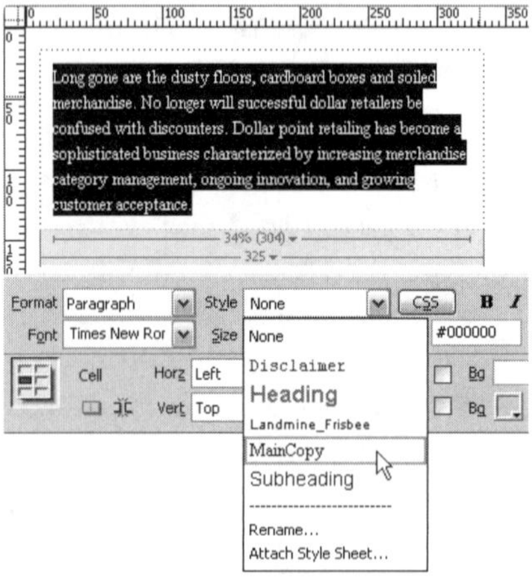

The text is formatted with the new style. Now again, keep in mind that you won't see any visible change on your page because you haven't specified your new format settings yet—you're going to do that right now.

3. In the CSS Styles panel, double-click your style; then in the CSS Rule Definition dialog box, make sure Type is selected in the Category list.

   Most designers like to set the Type category options because they want a lot of typographic control. One of the best things about this category is browser support: even old-timey browsers support the Type options.

4. Specify the Font, Size, and Color settings just as you would in the Property Inspector.

5. If you want to set italics for your text, use the Style pull-down menu.

   Instead of using the Italic button on the Property Inspector to manually set italics for your text, build this formatting into your style using the italics setting.

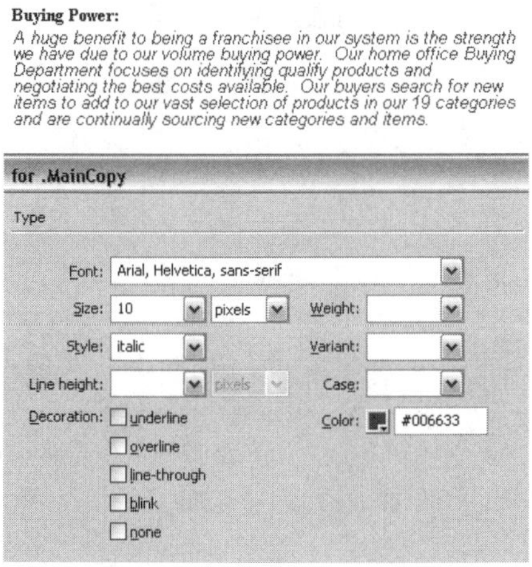

   Now that your Type options are in place, you'll set paragraph-related options for your style.

6. In the CSS Rule Definition dialog box, select the Block category.

   The Block category options provide additional traditional typography settings. These options control an entire paragraph (or block) of text.

NOTEWORTHY

All settings in the CSS Rule Definition dialog box are optional. Just set the formatting options that you want for your style and leave the rest as they are.

Rather than sticking with the values on the Size menu, try typing your own value.

7. Specify an alignment for your text by choosing a setting from the Text Align menu.

8. To indent the first line of your text paragraph, enter a value in the Text Indent field.

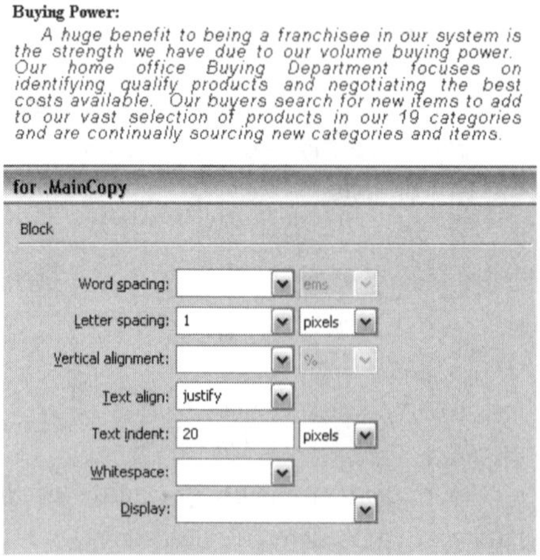

Keep in mind that the indent setting here indents only the first line of text in your paragraph. If you want to indent all the lines in your paragraph, use the Box category's Left Margin setting.

Now you'll set up your style to place a frame around your text.

9. In the CSS Rule Definition dialog box, select the Border category.

You can use the Border category to place a frame around your text. Here, you can set a style for the border, a color, and a line width. These options are also available for graphical elements that you may want to include on your page. For example, you may wish to put a border around an image.

10. In the Style pane, choose a style for your border from the Top pull-down menu.

You can choose from eight border styles, including Solid, Dashed, Dotted, and Ridge. Use the Same For All option to set the same style for all four sides of your page element, or use different styles on different sides.

11. In the Width pane, set the thickness of the border.

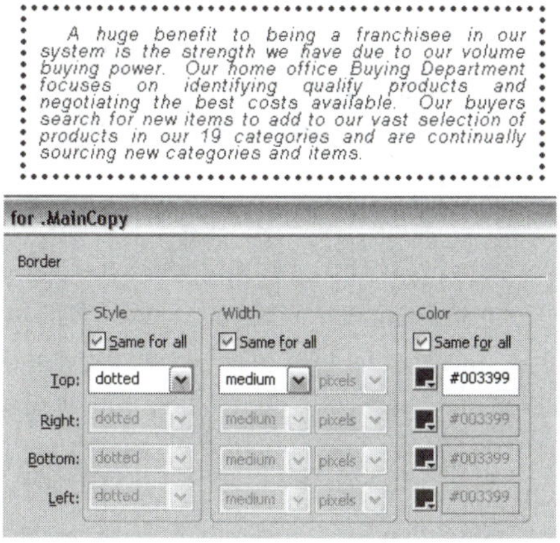

Select one of the preset thicknesses (Thin, Medium, or Thick) or enter a custom value. Choose Same for All if you want to use the same width for all four sides.

12. Set a color for your border by clicking the boxes in the Color pane.

    Clicking the color box opens Dreamweaver's color palette. Remember that you don't need to limit your color choices to this palette.

13. When you're done adding properties to your style, click OK in the CSS Rule Definition dialog box.

If you want to go back and make changes to your style—either to edit the settings you used or to add some new ones—use the Properties pane in the lower half of the CSS Styles panel, just as you saw in "Editing Your Styles" earlier in this chapter.

A second (and perhaps more straightforward) way to edit a style is to double-click it in the top pane of the CSS Styles panel. Doing so reopens the CSS Rule Definition dialog box, where you can pick up where you left off.

Redefining HTML Tags

In the previous section, you saw how to create your own custom Class styles. Being able to create your own styles can be a real power trip, so what if your now CSS-corrupt, power-hungry self wants to go beyond just creating styles—what if now you want to change the rules of HTML? Good news—you can use CSS to redefine existing HTML tags.

NOTEWORTHY

When you create custom Class styles (as you're doing here), you have to apply them to each element, one at a time, wherever you want to use them on your page. Sound like a drag? Maybe, but once you've taken the time to format your text, you'll then have total control over the text on your page (or even over your entire site, as we'll discuss shortly).

NOTEWORTHY

What you select on your page before applying your style is important. Single-clicking a paragraph will format the entire paragraph. Selecting a single letter, word, or sentence will format only that selection.

You can create as many custom Class styles as you want, but whether you like it or not, your page is going to be loaded full of HTML tags—paragraphs, lists, tables, and so on. In fact, every page element that you insert into your page uses HTML tags, and at least initially, the tags determine the formatting of your page. So instead of creating new styles from scratch, you can redefine existing tags using CSS.

Redefined HTML tags override the rules of HTML and provide a new set of formatting rules to follow.

When you redefine an HTML tag, what you're really doing is overriding your viewer's web browser preferences by sending the browser a new set of rules to follow. For example, let's assume that you want to change the look of all the main text on your page—say you want to change the formatting, such as the font family and type color. Main text always uses the Paragraph tag. The problem with the Paragraph tag (and many other HTML tags) isn't structural—it's cosmetic. So while you could create a new custom Class style to handle the formatting duties of your main copy, you'd then have to manually apply your new style to every paragraph. But since your text is already formatted with the Paragraph tag, why not just change the rules for the Paragraph tag? Doing this is a heck of a lot easier than doing all that manual formatting. It's pretty powerful stuff. Go on and flex—no one's looking!

My approach is to redefine as many HTML tags as I need and then go back and build extra Class styles needed to handle any additional content, such as a copyright line or figure captions.

Are you ready to give this a try? In this example, you'll see how to redefine the formatting for all the paragraphs on your page. But you can just as easily use these steps to redefine table content, lists, the look of hyperlinks, and anything else on your page that is defined with an HTML tag.

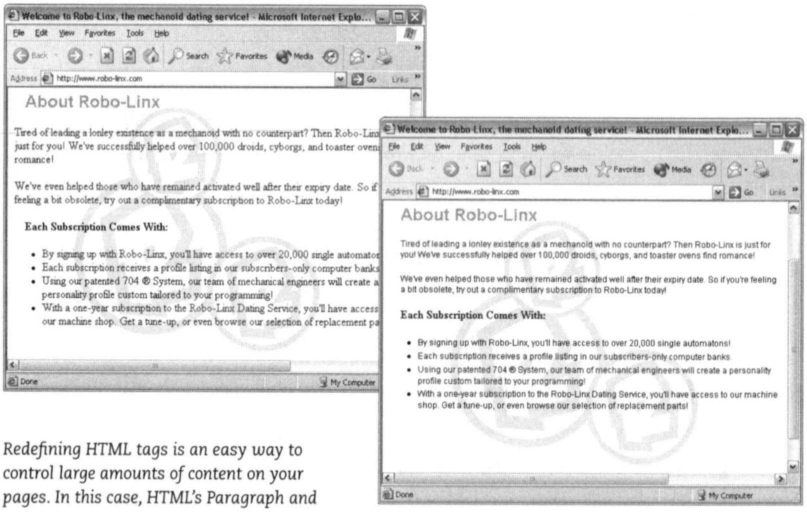

Redefining HTML tags is an easy way to control large amounts of content on your pages. In this case, HTML's Paragraph and Unordered List tags have been redefined to control most of the content's font and size.

Here's how to redefine an HTML tag:

1. At the bottom of the CSS Styles panel, click the New CSS Rule button.

2. In the New CSS Rule dialog box, set the Selector Type option to Tag and choose p from the Tag pull-down menu.

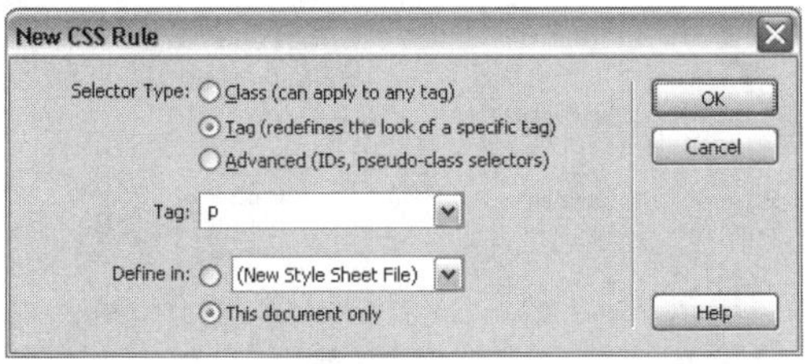

   The p setting refers to HTML's Paragraph tag. It's helpful to have a somewhat decent understanding of HTML, so that you know what tag to choose from the menu. Otherwise, open Dreamweaver's Reference panel (Window > Reference) for a helping hand.

3. At the bottom of the dialog box, set Define In to This Document Only; then click OK.

   Although you can use the New Style Sheet File setting with redefined HTML tags (it will create an external style sheet—something we'll look at later in this chapter), stick with This Document Only for now.

4. In the CSS Rule Definition dialog box that appears, specify any formatting settings that you want all paragraphs in your page to use.

   You saw how to use this dialog box earlier. For example, you may want all paragraphs to use a particular font and size (use the Type category). Or perhaps you want all paragraphs to start with a specific indent or a certain amount of letter spacing (use the Block category).

   Any properties that you set here will override the Paragraph tag's default formatting, and therefore tell your visitor's browser to display the tag in this new way. Any properties that you don't specify will revert to the tag's default style. For example, if you don't specify a font color, the color will be black, the text color's default. It's a CSS makeover dream come true!

5. When you're done setting your options, click OK.

NOTEWORTHY

If you want to delete a style you've created, select it in the CSS Style panel and click Delete CSS Rule at the bottom of the panel. Deleting a style will return the text's formatting to the next controlling style, in most cases, back to the default HTML formatting.

Right away, all paragraphs on your page reformat to reflect your new settings—no need to reapply them. Also, p now appears in the CSS Styles panel rule list, indicating that all paragraphs are now being controlled via the panel.

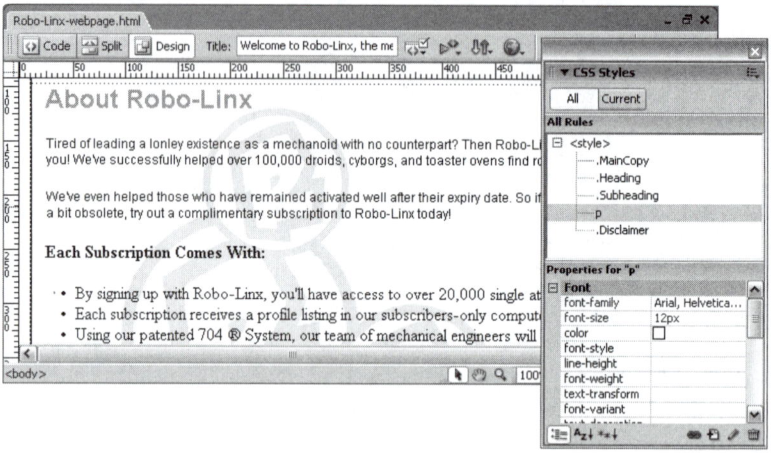

Pretty cool, huh? Don't get me wrong—Class styles are still amazing. But redefined HTML tags make the job of creating styles so easy, especially because they're already applied and being used. All you need to do is change the rules.

Using External Style Sheets

Dreamweaver + An external style sheet + Frothy cappuccino = One killer website!

I hope you and CSS have been getting along and having fun together. But up until this point, all the CSS work you've been doing has been within an embedded style sheet—that is, all your styles are being stored in a style sheet that resides within your current page.

Even though embedded style sheets are a great way to get introduced to CSS, there's one major reason to ditch them and move on to external sheets: Embedded style sheets can control only one web page at a time, while external style sheets can control your whole site—be it a 20-page site for your rockabilly-gangsta rap outfit or a 2,000-page e-commerce site. It all works the same way.

So why format each page one at a time when you can format your whole site using a single external style sheet file? You'll be back to the beach in no time!

An external style sheet is just a plain-text file that's been saved using the ***.css*** file extension. The text file must reside in your local root folder and be transferred when you publish your site live (in Chapter 4 we talked about uploading your site, along with any other files that are needed, to your remote site folder). To have the style sheet control

GIVE HTML THE HEAVE-HO—USE CSS TO CONTROL LISTS!

Just like the formatting of tables, headings, and other page elements, the formatting of lists is determined by HTML tags. But rather than being content with this vanilla formatting, consider using CSS to give your lists a makeover. Try dressing up your lists with custom bullets, using tiny graphics or symbols saved as JPG, GIF, or PNG files in your local root folder.

In this example, you'll set up an unordered list as you normally would, but then you'll use CSS to change the rules of the unordered list formatting. The process works the same for ordered lists as well.

Here's how to use CSS to control your lists:

1. Select the text on your page that you want to convert to a list.
2. In the Property Inspector, click the ordered or unordered list button. We're working with a bulleted list in this example, so click the Unordered List button.
3. At the bottom of the CSS Styles panel (Window > CSS Styles), click the New CSS Rule button.
4. In the New CSS Rule dialog box, set the Selector Type to Tag, and from the Tag pull-down menu, choose ul.

   In HTML, ul is the code that controls an unordered list.

5. Set Define In to This Document Only; then click OK.
6. In the CSS Rule Definition dialog box, select the List category.
7. Choose your bullet style either through the Type menu (for a predefined bullet character) or the Bullet image field, where you can browse to a custom graphic image.

   I recommend that you choose one of the first three bullet choices if you use the Type menu. Although you could choose a numeric (decimal), roman, or alphabetic value as your bullet character, this might cause confusion. If you're making ordered lists, it would make more sense to redefine the ordered list (ol) tag instead.

   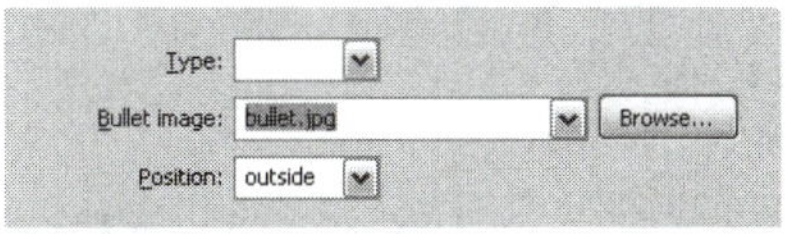

8. If your bulleted text is long enough to break onto another line, use the Position menu to specify whether the wrapped text aligns with the bullet's indent or with the page margin.

   Inside aligns the wrapped text to the page margin, and Outside aligns the text to the bullet's indent.

9. Before finishing, you can use any other category in the CSS Rule Definition dialog box to further control the look of your text. For example, to adjust the amount of space your bullets indent, select the Block category and enter a value in the Text Indent field. You can also set other formatting, such as font, color, and so on, at this point.
10. When you're done, click OK.

    The bulleted items on your page reformat to reflect your new formatting, and ul appears in the CSS Styles panel.

    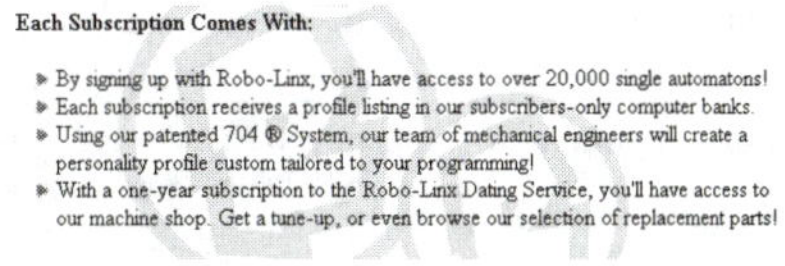

If you want to make changes to your formatting, use the Properties pane in the lower half of the CSS Styles panel, or double-click ul in the rules list to return to the CSS Rule Definition dialog box.

GEEK'S DELIGHT

Web browsers store external style sheets in their browser cache, meaning that your site will load faster where bandwidth is a concern. Usually, a CSS file's size is next to nothing, but sometimes those folks with antique browsers also have antique computers with matching antique Internet access. Caching your external style sheet will help speed up load time for those old-timers.

An external style sheet is simply a plain-text file that drives the look of several web pages.

NOTEWORTHY

Want to get into something really powerful? Using Dreamweaver templates and CSS together is like attaching a jet engine to your web site. If you define CSS styles in your template, they'll be ready to use in all your new pages. Now that's power! Check out Dreamweaver's templates in Chapter 13.

multiple pages, you'll have to connect your pages to it, a process that you'll learn about shortly. Because your pages will be linked to the style sheet file, you'll need to make any formatting changes there, not in your web pages. Then, like magic, you'll be able to update the formatting right across your site in seconds! External style sheets are by far the most powerful tools for harnessing the capabilities of CSS.

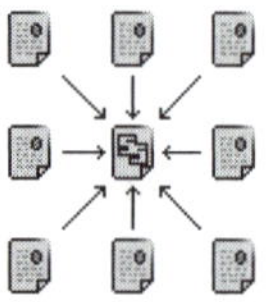

If you use an external style sheet for your site, you can connect an unlimited number of web pages to it. This means that you can control your entire site from a single file. Killer!

Exporting Embedded Sheets

You've seen how to create custom class styles, and you redefined some HTML tags. Only problem is that all your lovely styles have been created in an embedded style sheet—they're all trapped in your page and can be used only there. That's no good. As they say, if you truly love something, set it free.

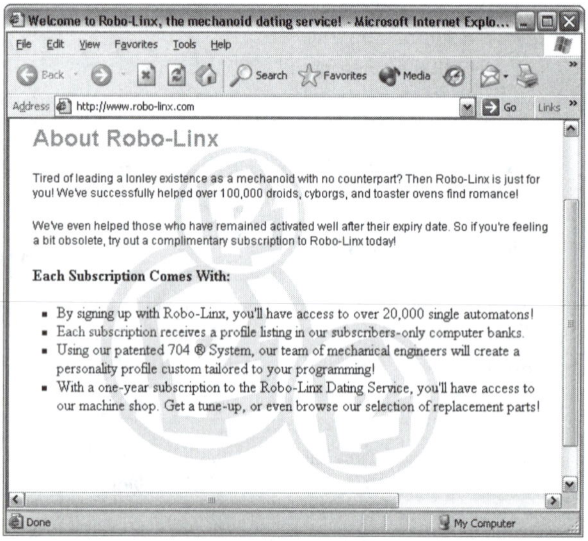

Unfortunately, the CSS styles applied here are available only to this page, because they're being stored in an embedded style sheet. They need to be exported to an external style sheet so they can be used throughout the site.

So how do you get your embedded styles out of your page so that you can use them in other pages throughout your site? No problem. You simply export your styles as an external style sheet.

Here's how it goes:

1. Choose File > Export > CSS Styles.

2. In the Export Styles as CSS File dialog box, navigate to where you want to save your styles and give your new style sheet a name.

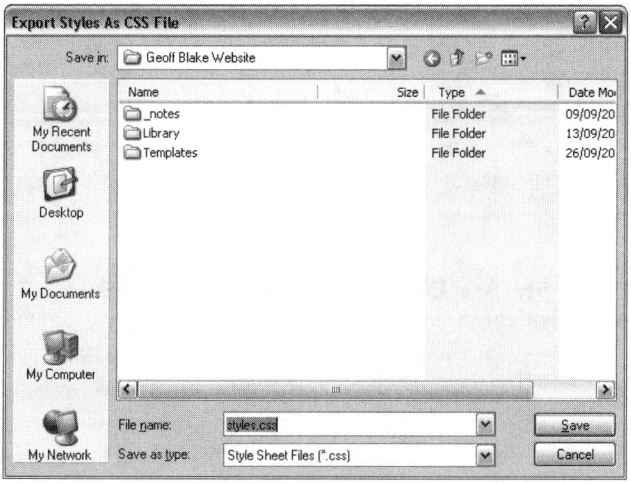

Make sure to save your style sheet inside your local root folder.

3. Click OK when you're done.

Dreamweaver saves the new style sheet file. The only bummer is that the embedded style sheet is left in your page—and your page doesn't link to your new style

You can always export your embedded styles as an external style sheet.

Save yourself tons of heartache and agony—use external style sheets whenever possible.

sheet automatically—so you'll have to delete your embedded style sheet from your page and link to your new external style sheet manually.

4. In the CSS Styles panel, click the <style> expander heading at the top of the upper panel (this header represents your embedded style sheet); then click the Delete Embedded Style Sheet button at the bottom of the panel.

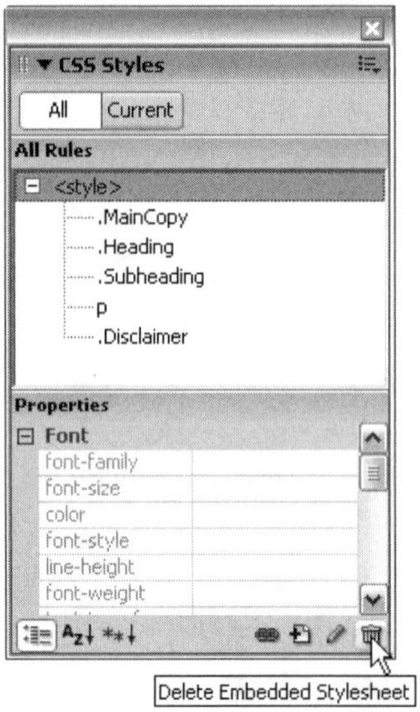

The embedded style sheet is deleted, and all your text reverts to its original vanilla formatting. Don't freak, though. In the next section, you'll see how to attach your new external style sheet to your page.

Creating an External Style Sheet from Scratch

Rather than creating styles in an embedded style sheet and then going through the process of exporting them, you can create your styles in an external style sheet right away and then attach your style sheet to your web pages later (this is my preferred method—just makes more sense to me). When working this way, it doesn't matter if you have any pages open in Dreamweaver, because the style sheet that you create won't be attached to any of your files just yet.

Here's how to build an external style sheet from scratch:

1. Choose File > New.

2. In the New Document dialog box that appears, select Basic from the Category column at the left, and select CSS from the Basic column in the middle; then click Create.

   Dreamweaver opens an empty style sheet file in Code view, ready for your new styles. Now, you could code your CSS styles by hand, but why do that when Dreamweaver's on the case? Instead, use the CSS Styles panel to build your styles, as you did earlier in this chapter. The process is exactly the same—only thing is, you'll have to look at that gnarly code as you work, because CSS files always are displayed in Code view only.

Connecting your pages to an external style sheet is where the CSS juice really kicks in.

3. Create any Redefined HTML or Class styles that you want in your style sheet.

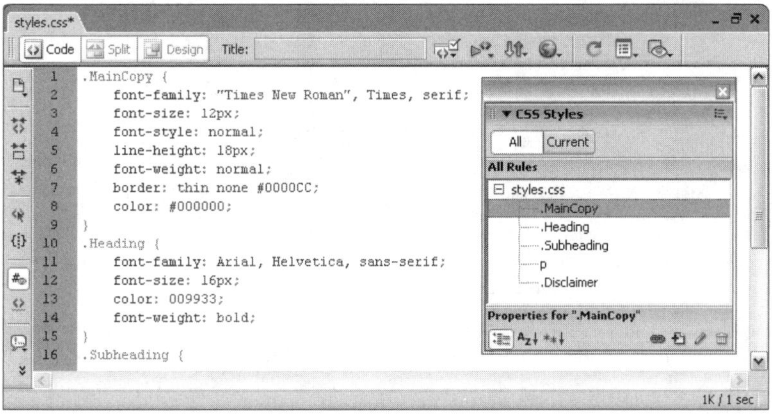

4. Save your style sheet by choosing File > Save As. Give your file a name, and make sure to save it in your site's root folder.

Now that you've created an external style sheet and loaded it full of styles to use throughout your site, what do you do with it? See the next section to find out how to link your pages to your external style sheet.

Linking to an External Style Sheet

Now that you've successfully created an external style sheet, you'll want to connect it to your pages in your site. Connecting to an external style sheet is where the juice really kicks in. You're about to see how to link an unlimited number of HTML files to a single text file that then controls all the text formatting in your site. It's time to go after that CSS flame!

Here's how to link to an external style sheet:

1. Choose File > Open, and navigate to the web page that you want to connect to your external style sheet.

   Once the web page is open, you're ready to link it to your external style sheet.

2. At the bottom of the CSS Styles panel, click Attach Style Sheet.

3. In the Link External Style Sheet dialog box, click Browse and navigate to the external style sheet you want to link to.

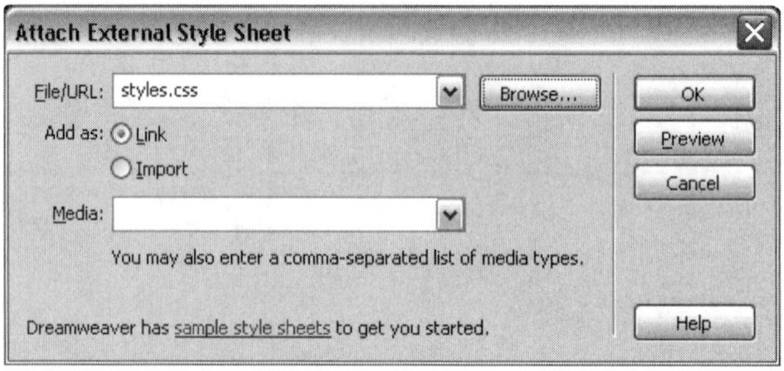

4. Set the Add As option to Link.

   Link is Dreamweaver's default. This will create a reference to the style sheet from your page. The Import setting is best used for importing styles from one style sheet into another style sheet, not for linking styles to your page as you're doing here.

5. Click Preview to see how the style sheet will affect your page. If you're happy with the results, click OK.

   The styles in the external sheet are added to the CSS Styles panel, and the formatting of your page's content (if it's being controlled by a style in the style sheet) updates to reflect the new formatting.

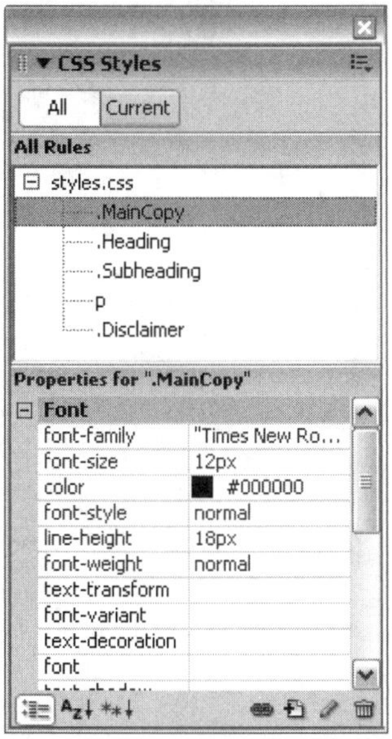

NOTEWORTHY

If you ever want to unlink a page from an external style sheet, select the style sheet name in the CSS Styles panel (it will end in .css) and click the Unlink CSS Style Sheet button at the bottom of the panel.

Now repeat these steps for each of the web pages in your site. Once all the pages in your site have been linked to your style sheet, you can exercise supreme power over all your text formatting from a single teeny-tiny text file: the external style sheet!

Making Sitewide Changes via CSS

Are you on cloud nine? Well, you should be, because you're about to see how to make formatting changes within your style sheet that will then instantaneously update right across your site—or at least across the pages that are linked to your external style sheet. The processing for making changes to your external style sheet is almost the same as that for making changes to your embedded style sheet, which you saw earlier. There are just a few extra steps.

When you make changes to your external style sheet, all pages that are linked to it instantaneously update.

Follow these steps to edit an external style sheet in Dreamweaver:

1. At the top of the CSS Style panel, make sure All is selected as the panel's mode.

2. In the All Rules pane at the top of the panel, double-click the name of the style sheet you want to edit.

   External style sheet names end in .css and are displayed as expandable and collapsible headings.

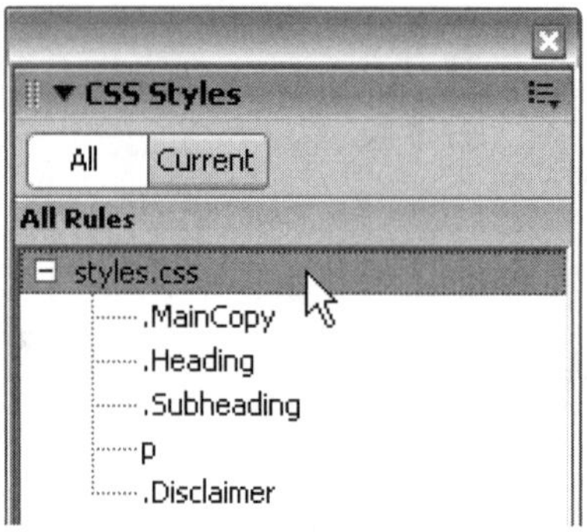

You can also edit your external style sheets by opening them directly in Dreamweaver. Choose File > Open or double-click your .css file in the Files panel, and you're on your way.

The CSS file opens for editing.

3. To make changes to your styles, use the CSS Styles panel just as you did earlier in this chapter.

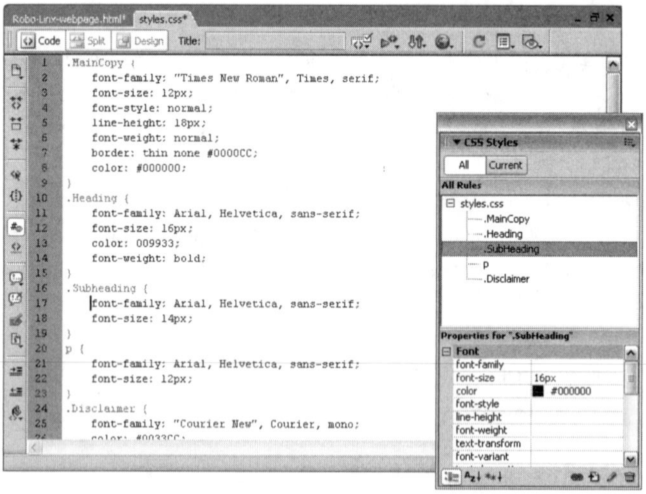

Use the Properties pane at the bottom of the panel to make your changes, or double-click a style to open the CSS Rule Definition dialog box.

You can even create new styles (both Class styles and redefined HTML styles) in your external style sheet by using the New CSS Rule button at the bottom of the CSS Styles panel. Just make sure that the New CSS Rule dialog box's Define In option is set to This Document Only. You want to make sure that any new styles you create are stored within the open CSS style sheet.

4. When your edits are complete, save your style sheet as you would any other file: choose File > Save.

Now here's the interesting part: Any page in your site that's linked to your style sheet updates to reflect your changes. The pages don't even have to be open in Dreamweaver! How's that for formatting bliss? That's what CSS is all about!

Unfortunately, learning CSS will not increase your chances of getting a date. Try a shower and a breath mint.

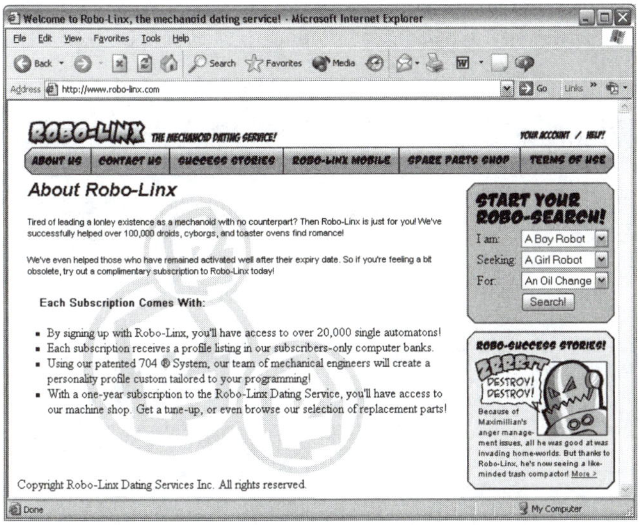

NOTEWORTHY

Here's a neat way to work: In Dreamweaver, open both an external style sheet and a page that uses that style sheet. As you make changes to your styles in the style sheet, save the file, and you'll see your changes reflected immediately. Even better, keep your web page running in a web browser in the background to preview changes you make to your style sheet.

SETTING DESIGN-TIME STYLE SHEETS

As you're building your pages, sometimes it's nice to get some space from CSS. With Dreamweaver's Design Time command, you can temporarily turn off the CSS formatting in your pages. Perhaps you just want to rough out raw pages, or maybe you're finding the CSS formatting distracting as you work.

With this command, you can set which external style sheets are visible, and which ones are hidden as you develop your page. Unfortunately, you can control only entire external style sheets. You cannot control the visibility of embedded style sheets and individual styles, which would be really handy to do.

If you want to use the Design Time feature, here are the steps:

1. Choose Text > CSS Styles > Design Time.

SETTING DESIGN-TIME STYLE SHEETS (CONT.)

2. In the Design Time Style Sheets dialog box that appears, specify which style sheets you want to show and hide:
   - To display a style sheet only during development, click the plus sign button above the Show Only at Design Time list.

   - To disable a style sheet during development, click the plus sign button above the Hide at Design Time list.

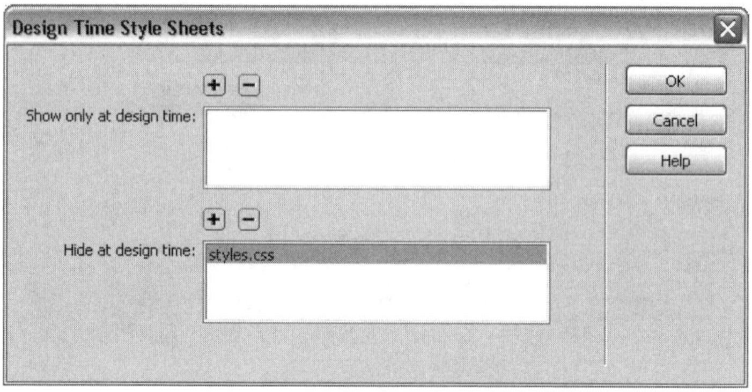

3. Click OK.

   The CSS Styles panel displays "design" beside any style sheets that you've set to Show Only at Design Time, and "hidden" beside any style sheets that you've set to Hide at Design Time.

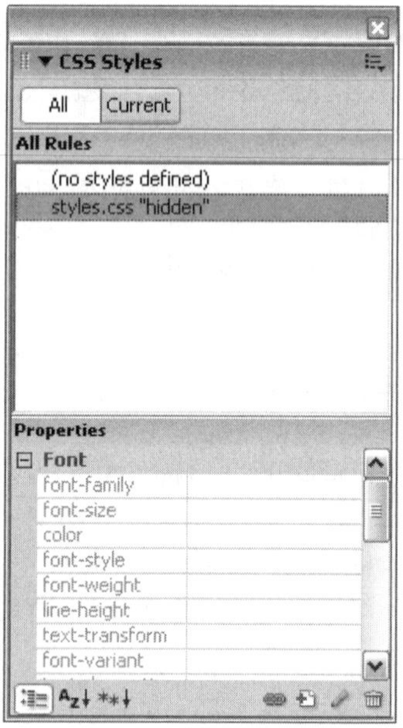

Keep in mind that the display of styles is controlled only in Dreamweaver. When you preview your pages in a web browser, all the styles will be visible—hence, the name ***design time***.

JUST THE GIST

Using CSS Styles

- CSS is a set of technologies that enhances ordinary HTML so that you can easily control the formatting of your web pages.
- When you apply a CSS style, Dreamweaver creates a reference from the text to the style. The text then simply follows the formatting rules for the style.
- When you edit a CSS style, all text that uses the style is automatically updated throughout your page.

Creating New Styles

- Although you can create styles with the Property Inspector, not all CSS options are available here. Instead, the Property inspector is much better suited for applying styles.
- Using the CSS Styles panel to create CSS styles gives you access to all available CSS properties in a single dialog box.
- To get started, click the New CSS Rule button at the bottom of the CSS Styles panel.
- Use the CSS Rule Definition dialog box's Category list to set attributes for your text.

Redefining HTML Tags

- You can specify new CSS rules for any HTML tags on your page. The new rules override your visitor's web browser preferences and display your page using the redefined style.
- To begin redefining an HTML tag, set Selector Type to Tag and choose the tag from the pull-down menu in the New CSS Rule dialog box.

Using External Style Sheets

- An external style sheet is a container of styles that's saved as a separate text file. It can be used to control the formatting of an unlimited number of pages.
- By default, Dreamweaver stores your styles in an embedded style sheet, which is a container of styles that resides in your current page. An embedded style sheet can control only the page that contains it.
- You can export embedded styles to an external style sheet so you can use them in your other pages. Choose File > Export > CS Styles.
- To use an external style sheet, you have to link to the style sheet from your page. Click the Attach Style Sheet button at the bottom of the CSS Styles panel.
- When you make changes to styles in your external style sheet, all pages linked to that style sheet update automatically throughout your site.
- To edit an external style sheet, double-click it in the top pane of the CSS Styles panel and then edit it as you normally would.

Chapter 9

Building *Hyperlinks*

STUFF YOU'LL LEARN IN THIS CHAPTER

The place is jumping. Are you ready for it? Great, 'cuz this chapter is all about getting hyperactive with hyperlinks in Dreamweaver. You'll get the what's-up on different path types and learn how to create links to all sorts of objects and elements. Strap on the rocket and let the caffeine buzz roar!

Understanding Hyperlink Paths: The Path to Tranquility

Does the prospect of building hyperlinks have you bouncing off the walls with hyperactivity? Try to remain calm and Zen-like. Deep breath and hold for five—this is vital stuff!

Hyperlinks are very important in web design. Without them, the World Wide Web would be a pretty boring place. After all, remember what the web is: a bunch of pages and sites that are all interconnected.

You've probably been surfing the web for a while now, so the concept of a link should make sense. The whole idea is ***click here, go there***. In other words, you click a link, and it takes you somewhere else. This means that a hyperlink has two parts: what the visitor clicks (the link's starting point), and where the visitor is taken (the link's destination). For a hyperlink to work, both the starting point and the destination must be in place.

Dreamweaver makes inserting hyperlinks into your pages easy, but they can be tough to troubleshoot when they don't work properly. So before you really get going with hyperlinks, it's critical to understand how they work.

A hyperlink has *two parts: what the visitor clicks* (the link's starting point), and *where the visitor is taken* (the link's destination).

Otherwise, you may find yourself with a site full of broken links and a gaggle of frustrated web surfers pounding on your front door. Broken links just scream amateur, so be careful.

The first thing you need to know is that there are different types of hyperlink paths. Think of paths as providing directions from one location to another. If you're in New York City and want to get to Berkeley, California, you follow a specific set of directions to get there. Similarly, you follow a specific route through your site's structure when you link from your ***index.htm*** file to your ***services.htm*** file, for example.

But just as when you travel from the Atlantic coast to the Pacific you can take interstate highways or local roads, when you build links you can choose from three types of paths—absolute paths, document-relative paths, and root-relative paths—depending on where you're linking to and the type of link you want to create.

GEEK'S DELIGHT

Every location on the web has a specific address, called a URL (uniform resource locator). This is similar to a house's street address. If you mail a letter to an incorrect address, it could wind up at the wrong house or get returned to you—which is exactly what happens when there's an error in a link to a web address.

Absolute Paths

How's your Zen state coming along? I miss the sugar, too. Let's make this quick so we can go raid the junk-food stash.

You can think of absolute paths as "hard" paths, because the entire destination is specified in the path. For example, http://www.tentonbooks/dw/paths.htm is an absolute path. See how the whole URL is specified? Whenever you're linking to another site, or to a page in another site, you must be sure to use an absolute path. You can also use absolute paths when linking to pages within your own site, although it means more work with no major advantage.

Here's a real-world example. If you were in New York City and wanted to visit Peachpit Press in Berkeley, you'd need Peachpit's full address, 1249 Eighth Street, Berkeley, California (send your Geoff Blake hate mail there—please, no live animals). If you were missing part of the address, then you wouldn't know where to go. For example, if you had only the 1249 Eighth Street part, then you'd be lost. It's the same with absolute paths. If an absolute path is missing part of the URL, your link won't work because it won't know where to go.

IMMINENT DOOM

Absolute paths are very sensitive. If they're off by even a single character, or if the content they're pointing to moves, they won't work.

Document-Relative Paths

Document-relative paths can be considered "soft" paths. Links that use document-relative paths don't include the full URL, but only the path that leads the current file to the linked file.

For example, let's say that your site includes a folder called ***htm***. Inside this folder, you have two files, ***news.htm*** and ***services.htm***. Because the two files reside in the same folder, when linking from one to the other, you can just link directly to the file name and leave out the part of the URL that is common to both files. So if you were linking from ***news.htm*** to ***services.htm***, your link would simply read services.htm. (You could use an absolute path—in which case your link would appear as http://www.yoursite.com/htm/services.htm—but that's kinda overkill, as most of the URL is common to both files.)

Let's go back to our Peachpit example. If I were giving you directions from your house to Peachpit and you already lived in Berkeley, I wouldn't have to tell you to travel from New York City to Berkeley, California—you're already there. Instead, I'd leave out the part of the directions that were common between New York City and your home address and Peachpit's address, and just tell you what you need to know: "Go to 1249 Eighth Street." Make sense?

NOTEWORTHY

Document-relative paths are most commonly used for linking to other pages within the same web site. Dreamweaver uses document-relative paths by default.

THE PATH TO DOCUMENT-RELATIVE WISDOM

Document-relative paths provide a very straightforward way to create links in your site. In fact, Dreamweaver uses 'em by default. However, if you look at a document-relative path in your page, you may find it a little hard to understand at first. So to calm your nerves, let's take a closer look at exactly how document-relative paths work.

The characters in a path tell the link where to go:

<table>
<tr><td>/</td><td colspan="2">Moves down one level in the structure</td></tr>
<tr><td>../</td><td colspan="2">Moves up one level in the structure</td></tr>
<tr><td colspan="3">Now let's take a look at a few examples. In each of these examples, assume that the page that's being linked from is called Linking_From.htm and that it resides in your site's htm folder.</td></tr>
<tr><td>pressroom/recent.htm</td><td>Starting in the htm folder, this path goes down into a subfolder called pressroom and links to the recent.htm page.</td><td>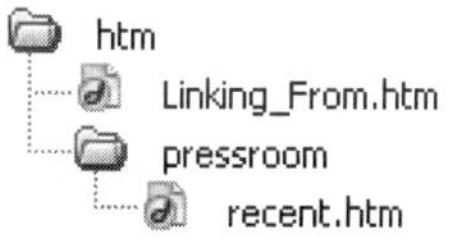</td></tr>
<tr><td>../index.htm</td><td>Starting in the htm folder, this path goes up one level to the site's top level (the root level) and links to index.htm.</td><td></td></tr>
<tr><td>../catalog/products/paper.htm</td><td>Starting in the htm folder, this path travels up one level to the site's root folder, down into a folder called catalog, and down into a second folder called products, and links to the paper.htm page.</td><td>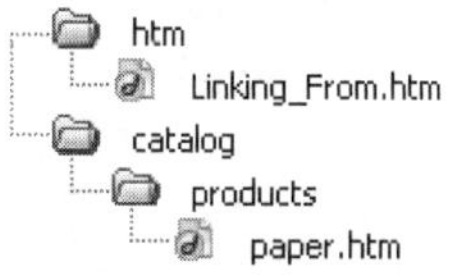</td></tr>
</table>

Making sense? Once you start inserting some links on your page, you'll see paths like these appear in the Property Inspector's Link field. Still confused? Don't sweat it. Once you see hyperlinks in action on your page, they'll become much clearer.

Root-Relative Paths

The trickiest of the three path types (and perhaps the least used) are root-relative paths. A root-relative path always begins at the site's root folder and then proceeds from there to the link's destination. For example, if you were creating a link from ***news.htm*** to ***services.htm*** and both files reside in a folder called ***htm***, just as before, the path would be /htm/services.htm. This link directs the path back to the beginning—the root folder (indicated by the initial forward slash)—and then starts its journey down through the site's hierarchy.

> **NOTEWORTHY**
>
> The nice thing about root-relative paths is that if you move files around in your site, you don't have to worry about broken links (because the path always starts back at the beginning). But when you're working on a site, Dreamweaver updates the links for moved files anyway.

Let's return to our Peachpit Press example. Let's say I'm giving you directions from the Empire State Building in New York City to Peachpit Press in Berkeley. My directions would begin at the Empire State Building at 350 Fifth Avenue in New York City, and they'd end at 1249 Eighth Street in Berkeley. You stop me and say, "But I don't live in New York City—I live in Nashua, New Hampshire." I then explain that the directions I have begin in New York City, not Nashua. So you have to first travel to the Empire State Building and then follow the directions to Berkeley.

Sound like a lot of extra traveling? Yeah, it can be. But if you want to use root-relative paths, you need to specify this approach when you define your site in Dreamweaver. Go to the Local Info category of the Advanced Site Definition window, discussed in Chapter 4 when you first defined your site.

Linkin' Stuff Up

Still jacked up on your caffeine high? If not, now's the time to top off the tank. Actually, creating a link in Dreamweaver is pretty straightforward. It's what goes on in the background that can get complicated—and that's why it's important to understand the different types of paths, which you just learned about.

When you create a hyperlink on your page, Dreamweaver inserts the necessary code for you.

When you create a hyperlink on your page, Dreamweaver inserts the necessary code for you, allowing you to remain in a visual design environment—Dreamweaver's Design view. Even in Design view, you can code your links by hand in the Property Inspector or create links through point-and-click dialog boxes.

If this is your first time out, point-and-click may be the best way to go—especially if you're working at home, and your household is as difficult to concentrate in as mine is: free-loading bum friends playing video games all day, Metallica performing live in the living room (word has it they'll play for food these days), and a three-ring circus on the driveway. Besides, the dialog boxes are really easy to use and almost impossible to mess up.

A hyperlink's starting point is usually a piece of text or a graphic. And from there, you can link to other pages in your site, other web sites, e-mail addresses, different locations on the same page—whatever is out there on the Internet. So forget the heavy metal and lion taming and let's see how to create some links.

Linking to Another Web Page

No matter what content or design elements you use in Dreamweaver, you really don't have a web site until you start linking your pages together. Until then, all you have is a folder of stand-alone pages. So here, you'll see how to begin connecting your pages to one another so that surfers can actually navigate your site.

To try out the process here, you'll need more than one web page in your site. If you've already created a few, perfect. If you've been working on just a single page, just choose File > Save As and save a copy of your file under a different name in your local site folder; you can then use that copy as your second page.

To create a link to another page in your site, follow these steps:

1. Select a piece of text or an image on your page that you want to set a hyperlink for.

   This will be the content on your page that will be clickable—the hyperlink's starting point.

2. In the Property Inspector, click the Browse for File icon beside the Link field.

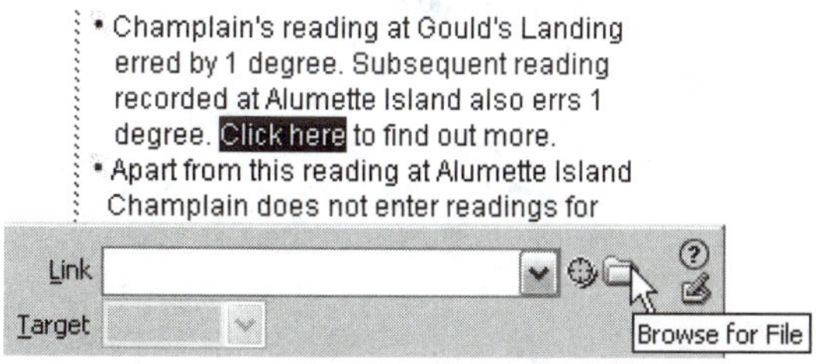

3. In the Select File dialog box that appears, navigate to and select the web page that you want the text or graphic to link to; then click OK.

NOTEWORTHY

You should always check for broken links before publishing your site live on the web. In Chapter 14, you'll see how Dreamweaver's built-in Link Checker command works—as the name implies, it checks all the links in your site for you.

You really don't have a web site until you start linking your pages together.

NOTEWORTHY

If you create a link on a new page that hasn't been saved yet, you'll receive a message saying that a file:// path will be used. This path will dig through your entire hard drive hierarchy and point to the linked file. Once the page is saved, the link will switch to a document-relative path. This is also the case if the file is outside the site directory—for example, if the local site is on drive C and you link to a file on drive D.

IMMINENT DOOM

If you try linking to a web page that isn't saved in your site's local folder, Dreamweaver warns that your link may not work when you publish your site. Just as when you try to insert a graphic that isn't saved in your site folder, Dreamweaver offers to copy the page to your site for you. If you choose No, your link will not work when you upload your site to the web.

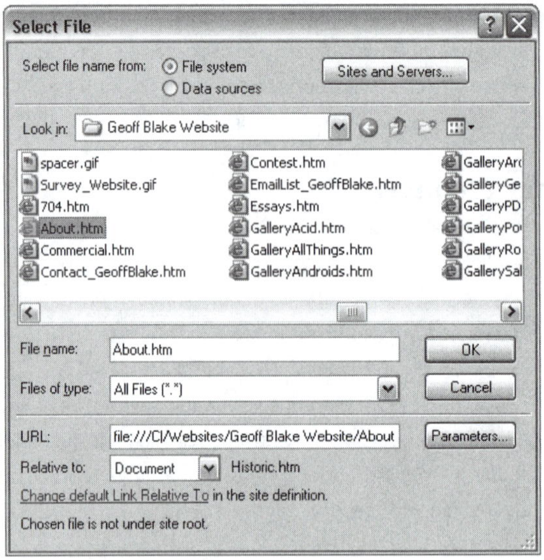

Dreamweaver creates a link to the web page. The Link field in the Property Inspector displays the hyperlink's path, and if you haven't changed the default Dreamweaver settings, you'll be able to see that your text is a hyperlink because the text will appear blue and underlined (the default formatting for a link).

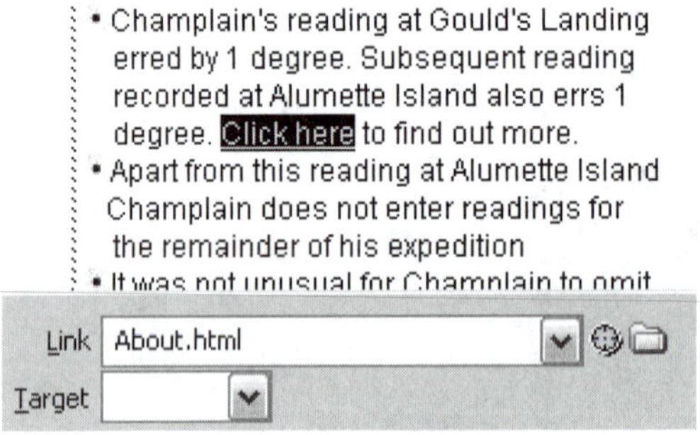

If you've set a link from an image, by default Dreamweaver places a blue border around it, indicating that it's clickable. Most designers don't like borders on their graphics, so if you want to remove it, set the Border field in the Property Inspector to zero. Even without a border, the image is still clickable.

4. If you want the link to open in a new browser window, from the Target menu in the Property Inspector, choose _blank.

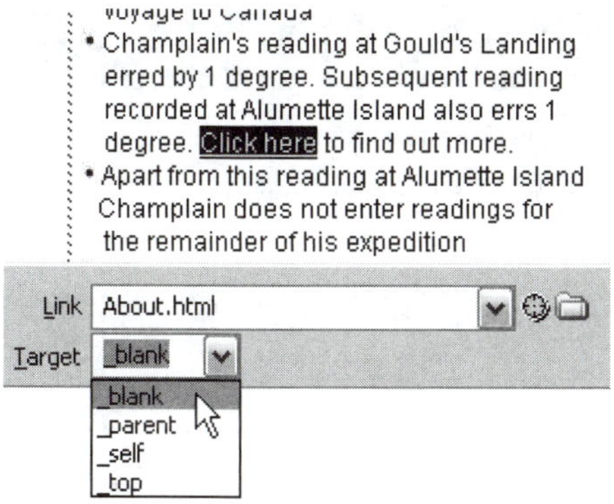

To test text-based links in Dreamweaver, hold down Ctrl+Alt (Windows) or Command+Option (Mac) and double-click your text. Unfortunately, this only works with text-based links. Holding down Ctrl+Alt (Windows) or Command+Option (Mac) and double-clicking an image will open your graphic in your external graphics editor.

By default, when a link is clicked in a web browser, the link's destination opens inside the same browser window. This is fine for links within your own site, but if you're linking to another web site, you may prefer for it to open in a new browser window, so that your site stays open in the background, making it easier for your visitors to stay there.

The other options on the Target menu relate to framesets, discussed in Chapter 7.

NOTEWORTHY

Keep in mind that when a visitor hovers the mouse over a link, the visitor can see the link's path on the browser's Status bar. Many experienced surfers use this technique to determine whether they want to follow a link or not, so consider naming files and folders usefully.

5. To test your hyperlink, preview the page in your web browser and click the link.

   If you ever want to remove a hyperlink from your page, just select the link's path in the Link field In the Property Inspector and press Delete.

CREATING LINKS WITH THE POINT TO FILE ICON

In addition to linking to files in your site by clicking the folder icon beside the Link field in the Property Inspector, you can take a more visual approach to creating hyperlinks: using Dreamweaver's Point to File icon.

When you use the Point to File icon, you simply select the text or graphic that you want to use as the hyperlink and then point to the file in the Files panel that you want to link to. It's a neat way to work. Take a swig from your cafe mocha and let's get started.

Here's how to create a link using the Point to File icon:

1. With your web page open, open the Files panel (Window > Files).

2. Select the text or graphic on your page that you want to set a hyperlink for.

   Again, whatever you select on your page will become clickable after the hyperlink is set.

3. In the Property Inspector, select the Point to File icon.

4. Drag the Point to File pointer to the web page or graphic in the Files panel that you want to link to. Then release the mouse.

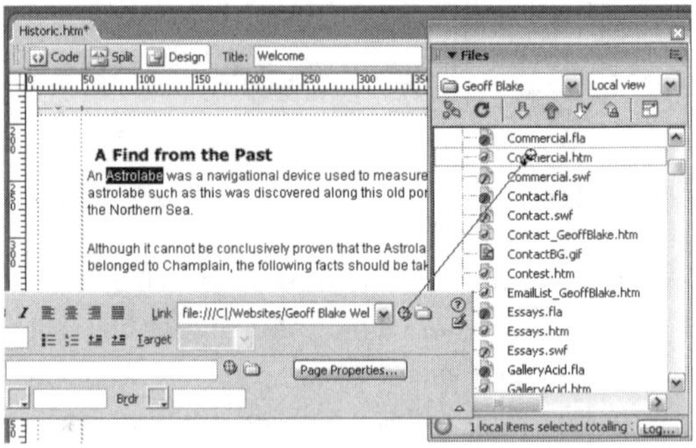

   You can also drag the pointer to something called an ***anchor***, which would appear elsewhere on the same page. We'll talk about anchors later in this chapter.

   When you release the mouse button over a link destination, Dreamweaver creates a path for the hyperlink in the Property Inspector's Link field. That's all there is to it.

Here's an even faster way to use the Point to File icon: Select the text or graphic on your page and then hold down Shift and drag from your selected text or graphic to the Files panel. The Point to File arrow will appear, and you can harpoon yourself a document in the panel. Now that's hyperspeed hyperlinking!

Linking to Another Web Site

Often, you'll want to link to another web site rather than to pages within your own site. You can link to another site from within your page contents, or you can create a Links page for your site, to contain all external links. It's all easy with Dreamweaver.

Here's how to create a link to another web site:

1. Select the text or image on your page that you want to set a hyperlink for.

2. In the Link field in the Property Inspector, enter the web site's URL.

Make sure you that type the web site's full URL, starting with `http://`. For example, type `http://www.tentonbooks.com`.

3. From the Property Inspector's Target menu, choose _blank.

Whenever you're linking to a location outside your site, you should consider setting Target to _blank, to open the link in a new browser window and keep your site open in the background. If you don't choose _blank, then the link's destination will open in the same browser window, meaning that your visitor will leave your site and be on to a new one without even realizing it.

When the Link field and Target menu are set, Dreamweaver creates the hyperlink to the web site.

4. Test your link by previewing your page in your browser and clicking your linked text or graphic.

What? Your link isn't working? Double-check that you've typed the URL into the Property Inspector's Link field correctly. If the link still isn't working, make sure you're connected to the web—you'll need to be connected for the link to work. If this tripped you up, go pour another coffee.

NOTEWORTHY

Rather than linking to a page in your site or to another web site, you may wish to link to other files—PDF files, audio files, and so on. You'll see how to do this in Chapter 11.

Linking to an E-mail Address

Hopefully, you're still buzzing with hyperlinks. Now for something really useful to include in your site. Have you ever clicked a Contact Us link on a web site and had your e-mail program open and begin a new e-mail for you? Ever wonder how the web site knew how to do all that? It's actually very simple. All you have to do is create something called a *mailto* link on your page—and you're about to find out how it's done!

Unscrupulous web marketers and spammers often use software programs called spiders to harvest e-mail addresses from web pages, newsgroups, and online forums. Perhaps a better way to have people contact you is to use a contact form, something you'll see how to create in Chapter 12.

To link to an e-mail address, try this:

1. Select the text or graphic on your page that you want to link to an e-mail address.

This could be a Contact Us button or some text that says, "Click here to e-mail us."

(continued on page 243)

Neither Peachpit Press nor Geoff Blake are liable for any damages, bodily or otherwise, resulting from consumption of an All-Nighter Buzz Float Blowout. Please consume responsibly.

GEOFF'S ALL-NIGHTER BUZZ FLOAT BLOWOUT

Are you thinkin' of pulling an all-nighter to cram in that web design project? You knew you shouldn't have played Halo II all afternoon, but you did anyway, didn't you? Well no worries, because with my specialty All-Nighter Buzz Float Blowout recipe, you'll be bouncin' off the walls straight on through 'til 5 a.m.! Get all buzzed out by following these steps.

How to make Geoff's All-Nighter Buzz Float Blowout:

1. You'll need some kind of bowl. Salad bowls are too small. Maybe something your mom would bake in, or if you're in a pinch, use a roasting pan.

2. Fill your bowl about one-third full with cola. I recommend the mega-caffeinated version, but if you've got only the cheap no-name stuff, just add two heaping tablespoons of white sugar and stir for about a minute.

3. Add a container of chocolate cake icing and mix the entire concoction until everything's nice and thick.

4. Now for the float part: Add three to five heaping scoops of chocolate ice cream. I prefer the kind with the chocolate chips, but it's really personal preference. Then pour in four to six cups of freshly brewed coffee. If you want to get fancy, you could get into flavored coffees, but if this is your first attempt, maybe play 'er straight for now.

5. Finally, the garnishing. I usually decorate my float with sprinkles, a Twix bar cut into pieces, or espresso beans if I'm feeling in the mood. Zig-zag some maple syrup across the top if you're trying to impress others with your culinary skills.

6. Serve, and enjoy!

The contrast between the cold ice cream and the hot coffee will have your taste buds hoppin'. And as for you, well just make sure there isn't anything breakable around. Happy all-night sugar high!

2. In the Link field in the Property Inspector, type `mailto:` followed by the e-mail address.

   For example, you could type `mailto:info@tentonbooks.com`.

3. If you want to force a subject line for the e-mail, type `?subject=` and then type a subject.

   For example, you might enter something like this: `?subject=Whachya Think of Ten Ton Dreamweaver?`

4. When you're done, press Enter (Windows) or Return (Mac).

   Dreamweaver sets the e-mail address link.

Go ahead and try it. Preview your page and click your link. Your e-mail program should launch and create a new e-mail for you, complete with the e-mail address and subject line.

When a visitor clicks your mailto link, the visitor's e-mail program will launch and begin a new e-mail, complete with your e-mail address and a subject line, if you specified one.

NOTEWORTHY

You can use the ability to set an e-mail's subject line to help you sort messages as your e-mail software receives them. For example, if you set the subject line to read Customer Service Inquiry, then in your e-mail program, you can create a filter that places any incoming e-mail with that subject line into a specific e-mail folder. Check your e-mail program's online help to see how to set this up.

SETTING LINKS WITH THE ASSET PANEL

Like CSS, the Asset panel is always gonna be there to help you with various page-building functions. It's back again, this time to help you maintain consistency in your hyperlinks.

The Asset panel tracks any URLs (such as a web site address or an e-mail address) that you've used in your site already. This saves you from having to remember long addresses, and it makes reusing them throughout your pages easy. The Asset panel tracks only URLs, though—not hyperlinks to other pages within your site.

Here's how to use the Asset panel to create a hyperlink:

1. On your page, select the text or graphic that you want to set a hyperlink for.

2. In the Asset panel, click the URL category button on the left side of the panel.

   A list of URLs that you've used throughout your site appears.

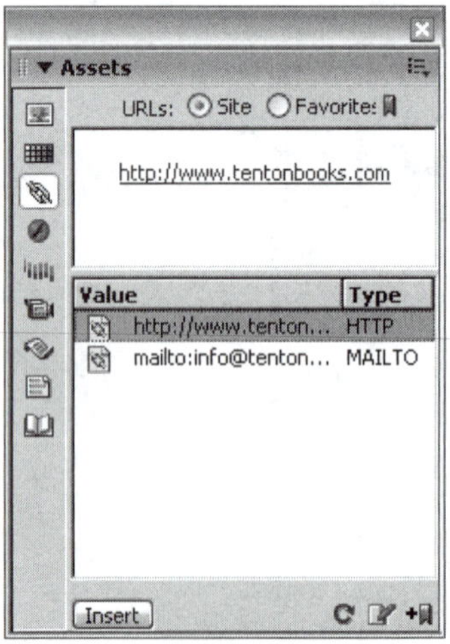

3. Click the Refresh Site List button at the bottom of the panel to ensure that the panel displays all the URLs used in your site.

4. Select the URL that you want to use; then click Insert at the bottom of the panel.

Linking to a Different Location on the Same Page with Anchors

You've seen how to create links to many different destinations, such as other pages and web sites. But wouldn't it be cool to not only link to a page, but to a specific location on a page? You may have seen this technique used on web sites that have glossary pages, where you click a letter at the top of the page and are taken to the corresponding alphabetical section that appears farther down the page. This technique is very useful in a variety of situations, and it uses something called an ***anchor***. You can think of an anchor as a placeholder on your page.

You first insert an anchor on your page to set your link's destination, and then you create a link from somewhere else on the page to that anchor. Anchors are really useful on longer pages, where a lot of scrolling would otherwise be required.

To help your visitor navigate your page easier, it's always a courtesy to include "back to top" links on pages that use anchors. That way, your visitor can easily jump back to the top of your page rather than having to scroll.

Here's how to creates links with anchors, including a link to return the visitor to the top of the page:

1. On your page, place the cursor where you want to insert an anchor. (Wherever you place your insertion point will be considered the link's destination.)

2. Choose Insert > Named Anchor.

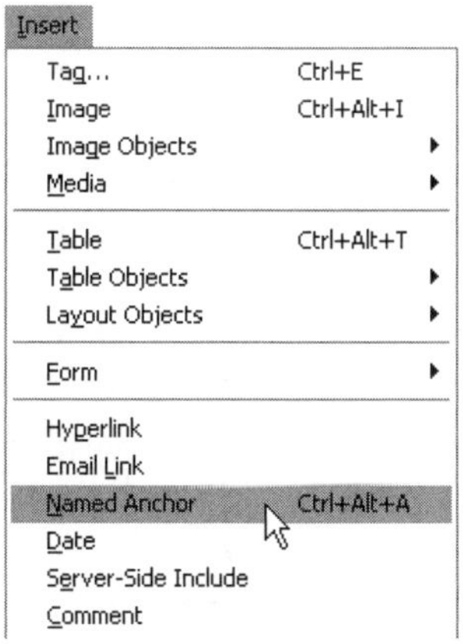

   You can also insert an anchor by clicking Named Anchor in the Common category of the Insert bar (Window > Insert).

NOTEWORTHY

Anchors are not placed permanently on your page. If you accidentally insert the anchor in the wrong spot or if you want to move it to a different place on the page, just drag it to a new location or cut and paste it.

3. In the Named Anchor dialog box that appears, enter a name for your anchor; then click OK.

An anchor name is just a way to distinguish multiple anchors that appear on your page. Anchor names can be whatever you want, but cannot contain spaces—but if you really need one, try using an underscore instead.

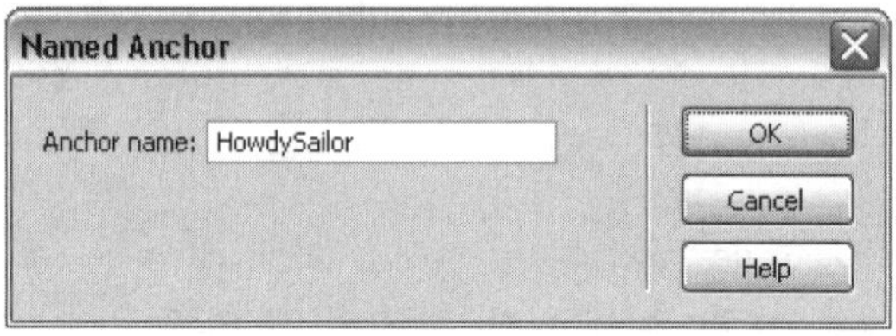

Dreamweaver inserts the anchor symbol (a gold shield with an anchor icon) on your page beside the cursor. If you don't see the anchor symbol, choose View > Visual Aids > Invisible Elements.

Now you're ready to create the link to the anchor.

4. Scroll back to the top of your page and select the text or graphic that you want to link to the anchor.

5. Choose Insert > Hyperlink.

6. In the Hyperlink dialog box that opens, choose your anchor from the Link pull-down menu; then click OK.

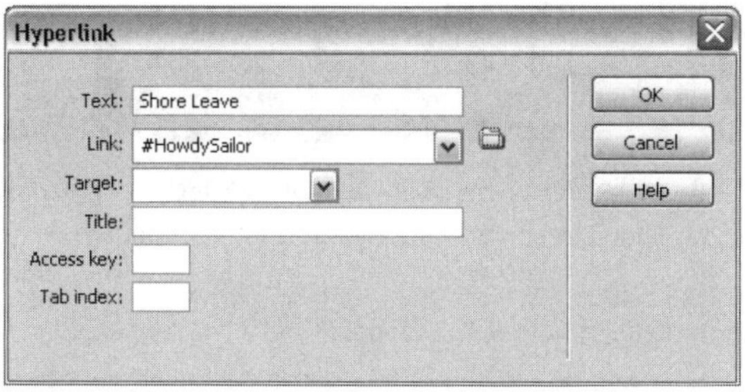

Dreamweaver sets a link to your anchor from the text or graphic you selected.

Now create a link to return the visitor to the top of your page.

7. Click at the top of your page and choose Insert > Named Anchor.

8. In the Named Anchor dialog box that appears, type a name for your new anchor; then click OK.

   The first anchor you inserted will scroll your visitor down the page. This second anchor, which is completely separate from the first, will now send them back to the top of the page. So make sure to use a new name for your anchor—for example, name it `top`.

   Now you're ready to create the link that will navigate the visitor back to the top of your page.

9. Scroll down to where you inserted your first anchor on your page and type `Back to top`.

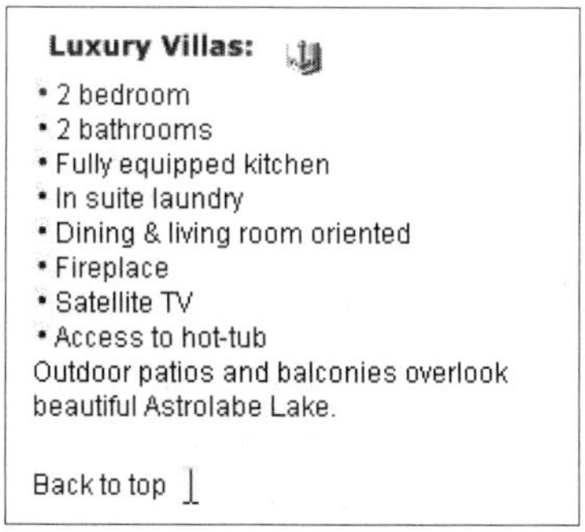

10. Select the "Back to top" text; then choose Insert > Hyperlink.

11. In the Hyperlink dialog box that appears, choose your "top" anchor from the Link pull-down menu; then click OK.

    The link back to the top of your page is created. To test the links to your anchors, preview your page in your web browser.

LINKING TO A SPECIFIC LOCATION ON ANOTHER PAGE

Anchors are useful not only for linking to a specific spot on the current page. You can also use them to link to a location on another page.

Here's how to use anchors to link to other web pages:

1. Open the page that you want to link to and place the cursor on your page where you want to insert the anchor.

2. Select Insert > Named Anchor.

3. Enter a name for your anchor in the Named Anchor dialog box that appears and click OK.

   Dreamweaver inserts the anchor symbol on your page. Now that the anchor's been placed—your link's destination—you're ready to link to it. You're done with this page, so it can be closed.

4. Save and close the page.

5. Open the page that you want to link from and select the text or graphic that will become the hyperlink.

6. In the Property Inspector, click the folder icon beside the Link field and navigate to the file you're linking to; then click OK (Windows) or Choose (Mac).

   The file name appears in the Link field.

7. Click after the file name in the Link field, type a number sign (#), and then type the name of your anchor.

   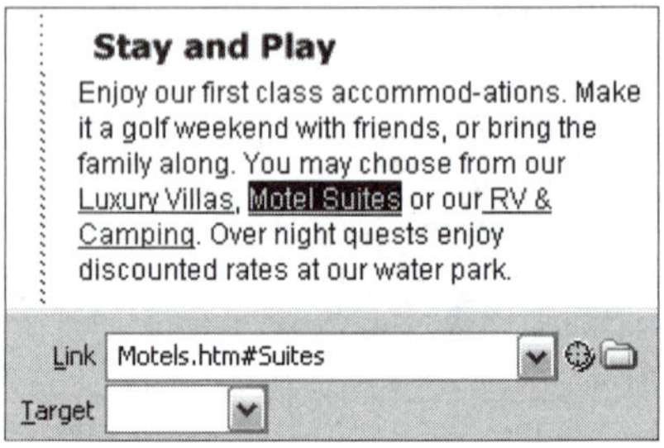

   Links are case sensitive, so make sure you use the same capitalization as you used when you named your anchor.

   Dreamweaver creates a link from your selection to the anchor and page that you specified. To test your link, preview the page in your web browser.

Hyperlink Formatting: Beyond Black Coffee

Default text-based hyperlinks look kinda boring: blue and underlined—whoopy-doo. So we gotta get them looking a little more twenty-first century—and again, Cascading Style Sheets formatting saves the day. If you've been paying attention for the past few chapters, this should come as wonderful news.

For hyperlink formatting needs, Cascading Style Sheets formatting again saves the day.

Getting Started with Hyperlink Formatting

To get started with hyperlink formatting, you'll use Dreamweaver's Page Properties dialog box. By starting here, you can control the look of all the hyperlinks on your page in one shot. This makes it easy to control fonts, colors, and other attributes of your hyperlink text.

Here's how to use the Page Properties settings to control your links:

1. Choose Modify > Page Properties.

2. In the Page Properties dialog box that appears, click the Links category at the left.

3. To change the typeface and size of your links, use the Link Font and Size menus.

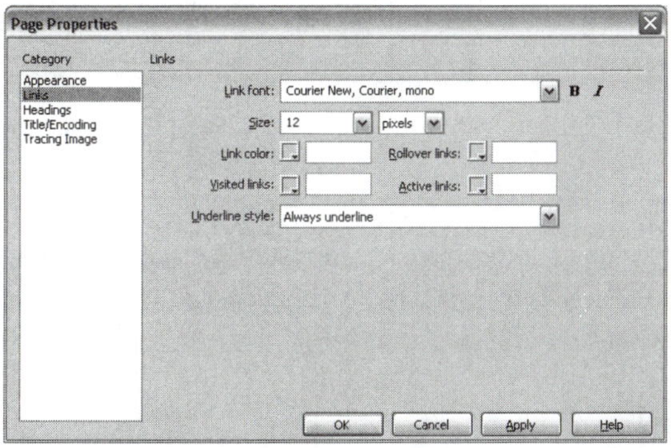

4. To control the color of your links, use the Link Color, Visited Links, Rollover Links, and Active Links fields.
   - **Link Color:** Link Color sets the color for all active links on your page. If you leave this option unset, then your links will appear in blue, the default.

   - **Visited Links:** To control the color of links that have already been clicked, set a color for Visited Links. Setting different colors for Link Color and Visited Links helps your visitors remember where they've already navigated to.

NOTEWORTHY

Seriously consider using a different color for visited links. It can be difficult for visitors to remember where they've already been on your site, so help them out by providing a visual reminder.

- **Rollover Links:** Add some interactivity to your page by setting a color for Rollover Links. Whenever your visitor moves the mouse over the hyperlink, the text will change to this color.

> **IMMINENT DOOM**
>
> If you decide to use the Show Underline Only on Rollover option, make sure you use a different text color for your hyperlinks than you used for your page text. Otherwise, visitors will have no idea where the hyperlinks are on your page.

- **Active Links:** Use the Active Links setting to control the color of a link when the user's mouse clicks it. The color flickers very quickly, and it's hardly noticeable, so many designers (myself included) usually don't bother with it. (If anything, I'll set this color to the same value that I used for Link Color.)

5. To really add some interactivity to your links, choose an option from the Underline Style menu.

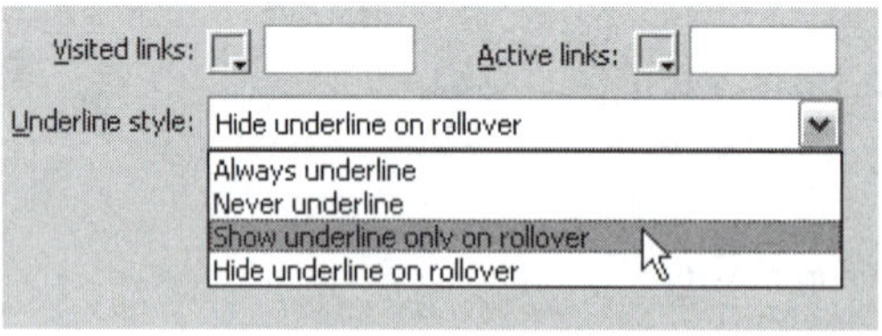

Your choices are Always Underline, Never Underline, Show Underline Only on Rollover, and Hide Underline on Rollover. Having an underline appear only when the visitor's mouse moves over the link (Show Underline Only on Rollover) is a very popular choice for web designers.

6. Once your formatting is complete, click OK to close the Page Properties dialog box.

Depending on the settings you've chosen in the Page Properties dialog box, you'll see some styles appear in the CSS Styles panel. In the next section, you'll see how to control your link formatting directly with CSS.

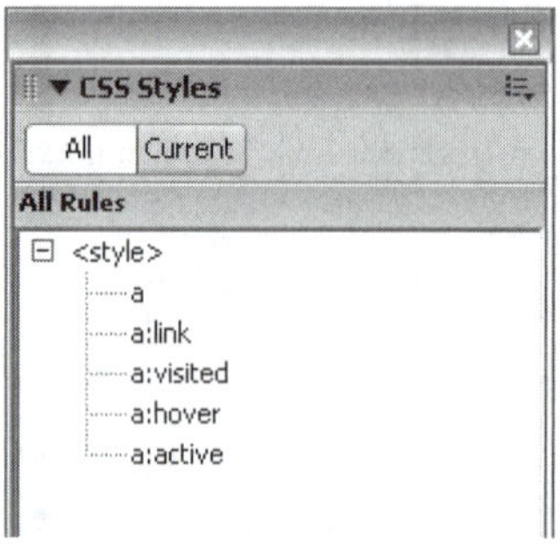

CSS is back, this time to help you with hyperlink formatting.

Controlling Link Formatting with CSS

As mentioned in the previous section, depending on your settings in the Page Properties dialog box, a number of new styles will appear in the CSS Styles panel. You may see any combination of a, a:link, a:hover, a:active, and a:visited.

These styles that Dreamweaver created are all contained within an embedded style sheet—remember your date with CSS in Chapter 8? Everything you saw there applies, so if you want to make further changes to your hyperlink styles, add new attributes, or—best of all—export your hyperlink styles to an external style sheet, the process is the same as you saw in Chapter 8.

You can edit the CSS styles that control your hyperlinks just like any other CSS styles. In fact, everything you learned about Cascading Style Sheets in Chapter 8 applies here.

NOTEWORTHY

Exporting your hyperlink styles means you'll be able to control the look of your hyperlinks right across your site—which is totally killer.

GETTIN' A GRIP ON ROLLOVER STATES

The CSS Style	Also Known As
a:link	A link's up state: the style of a hyperlink before it has been clicked by the visitor.
a:hover	A link's over state: the appearance of a hyperlink when the user's cursor moves over it.
a:active	A link's down state: the style of a link when it's selected by the user.
a:visited	A link's visited state: the appearance of the hyperlink after it has been clicked by the visitor.

Using Rollover Images to Identify Links

A common web design feature is the rollover image—a button or graphic that changes appearance whenever the visitor's mouse pointer hovers over it.

A common web design feature these days is the rollover image—that is, a button or graphic that changes appearance whenever the visitor's mouse pointer hovers over it. Keep in mind that a rollover image isn't necessarily a hyperlink. However, you can use rollover images to identify hyperlinked graphics, just as you can use color or underlining or other formatting to identify hyperlinked text.

Rollovers are so common, in fact, that many surfers now expect a site's main navigation bar to include them. Rollovers are easy to create in Dreamweaver, and they add a nice level of interactivity to your site.

Yeah, I'm a grumpy tart without coffee. Here's an example of two graphics that'll be used in a rollover: the left one before the rollover and the right one after. Remember that both have to be the same size, and most important, bring coffee!

Before you begin, you'll need some graphics. Because the image is going to change when your visitor moves the mouse over it, you'll need two graphics: one for the image as it normally appears, and one for the image as it appears when the visitor's cursor is over it. You can use images you already have, or you can create your own. Regardless, make sure that both the normal and rolled-over graphics have the same dimensions. Otherwise, your image will appear distorted when the visitor moves the mouse over it. If you want to find out how you can create your own buttons—for a navigation bar, for instance—see the sidebar "How to Make Your Own Buttons" later in this chapter.

Here's how to add rollover images to your page:

1. Place your cursor on your page where you want to insert the rollover graphic.

2. Choose Insert > Image Objects > Rollover Image.

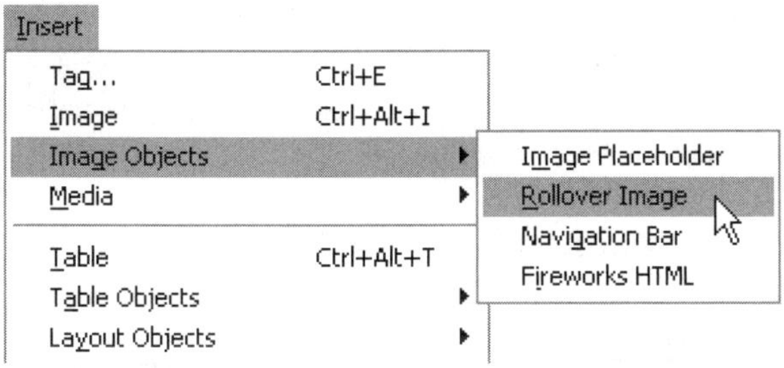

Choosing Rollover Image from the Insert submenu brings up a dialog box with options for your rollover.

3. In the Image Name field in the Insert Rollover Image dialog box that appears, specify a name for your rollover.

4. Click the Browse button beside the Original Image field to specify the graphic that will be used as the normal image.

   This is the idle graphic that will be seen when there's no interactivity from the user—called the rollover's up state.

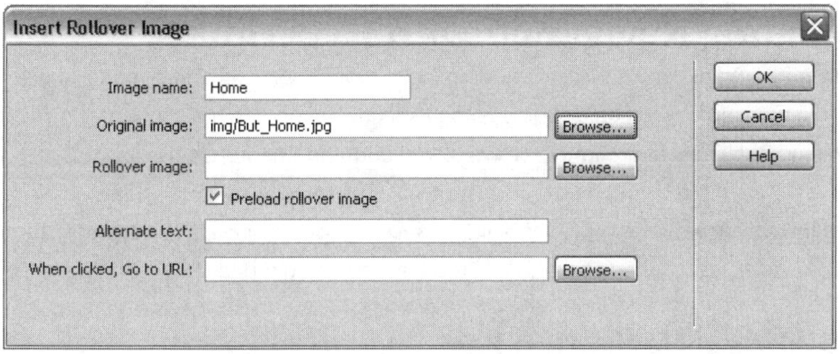

5. Click the Browse button next to the Rollover Image field to select the image for the button's over state.

   This graphic will appear when the visitor's mouse rolls over the button.

6. If you want, specify some alternative text in the Alt field, then set the button's hyperlink in the When Clicked, Go to URL field.

   Your rollover image doesn't have to have a hyperlink attached to it, but if you leave the When Clicked, Go to URL field in the Insert Rollover Image dialog box blank, Dreamweaver will insert a number sign (#) in the field, indicating a null link.

Some browsers (such as Internet Explorer in Windows) will jump the visitor to the top of the page when the visitor clicks a null link. To avoid this jumping behavior, type `javascript:;` in the URL field. This code will prevent the page from scrolling to the top when the visitor clicks your rollover image

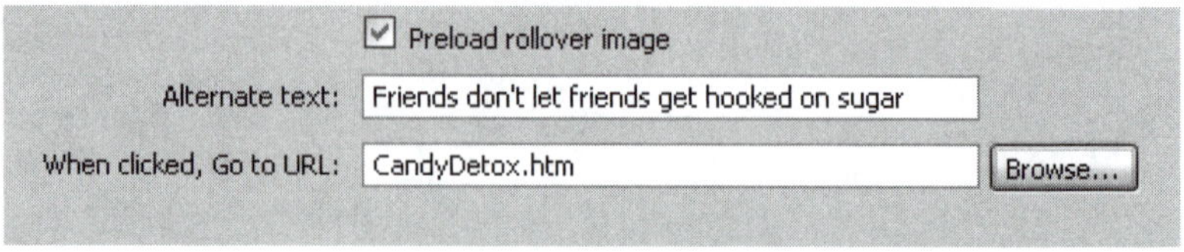

7. When your rollover settings are complete, click OK.

Hyperlinks are key to building navigation systems.

The rollover is inserted onto your page, but unfortunately you won't be able to see the effect in Dreamweaver. To see it work, save your page and preview it in your browser.

8. Save your page. Then preview your work in your browser.

Building Navigation with Hyperlinks

You've been linking from text and perhaps a graphic or two. But hyperlinks are also key to building navigation systems, such as a navigation bar or a secondary navigation system, such as a sitemap, which we talked about in Chapter 3.

Dreamweaver provides tools for building several types of navigation systems for your pages. You certainly don't have to use them all, but it's good to know what's available.

Building a Navigation Bar

In the last section, you saw how to create rollovers. If you want a whole navigation bar, complete with rollover buttons and hyperlinks, you could be in for a lot of work—so to speed things up, Dreamweaver offers the Navigation Bar command. Using this fella, you can quickly construct a horizontal or vertical nav bar, and also have Dreamweaver set up all your rollovers for you. Not only does this make building nav bars fast, but it also makes it easy to keep consistency across the pages in your site.

To create a navigation bar with rollovers, you'll need several sets of buttons to use: one for each of the four button states that are available with this command. To learn more about creating buttons, see the sidebar "How to Make Your Own Buttons" later in this chapter. Once you have some button images ready to go, you're set to begin building your navigation bar.

Creating a navigation bar in Dreamweaver is not only easy, but it also adds consistency to the pages throughout your site. With Dreamweaver's Navigation Bar command, you can easily create links and rollover buttons for a vertical nav bar, or for a horizontal one, as seen here.

Follow these steps to build a navigation bar:

1. Open the initial page that you want to place your navigation bar on.

Honestly, I set images only for a button's up and over states, but it is, of course, up to you.

2. Place your insertion point where you want the navigation bar to appear and choose Insert > Image Objects > Navigation Bar.

   You can also use the Insert bar (Window > Insert) to place a navigation bar on your page. In the Common category on the Insert bar, click the Images pull-down menu and choose Navigation Bar.

   The Insert Navigation Bar dialog box appears.

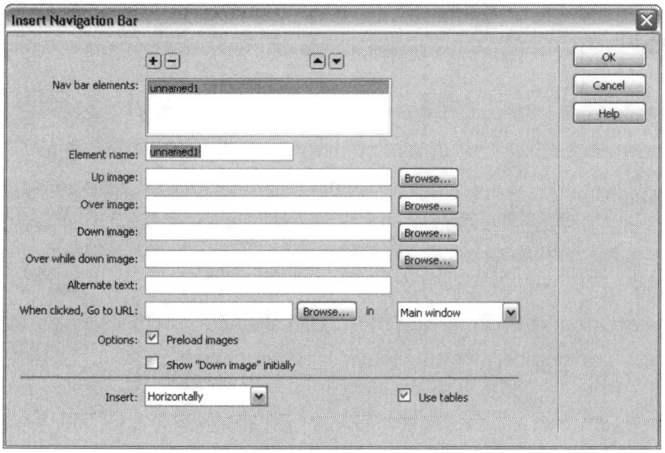

3. In the Element Name field, enter a name for the first button on your navigation bar.

   For instance, you might want to create a button that your users can click to get back to your site's main page. For this button, you could enter the name **Home**.

4. Click the Browse button beside the Up Image field and navigate to the graphic that you want to use for your button when it's idle on your page.

   A button's up state is its appearance on your page when there's no interaction from the visitor.

5. The next three button states are optional. If you want to specify different button images for Over Image, Down Image, and Over While Down Image, do so now.

   Refer to the sidebar "Gettin' a Grip on Rollover States" earlier in this chapter for a description of each of these button states.

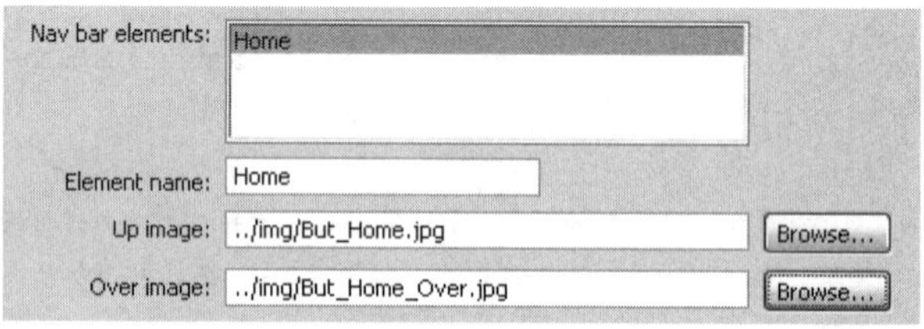

6. If you want, insert an entry for Alternate Text. (Alternative text is a short text message that will appear when your visitor rolls the pointer over the graphic.)

7. When Clicked, Go to URL field, specify where you want the navigation button to jump the visitor to.

   It's much easier to click the Browse button than to remember the URL, unless it's an easy one. Also, if you're using your navigation bar in a frameset (remember Chapter 7?), you can specify what frame you want the linked file to open in using the In menu (to the right of the Browse button).

8. To add more buttons to your navigation bar, click the Add Item button at the top of the dialog box and repeat steps 3 through 7 for each button.

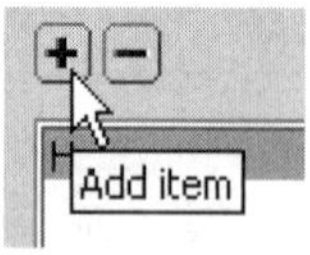

9. Make sure to leave Preload Images turned on, and check Show Down Image Initially if you want the button's down state to appear first, instead of its up state.

Preloading images is highly recommended. Remember that a single button on your navigation bar actually uses several graphics. Loading them before they're needed ensures smooth rollover transitions. Otherwise, the graphics will load as your visitor moves the mouse over a button, which slows down your site's interactivity.

Also, rather than initially showing your button's up state, you may prefer to show the button's down state. For example, on your Services page, you may want the Services button on the navigation bar to appear in its down state. This approach helps your visitors navigate your site by providing them with visual cues.

10. If you want to rearrange the buttons in your navigation bar, use the Move Item Up in List and Move Item Down in List buttons at the top of the dialog box.

11. Use the Insert menu at the bottom of the dialog box to set either a horizontal or vertical navigation bar.

12. To use a table to hold your navigation bar, check the Use Tables option at the bottom of the dialog box.

    I strongly recommend using a table to hold your navigation bar. If you leave the Use Tables option unchecked, the navigation bar elements will be placed directly on your page as loose graphics, making it very difficult for you to select, move, or copy your navigation bar. In the next section, you'll see how using tables to hold your navigation bar comes in really handy.

13. Once your settings are complete, click OK.

    Dreamweaver inserts your navigation bar on your page where you originally placed your insertion point.

If your nav bar doesn't look like you want it to, you can always make changes to it. Click anywhere inside the nav bar and choose Modify > Navigation bar. Dreamweaver will display the Insert Navigation Bar dialog box, where you can make your changes. Once your changes are complete, click OK.

NOTEWORTHY

Dreamweaver lets you insert only one navigation bar per page. If you attempt to insert another, it won't let you but instead asks if you want to make changes to the current navigation bar.

HOW TO MAKE YOUR OWN BUTTONS

Do you want to create custom buttons for your site? Here's how to create a group of buttons that all have a similar look, so they can be used in the main navigation bar throughout your site. You can then follow the same procedures to create a second set of buttons that you can use as rollover images.

Here's how to create your own button graphics:

1. Launch your external graphics program—Fireworks is a great choice since you may already have it, if you bought the whole Studio suite—and create a new document whose dimensions are set to the size of the button you want to create.

   Try 75x20 or 100x30. Once you do this a few times, you'll get a feel for how large or small you want your buttons.

2. Use any of your program's painting tools, filters, or special effects to create the look of the button.

   This is the creative part. Maybe you want your buttons to look futuristic, or maybe like they're carved out of stone. Whatever the theme of your web site, try to carry it through to your buttons. Also, many programs come with prebuilt button features. For example, Photoshop's Styles palette contains many prebuilt button designs. These make it easy to build a set of buttons very quickly.

3. Using your program's Text tool, type the button's text label on the button image.

   This is where you type `Home`, `Contact`, or whatever label you want to use for your button.

4. When your button is complete, save it as either a JPEG or GIF image in your local site folder.

   Turn to the guidelines in Chapter 10 for optimizing your graphics. It may take a bit of tweaking to get the best quality with the lowest possible file size for your image.

5. Continue creating more buttons by selecting your button image's text label with the Text tool and entering a new label; then save the button under a different file name. Repeat this process until you have all the buttons that you want for your navigation bar.

6. If you want a second set of buttons to be used as rollover images, go back to step 1 and begin creating an alternative set of buttons.

   This second set of buttons will be used for your buttons' over state, so consider using the original buttons with a different color or applying some sort of special effect. Also, make sure that your rollover buttons are the same dimensions as your original buttons.

Now that you have a set of buttons, you can use them with Dreamweaver's Rollover Image and Insert Navigation Bar commands.

Can't be bothered creating your own buttons? There are nearly endless resources for free buttons online. To get started, check out prodraw.net/button or buttonland.com.

Adding a Navigation Bar Throughout Your Site

Now that you've built a navigation bar, you'll likely want to use it on other pages in your site. You could try copying and pasting your nav bar into other pages, but if the page you're pasting to is saved in a different folder in your site than your original page, you'll be left with nothing but a bunch of busted links and broken images, because all the graphic paths and hyperlinks will now be pointing to incorrect locations.

Once you've saved your navigation bar as a library item, you can insert it throughout your site and not worry about links and images not working.

So rather than copying and pasting, a better approach is to save your navigation bar as a library item. Remember libraries from Chapter 5? Once you've saved your navigation bar as a library item, you can insert it throughout your site and not worry about links and images not working.

Here's how it's done:

1. Insert a navigation bar on your page, as you did in the previous section.

2. Open the library by choosing Window > Assets and then clicking the Library category in the button column on the left.

   Now you need to add the navigation bar to the library.

3. Select your navigation bar on the page.

   Here's where using a table to hold your navigation bar really pays off. To select your entire navigation bar, all you need to do is select the table. Probably the easiest way to do this is to click anywhere in the nav bar and then click the `<table>` button in the Tag Selector area of the Status bar, at the bottom left.

   If you didn't use a table to hold your navigation bar, you can still play along. Click a button in your navigation bar to select it; then click the <p> button in the Tag Selector. This will select all the buttons in the nav bar for you

4. At the bottom of the Library pane, click the New Library Item button.

   The navigation bar appears in the library as an untitled library item.

5. Give the nav bar a name and press Enter (Windows) or Return (Mac).

6. In the Update Files dialog box that appears, click Update.

   Now the navigation bar is ready to be placed on the other pages in your site.

7. Open the page that you want to insert your navigation bar on.

8. Place your insertion point where you want the navigation bar to appear and click the Insert button at the bottom of the Library pane.

   Dreamweaver inserts the navigation bar on your page, with the graphics and hyperlinks intact.

PLACING BREADCRUMBS—

Many web sites display a series of links at the top of the page, giving visitors a trail back to where they started, usually the home page. These links are known as breadcrumbs, and they're a very useful secondary navigation system, allowing visitors to navigate via the site's structure rather than from the main menu.

Listed in category: Collectibles > Advertising > Candy & Nuts > Other Candy, Nuts

Here's an example of breadcrumbs from eBay.com.

Dreamweaver comes with two basic prebuilt breadcrumb bars that you can insert on your page, so you can get started with breadcrumb navigation right away, without having to create your own from scratch.

To use Dreamweaver's prebuilt breadcrumbs, you'll be using the Snippet panel. You haven't seen this panel yet, but it contains prebuilt code blocks for page elements, such as page footers and navigational elements.

Now, what hierarchy do you use to insert the placeholders for your page links? That is, the visitor can come to the current page from any number of different directions or pages. How do you set up the default breadcrumb bar to anticipate whatever series of breadcrumb trails your visitor will follow? This relates directly to the type of structure you're using for your web site. If you'll recall back to Chapter 3, there are four main structural types: linear, hierarchical, spoke-and-hub, and full-web. Keeping these structural types in mind, breadcrumbs would be easiest to implement with the linear sites. They'd also be easy to use with a hierarchical structure, where the first breadcrumb entry would be the home page, the second breadcrumb entry is the landmark page, and the third a content page. Breadcrumbs could also be used in a spoke-and-hub model, although it would be tricky to implement; and finally breadcrumbs would be unusable in a full-web structure, because in a full-web set-up, there's actually no structure because each page links to every other page. Keep this in mind as you add breadcrumbs onto your page. And remember, breadcrumbs may not be well suited to the type of site you're creating.

Here's how to insert breadcrumbs on your page:

1. Place your insertion point on your page where you want to insert your breadcrumb bar.

2. Open the Snippets panel by choosing Window > Snippets.

3. In the Snippets panel, expand the Navigation folder, then expand the Breadcrumb folder.

Image Maps Revealed

Have you ever visited a site that contained a single graphic with several links in it? These elements are called image maps. In an image map, an image is divided into multiple clickable areas, or hotspots, that the visitor can use to navigate your site.

Image maps are handy navigation tools, especially when created using graphics that contain some sort of boundaries, like a collage or an actual map, so the visitor knows where to click to activate a particular link. For instance, the visitor might click an area of a collage of products to go to the section of the web site that features that particular product.

Automatically create breadcrumbs with Expert Breadcrumbs, a Dreamweaver extension available from Kaosweaver (kaosweaver.com).

SORTA LIKE A CANDY TRAIL, RIGHT? (CONTINUED)

The Breadcrumbs folder contains two types of formatting that you can use for your breadcrumb paths: Angle Bracket Denotes Path and Colon as Separator. Both work exactly the same, so the only difference is aesthetic.

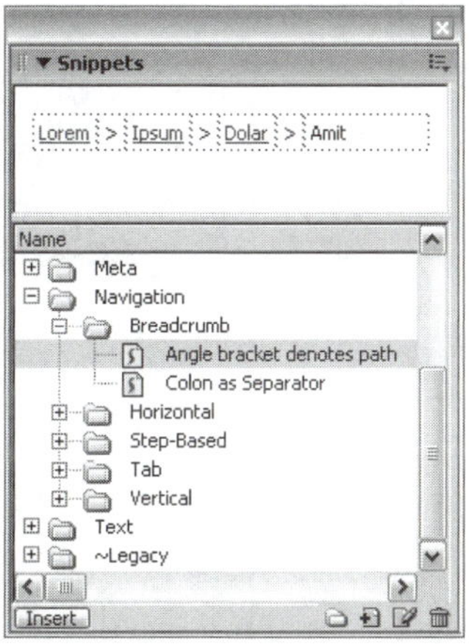

4. Select the type of breadcrumb path you want; then click Insert at the bottom of the panel.

   Dreamweaver inserts the breadcrumb navigation bar on your page. Even though your breadcrumbs are prebuilt Dreamweaver page objects, they're just ordinary text contained in a table. They're contained in a table to make it easier to control their position on your page. If you're using CSS to control the look of your hyperlinks, the breadcrumb links will take on this formatting as well.

   All that's left now is to change the text on the breadcrumb bar and set the correct hyperlinks.

5. Select the first piece of text in your breadcrumb bar and type the correct structural heading.

   Most likely, you'll type **Home**, as your home page is at the top of your site's structure.

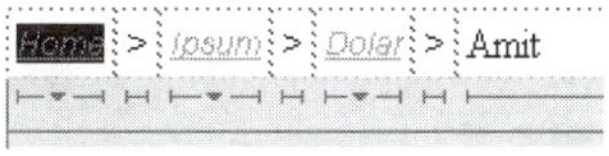

6. With the text still selected, set a link for your structural heading using the Property Inspector's Link field.

7. Continue entering structural headings and setting their links until your breadcrumb bar is complete.

That's about all there is to inserting breadcrumbs on your page. If you're not sure whether to use them, remember how back in Chapter 3 we talked about including several ways for surfers to navigate your site. Breadcrumbs would make a lovely addition.

Here's how to create an image map:

1. Select the graphic on your page that you want to add hotspots to.

2. At the bottom left of the Property Inspector, click the hotspot shape tool that you want to use.

   You can create rectangular, circular, or polygonal hotspots.

3. If you have Dreamweaver's Accessibility preferences turned on, you'll be asked to add alt text to your image when you click a hotspot tool. You can add alt text now, or you'll have an opportunity to add it in a moment. Click OK to continue.

4. Drag the cursor over the image to create the hotspot.

5. To make adjustments to your hotspot, use the Hotspot Pointer tool at the bottom left of the Property Inspector. Drag the hotspot's resize handles to make the area larger or smaller, or drag in the middle of the hotspot to move it around in the image. If you trash your hotspot by accident, just press Delete and start again.

6. In the Property Inspector's Link field, set your hotspot's hyperlink.

   As soon as you drag with a hotspot tool, the Property Inspector switches to provide hotspot options so you can enter your settings.

   You create links for hotspots in the same way as you create links for text or images.

GEEK'S DELIGHT

You may have heard the terms client-side image map and server-side image map. Client-side maps are stored within an HTML document, and server-side maps are stored on a server. If you have heard these terms and find them confusing, forget about 'em and just make your image maps in Dreamweaver as described in this section. If you've never heard these terms before, inconspicuously scribble out this note and move on.

In an image map, an image is divided into multiple clickable areas, hotspots, that the visitor can use to navigate your site.

7. To open the link in a new browser window, choose _blank from the Target menu. If you want, set a Target option and enter alternative text in the Alt field.

It's a really good idea to provide alternative text for your hotspot. Your visitors won't see the hotspot shape, but alternative text will let them know that they can click the image. It can also give them an idea of where the link will take them.

I often create clickable areas on a single graphic that is made from several button images. Visitors think they're clicking buttons, but they're actually clicking image map hotspots.

8. To add more hotspots to your graphic, repeat steps 2 through 7. When you're done, click outside your image.

Wanna test your work? Then get previewin' your page in a browser. Hover your cursor over your image map, and your alt text will appear. Give 'er a click, and you'll be whisked away to your hotspot's destination.

Building a Linked Site Structure

As you begin building links and establishing your site's hierarchy, it won't take long for you to realize that you should have put two spoonfuls of sugar on your cereal this morning rather than one. The work can get tedious—and confusing—if you haven't planned out things properly ahead of time. Determining your site's structure and the number of pages you'll need and what your pages should be called are all issues that are tough to tackle during the construction stage of site design. That's why we spent so much time in Chapter 3 talking about the importance of planning everything out upfront.

So in this section, we'll assume that you've planned your entire site structure: that you know exactly what pages need to be created, where they should be saved, and what they'll contain. We'll also assume that you have a single, well-designed page layout that you want to use as the basis for the rest of your site. What you'll be doing here is transforming that plan into a fully operational site.

Incorporating Hyperlinks in Your Design

Before you delve deeply into building a full-blown site, it's critical that you establish your initial page layout. You'll save yourself tons of time if you do. Your initial layout should include text, graphics, primary and secondary navigation tools, CSS, tables, frames, and other elements. But most important, your initial layout has to have hyperlinks, which you'll see how to incorporate in this section.

You'll start by creating a site hierarchy made up of linked dummy files; then you can replace those dummy files with real pages.

Here's whatcha do to build your site hierarchy and link your pages:

1. Open the Files panel (Window > Files).

2. Do one of the following:
   - To create your dummy file at the top level (the root level) of your site, right-click (Windows) or Control+click (Mac) a blank part of the panel and choose New File.

   - To place your dummy page in a particular folder, right-click (Windows) or Control+click (Mac) directly on the folder's icon and choose New File.

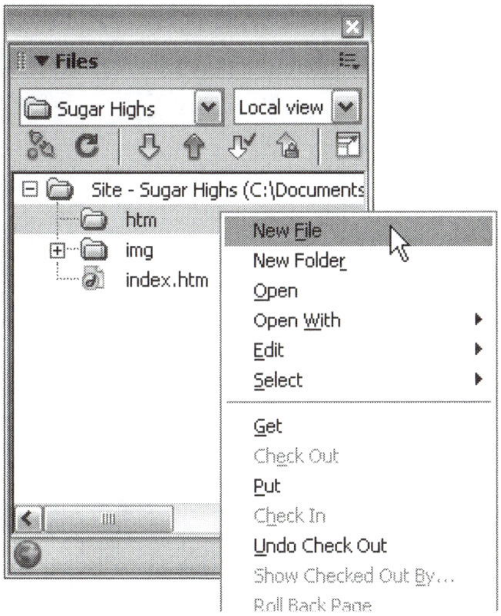

Dreamweaver creates an empty dummy page for you in your site.

Remember that you can always drag documents around in the Files panel to reorganize them, so if you created your dummy file in the wrong location, just drag it into the right folder.

3. In the Files panel, name your page in accordance with a page needed in your site structure.

   For example, if you know you'll need a page in your ***htm*** folder called ***services.htm***, then name your new file accordingly. Also, make sure to set the extension to either .htm or .html, and remember to be consistent!

   You've now created a blank page that will hold the place of your real ***services.htm*** page, which hasn't been created yet. If you open your dummy page (by double-clicking in the Files panel), it will be empty. You'll be using this empty page as a placeholder when you create your hyperlinks.

4. Continue creating new files and naming them accordingly until you've created your entire site structure.

   When you're done, you'll have an entire web site made up of empty, dummy pages. Well, it's not really a web site yet, because none of the pages connect to each other. That's up next.

IMMINENT DOOM

Absolutely avoid special characters in file and folder names. There's a very high chance that they won't be interpreted properly online. Also avoid using spaces in file and folder names. Even though they're replaced by %20, it's better to err on the side of caution.

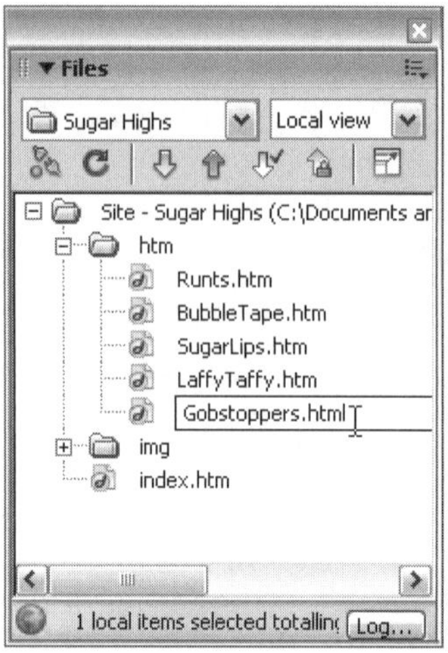

5. Open the page that contains the layout design that you want to use throughout your site.

   This is the page that you've been working on all along, which contains your graphics, text, and layout that you plan to use as the basis for other pages in your site. You'll now set hyperlinks on your page to the dummy pages in your site.

NOTEWORTHY

Of course, if you know the path to the file you're linking to, you could type it into the Link field by hand. Be careful though. One missed character or a typo, and your link won't work.

6. Select the first image or piece of text on your page that you want to set a hyperlink for.

   Typically, you'll select the first button on your main navigation bar, but you could select any text or graphical element that will link to another page in your site. Really, it doesn't matter where you begin, as eventually you'll be getting to all the hyperlinks on your page.

7. In the Property Inspector, click the Browse for File icon beside the Link field.

8. In the Select File dialog box that appears, navigate to and select the web page that you want the text or button to link to; then click OK (Windows) or Choose (Mac).

   Dreamweaver creates a link to the dummy web page. Of course, right now the page is empty. What's important here is the file name of the page—you're building hyperlink paths to the pages in your site.

9. Continue setting the hyperlinks in your page that will connect to other pages in your site. When you're done, save your file.

   For example, set the links for your main navigation bar and other page elements, so that all links from your page have been set.

10. Test your design in various browsers and platforms to make sure it works.

    It's better to catch a design flaw at this stage, where it appears in only one file, than at the end, when the design's been used throughout countless pages of your site.

Now, with all your hyperlinks set, you're ready to start replacing your dummy pages with real web pages. This is what I call ***rolling out*** the design.

IMMINENT DOOM

If you begin overwriting dummy files in your site before building your initial page design exactly as you want it—this includes inserting text, placing graphics, and setting all the necessary hyperlinks—then you'll have to open each page in your site one at a time and manually make any adjustments. Depending on the size of your site, this could be anywhere from an afternoon's worth of work to several days'. Be sure that your initial page design is exactly what you want before rolling it out across your site.

Rollin' Out Your Hyperlinked Site Design

You've set hyperlinks in your original design page and tested it in a few target browsers, making any necessary tweaks. You're now ready to roll out your hyperlinked page design across your site.

Essentially, what you have at this point is a single, well-designed page that's linked to a bunch of empty dummy pages in your site. What you need to do now is replace all those dummy pages with the layout that you've so laboriously created.

To roll out your hyperlinked design, follow these steps:

1. From your original design page, choose File > Save As.

2. In the Save As dialog box that appears, select the first dummy file in your site's structure; then click Save.

   You're overwriting the first dummy file with your design page. The empty page will be replaced with your design page, but the file name (which was used to establish hyperlinks) remains.

3. Dreamweaver will ask you to confirm that you want to overwrite the file. Click Yes to continue.

   The empty dummy file is replaced with the layout design page.

4. Choose File > Save As again and select the next file in your site's structure. Click Save and, when prompted, click OK to overwrite the dummy file.

5. Continue overwriting the dummy files in your site structure until they've all been replaced with your design page.

   When you're done, you'll have a fully working web site. Congratulations!

6. Preview your site in your browser to see how it looks. Click your navigation buttons to go to the various pages in your site to make sure your links are working.

   Once your site's humming, you're ready to insert each page's unique content.

7. Open each page and insert the appropriate content on each.

   For example, on your home page, you'll probably want some kind of welcome message. On your products page, you can insert the appropriate graphics and text for your products, and so on.

Hopefully you can now see why it makes sense to spend the time up front designing a single page that looks and functions exactly as you want. Imagine at this point that you decide that you want every page to include breadcrumb navigation, but breadcrumbs weren't used in the original design. Now you're faced with the task of opening every single page and inserting breadcrumbs, one at a time. There goes your weekend. So again, before rolling out, make sure your design is exactly what you (or your client) is after.

JUST THE GIST

Understanding Hyperlink Paths

- Absolute paths point to their destination by using a full URL, such as http://www.tentonbooks.com/dw/paths.htm.
- Document-relative paths exclude the part of the URL that is common to the link's starting point and destination.
- Root-relative paths always begin by returning to the site's root folder; then the path leads down through the structure to the link's destination.

Creating Hyperlinks

- To link to another page in your site, use the Browse button beside the Link field in the Property Inspector.
- When linking to another web site, be sure to enter the site's full URL (including `http://`) in the Property Inspector's Link field.
- To create a hyperlink to an e-mail address, enter `mailto:` and then the e-mail address that you want to link to.
- Insert and link to anchors to provide navigation to different locations within a page.

Formatting Hyperlinks

- To begin formatting the look of your hyperlinks, use Dreamweaver's Page Properties dialog box.
- Because hyperlink formatting uses Cascading Style Sheets, you can make further edits to your link formatting through the CSS Styles panel.
- Use rollover images on your page, replacing one graphic with another, to add interactivity to your pages.

Adding Hyperlink Navigation Features

- To create navigation bars quickly, use Dreamweaver's Navigation Bar command, which allows you to set rollovers and hyperlinks for each button you include. To use your nav bar on other pages, make sure to save it as a library item.
- Use an image map to place multiple hyperlinks, called hotspots, on a single image. This saves you from having to slice an image into smaller pieces when more than one link is needed.

Building a Linked Site Structure

- To build a site that has both a solid structure and a consistent design, begin with a single, well-designed page. Then create dummy pages in your structure as placeholders for the real pages that will replace them once they've been designed.
- From your page that contains the initial layout, create hyperlinks to the dummy pages in your site.
- Replace all the dummy pages in your site by overwriting them with the page that contains your design. Then add your actual content to your pages.

Chapter 10

ADDING and *Adjusting* GRAPHICS

STUFF YOU'LL LEARN IN THIS CHAPTER

All right space cadets, this chapter's all about your first space flight with graphics. Your journey starts with a mission briefing—that is, getting a handle on how graphics work on the web. You'll find out about file formats, image resolution and other graphics fundamentals. From there, you'll be strapped into your seat and blasted into the world of web graphics head-on. You'll see how to import 'em, manipulate 'em, modify 'em, and more! Hop into your Saturn V and hang on for the ride!

Understanding Graphics and the Web

Before heading off into the final frontier, you've gotta take some time and prep for your mission. Let's start at the beginning. When the World Wide Web was conceived, it was built to handle only text-based documents. But obviously, the web has grown far beyond that, making it primarily a visual environment. This is why graphics are so important in web design. In fact, you'll discover that graphics are used everywhere: navigation bars, bullet points, buttons, icons, and more. Just surf the web a bit, and you'll see how vitally important graphics are to web design.

Now before stepping onto the launch pad, you need to understand a few fundamentals: namely, the difference between the two main types of graphics—raster and vector—and the types of image file formats that you can use in your site. We'll talk about these issues (and a few others); then you'll begin to learn how to use graphics in your site. Sit back and enjoy the mission briefing—you'll be in low earth orbit in a matter of pages!

Graphics are used ***everywhere*** *on the web: navigation bars, bullet points, buttons, icons, and more.*

Graphics Come in Two Flavors: Raster and Vector

Graphics all boil down to just two flavors: raster and vector. We talked a bit about this in Chapter 1, when we discussed the web design puzzle, but that was way back when you'd just signed up for flight school, so here's a little refresher.

When I first found out that vector images were math based, I nearly fell off my chair. What—was I supposed to draw with a calculator in hand? Thankfully, vector-drawing programs handle all the math in the background, so you don't have to see it.

Raster graphics are pixel-based images such as photographs, artwork, film stills, or any image that you've scanned into your computer. Because they're pixel-based, issues like resolution, quality, and file size may be problems—unless you have a fairly good foothold on how these things work.

Raster graphics are made up of a grid of pixels, like tiles in a mosaic. Maybe Buzz and the gang found ancient mosaics on the moon—oh, conspiracy!

Vector graphics, on the other hand, comprise images such as logos, clip art, line drawings, cartoons, or any other image that's made up of solid areas of color. Rather than pixels, vector graphics consist of mathematical lines, curves and arcs. Because math is being used instead of pixels, quality is never an issue, and file sizes are much more manageable.

Vector images, like this cartoon space capsule, are composed of mathematically calculated lines and arcs. No calculator needed, thank goodness!

The differences between raster and vector graphics should be fairly straightforward. But there is a sticky spot. All the graphics that you want to use on your web site must be raster images, unless you're building a Flash-based web site (which we're not doing here). So what if you have a vector-based logo or line drawing that you want to use in your site? Well, you'll have to convert it to a raster image and save it in a file format suitable for the web. To do that, just open your vector image in a raster image editor, like Photoshop or Fireworks, to commit it to pixels. And as for file formats, keep readin'!

NOTEWORTHY

Macromedia Flash is a vector-based design tool that's really turned web design on it's ear, allowing you to nearly forget about HTML and traditional web design and build pages in a much more visual environment. Flash has a fairly steep learning curve, but if you want to take your web design skills further, it's well worth getting into.

File Formats for the Web

There are a lot of graphic file formats out there—so many that you'd easily run out of fingers and toes a few times over. However, you'll use JPEG and GIF images for most of your graphics work. You may sometimes use PNG, though earlier versions of Internet Explorer and Netscape do not support it, and SWF, though the user must have Flash Player installed to view graphics saved in that format (98 percent of all computers have some version of Flash Player installed). Internet Explorer and Firefox (at least the Windows versions) also support BMP and TIF images; however, considering the size of most TIF and BMP images, it is a good idea to use a graphics editor and convert them to JPG, PNG, or GIF. All other graphic file formats that you may encounter will not be usable in your web site. If you have an image in a different format, you'll have to resave it, most likely as a JPEG or GIF file.

You'll use JPEG and GIF images for most of your graphics work.

THE JPEG FORMAT

The JPEG (Joint Photographic Experts Group) format was built to handle images that are made up of millions of colors, making it perfect for images like photos or artwork—in other words, raster images. JPEGs apply compression to your images to help keep the file size small, but image quality is sacrificed to do so. This means that if a high amount of compression is used, a small file size may be achieved, but this will result in a fairly poor-quality image.

Therefore, you'll always be striking a balance between an image's file

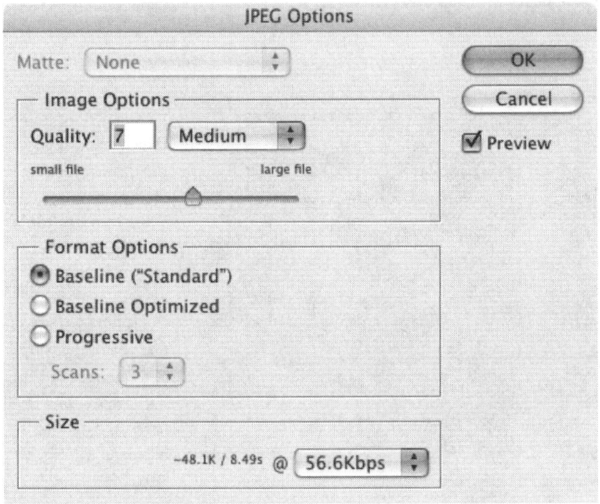

The JPEG file format reduces an image's file size by applying quality compression to it. Compression is measured on a scale from 0 (low quality) to 12 (maximum quality).

NOTEWORTHY

Think of file formats as different tools that can perform different tasks. Some may support millions of colors, while others may support animation or transparency. The file format you choose will depend on what you're trying to achieve.

size and it's quality. This process is called ***image optimization***, and it's a process that you'll probably go through with each image that you want to use in your site. For more on image optimization, see "Prepping Your Graphics" later in this chapter.

IMMINENT DOOM

Because the JPEG file format sacrifices quality for file size, every time you open a JPEG in your image editing program, change it, and then resave it as a JPEG file, you're reapplying compression to your image. Repeatedly doing this will eventually result in a very poor quality—and practically unusable—image.

THE GIF FORMAT

Like JPEG, the GIF (Graphic Interchange Format) file format compresses images, but GIF does so by controlling the number of colors used in the image, up to a maximum of 256 (the fewer the colors, the smaller the file size). Because photos and artwork use a huge number of colors, GIF isn't well suited for those types of images. Instead, GIF is suitable for anything that has a simple color makeup—vector images that need to be rasterized for use on your site.

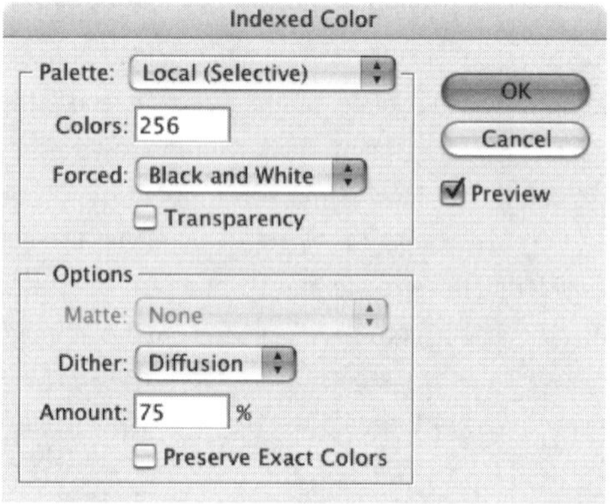

When GIF is on the case, you can minimize an image's file size by specifying the number of colors used. This isn't so hot for graphics that use a lot of colors—for instance, photos—but it's perfect for images that use only a few colors.

JPEG files may use either the .jpg or .jpeg file extension. Either way, they work the same.

GIF also has a few other tricks up its sleeve. For one, the GIF file format supports animation. An animated GIF image would actually contain several graphics that play in sequence, just like a flipbook. They were all the rage way back in Galileo's time, but with the advent of Flash, animated GIFs are pretty much washed up and outta work. You can also use GIF files when you want transparency in your image. Transparency is most useful when you want your image's background to be clear rather than white, so that your web page's background shows through.

IMMINENT DOOM

Saving a photo using the GIF file format will usually result in a very poor quality image. Remem-ber that GIF removes color from images to reduce file size—and photos use millions of colors.

Using the wrong file format for the job can result in some less desirable results. The Buzz on the right looks great—he's using the JPEG file format. But the Buzz on the left is lookin' a little homesick—this is because GIF has removed all but a few colors.

THE PNG FORMAT

The up-and-comer in web graphics is the PNG (Portable Network Group) file format. It comes loaded with features that give both JPEG and GIF a run for their money. Just like GIF, PNG supports transparency, and like JPEG, it can handle a variety of color methods. This makes PNG a sort of "best of" compilation for JPEG and GIF settings, making it perfect for both raster and vector-based images.

Read all about the PNG file format at webmonkey.wired.com/webmonkey/99/09/index0a.html?tw=design.

So why not ditch JPEG and GIF and go with PNG for all your web graphics? Well, the bumble-bee in PNG's flight suit is that not all its features are fully supported by major web browsers yet. PNG can do quite a bit, but your visitors may not be able to see its handiwork, so it's best to stick with JPEG and GIF, at least for now. But keep your eye on PNG—it promises to be one heck of a file format, and with support from the World Wide Web Consortium and the major software vendors, it won't be long until PNG images are firing on all cylinders.

THE SWF FORMAT

The SWF (Shockwave Flash) file format is used when exporting Flash files for use on the web. A great feature of the SWF format is that it's vector based, keeping file size very small. The only catch is that the visitor must have the Flash Player plug-in installed, so the browser can display SWF files—but nearly all web browser these days have the Flash Player plug-in, so incorporating Flash content into your site is not nearly the problem it used to be.

Flash was originally intended to create animations for the web. But pioneering designers realized that an animation can be a single frame, allowing them to create static, scalable vector graphics. In addition, SWF files can even contain raster images, MP3 quality audio, and short video clips, broadening the possibilities even further. In fact, Flash is now often used to create full applications.

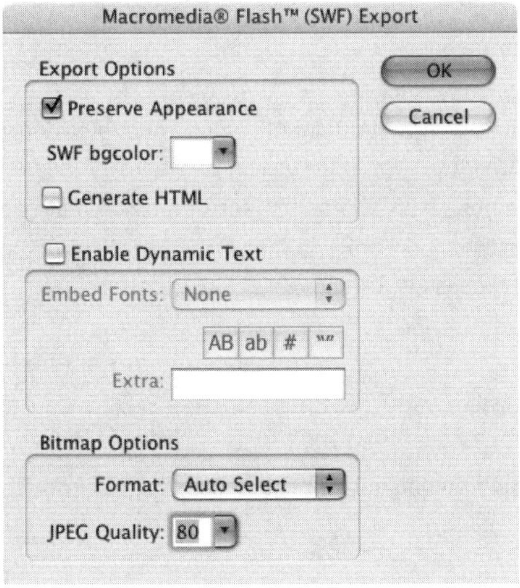

You gotta love Flash, which means you gotta love the SWF format, which is the go-between for getting your animations out of Flash and into Dreamweaver.

Image Resolution Revealed

Raster images possess a quality setting, called the image's resolution, usually defined in dots per inch. The higher an image's DPI, the better the image quality, and the larger the file size.

One of the most difficult aspects of working with graphics on the web is wrapping your brain around image resolution. This can be a complicated subject, and all the misinformation out there makes it even tougher to understand. So before going any further, let's take a quick look at how image resolution works.

As mentioned earlier, at least for now, all the images on your web site will be raster graphics, and you'll be sticking with JPEGs and GIFs. These two file formats build images out of a grid—or map—of pixels (which is why they're called *bitmaps*).

Raster images also possess a quality setting, called the image's resolution. Resolution can be defined in several ways, but the most common is DPI, or dots per inch. Theoretically, the higher an image's resolution, or DPI, the better the image quality, and thus the larger the file size. Standard resolution in the print world is 300 DPI, but we're in the web design world here, so you're about to catch a lucky break. All images in your web site need be only 72 DPI, which also means they will have nice, small file sizes. Why 72 DPI? Because that's the maximum resolution that most consumer-grade monitors can display.

> **IMMINENT DOOM**
>
> Using images in your web site that have a resolution higher than 72 DPI will not improve the image's quality. You're still viewing the image through a 72-DPI interface: your monitor. Using a higher DPI will only bloat your image's file size, resulting in an unnecessarily slow download time.

Prepping Your Graphics

Because graphics make up the heaviest part of a page's download, it's important to prepare them properly for use on the web. Preparing your images for use on the web is called image optimization. Image optimization is the process of balancing an image's quality with its file size, and if you ignore image optimization, you're likely in for a crash landing. Because the web is all about speed, you'll want your images firing off the launch pad as quickly as they can. This means that your file sizes will have to be as small as possible, while still keeping your images looking good.

You'll be optimizing your images in your graphics program of choice. (See the sidebar "The Lowdown on Image Editors" in Chapter 1 for a discussion of the image editors available.) I use ImageReady (which comes with Photoshop) for optimizing, but you may prefer a different program, such as Fireworks or Paint Shop Pro. Regardless of the graphics program you use, the overall process is the same.

Here's how to optimize your images:

1. Open your image in your graphics editor.

2. Access your program's save or export commands to begin the process of optimizing your image.

Some graphics programs, such as ImageReady and Fireworks, have a palette that's used for optimizing images. Other programs, such as Photoshop and Paint Shop Pro, do their optimizing as they're saving an image. You'll have to check your particular graphics program.

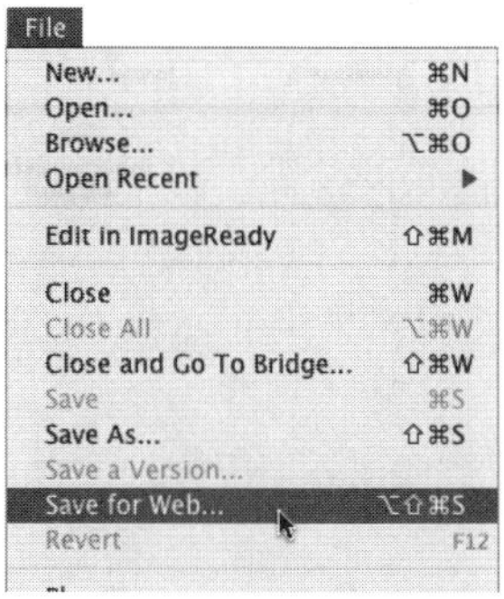

3. Choose a file format , JPEG or GIF, and set your program's controls to this format.

   Here's my rule of thumb for choosing the file format: If it's a raster graphic, chances are JPEG is the best choice. If the image originated as a vector graphic, odds are GIF will be my choice. This rule doesn't always hold, but it's a good guideline.

4. Adjust your JPEG or GIF settings to add or remove quality from your image, thus altering the file size.

   This is the balance between quality and file size that we've been talking about. You don't want to lose too much quality, but you also don't want to unnecessarily bloat the file size. Good graphics programs provide an easy-to-follow interface where you can make your tweaks, and they also give you a live preview so that you can see what you're going to get.

As with everything in web design, shoot for a least common denominator. In the case of optimizing web graphics, assume that visitors to your site will be running a 56K modem.

5. Once you've achieved a good balance between file size and quality, save your image in your local site folder.

   Because there are so many variables involved, it's hard to give you an exact file size to shoot for. But to give you a ballpark, you could crunch a small 100x30 pixel button down to, say, 2 or 3 kilobytes or even less, and a 300x200 pixel photo down to 40 kilobytes or even smaller.

   With your image optimized and saved in your site's folder, it's ready to be inserted into your web page.

Keep in mind that image optimization is a bit of an art. If you find your graphics looking poopy, try again and keep at it. The more images you optimize, the better you'll get at it.

FINDING GRAPHICS TO USE IN YOUR WEB SITE

Where can you find graphics to use in your site? Some obvious choices are to take your own photos with your digital camera or, if you have some printed material that you want to use, dust off your scanner and put it to good use. And for graphics like buttons, logos, and icons, try your graphics editor. Many top-notch graphics programs come with commands and prebuilt styles for creating your own buttons and navigational elements.

If you're feeling a bit of a creative block, consider searching for free buttons and graphics online. Many sites, such as flashbuttons.com, offer free or reasonably priced graphics specifically for use on web pages.

Of course, you can find photos and other types of graphics on the web, too. You can use a stock image service like gettyimages.com or thinkstock.com, or you could take a slightly more cost-effective approach. For example, did you know that Google has an images-only search tool? Just go to Google.com, click Images at the top, and then type what you're looking for. The results page will display thumbnails of any image results. Always be careful about using graphics off the web, though. It may be easy to download them from Google or swipe them from someone else's site, but many images are protected by copyright.

Using Graphics on Your Dreamweaver Pages

Once you have some graphics and have saved them in the appropriate format—here, JPEG or GIF—actually getting them onto your page is fairly easy. What you may find difficult is getting your images positioned where you want them. Thankfully, Dreamweaver has a few tricks up its sleeve to help you, as you'll soon see. But let's start with something easy: setting a graphic for your page's background.

Using a Graphic as a Page Background

Many sites on the web use either a colored or graphical background on their pages. This makes the site look a little more interesting, and also plays a part in a site's overall design and branding

Keep a high contrast between your background and your page text, to keep your page legible.

In designing your page's background, keep a few things in mind. If you're going to use a color, don't choose anything too bright. You don't want your visitor's head to explode, so choose a color that's easy on the eyes. If you decide to use a graphical background, be very cautious. Background graphics can easily render a page's text illegible—a major frustration for web surfers. Keep a high contrast between your background and your page text, and you shouldn't have a problem.

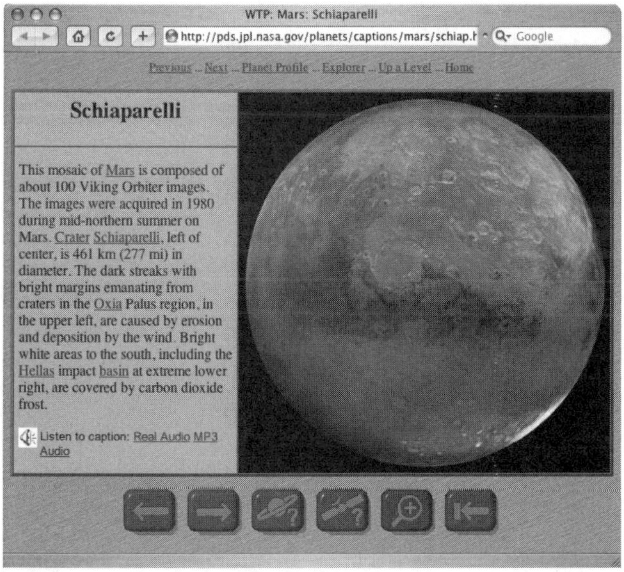

:This page uses a subtle background graphic: a brushed metal look. Even though the page may look like it has one massive image in the background, effects like this can usually be created with a single, tiny graphic.

Here's the sort of background image to avoid.

Here's how to set your page's background:

1. Choose Modify > Page Properties.

   The Page Properties dialog box appears.

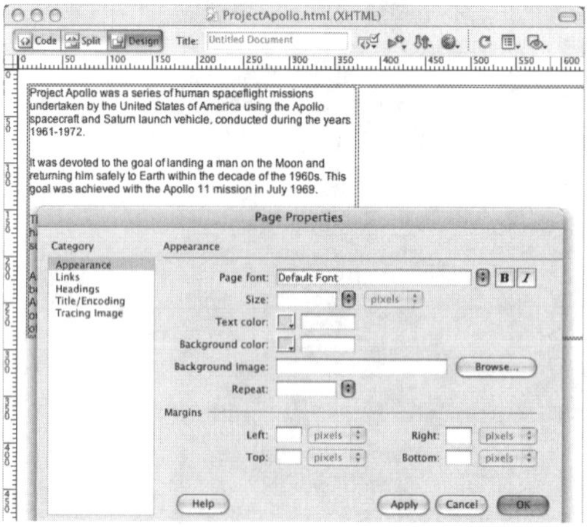

2. In the Appearance category at the left side of the dialog box set your page's background by doing one of the following:

   - To change your page's background color, click the color swatch next to Background Color. Dreamweaver's 216 web-safe color palette opens. You can select a color from this or any other color palette.

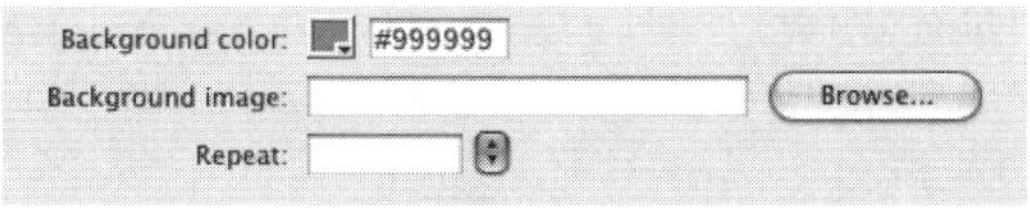

- To set a background image, click the Browse button next to the Background Image field and navigate to the image that you want to use.

3. Click OK.

   The background of your page changes to reflect your settings. If you chose to use a background image, the image appears behind your page's content and tiles horizontally and vertically. Because of this tiling behavior, many designers choose a patterned background image with no discernable edges—sorta like the patterned tiles on your kitchen floor.

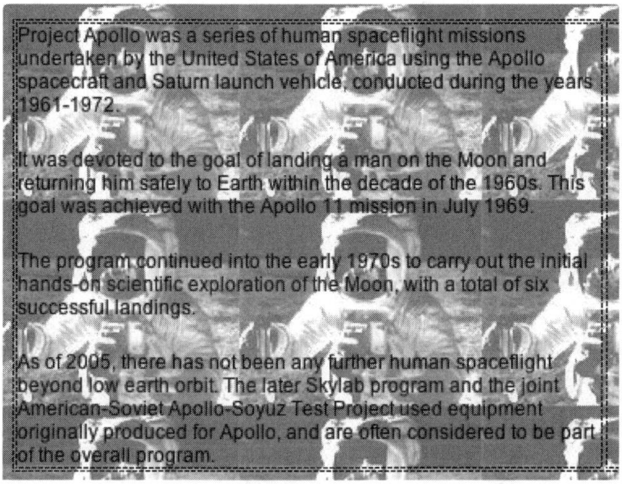

   Notice too that the CSS Styles panel (if it's set to All mode) displays a new style: body. Options set for the background are actually controlled by CSS. For more on using CSS to control your page's background, see "Controlling Your Page Background with CSS."

4. If you want to modify the background, do one of the following:

   - To choose a different background for your page, choose Modify > Page Properties to return to the Page Properties dialog box, where you can change your settings.

- To fine-tune the background and the way it works with your web pages, open the CSS Styles panel and follow the steps in "Controlling Your Page Background with CSS."

Controlling Your Page Background with CSS

Now that you have a background on your page, you may wish to make further modifications. The background for your page is always controlled by HTML's <body> tag. So when you set a background through the Page Properties dialog box, Dreamweaver creates a redefined HTML tag for you. By making changes to the rules that govern the <body> tag in CSS, you can control how the image tiles, whether the background image scrolls with the page, and a few other neat options not available in the Page Properties dialog box.

To change your page background via CSS, follow these steps:

1. Open the CSS Styles panel (Window > CSS Styles) and set the panel's mode to All.

2. In the All Rules pane at the top of the panel, double-click the body style.

3. In the CSS Rule Definition dialog box, select the Background category.

   The Background settings control graphics and color that appear behind objects on your page.

   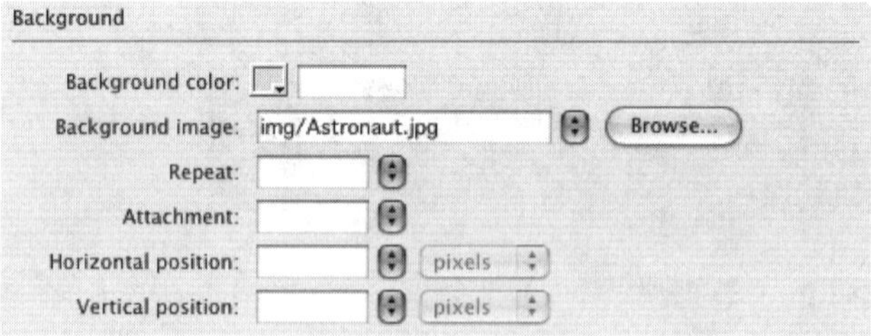

4. To change the color or image being used in the background, do one of the following:

   - Click the Background Color swatch and choose a new color.

   - Click the Browse button beside the Background Image field and navigate to the new background image.

5. If you're using a background image, you can make some additional adjustments:

- To control the tiling behavior of your background image, choose an option from the Repeat pull-down menu.

Repeat tiles the graphic as it normally does (both horizontally and vertically), Repeat-X tiles the graphic only horizontally, and Repeat-Y tiles the graphic only vertically. No Repeat disables the tiling behavior of your background graphic.

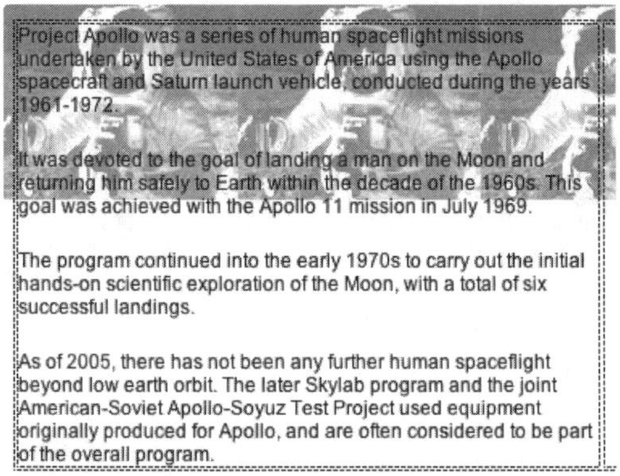

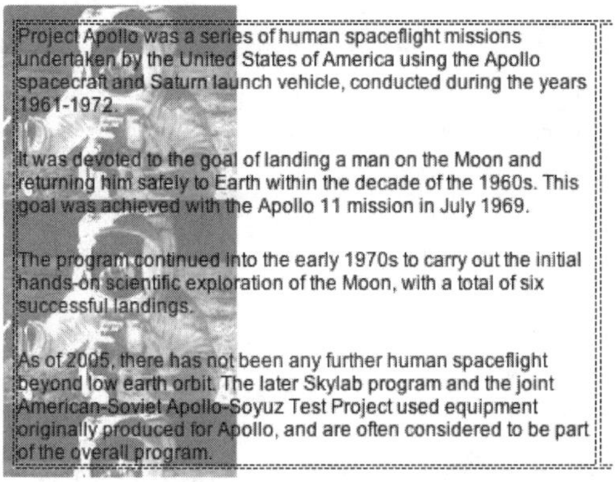

- To specify whether the background image scrolls with your page contents or remains fixed when the visitor scrolls down your page, choose an option from the Attachment menu. Note, though, that the user's browser ultimately controls how the page scrolls.

- To control the horizontal and vertical placement of your background image, choose options for Horizontal Position and Vertical Position.

You can place your image at the left, right, top, or bottom of the page, and center it vertically and horizontally. You can also enter a specific value, in pixels, to move the background image.

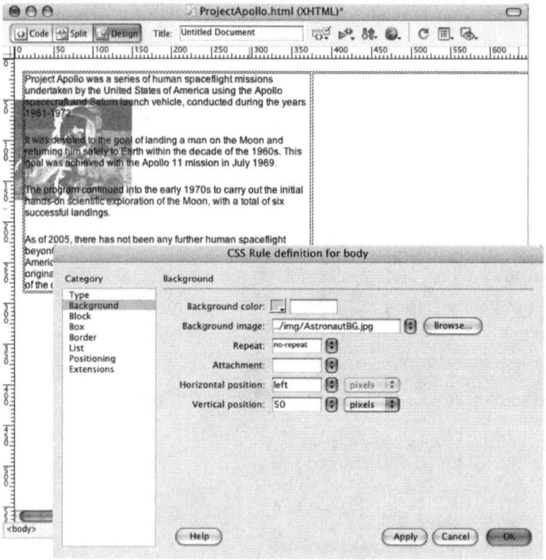

6. When you're done modifying your background, click OK.

   Your changes are applied to the background of your page.

Now let's start thinking a little grander here. In Chapter 8, you saw how to work with external style sheets. Wouldn't it be great if you could control the background of all the pages in your site from a single style? Well, you can! In your external style sheet, create a new rule for the <body> tag; then set the appropriate options in the Background category, just as we did here. Once that's done, link all your pages to the external style sheet, and you're ready to go.

Also, you can specify a background for just a single style rather than for the entire page. For example, you can set a yellow background behind all of the Heading 1 elements on your page. If you've already set a background color for your page, both the style's background and the page background will appear. If you have some CSS styles kicking around from Chapter 8, try setting options in their Background category. This will result in a background appearing behind only the space that the style occupies on the page. CSS's parlor tricks are endless!

Placing Images on Your Page

Before placing images on your page, make sure that all your graphics have been copied to your site folder.

Now you're ready to insert images on your page. Before you begin, make sure that all the graphics that you want to use have been copied to your site folder; otherwise, you'll have serious problems when you go to upload your pages to your remote site. We'll talk about possible problems that may arise in a bit, but first, let's get droppin' graphics onto your page.

Here's how to insert an image on your page:

1. Click where you want to insert an image.

2. Choose Insert > Image.

You can also use the Insert bar (choose Window > Insert) to place images on your page. In the Common category of the Insert bar, click the Images button.

3. In the Select Image Source dialog box that appears, navigate to the image that you want to insert, select it, and click OK (Windows) or Choose (Mac).

If you're inserting an image on a new, blank page that has not yet been saved, Dreamweaver displays a warning indicating that a file:// path will be used until you save. Once your page is saved, the file:// path is replaced with something called a relative path.

Just like external style sheets, images are referenced files, meaning that Dreamweaver creates a path between a page and an image file when you insert a graphic. If you haven't saved your page yet, Dreamweaver can't create a path. We'll talk more about file paths in the next section.

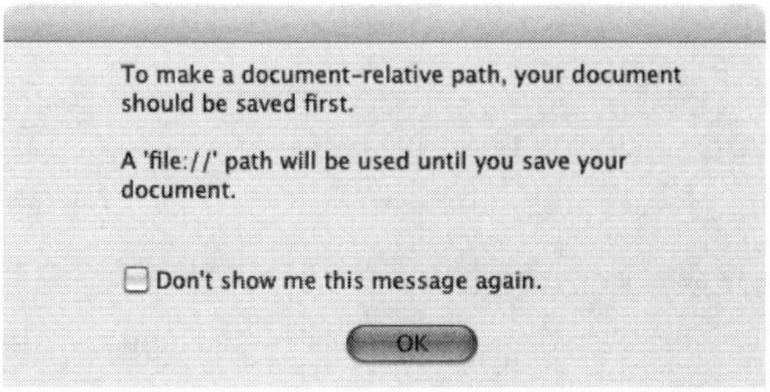

If you try to insert a graphic that isn't saved in your site's local folder, Dreamweaver displays a dialog box warning you that this could cause problems. This dialog box also offers to copy the image into your site's folder for you. Make sure to choose Yes.

It's always a good idea to save your page before inserting graphics to avoid any potential problems.

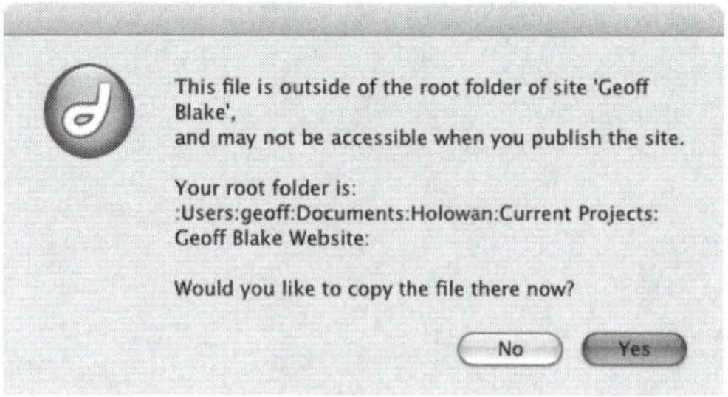

IMMINENT DOOM

Choosing No when Dreamweaver offers to copy an outside image to your site's local folder could be disastrous. Your page may look fine on your computer, but the image will not transfer when you upload your site to the web. This means that your graphic will be missing when surfers visit your site. To avoid this problem, always copy all your graphics into your site's local folder before inserting them on your page (see Chapter 4 for details).

4. The Image Tag Accessibility Attributes dialog box appears. Enter any accessibility information you want; then click OK.

   The image appears on your page where you originally placed your insertion point.

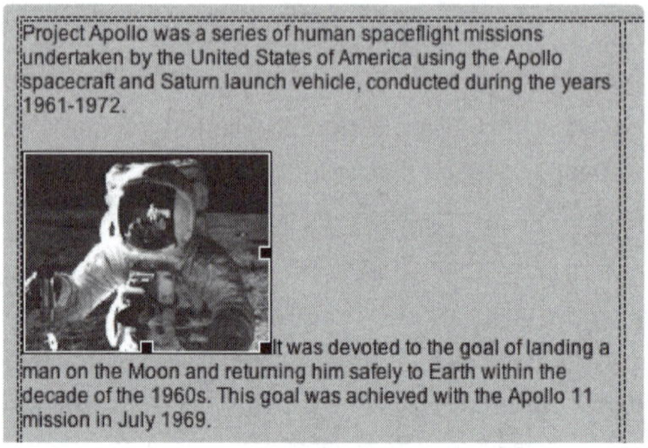

   Now, depending on the size of the image and where you placed your insertion point, your image may not appear as expected. We'll talk about how to adjust your image's placement shortly.

UNDERSTANDING THE IMAGE SOURCE

When you insert a graphic into your web page, the graphic is not embedded in your page. Instead, Dreamweaver creates a reference to the source graphic file.

Always remember that when you insert a graphic, the graphic is not embedded in your page. Instead, Dreamweaver creates a reference to the source graphic file. This is fundamental. If you make a change to the original image source file (the one sitting in your site's local folder), the graphic will be updated automatically on any page where it's used, because those pages are simply referencing the source file. This is similar to the way Cascading Style Sheets works.

If you change the name of your graphic in Dreamweaver's File panel, a dialog box will appear asking you to update all the references to the graphic. Click Update, and Dreamweaver will handle all your image references for you.

INSERTING GRAPHICS FROM THE ASSETS PANEL

As you've seen in previous chapters, Dreamweaver's Assets panel is one handy fella. And it's back here again to help you with your graphics. The Assets panel lists any images that you've saved in your local site folder and offers to place them on your page for you. Not only will this help keep consistency throughout your web pages, but it makes working with graphics in Dreamweaver a breeze.

And here's something else the Assets panel will do for you: I don't know about you, but I have an awful time remembering the differences between my graphics files. I can't remember what the heck the difference is between LunarOrbit02A.jpg and LunarOrbit02B.jpg, for example. Thankfully, when you select a graphic in the Assets panel, Dreamweaver displays a preview so you can see the image before you insert it on your page. This makes finding the graphic you're after super-easy.

Double-clicking a graphic in the Assets panel opens the image in your external graphics editor.

Follow these steps to insert a graphic from the Assets panel:

1. Click your page where you want to insert your graphic.

2. In the Assets panel, click the Images Category button on the left.

   The Images category appears, listing all the images that are saved in your site's local folder.

3. In the list of images in the bottom half of the panel, select the image that you want to insert.

   A preview of the image appears in the top pane of the Assets panel, helping you find the right image.

4. At the bottom of the Assets panel, click the Insert button, or drag the image from the panel to your page and drop it where you want it.

5. The Image Tag Accessibility Attributes dialog box appears. Enter in any accessibility information you want and then click OK.

   The image appears on your page.

IMMINENT DOOM

If you change a graphic's name in the Files panel and don't click Update, the path between the web page and your graphic will be broken—meaning that your image will not appear on your page.

Be careful if you monkey with any of your site files outside of Dreamweaver. If you were to quit Dreamweaver and then open your site folder on your hard drive and change file names, move files around, or delete files, then the next time you launch Dreamweaver, all the links to your graphics would be lost.

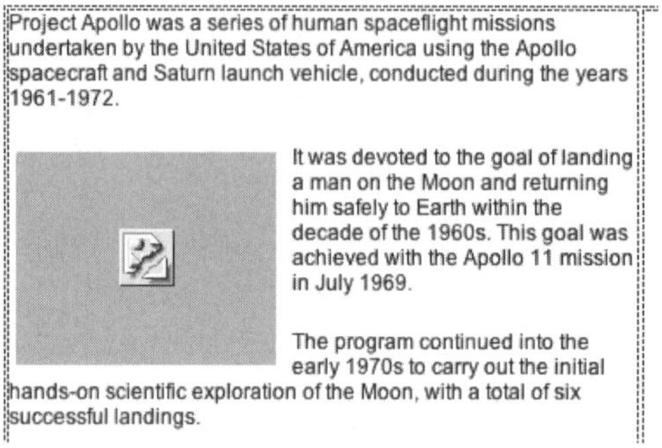

If you rename or move a graphic outside of Dreamweaver, the connection between your web page and the image will be broken. To avoid seeing the missing image icon, keep a clean nose and use the Files panel in Dreamweaver to move and rename your images.

So be careful with your graphic references. If you need to rename or delete graphics in your site, make sure to do it through the Files panel, so Dreamweaver can help you manage all references to your graphics.

Because the images in your web pages are really just references, you can also easily swap one graphic for another, replacing the old graphic with a new one.

GEEK'S DELIGHT

By default, Dreamweaver creates a link to an image like this: img/Astronaut.jpg. But rather than using that type of path, you could type something like this in the Property Inspector's Src field: http://www.tentonbooks.com/img/test.jpg. This would link you directly to an image file, even if it's being used in another web site. This is called hot linking. It's okay to do this with your own sites, but it's a no-no to hot link to other people's images because it eats up their site's bandwidth.

Here's how to replace a graphic:

1. On your web page, double-click the graphic that you want to replace.

   You can also select the graphic on your page and then, in the Property Inspector, click the folder beside the Src field.

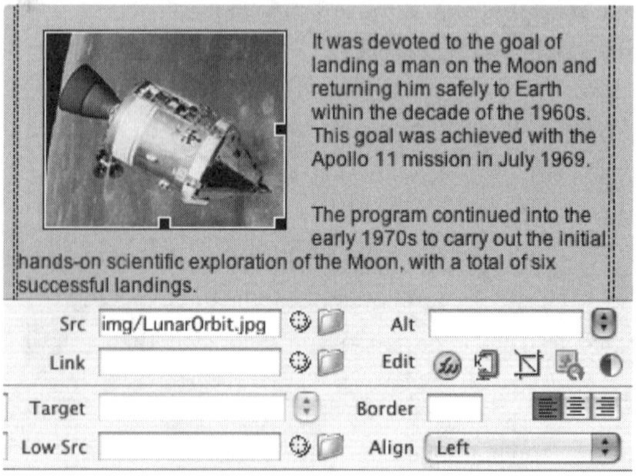

2. In the Select Image Source dialog box that opens, navigate to the new image that you want; then click OK (Windows) or Select (Mac).

   The old image is replaced with the new image.

Finally, because all graphics are referenced, all your images—every last one of them—will have to be uploaded when you publish your site to the web. Remember back in Chapter 4, you saw that Dreamweaver will upload your entire site in one shot for you, so you don't have to upload your files one at a time. But make sure to double-check that everything uploads. If you miss a graphic, it won't be displayed on your site. Instead, your site's visitors will see an empty image placeholder, which looks ***really*** amateurish.

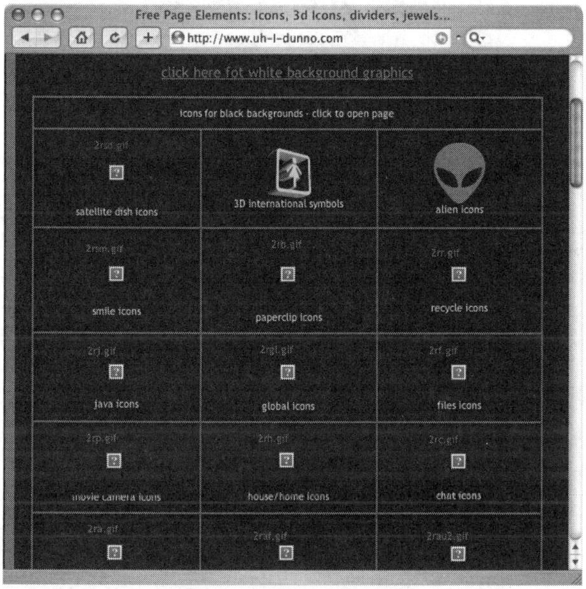

A missing graphic on a live web page is a major design faux pas. It's really important to upload all your graphics to your remote site and test every page in your site to make sure that all your images are loading correctly.

Controlling Images on Your Page

Now that you have a graphic or two on your page, you'll probably want to make some adjustments—things like the alignment of your image, its size, and so on.

Whenever a graphic is selected on your page, the Property Inspector displays settings you can use to adjust the image. This makes manipulating your images easy; however, just as for text, you can also use CSS to control your images.

CSS offers more precise settings to control your images than does the Property Inspector. To see how to use CSS to control your images, see "Using CSS to Control Your Images" later in this chapter.

Setting Basic Image Properties in Dreamweaver

You'll start with the simple approach to controlling your images: the Property Inspector. Before starting, make sure to expand the Property Inspector by clicking the expand/collapse arrow (in the bottom-right corner of the Property Inspector) so that you can see all the available image settings.

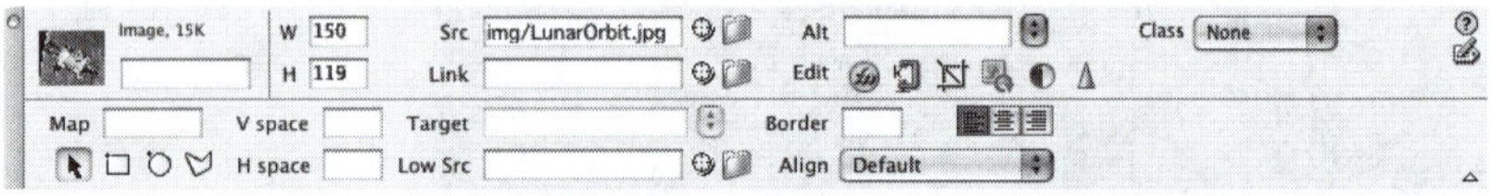

Behold the Property Inspector, complete with image editing options. When you select an image, these settings appear in the Property Inspector, as will a thumbnail of your graphic, in the top-left corner. Other commands of interest include the image map tools just below the image thumbnail and the editing tools.

Here's how to adjust the properties for your image:

1. Click the graphic on your page to select it.

   Image-related settings appear in the Property Inspector.

2. To put a frame around your image, set a pixel value in the Property Inspector's Border field.

   As soon as you type a value in the field and press Enter (Windows) or Return (Mac), a frame appears around your image. If you want to remove the frame, type **0**.

3. To adjust the horizontal position of your image, use the Left, Center, and Right options.

   These alignment settings work best if your graphic is sitting on a line by itself, without any text beside it. If there is text on the same line, the graphic and the text will take on the same alignment setting. In the figure, the image has been centered between the page margins.

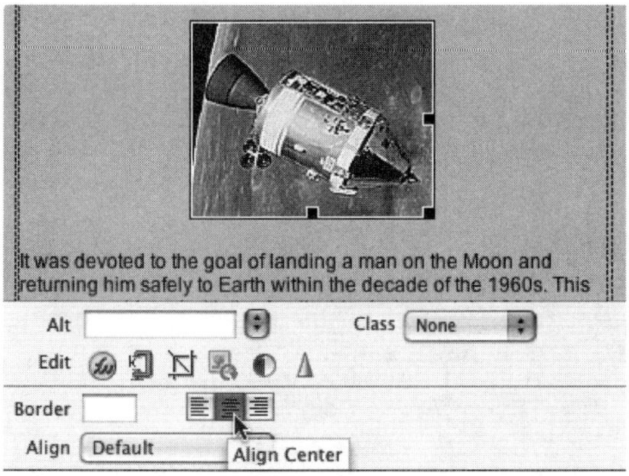

4. To control the vertical alignment of your image, choose a setting from the Align menu.

   The vertical alignment is the position of the graphic in relation to text that sits on the same line. Here are the options:

   Baseline: Aligns the image's bottom to the baseline of the text. The baseline is the imaginary line that the text sits on.

   Top: Aligns the image's top to the top of the text or to the top of another graphic.

   Middle: Aligns the image's middle to the text's baseline.

   Bottom: Strangely enough, Bottom is the same as Baseline, which aligns the bottom of the image to the bottom of the text. Why have two commands that do the same thing? I'm wondering the same thing.

   Text Top: Aligns the top of the image to the top of the text.

   Absolute Middle: Aligns the image to the text's vertical center (as opposed to its baseline, as with Middle).

   Absolute Bottom: Aligns the image to the bottommost text element, which includes descenders (the parts of letters that fall below the baseline, such as the tail on a lowercase *p* or *y*).

   Left: Moves the image to the left, allowing text to flow around its right side.

Right: Moves the image to the right, allowing text to flow around its left side.

I stick with Left most of the time.

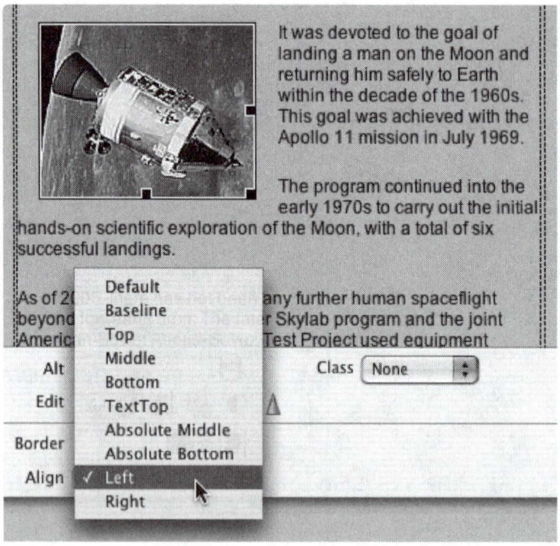

NOTEWORTHY

You can use the Property Inspector's Low Src field to set a lower-quality image to load in the visitor's browser while a higher-quality image is downloading. For instance, you might use a black-and-white version of your image, with a lower resolution to appear as a preview until the high-quality image is fully loaded. Personally, I've never bothered with this because it causes an unnecessary download. If you do a good job of optimizing your images in the first place, they should download quickly enough.

Using CSS to Control Your Images

You may have noticed that the image settings in the Property Inspector are quite limited. But once again, CSS rides to the rescue. CSS saved the day with text formatting, and it's a hero again with graphics. Using CSS with graphics gives you superior control over your images and their placement on your page.

CSS gives you superior control over your images and their placement on your page.

Before starting, make sure that you have the CSS Styles panel open (choose Window > CSS Styles) and that it's set to All mode. Also, remove any settings in the Property Inspector that had been previously set to control your image. This will ensure that it'll be nothin' but pure CSS controlling your graphic. To use CSS to control your images, you're going to create a new style specifically for this purpose.

To use CSS to control your graphics, follow these steps:

1. At the bottom of the CSS Styles panel, click the New CSS Rule button.

2. In the New CSS Rule dialog box that appears, set Selector Type to Class and enter a name for your new style in Name field.

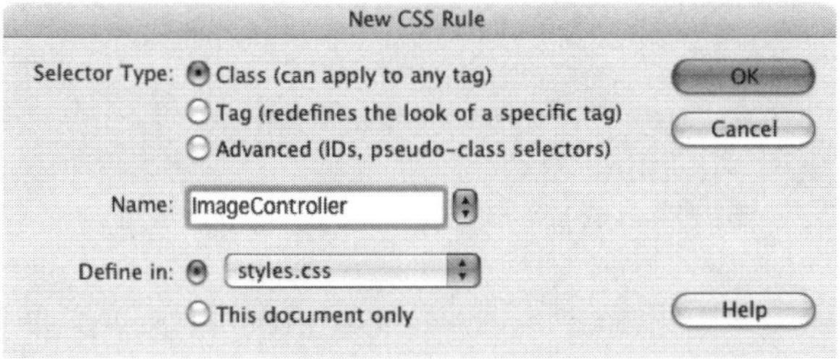

3. In the Define In field, specify where your new style should be saved; then click OK.

   You saw how this works in Chapter 8. You can save your new style in either an external style sheet (select the top option and enter a location) or in an embedded style sheet (select This Document Only).

4. In the CSS Rule Definition dialog box that appears, click OK.

   It may seem odd to click OK without setting any options, but stick with me here. The easiest way to work with CSS and images is to apply your new style to an image first and then go back and add your settings. That way, you can see their effects as you work.

5. Back on your page, click your graphic to select it.

6. From the Class pull-down menu in the Property Inspector, select your new style.

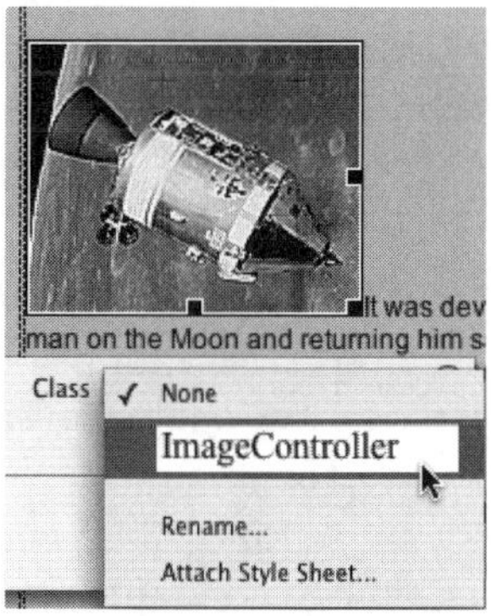

   This attaches your new CSS style to your image—the image is now being controlled with CSS. This is just like applying a style to text, only this time you're applying a style to a graphic.

7. In the top pane of the CSS Styles panel, double-click your CSS style.

   Dreamweaver returns you to the CSS Rule Definition dialog box.

8. In the CSS Rule Definition dialog box, click the Box category on the left.

   The Box category contains the settings to control the position of your graphic on the page and the amount of space around it.

9. To set your graphic's position, choose an option from the Float menu; then click Apply at the bottom of the dialog box to preview your results.

   Setting the Float menu to Left allows text to flow around the graphic's right side. Setting the menu to Right allows text to flow around its left side.

   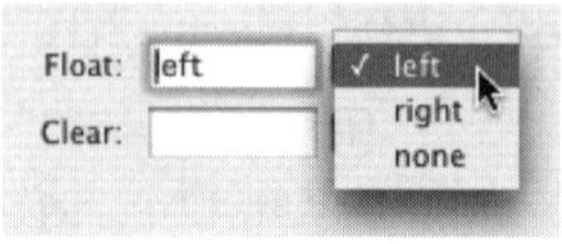

   When you click Apply, your graphic moves to the right or left, and any text on your page wraps around your graphic. This is similar to choosing Left or Right from the Align menu in the Property Inspector, except now you're controlling your graphic's alignment via CSS.

10. To insert space between your image and the text on your page, insert values in the Margin fields.

    You can use the same value for the margin on all four sides of your image by checking Same for All, or you can set a value for each side. Click Apply to see the Margin settings applied to your image.

11. To apply a frame around your image, select the Border category in CSS Rule Definition dialog box and use the pull-down menus to set the frame's style, width, and color. Click Apply to preview the Border effect in your page.

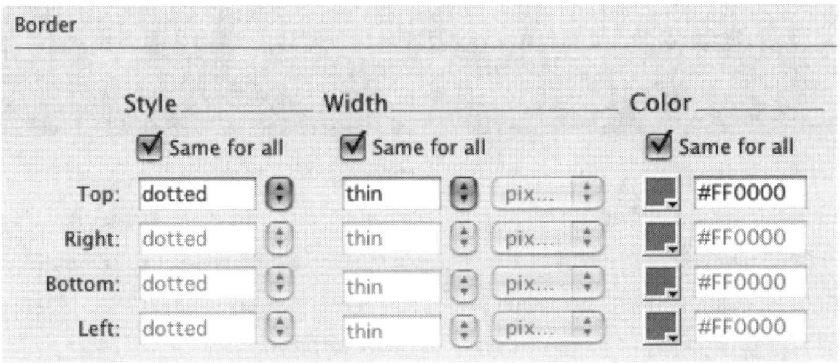

12. To insert some space between your graphic and its border, return to the Box category and insert a value for Padding.

    Just as with the Box category's Margin setting, you can specify the same value for all four sides or set individual values.

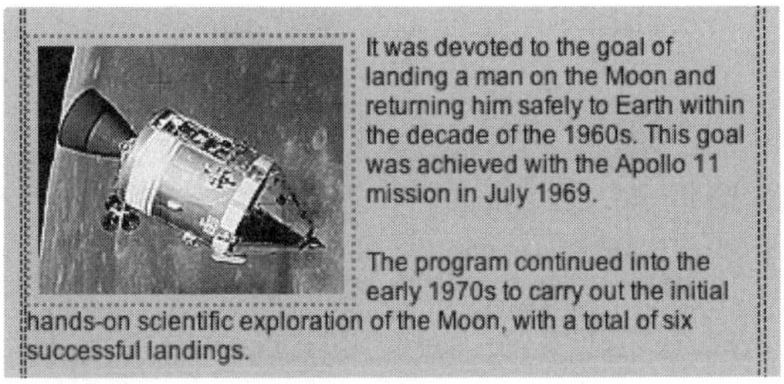

13. When you're happy with the placement of your graphic, click OK to close the CSS Style Definition dialog box.

    If you need to do a little more tweaking to get your graphic just as you want it, no problem. Just double-click your style in the CSS Styles panel again and continue fiddling with your settings until the image is placed exactly where you want it.

Now imagine defining a few CSS styles to control the various positions of images on your page, but saving them in an external style sheet. You could then control all the images on all the pages in your web site from just a few styles. How's that for mega-control over your graphics?

USING A TRANSPARENT GIF FILE TO ALIGN AND SPACE OUT OBJECTS

Are you finding it tough to control the placement of your text, graphics, and other page elements? Cascading Style Sheets help a lot, but the problem with CSS is that not all browsers support it. If this is a concern, you may want to consider an alternative to help you control your page content—namely, using a transparent GIF file to help align and space out objects on your page.

Here's how to insert a transparent GIF file to help space out graphics and other objects on your page:

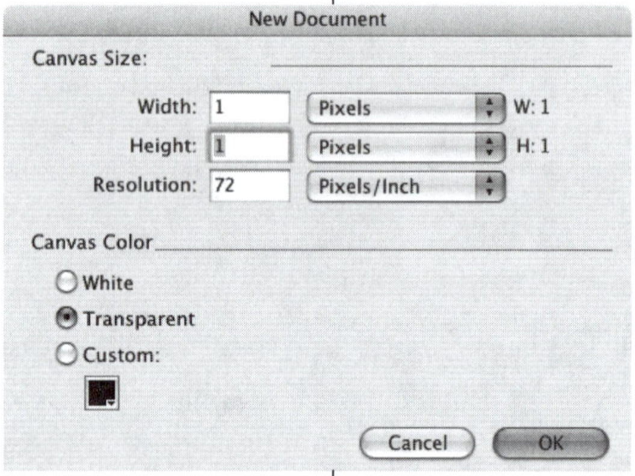

1. Using your graphics program, create a new 1x1-pixel image.

   When you create your new graphic, make sure to set your new image's background (sometimes referred to as the canvas) so that it is transparent.

2. Save your image as a GIF file in your site's local folder. Name it ***Spacer.gif*** or ***Transparent.gif*** (or something like that) to help you remember that it will be used to space out objects on your page.

3. Head back to Dreamweaver and insert your transparent GIF file into your page wherever you're having spacing problems.

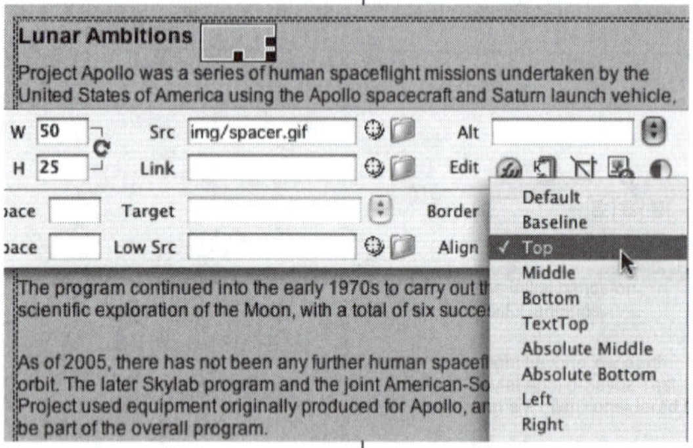

For example, you can use your GIF file to control the space between paragraphs by inserting it after the last word in each paragraph. Or if you want some space between an image and some text, insert it between the two.

4. Use the Property Inspector's Width and Height settings, as well as any other options in the Property Inspector, to control the size and alignment of your GIF file.

Changing the size of your GIF file will force your page objects to move, helping you control their position. Don't worry about distorting your transparent GIF file—there's nothing to distort, because it's transparent!

Resizing Images Inside Dreamweaver

When you insert a graphic into your page, you may find that the image appears larger or smaller than you want. In these situations, you can always resize your image so that it fits into the space that you want it to occupy.

You can resize your image in Dreamweaver, but you should do so cautiously. The problem with resizing in Dreamweaver is that it's very easy to accidentally distort your image—to end up with what I call the "carnival fun-house mirror effect." As an alternative, consider resizing your image in your external graphics editing software. If you have Fireworks, for instance, all you have to do is click the image and then click the Fireworks logo that appears in the Properties Inspector. This brings up Fireworks and allows you to edit the image and then return to (and automatically refresh) Dreamweaver—a very easy and clean way to do this and other image editing tasks, and you'll also be able to control the quality of your image. For more on resizing your graphic with your image editor, see the sidebar "Geoff's Method for Resizing Images" later in this chapter. For now, let's look at how to resize in Dreamweaver.

You can resize your image in Dreamweaver, but you should do so cautiously because it's very easy to accidentally distort your image

IMMINENT DOOM

Always keep a backup copy of all your original graphics. If you goof up, you can always revert to the original graphic and start again. Otherwise, once you make a change to your image, it's changed for good.

To resize your graphic in Dreamweaver, follow these steps:

1. On your page, select the image that you want to resize.

   When you select an image in Dreamweaver, the Property Inspector displays the graphic's width and height in pixels. You'll also notice that resize handles appear on the right and bottom and in the bottom-right corner of the image.

2. Using the image's resize handles, drag to make the image larger or smaller.

   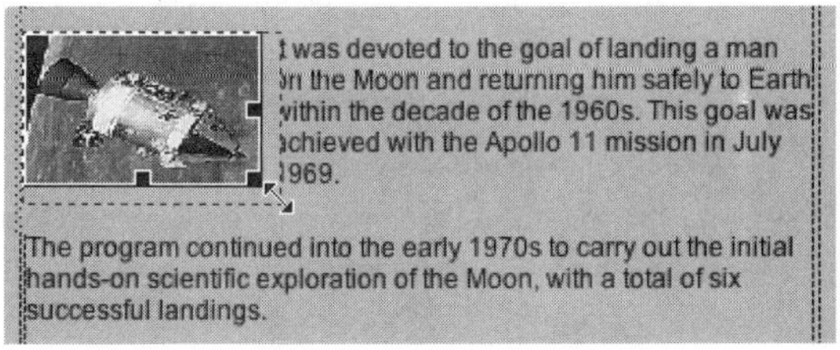

   Your image resizes on your page. To avoid distorting your image, hold down the Shift key as you drag the bottom-right resize handle. This scales your image's width and height proportionally.

   Rather than visually sizing your image, you can enter values in the Width and Height fields in the Property Inspector, although it's pretty tough to know what values to enter without causing image distortion. The values that you type in the Property Inspector are measured in pixels. However, you can also type your values using pc (picas), pt (points), in (inches), mm (millimeters), or cm (centimeters). Dreamweaver will convert values typed in any of these measurements back to pixels

NOTEWORTHY

Changing the size of your image onscreen does not change the image's file size or have an impact on download time. For example, if you make your image smaller on your page, only its appearance changes. The image's file size (and therefore its download time) are unaffected. To reduce an image's file size, you have to resize the source image in an external image editing program and then reload it into Dreamweaver.

3. If you want to reset the image to its original size, click the Reset Image to Original Size button to the right of the Width and Height fields.

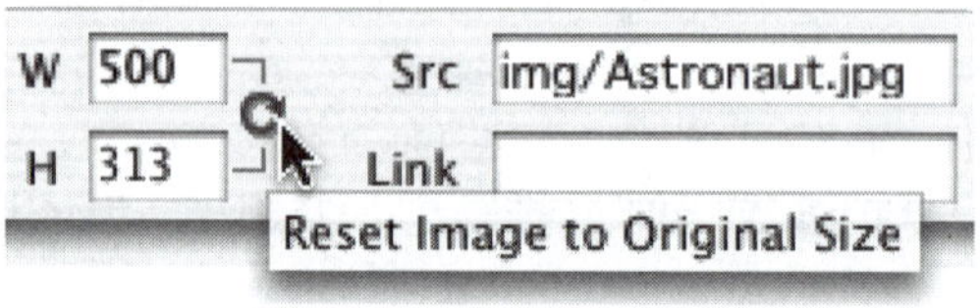

The image is restored to it's original width and height—assuming that you haven't clicked the Resample button.

4. If you're happy with the image's appearance and want to permanently change the image, click the Resample button in the Property Inspector.

Be very careful here. Once you click Resample, that's it; your image's source file is permanently changed.

Personally, I'd much rather manually control the image using my external graphics editor, so I avoid using Resample in Dreamweaver.

5. Dreamweaver warns you that you're permanently changing your image. Click OK to continue.

Resample adds or removes pixels to clean up some of the distortion caused by resizing an image in Dreamweaver. This helps give the image a sharper appearance.

Bear in mind that once you've used the Resample button, you cannot reset the image to its original width and height. This is because Resample permanently changes the size of your original image file sitting in your site folder. Therefore, the image will change on any other pages where it's being used, too. Deadly.

Dreamweaver's Built-in Image Editing Commands

Dreamweaver has a few built-in image editing commands in addition to the resize options. From within Dreamweaver, you can crop, sharpen, and manipulate the color in your images. These tools are great for quick, on-the-fly image editing, but the commands are limited.

*Dreamweaver's **built-in image editing tools** are great for quick, on-the-fly editing, but the commands are **limited.***

Further, when you use Dreamweaver's built-in editing tools, you're permanently changing your original graphic file. A better approach is to use an external graphics program to handle all your image editing. However, if you don't have any image editing software installed on your computer, you won't have much choice—but at least you'll be able to make changes to your images with Dreamweaver's tools.

Here's how to use Dreamweaver to manipulate your images:

1. Select the image on your page that you want to edit.

   The Property Inspector displays all the available image-related settings.

2. To crop your image—that is, to trim away any unwanted areas—do the following:

   a. Click the Crop button in the Property Inspector.

   b. Dreamweaver warns you that you're about to permanently change your original image's source file. Click OK to proceed.

   c. Drag the crop handles that appear around your image to size the crop frame to indicate what areas to keep and which to cut away.

IMAGE EDITING TOOLS IN THE PROPERTY INSPECTOR

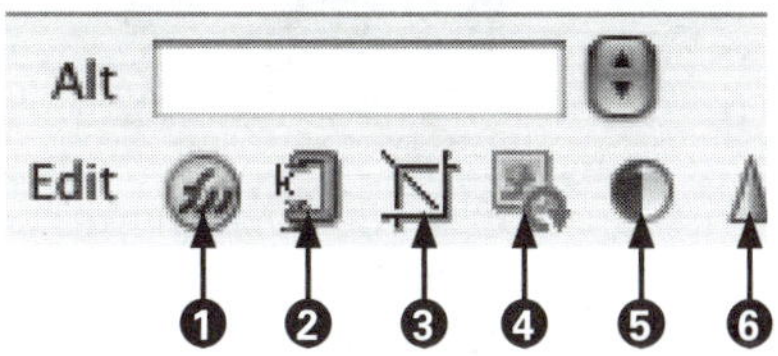

(1) Edit in External Image Editor **(2)** Optimize in Fireworks **(3)** Crop **(4)** Resample Image **(5)** Brightness and Contrast **(6)** Sharpen

You can undo your crop if you're not happy with your results. Just choose Edit > Undo.

d. Press Enter (Windows) or Return (Mac) to apply the crop. Any areas outside of the crop frame are removed.

3. To adjust the color in your image, do the following:

   a. Click the Brightness and Contrast button in the Property Inspector.

   b. When Dreamweaver warns you that you'll be making permanent changes to your image, click OK.

   c. In the Brightness/Contrast dialog box that appears, use the sliders to adjust your image.

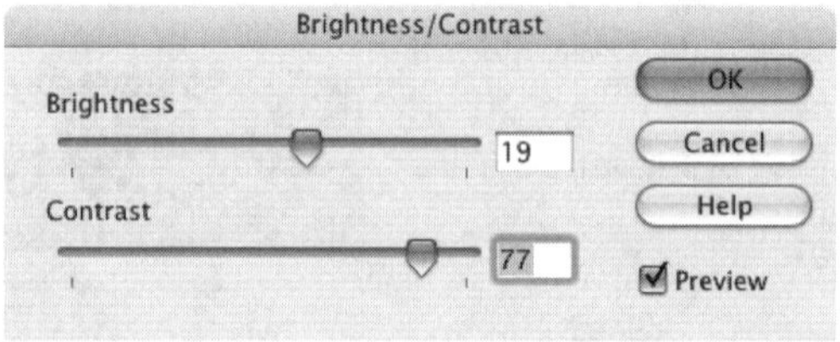

   d. When you're happy with the way that your image looks, click OK. The settings are applied to your image.

4. To make your image sharper, do the following:

   a. Click the Sharpen button in the Property Inspector.

   b. Dreamweaver warns you that you'll be making permanent changes to your image. Click OK to continue.

   c. In the Sharpen dialog box that appears, drag the slider to adjust the amount of sharpening. As you drag, you'll notice that the amount of contrast around the edges of objects in your image increases or decreases. Be careful, though. Oversharpening makes your image look pixilated and of lower quality.

   d. Click OK when you're done. Dreamweaver applies the sharpening to your graphic.

Editing Graphics Outside Dreamweaver

An external image editor is a much better tool than Dreamweaver for manipulating your graphics. After all, Dreamweaver is a web design program, not an image editor. An external image editor will give you a much wider range of commands. For example, you'll be able to manipulate color in more ways, insert text, apply special effects filters, and do pretty much anything else your creative mind can cook up.

To make your work easier, it's a good idea to set up your graphics program of choice as your default image editor in Dreamweaver. Macromedia Fireworks is already set up as the default editor, but you can set another image editor if you prefer.

Here's how to set up the default external editor in Dreamweaver:

1. Choose Edit > Preferences (Windows) or Dreamweaver > Preferences (Mac).

2. In the category list on the left, select File Types/Editors.

   You'll start by setting the default external editor for JPEG images.

3. In the Extensions list in the File Types/Editors pane, select .jpg .jpe .jpeg.

4. Above the Editors list on the right, click the Plus button.

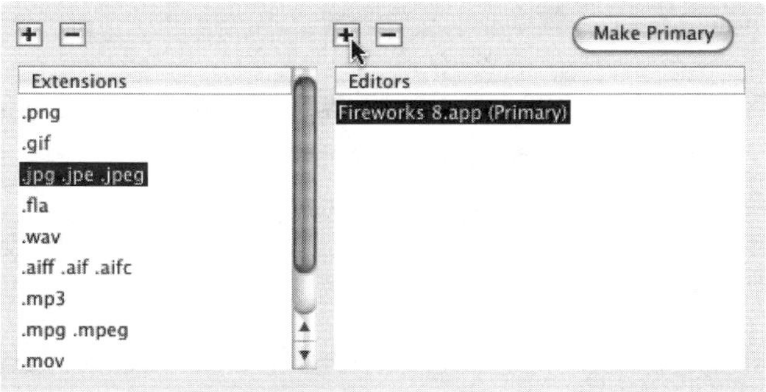

5. In the Select External Editor dialog box that appears, navigate to the graphics program that you want to set as your new JPEG editor. In Windows, select the program by clicking its .exe file. On the Mac, select the program file itself. Then click Open.

6. To set your external editor as the primary JPEG image editor, click the Make Primary button.

7. You'll most likely want to use the same external editor for GIF and PNG files as well, so repeat these steps to set your image editor as the primary editor for those file types, too.

8. Click OK to close Dreamweaver's preferences.

Now that you've set a new external image editor, you can easily use it as you're building your pages and inserting images.

A faster way to launch your external editor from Dreamweaver is to hold down Ctrl (Windows) or Command (Mac) and double-click your graphic.

Here's how to launch your external image editor from Dreamweaver.

1. Select the image on your page that you want to edit.

2. In the Property Inspector, click the Edit button.

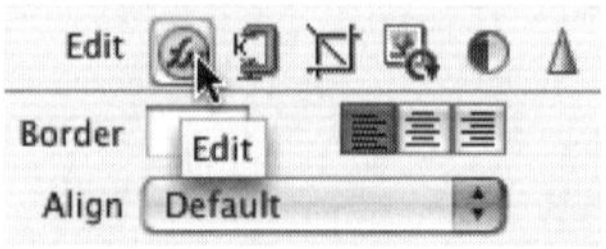

   Your external editor launches and opens the graphic for editing. Here's where the really powerful stuff starts happening.

3. Make any changes to your image that you want.

   You can use any tools that your image editor possesses—filters, color effects, text, and so on. Just remember to keep your image's resolution at 72 DPI. Other than that, go wild!

4. Save your file, and go back to Dreamweaver.

   The image instantly updates on your page. How did it do that? Remember that your image is a referenced file. You changed the original source file, so the image not only changed on your current page, but it was updated on any other pages that use it, too.

SPACE RACIN' WITH FAVICONS

You may have noticed while browsing the web that many sites have a unique icon appearing beside the URL in the browser's Address field. This is a favicon (short for Favorites icon), and they're all the rage on the web these days.

Here's a favicon in action, for geoffblake.com.

A favicon is a great way to help brand your site, because your icon will not only show up in your visitor's browser's Address field, but it will also appear in the visitor's Bookmarks or Favorites menu and toolbar.

Are you interested in creating your own favicon image and adding it to your site? It's really easy—just follow these steps:

1. In your graphics program, create a new 16x16-pixel image. Within this image, use all your creative might to create an icon to use as your favicon.

   Keep your favicon simple: 16x16 pixels isn't a whole lot of space to design in, so try not to create something with too much detail—a silhouette of your company's logo, perhaps.

2. Save your graphic in your local site's root folder as a JPEG, GIF, or PNG file and make sure to name it favicon—otherwise, it won't work.

   Back in Dreamweaver, you'll have to insert some HTML code by hand—gasp! Don't worry, it's actually very easy. Just follow these steps and remember to breathe.

3. In Dreamweaver, switch to Code view by clicking the Show Code View button on the Document toolbar.

4. In your page code, click just before your page's </head> tag and enter the following code:

```
<link rel="shortcut icon" href="http://www.url.com/favicon.gif"/>

<link rel="icon" href="http://www.url.com/favicon.gif"/>
```

To find out more about favicons, check out favicon.com.

> **NOTEWORTHY**
>
> Unfortunately, Internet Explorer for the Mac does not support favicons. Other popular browsers on both Windows and Mac support 'em just fine.

SPACE RACIN' WITH FAVICONS (CONTINUED)

```
<!DOCTYPE html PUBLIC "-//W3C//DTD XHTML 1.0 Transitional//EN"
"http://www.w3.org/TR/xhtml1/DTD/xhtml1-transitional.dtd">
<html xmlns="http://www.w3.org/1999/xhtml">
<head>
<link rel="shortcut icon" href="http://www.geoffblake.com/favicon.gif" />
<link rel="icon" href="http://www.geoffblake.com/favicon.gif" />
<meta http-equiv="Content-Type" content="text/html; charset=ISO-8859-1" />
<title>Untitled Document</title>
</head>
```

Make sure that you replace www.url.com with your site's URL.

5. Save your page.

   Now the unfortunate part is that any page that you want to use your favicon on has to have this code, so you may spend the rest of the afternoon copying and pasting this code into all the pages in your site.

6. Once the code has been inserted into all the pages in your site, upload your pages and your favicon graphic to your remote site.

Your favicon will now appear in the web browser's Address field, and in the Favorites or Bookmarks menu when someone bookmarks your site. Now that's high orbit!

GEOFF'S METHOD FOR RESIZING IMAGES

Resizing images can be tricky business. As you saw earlier, it's really easy to accidentally distort images if you're sizing them in Dreamweaver, so most designers usually develop their own approach to resizing images in their external graphics program.

Here is the approach that I use when I'm resizing graphics for my web pages. You certainly don't have to do it my way, but if you're a newbie, this will at least get you started.

Here's my technique for resizing images:

1. In Dreamweaver, manually size the image to occupy the space that you want it to fill.

You can either manually drag the image's resize handles or enter values in the Width and Height fields in the Property Inspector. At this point, don't be concerned about image quality, even though you're getting that carnival fun-house mirror effect.

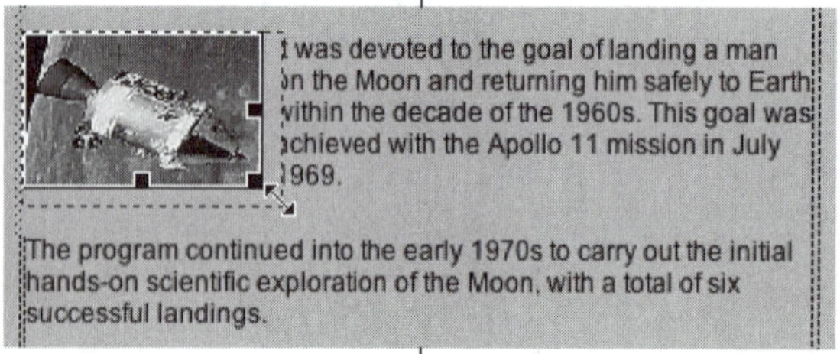

GEOFF'S METHOD FOR RESIZING ... (CONTINUED)

All you're after at this point are the pixel dimensions that you want the image to have on the screen.

2. Once your image is sized, note the image's Width and Height settings in the Property Inspector.

   Now you know what size your image needs to be, and you're ready to edit the image in your external editor.

3. Click the Edit button in the Property Inspector to launch your image editor.

4. In your image editor, create a new, blank document set to the size you noted back in step 2. Also, make sure that your new image's resolution is set to 72 DPI.

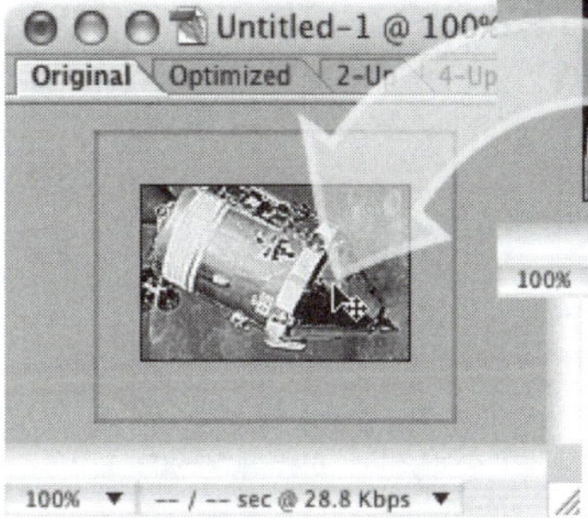

5. Using your program's arrow tool (called the Pointer tool in Fireworks and the Move tool in Photoshop and ImageReady), drag your original graphic into your new image window.

6. Close your original graphic.

7. Within the new image window, scale and move your image until it's set the way you want.

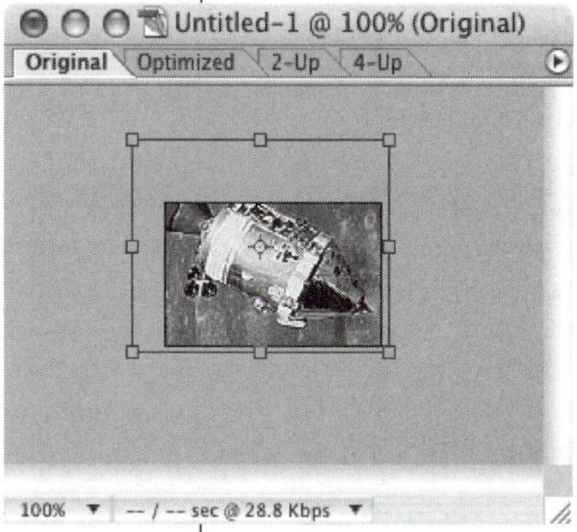

   Most graphics programs offer a way to do this. Photoshop and ImageReady both have a tool called Free Transform (Edit > Free Transform). If you're using Fireworks, just drag the corners of the blue frame that appears around your graphic. To scale your image proportionally, hold down Shift as you drag from the image's corner.

8. Once your image is correctly sized, choose File > Save As.

   What you'll be doing here is overwriting your original graphic with your new graphic. Before replacing your file, it's always a good idea to make a backup copy, just in case you goof.

GEOFF'S METHOD FOR RESIZING ... (CONTINUED)

9. Be sure you've made a backup copy of your original graphics file. Then navigate to your site's local folder, select your old graphic file, and then click Save.

   Clicking your old graphic file ensures that it will be overwritten. Just make sure that you're overwriting it with the same file format (JPEG, GIF, or PNG). Overwriting your original graphic not only toasts the old graphic. but it also means that your new graphic will now appear in Dreamweaver.

10. Head back to Dreamweaver.

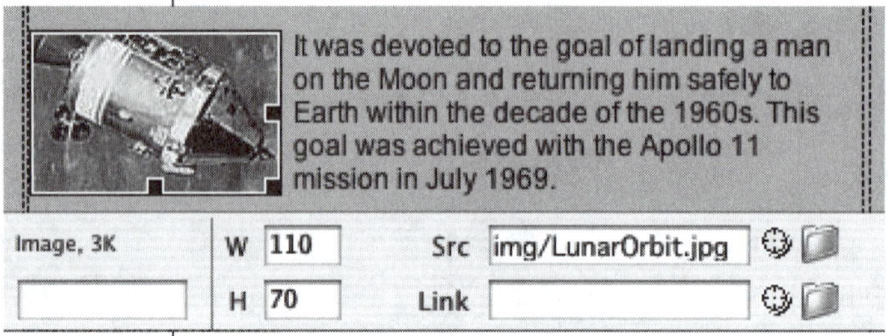

   Your updated graphic will now appear.

11. If you're not happy with your graphic, go back to your graphics program and make additional changes.

Often, I'll spend lots of time tweaking and refining my site images in this way, going back and forth between my graphics program and Dreamweaver—and, of course, my web browser—to see how my images will appear on the web.

Now there's a heck of a lot more than this to resizing images and understanding image resolution.

JUST THE GIST

About Raster and Vector Graphics

- Raster graphics are made up of tiny blocks of color called pixels. Examples of raster images include photos, scans, and artwork.
- Vector graphics are built out of mathematically calculated lines and curves. Examples of vector images include logos, clip art, and cartoons.

About Web File Formats

- The JPEG file format supports millions of colors, making it suitable for photographs. It reduces file size by sacrificing image quality.
- The GIF file format reduces file size by removing color from an image, making it suitable for graphics with few colors, such as logos and clip art.
- Because of its superior performance, the PNG format may someday replace JPEG and GIF, but it is not yet widely supported by popular web browsers.
- The SWF file format is used when exporting Flash files, which are vector-based animations, for use in Dreamweaver.

About Image Resolution

- Resolution is measured in DPI, or dots per inch.
- Raster images that you use in your web site need be only 72 DPI.

Setting Your Page Background

- Choose Modify > Page Properties to change your page's background.
- Ensure that your page background complements your site design and leaves your page text readable.

Inserting Images

- To insert a graphic, choose Insert > Image.
- Insert only images that have been saved in your site's local folder. Otherwise, they won't appear when you upload your site to the web.
- Images that are inserted into your web page are referenced files—they're not embedded.
- If you break the link to an image (by moving the image, renaming it, or deleting it outside of Dreamweaver), the image won't appear on your page.

Controlling Images on Your Page

- Use the settings in the Property Inspector to control your images. For a finer level of control, use CSS to manage your images.
- To resize your images, drag the resize handles that appear on the bottom, right, and bottom-right edges when you select a graphic.
- Clicking the Resample button on the Property Inspector cleans up a resized image, but doing so also permanently changes the image's source file.
- Dreamweaver comes with a set of built-in tools to modify your images. These allow you to make fast changes to your graphics without leaving Dreamweaver.
- A better way to modify your images is to use an external graphics editing program.

Chapter 11

ADDING Multimedia and Interactivity

STUFF YOU'LL LEARN IN THIS CHAPTER

As you no doubt have witnessed, the web these days is less and less about static design and more about a dynamic, interactive experience for surfers. And what's a dynamic, multimedia experience without sound, video, and Macromedia Flash animation? Not only will this chapter show you how to use these in your site, but you'll also see how to use Dreamweaver's ready-made actions, called behaviors, along with the Dreamweaver's timeline. Your pages will never be the same!

Getting Started with Multimedia

Nothing spices up a web site like a little multimedia. Multimedia typically comes in three flavors: audio, video, and Macromedia Flash.

Audio, or sound, can help establish an overall atmosphere and environment for your pages, and it's also great for voice-overs (a message from the CEO, for example). You can also provide downloadable audio files at your site: music, samples, speeches, and more.

If you're totally bummed out about video on the web, just go into hibernation for five years. The web you'll awaken to will be totally transformed—we'll all be watching reruns of American Idol *online and laughing at the funny clothes and haircuts. Oh wait—I already do that.*

Video on the web can be tricky. The basic problem is file size: Broadcast-quality video is massive—around 1 GB for just five minutes of footage—and even today's fastest connection speeds choke under that weight. Nevertheless, short videos, especially videos with small physical dimensions, work well on the web and are easy to incorporate with Dreamweaver.

NOTEWORTHY

You can build an entire web site in Flash, but that's another story. You'll need the Macromedia Flash application and a strong understanding of many of the topics discussed in this book.

Plug-in and Play

A plug-in is an add-on program that extends the abilities of much larger programs—in this case, web browsers. Your visitors will need to have plug-ins installed to play the multimedia files on your site. For instance, for visitors to see any Flash content you've used in your site, they must have the Flash Player plug-in installed on their computers. According to a June 2005 online survey, conducted by NPD (a market research firm), 97.6 percent of Internet users have the Flash Player plug-in (macromedia.com/software/player_census/flashplayer). That's more users than those who have Adobe Acrobat Reader (used to view PDF files).

For *Flash, audio,* and *video* to work for your visitors, your visitors will need to have *multimedia plug-ins* installed.

For audio and video to work, your visitor must have one of three popular media plug-ins installed: Windows Media Player, QuickTime Player, or RealPlayer. In fact, these are not only browser plug-ins, but also stand-alone players that can be used to play music and videos outside of web browsers. The tough part with audio and video is that you won't know which of the three plug-ins a visitor will have. Because the Flash Player plug-in has a huge installed base, many web page designers have begun using it for audio and video as well as animated content. You may want to consider doing this for your sites.

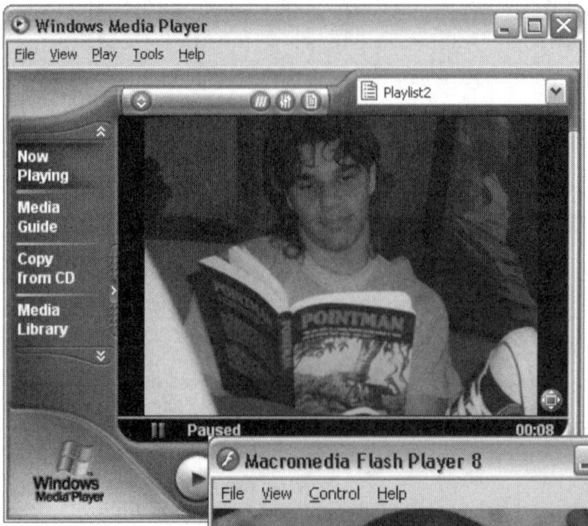

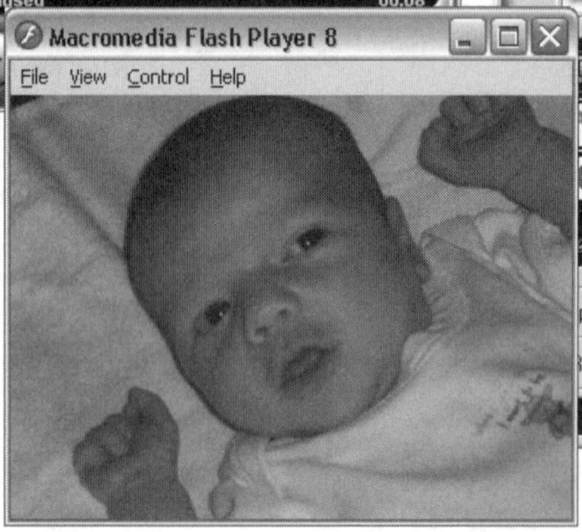

Even though Windows Media Player, QuickTime Player, RealPlayer, and Flash Player are the standard media plug-ins for web browsers, they're also stand-alone media players that can be used on their own to play video and audio files, as seen here.

Inserting Multimedia

Now you're ready to begin inserting multimedia objects on your page.

We'll start with Flash. You'll see not only how to insert a Flash movie, but also how to set properties for it so that it plays back for your visitor as you want it to. Then you'll see how to work with audio and video, both of which work in a similar manner.

Inserting Flash Files

You're ready to insert Flash movies on your Dreamweaver page. Flash movies are typically created in the Macromedia Flash program and saved as SWF (Shockwave Format) files. You then insert these SWF files on a web page just as you insert a graphic.

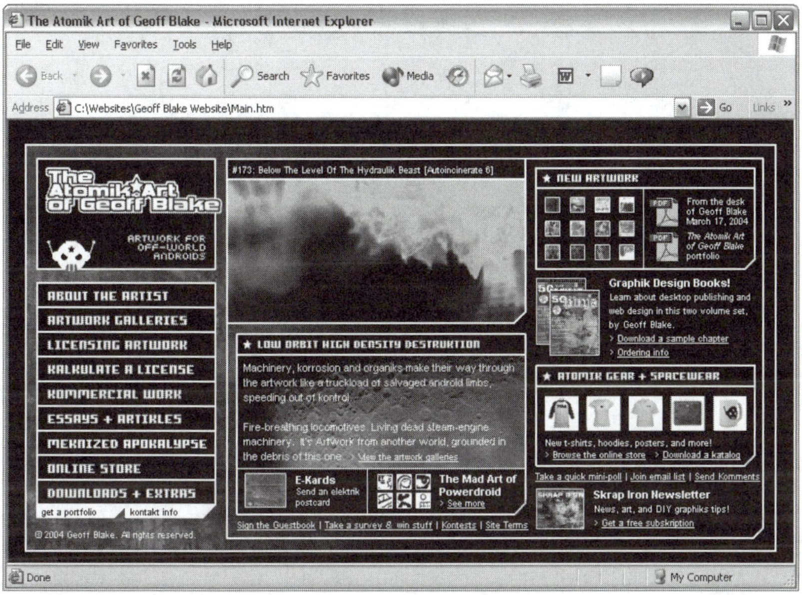

You can insert a Flash movie, saved in the SWF format, on your page in Dreamweaver. Even though the Flash movie may contain its own content, like graphics, buttons, and so on, you can combine it with content in your Dreamweaver page.

A cool thing about working with Flash is that once you've place a movie on your web page, you can move it and manipulate it just as if it were a static graphic. And when you preview your page in a web browser, you'll see the animation play within your page layout.

Even if a visitor to your site doesn't have the Flash Player plug-in, they'll be prompted to download and install it, so really, you shouldn't hesitate to incorporate Flash into your web site.

IMMINENT DOOM

If you're working on a Mac, make sure your media files—both audio and video—have a file extension. If you leave off the extension when you upload your site, your media files won't work!

As a designer, you should have popular multimedia plug-ins installed for testing purposes, just as you should have multiple browsers available.

NOTEWORTHY

The file format and extension are a little confusing. Flash files use the .swf extension, which stands for Shockwave Flash. However, another Macromedia program, Director, creates Shockwave files, but they use the .dcr extension.

NOTEWORTHY

When using any sort of multimedia on the web, remember this golden rule: Your multimedia must have a purpose. Using Flash, audio, or video on your site simply because you always wanted to create a spinning logo or just to show off your collection of background music won't cut it. You should use it only if you've determined that the experience the particular media provides is the best way to communicate with your audience.

Here's how to insert a Flash movie:

1. Open your page in Dreamweaver and place the insertion point where you want to insert the Flash file.

   You can insert Flash files anywhere on your page. For example, if you're using layers to control your page layout, click inside the layer that you want to contain your movie.

2. Choose Insert > Media > Flash.

Lookin' for some free Flash content for your site? Get started at flashbuttons.com and freeflashlogos.com.

3. In the Select File dialog box that appears, navigate to and select the SWF file that you want to insert; then click OK (Windows) or Choose (Mac).

4. If you have Dreamweaver's accessibility features turned on, the Object Tag Accessibility Attributes dialog box appears. Fill in the Title, Access Key, and Tab Index fields to give your users an alternate way to access and view your media, then click OK.

   What do these accessibility attributes mean?

   Title: Similar to the Alt tag, it gives your page elements a name and description that your users can view.

   Access Key: Provides a keyboard shortcut that moves users directly to an element on the page.

   Tab Index: Establishes a sequential order in which page elements are accessed using the Tab key.

NOTEWORTHY

Because Flash has been misused so often, some web browsers now have extensions and plug-ins to block Flash content—for instance, Firefox's Flashblock. If you want to include Flash movies in your site, consider building an opening splash page for your site that lists your site's optimal requirements, including the Flash Player plug-in.

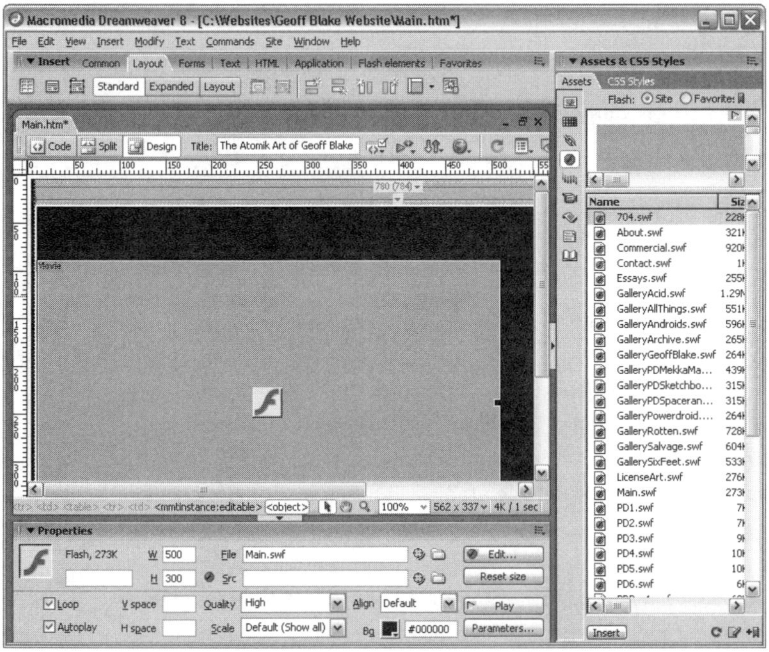

Dreamweaver inserts the Flash file onto your page, leaving an icon of a plug-in as a placeholder. Unlike with Flash Text and Flash buttons, Dreamweaver doesn't display the contents of a Flash file after it's been inserted.

5. To see your Flash file in action, click the Play button in the Property Inspector.

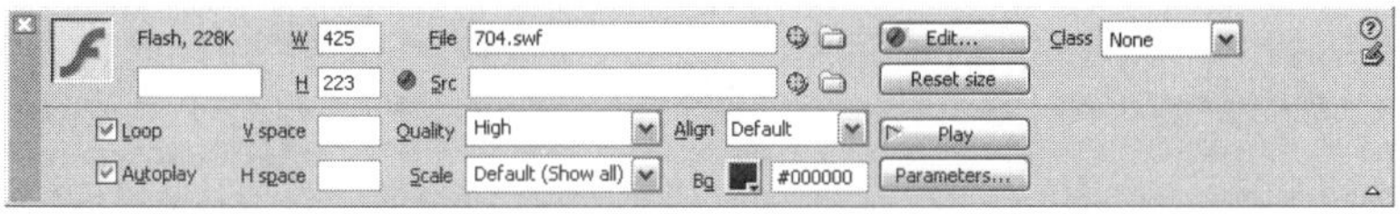

The Flash file plays within Dreamweaver. It's much better, however, to preview your Flash file in a web browser. That way, you'll have a better idea of what your visitor will see.

Now that you have a Flash file inserted into your page, you're ready to set its properties.

If you've inserted more than one Flash file on your page and you want to view them all at once, press Control+Alt+Shift+P (Windows) or Shift+Option+Command+P (Macintosh).

6. In the Property Inspector, use the W (width) and H (height) fields to specify the size of the area that your Flash movie will occupy on your page.

When you first insert a Flash file, Dreamweaver sets the width and height of the movie for you. Note that these fields do not necessarily set the width and the height of the Flash movie, but only of the page area that the Flash movie will occupy. You'll specify the relationship between the movie size and the page area when you use the Scale option, as you'll soon see.

7. Click Loop if you want to make the movie play continuously in your visitor's browser.

   If Loop is unchecked, then the movie will play through once and then stop.

8. To make the movie play automatically as soon as it loads into the visitor's browser window, select Autoplay.

   In other words, with Autoplay checked, the user won't have to click a Play button to start the movie; it will begin playing on its own.

9. To add some space between the Flash movie and other objects on your page, insert values for V Space and H Space.

   Just as for graphics, adding horizontal or vertical spacing pushes text, graphics, and other page objects away from your Flash file.

10. Use the Quality pull-down menu to set the playback quality of your Flash movie, and thus the speed at which it is rendered on your visitor's screen.

    Low makes the movie play faster, but sacrifices quality.

    Auto Low plays the movie faster, but improves the movie's quality if possible.

    Auto High places more importance on the movie's quality, increasing playback speed if possible.

    High produces the highest-quality movie; use it when you're not concerned about playback speed.

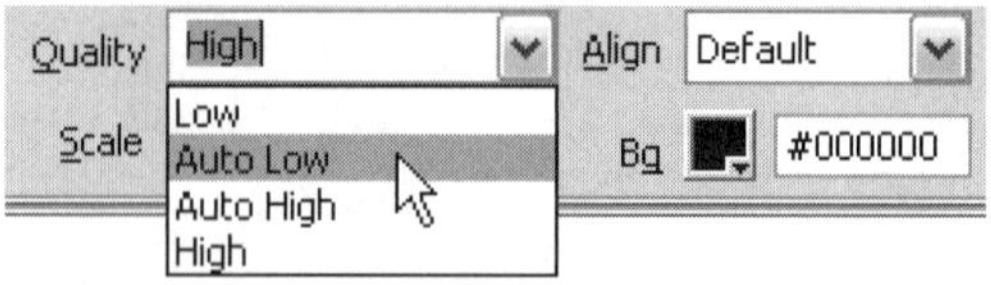

11. Choose an option from the Scale menu to control the way your Flash movie occupies the space on your page. The options are as follows:

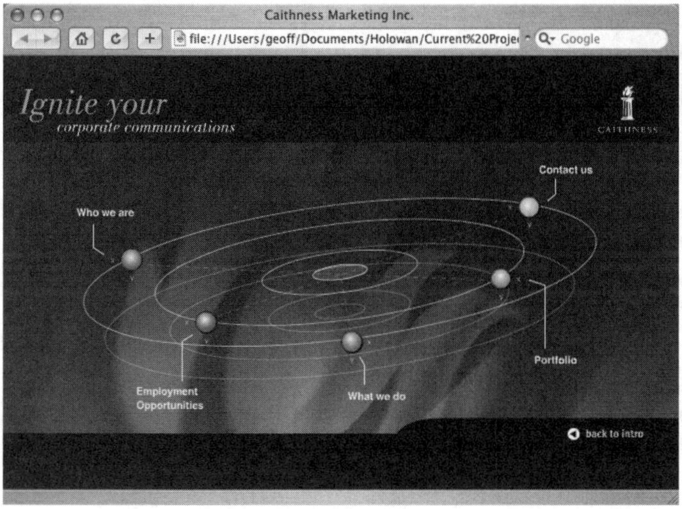

Default (Show All) displays the entire contents of your Flash movie in the area specified in the Property Inspector's W (width) and H (height) fields without distorting the shape of the movie. Any extra space around the movie is filled with the color specified in the Property Inspector's background color field.

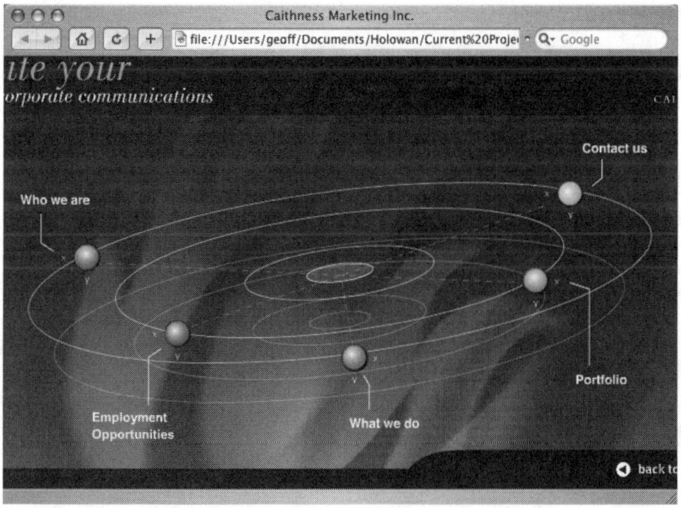

No Border completely fills the specified area without distortion, but doesn't show any background color. The movie will be cropped if necessary for it to occupy the entire area with the correct proportions.

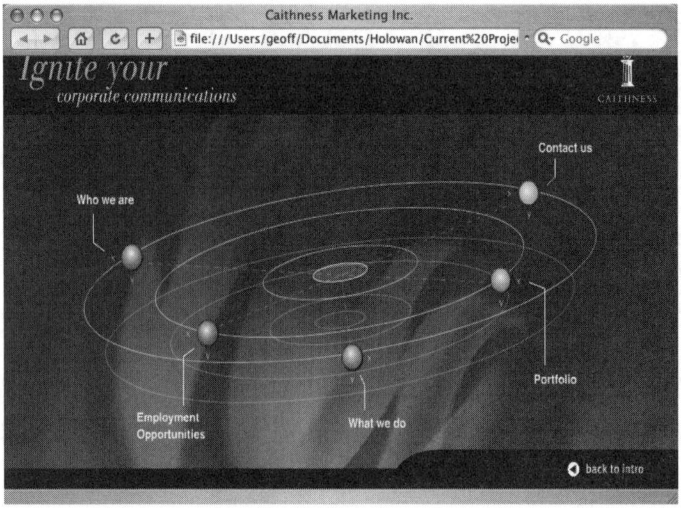

Exact Fit fills the entire specified area, but instead of filling empty space with background color or cropping the movie to maintain its proportions, this option distorts the Flash file so that it fills the specified area on your page.

12. Use the Align menu to set the horizontal and vertical alignment of your Flash movie.

    The alignment options available in the Property inspector's Align menu are the same for Flash movies as they are for graphics.

13. Use the Property Inspector's Bg field to set a background color for the movie area.

    The background color appears in the visitor's browser whenever the movie isn't playing, and it may also appear during the movie depending on the option you choose from the Scale menu.

INSERTING DIRECTOR SHOCKWAVE FILES

Inserting Director Shockwave files is similar to inserting Flash files, but with just a few differences. Most notably, when you insert a Shockwave file, Dreamweaver won't read the file's dimensions and instead places the file on your page at 32x32 pixels—no good. So when inserting Shockwave files, you need to manually insert the dimensions of the file after it's on your page.

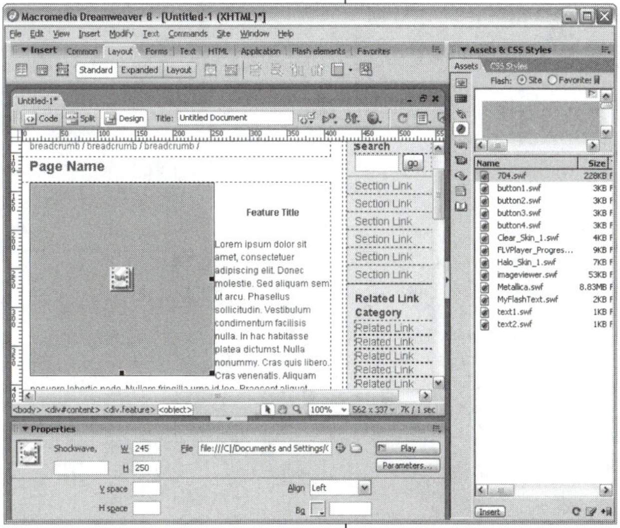

Inserting a Shockwave file into your Dreamweaver page is similar to inserting a Flash file, although you'll have to manually set the Shockwave file's width and height.

To minimize the hassle, open your file in Director and choose Modify > Movie > Properties. See the Stage Size values? Burn them into your memory. When you've resized your file, head back to Dreamweaver to insert it.

Here's how to insert a Shockwave file:

1. Open your page in Dreamweaver and place the insertion point where you want to your Shockwave movie to appear.

2. Choose Insert > Media > Shockwave.

3. In the Select File dialog box that appears, navigate to your Shockwave file, select it, and click OK (Windows) or Choose (Mac).

   Don't forget that Shockwave files use the DCR file extension.

4. If you have Dreamweaver's accessibility features turned on, the Object Tag Accessibility Attributes dialog box will appear. Complete the dialog box and click OK.

   Dreamweaver inserts the file on your page as a 32x32 pixel Shockwave icon.

5. In the Property Inspector, set the correct size of your Shockwave file in the W (width) and H (height) fields.

   What, you forgot? Geez, that means a trip back to Director to find out the correct size. Don't worry—I do that all the time!

6. Proceed as when inserting a Flash file.

   The other options in the Property Inspector are the same as for Flash files, except there aren't as many.

Adding Audio

You can add audio to your site in two ways: by linking to an audio file or by embedding the file in your web page.

You can add audio to your site in two ways. The simplest way is to provide a link on your page to an audio file that surfers can download and listen to at their leisure. When a visitor downloads the audio file, the visitor's audio software will kick in and play it, so you don't have to worry about what plug-ins are installed.

You can also embed an audio file on your page, so that it plays within your site. You can set the audio file to *stream*—that is, to begin playing before it's entirely downloaded, so that your visitors hear it more quickly after they open your web page. Streaming audio is useful, for instance, if you want to include background music on your site.

Stuck for audio and sound effects for your site? Flashkit.com has a massive library of sound effects and background loops (as well as lots of other web-related content). Also check out sound-effects-library.com.

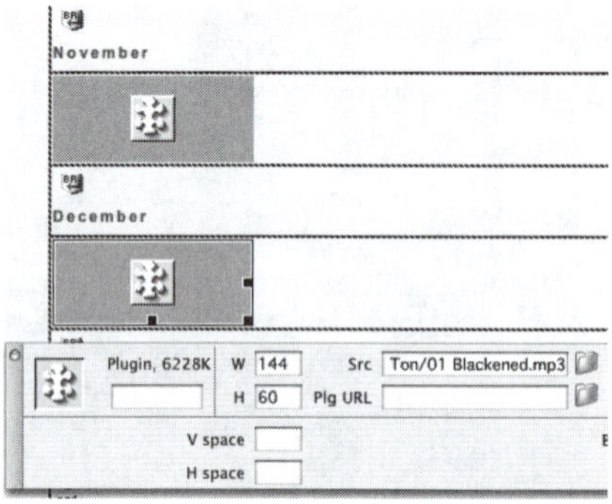

Inserting audio into Dreamweaver is easy. You'll see only the plug-in icon on your page as you work in Dreamweaver, but when you preview the page in a browser, you'll see your media player's controls instead.

NOTEWORTHY

Whether you're providing a link to an audio file or streaming it, don't forget that just like other files used in your site, audio files will need to be uploaded when you publish your site to the web. Otherwise, your audio won't work.

When you go this route, you'll be relying on the visitor to have one of the three media browser plug-ins installed; whatever plug-in the visitor has will then appear as an object on your page. The plug-in will give the visitor stop, rewind, and play controls to play the sound file. However, since you can't know which audio plug-in your visitor will be using, you won't know exactly how your page will look (if you're as concerned about page design and aesthetics as I am, this can be a real issue).

Probably the best fix is to use Flash's SWF format for your audio. As discussed earlier, the SWF format relies on the Flash Player plug-in, so you can forget about plug-in compatibility issues and awkward audio controls. However, you'll need to create your sound files using the Flash application.

Whether you link to audio files or embed them, MP3 is the simplest, cleanest format to use. It's the standard for audio on the web, and any media software can play it, so your visitors should have no problems hearing your audio. Even so, if you're offering audio files for download, you should provide several audio formats, such as WMA and WAV, so surfers can choose the file type they prefer.

Here's how to link to an audio file:

1. On your page in Dreamweaver, select the text or graphic that you want to use to link to the audio file.

   If you're linking from text, it's a good idea to type the size of the audio file so surfers know what kind of download they're in for.

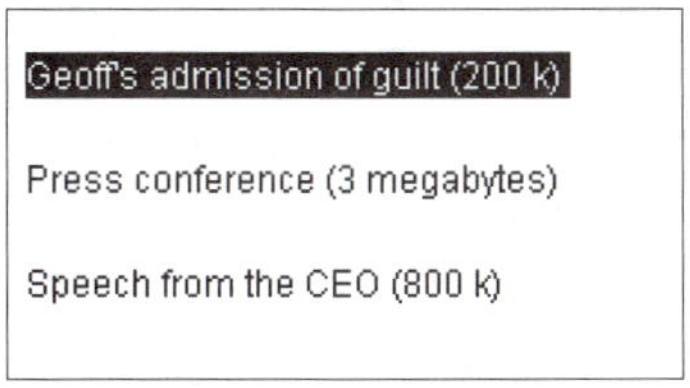

2. In the Property inspector, click the Link field's folder icon.

3. In the Select File dialog box that appears, navigate to and select the audio file that you want to link to; then click OK (Windows) or Choose (Mac).

   Dreamweaver creates a link to the audio file.

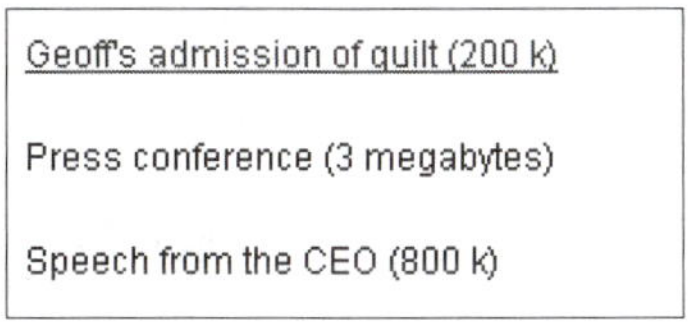

Here's how to embed an audio file:

1. On your page in Dreamweaver, place the insertion point where you want to embed the audio file.

2. Choose Insert > Media > Plugin.

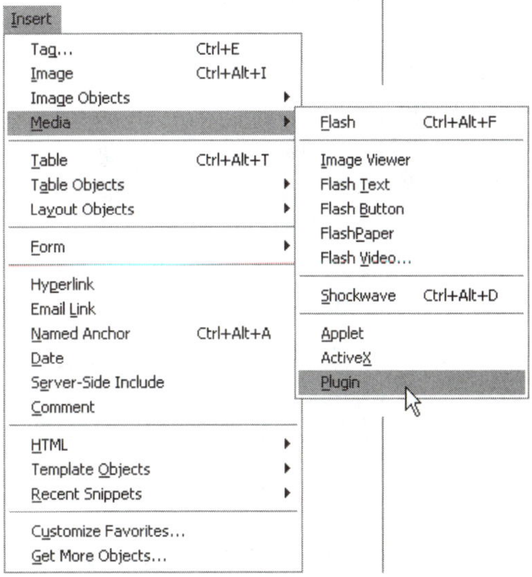

NOTEWORTHY

If you want to provide audio files in multiple formats, consider Apple's QuickTime Pro (not to be confused with the free QuickTime Player). At $30, it's a pretty cheap fix for converting sound files to different formats. Check it out at apple.com/quicktime for more.

Don't use MIDI music on your site, or I'll come to your house and take away your computer.

3. In the Select File dialog box that appears, navigate to and select the audio file that you want to embed; then click OK (Windows) or Choose (Mac).

   Dreamweaver inserts the embedded audio file on your page. It appears as a 32x32-pixel plug-in placeholder.

4. In the Property Inspector, set the embedded audio file's width and height.

   The values that you enter determine the size of the player controls that will appear on your page. Most player plug-ins should work with width and height values of 144x60. If you want to remove the player controls, set the width and height to 0. Keep in mind, though, that removing the player controls means your visitors will have no way to turn off the audio other than turning off their speakers—*or leaving your site*.

5. To play your embedded sound in Dreamweaver, click the green Play button in the Property Inspector.

   When you click Play, Dreamweaver displays the plug-in audio interface on your page. Just click the interface's Play button to hear your embedded sound file.

Adding Video

As with audio, you have two choices for adding video to your site: link to a video file or embed the file in your web page.

Just as with audio, you have two choices for working with video in Dreamweaver: Let visitors download and play the video on their own—the simple and easy approach—or embed the video on your page. When your embedded video streams, the visitor can begin watching the clip right away. Unfortunately, streaming playback is often choppy until the clip has been fully loaded. And then there's the issue of browser plug-ins, just as with embedded audio.

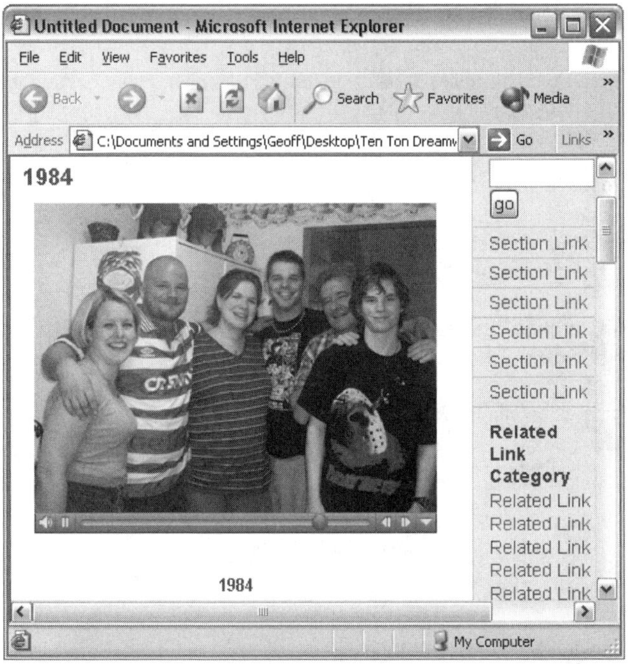

When using video in your site, you can either create a hyperlink to it, which allows visitors to download it and play it, or you can embed it in your page and stream it to your viewers, as seen here.

Just as with audio, if you want to reach the maximum number of web surfers, offer your video clip in a few different formats, such as MOV and MPEG, so that visitors can choose their format of preference before downloading. And as with any files, be sure to upload any movie clips you use to your web server when you publish your site.

Here's how to link to a video clip:

1. On your page in Dreamweaver, select the text or graphic that you want to link to the video.

   If you're linking from text, type the file size of the video that your visitors will be downloading, as a courtesy to let surfers know what they're in for before they start downloading.

2. In the Property Inspector, click the Link field's folder icon.

3. In the Select File dialog box that appears, navigate to and select the video file that you want to link to; then click OK.

   Dreamweaver creates a link to the audio file.

Here's how to embed a video clip on your web page:

1. On your page in Dreamweaver, place the insertion point where you want the video clip to appear.

2. Choose Insert > Media > Plugin.

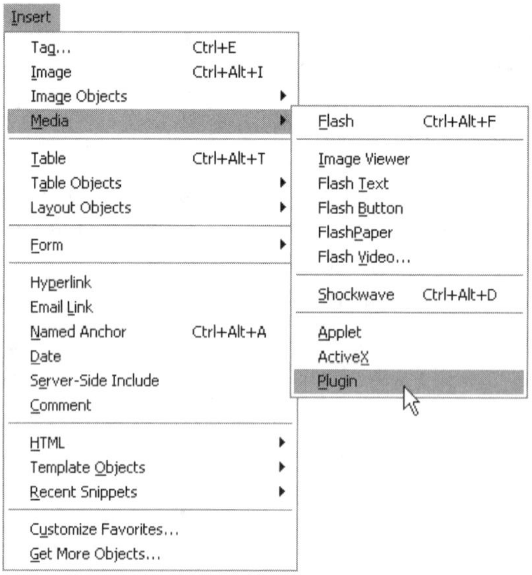

3. In the Select File dialog box that appears, navigate to your video clip, select it, and click OK.

   Dreamweaver inserts the video clip on your page as a 32x32-pixel plug-in placeholder.

4. With your clip still selected, set width and height values in the Property Inspector.

   Unlike the width and height for a graphic, the width and height values here won't scale your video clip. Instead, the values determine how much of your movie will be cropped and how much area will be visible.

   You'll probably want your movie to play back at its intended size. To figure this out, you'll have to open your movie in your media player and find its dimensions. Then enter these values in the Property Inspector.

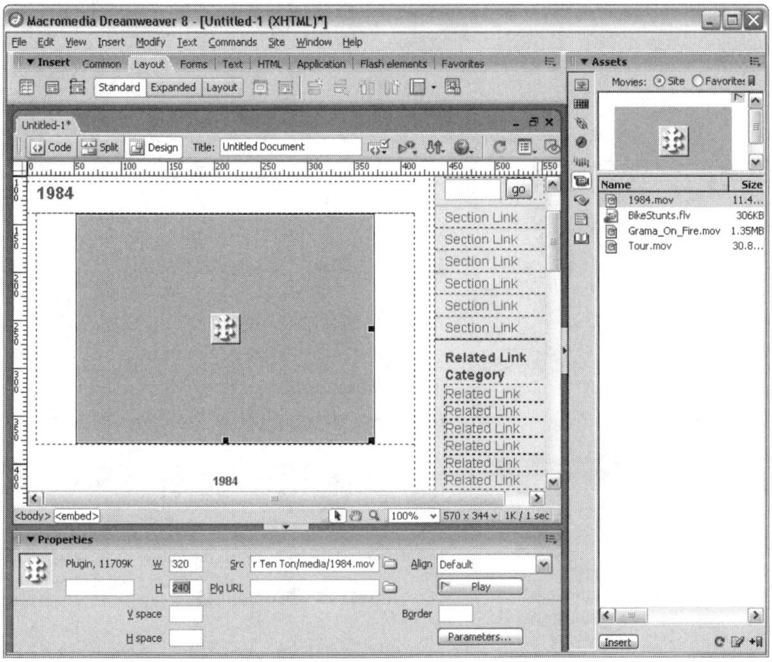

5. Click the green Play button in the Property Inspector to view your movie directly inside Dreamweaver.

DELIVERING FLASH VIDEO IN YOUR WEB PAGES

As you've seen in both the audio and video discussions in this chapter, working with media can be tricky business due to the plug-in issue. We talked about the possibility of using the Flash Player plug-in to deliver embedded audio. You can also use it to deliver video, by using a relatively new file format called Flash Video. Your video file will first need to be converted to Flash Video's FLV format. This can be done with the Flash 8 Video Encoder, which ships with Flash 8. Once your video's been converted, it can be easily inserted into Dreamweaver.

Rather than inserting traditional video files on your page, which is a game of hit-and-miss with the three popular browsers, you can go with Flash Video's FLV format, which relies on the Flash Player plug-in.

Here's how to insert a Flash Video:

1. On your page in Dreamweaver, place the insertion point where you want to insert your video and choose Insert > Media > Flash Video.

2. In the Insert Flash Video dialog box that appears, set the Video Type pull-down menu to Progressive Download Video.

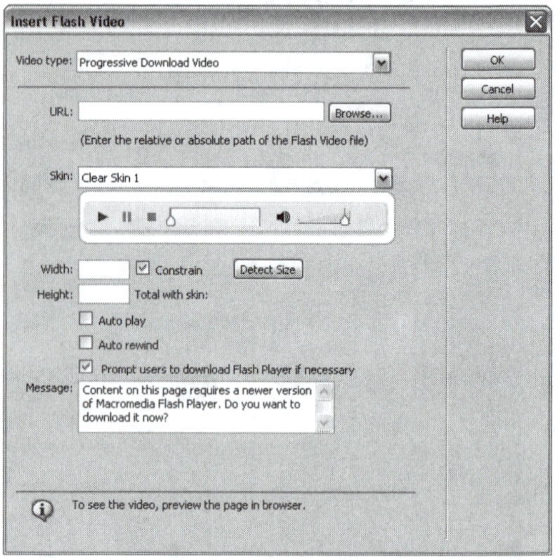

You can also use Streaming Video, but the process is more involved. For more on streaming Flash Video content, check out: macromedia.com/software/flashcom/fvss.

3. Click the Browse button next to the URL field; then in the Select File dialog box that appears, navigate to your FLV file, select it, and click OK (Windows) or Choose (Mac).

   If you're working on a Mac and your FLV file is located two or more directories away from your HTML file, you must use an absolute path for your Flash Video to work—for example, http://www.yoursite.com/media/flash/flashvideo.flv.

4. From the Skin pull-down menu, choose the appearance for the video's player controls.

   The video player's skin is the interface style that users see when they play your video.

DELIVERING FLASH VIDEO IN YOUR WEB PAGES (CONTINUED)

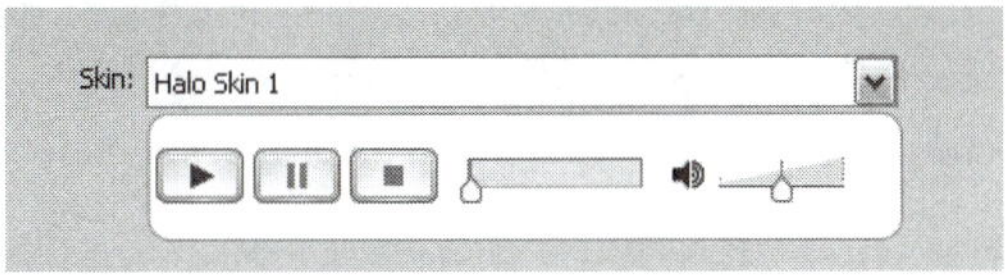

5. Use the W (width) and H (height) fields in the Insert Flash Video dialog box to set the size of your video in pixels.

   Even better, click the Detect Size button to have Dreamweaver load the video dimensions for you. If Dreamweaver can't find the video's size, you'll be prompted to type the values yourself.

6. Select the Auto Play and Auto Rewind check boxes if you want your video to play as soon as the page loads and then return to the beginning as soon as it has played through.

7. Make sure that Prompt Users to Download Flash Player If Necessary is checked.

   Code will then be inserted to check to make sure that visitors have the correct Flash Player plug-in installed when your page loads in their browsers. If they don't, they'll be prompted to download the latest version of the player. You can use the Message field to customize the prompt that visitors receive.

8. Click OK when you're done.

   Dreamweaver inserts the Flash Video on your page.

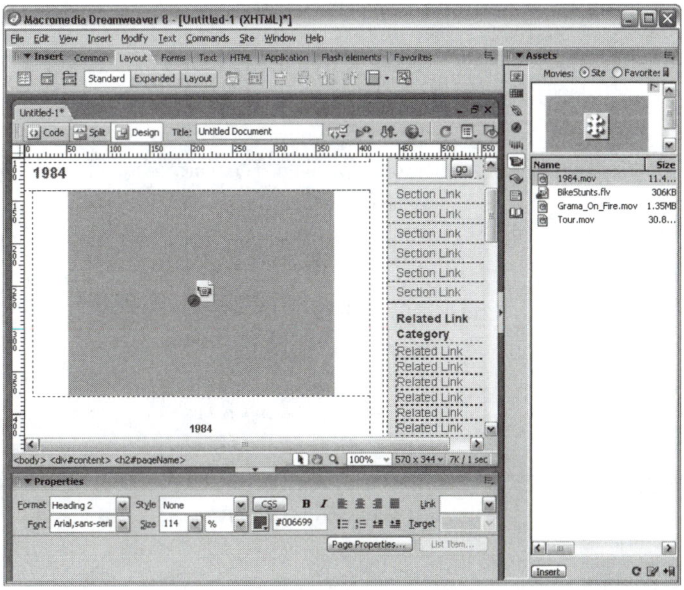

To see the video play, you'll need to preview your page in a web browser. If you want to make any further adjustments to your Flash Video, use the options that appear in the Property Inspector.

When you insert Flash Video on your page, Dream–weaver automatically generates two SWF files and saves them in your site, in the same folder as the current web page. The first SWF file contains the video player, and the other contains the player skin. So a Flash Video actually requires four files: the FLV file, two SWF files, and the web page that the Flash Video is inserted into. Make sure that all of these files are uploaded to your server when you're ready to publish your site.

If you're considering offering video content on your site, seriously consider Flash Video. For lots more information, check out the Flash Video Development Center at macromedia.com/go/flv_devcenter.

Using Behaviors to Add Interactivity

Dreamweaver's behaviors are prewritten functions that have been packaged into simple, easy-to-use commands, and they pack a wallop of interactivity for your pages.

Ready to really spice up your pages? Dreamweaver's behaviors are just the thing. Behaviors are prewritten functions that are packaged into simple, easy-to-use commands. They do cool stuff like open pop-up menus, windows, and messages, and can even check your visitors' browsers and plug-ins. If you haven't worked with behaviors yet, you're in for a treat!

Like most Dreamweaver commands, behaviors are available through a series of dialog boxes. In other words, you can set up your behaviors with a handful of mouse clicks without knowing a thing about how to create them.

> **GEEK'S DELIGHT**
>
> Dreamweaver's behaviors are written in JavaScript, a scripting language used within in HTML code. JavaScript is used to add interactivity to web pages—rollovers, pop-up windows, and much more. JavaScript is completely different from Java (which is a programming language as opposed to a scripting language).

You do, however, need to know a few things about behaviors before you get started. First, they're always attached to an object on your page—a graphic, a piece of text, or even to the page itself. Second, each behavior has two parts: an event and an action. Remember the classic scene in ***Indiana Jones: The Temple of Doom*** when Indy, in the temple, swaps a bag of sand for the golden idol? The removal of the idol from the pedestal was the triggering ***event*** that fired off the ***action***, in this case the booby trap of arrows and spears that flew from the walls. Behaviors work the same way in Dreamweaver. The trigger is usually some sort of involvement on the user's part—perhaps clicking a link or moving the cursor over a specified area. The action might be the appearance of a pop-up window or the showing or hiding of page content. So think of behaviors as if you're setting a booby trap: When the event is triggered, the trap is sprung.

Attaching Behaviors

I hope you're stoked and ready to start using behaviors on your web pages. As already mentioned, you attach a behavior to an object on your page—to a graphic or some text or to the page itself. You create the behavior and add it to your page in Dreamweaver's Behaviors panel. The panel also lists any events and actions that have been applied to the selected object and allows you to make changes to them, too.

Each of the 27 behaviors that are available in the Behaviors panel has its own unique dialog box where you can set the parameters for the effect and make any adjustments down the road. Because there are so many behaviors—each functioning uniquely—we won't be exploring all of them here. However, the sidebar "Meet 27 New Friends—A Rundown of Dreamweaver Behaviors" describes each behavior so you'll know what each one does. Here, we'll walk through the setup for one of the most popular behaviors, Swap Image, so you can see how behaviors work in Dreamweaver.

INSERTING JAVA APPLETS—NOT TECHY AT ALL!

Have you ever heard of Java applets? An applet is a tiny program that runs in your web page and that offers your visitors some kind of interactive content. For example, you might want a stock ticker on your web site, a quote of the day, or news headlines. These sorts of constantly updating, interactive objects are handled by applets.

Now don't confuse Java applets with JavaScript—they're totally different. Java is a stand-alone programming language, whereas JavaScript is a scripting language used within the HTML code of your web pages.

But here's the good news: You don't need to know Java to use Java applets. You can insert Java applets on your page, just like you insert graphics, movies, or audio. Because the applet is a self-contained program, all you need to do is insert it, and you're away.

Where can you get Java applets? Search the Internet—there are countless numbers of them available for free online. Try starting with javaboutique.com or javafile.com.

Once you've found an applet that you want to use, download it and save it in your site's local folder. Now you're ready to insert the applet on your page.

Here's how to insert a Java applet:

1. On your web page in Dreamweaver, place your cursor where you want to insert a Java applet.

2. Choose Insert > Media > Applet.

3. In the Select File dialog box that appears, navigate to your applet (always saved as a CLASS file), select it, and then click OK (Windows) or Choose (Mac).

   Dreamweaver inserts the applet as a 32x32-pixel Java icon on your page.

Most applets that you download come with setup instructions. You'll need to read those files to see what size it is, and what other Property Inspector options you need to for the applet to function properly.

When you publish your page, make sure to upload the applet's CLASS file, as well as any additional files that the applet requires, such as graphic files.

One of the most common behaviors used on web pages is Swap Image, otherwise known as a rollover. Here, the flowers change color when they're selected. It's simple interactivity like this that makes an otherwise plain web site interesting.

> **NOTEWORTHY**
>
> Browser compatibility has long been an issue with JavaScript functions, and therefore with Dreamweaver behaviors. But fortunately, Dreamweaver looks after browser compatibility issues for you, as you'll see in the exercise here.

The Swap Image behavior is applied to a graphic to create a rollover effect, which switches one graphic for another when the visitor's cursor rolls over it. You might remember using Dreamweaver's Rollover Image command in Chapter 9—it achieves the same effect as Swap Image. But Swap Image adds a bit of a twist: You can control the rollover effect for a group of images all at once.

Here's how to add a behavior to your page:

1. Choose Insert > Image to insert a graphic on your page. In the Select Image Source dialog box that appears, navigate to and select a graphic to use; then click OK.

2. In the top-left corner of the Property Inspector, enter a unique name for your graphic.

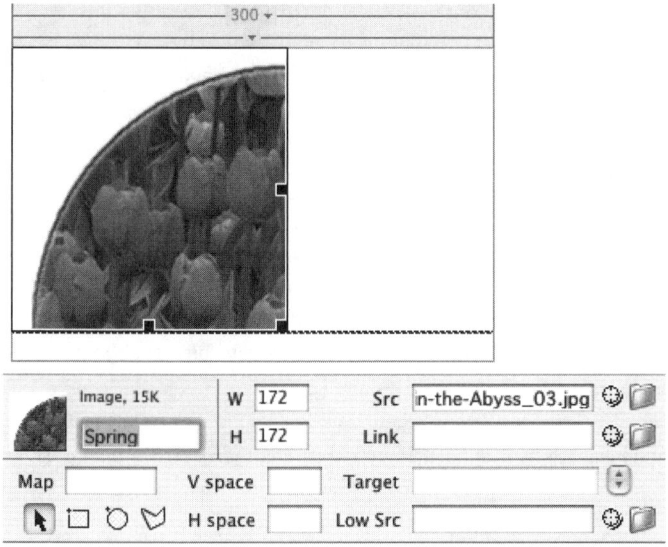

The name will allow the behavior to locate and affect the graphic on your page independent of any other images on your page. Names cannot use special characters or spaces and must begin with a letter. Keep in mind, too, that names are case-sensitive.

3. Repeat steps 1 and 2 to add a few more graphics to your page.

   Once each graphic has its own unique name, you're ready to begin applying behaviors to them.

4. Select the graphic that you want to attach the behavior to.

5. Choose Window > Behaviors to open the Behaviors panel.

6. In the top-left corner of the Behaviors panel, click the Show Set Events button.

The Behaviors panel has two view modes, Show Set Events and Show All Events, which are controlled by the two buttons at the top left of the panel. When you're getting started with behaviors, you'll find it easiest to work in Show Set Events mode.

7. Click the Add Behavior button (the Plus button) at the top of the panel.

   As you can see, there are many actions available in Dreamweaver.

   However before setting an action, you'll specify the target browser for your behaviors. As mentioned earlier, Dreamweaver handles browser compatibility for you, freeing you to focus on page design.

8. In the menu that appears, choose Show Events For; then select your target browser from the submenu.

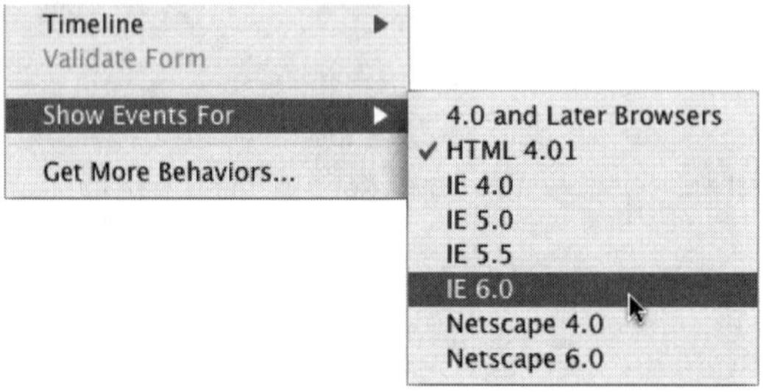

Even though Dreamweaver allows you to choose a target browser for your behaviors, you still should test your effects in multiple browsers—and if possible, on both Windows and Mac computers.

   Selecting an earlier browser version ensures that your page will be widely compatible, but only a few actions will be possible. Choosing a newer target browser makes more behaviors available, but your page may not function properly in older browsers. Because Netscape and Internet Explorer interpret JavaScript slightly differently, you can specify only one or the other, not both at the same time.

   You have to set your browser compatibility only once; then you're ready to go. If you wish, you can leave the browser setting alone and use Dreamweaver's default (HTML 4.01).

   Now you're ready to apply your behavior.

9. Click the Add Behavior button in the Behaviors panel again and choose Swap Image.

   Some choices in this menu will appear dimmed depending on the target browser you chose. The page object that you're attaching the behavior to (in this case, an image) also limits the actions available.

10. In the Swap Image dialog box that appears, from the Images list, choose the graphic that you want the behavior to affect.

    The Images list shows all the graphics that are currently on your page, which helps you tell the difference between your graphics as you're applying the Swap Image behavior. Just make sure that the graphic you selected in step 4 is selected in the list.

11. Click the Browse button beside the Set Source to field; then navigate to the image that you want to swap in when the rollover effect is triggered.

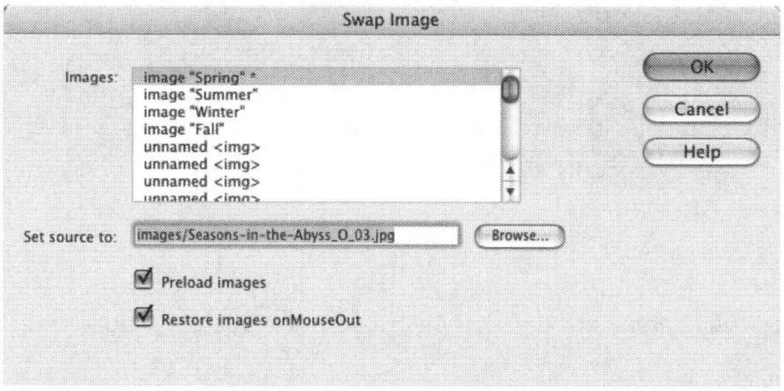

12. Make sure that Preload Images and Restore Images OnMouseOut are both checked; then click OK.

    Preloading your rollover images ensures that the rollover image will be loaded into your visitor's browser cache, so that there won't be a delay when the behavior is triggered.

    Restore Images OnMouseOut swaps out the rollover image for the original image when the visitor moves the cursor away from the graphic; this option adds a second action to your image: Swap Image Restore.

    When you click OK, both Swap Image and Swap Image Restore appear in the right column of the Behaviors panel. In the left column of the Behaviors panel, the default event for each action is displayed. The default event is determined by both the object that you attached the behavior to and the target browser that you're using.

NOTEWORTHY

Just like when you use Dreamweaver's Rollover Image command, make sure that the rollover image you choose has the same dimensions as the original graphic. Otherwise, the rollover image will appear distorted when it's swapped in.

IMMINENT DOOM

When some behaviors are used—for example, Set Nav Bar Image—Dreamweaver inserts a null link, which appears as "javascript:;" in the Property Inspector's Link field. Null links are used when a hyperlink is required for the behavior to work, but when the user isn't actually taken to a new destination. If you remove the null link, Dreamweaver warns you that the behavior will also be removed from the object. If this is not what you want, choose Edit > Undo; otherwise, you'll have to rebuild your behavior manually.

13. To add the Swap Image behavior to another graphic on your page, select it; then repeat steps 9 to 12.

    Now that your behavior is complete, you're ready to test it. Unfortunately, you can't preview the effects of behaviors in Dreamweaver. To see them in action, you need to save your page and preview it in your web browser.

Note that a single object on your page can have multiple behaviors applied to it. For example, you can set up an effect so that when a visitor moves the cursor over a graphic, Swap Image is triggered, and then when the visitor clicks, a pop-up window appears.

You can add as many behaviors as you want. In fact, you can even set up your page so that two or more actions share the same triggering event. For instance, you can set up your behavior so that when a visitor moves the cursor over a graphic, the Swap Image behavior and a pop-up window are triggered at the same time. When actions share the same events, the order in which they're triggered is determined by the order in which the actions appear in the Behaviors panel. Actions at the top of the panel are triggered before the actions that come later. You can rearrange the sequence of your behaviors by clicking the Move Event Value Up and Move Event Value Down buttons at the top of the panel.

As you preview your behavior, you may find that you want to tweak it. Or perhaps the behavior isn't triggering at all. In either case, you'll have to head back to Dreamweaver and edit your behavior. In the next section, you'll see how to do just that.

MEET 27 NEW FRIENDS—A RUNDOWN OF DREAMWEAVER BEHAVIORS

Yup, there's a ton of these bad boys in Dreamweaver—27 in all. Let me do some brief introductions so you can get to know who's who.

Call Javascript: Allows you to type your own custom JavaScript code for execution in your site visitor's web browser. You'll need to understand JavaScript to use this one.

Change Property: Dynamically changes the properties of images, forms, layers, and more. For example, you can make the background color of a layer change when the visitor's cursor moves over it.

Check Browser: Detects the type of browser the visitor is using and redirects the visitor to a specific URL. This behavior is useful if you've built two versions of your site that are optimized for two different browsers.

Check Plugin: Checks the visitor's browser to see if appropriate media plug-ins required to view your site are installed. You can display URLs depending on whether the plug-ins are installed.

Control Shockwave or Flash: Lets you play, stop, rewind, or jump to a specific frame in a Shockwave or Flash movie when you attach this behavior to a piece of text or a graphic on your page—allowing you to control the movie's playback from anywhere on the page.

Drag Layer: Allows the visitor to drag layers (and their contents) around the screen. With this behavior, you can create games, customizable interfaces, and much more.

Go to URL: Sets a link to trigger using a variety of events, including when the visitor moves the cursor over an object or when a page loads (normally, a hyperlink must be clicked to open its destination). More than one destination can be set with Go to URL—useful within a frameset where you want to control the contents of two or more frames from a single link.

Hide Pop-Up Menu: Used with Show Pop-Up Menu, discussed below.

Jump Menu: Allows you to edit form-based jump menus, also known as pull-down menus.

Jump Menu Go: Adds a Go button beside a jump menu.

Open Browser Window: Creates a pop-up window. You can control what appears in the window, as well as the properties for the window, such as its size and whether it includes scrollbars and a navigation bar.

Play Sound: Triggers audio on your web page when any of a variety of events occurs.

Popup Message: Creates a pop-up window that contains whatever message you want. This behavior can be useful to relay important information about your site to your visitors (although they may get confused and think that the warning is coming from their computer system, not your site).

Preload Images: Ensures that all required images have been downloaded for the user when you're using other behaviors to control the display of images in your web page (for example, in the case

MEET 27 NEW FRIENDS—A RUNDOWN OF DREAMWEAVER BEHAVIORS (CONTINUED)

of rollovers). This behavior prevents disruptions as visitors are using your site.

Set Nav Bar Image: Controls the display of a selected button in a navigation bar as well as the display of the other buttons.

Set Text of Frame: Dynamically replaces the content of a frame with new code that you specify in the behavior's dialog box. Any valid HTML code will work. Whenever the action is triggered, the frame's content is replaced with the code you set.

Set Text of Layer: Works just like Set Text of Frame, but dynamically replaces the contents of a layer with new code that you specify.

Set Text of Status Bar: Sets a scrolling message on the status bar of the visitor's web browser. Often, however, experienced web surfers rely on the status bar to display hyperlink destinations before they decide to click them.

Set Text of Text Field: Similar to Set Text of Frame and Set Text of Layer, except only text (and not HTML code) can be used. This behavior can be used to show an example of how a particular text field must be filled out—for example, a date field that should appear as mm/dd/yy.

Show Pop-Up Menu: Creates pop-up menus on your page. When Show Pop-Up Menu is used, the Hide Pop-Up Menu behavior is automatically inserted.

Show-Hide Layers: Allows you to control the visibility of layers—and therefore their contents—on your page. You can use this behavior to add a pop-up navigation system and messages that appear and disappear, for instance.

Swap Image: Allows you to create an image rollover that affects a selected image or other images on your page. The Swap Image Restore behavior is automatically inserted whenever Swap Image is used.

Swap Image Restore: Returns a rollover graphic to its original display.

Go to Timeline Frame: Jumps to a specific frame within the timeline animation.

Play Timeline: Plays a timeline that has been inserted on the current page.

Stop Timeline: Stops a timeline animation that is currently playing on your page.

Validate Form: Ensures that the visitor has filled in a web-based form correctly before it's submitted.

If you want to go beyond the 27 preset behaviors in Dreamweaver, you can search out more on the web. Start by visiting the Dreamweaver Exchange web site (www.macromedia.com/cfusion/exchange/). Choose Get More Behaviors at the bottom of the Add Behavior menu in the Behaviors panel. Your web browser will launch, and you'll be taken directly to Dreamweaver Exchange, where you can search for behaviors by type, learn about what's available, and download the necessary installation files.

Editing an Attached Behavior

You can edit your behaviors at any time in Dreamweaver. For example, you may want to change some of the parameters that you set in the behavior's dialog box. Or maybe you want to use a different rollover image, or tweak the size of a pop-up window. Or you may want to change the event that triggers a behavior's action. No problem at all.

You can edit your behaviors at any time in Dreamweaver.

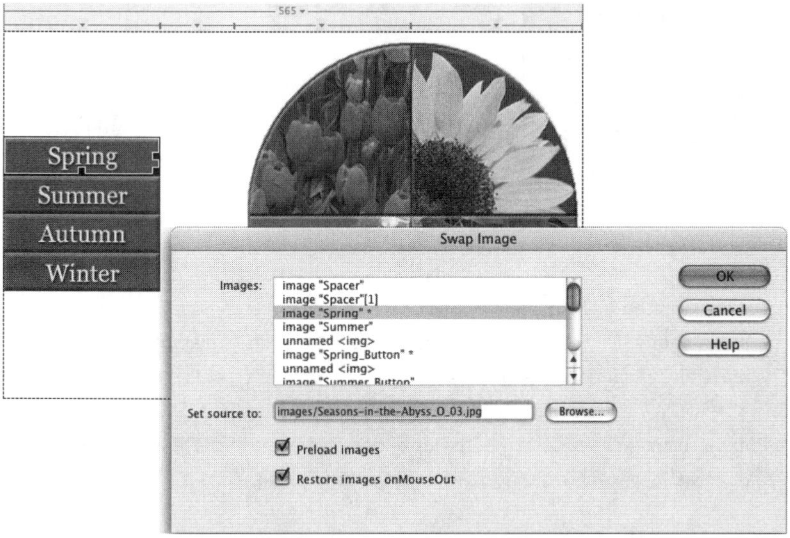

Editing behaviors is downright easy! Here, a new rollover image is being set in the Swap Image dialog box. Use the Action menu or double-click your behavior's Event to get the party started!

Here's how to edit a behavior:

1. Select a page object that has the behavior attached to it that you want to change.

   The Behaviors panel will display the event and action that are attached to the object.

2. If you want the behavior to be triggered by a different event, click in the left column of the Behaviors panel. In the pull-down menu that appears, select a new event to trigger the action.

Remember that the events available in the pull-down menu are determined by the target browser that you're using. If the event you're looking for doesn't appear, try changing the target browser to a more recent version.

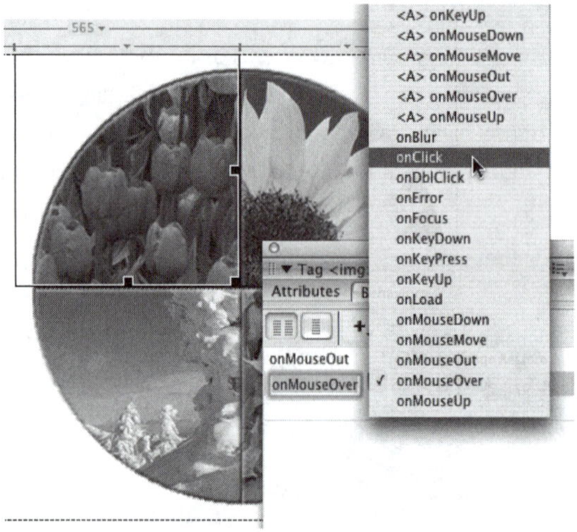

3. If you want to make a change to your action's parameters, double-click the action in the right column of the Behaviors panel. In the action's dialog box that appears, make any changes to the parameters that you previously set; then click OK.

4. If you want to remove the behavior entirely, select it in the Behaviors panel and click the Remove Event button at the top of the panel.

Creating Animation with Timelines

Timelines allow you to reposition objects on your page and control their sequence, to create animations.

You saw how easily you can add interactivity to your web pages with behaviors. Now you'll see how to add a different type of interactivity: animation! Animation is made possible in Dreamweaver through the use of timelines, which allow you to reposition objects on your page and control their sequence. You can also use timelines to trigger behaviors according to timing that you set.

You can set up timing so that surfers experience effects in a certain order. For example, maybe you want a message for your visitor to drop down from the top of the browser window, hover for a moment, and then be whisked away. Or maybe you want an object to zoom across your screen whenever a visitor clicks a specific button. This level of interactivity is no problem with Dreamweaver's timeline commands.

Any content that you want to animate must be contained in a layer. A timeline can contain as many layers as you want, which means the level of interactivity and the complexity of your animations is limited only by your imagination.

The timeline is made up of frames, just like the frames in a traditional animation. Whenever you want a change to occur in your animation—perhaps you want the object in the animation to change direction, size, or stacking order, for example—you insert a keyframe, which then sets the change within the overall timeline.

A nice thing about timelines in Dreamweaver is that they don't rely on any additional technologies like plug-ins. To view your animation, all your visitors need is a version 4 browser or later. That makes life easy for us designers.

Creating a Basic Animation

To create animations on your page, you use the Timelines panel (Window > Timelines). The Timelines panel contains a grid of cells, each of which represents a frame in the animation. Each row of cells is a channel in the timeline, and each channel can contain its own animation. This means that you can have multiple animations happening at the same time, without one interfering with the others. Each column of cells represents a specific point in time on your timeline (measured in seconds). As you add animations to the Timelines panel, they appear as horizontal purple bars, which you can adjust until your animation is set exactly as you want.

To use Dreamweaver's timeline, you'll need a layer on your page to animate.

To use Dreamweaver's timeline, you'll need a layer on your page to animate. So before you get started with timelines, you'll first create a layer and give it some content.

THE TIMELINES PANEL

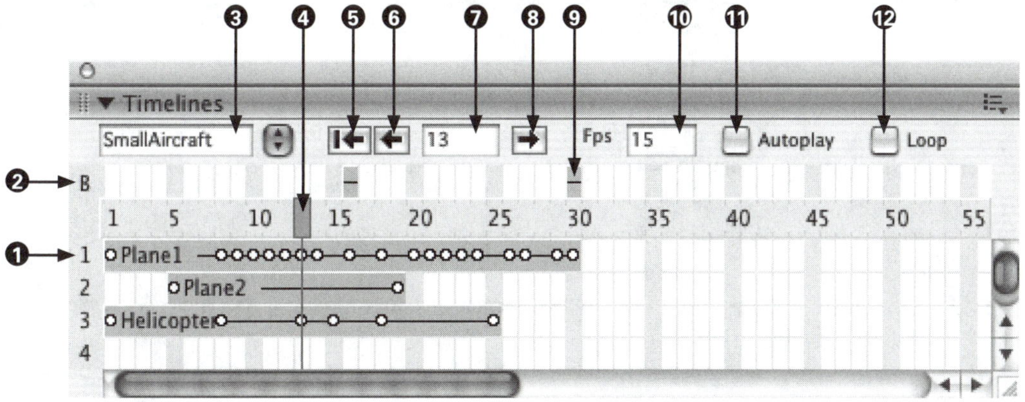

(1) Animation channel **(2)** Behaviors channel **(3)** Timeline pull-down menu **(4)** Playhead **(5)** Rewind to Beginning **(6)** Rewind **(7)** Current frame **(8)** Play **(9)** Behavior marker **(10)** Frame rate **(11)** Autoplay **(12)** Loop

Here's how to animate a layer:

1. Click the Draw Layer button in the Layout category of the Insert bar; then draw a layer on your page.

2. Add some content to the layer and set any options that you want in the Property Inspector.

   For example, you might insert your web site's logo on the layer with the idea of having it fly across your page. In the Property Inspector, you would then specify the size, stacking order, background color, and any other layer settings.

   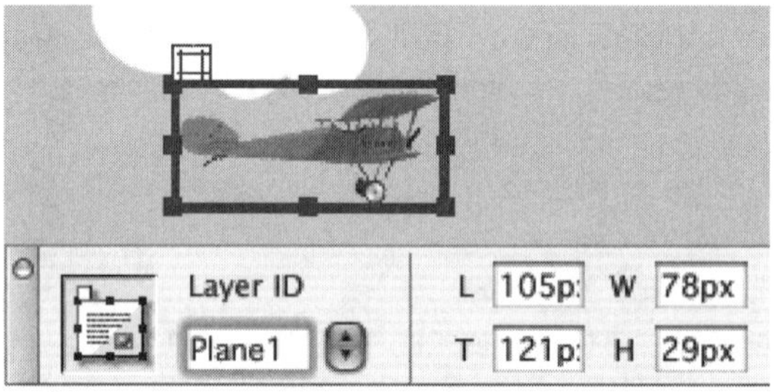

   Once you have a layer containing some content, you're ready to add it to Dreamweaver's timeline.

3. On your page, move your layer to where you want it when the animation begins.

   For example, you might want your logo to come swooping in from the top-left corner. Therefore, you'd position the layer at the top left of your page, where it should be before the animation sequence starts.

4. Open the Timelines panel by choosing Window > Timelines.

5. Add your layer to the timeline by choose Modify > Timeline > Add Object.

   When the layer is added, Dreamweaver displays a message detailing the layer attributes that can be animated in the timeline. This message will appear every time you add a layer to the timeline, so if you want to disable it, select Don't Show Me This Message Again and click OK to continue.

   Dreamweaver adds the layer to the timeline, as indicated by a purple bar. New animations are always 15 frames long by default, with white circles at each end that represent keyframes: the beginning and end of a movement.

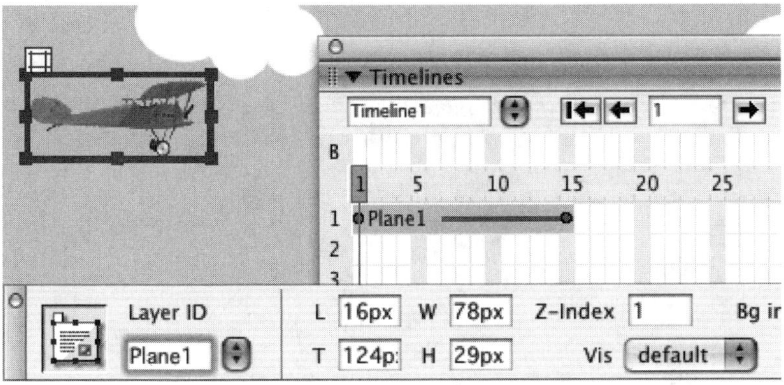

Next, you'll set the position for where the layer should be at the end of the animation.

6. Click the keyframe at the end of the purple bar in the Timelines panel.

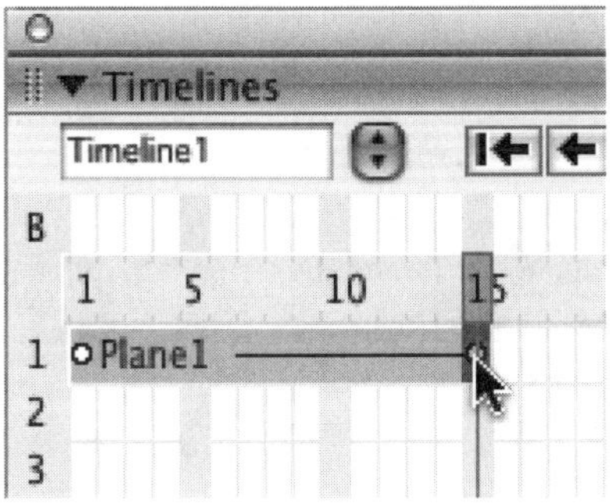

This keyframe represents the end of the animation.

7. Drag the layer on your page to where you want it to appear when the animation ends.

   When you drag your layer to a new position, Dreamweaver draws a path on your page, indicating where the animation begins and ends. That's how easy it is to animate objects in Dreamweaver!

8. To preview your animation, click and hold the Play button at the top of the Timelines panel.

   You can preview your animations directly in Dreamweaver without having to open the page in a browser. If you were to open your page in a web browser, you'd find that the animation doesn't play. This is because no controls on the page have been set up yet to play the timeline.

9. If you want to add a second animation to your page, repeat these steps with a new layer.

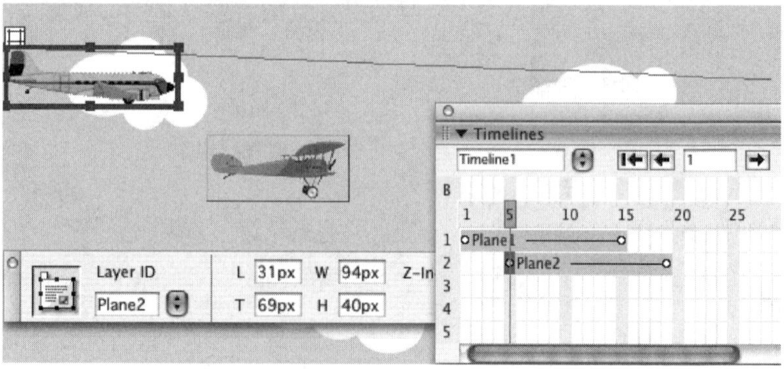

When new animations are added, they're inserted into their own channels in the Timelines panel. With two or more animations in the Timelines panel, you can drag each to the left or right to set their timing in relation to one another. For example, you might want the first animation to begin playing right away, and have the second animation starts five frames later.

Modifying Your Animation

Now you'll see how easily you can make changes to your timeline so that your animation plays back just as you want for your visitors. You'll see how to set your animation so that it plays more slowly or quickly, begins playing automatically as soon as it's loaded into a web browser, or loops indefinitely. You'll also see how to adjust keyframes.

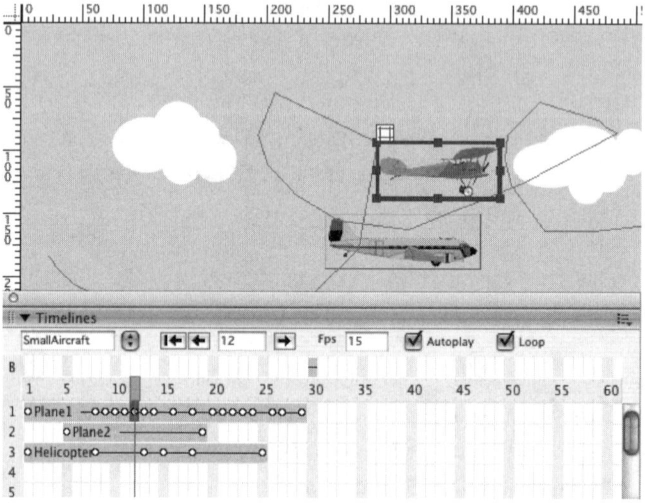

Make your timelines even more interesting by adding keyframes, setting the timeline to play automatically, and tweaking it in other ways.

Here's how to modify your animation:

1. To adjust your animation's frame rate (that is, the speed at which it plays back), enter a new value in the Fps field at the top of the Timelines panel.

   Decreasing the frame rate plays the animation more slowly; increasing it plays the animation more quickly. Keep in mind, though, that the actual frame rate your visitors will see depends on their browser, computer speed, and Internet connection. If the playback speed is important, test your animation on different computers that use a variety of connection speeds so that you can find a frame rate that meets your needs. For most animations, though, the default setting of 15 fps is fine.

2. Select Autoplay to have your animation play as soon as the page opens in your visitor's web browser.

RECORDING ANIMATIONS FREEHAND

Sometimes, you may want your layer object to follow a specific path around your page. Rather than creating an animation path within the Timelines panel, you may find it easier to drag out your own animation path and have Dreamweaver create all the required frames and keyframes that your animation needs.

To create a path by dragging, follow these steps:

1. Select the layer that you want to animate and move it to where you want the timeline to begin.

2. Choose Modify > Timeline > Record Path of Layer.

3. Drag the layer around on your page to draw the path that the animation should follow. When you're done, release the mouse button.

   As you drag around your page, you'll see a series of gray dots, indicating the path of your animation. When you release the mouse, Dreamweaver inserts the animation in the Timelines panel, complete with the necessary number of frames and keyframes.

4. Preview your animation by clicking and holding the Play button at the top of the Timelines panel.

If you want to tweak your animation, you can go back and manipulate your keyframes, which you'll see how to do in "Modifying Your Animation."

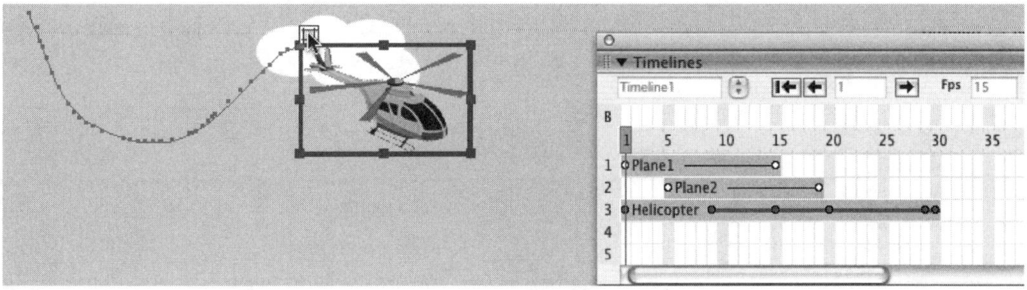

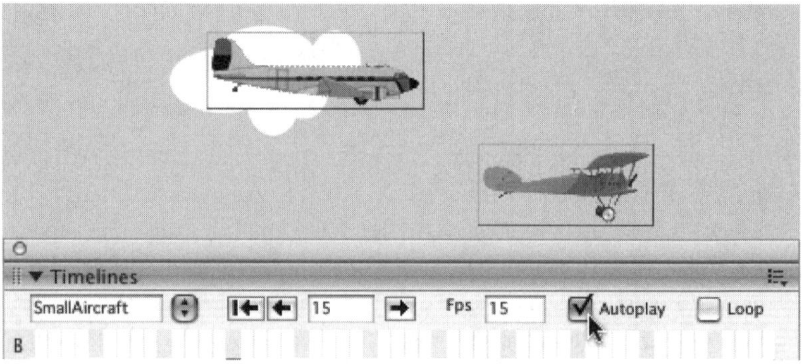

When Autoplay is selected, Dreamweaver displays a message indicating that the Play Timeline behavior has been added to control the timeline.

Rather than using Autoplay, you can set objects on your page to control the playback of a timeline. For example, maybe you want the animation to play when the visitor performs some sort of action, like clicking a button or hyperlink. To see how this is done, head down to "Using Behaviors with Timelines."

3. If you want your animation to loop continuously, select the Loop setting.

   When looping is selected, Dreamweaver displays a message informing you that the Go to Timeline Frame behavior has been added.

4. If you want to increase or decrease the length of your animation, drag the keyframe at the end of the animation timeline.

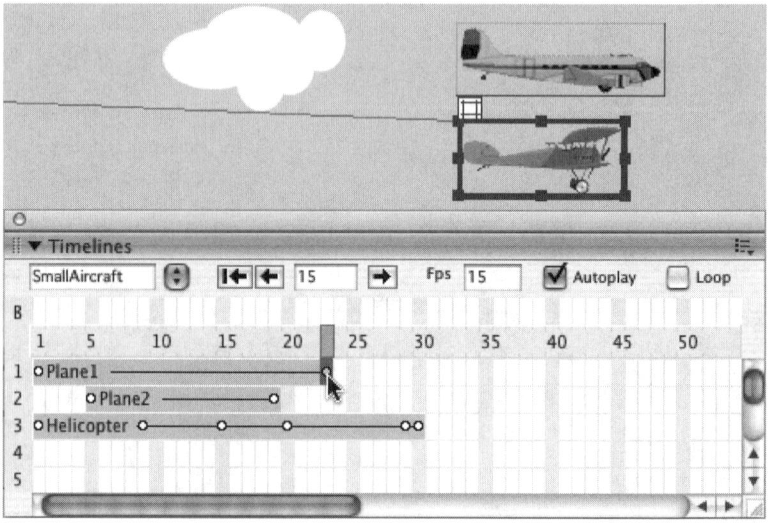

NOTEWORTHY

If you've set your timeline to loop, you can control the number of times the animation repeats by editing the Go to Timeline Frame behavior. Double-click the Go to Timeline Frame behavior in the Behaviors panel; then in the dialog box that appears, enter a value in the Loop field.

Dragging toward the left removes frames, therefore shortening the length of the animation. Dragging toward the right adds frames, increasing the animation's length.

5. To add a keyframe to your animation, click the timeline where you want the keyframe to appear; then choose Modify > Timeline > Add Keyframe.

   A white circle representing the keyframe is added to the timeline.

   Keyframes are needed whenever something in the animation changes, such as the layer object's position or properties. You can reposition a keyframe on the timeline by dragging it to the left or right, which affects the animation's timing. With the keyframe selected in the timeline, you can make changes to the layer that it controls.

6. To have your animation play in an arc, drag the layer object to a new location on the page. The animation path on your page will curve to adjust to the new keyframe's position.

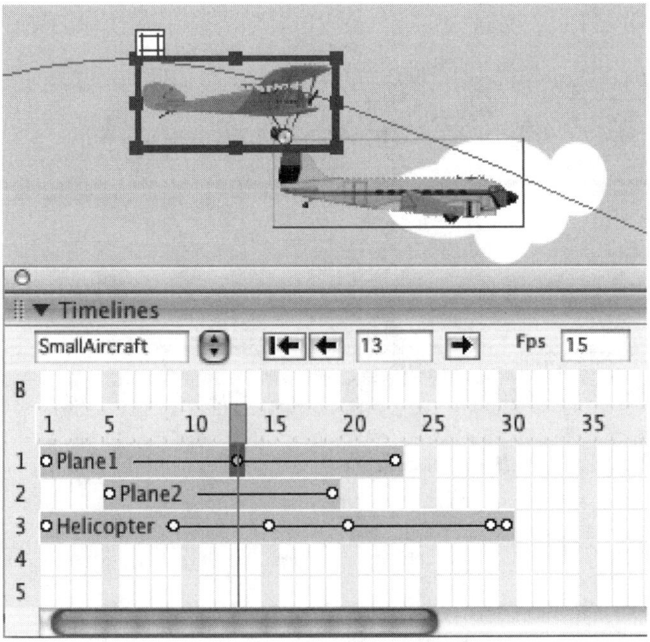

7. Use the options in the Property Inspector to change the layer's dimensions, visibility, and stacking order.

   Even when a layer is being animated with a Dreamweaver timeline, you can make changes to it. If you change the layer's size, for example, when the animation is played back, the layer will appear to shrink or expand as the timeline plays. You can achieve some very interesting effects by changing layer properties.

8. If you want to remove frames or keyframes in your timeline, choose Modify > Timeline; then choose either Remove Frame or Remove Keyframe. Dreamweaver will remove the frame or keyframe from your animation, shortening the timeline by one frame.

If you selected the Autoplay option, preview your animation in your browser to see how it works. If you didn't use Autoplay, just click and hold down the Play button at the top of the Timelines panel to see your work.

Using Behaviors with Timelines

In the previous section, you saw how you can use Autoplay to make your animation begin playing right away for your visitors. But rather than using Autoplay, you could control the playback by using a few Dreamweaver behaviors. For instance, you could set your animation to play only when the visitor performs some kind of action, like clicking a link or rolling the cursor over a graphic. You can also set up behaviors within the timeline, so that they trigger when a specific point in the timeline is reached.

You can control your animation with a behavior. You can also set up behaviors within the timeline, so that they trigger when a specific point in the timeline is reached.

Adding behaviors to your timelines allows you to sequence the interactivity on your page. When behaviors are added to the timeline, they appear as markers in the Behavior channel at the top of the Timelines panel.

Here's how to control the playback of your timeline using behaviors:

1. On your page, select the object that you want to use to trigger the playback of your timeline.

   For example, you could select a graphic that looks like a Play button, or a piece of text that says "Click here to play animation."

2. Be sure that Autoplay is turned off at the top of the Timelines panel.

3. In the Behaviors panel, click the Add Behavior button; then in the menu that appears, choose Timeline > Play Timeline.

4. In the Play Timeline dialog box that appears, choose the timeline whose playback you want to control from the Play Timeline pull-down menu; then click OK.

   Dreamweaver loads the behavior into the Behaviors panel. At this point, you can choose a different triggering event from the pull-down menu in the left column, which you saw earlier in this chapter.

5. Test your page in your browser. When your page loads into your browser, click the object that you set the behavior for.

   The animation should begin playing.

In addition, you can set up behaviors to jump to a specific frame in the timeline and to stop the timeline. In the Add Behavior menu in the Behaviors panel, choose the Go to Timeline Frame and Stop Timeline behaviors from the Timeline submenu.

You can also set up behaviors in your timeline so they are tripped by the timeline itself when the animation reaches a specific frame.

Here's how to add a behavior to your timeline:

1. In the Timelines panel, click a frame in your animation to select it.

2. Choose Modify > Timeline > Add Behavior to Timeline.

   Dreamweaver displays a message indicating that the Behaviors panel will need to be used to add a behavior to the timeline.

3. In the Behaviors panel, click the Add Behavior button; then choose an action from the menu that appears.

   From this point forward, you set a behavior just as you did earlier in this chapter. You might, for example, want a browser window to open when the animation reaches a certain point, or to make other layers on your page visible or hidden.

4. The dialog box for the behavior you chose appears. Set the parameters that you want; then click OK.

   When you click OK, the action appears in the Behaviors panel as usual, but notice the event in the left column. It's set to trigger on a specific frame in your animation. Also take a look at the Timelines panel. The first channel is marked with a B, indicating the Behaviors channel. Whenever a behavior is set for a specific frame, as is the case here, a marker appears in this channel. This marker is helpful if you need to go back and make adjustments to your timeline behavior later.

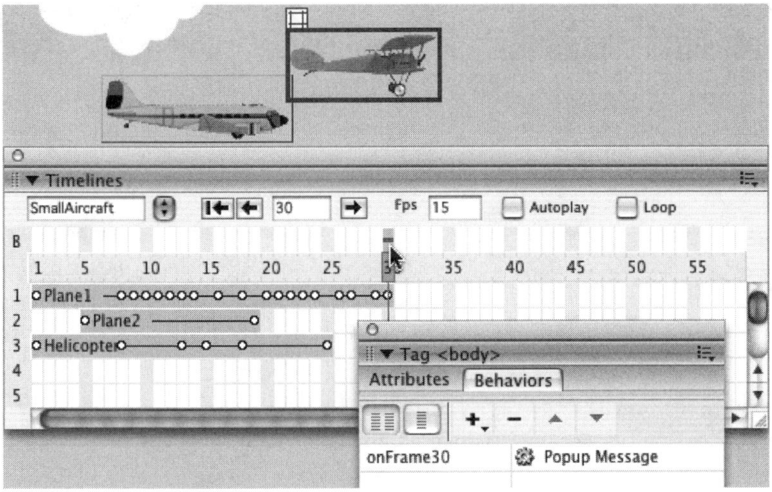

5. If you want to adjust your behavior, select the marker in the Behaviors channel in the Timelines panel; then in the Behaviors panel, manipulate your behavior's event or action, as you saw earlier in this chapter.

6. If you want to delete a behavior that you've added to the timeline, select it in the Behaviors channel; then choose Modify > Timeline > Remove Behavior.

   The behavior marker is removed from the Timelines panel.

7. Once you have a behavior or two set up in your timeline, view your page in a web browser to make sure that the behavior is being triggered as you want.

There it is: timelines controlled by behaviors, and timelines triggering behaviors. Whether used together or by themselves, behaviors and timelines add a lot of interactivity to your pages. They can help make your site a more enjoyable place to visit.

JUST THE GIST

Inserting Flash Files

- To insert Flash files on your page, choose Insert > Media > Flash.

- Use the options available on the Property Inspector to control your Flash files—most important, Quality and Scale.

Adding Audio

- Linking to audio files is the easiest way to incorporate sound into your site. Use the Link field in the Property Inspector to link to an audio file.

- When you embed an audio file, the visitor's media player controls appear on your page, allowing the visitor to play the sound file. To embed a sound file, choose Insert > Media > Plug-in.

Adding Video

- Linking to video allows visitors to download the video file to their computers, minimizing compatibility issues. Use the Property Inspector's Link field to specify the path to the video clip that you want to link to.

- When you embed video in your page, you can make it stream, so the visitor can view it as it loads on the page. To embed video, choose Insert > Media > Plugin.

Using Behaviors to Add Interactivity

- Dreamweaver's behaviors are JavaScript functions that you insert by clicking. They're available from the Behaviors panel (Window > Behaviors).

- Behaviors have two parts: an event and an action.

- To add a behavior, select an object on your page; then choose a behavior from the Add Behavior menu.

- To set a new event to trigger your behavior's action, use the pull-down menu in the left column of the Behaviors panel. To change an action's settings, double-click it in the right column of the panel to open its dialog box.

Creating Animation with Timelines

- Timelines let you animate objects in Dream–weaver, by sequencing events and special effects. All animations are created in the Timelines panel (Window > Timelines).

- Keyframes are needed whenever there's a change in the animation.

- Any object that you want to animate on your page must be contained in a layer. To add a layer and its contents to the timeline, choose Modify > Timeline > Add Object to Timeline. To animate a layer, click the animation's last frame in the Timelines panel; then move the layer to a new position on your page.

Using Behaviors with Timelines

- To use a behavior to control a timeline, use the behaviors in the Add Behavior > Timeline submenu: Go to Timeline Frame, Play Timeline, and Stop Timeline.

- To have a timeline trip a behavior, click a frame in the animation, choose Modify > Timeline > Add Behavior to Timeline, and use the Behaviors panel to set the behavior of your choice.

Chapter 12

BUILDING Forms

About Forms

You've probably filled out lots of forms online. Maybe you've filled out an online survey or purchased items from Amazon or eBay. Even just signing into your Hotmail account with your username and password is filling out a form.

STUFF YOU'LL LEARN IN THIS CHAPTER

In this chapter, you'll find out all about working with forms in Dreamweaver. You'll learn what's involved in ensuring that your form functions properly when data is submitted. Then you'll see how to insert all sorts of form objects on your page, including text boxes, radio groups, check boxes, and, of course, Reset and Submit buttons. Finally, you'll see how to use Dreamweaver's Validate Form behavior to ensure that users fill out your form correctly.

So you may already know that forms are a means of collecting various types of information supplied by visitors to a web site. For instance, you can use forms in your site to create a questionnaire or a guest book or to build database-driven pages. You may not know, however, that a form consists of two parts: what your visitor sees in the browser, and the back-end setup that runs on your web server and that handles the form content when the visitor submits it.

Forms are a means of collecting various types of information supplied by visitors to a web site.

Dreamweaver makes building the front-end aspects of a form—what site visitors see in their browsers—easy. As you'll see, you can quickly insert various form objects, such as text fields, pull-down menus, and check boxes. Dreamweaver also lets you easily validate the information that a user inserts in your form, to make sure that the form is completed properly.

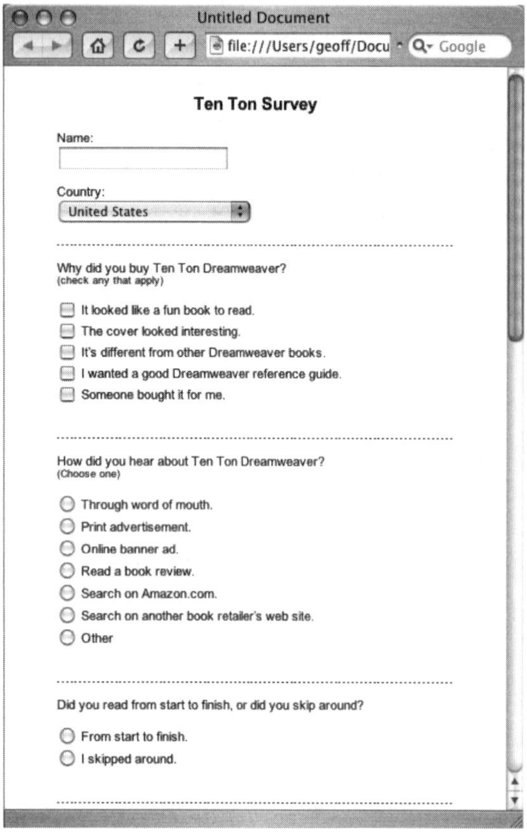

Forms provide a way for you to collect information about your web site visitors. For instance, you can use forms to create a guest book, a simple poll, or a survey like this one. To try this form in action, go to tentonbooks.com

But the back-end aspect of forms—which is required if the form is to work—can get a little hairy, especially if you're brand new to forms and web design. When your form has been filled out and the user clicks Submit, the content entered in the form is sent to a script that's installed on your web server, where it's then processed. Some back-end processing is handled by server-side technologies such as PHP, Macromedia ColdFusion, or Microsoft ASP.net, while others rely on simpler CGI (common gateway interface) scripts. The type of back-end programming and data processing that occurs depends on the type of form and site you're working with. In some cases, simple scripts compile the form data and send the information to an e-mail address. Other, more complex scripts collect the information in a database or build a web page for the visitor based on the information that the visitor provides.

Now if you're starting to feel a little woozy, don't worry. Many Internet service providers these days offer free CGI scripts and a whole bunch of other goodies for their clients. Or if you're working within a company, your system administrator should be able to help you set up whatever you need. In either case, if you want to use forms on your site, you'll be given a URL to the server-side application. All you do in Dreamweaver is set a hyperlink from your form to the application. Easy as pie.

Inserting Form Fields

Just as with every other part of your web site, you should plan what you want to create before you create it.

So are you ready to start building a form? Just as with every other part of your web site, you should plan what you want to create before you hunker down to create it. Otherwise, you'll find yourself going back and adding new elements and modifying ones you've already put on your form. So sit down with your form in mind and figure out the best way to build it—that is, what form fields will you need for the various parts of your form?

In this section, you're gonna see it all: text fields, check boxes, radio buttons, lists, pull-down menus, file fields, Reset and Submit buttons—everything you need to build a form from the ground up. But first, you have to create the form area on your page. This is the area that will hold all your form fields.

Here's how to start a form:

1. On your web page in Dreamweaver, click to place the insertion point where you want to insert the form.

   This could be in a layer, inside a table cell, or directly on your page.

2. Choose Insert > Form > Form.

   If a warning appears saying that invisible elements must be turned on, click OK; then choose View > Visual Aids > Invsible Elements. This warning will not appear if invisible elements are already turned on.

   A red frame appears on your page, indicating the form area. You'll insert all your form fields in this area.

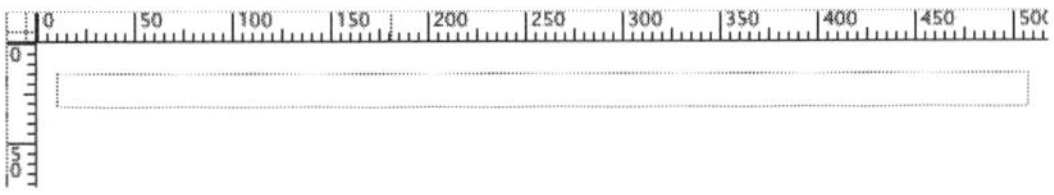

3. In the Property Inspector, enter a name for your form in the Form Name field.

   If you wish, you can leave your form with the default name, or you can type your own. Form names are used when referencing a form in JavaScript or other scripting languages.

4. In the Property Insector's Action field, enter the path to your form's back-end application or script.

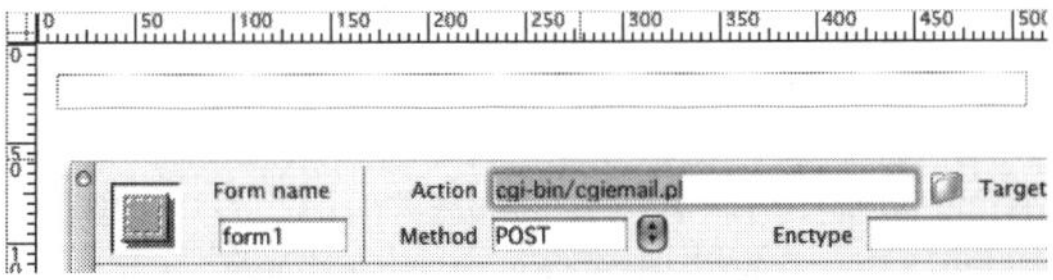

   The Action field determines what happens to the form data when the user clicks Submit. You may need to contact your ISP or system administrator for this information. If you don't yet know what to put in this field, you can leave it blank and fill it in once your form is complete and you've spoken with your ISP or system administrator.

5. Use the Method pull-down menu to specify how the form data will be sent to the web server.

NOTEWORTHY

You don't have to start by creating a form area on your page. Instead, you can insert a form object, such as a text field or a check box, and Dreamweaver will prompt you to insert a form along with it.

The Method pull-down menu defaults to Post, which is the most frequently used option for submitting a form. Post allows an unlimited file size to be sent to your server. However, in your particular setup, you may need to use Get, which limits the amount of data that may be submitted.

> **NOTEWORTHY**
>
> If you want to use a table to control your form, click to place the insertion point inside your form's red frame and choose Insert > Table. In the Table dialog box that appears, enter the number of rows and columns that you need for your form, as well as the width of your table. If you planned your form as we discussed earlier, you should have a good idea of the size of table that you'll need to control your form. How many fields do you plan to use? Placing each field on its own row is usually easiest.

Again, your system administrator or Internet service provider should be able to tell you which method is required for your particular configuration.

6. If necessary, use the Enctype pull-down menu to set the encryption type for submitted form data.

This setting determines what format submitted data is sent in, so the application or script on your web server will know how to handle it. For example, you'll need to use this setting if your form will allow users to upload files. Check with your system administrator or Internet service provider for details.

With your form set up, you're ready to begin inserting form fields. Some designers use tables to help line up the text and fields in their forms. You can use this approach, or you can control the positioning of your fields via CSS after you've inserted them on your page. Remember: Tables may be fast and easy upfront, but CSS makes content a heck of a lot easier to manage down the road. For more on using CSS to control your forms, see the sidebar "Controlling Form Objects with CSS" later in this chapter.

Whenever you want a field for the user to type in, you insert a text field.

With the form area now set on your page, you're ready to begin inserting the fields that you want. We'll start with the easiest first—text fields—and then go from there.

Inserting Text Fields

Often, you'll want a field where the user of your form can type content—the user's name or e-mail address, for example, or comments or a message. Whenever you want a field for the user to type in, you insert a text field.

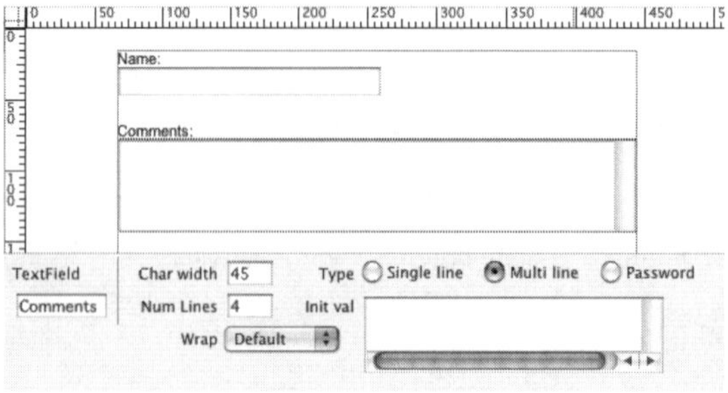

Text fields allow the user to enter alphanumeric content into your form, such as the person's name, comments, and zip code. Text fields come in several flavors, including single line and multiline, as seen here.

Text fields come in three flavors: single line, multiline, and password. Single-line text fields are perfect for short bits of information, like a name or zip code. Multiline text fields give the user a larger space to type in, so they're well suited for comment fields, for example. Any content that's typed in a password field appears as a row of asterisks (Windows) or dots (Mac).

NOTEWORTHY

Information entered in a password field isn't encrypted—it simply appears as a row of asterisks (Windows) or dots (Mac) on the form. For data transmission to be secure, the web server must be configured with a security certificate, so that data can be transmitted via Secure Socket Layer (SSL). Certificates must be purchased from a third party (like VeriSign) and installed on the web server. When a page is secure, the URL will start with https:// and most browsers will display a lock icon (or something similar) at the lower right of the browser window.

Here's how to insert a text field:

1. Click to place the insertion point where you want to insert the text field.

2. On Dreamweaver's Insert bar, open the Forms category.

   If the Insert bar isn't visible, choose Window > Insert to display it.

3. In the Forms category of the Insert bar, click the Text Field button.

   If you have Dreamweaver's accessibility controls turned on (they're on by default), Dreamweaver displays the Input Tag Accessibility Attributes dialog box. For more on creating forms with accessibility, see the sidebar "Creating Forms with Accessibility" later in this chapter.

   Dreamweaver inserts a text field on your page.

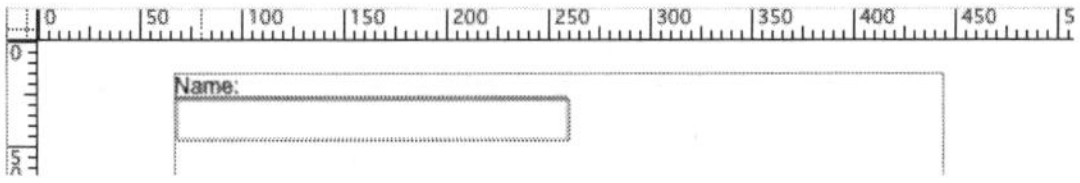

4. In the Property Inspector, give your text field a name in the TextField field.

   Dreamweaver gives all inserted fields a default name—in this case, TextField. You can leave these default names, but a more descriptive name is often better. For example, if you're providing a text field for the user's e-mail address, name the field E-mail. For more on naming fields, see the sidebar "Naming Form Fields" later in this chapter.

5. Set the width of your text field by entering a value in the Char Width field.

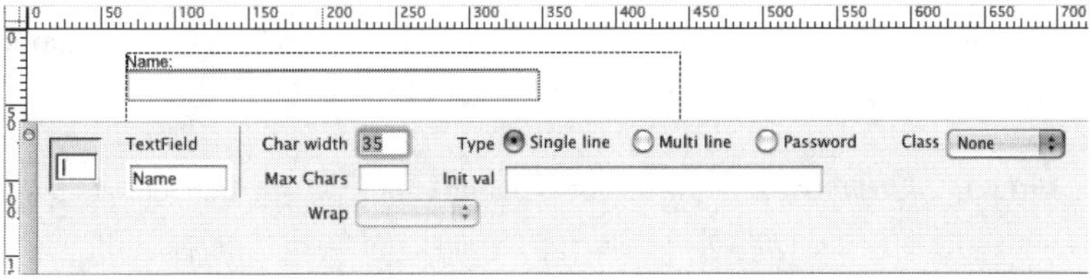

You can leave the width set to its default value or enter a new value. Unlike with most other page elements in Dreamweaver, text field width is not measured in pixels, but in character widths. This means that setting the text field width is hit or miss. However, even though you can control text field width here, the visitor's web browser really determines the size. Therefore, as always, it's important to preview your work.

6. If you want to control the number of characters that the user can insert in the text field, enter a value in the Max Chars field.

   You can use this setting to help ensure that the user correctly enters information such as a zip code or telephone number, or to limit the length of comments.

NOTEWORTHY

When creating a multi-line text field, rather than inserting a text field and then setting it to Multi Line in the Property Inspector, you can click the Text Area button in the Forms category of the Insert bar, and Dreamweaver will insert a Multi Line text field for you.

7. Select a Type option to specify the type of text field you're creating.
   Single Line: Use this setting if you want the user to enter only a single line of text. This option is useful for names and e-mail addresses, for instance.

   Multi Line: When you choose Multi Line, the height of the text field (also called the text area) expands, giving the user additional room to type. You can use this option to provide an area where the user can enter comments or ask a question, for example.

   Password: Select Password if you want the user to enter a password. Any characters that the user types appear in the text field as asterisks (Windows) or dots (Mac).

   Remember that the Password setting does not encrypt data when it's submitted; the data appears as asterisks or dots, but only on the form page. When the form is submitted, the data can be read by whatever page is set in the action.

8. If you choose Multi Line as the field type, choose an option from the Wrap pull-down menu to determine how the text field handles wrapped text.
   Default: Allows the visitor's web browser to determine how the text wraps within the text field.

   Off: Shuts off text wrapping. The user can keep typing, and the text won't move to a new line until the user presses Enter (Windows) or Return (Mac).

   Virtual: Wraps the text in the text field on the user's screen, but submits the entry to the web server as a single, unbroken line of text.

Physical: Wraps the text in the text field on the user's screen and retains all the line breaks when the form is submitted to the web server.

9. If you want text to appear by default in the text field, type the entry in the Init Val field.

   Init Val—short for initial value—is useful when you want to show visitors a default value (if you expect them to enter a particular value) or an example of how text should be inserted in a field. For instance, you might enter the formatting of the date: dd/mm/yy.

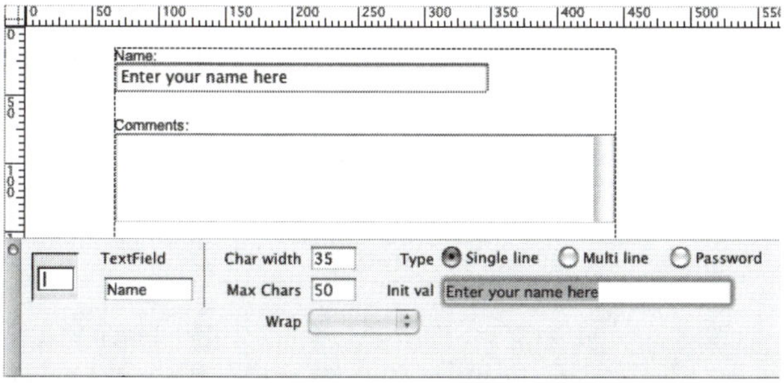

NAMING FORM FIELDS

As you're building your form, you may want take some care with the names of the fields that you insert, instead of leaving the names that Dreamweaver uses by default or choosing unspecific names like Textfield or Checkbox2. Names can be especially important when you're handling the data after the user submits it to the web server.

The web server receives the form entries as text-based data. The names of the fields appear, followed by an equal (=) sign, followed by the content that the user entered. For example, if your form contains a text field named E-mail and a user fills in your form with `info@tentonbooks.com` and clicks Submit, on the back-end that field will appear as E-mail=info@tentonbooks.com.

Therefore, when naming your fields—from text fields, to check boxes, to pull-down menus—choose names that will help you read the content or enter the data in a database.

CREATING FORMS WITH ACCESSIBILITY

You should build your forms so they are as user friendly as possible, including those with disabilities. To help you, Dreamweaver includes accessibility options for many types of page elements, including forms.

You don't have to use these features, but more and more web designers are creating pages for visitors on the web who have impaired vision, reading disabilities, or other special needs.

With accessibility turned on, Dreamweaver displays the Input Tag Accessibility Attributes dialog box whenever you insert a form object (the dialog box will not appear when jump menus and radio groups are inserted, however).

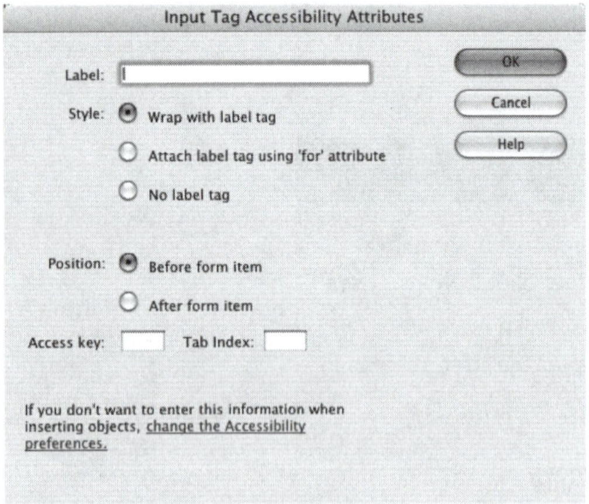

Add accessibility features to your forms to ensure that users with disabilities can use them. It all starts in the Input Tag Accessibility Attributes dialog box.

Here's how to set the Input Tag Accessibility Attributes dialog box:

1. In the Label field, enter the text that you want to appear on the page beside the field.

   For example, if you're inserting a field where you want the user to type his or her name, your label might be First Name and Last Name. Unlike the text that everyone can see on your web page, this label can be read aloud by screen reader software, depending on the label tag you choose in the dialog box.

2. Select a Style setting to determine how your label tag should be handled in your page's background code.

   Wrap with Label Tag: This option encloses the label and form element in a single container in your code, within the <label></label> tag pair. However, you can't position the label anywhere you want to with this tag, and it's not always fully compatible with screen readers.

   Attach Label Tag Using 'For' Attribute: This option is useful if the label and form element are separated, perhaps by table cells that are being used to control the layout of the form. It's also the most compatible with screen readers. In the code, it inserts an attribute in the <label> tag to connect it to its associated form element. For example, your code would appear as `<label for="textfield">First and Last Name</label><input type="text" name="textfield" id="textfield" />`.

   No Label Tag: Doesn't use a label tag at all. If you use this option, screen readers will not be able to read your label. Therefore, the code appears as `First and Last Name<input type="text" name="textfield" />`.

CREATING FORMS WITH ACCESSIBILITY (CONTINUED)

3. Select a Position setting to determine whether the label appears before the form item or after it.

4. If you want, in the Access Key field, enter a single character to act as a keyboard shortcut for the form object.

   The access key is useful for giving disabled users a way to jump from one part of a form to another. When viewing the form, the user will need to press a modifier key, such as Ctrl or Alt (Windows) or Command or Option (Mac), as well as the shortcut key to be taken directly to the field. The modifier key needed is determined by the user's platform and browser.

5. If you want, insert a numeric value in the Tab Index field to set the field's tab order.

   If you set values in the Tab Index field for the fields in your form, the user will be able to press the Tab key to cycle through your form fields in the order that you establish. For this feature to work correctly, you need to set incremental values for all the fields in your form.

Inserting Check Boxes

Use check boxes when you want site visitors to select multiple items in a list. For example, you might ask your visitors to select their preferred types of music from a list of popular music styles. Visitors could then check any music styles that they enjoy, leaving the styles they don't enjoy (speed demon death metal, of course) unchecked. In a list of check boxes, the user can check or leave unchecked as many items as they like. To let visitors know their options, you may want to preface the list with the message, "Check any that apply."

Use check boxes when you want site visitors to select multiple items in a list.

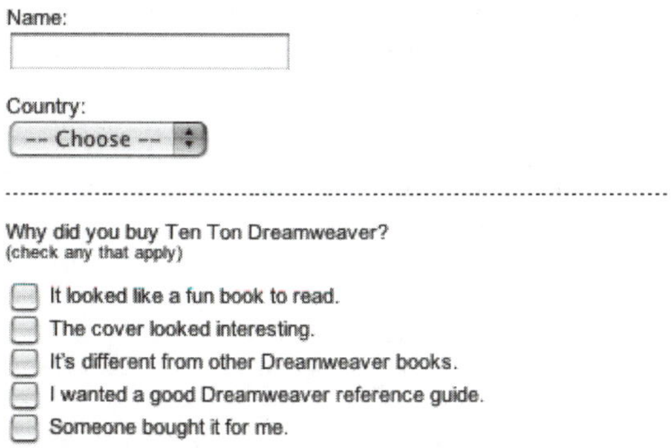

Check boxes allow the user to make multiple selections in a group of choices. Whenever you include a group of check boxes, it's a good idea to include an instruction that says "Check any that apply."

If you want to set up your list of items so that the user can select only one item, insert a group of radio buttons instead of check boxes. You'll see how to work with radio buttons in the next section

NOTEWORTHY

People often confuse check boxes and radio buttons. From a group of check boxes, you can select as many items as you want, and from a group of radio buttons, you can select only one.

Here's how to insert check boxes:

1. Click to place the insertion point where you want the check box to appear.

2. In the Forms category of the Insert bar, click the Checkbox button.

   Dreamweaver inserts a check box where you placed the cursor.

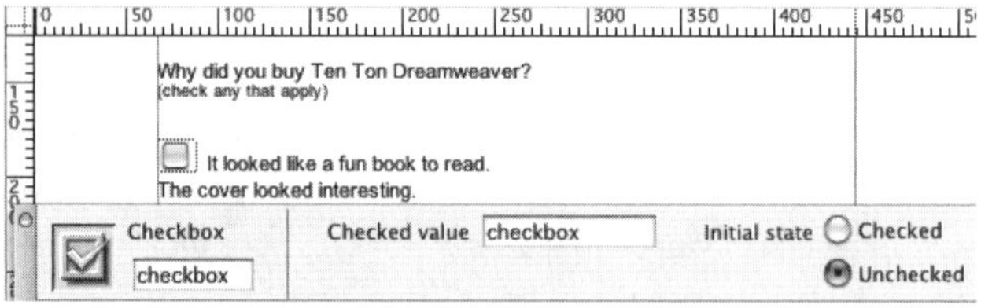

3. In the Property Inspector's Checkbox field, give your check box a name.

   Dreamweaver inserts a default name, but you'll most likely want to change it.

4. In the Checked Value field, type the field entry that will be submitted to the web server.

   As you saw in the sidebar "Naming Form Fields," when a text field is submitted to a web server, the content that the user enters in the field is displayed after the field's name and an equal sign. But with check boxes, the user doesn't make an entry. Therefore, the text that's set in the Checked Value field is the entry that's submitted to the server.

   For example, you might name your check box `Favorite_Music` and set the check box's value to **`Ambient`**. On the back-end, the form data would appear as Favorite_Music=Ambient.

5. Select an Initial State setting to specify whether the check box is initially checked or unchecked for the user.

6. To add more check boxes to your form, repeat steps 1 through 5.

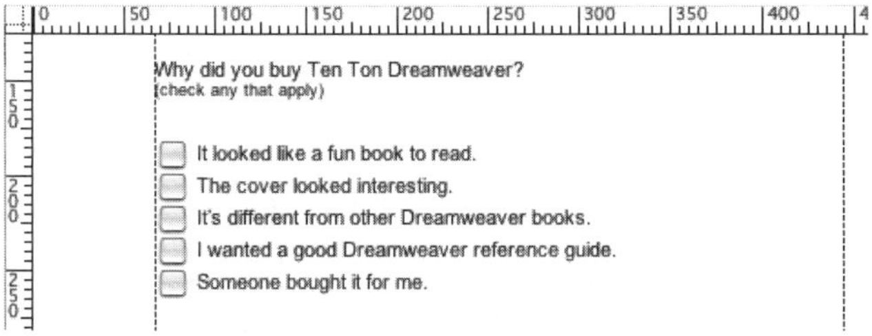

Inserting Radio Buttons

Radio buttons may seem similar to check boxes initially; however, while the visitor can select multiple check boxes, only one radio button within a group can be selected at a time. For example, you might ask site visitors what time zone they live in: Pacific, Mountain, Central, Eastern, or Atlantic. You can then set up a group of radio buttons so your visitors can make only one choice.

While the visitor can select multiple check boxes, only one radio button within a group can be selected at a time.

You restrict the user to only one selection by using the same name for each radio button in the group. Then when the user selects a radio button in the group, any previously selected radio button is automatically deselected. Although you can insert radio buttons individually, to make sure that each radio button in a group uses the same name you can use Dreamweaver's Radio Group command.

NOTEWORTHY

If you want to insert radio buttons individually, use the Radio Button command on Dreamweaver's Insert-bar. This approach is useful if you've added a radio group, but you've forgotten an item or two. After inserting the radio button, you can select it and set the options that appear in the Property Inspector.

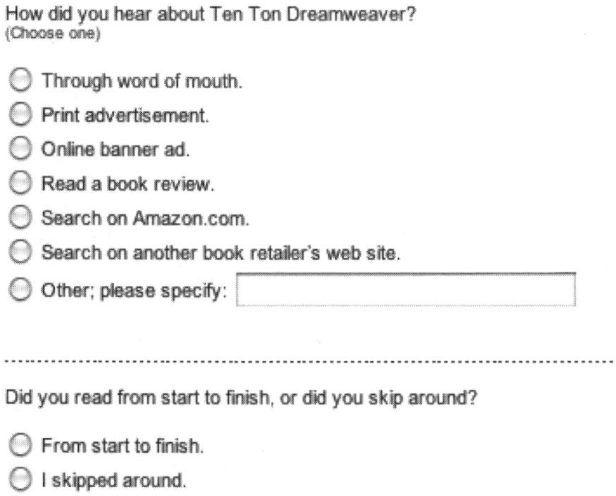

Radio buttons may look similar to check boxes; however, the user can select only a single button within a group of choices.

Here's how to insert a set of radio buttons:

1. Click to place the insertion point where you want the radio button to appear.

2. In the Forms category of the Insert bar, click the Radio Group button.

3. In the Radio Group dialog box that appears, enter a name for your radio group in the Name field.

4 In the Radio Buttons box, click the first Radio entry in the Label column; then give your first radio button a name.

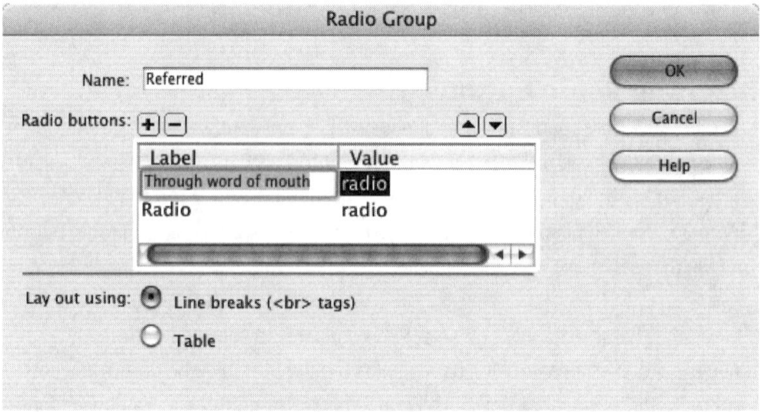

5. Click Tab to move to the Value column; then enter a value for the first radio button.

   As with check boxes, a radio button's value is returned to the server when the user selects the button.

6. Click Tab again to move to the second radio button and repeat steps 1 through 5.

7. If you need additional radio buttons for your radio button group, click the + (plus) button at the top of the Radio Buttons box.

   To remove any unwanted radio buttons, select them in the Radio Buttons box and click the – (minus) button.

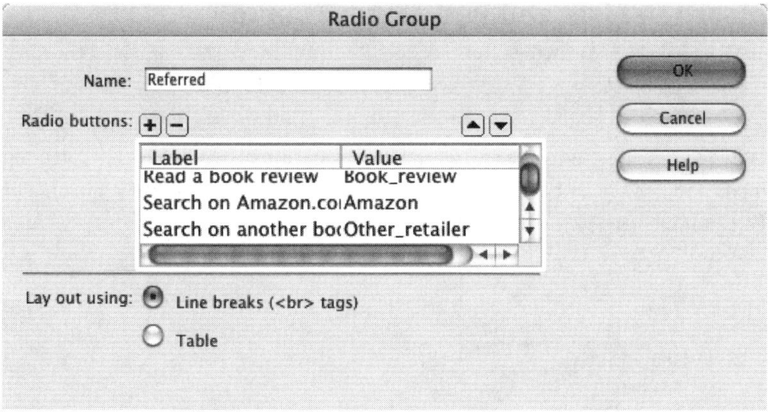

8. Select a Lay Out Using setting at the bottom of the dialog box to determine how your radio group is controlled on your page.

   You can set up your radio group so that your entries are separated by forced line breaks (
 tags) within a single paragraph, or organized into a table. If you use a table, each radio button is placed in its own row.

9. Click OK when you're done.

   Dreamweaver inserts the group of radio buttons onto your page. If you want to make further changes to your radio buttons, just select them and use the settings in the Property Inspector.

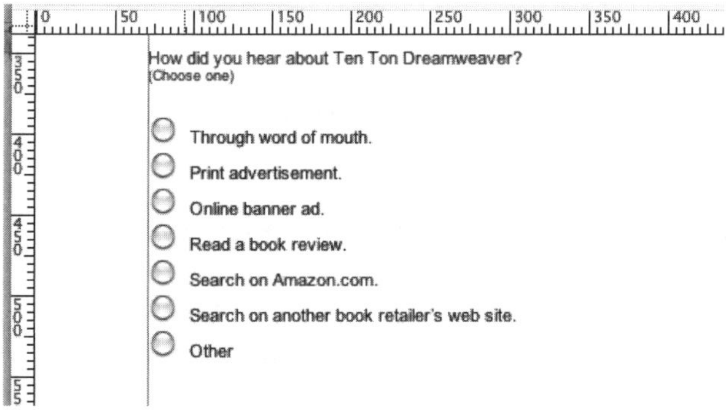

IMMINENT DOOM

If you select a radio button in a group and change its name in the Property Inspector, it will no longer be associated with the group, meaning that the set of radio buttons will not work as expected.

Inserting Lists and Pull-Down Menus

A list appears as a scrollable set of options, and the user can select more than one option. A pull-down menu is also a set of items, but the user can't make multiple selections.

Lists and pull-down menus work exactly the same way. The only difference is their appearance on the screen and the amount of space they take up. A list appears as a scrollable set of options on your form, and the user can select more than one option before clicking Submit. A pull-down menu is also a set of items; the user can open the menu and choose an option, but unlike with lists, the user can't make multiple selections from a pull-down menu.

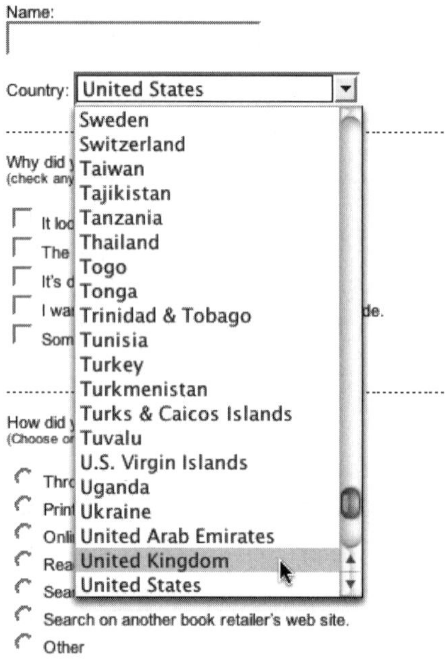

Pull-down menus can offer the user many choices, but when they're closed, they take up very little space on the page.

A nice thing about lists and menus is that they let you control the choices that the user can make. For example, you can ask the user to select a state from a menu of the 50 states in the USA, and so ensure that when the form is submitted to your web server, the state appears in the format that you want (abbreviated, for example).

Here's how to insert a list or menu:

1. Click to place the insertion point where you want the list or menu to appear.

2. In the Forms category of the Insert bar, click the List/Menu button.

   Dreamweaver inserts a blank pull-down menu on your page.

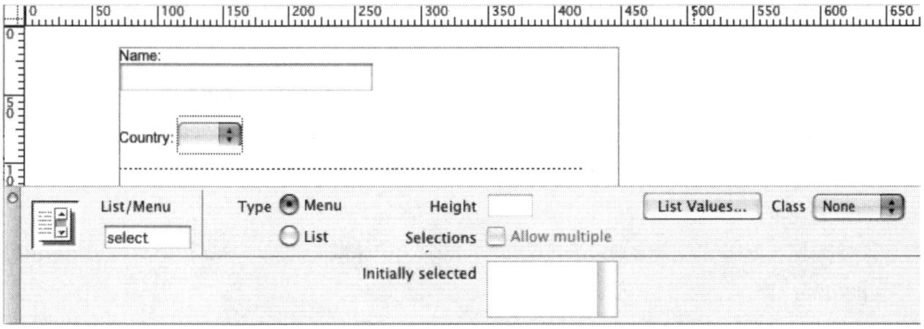

Clicking the List/Menu button will insert this handy "starter" menu on your page.

3. In the Property Inspector, enter a name for your list or menu in the List/Menu field.

4. Select a Type setting to specify whether your form object will be a list or a pull-down menu.
   Menu: Creates a pull-down menu.

   List: Creates a selection list.

   If you choose List, the Height and Selections options become available. In the Height field, enter the number of rows that you want your list to display on the page. A scrollbar will appear to display any rows that are not visible. Use the Selections option to specify whether the user can make multiple selections in the list.

5. Click the List Values button in the Property Inspector to add items to your list or pull-down menu.

6. In the List Values dialog box that appears, click the Item Label column and type the first entry for your list or pull-down menu.

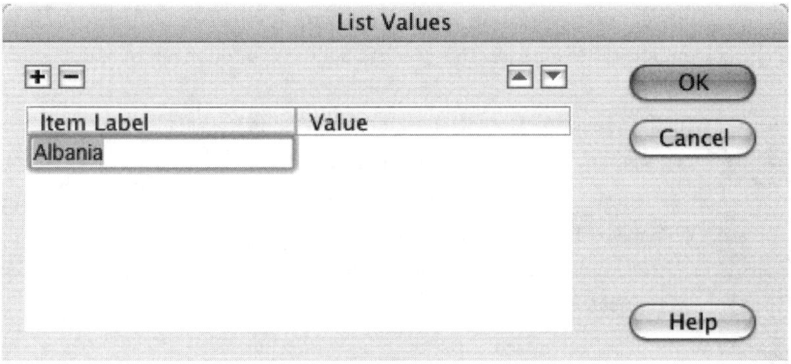

NOTEWORTHY

If you allow multiple selections in your list, users can Shift-click or they can Ctrl-click (Windows) or Command-click (Mac) to make selections. You may want to include a text message in your form letting users know they can do this.

7. Press the Tab key to move to the Value field; then type the value for your entry.

   Just as with check boxes and radio buttons, the value is the data that will be submitted with the form. For example, your list item may read United States (what the user sees), but the value returned to the server may be USA.

8. Press Tab again to continue with the next entry. Continue adding list items and values.

9. When you're done, click OK.

10. In the Property Inspector, choose one of your list or menu items from the Initially Selected box to specify which of your items appears selected by default.

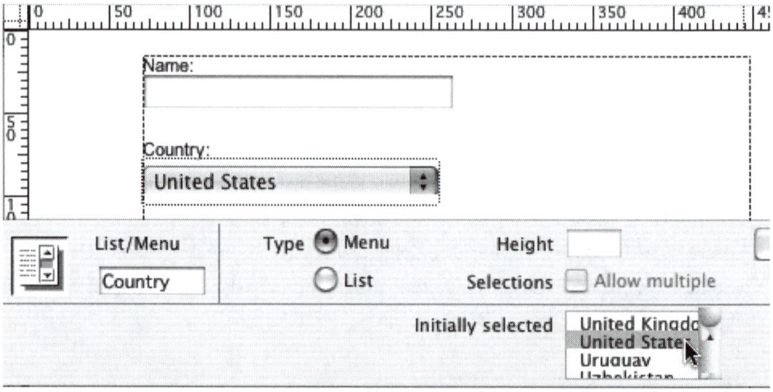

CREATING A HYPERLINK JUMP MENU

As you've surfed the web, you may have seen sites that use pull-down menus as navigational aides. For example, after you open a pull-down menu and choose an option you might be whisked away to a new page in the site (or to an entirely different site). This setup is achieved through jump menus.

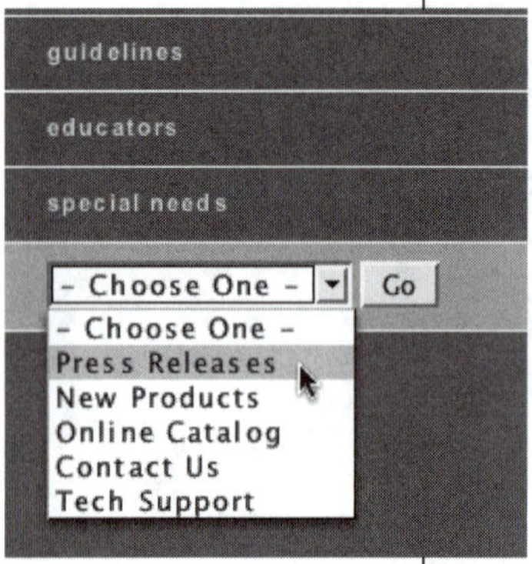

Jump menus are a handy navigational option to consider. A menu can contain as many items as you want, each of which links to its own destination.

Here's how to insert a jump menu:

1. Click to place the insertion point where you want the jump menu to appear.

2. In the Forms category of the Insert bar, click the Jump Menu button.

CREATING A HYPERLINK JUMP MENU (CONTINUED)

3. In the Insert Jump Menu dialog box that appears, in the Text field, enter a name for the first item in the menu.

4. In the When Selected Go to URL field, type the destination for your menu item.

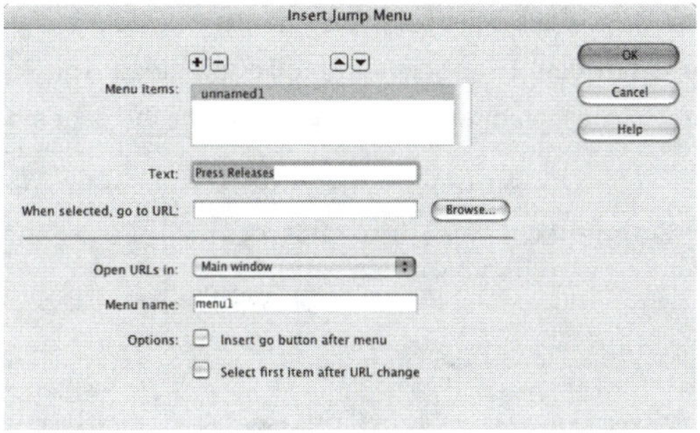

   You can either type the URL of a web site or use the Browse button to navigate to a page within your current site.

5. Do any of the following:
   - To add entries for your jump menu, click the Add Item button (+) at the top of the Menu Items list.
   - To remove menu items, click the Remove Item button (-).
   - To reorder your menu items, use the Move Item Up in List and Move Item Down in List buttons.

6. If you're working in a frameset, use the Open URLs In pull-down menu to specify where the URLs will open. (This setting only works within a frameset.)

7. In the Menu Name field, enter a name for your jump menu; then select an Options setting.

   Insert Go Button After Menu: Adds a Go button to the right of the jump menu.

   Select First Item After URL Change: Sets the jump menu back to the first item after the user has used it to jump to a destination. This option is useful only if a frameset is being used.

8. When you're done, click OK.

The jump menu is inserted on your page. To edit a jump menu after it's been inserted on your page, open the Behaviors panel (choose Window > Behaviors) and double-click the Jump Menu action. The Jump Menu dialog box opens, where you can make your changes.

Inserting File Fields

File fields are a neat addition to forms. They allow the user to upload a file to the web server when submitting a form. You can use file fields in a guest book, for example, where you want the user to upload a photo.

File fields allow the user to upload a file to the web server when submitting a form.

When you insert a file field, Dreamweaver adds a browse button, which the user can use to navigate to and select the file to upload. This file can be a text file, a spreadsheet, a graphic, or any other type of file on the user's computer.

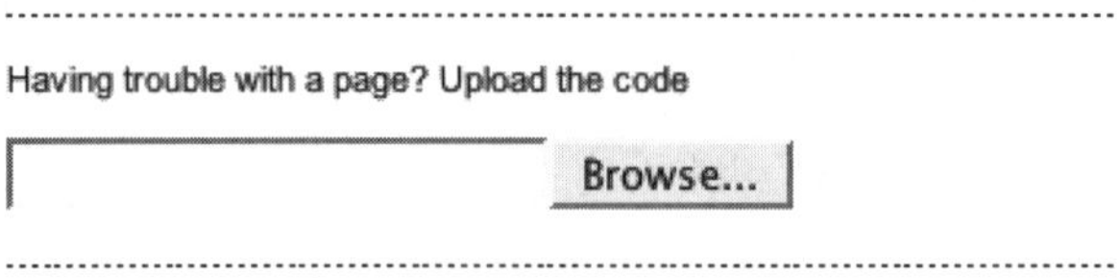

File fields allow users to upload files when they submit forms. Dreamweaver makes inserting file fields easy; however, for a file field to work correctly, the application or script that processes the form on the back end must be able to handle file uploads.

If you want to include a file field in your form, the application or script running on the web server that will collect all the form data must be able to accept file uploads. Also, your form's method must be set to POST, which you saw how to do in "Inserting Form Fields" earlier in this chapter. If you're uncertain about these settings, contact your system administrator or Internet service provider.

Here's how to insert a file field:

1. Click to place the insertion point where you want the file field to appear.

2. In the Forms category of the Insert bar, click the File Field button.

   Dreamweaver inserts the file field in your form.

   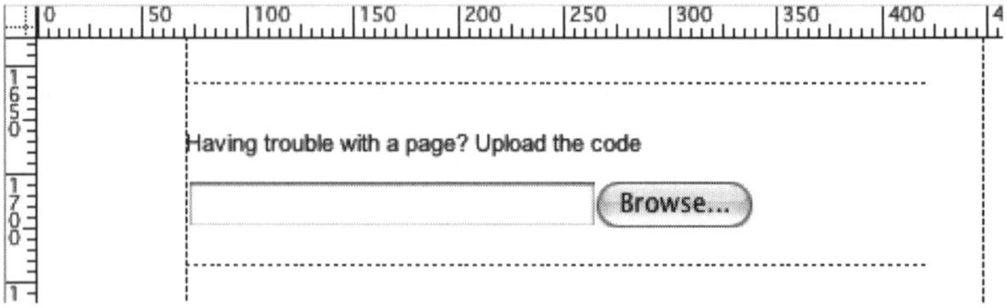

3. In the Property Inspector, enter a name for your file field in the File Field Name field.

4. If you want, use the Char Width and Max Chars options to set the width of your file field and the maximum number of characters it can hold.

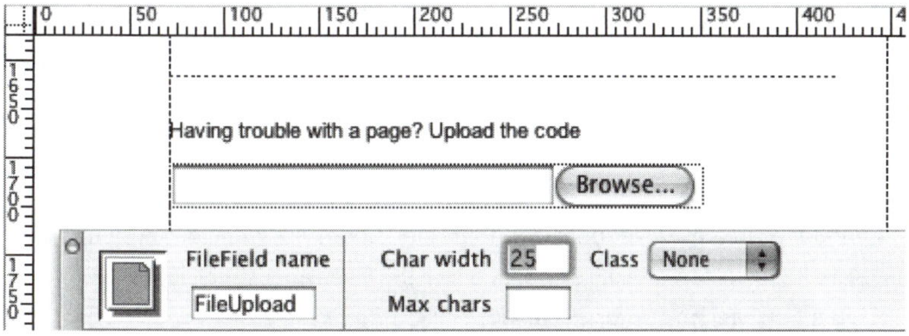

Typically, forms include two buttons: a Submit button and a Reset button.

Inserting Reset and Submit Buttons

You'll want a way for the user to submit your form to you. For this, you'll need to insert some buttons. Typically, forms include two buttons: a Submit button and a Reset button.

The Submit button triggers the link that you learned how to set in the Property Inspector's Action field in "Inserting Form Fields" earlier in this chapter. The link starts the application on your web server, which then receives the form data. The Reset button clears away all the entries that have been made in the form and resets all the fields to their default settings.

> **NOTEWORTHY**
>
> Form buttons don't have to only submit and reset forms. In fact, you can set them to do any number of things. After you've inserted a button, you can select it and set a behavior for it using Dreamweaver's Behavior panel. You can make a button open a URL, display a pop-up message, and more. Or you can delve into the world of JavaScript and make buttons do all kinds of wonderful things, like calculate sales tax, for example.

Here's how to insert a button in your form:

1. Click to place the insertion point where you want the button to appear. Usually, buttons appear at the bottom of a form.

2. In the Forms category of the Insert bar, click Button.

   A button is inserted in your form, with the default label "Submit." You'll see how to change this shortly.

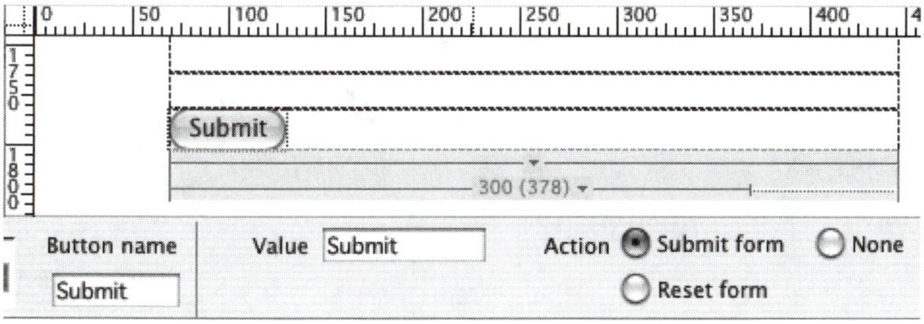

3. In the Property Inspector, enter a name for your button in the Button Name field.

4. If you want to change the text that appears on the button, enter the new text in the Value field.

   For example, if you want your button to say Reset, or Go, or Giddy Up Cowboy, enter the text in the Value field.

5. Use the Action setting to specify the appropriate action for your button.

   Your button can either submit or reset a form. However, you can also use it to trigger a Dreamweaver behavior. To trigger a behavior with your button, make sure it's selected on your page, and use the Behaviors panel, just as when you set a behavior on text or a graphic.

6. Repeat steps 1 through 5 to add any other buttons into your form.

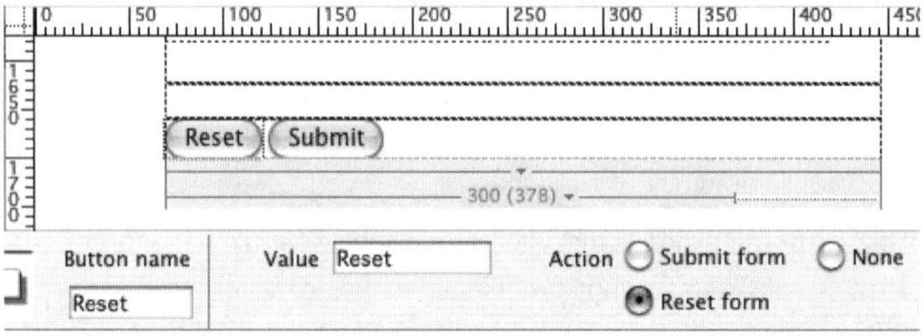

Ensuring That Your Form Is Completed Correctly

You've worked hard to create your form. The last thing you need is for a buncha yahoo users to go and mess it up by not filling it in as you'd intended! Dreamweaver provides a tool for you to control the type of data inserted in your form: the Validate Form behavior. For example, if you ask the user to provide a zip code, you can ensure that the user inserts only numbers, not letters. If you ask for an e-mail address, you can make sure that the user actually inserts an address.

To ensure that your form is filled out as you intend, you can use Dreamweaver's Validate Form behavior. As you can see here, if users don't insert form content properly, they can't submit the form.

INSERTING IMAGE BUTTONS

Rather than using plain buttons in your forms, you can customize your buttons to match the design of your site. Dreamweaver lets you insert any image you like and set it to control your forms.

Here's how to insert an image button:

1. Click to place the insertion point where you want the button to appear.

2. In the Forms category of the Insert bar, click the Image Field button.

3. In the Image Source dialog box that appears, navigate to and select the image that you want to use for the button; then click OK.

   The image button is inserted into your form.

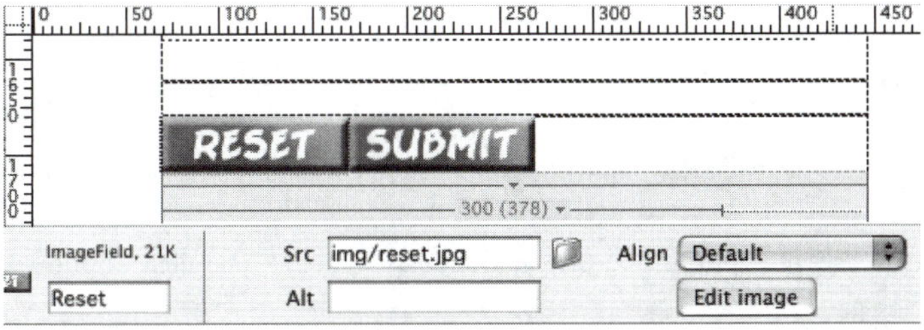

4. Use the Property Inspector's Image Field field to give your button a name.

   If you want your image button to function as a Submit button, for instance, type Submit in the Image Field field. You can also set a Dreamweaver behavior to make the button function.

5. Add alternative text for your image button by entering text in the Alt field.

The Validate Form behavior not only enforces the rules for entering data in a form, but it also keeps data consistent so it can be easily compiled at the back-end.

The Validate Form behavior not only enforces the rules for entering data in a form, but it also keeps data consistent so it can be easily compiled at the back-end. Only entries made in text fields can be validated; other field types don't allow users to insert their own content.

Here's how to validate a form:

1. Select your form by clicking the `<form>` tag in the Tag Selector on Dreamweaver's Status bar.

   The `<form>` tag in the Tag Selector will actually appear as `<form#` followed by the name that you gave your form when you inserted it.

2. If it's not already on screen, open the Behaviors panel (choose Window > Behaviors).

3. From the Add Behavior menu in the Behaviors panel, choose Validate Form.

4. In the Validate Form dialog box that appears, select a text field from the Named Fields list.

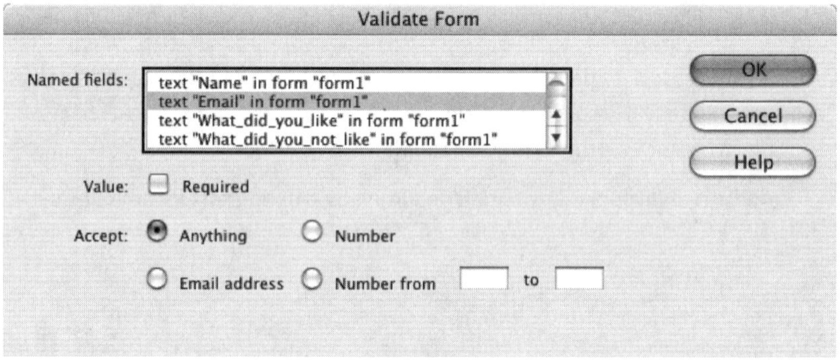

5. If you want the selected field to be a field that the user must fill in, select Required for the Value option.

6. For the Accept option, select the type of data that the field will accept.

   Anything: Allows the user to enter any type of data in the field.

   Email Address: Accepts only an e-mail address as an entry.

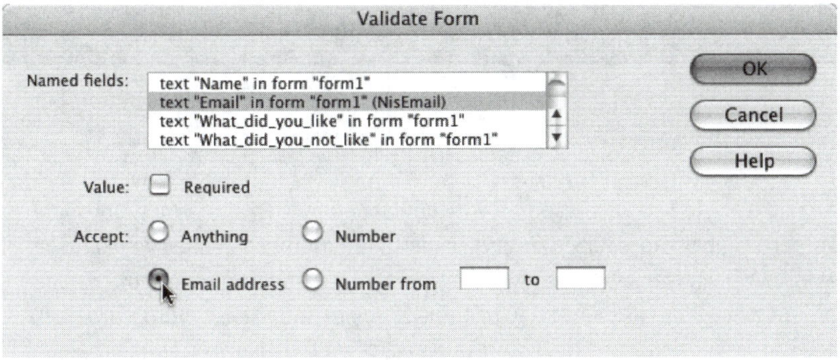

Number: Allows only numbers to be entered in the field.

Number From: Accepts a number only if it falls within the specified range of numbers.

7. If you want to validate another text field, select it in the Named Fields list and repeat steps 5 and 6.

8. When you're done, click OK.

   The Behaviors panel displays the onSubmit event, with the Validate Form action. This means that the form will be validated when the user clicks the form's Submit button.

NOTEWORTHY

If you want to validate an individual field rather than the entire form, you can do so. Select the text field that you want to validate; then set the Validate Form behavior for it.

CONTROLLING FORM OBJECTS WITH CSS

As you're inserting form objects, you may notice that when they're selected, the Property Inspector displays a Class pull-down menu. If you've created some custom Class CSS styles in your document, you can use this menu to assign a style to the form object. See where this is going? You can use CSS styles to tightly control the positioning and appearance of your form elements on your page. In fact, using CSS is the best way to control your forms.

For example, you may want to control the spacing around your form objects, or control the background or border color of your elements. Or you may want to redefine the HTML `<form>` tag to control aspects of your entire form. Either way, using CSS to control your form and form objects is exactly the same as using it to control text or other elements on your page—it's all handled in the CSS Styles panel. You use the settings that are available in the CSS Rule Definition dialog box (which appears when you double-click a style in the CSS Styles panel), just as you do when controlling other objects on your page.

JUST THE GIST

About Forms

- Forms let you collect information supplied by visitors to your site.
- A form consists of two parts: what the user interacts with in the web browser, and an application or script that runs on your web server that handles submitted data.
- For a form to work correctly, a back-end application or script must be set up. Consult your system administrator or Internet service provider for details.

Inserting a Form

- Insert a form by choosing Insert > Form > Form.
- Use the settings in the Property Inspector to determine how your form interacts with the application or script running on your web server.

Inserting Form Fields

- Text fields allow users to type their own content directly on your form. To insert a text field, click the Text Field button in the Forms category of the Insert bar.
- You can set text fields as single-line fields, multiline fields, or password fields.
- Check boxes allow users to make multiple selections from a group of choices. To insert a check box, click the Checkbox button in the Forms category of the Insert bar.
- Radio buttons restrict users to only one selection in a group of choices. To set a group of radio buttons, click the Radio Group button in the Forms category of the Insert bar, or insert them individually using the Radio Button button, also on the Insert bar.
- Lists and pull-down menus work the same way; the only difference is their appearance. Lists appear as a scrolling series of options; pull-down menus appear as a drop-down list of options. To insert a list or pull-down menu, click the List/Pull-down button in the Forms category of the Insert bar.
- File fields allow users to attach files from their computers when they submit the form. For a file field to work on your page, the application or script running on your web server must be able to handle uploaded files.
- Reset and Submit buttons allow users to clear their forms or submit forms to your web server. You can also use Dreamweaver's behaviors to set many other commands. To insert a button, click Button in the Forms category of the Insert bar.
- Set the options for your forms fields in the Property Inspector.

Ensuring That Your Form Is Completed Correctly

- To ensure that your form is filled out as you intended, you can use Dreamweaver's Validate Form behavior. The behavior works only on text fields, as the other types of form objects don't allow users to add their own content.
- To add the Validate Form behavior, select the `<form>` tag on the Tag Selector; then choose Validate Form from the Behavior panel's Add Behavior menu.

Chapter 13

Building *Template-* Driven Pages

Getting Started with Templates

Here it is—one of the coolest, if not the coolest, functions in Dreamweaver: templates! You may be familiar with templates in other software programs, such as Microsoft Word. Templates in Dreamweaver are similar, but much, much more powerful.

STUFF YOU'LL LEARN IN THIS CHAPTER

You've seen a lot of cool stuff in Ten Ton Dreamweaver, but there's one very powerful feature that hasn't been discussed: templates! Without a doubt, templates are the most powerful tool for building, maintaining, and updating sites in Dreamweaver with the least amount of effort, regardless of the size of your site. In this chapter, you'll see not only how to build templates, but also how to designate areas of your page as editable or locked. From there, you'll see how to build template-driven pages, make sitewide changes—and a whole lot more. This is it: one of the best Dreamweaver features has been saved for the end!

A Dreamweaver template is a file that's used to drive the content and layout of any number of web pages. But this is where the similarity between Dreamweaver templates and traditional templates ends. In Dreamweaver, templates contain special areas called editable regions. On pages that are based on a template, these regions are the only editable areas on the page—all other areas of the page are locked.

Dreamweaver templates contain editable regions. On pages based on a template, these regions are the only editable areas on the page—all other areas are locked.

Therefore, you can build a site with a consistent overall layout controlled by a single template file, and designate editable areas where the individual pages in the site can hold their own unique content. Any changes you make to the template are automatically applied to any pages that use it. This is precisely the same

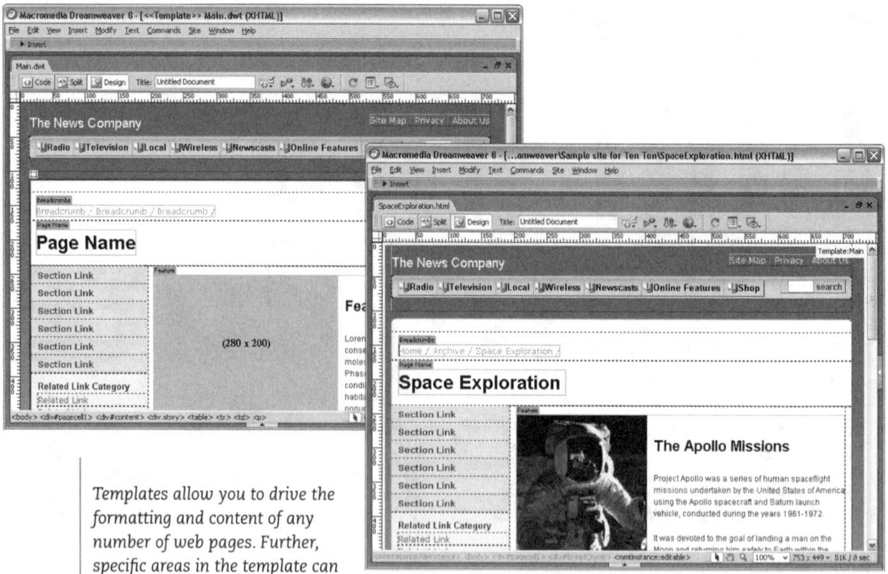

Templates allow you to drive the formatting and content of any number of web pages. Further, specific areas in the template can be designated as editable regions. As you can see in this example, the breadcrumb links, page name, and feature article (which contains a photo and text) are contained within editable regions, meaning they're fully editable in any page that's based on the template. All other areas on the page are locked.

Co-workers with no web experience can also update a web site with Macromedia Contribute. Check out macromedia.com/software/contribute to find out more.

concept underlying your ability to manipulate items in Dreamweaver's Library panel (which you saw in Chapter 5) and control page layout and formatting with CSS (discussed in Chapter 8). In fact, using templates, the Library panel, and CSS together is a sure way to easily wield complete control over your entire site, without even breaking a sweat.

Templates make managing and maintaining sites a breeze.

If you're a designer working on your own, templates make managing and maintaining sites a breeze. But if you're working with a group of people who are all contributing to a site, templates really shine. Consider this: Maybe a few co-workers will be regularly adding and updating content on the company's web site—small changes like making monthly updates and listing new products—but none of them really know much about web design. To prevent anyone from inadvertently causing damage or altering areas of the page that they shouldn't change, you can build a template to control all the pages in the site. You can then set up the pages so that the group can edit only certain areas of each page, and you can lock other areas so that the group can't change them. Even someone with no Dreamweaver or web experience will be able to update the site. You, on the other hand, will have *master control* over the entire web site, so that when larger changes need to be made (new pages, an updated navigation bar, and so on), you can make the changes in the template and update the entire site faster than you can say "Can I have a raise?" All your co-workers will think you're a web genius, and all you have to do is dog-ear this chapter in *Ten Ton Dreamweaver* in case you run into problems!

Sound powerful? It is—and it's my favorite Dreamweaver topic! So let's stop talkin' and see what templates can do for your sites.

Creating a Template and Inserting Editable Regions

So you're ready to roll with templates. The best approach to creating templates is to begin with a finished page that you want to use as the basis for the other pages in your site. This finished page will then be converted to a template and used to drive the look and layout of the other pages.

The best approach to creating templates is to begin with a finished page that you want to use as the basis for the other pages in your site.

The completed page should contain all the design and layout elements that you want to use throughout the site. For example, it should contain primary and secondary navigation controls, your site's name and logo, and any other elements that you want to appear on each page throughout your site.

In addition, it should contain dummy content (dummy text and images) that will then be marked as editable once the page has been converted to a template. In the pages that are derived from the template, this dummy content can then be replaced with the actual content that you want to appear on each page.

NOTEWORTHY

You don't have to start with a completed page when working with templates—doing so just makes creating your template easier. But if you like, you can start with a new, blank template and begin building a page layout within it. Just choose File > New; then in the New Document dialog box that appears, choose Template Page from the Category list and HTML Template from the Template Page list. Click Create, and you're away.

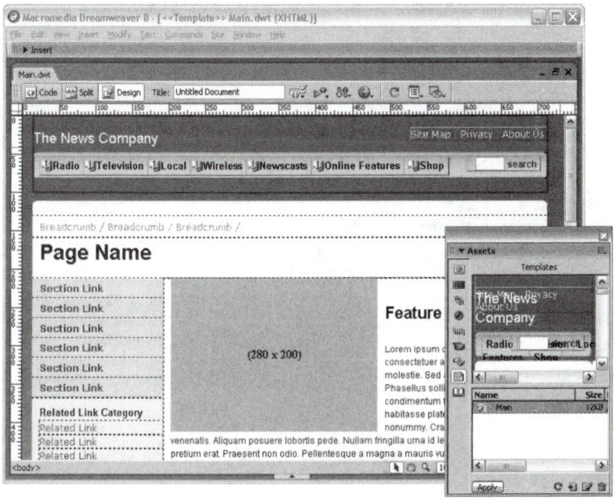

Although any page can be saved as a template, usually it's best to start with a page that contains all the elements (logos, nav bars, buttons, and so on) that you want on all of your pages. Once a page has been converted to a template, it appears in the Templates category of the Assets panel.

When you have a finished page containing dummy content, you're ready to convert it to a template and begin inserting editable regions.

Here's how to create a template and insert editable regions:

1. Open the finished page that you want to use as a template.

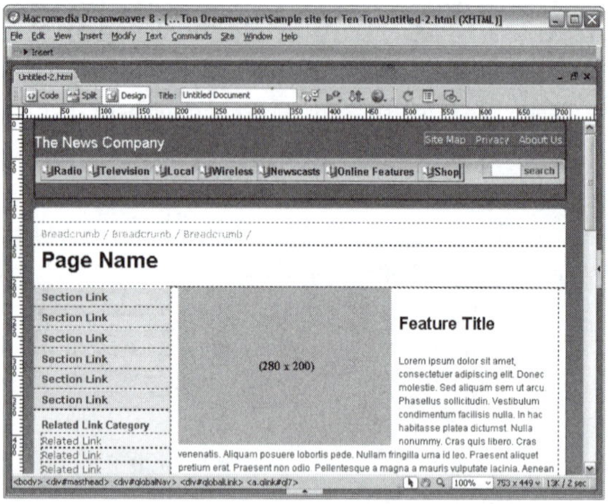

2. Choose File > Save as Template.

3. In the Save as Template dialog box that appears, set the Site pull-down to the local site that you're adding the template to; then in the Save As field, enter a name for your template. Click Save when you're done.

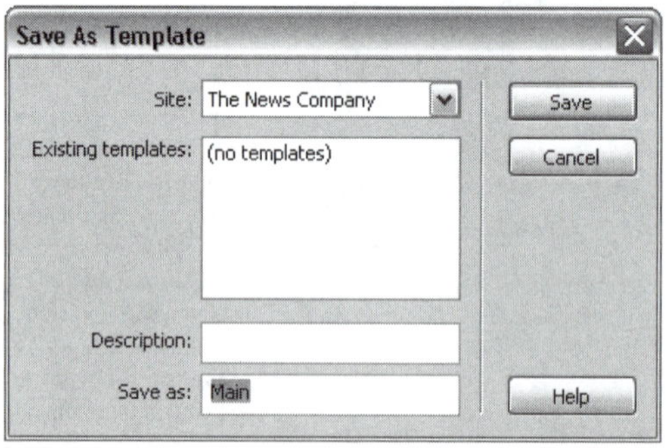

If you want, you can also enter a description for your template in the Description field. When you click Save, a message may appear asking you to update your links. Click Yes to continue.

Dreamweaver saves your template as a .dwt file inside your site's local folder, inside the Templates folder, which is automatically created. On your page's title bar, you'll see <<Template>>, which indicates that your page has been converted to a Dreamweaver template file. Now that you have a template, you're ready to begin adding editable regions to it.

IMMINENT DOOM

Make sure to leave any templates that you create inside your site's Template folder. If you move templates out of the folder, or move the folder itself, any template-driven pages in your site won't be able to update.

4. Select the page element that you want to set as an editable region.

   The content that you select will be marked as an editable area on any pages that use the template. For example, you might select a heading at the top of the page, a graphic, a table cell, a layer, or contents within a table cell or layer.

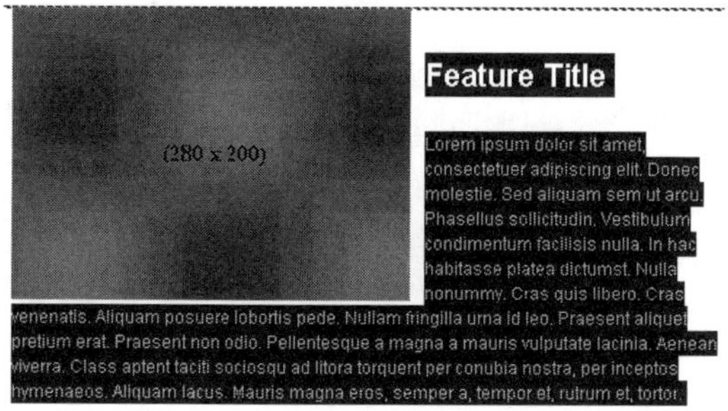

5. Choose Insert > Template Objects > Editable Region.

   In addition to inserting editable regions, you can use other regions, called optional and repeating regions, which we'll talk more about in "Customizing Templates with Other Region Types."

6. In the New Editable Region dialog box that appears, give your editable region a name; then click OK.

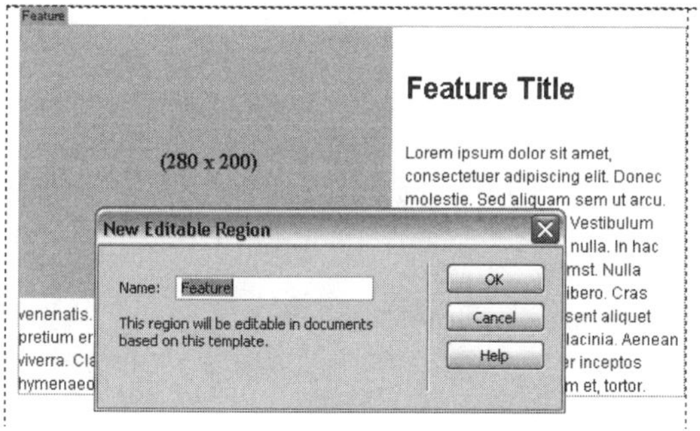

   A turquoise frame appears around the object you selected, with a tab that displays the editable region's name.

7. Continue selecting page elements and marking them as editable regions in your template until you've set all the editable regions you'll need.

You can add as many editable regions as you like. If you realize that you need more editable regions later, you can always add more.

8. If you want to remove an editable region in your template, select it by clicking the tab at the top left; then choose Modify > Templates > Remove Template Markup.

9. Once you've added the editable regions that you need, save your template by choosing File > Save.

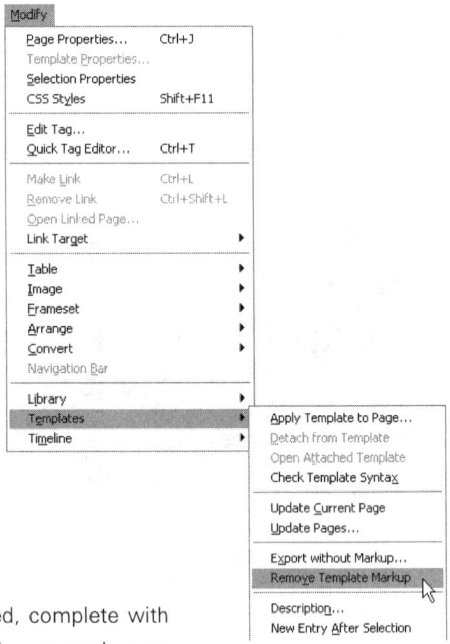

Now that you have a template created, complete with editable regions, you can begin building pages in your site that are driven by the template.

Building a Template-Driven Page

The whole point to using templates in Dreamweaver is to control multiple pages in your site—so that's exactly what you'll do here. You'll create a new, untitled document with your template applied to it.

Once the template has been applied, your new page will take on all the content and formatting of the template. Further, you'll be able to manipulate any areas on your page that have been specified as editable regions—you'll be able to change the dummy content to the actual content that you want on the page.

Here's how to apply your template to a new page:

1. Choose File > New.

2. In the New Document dialog box that appears, click the Template tab at the top.

   On the Templates tab, in the Templates For column, you'll see a list of all the current sites that you've defined in Dreamweaver. When you click a defined site, any templates that you've created for that site appear in the center column, along with a preview of the template, on the right.

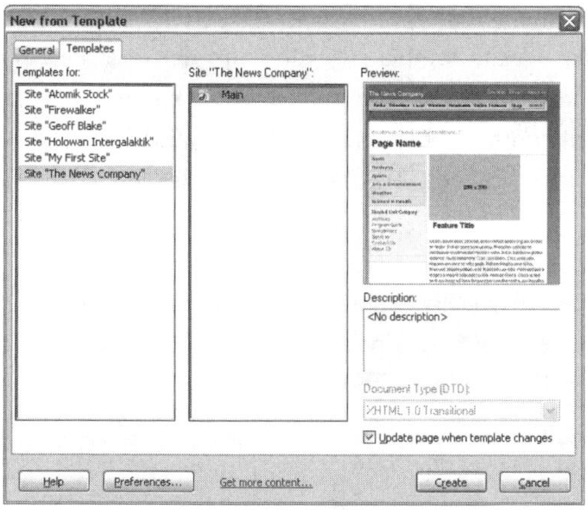

3. In the center column, select the template that you want to base your new page on; then click Create at the bottom of the dialog box.

   A new, unnamed web page is created. It looks identical to your template, but you can tell that it's a new web page by the title bar, which displays Untitled-1 (as opposed to <<template>>, which you saw earlier).

   You'll also notice a yellow frame around your page, with a tab at the top right displaying the name of the template that's controlling the page. This tab is especially helpful when you're using several templates in your site. Any editable regions that you inserted into your template also appear on the new page. You'll be able to manipulate content inside these editable regions, but you won't be able to select anything that appears outside them.

   With your template applied to a new page, you're ready to work within the editable regions.

An even faster way to create a template-driven page is to open the Assets panel (Window > Assets), click the Templates category on the left, and then choose New from Template from the Assets panel menu.

4. Click inside the first editable region on your page and begin manipulating the content.

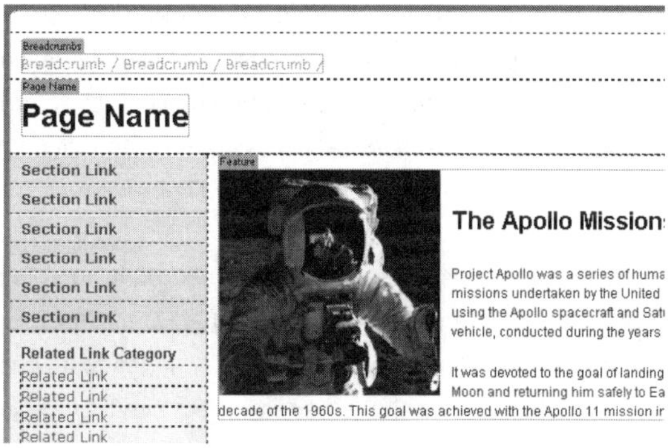

What you marked as an editable region in the template determines what sorts of changes you can make on the template-driven page. For example, if you marked a table cell or a layer as an editable region, you'll be able not only to adjust the contents of that container, but also to set any options you like in the Property Inspector. Working within editable regions is just like working in a regular Dreamweaver page.

Once you've made changes to your editable region, you're ready to save your file and preview it in your browser to see how it's looking. Saving and previewing a template-driven page is no different than saving and previewing a regular Dreamweaver page.

5. Choose File > Save, give your page a name, and then click Save.

6. To preview your page, choose File > Preview in Browser; then choose your target browser.

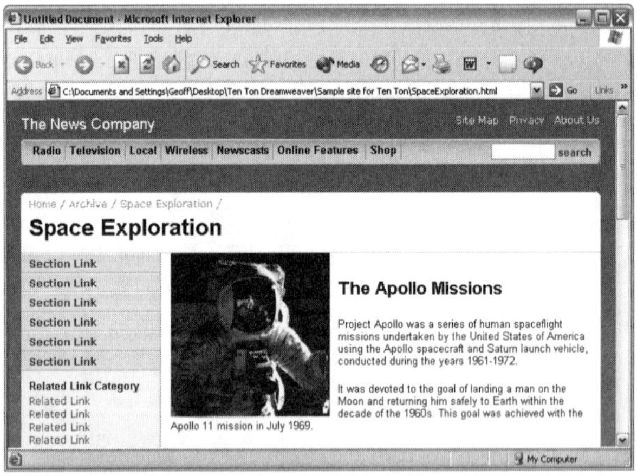

You can create as many pages based on your template as you need, and you can always add more in the future.

Now you can apply your understanding of how to create a template-driven page and how to manipulate editable regions to build additional pages for your site. You can create as many pages as you need, and you can always add more in the future. You can even use *nested templates*—that is, a template that's controlled by another template. You'll see how in "Working with Nested Templates."

With several pages controlled by your template—or even just the one that you've created here—you're ready for the best part about templates. In the next section, you'll go back to your template, make some changes to its content and formatting, and then automatically update all the pages in your site that are under the template's control.

APPLYING TEMPLATES TO EXISTING PAGES

You don't have to start with a new, untitled document when you're creating new pages based on your templates. In fact, you may have pages in your site that you've already created, and now you want your new template applied to them.

However, when you apply a template to an existing page, Dreamweaver attempts to match the page's content to the template's editable regions. If your existing page doesn't contain editable regions with names identical to those in your template—which is often the case—Dreamweaver opens the Inconsistent Region Names dialog box and asks you how you want to handle the mismatched content. You can move the content into one of the template's regions, or you can delete it, but either way, you have to do something with the content—you can't leave it mismatched. Thankfully, the Region Names dialog box makes it easy to handle content in these types of situations.

Here's how to apply a template to an existing page:

1. Open the existing page that you want to apply the template to.

2. If the Assets panel is not already open, choose Window > Assets to open it; then click the Templates category in the column of buttons on the left.

   When the Templates category opens, any templates that you've created for your current site will be listed in the lower half of the panel. The top portion of the panel displays a preview of the currently selected template. If you don't see any templates listed in the Assets panel, click the Refresh Site List button at the bottom of the panel.

3. From the list in the Assets panel, select the template that you want to apply; then click the Apply button.

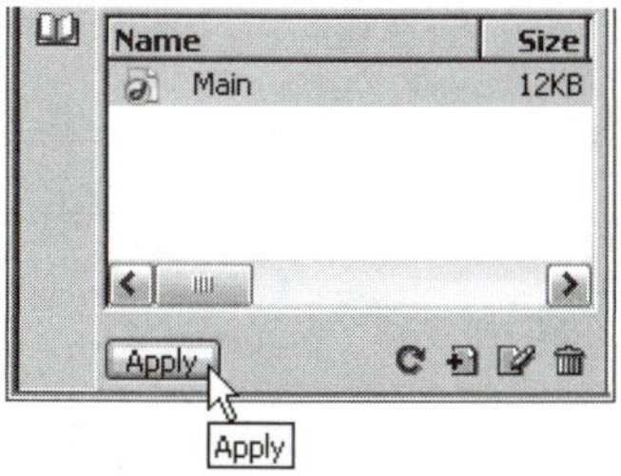

   If your existing page already contains content, Dreamweaver will display the Inconsistent Region Names dialog box.

APPLYING TEMPLATES ... (CONTINUED)

4. In the Inconsistent Region Names dialog box, select the first piece of mismatched content from the list in the dialog box.

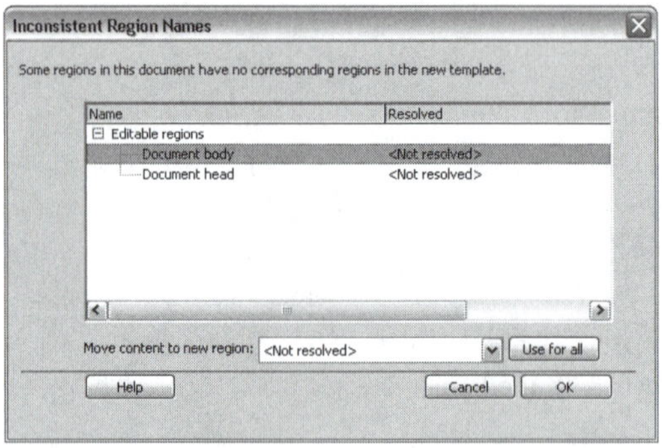

5. From the Move Content to New Region pull-down menu, select a region to move the mismatched content to.

   Regions that appear in the pull-down menu are determined by the regions that are available in the template that's being applied. If you don't want to map your page's content and instead want to delete it, choose Nowhere.

6. If your page contains other mismatched elements, select the next item in the list at the top of the dialog box and use the Move Content to New Region pull-down menu to indicate where it should be placed. If you want all mismatched content handled the same way, click the Use for All button. When you're done, click OK.

   The template is applied to your page, and the previously mismatched content is moved to the regions you specified, or it's removed entirely if you chose to delete it.

With the template applied, your page is now under its control.

DELETING TEMPLATES: TAKIN' OUT THE TRASH

Although you can delete a template that you've created and applied to pages, doing so may yield some unexpected results. First, of course, any pages that are being controlled by the template can no longer be updated by the template. What's more, even with the template removed, only areas that appear within editable regions on the formerly template-based pages will be editable. All other areas of the page will remain locked.

If you want to be able to make changes to these locked areas, you first have to unlock them by detaching the page from its template (even though the template has been deleted). Wacky?

Here's how to delete a template:

1. Open the Assets panel (choose Window > Assets); then click the Templates category in the column of buttons on the left.

2. In the lower half of the Assets panel, select the template that you want to delete; then click the Delete button at the bottom of the panel.

3. In the message window that Dreamweaver displays, click Yes to confirm that you want to delete your template.

Other times, you may no longer want a page to be under the control of your template. You can easily disconnect a page from its template at any time. Once a page is disconnected from the template, all the previously locked areas become fully editable.

To disconnect a page from its template, choose Modify > Templates > Detach from Template.

Updating Templates to Make Automatic Sitewide Changes

You've seen that templates are very easy to work with and, at the same time, are very powerful. But now, with a template up and running and controlling a few pages in your site, you're ready to see their real power. After you see this, you'll never build web sites without templates again—it's that cool!

When you update your pages, they change to reflect the modifications that you made in your template while also retaining the content that you placed in their editable regions.

You're about to see what happens when you open your original template and make a few changes to it (maybe you're changing some formatting, setting some hyperlinks, or adjusting some formatting). When you save your template, Dreamweaver will ask you if you want to update the pages that the template controls. When you update your pages, like magic, they change to reflect the modifications that you made in your template while also retaining the content that you placed in their editable regions. The results are totally amazing—and totally easy to achieve. And, of course, you can make changes to your template and update your site whenever you want.

When you want to update your template, you should first close any pages driven by that template that are open in Dreamweaver. If you leave pages open, you may run into problems—check out the sidebar "Save Yourself a Headache—Close Your Pages Before You Update."

Here's how to update your template:

1. Close any pages that use the template that you want to update.

2. In the Templates category of the Assets panel, double-click the template that you want to update.

   Dreamweaver opens the original template file for editing. Don't forget—you can tell that you're in the template file by the <<Template>> designation on the title bar.

3. Make any changes that you want to your template.

   For example, on the site's main navigation bar, you might set hyperlinks to your new template-driven pages that you created in the preceding section. You might also add some text and formatting or insert new images that you want to appear throughout your site.

Do not make changes here to objects within the editable regions that you've set. To edit an object within an editable region, you need to work within the template-driven page itself, not the template file. If you make changes within an editable region in your template file, your changes will not be applied across the pages in your site—only changes made outside the editable regions will be applied.

4. When your changes are complete, choose File > Save.

   Dreamweaver displays the Update Template Files dialog box, asking you if you want to update pages that use the template.

5. In the Update Template Files dialog box that appears, click Update.

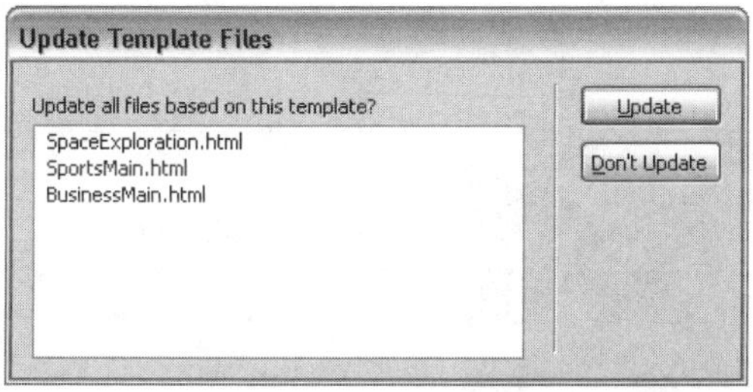

   The Update Pages dialog box appears as Dreamweaver updates any pages that are driven by the template. This is the same dialog box that appears when you update library items, which you saw in Chapter 5.

6. To see a log that reports the number of files updated and any problems that Dreamweaver encounterd, select the Show Log check box.

   The bottom of the dialog box expands to show the update log.

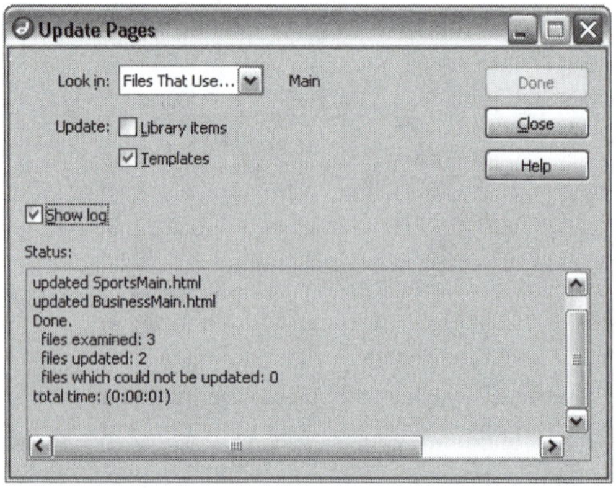

NOTEWORTHY

If you're working on a template-driven page and you're not sure whether it's been updated, you can manually update it by choosing Modify > Templates > Update Current Page.

7. When the update is complete, click Close.

8. Close your template; then preview the pages that the template controls.

   If you have your browser window open, just click its Refresh button. Otherwise, you'll have to open one of your pages in Dreamweaver and then choose File > Preview in Browser.

SAVE YOURSELF A HEADACHE—CLOSE YOUR PAGES BEFORE YOU UPDATE

You don't have to close any pages you have open in Dreamweaver before editing the template that controls them, but there's a really good reason to do so.

After you make changes to your template and save it, any pages that use the template are automatically updated, as you saw. However, if you leave a page open in Dreamweaver when you save and update your template, the changes will appear in the open page, but the page won't automatically be saved. You'll see an asterisk on Dreamweaver's title bar and on the document tab, to remind you that the page has been changed but hasn't been saved. You must maually save the page before your changes can be previewed.

Doesn't sound like too much of a problem, but it can be. A guy I used to work with scrapped his entire site—deleted it and emptied his Recycle Bin—and started his site all over again because he couldn't figure out why his pages weren't updating. Turns out he had *all* his template-driven pages open in Dreamweaver when he did his update. Because he didn't realize he had to save his pages manually, his changes didn't show up when he previewed the pages in his browser. Of course, he realized his mistake after he'd started over—talk about a bad day at the office! So to keep things easy, just make sure to close any open pages in Dreamweaver before you begin making your changes to your template.

Working with Nested Templates

Throughout this chapter, you've been getting familiar with Dreamweaver's template feature—hope you're getting along with your new best friend! You've seen a lot of the flexibility of templates (and you'll see even more in the upcoming sections), but nothing else quite matches the ability to create nested templates. Put simply, a nested template is a document that controls pages in your site (just like a regular template), but which itself is under the control of another (master) template.

A nested template is a document that controls pages in your site, but which itself is under the control of another template.

Imagine this: You've set up a site whose pages are being driven by a template. Now you want a special section in the site that will use much of the same formatting as the rest of the site, but which also provides a formatting framework of its own—perhaps you want an online store within your site or a subsection that contains hands-on tutorials. You can set up a master template to handle the overall formatting of your site and then create a nested template to drive the formatting of your site's special section. When you make a change in your master template, that change then ripples down to your nested template and is applied to any pages that the nested template controls.

You can set up as many nested templates as you want—templates controlling templates controlling templates—as many as you need to control the site you want to build.

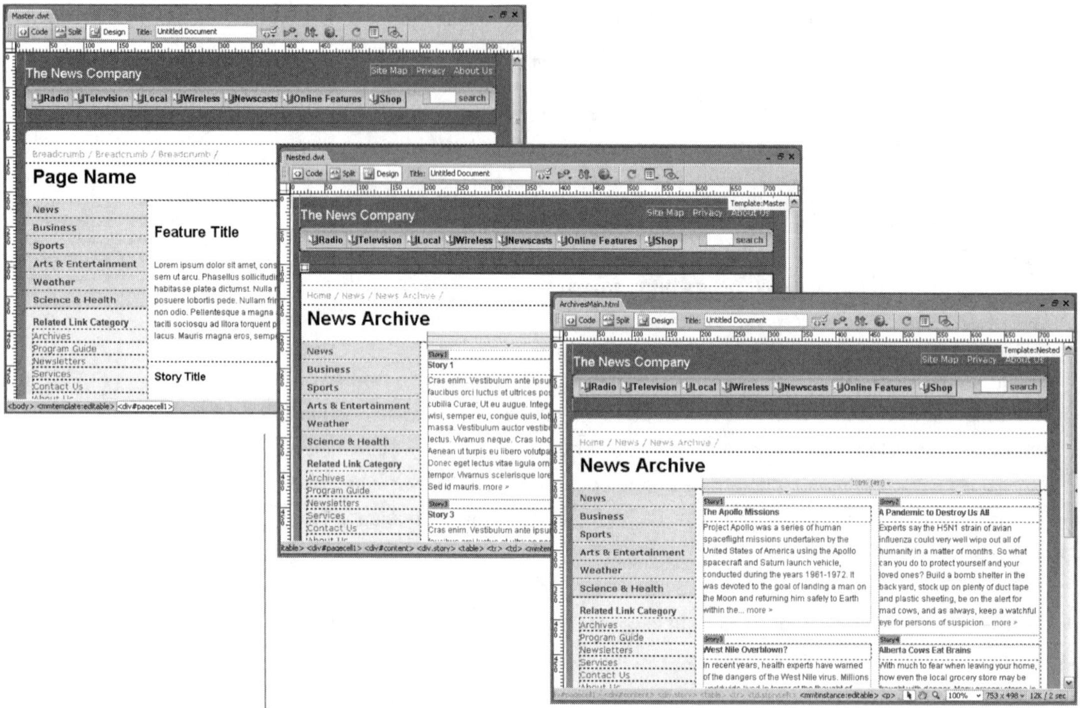

Nested templates allow you to create a second level of control in your web site. Normally, a master template controls the outermost page content (such as navigation controls and site-branding elements), while a nested template controls content within the page's main area. A page that's driven by the nested template contains content specific to that page, like text and graphics.

To begin, you'll have to set up the master template. The master template can be a template that you've already created, or it can be a new, blank file.

Here's how to set up a nested template:

1. Open the file that you want to use as the master template; then choose File > Save as Template.

2. In the Save as Template dialog box that appears, use the Site pull-down menu to choose the site in which you want to save your template; then, in the Save As field, enter a name for your template. Click OK when you're done.

3. As you did earlier, insert any editable regions that you want in your template by selecting page content and choosing Insert > Template Objects > Editable Region.

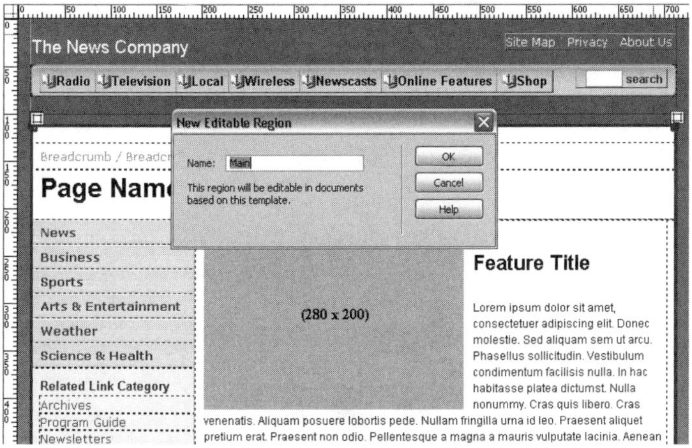

These editable regions will be the only editable areas in your nested template. All other areas of the page will be locked, just like locked areas in a regular template-driven page.

4. When you've created the editable regions that you want, choose File > Save.

   Now you're ready to create your nested template.

5. If it isn't already visible, open the Assets panel (choose Window > Assets); then click the Templates category button on the left.

6. In the Templates category of the Assets panel, select the template that will control your nested template; then from the Assets panel menu, choose New from Template.

   A new document is created with your template applied to it.

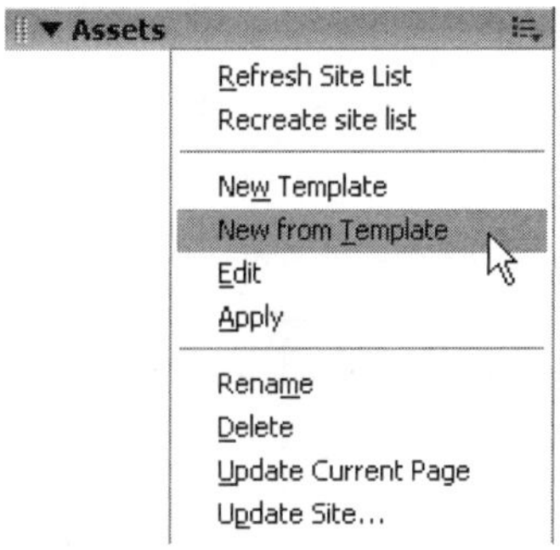

7. Choose File > Save as Template. In the Save as Template dialog box that appears, give your nested template a name; then click OK.

A nested template is created automatically whenever you save a template-driven page as a template. Even though your page is now a template, you'll be able to edit only the content that resides in your master template's editable regions, as discussed earlier. Within the editable regions, you'll also be able to insert additional editable regions for the pages that will be driven by your nested template. You can also insert optional and repeating regions, which we'll talk about in the next section.

8. In the nested template, make any changes to the editable regions that you want and insert any editable regions that you need. When you're done, choose File > Save.

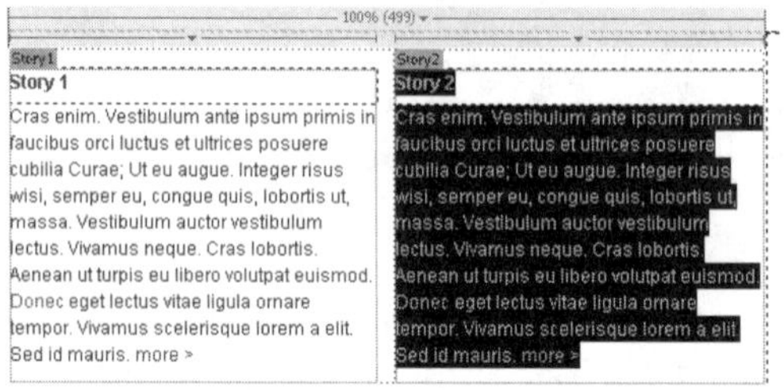

As you begin inserting regions within your master template's editable regions, an orange outline appears around the master region, to help you distinguish between the editable regions in your master template and those in your nested template.

If you don't insert any regions into your master template's editable regions, those regions remain outlined in blue, and they'll appear as editable regions in pages that are based on your nested template. In other words, they're *passed through* to the pages that are driven from your nested template.

9. Create a new page based on your nested template.

You've already done this a few times. You can choose File > New and create a new document from the Templates tab, or you can select your nested template in the Assets panel and choose New from Template from the Assets panel menu.

10. On your new page, you can now make changes to the content that sits inside the editable regions that you set in your nested template or inside editable regions that are being passed through from the master template.

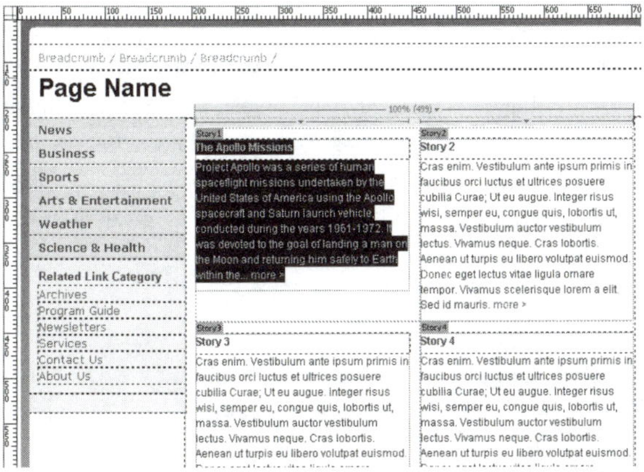

You can now start creating as many pages based on your nested template as you want. The master template drives the nested template, and the nested template drives your site's pages. If you make a change in the nested template, it will be reflected in the driven pages; and if you make a change in the master template, it will be reflected in the nested template and the driven pages. How awesome is that? Just think of the possibilities!

Customizing Templates with Other Region Types

So by now, you should really be hoppin' with templates. I told you they were the coolest part of Dreamweaver! But there's more! So far, you've been working only with editable regions. As you've seen, editable regions are very useful for limiting the changes that a template user can make. However, you can enhance your templates with other types of regions as well.

In this section, you'll see how to set optional regions, which are regions that the template user can choose to either hide or display—perfect for page elements that you may want to appear on some pages but not on others. You'll also see how create a region with an attribute that's editable. For example, maybe you want to allow the person who's editing a template-driven page to change a graphic, but you don't want the person changing the image's width or height or the hyperlink that's been set. You can do this by setting an editable attribute. Finally, you'll see how to work with repeating regions—areas in a template that can be duplicated as many times as needed on pages that are based on the template.

Setting Optional Regions

In a template-driven web site, any page elements that appear in the template will appear in all pages controlled by that template—that is, unless you insert optional regions into your template. Optional regions are areas in the template whose visibility can be controlled by the person working on the template-based pages—in other words, the user can literally turn the optional region and its content on or off.

A person working on pages that contain an optional region can turn the optional region and its content on or off.

Optional regions allow you to literally turn page content on and off. On the page shown here, the person working on the page can turn the template element for the graphics that accompany articles on or off, depending on whether a graphic is needed for a particular article.

For example, maybe you want to display a New Product logo only beside recently added products on your web site. In the template, you would set up the logo to appear beside all the products, but you would set up the template so that in the pages that the template controls, you could turn the logo display on or off depending on whether the product is new.

You can implement more advanced functionality with optional regions as well. For example, you can set an optional region's visibility depending on certain conditions in the visitor's web browser. This advanced functionality requires hand coding and an understanding of the template expression language. If you'd like to find out more, visit macromedia.com/devnet/dreamweaver/articles/template_parameters.html.

Here's how to insert an optional region:

1. In your template, select the page object whose visibility you want to control in an optional region.

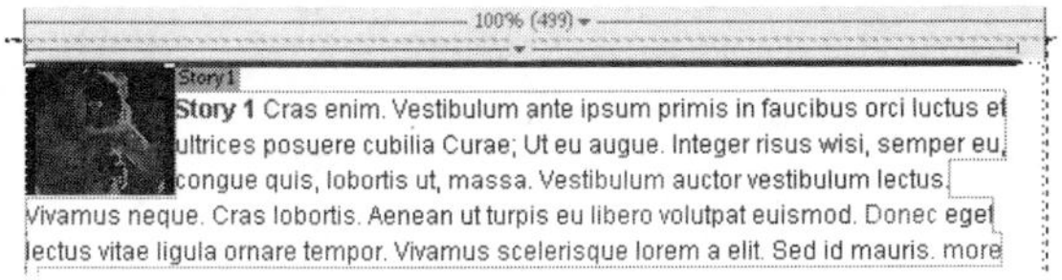

You can select a graphic, a layer, text, or any other page element that you want.

2. Choose Insert > Template Objects > Optional Region.

3. In the New Optional Region dialog box that appears, give your optional region a name.

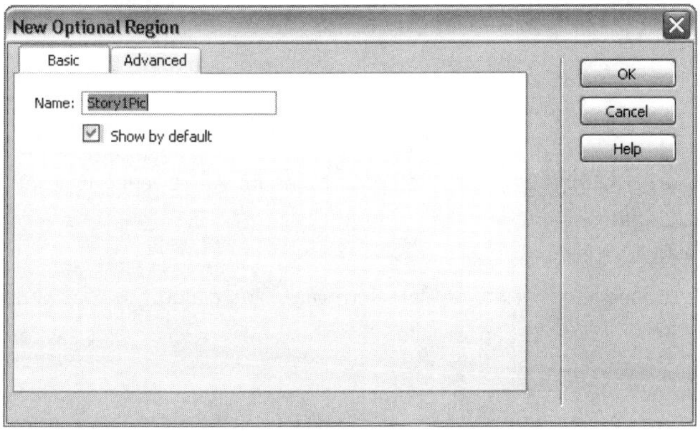

This name will appear in pages that are being controlled by the template, so you should make the name descriptive.

4. Select or deselect the Show by Default check box; then click OK.

If you turn on Show by Default, your selected page object will appear by default on template-based pages. If you turn it off, the object will be hidden by default. Either approach will work, though you'll probably want the default setting to be the one you'll use most often.

When you click OK, Dreamweaver places a light blue frame around your selected page object, with a tab at the top that contains your optional region's name, preceeded with *If*.

5. Continue adding optional regions by repeating steps 1 through 4.

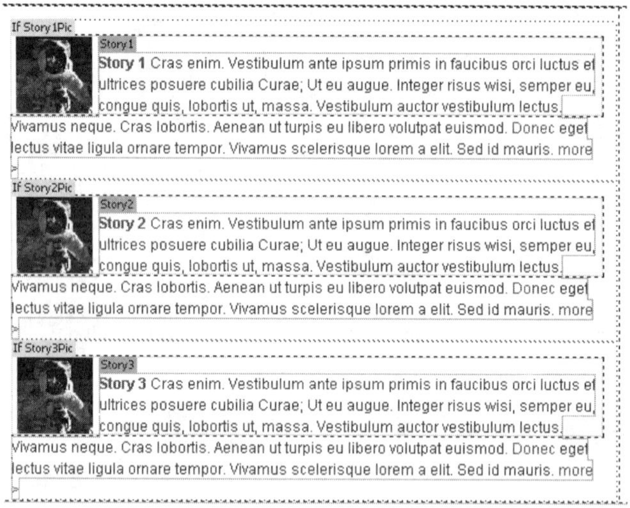

Once you've created all the optional regions you need, you're ready to save your template and update your pages.

6. Choose File > Save; then in the Update Template Files dialog box that appears, click Update. In the Update Pages dialog box that appears, click Close when the update is complete.

   With your template-based pages updated, you can now control the visibility of your optional regions from each page controlled by the template.

7. Open a page that is being controlled by your template by either choosing File > Open or double-clicking the page in the Files panel.

8. In your open page, choose Modify > Template Properties.

9. In the Template Properties dialog box that appears, select the optional region whose visibility you want to control; then at the bottom of the dialog box, click the Show check box. Click OK when you're done.

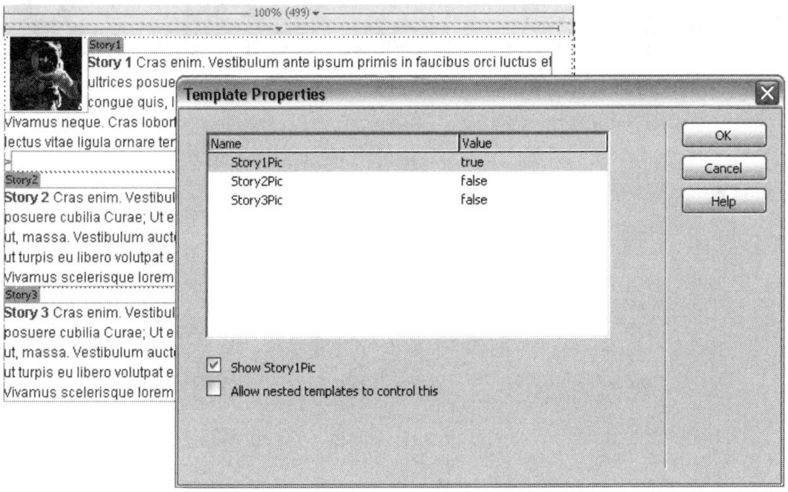

When you click OK, the visibility setting is applied to the object that appears within the optional region. For example, if your page object's visibility was turned on by default and you unchecked the Show check box in the Template Properties dialog box, then the page object would disappear.

Setting Editable Tag Attributes

As you've seen, content that resides in an editable region is fully editable. That may be fine for most areas in your template, but sometimes you may want more detailed control over what, specifically, is editable within a region.

An editable attribute determines what's editable in an editable region on a template-driven page, and what isn't.

For example, you may want people working with your template-based pages to be able to change a graphic, but you don't want them to be able to change the graphic's width and height. In other words, you want very specific aspects of a page object to be editable, but you want to retain control over the other aspects. To set up your pages in this way, you can create an editable attribute, which determines what's editable in an editable region on a template-driven page, and what isn't.

The only catch here is that to use editable attributes, you need a decent understanding of HTML tags and the attributes and values that can be used in each. If you're not handy with HTML coding, you may find Dreamweaver's Reference panel (choose Window > Reference) helpful when setting editable attributes.

Here's how to set an editable attribute:

1. Select the page element whose attribute you want to make editable.

INSERTING EDITABLE OPTIONAL REGIONS

Optional regions are very useful not only for keeping your pages consistent, but also for making updating easy for people working on your template-driven pages. However, you may have noticed something: the content inside optional regions isn't editable!

What if you want to set up a template region whose visibility can be controlled, but also whose content is editable? What you need is an editable optional region.

To insert an editable optional region, follow these steps:

1. Select the page element that you want to set as an editable optional region.

2. Choose Insert > Template Objects > Editable Optional Region.

3. In the New Optional Region dialog box that appears, enter a name for the editable optional region; then set the default visibility of the region with the Show by Default option. Click OK when you're done.

   Dreamweaver inserts the editable optional region into the template; it appears as an editable region within an optional region, indicated by the two tabs at the top left of the region.

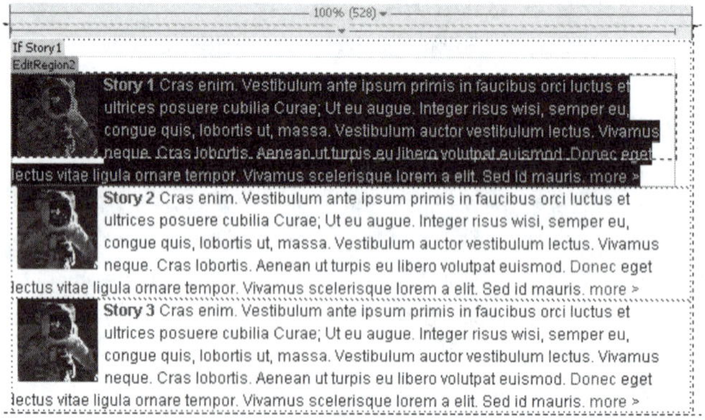

4. Dreamweaver gives the editable region a default name. To change it, click the editable region's tab; then rename the region in the Property Inspector.

When your template is saved and your pages have been updated, you can control your editable optional region's display through the Template Properties dialog box, just as before. When an editable optional region is displayed, you can edit its contents just as you normally would.

For example, you might select an image, table, or layer.

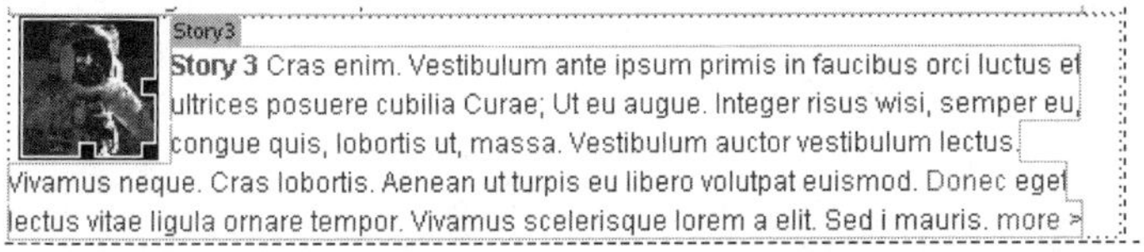

2. Choose Modify > Templates > Make Attribute Editable.

3. In the Editable Tag Attributes dialog box that appears, open the Attribute pull-down menu and select the attribute that you want to make editable.

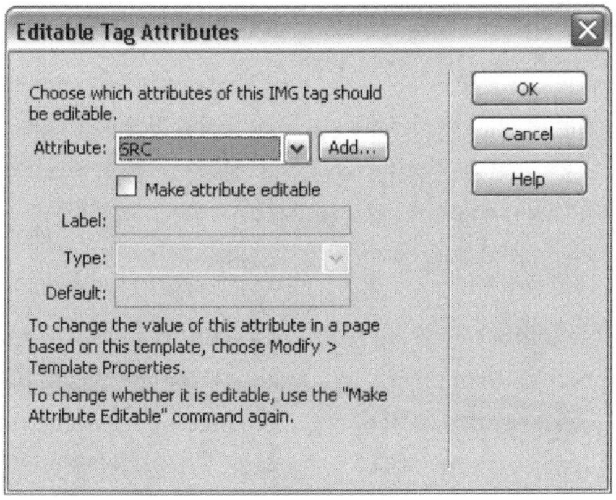

If the attribute that you want to change is not listed in the pull-down menu, click the Add button. In the dialog box that appears, type the attribute that you want to set; then click OK. The attribute you enter must be a valid attribute for the tag you selected. That's why knowing HTML (or keeping the Reference panel handy) is important here.

4. Select the Make Attribute Editable check box.

When this option is selected, the Label, Type, and Default fields become available.

5. In the Label field, type a unique name for your editable attribute.

The label is just like a name for an editable region. Users of the template-driven pages will use the name you use here to identify an object on the page whose attributes are editable. Therefore, make the name descriptive.

6. Select an option from the Type pull-down menu.

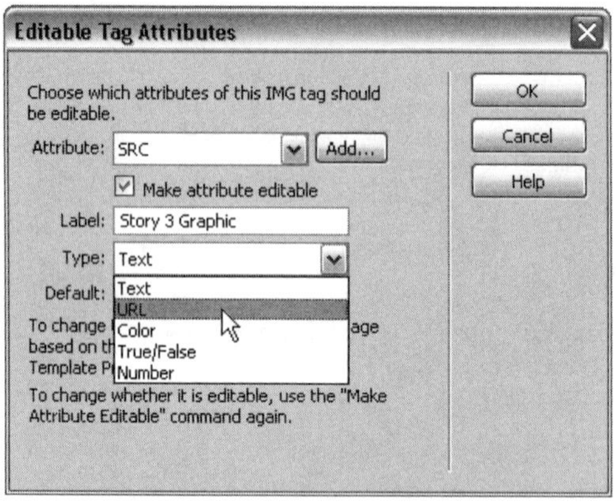

Text: Choose Text if the editable attribute's value is text based. For example, use Text if you're making a table cell's valign attribute editable. When Text is selected, a text box will appear in template-driven pages where the user can type a valid value for the attribute—in this case, Top, Middle, Bottom, or Baseline.

URL: Use URL if the editable attribute's value requires a path to a file. For example, you might make the src attribute of an image editable. Template-based pages would provide a field with a browse icon, where the user could specify a path to a graphic; all other attributes for the image would be locked.

Color: Set Color if the editable attribute requires that a color be specified. If you're making the bgcolor attribute of a table cell editable, for example, then with Color set, Dreamweaver's color picker will appear in the template-driven page so that the user can specify the background color.

True/False: Use the True/False setting when your editable attribute's value is either true or false (called a Boolean attribute). For example, you could set an inserted audio clip's hidden attribute so that it can be controlled within the template-driven pages.

Number: Select Number when a numeric value is needed for the editable attribute. For example, if your editable attribute is a table's width attribute, the user of the template-based page will be able to enter a numeric value.

7. In the Default field, set a default value for your editable attribute; then click OK.

   The default value will be the value that's initially set for your tag. For example, it could be the initial background color of a table cell or the initial width and height of a graphic.

Now you're ready to manipulate the editable attribute within a template-based page. First, though, you need to save your template and update your pages.

8. Choose File > Save; then in the Update Template Files dialog box that appears, click Update. In the Update Pages dialog box, click Close.

   You can now set values for your editable attribute.

9. Open a page that is being controlled by your template, either by choosing File > Open or double-clicking the page in the Files panel.

10. In your open page, choose Modify > Template Properties.

    The Template Properties dialog box that appears lists all available properties and their default values.

11. Select the editable attribute whose value you want to manipulate; then at the bottom of the dialog box, set a new value. When you're done, click OK.

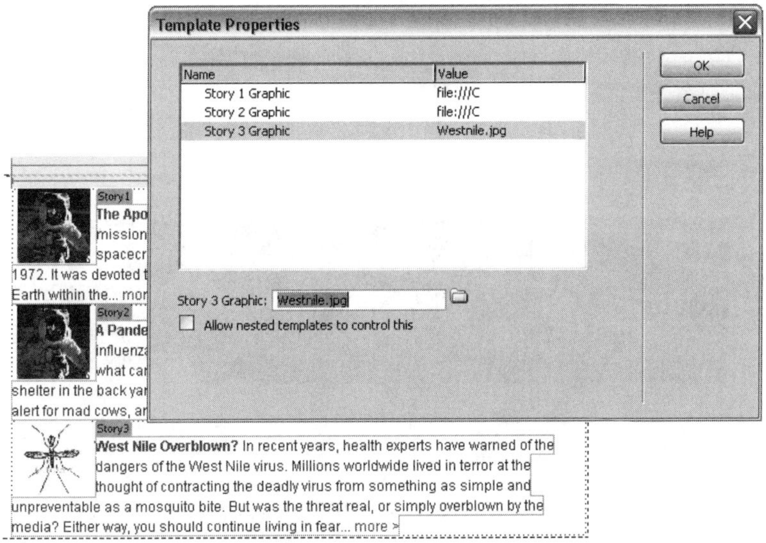

The type of value you set for your editable attribute back in Step 6 determines the type of setting you can make. For example, if you chose Text, a text box appears; if you chose Color, a color picker appears; and so on.

When you click OK, the value is applied to the page element associated with the editable attribute.

Setting Repeating Regions

Repeating regions are areas in your template that can be duplicated as often as they're needed on pages that use the template. For example, the template for a newsletter could control the look and formatting of an article, including its headline; then the article object could be placed inside a repeating region. The newsletter's editor can then duplicate the region on template-based pages as many times as there are articles on that page. The template controls what repeats, but the user controls the number of times the object is repeated on the pages that the template controls.

Repeating regions are areas in your template that can be duplicated as often as they're needed on pages that use the template.

To make the content in a repeated region editable, you can insert an editable region inside a repeating region. Otherwise, you can simply set the region to repeat in its entirety.

Repeating regions often are used inside tables, to repeat rows as often as they're needed. For this purpose, Dreamweaver includes a separate command, discussed in the sidebar "Constructing a Repeating Table."

Here's how to set up repeating regions in your template:

1. Select the area in your template that you want to set as a repeating region.

   You can select any page element or group of page elements that you want to repeat.

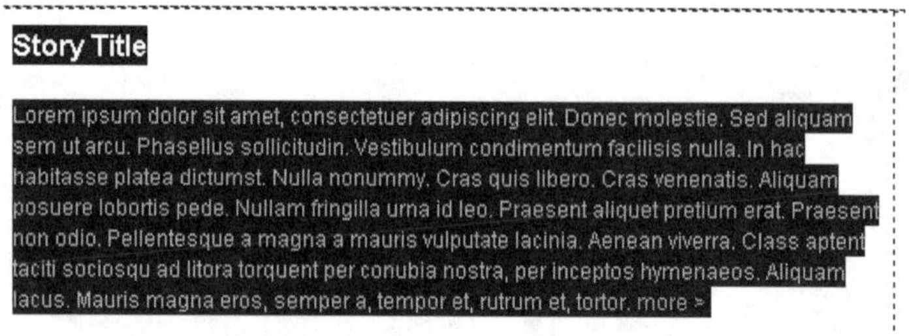

2. Choose Insert > Template Objects > Repeating Region.

3. In the New Repeating Region dialog box that appears, give your repeating region a unique name; then click OK.

   Dreamweaver outlines your repeating region in a light blue frame with a tab at the top left that displays Repeat: and your repeating region's name.

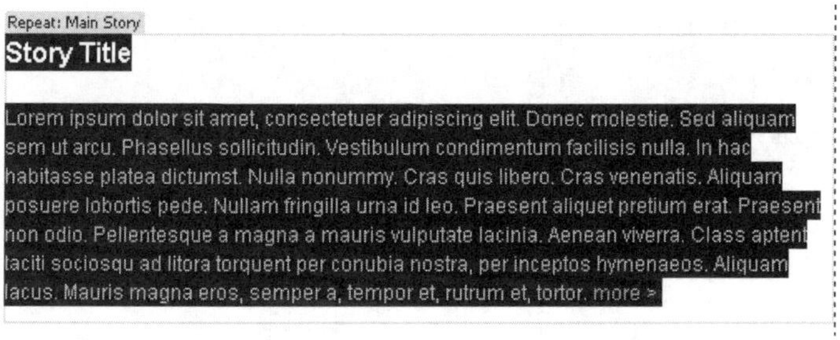

4. Do one of the following:

    - If you want the content in your repeating region to be editable, then you must insert an editable region inside your repeating region. With your repeating region content still selected, choose Insert > Template Objects > Editable Region. In the New Editable Region dialog box, give your editable region a name and click OK. Then choose File > Save. Dreamweaver outlines your editable region in a turquoise frame.

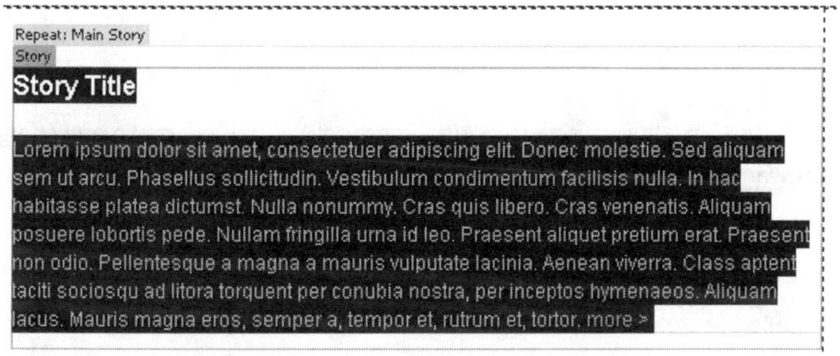

    - If you simply want to be able to duplicate the editable region's existing content in your template-based pages, choose File > Save.

5. In the Update Template Files dialog box that appears, click Update. In the Update Pages dialog box, click Close.

6. Open a page that is being controlled by your template, either by choosing File > Open or by double-clicking the file in the Files panel.

   In your template-driven page, you'll see the light blue tab containing Repeat*:* and the name of your repeating region, as well as plus (+), minus (–), and up and down controls. You can use these controls to duplicate, delete, and change the order of the repeated entries on your page.

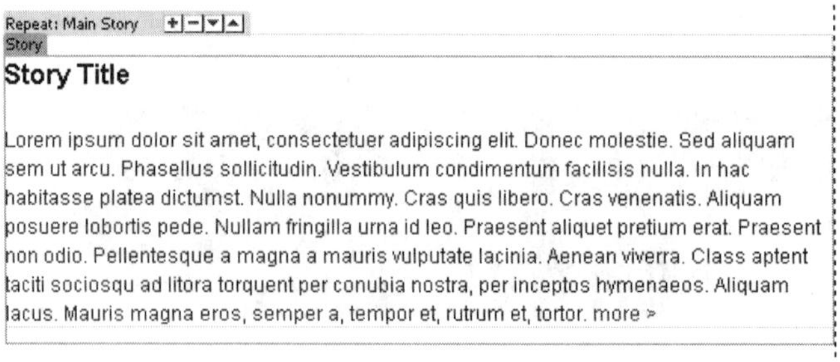

If you don't see the plus (+), minus (–), and up and down controls in your template-based pages, choose View > Visual Aids > Invisible Elements.

7. Do any of the following:
   - Click the plus (+) button to duplicate the content in your repeating region.
   - Click the minus (–) button to remove a repeating region entry. You can remove an entry only from an area that is editable—just be sure to click inside it first.
   - Use the up and down arrows to change the order of your repeating region entries. Reordering applies only to repeating regions that also contain editable regions; first click inside the region that you want to reorder before using the up and down arrows.
8. If you inserted an editable region inside your repeating region, make any changes that you want to the content contained in the region.

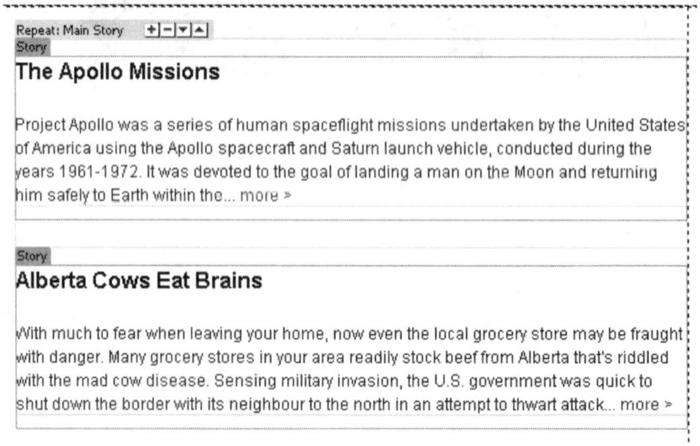

CONSTRUCTING A REPEATING TABLE

Repeating regions often are used in tables. For instance, you may want to control the look of a table that will contain a list of products, but you want the number of products included to be determined on the template-driven page. By creating a repeating table, you can set up the formatting of the table and then allow the user of the template-based pages to determine the number of rows in the table.

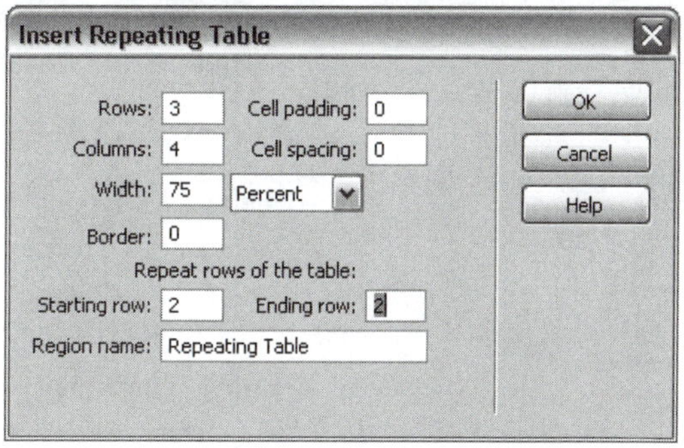

Here's how to insert a repeating table:

1. In your template, place the cursor where you want to insert the repeating table.

2. Choose Insert > Template Objects > Repeating Table.

3. In the Insert Repeating Table dialog box that appears, set values for the number of rows and columns, the table's width, border, cell padding, and cell spacing.

   Carefully think about the number of rows you add. You have to consider not only how many rows you want to set to repeat, but also how many rows you want to remain stationary. For example, you might want two rows that repeat and a header row and a footer row that remain stationary.

4. In the Starting Row and Ending Row fields, insert the row numbers for the rows you want to allow the template user to repeat.

   For example, if you want the first two rows in your table to repeat, set Starting Row to 1 and Ending Row to 2. If you want just the first row to repeat, set both the Starting Row and the Ending Row fields to 1. The rows that you set to repeat must be contiguous. You can't, for example, make row 1 and row 3 repeat with this command.

5. Type a descriptive name in the Region Name field; then click OK.

   The repeating table is inserted into your template, with editable regions inserted automatically into each cell in the rows that you set to repeat. Any content you enter into the editable regions will be editable on template-driven pages, while any content you insert into the remaining cells in your table will be locked.

6. Save your template and update your pages; then in your template-driven pages, use the plus (+), minus (–), and up and down controls just as for repeating regions.

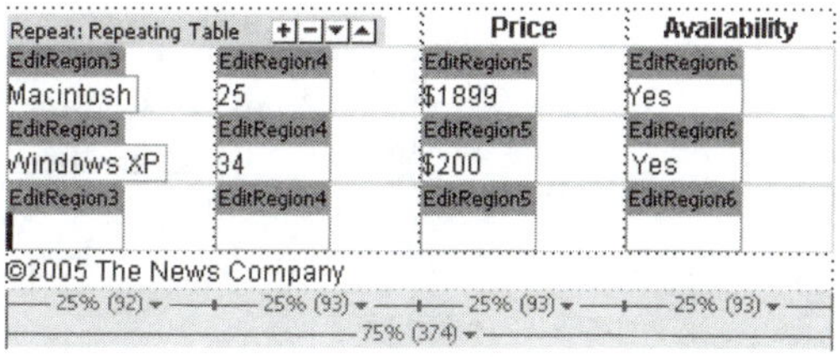

JUST THE GIST

Started with Templates

- Templates in Dreamweaver are used to drive the content and layout of multiple pages in your web site.

- Templates contain areas called editable regions. On a page controlled by a template, the content within editable regions can be edited. All other areas of the page are locked.

Creating Templates

- To create a template, a good approach is to first create a page that you want to use as the basis for other pages in your site. Include placeholder content for text and images that will be replaced with actual content in the template-driven pages.

- To create a template, choose File > Save as Template.

- To insert an editable region, select the content that you want in the region and choose Insert > Template Objects > Editable Region.

- To create a new page based on a template, choose File > New, select a template, and click Create.

Updating a Template

- Any changes made to elements in a template that do not reside in an editable region automatically update on any pages based on the template.

- Before updating a template, it's a good idea to close any pages based on the template that are open in Dreamweaver.

- To update a template and the pages it controls, open the template, make changes, and save the file. Then click Update.

Working with Nested Templates

- A nested template is a template whose content and formatting is controlled by another template.

- To create a nested template, open an existing template and choose File > Save as Template. A nested template is created automatically whenever you save a template-driven page as a template.

JUST THE GIST (CONTINUED)

- Only areas that appear within editable regions in the master template are editable in a nested template.

Customizing Templates with Other Region Types

- Optional regions are areas in a template that can be turned on and off, depending on whether you want the element in the region to appear on a page. To insert an optional region, choose Insert > Template Objects > Optional Region.

- Set editable attributes to control which aspects of an editable region can be edited and which are locked. To make an attribute editable, choose Modify > Templates > Make Attribute Editable. Then set the attribute you want to make editable and the type of value that the attribute will accept.

- Repeating regions are areas in the template that can be duplicated as often as they're needed. A repeating region can be set to contain an editable region. To set a repeating region, choose Insert > Template Objects > Repeating Region.

Chapter 14

Managing and Maintaining Your SITE

STUFF YOU'LL LEARN IN THIS CHAPTER

In this chapter, you'll see how to prepare your site for the web by checking your links, organizing your files, and running reports. Then you'll finally get this baby online. You'll also see how to manage your site once it's live, updating links sitewide, hiding files during maintenance operations, keeping your local and remote sites synchronized, and managing the remote site. You'll see how to work with others, using Design Notes and checking files in and out, to keep your site up-to-date. Then it's time to add metadata to your pages and submit your site to the search engines.

Getting Ready to Publish

You've seen it all, you've done it all! Now you should have a wonderfully designed site complete with text, hyperlinks, graphics, and CSS. You're finally ready to take all your hard work and post it online for the world to see. But wait—don't jump the gun. Your site needs a few final touches—maintenance touches, that is.

Before you publish your site, you should do a little housekeeping to ensure that your site's in the best possible condition. In this section, you'll see how to check your entire site for broken links using Dreamweaver's handy Link Checker utility. Then you'll see how to keep your files organized within your local site and how to generate reports on various aspects of your site. When everything's looking rosy, you'll be ready to upload the works and retire!

To keep your site free of broken links, use Dreamweaver's Link Checker.

Checking for Broken Links Sitewide

The first order of business before you upload your site is to ensure that all the hyperlinks in your site work. Broken links on the web are a regular occurrence for most of us, and isn't it frustrating? Not only that, but broken links make your site seem less pro.

> **NOTEWORTHY**
>
> You can also check links within a single page. Choose File > Check Page > Check Links. The Link Checker tab of the Results panel appears, listing any links that are broken in the current page. You can fix your broken links just as you can when you check links with the Link Checker sitewide.

To keep your site free of broken links, use Dreamweaver's Link Checker. With this utility, you won't have to manually search your site for broken links—and it's mindlessly simple to use!

Here's how to check for broken links across your site:

1. Choose Site > Check Links Sitewide.

   The Results panel appears, with the Link Checker tab open, and Dreamweaver begins scanning your site for broken links.

   If any broken links are found, Dreamweaver lists them on the Link Checker tab. The file that contains the broken link is listed in the column on the left, and the broken link within the file is listed in the column on the right.

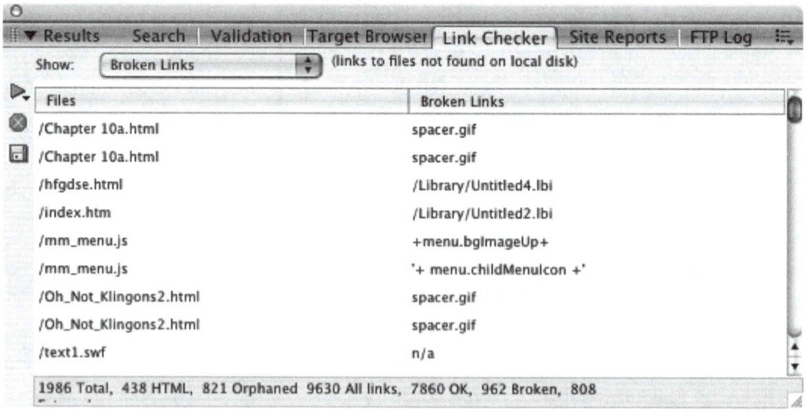

2. To fix a broken link, click it in the Broken Links column; then click the folder icon that appears.

3. In the Select File dialog box that appears, navigate to and select the correct file that the hyperlink should point to; then click OK (Windows) or Choose (Mac).

   The fixed link is removed from the list.

4. Set new destinations for any other broken links that appear in the Link Checker.

CHECKING FOR UNUSED FILES

Sometimes, files that at one time were needed wind up orphaned, with no pages in the site linking to them. Orphaned files used to be a pain in the butt to find and so often needlessly took up web space. Thankfully, Dreamweaver's Link Checker has a function to search for orphaned files.

Here's how to check for orphaned files:

1. Choose Site > Check Links Sitewide to run the link checker.

2. On the Link Checker tab of the Reference panel that appears, choose Show > Orphaned Files.

   Dreamweaver creates a list of all the files in your local site that do not link to other pages.

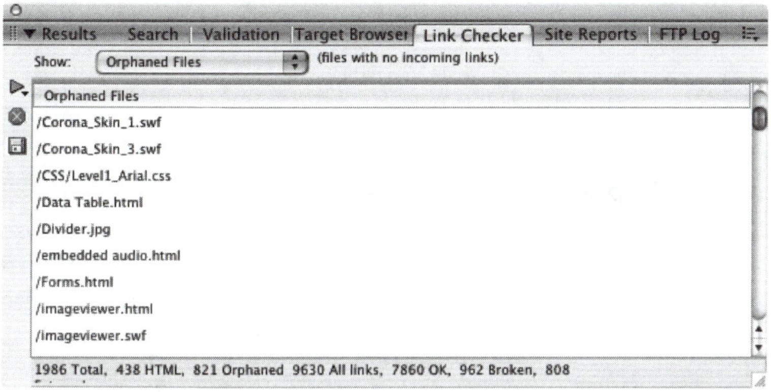

3. To remove a file, select it in the list and press Delete.

NOTEWORTHY

From the Show menu on the Link Checker tab of the Results panel, you can choose External Links to display a list of external links. Dreamweaver doesn't check external links for you, but you can use the list to check them manually.

Keeping Your Site Organized

When you want to reorganize the files in your local site, you can do so directly in Dreamweaver's Files panel (choose Window > Files). When you work in the Files panel, Dreamweaver monitors and updates links to pages as they move. For instance, if you want to move a file from one folder in your local site to another folder, you just drag it to the new location. When you do, Dreamweaver will display the Update Files dialog box, which asks if you want to update any links to the file. Make sure always to click Update, and you won't have any problems with broken links.

You can reorganize the files in your local site directly in Dreamweaver's Files panel.

If you want to rename a file in your site, just highlight it, click it again (or press F2), and enter the new name for your file. Again, Dreamweaver displays the Update Files dialog box, asking if you want to update hyperlinks to the file. Click Update, and you're good.

If you want to remove a file from your site completely, highlight the file's name in the Files panel and press Delete. Dreamweaver warns you if any pages in your site currently link to the file and asks if you're sure you want to delete the file. Click Yes to confirm. After you delete a file, it's a good idea to run Dreamweaver's Link Checker, discussed earlier in this chapter, to ensure that your site doesn't contain any broken links.

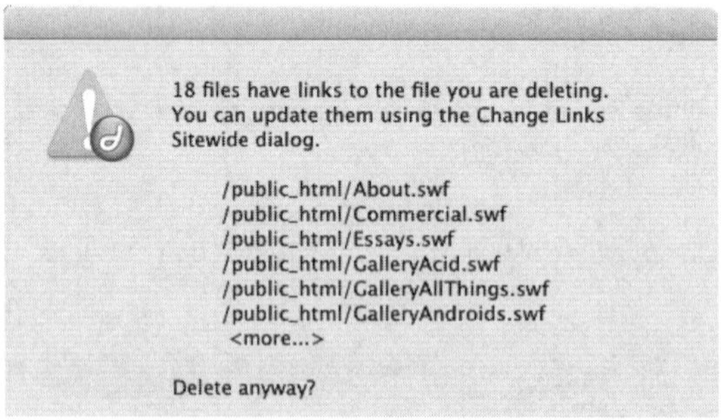

When you delete a file in the Files panel that other pages link to, Dreamweaver warns you of the potential problem.

Running Reports on Your Site

Use Dreamweaver's Site Reports function to collect information about your site.

Dreamweaver provides a handy little function called Site Reports, which you can use to collect information about your site. For example, you can use Site Reports to generate a list of documents in your site that were modified within a certain timeframe, or to ensure that all the images in your site have alternative text set for them.

Reports come in two flavors: workflow reports and HTML reports. Workflow reports are useful when you're working with a group of designers on a site. HTML reports come in handy when you want to ensure that your pages are functioning at their best. For example, you can use HTML reports to help clean out unnecessary background page code or to ensure that your pages comply with current accessibility standards for those with disabilities.

When you run a report of either type, Dreamweaver displays the results on the Site Reports tab of the Results panel, where you can then make adjustments to your pages.

Here's how to run a report on your site:

1. Choose Site > Reports.

2. In the Reports dialog box that appears, choose what you want to run a report on from the Report On pull-down menu.

   Current Document: Runs the report on a page currently open in Dreamweaver.

   Entire Current Local Site: Runs the report on your entire site.

   Selected Files: Runs the report on files that are currently selected in the Files panel.

   Folder: Runs the report on a particular folder in your site.

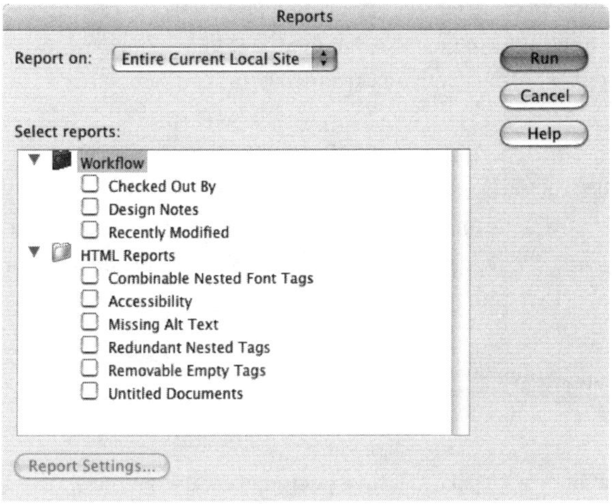

3. From the Select Reports window, select the reports that you want to run. Reports are organized into two groups: Workflow and HTML Reports.

   Checked Out By: Generates a list of all the files that have been checked out by a member of a design team. For more about working with a design team, see "Working with a Team" later in this chapter.

   Design Notes: Generates a list of all the Design Notes that have been used throughout a site. For more on Design Notes, see "Using Design Notes" later in this chapter.

   Recently Modified: Creates a list of documents that have been modified within a certain number of days or within a specified time frame.

   Combinable Nested Font Tags: Generates a list of documents whose background code contains nested font tags.

Accessibility: Checks whether pages are in compliance with current accessibility standards.

Missing Alt Text: Creates a list of files that contain images that do not have alternative text set for them.

Redundant Nested Tags: Generates a list of files whose background code contains unnecessary nested tags.

Removable Empty Tags: Finds empty tags in the background code of pages that are no longer needed.

Untitled Documents: Checks pages to see if they have been given a page title, or if they use the default name: Untitled Document.

When you choose some reports, the Report Settings button at the bottom of the dialog box becomes available, so you can set parameters for your report. If you're running more than one report, you'll need to set each report's parameters separately, by selecting the report in the list and then clicking the Report Settings button.

4. If the Report Settings button becomes available, click it to set parameters for your report.

   The dialog box that appears displays different settings depending on which report you're running. For example, if you're running the Recently Modified report, you can specify how many days old the files you want listed should be or have the report return files based on when they were created.

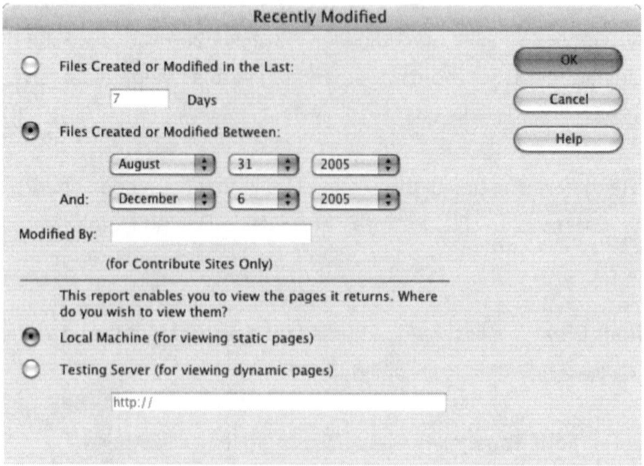

5. When you're ready to run your reports, click Run.

   Dreamweaver opens the Site Reports tab of the Results panel and begins running your selected reports. Any results are listed on the Site Reports tab.

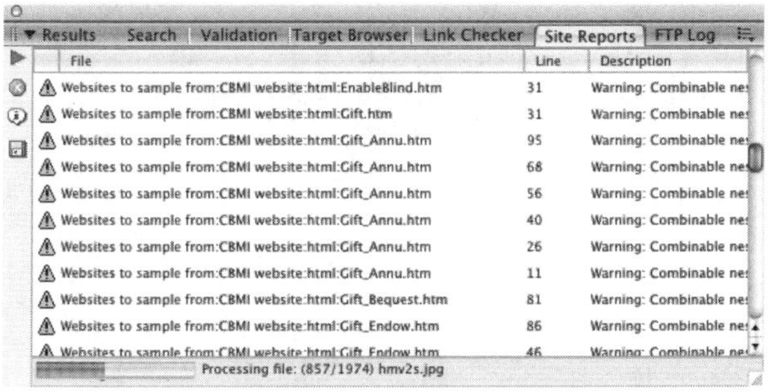

6. To fix an error picked up by a report or to view a document that contains a report result, double-click the file in the Results panel.

   Dreamweaver opens the file, where you can make any necessary adjustments.

Publishing Your Site

Now you've done the preliminaries—you're finally ready to publish your site live to the web. Get the champagne ready!

You're going to have two versions of your site: one that resides on your computer (the local site), and one that's live on the web (the remote site).

Way back in Chapter 4, we discussed how to set up your local and remote sites and how to upload and download files between your local and remote sites—for the full story of how to publish your site, make a return trip to that chapter.

Remember that you're going to have two versions of your site: one that resides on your computer (the local site), and one that's live on the web (the remote site). Whenever you need to update your site, you do so on the local version and then upload your changes to the remote site.

When you're ready to transfer your site, you'll need to connect to your remote web space. In the Files panel, make sure that the Show menu at the top left is set to the local site that you want to upload. Then, on the toolbar at the top of the Files panel, click the Connects to Remote Host button. Dreamweaver connects to your remote site and displays it on the left side of the Files panel; your local site is displayed on the right.

If the Files panel appears as a single narrow column, you can expand it so it's easier to work with. Click the Expand to Show Local and Remote Sites button on the File panel's toolbar.

Once you can see both your local and remote sites in the Files panel, you're ready to begin transferring files. If you want to upload your entire site, select your local site's folder (which appears at the very top of the file list) and then click the Put File(s) button on the toolbar. If you want to upload only a few files, select them in the local view and either drag them into the left column or click the Put File(s) button.

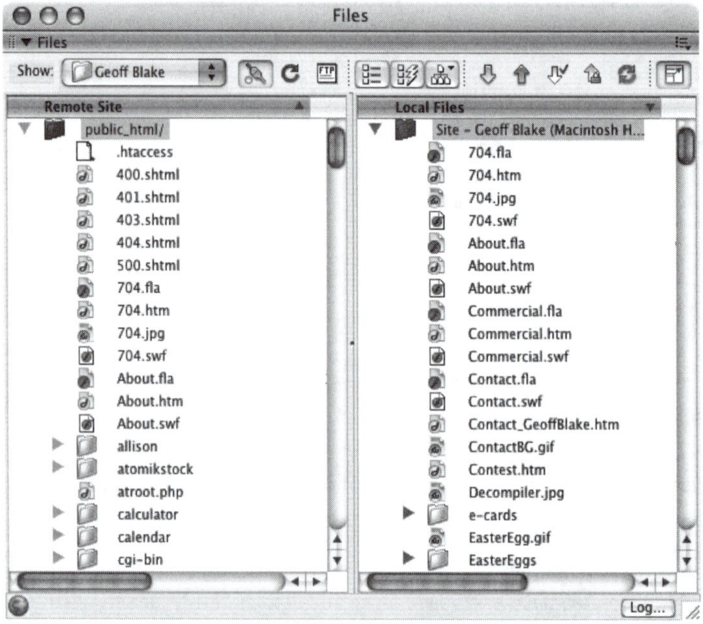

The Files panel, ready for publishing action—local files on the right, remote files on the left. How do you transfer files back and forth? Just drag and drop.

If the files you're uploading include dependent files, Dreamweaver will display a message asking if you want to include them in the file transfer. Remember: Dependent files are needed for the selected files to be viewed properly. They may be images, media files, or style sheets, for instance.

IMMINENT DOOM

A side effect of the age of technology is impatience: Surfers don't want to wait for a site to load. Be sure to preview your live site not only to see how it looks, but also to see how fast it loads. To do this, you must preview your remote site—not just your local one. Your local site may run very quickly on your machine—but the remote site may be another story.

If you want to upload only files that have been recently changed, but you're not sure which files need to be transferred, you can use Dreamweaver's Synchronize function. You'll see how in "Synchronizing Your Local and Remote Sites" later in this chapter.

Maintaining Your Site

So just because your site's been uploaded doesn't mean you can hang up your web designer hat and go be a cowboy or a fairy princess. The work of a designer is hardly ever done for long. For example, your client or boss may come along with a round of changes and updates for the site—time to get back on the job!

Fortunately, Dreamweaver makes maintaining your site easy, by providing the tools you need to keep your live site alive and running smoothly.

Changing Links Throughout Your Site

Sometimes, you may want to change the destination of a hyperlink throughout your site—for instance, after you delete a file from your site, or after your site is reorganized, with pages added, shuffled around, or in some other way changed.

To update all your links, use Dreamweaver's Change Link Sitewide command.

To help you update all your links, Dreamweaver provides the Change Link Sitewide command.

Here's how to change a link across your site:

1. Choose Site > Change Link Sitewide.

2. In the dialog box that appears, enter the hyperlink that you want to change in the Change All Links To field.

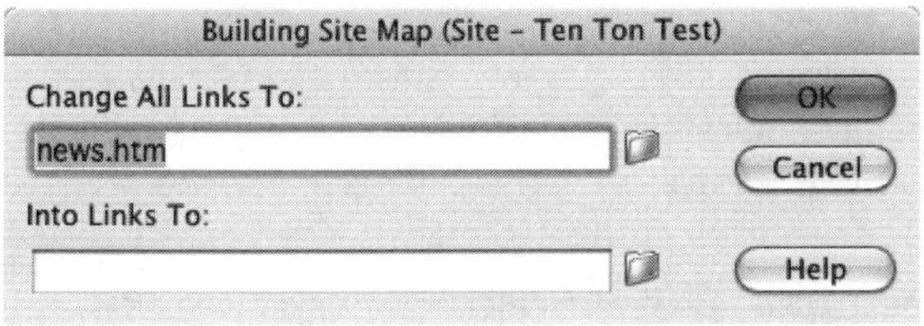

3. In the Into Links To field, enter the new hyperlink destination.

   All links that point to the destination that you entered in step 2 will change to point to the destination that you specify here.

4. Click OK.

   Dreamweaver updates all the links in your site that pointed to the previous destination.

Keep in mind that when you use the Change Link Sitewide command, the changes are made to your local site, not to your remote site. Therefore, you'll need to upload to the remote site any files that have changed. To see how to keep your local and remote sites the same, check out "Synchronizing Your Local and Remote Sites" later in this chapter.

Hiding Folders

As you're working on updating your site, you can save a lot of time by enabling cloaking. If a file or folder in your site is cloaked, it will be ignored by certain site functions, such as Put (uploading) and Get (downloading). For example, if you have folders of PDF and MP3 files already uploaded to your web space, there's no sense in uploading them again when you update a few pages on your site, if these files haven't also been changed. So to save time, you can cloak these folders.

If a file or folder in your site is cloaked, it will be ignored by certain site functions.

To take advantage of cloaking, make sure it's turned on in the Site Definition dialog box's Cloaking category. It's on by default, so if you didn't turn it off, you should be fine.

Here's how to cloak a file or folder:

1. In the Files panel, select the files or folders that you want to cloak.

2. Do one of the following:
   - In Windows, choose Site > Cloaking > Cloak.

   - On the Mac, open the Options menu at the top right of the Files panel and choose Site > Cloaking > Cloak.

   A red strikethrough appears across the file or folder icon, indicating that it's cloaked. Dreamweaver will now ignore this item during site operations.

To uncloak a file or folder, select it and choose Site > Cloaking > Uncloak. To uncloak all files or folders for your site, choose Uncloak All.

Synchronizing Your Local and Remote Sites

Once you've completed a round of updates, it can be tough to remember which files have been changed and need to be uploaded, and which ones are fine, especially when it's 4 a.m. Take the hassle out of updating with Dreamweaver's Synchronize command.

Essentially, in synchronizing, Dreamweaver compares your local site (or selected files within your site) with your remote site. If Dreamweaver finds any files that are more current than their counterparts, it will overwrite those older files so that the local and remote sites are in sync. Very handy.

If Dreamweaver finds any files that are more current than their counterparts, it will overwrite those older files.

Here's how to synchronize your local and remote sites:

1. In the right pane of the Files panel, right-click (Windows) or Control+click (Mac) and choose Synchronize.

2. In the Synchronize Files dialog box that appears, choose an option from the Synchronize menu to sync either the selected files in the Files panel or the entire site.

3. From the Direction pull-down menu, choose how you want to transfer your files.

   Put Newer Files to Remote: Uploads any local files that are more current than the remote files.

   Get Newer Files from Remote: Downloads remote files that are more current than the local files.

   Get and Put Newer Files: Overwrites older files in either direction locally or remotely.

4. Click Preview.

   The Synchronize dialog box appears, giving you get a last chance to verify that you're doing what you want to.

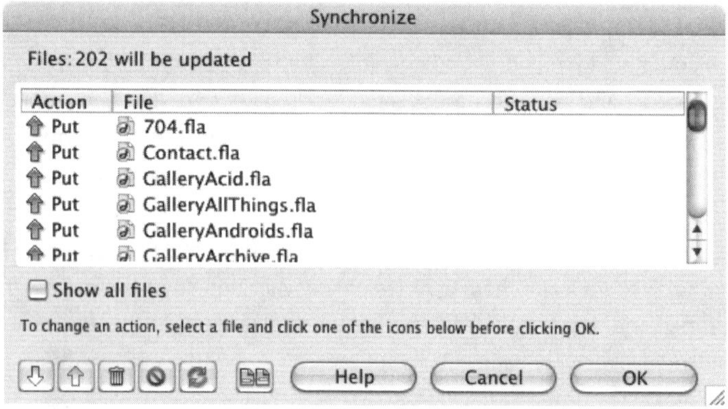

5. To change the action on a file, select the file and click the buttons at the bottom of the Synchronize dialog box.

   Mark Selected Files to Get the Remote Version: Replaces local files with their remote counterparts.

   Mark Selected Files to Put the Local Version: Replaces remote files with their local counterparts.

   Mark Selected Files for Deletion: Removes any selected files from both the local and remote sites.

   Ignore Selected Files During This Synchronization: Leaves any selected files out of the synchronization.

   Mark Selected Files as Already Synchronized: Sets the status of selected files as synchronized, removing them from the file list (unless Show All Files is checked).

   Compare the Remote and Local Versions of the Selected Files: Launches Dreamweaver's File Comparison utility.

6. When you're ready, click OK and bust a move.

SYNCHRONICITY WITHOUT SYNCHING

If you want to see which files on your local and remote sites are outdated without actually transferring anything, in the Files panel choose Edit (Windows) or Option > Edit (Mac) and then choose either Select Newer Local or Select Newer Remote.

Dreamweaver selects the newer local or remote files (depending on the option you chose). At this point, you can decide which files to transfer—or maybe you just want to review the list to see which files have recently changed before doing a full transfer. In the latter case, when you're ready, just click the Get or Put button at the top of the Files panel to perform the transfer.

Managing the Remote Site

You sometimes may need to move files around in your remote site, rename them, or remove them completely.

Just as for your local site, as you saw earlier in "Keeping Your Site Organized," to move a file or folder in your remote site, you drag it to a new location within your site structure directly in the Remote Site column of the Files panel. Dreamweaver will ask you to confirm that you want to move the file. Click Yes to continue. Keep in mind, though, that when you move files in your remote site, Dreamweaver does not automatically update your hyperlinks as it does when you move files in your local site.

When you move files in your remote site, Dreamweaver does not automatically update your hyperlinks as it does when you move files in your local site.

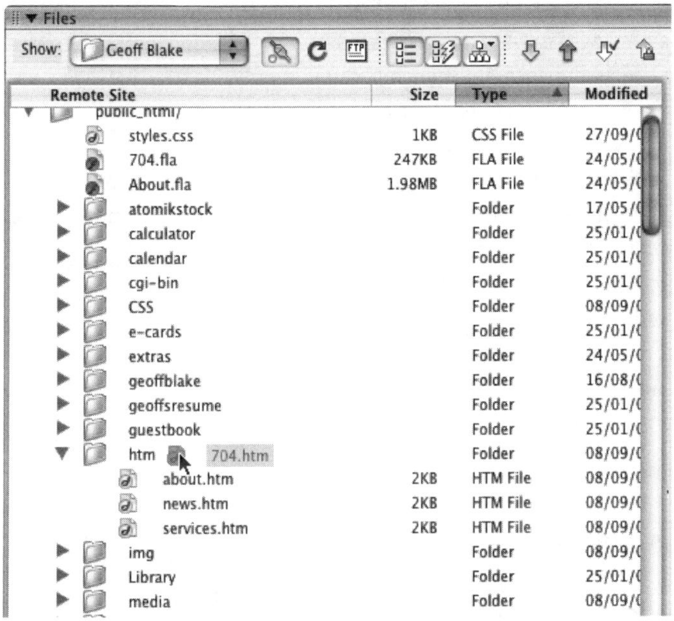

Wanna organize some files in your remote site? No problemo. In the Files panel's Remote Site column, you can rename files, delete them, or drag them to a new location, as you can see here.

You can also rename a file in your remote site from the Files panel just as you can for your local site, but again Dreamweaver won't update any hyperlinks for you.

And what if you want to completely remove your entire site, maybe for heavy-duty maintenance, or perhaps because it's old and no longer needed? To do that, select the remote site folder at the top of the Remote Site list in the Files panel and press the Delete key. Hey, it's quick and humane.

Working with a Team

Many times, web design isn't a lonely pursuit but, rather, a team sport. Many medium- and large-sized organizations use near-army-sized groups of designers, developers, and programmers, all working in their fields of expertise.

Remember: There's no "I" in team.

What binds all this talent together is the web site they're working on and the common tool they all use: Dreamweaver. Dreamweaver provides a couple of features to aid the growing number of designers working in a team environment.

Using Design Notes

Whether you're working as a part of a design team or all by your lonesome, Design Notes provide a great way to keep track of those bits of information that usually wind up scribbled on scraps of paper. A document's status, a project's deadline, edits, and communication between team members all can be stored in Design Notes.

Design Notes provide a great way to keep track of information related to a file.

When you add a Design Note to a document (they work on your web pages, graphics, and other files), Dreamweaver creates a _notes folder in your site folder and a corresponding file with the .mno extension.

NOTEWORTHY

The _notes folder won't appear in the Files panel.

Here's how to add a Design Note to a page:

1. Open the document that you want to add the Design Note to.

2. Choose File > Design Notes.

   The Design Notes dialog box opens to the Basic Info tab.

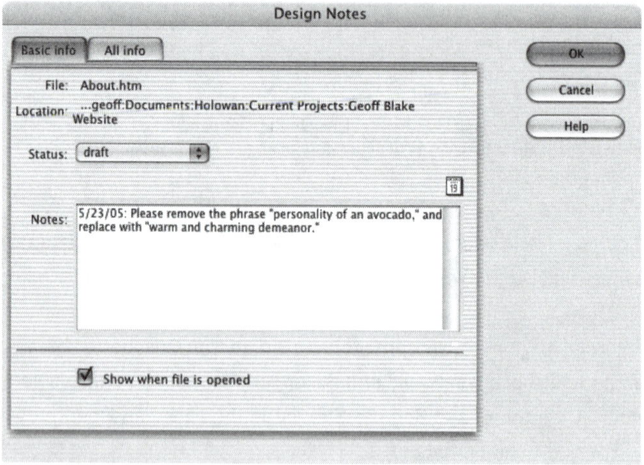

You can use the Status menu to communicate with other team members about the document's progress. You can also add notes at the bottom of the dialog box. To have the Design Note open automatically, select the check box at the bottom of the dialog box.

If you want to add your own menu items to the Status menu, follow these steps:

1. Open the Design Notes dialog box and switch to the All Info tab.

2. Click the Add Item button (the plus sign).

3. In the Name field, type **status**.

4. In the Value field, type the custom menu item text.

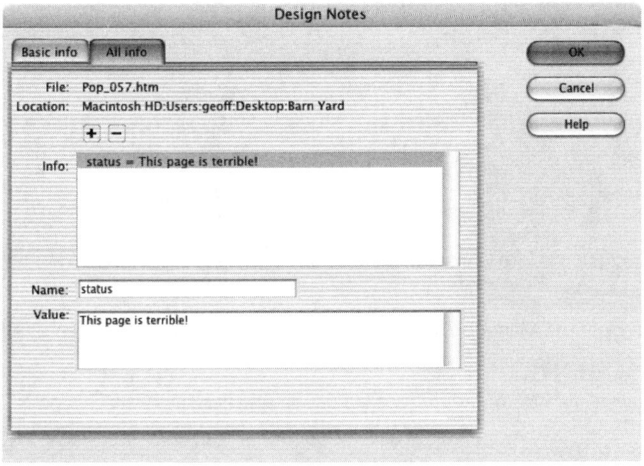

5. To test your new menu item, click the Basic Info tab.

   The Status menu should be set to your new option. Unfortunately, Dreamweaver allows only one custom status option.

You can also set up the Files panel to display the Design Note icon for files that contain Design Notes:

1. Choose Site > Manage Sites.

2. Select your site and click Edit.

3. In the Site Definition dialog box that opens, click the File View Columns category on the left.

4. In the list that appears, select Notes. In the Options category toward the bottom of the dialog box, select Show.

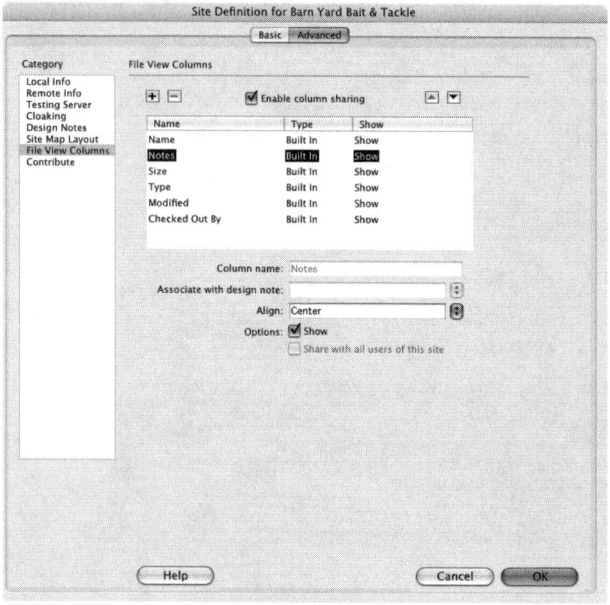

5. Click OK to close the Site Definition dialog box.

6. At the bottom of the Manage Sites dialog box, click Done.

You can also add a Design Note to a file directly in the Files panel. Right-click (Windows) or Control+click (Mac) the file and choose Design Notes.

A Notes column is now added to the Files panel. Any file that has a Design Note attached to it will display an icon in this new column. You can then double-click the Design Note icon to open the note for that file.

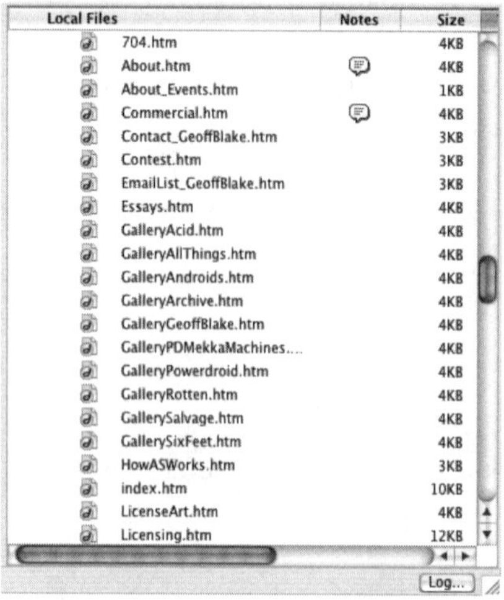

Checking Files In and Out

Dreamweaver provides the ability to check files in and out to ensure that team members don't overwrite each other's work as they build and update a web site. This feature also allows team members to see who's working on a particular file, so they know who to strangle when they're waiting for a file to become available.

To use Dreamweaver's Check In/Check Out feature, all team members must have the Check In and Check Out setting activated for the site they're working on, and Design Notes turned on.

Here's how to set up Check In/Check Out:

1. Open the Manage Sites dialog box by choosing Site > Manage Sites.
2. Select the site that you want to activate Check In/Check Out for and click Edit.
3. In the Category list on the left, click Remote Info.
4. Select Enable File Check In and Check Out.
5. Select Check Out Files When Opening.
6. Enter your name and e-mail address.

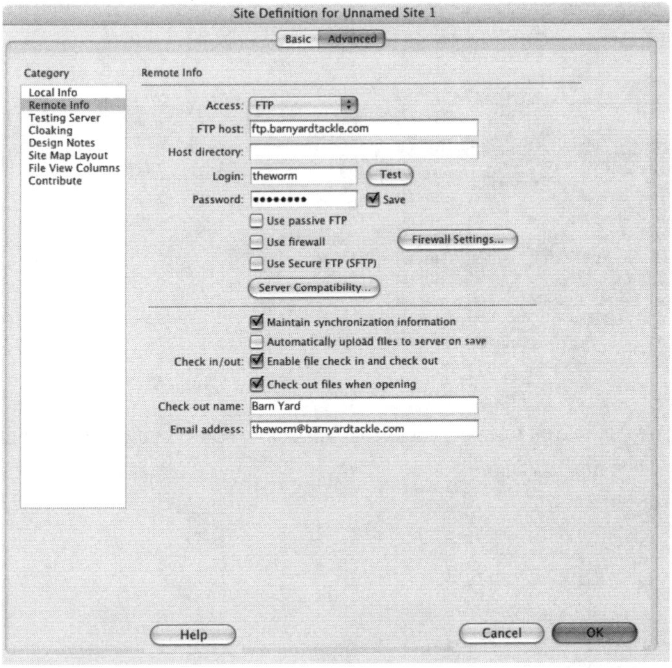

Dreamweaver's Check In/Check Out feature ensures that team members don't overwrite each other's work and allows team members to see who's working on a file.

With Check Out Files When Opening selected, when you double-click a remote file, it will automatically check itself out and download to your machine. By adding your name and e-mail address, you enable other team members to see who has a file checked out, and they can contact you directly from Dreamweaver. Pretty organized, huh?

IMMINENT DOOM

All team members must use Dreamweaver's Files panel to upload and download their work. That's how Dreamweaver tracks the Check In/Check Out status of files. If a team member uses an external FTP client, there's a very high probability that files will be overwritten accidentally.

With Check In/Check Out set up on your computer and your team members', here's how to check files in and out:

1. Check the Files panel to make sure that you're connected to your remote site.
2. From the Remote Site list on the Files panel, select the files you want to check out; then click the Check Out icon on the Files panel toolbar.
3. Dreamweaver will ask if you want to include dependent files. Choose Yes to get dependent files and No to dismiss the dialog box without getting the dependent files.

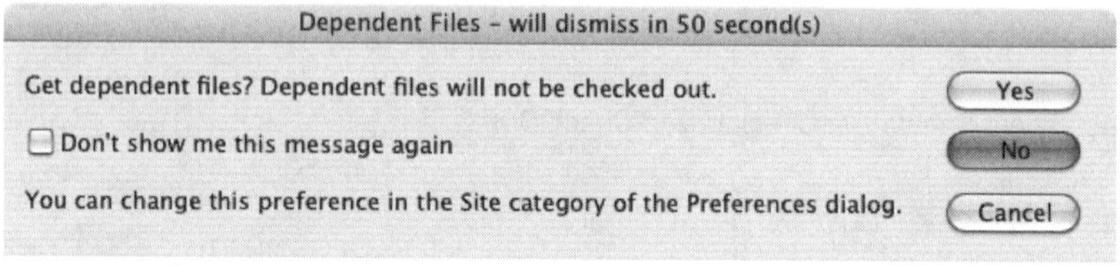

In your Files panel, a green check mark will appear beside the files you've checked out. Your colleagues will see a red check mark beside those same files, and in the Checked Out By column, your name will appear.

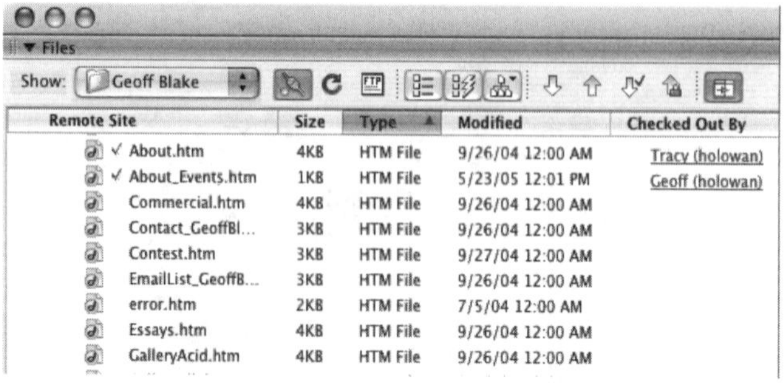

4. After you're done with the files, check them back in by clicking the Check In button on the Files panel toolbar.

Preparing Your Site for Search Engines

Those who are new to web design always seem eager to add their site to as many search engines as possible, as soon as possible. While certainly adding your site to the search engines is a good idea, hitting all the major search engines is very labor intensive. Savvy marketers know this and prey on the naïve by offering services that bulk submit web sites to all the search engines. However, paying to have your site bulk submitted is usually not worth the cost.

Paying to have your site bulk submitted to all the search engines is usually not worth the cost.

A much better approach is to manually add your site to search engines because you'll then have direct control over the descriptions and other information that the engine asks for. Most search engines provide a way to add your site to their databases. You may need to do a little hunting, but you'll usually find a link that says something like "Suggest a Site" or "Add a Site." Each search engine also will want slightly different information about your site.

Then the big question: How many search engines do you submit your site to? Some marketers feel that a site should be added to as many search engines as possible, while others argue that only the top 10 search engines really matter. The truth is, nobody knows for sure. It all comes down to you. Do you mind sitting in front of your computer for a day or so manually submitting your site to every search engine you can find, or are you happy with just hitting the biggies?

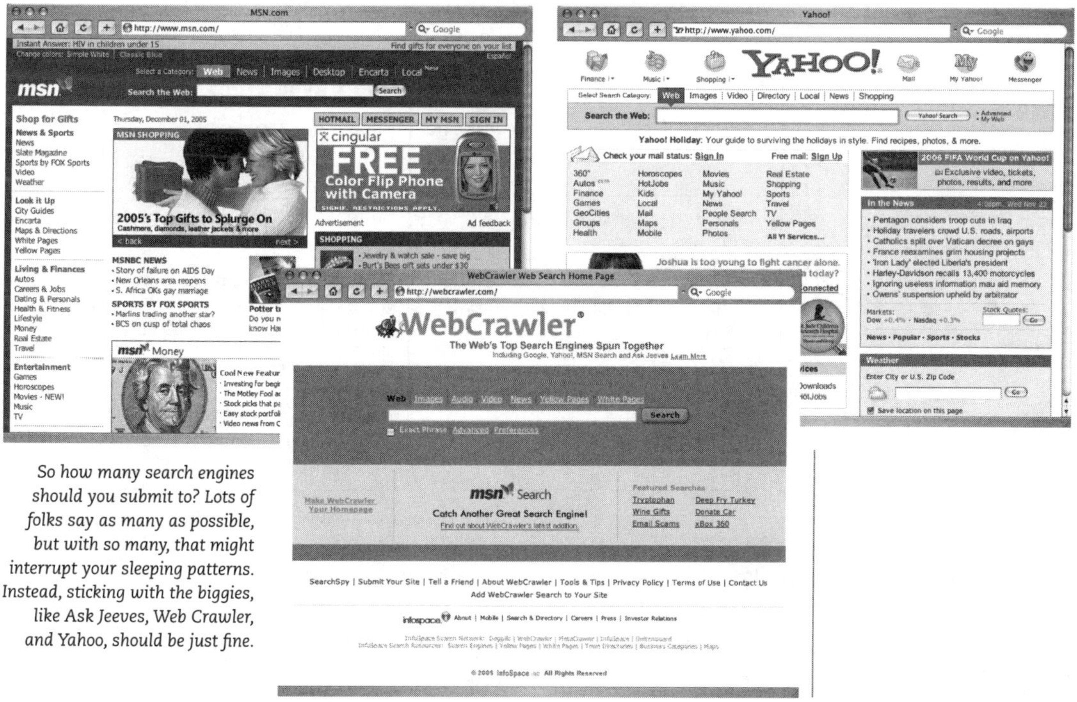

So how many search engines should you submit to? Lots of folks say as many as possible, but with so many, that might interrupt your sleeping patterns. Instead, sticking with the biggies, like Ask Jeeves, Web Crawler, and Yahoo, should be just fine.

Search engines use a site's keyword and description metadata to identify and categorize your site.

Before you submit your site to the search engines, you'll need to insert metadata into your Dreamweaver pages. A page's metadata, which is stored in the page's <head></head> tag pair, is the information that search engines use to identify and categorize your site. You can enter two types of metadata: keywords and a description.

Keywords are words or phrases that describe your site. For example, if you had a fan site dedicated to the movie *The Matrix*, your keywords might include *Neo*, *The Matrix*, *Wachowski brothers*, *Morpheous*, and *Trinity*. Usually, you start with very specific keywords and work your way toward the more vague.

NOTEWORTHY

Search engine spiders thrive on <head></head> tag content, so make sure to take the time to thoughtfully construct your metadata.

A site's description is a paragraph detailing the contents of the site. So in our *Matrix* fan site example, the description might read, "An online network of *Matrix* fans sharing ideas and theories related to the *Matrix* trilogy. Read about *The Matrix* comic books and video games and the philosophy behind the world of *The Matrix*."

MEGA META DO'S AND DON'TS

The techniques marketers use to place high in search rankings are always changing. I'm suggesting that you play with a clean nose and avoid some of the shadier search engine trickery—which, by the way, most search engines are on to. If a search engine runs into any of these shady techniques, odds are it will treat your site as spam and drop you from its index.

Do It!	**Don't Even Think of It!**
Use carefully selected keywords and a well-written description.	Repeat the same content over and over in your keywords and descriptions.
Make sure you use a descriptive page title.	Repeat the same word a zillion times in your page title.
Set up lots of links into and out of your pages, especially links to external sites.	Find out what the most popular keywords are (Viagra anyone?) and insert them into your keywords list.
Place keywords directly within your page content, and use descriptive alt tags on images.	Repeat the same keyword over and over at the bottom of your page, with the text color set to the same color as your page's background.

Here's how to set up your site for search engines:

1. Open the page that you want to add metadata to.

   You can add metadata only to your site's opening index page, or you can add metadata to all the pages in your site.

2. To add keywords to your page, choose Insert > HTML > Head Tags > Keywords.

3. In the Keywords dialog box that appears, type the keywords that you want to insert in your page, separated by commas; then click OK.

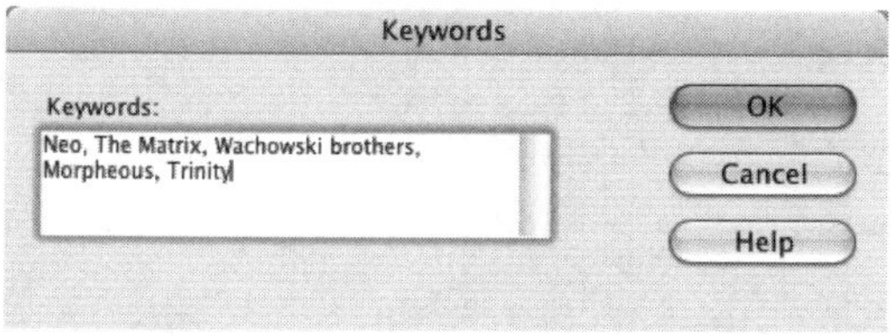

Dreamweaver adds the keywords to your page in the background code.

4. To add a description to your page, choose Insert > HTML > Head Tags > Description.

5. In the Description dialog box that appears, enter your site's description; then click OK.

   The description is added to your page's background code.

6. Save your page and upload it to your remote site.

   You're now ready to add your site to the search engines. In this example, you'll add your site to Google.

7. Launch your browser and navigate to www.google.com.

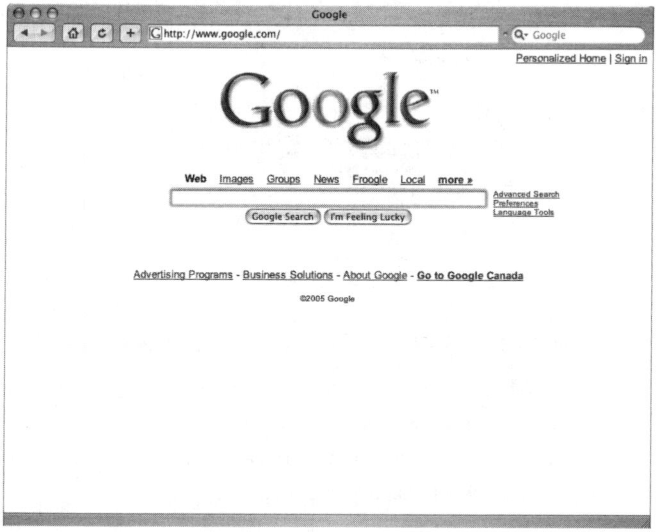

8. On the main Google page, click About Google.

9. On the page that appears, under the For Site Owners heading, click Submit Your Content to Google.

10. On the next page that appears, click Add Your URL to Google's Index.

11. On the page that appears, follow the on screen instructions to submit your site.

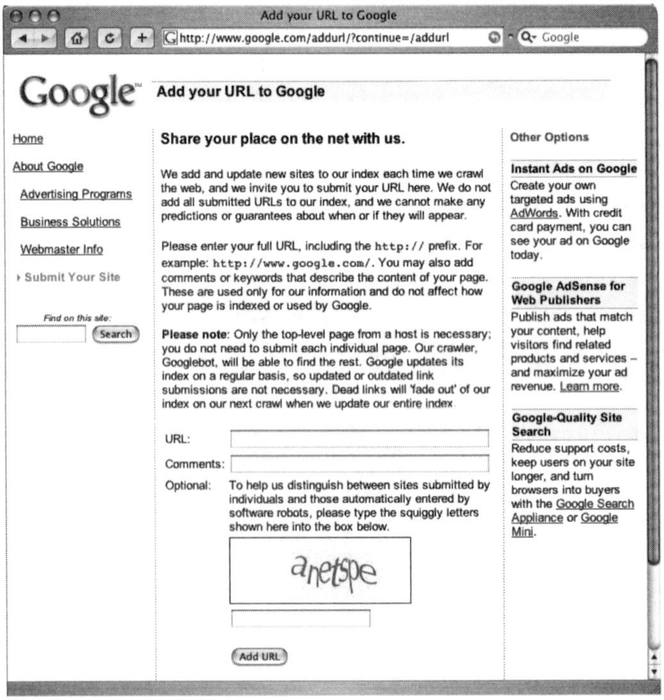

To add your site to other search engines, you'll follow a similar process. When you open the search engine in your browser, look for an Add a Site link (or something similar). Keep in mind that some search engines allow you to submit your site for free, while others charge a listing fee.

After you've submitted your site, it may take a long time for your site to show up in the search engine. Don't be surprised if it takes six months or longer. Bummer? Yup. But the major search engines are so inundated with requests to add sites that they have a difficult time keeping up.

GETTING OBSESSIVE ABOUT SITE RANKING

Some site owners are downright obsessive about having their sites rank high in search results. Their thirst to be at the top of the list drives them to endlessly tinker with page content and metadata until they figure out how a particular search engine is categorizing their pages.

But is this obsession with attaining higher and higher search placement necessary? Are search engines the only way to generate traffic on your site? Of course not. Here are a few things to think about:

- Surprisingly, most web surfers don't know how to search! Most surfers use search criteria so broad and unspecific that the odds of your page turning up are something close to a shot in the dark.
- What about your competitors for those coveted first few ranking positions? Everyone with a site similar to yours is trying to do the exact same thing you are, and the number of sites being added to search engines daily is enormous. The search engines can't keep up with demand.
- Consider the type of site you have. Let's say you run a local deli. You want a web site so customers can view upcoming specials, place large orders, and view a calendar of upcoming events. But do you need to add your site to a worldwide search engine like Google? Why would someone in southern Italy be interested in your small deli? You're just cluttering up major search engines with content that isn't useful to most surfers. What makes more sense is to add the site to a local online community directory.

This is not to say that you shouldn't add your site to the major search engines, assuming it's suited to an international audience. Go for it. Just don't spend too much time on it, and don't expect to see your site added by the end of the business day.

IMMINENT DOOM

Using shady search ranking techniques, like loading your page content with repeated keywords, is a sure way to get your site dumped from the search engines. These techniques are considered spamming.

JUST THE GIST

Getting Ready to Publish Your Site

- Dreamweaver's Link Checker makes it easy to test all the links in your site. Choose Site > Check Links Sitewide.
- To fix a broken link, click it in the Results panel; then use the folder button to specify a new hyperlink destination.
- You can use the Files panel to keep your site organized. Drag files to move them. Click files to rename them. Press Delete to delete selected files.
- Reports are useful for gathering information about the files in your site. Choose Site > Reports; then select the type of report you want to run.

Publishing Your Site

- To publish your site, connect to your remote web space by clicking the Connects to Remote Host button at the top of the Files panel.
- To upload the whole site, select your site's local site folder; then click the Put File(s) button. To upload individual files, select them in your local site and either drag them to the remote site or use the Put Files(s) button.

Maintaining Your Site

- To update hyperlink destinations across your site, choose Site > Change Link Sitewide.
- When uploading content to your remote site, you can tell Dreamweaver to ignore certain files or folders by cloaking them; choose Site > Cloaking > Cloak.
- Synchronizing ensures that the local and remote sites are exact duplicates. Dreamweaver compares the local and remote sites and transfers any files that need to be updated.
- Many of the functions that you can perform on your local site in the Files panel can also be performed on a remote site in the Files panel. However, when you move or rename a file in your remote site, Dreamweaver will not update hyperlinks automatically for you.
- To remove a site from its live web space, select the remote site folder at the top of the file list and press Delete.

Working with a Team

- Use Design Notes on your own or within a design team to attach notes to your files that indicate their status, deadline, edits, and so on.
- The ability to check files in and out ensures that team members won't overwrite each other's work. Select Enable Check In and Check Out in the Remote Info category of the site's Site Definition dialog box.

Preparing Your Site for Search Engines

- Search engines use your site's keywords and description—its metadata—to index your site. To insert metadata, choose Insert > HTML > Head Tags and then choose Keywords or Description.
- Adding your site to the search engines is a good idea, but it does not guarantee high traffic.

Index

C

D

E

F

G

H

I

J

K

L

M

N

O

P

Q

R

S

T

U

V

W

Z